1988

RECOVERING THE WORD

Recovering the Word

ESSAYS ON NATIVE AMERICAN LITERATURE

Edited by

BRIAN SWANN
and
ARNOLD KRUPAT

UNIVERSITY OF CALIFORNIA PRESS
Berkeley   Los Angeles   London

Joel Scherzer's "Strategies in Text and Context: The Hot Pepper Story" appeared in an earlier version in *Journal of American Folklore* 92: 364, 1979. Reproduced by permission of the American Folklore Society.

David Brumble's "Sam Blowsnake's Confessions: *Crashing Thunder* and the History of American Indian Autobiography" appeared in *The Canadian Review of American Studies* 16/3, Fall 1985.

Duane Niatum's "On Stereotypes" appeared in an earlier version in *Parnassus*.

Thanks to these journals for permission to reprint.

University of California Press
Berkeley and Los Angeles, California

University of California Press, Ltd.
London, England

Library of Congress Cataloging-in-Publication Data

Recovering the word

Bibliography: p.
Includes index.
1. American literature—Indian authors—History
and criticism.   2. Indian literature—History and
criticism.   3. Oral tradition—United States.
4. Indians in literature.   I. Krupat, Arnold.
II. Swann, Brian.
PS153.I52R43   1987   897   86–19150
ISBN 0-520-05964-6 (pbk. : alk. paper)

Printed in the United States of America

1 2 3 4 5 6 7 8 9

For Roy Harvey Pearce

Contents

INTERPRETING THE MATERIAL: ORAL AND WRITTEN
Oral

Written

CONTENTS

Introduction

THE EDITORS

I

While the serious study of Native American literatures by anthropologists and linguists is still less than a century old, such study by those outside the social sciences is considerably younger. Social-scientific attention to the rich Native literary heritage may be dated from somewhere around the turn of the present century and the pioneering efforts of Franz Boas and his students, whose researches provided the linguistic and cultural bases for study of a kind that could go beyond mere impressionism. Yet, it must be said that the first literary students of Indian song and story, contemporaries of Boas like Mary Austin, Natalie Curtis Burlin, and George Cronyn, were indeed largely impressionistic—rather than "scientific"—in their judgments. Indeed, granting in advance the possible exceptions to so recent a demarcation, it might even be said that a fully informed awareness of the problems and possibilities of this heritage on the part of students of literature dates from no earlier than 1975 and the publication of Abraham Chapman's valuable collection of critical essays, *Literature of the American Indians*. By that time, of course, a new generation of social scientists interested in Indian literatures was at work. We think here particularly of the pioneering studies of Dell Hymes and Dennis Tedlock, which raised exactly those questions of poetics and performance, of transcription, translation, and interpretation which students of literature were prepared to engage.

Or were they? For might there not be dangers in welcoming Native literatures into classroom discussion or journal debate as

1

though they were "just like any other," just like what "we" English teachers were familiar with? It soon became apparent that what Arnold Krupat has described as the question of identity and difference in the criticism of Native American literatures—regardless of whether the issue was thought of in that way or not—would have to be taken into account. Karl Kroeber's *Traditional Literatures of the American Indian,* appearing in 1981, offered essays by Kroeber himself and by Jarold Ramsey which treated Native American literatures as very much like what the student of the Western literary tradition was familiar with, as well as essays by Tedlock, Hymes, and the folklorist Barre Toelken that gave full play to the difference of Indian lyric and narrative expression.

Broadly speaking—and we are obviously speaking broadly here—it was in this context that Brian Swann produced *Smoothing the Ground* in 1983. By gathering in one place a wide range of essays by many of the best critics then working on Native American traditional and oral, as well as written literary expression, *Smoothing* provided a sophisticated introduction to the study of a range of Native American literatures. While being literary in emphasis it was also scientific, which is to say, linguistically and ethnographically informed. There has been other work along these lines: we mention here in particular Ramsey's collection of essays, *Reading the Fire* (1983), and Andrew Wiget's *Critical Essays on Native American Literature* (1985), which includes a selection of essays on all aspects of the subject, and *Native American Literature* (1985), a survey of traditional-oral and contemporary-written Indian literature.

The present volume continues the project begun in *Smoothing the Ground.* It also attempts to go beyond it, and thus to indicate the current "state of the art" in the criticism of Native American literatures. Although it is the case that the current "back to basics" mood of official America would imply that little of excellence on this continent derives from those who are non-WASP and non-male, thus providing virtually no institutional encouragement to the study of the subject of our concern, nonetheless developments in the area of Native American studies have been rapid and extensive. Our central intention is to help literary people take seriously what Dell Hymes has been saying for years, and recognize the dangers of offering interpretations of texts whose grammar and syntax are unknown to them. Like it or not, we need to face not only the truth (which we hold to be self-evident) but also the consequences of what William Bevis told us just over a decade ago, and recognize that "We won't get Indian culture as cheaply as we got Manhattan" (1975: 321). That is to say, literary people have for a long time mined the work of Boas and Sapir, of Paul Radin, Washington Matthews, and Melville Jacobs: why should they now not examine the contemporary research of anthropologists like Donald Bahr and Joel Sherzer; of linguists like William Bright, M. Dale Kinkade, or Anthony Mattina? In similar fashion, we must see that even social scientists willing to pay the highest price for Indian culture (in time and effort) can no longer offer commentary on the linguistic structure and cultural function of Native literatures without a more sensitive awareness of the dramatic effectivity, indeed, the grace and beauty of particular performance-events.

In this book, then, linguists and poets, folklorists and literary theorists, anthropologists and professors of English meet on the common ground of concern for the appreciation and elucidation of Native American song and story. The best contemporary criticism of Western literatures does not live by literature alone, seeking insights of a more specifically historical, philosophical, psychoanalytic, and linguistic kind for its commentary, and it seems high time to bring such interdisciplinary sophistication to bear on Native American literatures.

Our interdisciplinary commitment means that the reader will discover in this book a wide variety of perspectives, and thus also a wide variety of critical discourses. These range from the technical terminology of the professional linguist as in, for example, M. Dale Kinkade's account of a Salishan tale, to the vocabulary derived from contemporary Continental theory in the chapter by Arnold Krupat, to the less technical, more informal discourse of poet-scholars like Paula Gunn Allen, Duane Niatum, Howard Norman, and Brian Swann. Readers will find themselves more comfortable with one or another type of discourse, and less comfortable with others. We would urge our readers, however, to consider seriously stylistic modes that must at first seem alien or perhaps even hostile to their own habitual manner of speaking. We believe it is a mistake for anyone to assume (consciously or unconsciously) that there might

3

be some master discourse—a speech for all seasons—adequate in every way for every aspect of Native American literary expression. Academic discourse, because of its highly specialized nature, may tend to exclude those untrained in the specializations it invokes: yet it may be the case that some phenomena can only be accounted for or explained by a highly complex, technical vocabulary. In just the same way, "ordinary language" commentary, while it may appeal to the widest range of interested persons, may nonetheless have to equivocate or avoid certain phenomena whose precise nature can only be explicated technically.

This is only to say that we have tried in this book to be open to many different kinds of work in many different kinds of descriptive, interpretive, and appreciative languages, and that we have included every essay we found powerful and effective—regardless of the fact that one or another of us might not, himself, have cared much for some particular ways of working. Youthful as Native American Studies are, we would argue that such eclecticism remains useful; we recognize, however, the logic of the argument that such eclecticism (which has been the rule thus far for the Chapman, Swann, Kroeber, and Wiget collections) has outlived its usefulness. Perhaps the critical anthologies to follow this one will indeed support the view that Native American Studies are ready for distinctively Marxist, feminist, structuralist, and post-structuralist essays, thereby approaching (for better or worse) the condition of American Studies generally.

These theoretical speculations apart, it is our practical hope that the essays which follow will aid the understanding of the sophisticated general reader whose awareness of Native American literature may until now have been clouded by stereotypes, and also that of the professional student whose understanding may have been limited by narrowly disciplinary constraints. A few of our selections were first prepared as lectures; others are reprinted from original appearances in journals. Of these, most have been substantially revised for their publication here, while the majority of the selections have been prepared especially for this volume. The collaborations between Joel Sherzer and Donald Bahr with Brian Swann, we would particularly note, offer a kind of dialogue between the social scientist and the poet that has rarely taken place before, one that may encourage future efforts along these lines.

II

In the broadest fashion, all the essays in this book may be considered as addressing the linked and overlapping issues of the *presentation* and *interpretation* of Native American literatures. Inasmuch as traditional Native American literary art is oral, dramatic, performative, an event not an object, the first question for anyone interested in it is the question of how to *present* it for appreciation and study. Are videotapes or films the only (approximately) accurate modes of presentation, as Andrew Wiget, following the lead of Larry Evers's work, very nearly suggests? Or do more text-oriented approaches (as pioneered by Hymes and represented here most rigorously by M. Dale Kinkade) also constitute a legitimate *mythography*, one which, while attenuating the *experience* of oral performance, nonetheless may provide a more solidly secured linguistic base for its *comprehension*. Dennis Tedlock has argued that there is no such thing as prose except as a function of the written page, and Dell Hymes has presented strong arguments for the retranslation in verse format of the many Native narratives that have appeared in prose paragraphs. Is verse presentation therefore inevitable to convey what we may call the poeticity or dramatic effectivity (there are only awkward phrases to name the force and charm of oral narrative) of Indian literary expression? Anthony Mattina's essay brilliantly argues for multiple mythographic methods, demonstrating in particular the possibilities for the prose of what he has called "Red English." Howard Norman, who has produced some wonderful verse translations from the Swampy Cree, here also offers a prose version of a Cree trickster narrative.

Related to the issue of presentation, there is the matter of *translation,* of how, regardless of the physical format chosen, the strictly verbal portion of Indian performances might best be rendered in English. Is there some *via media* possible between the strict but sometimes stiff literalism often found in the renditions of social scientists, and the "poetic" but perhaps inaccurate free versions of the poets and professors of English—who may achieve a certain literary flavor at the expense of authenticity, denying, it may be, the difference of another culture? The first section of this book offers essays of a *theoretical* nature which consider these questions and others related to them, while the following section offers examples of contemporary mythographic *practice* based on recently recorded performances from the Kuna (Sherzer, with Brian Swann's "Note" on translation and collaboration), the Pima (Bahr, with a version by Swann), the Hopi (Wiget), and the Upper Chehalis (Kinkade). Subsequent essays work from a wide range of older texts.

Of course, once we have a body of inscribed and anglicized "Indian" songs and stories, questions arise: What to make of them, how to understand them? How do they interpret the natural and cultural worlds of the people who tell and retell them? What was their traditional function? What did they teach those who repeatedly loved to hear them? What do they teach us, who encounter them perhaps for the first time? And, as Paul Zolbrod's essay reminds us to ask, how do they relate to artistic expression of a nonverbal kind? In the next sections of this book, Carter Revard comments on the "naming ceremonies" of his own Osage people; Julian Rice comments with ethnographic and linguistic sensitivity on stories from the Lakota, and Howard Norman offers an account of some stories told of Wesucechak, the Swampy Cree trickster figure. The Native American trickster Coyote trots all through these pages to be examined generally by the eminent linguist William Bright, and specifically among the Navajo by the folklorist Barre Toelken, whose work with Yellowman has already achieved the status of indispensable text.

For all the many cultural things Native peoples lost as a result of the European invasion of America, one of the cultural things they received was the technology of writing as a means of preserving experience and knowledge. By the late nineteenth century, there were already a considerable number of written texts by Indians, most of them attempts to comment on events, personal and tribal, which the white conquerors considered important to their own sense of "history." By the early part of the twentieth century, many more Native Americans had expressed themselves in writing, in most cases as a result of the urgings of "science," particularly that *nuova scienza* that called itself *anthropology*.

The first Native American "novelist" may have been Elias Boudinot in 1823 with *Poor Sarah* . . . , or John Rollin Ridge, who in 1854 published the fictional account of the *Life and Adventures of Joaquín Murieta*. According to Andrew Wiget, Ridge was "the first Native American to publish a volume of poetry," in 1868 (1985:57).

By the 1930s there were a number of serious Indian artists composing novels, poems, and autobiographical texts in English. Although these were constructed upon formal principles that were European and print-derived, sensitive students could also discern in them the influences of the oral tradition. Difficult as it might be to distinguish formally between ancient, Indian modes of oral expression and later, written, Western modes, it was easy enough to see perceptions and concerns—a thematic dimension—that were unique to the Native American artist.

The final section of this book offers commentary on several texts. The earliest of these, historical and anthropological in inspiration, are collaboratively composed; the later texts, literary in inspiration, are individually composed.

We are pleased to reprint in revised form an essay by Dr. Rudolf Kaiser of Germany tracing the complex history of Chief Seattle's well-known speech. We also reprint an essay by H. David Brumble, one of the foremost American students of Indian autobiography, on Paul Radin's *Crashing Thunder*. Issues of major importance to contemporary Native American poets and novelists are examined in thoughtful work by Paula Gunn Allen, William Bevis, and Duane Niatum.

III

Once we had decided that an eclectic collection was permissible at this stage of the study of Indian literature, we simply invited all those whose work we had seen or heard of to contribute essays; we also advertised the project so that those whose work we did not know might also contribute. From the work that was submitted, we selected what appeared to us to be the best. The essays in this book, we believe, fairly represent a good deal—if, inevitably, not all—of the most interesting work currently being done by social scientists and literary critics on Native American literatures. We hope students and younger critics of Native American literatures will want to build on what appears here—but we also hope they may want to pursue some roads not taken by our contributors. To this end, we would like for a moment to become our own critics and offer a portrait, however sketchy, of needs and opportunities for further study.

We might begin by noting that Barre Toelken's contribution raises the issue of what an acute early reader of his essay spoke of to us as "classified research in the humanities." Indeed, this is an excellent description of an aspect of Native American literary studies that has long since dropped out of the study of the wholly secularized realm of Western literary studies. It might, for example, be worth pursuing the relationship between the Western scientist-critic whose curiosity is boundless, and the Native subject/object of his study who regards such boundlessness as offensive at best; lunatic or blasphemous at worst. This would also require scientist-critics to question themselves more rigorously concerning the epistemological status of Indian myth and literature (or myth-as-literature)—that is, to ask themselves whether (and how) they find the songs and stories they study to be "true" and/or effective as equipment for living, in a traditional, humanistic, or Kenneth Burkean fashion; or whether they find them to be fascinating but quite irrelevant in these regards. Both social scientists and literary people concerned with Native American literature—and we think this is equally, if differently, true for Native and non-Native people—have to ask themselves what the source of their concern actually is. Indian literatures have been appealed to as a repository of enduring value, a source of inspiration and renewal—and also as one more value-neutral subject/object of science. Without entering upon a debate as to the validity of these various approaches, we would only say—once more—that researchers can only gain by questioning the intention, function, and goals of their research.

Let us note, too, that the Indian as an individual is not much examined in these essays. The early part of the twentieth century saw the development of both structural-functional anthropology and culture-and-personality anthropology as supplemental or antagonistic to the Boasian commitment to a (possibly naive) empiricism and descriptivism. Looking at the essays in this book, it seems clear that, so far as the study of Indian literatures is concerned, structuralism, with its concern for principles of organization and function, has won out; culture-and-personality's interest in behavior—the components of individual action, or, in this context, performance—are very little considered. This means that the implications for the study of Native American literatures in the work of, say Claude Lévi-Strauss have been deeply considered; meanwhile, the (possible) implications for such study in the work of A. I.

Hallowell (see, for example, the essays collected in his *Culture and Experience,* 1955), the "ethnopsychiatrist" Georges Devereux, or even Edward Sapir (far more the individualist than the side of him represented in the Sapir-Whorf theory of language alone might suggest), have been scanted. In the latter regard, it seems to us—we are not linguists or social scientists—that the Sapir-Whorf theory of the way in which cultures are encoded in language may help give some specific inflections to the observation that language writes man, as structuralists and post-structuralists are fond of saying. It may also bear on the question of what is "traditional" and what is "individual" in the work of any given singer, teller, or, for that matter, writer.

A great deal has been done in the study of Native American literatures. Much remains to be done. We hope this book will present to the reader some of the best of recent work, and suggestions for future research.

New York   Brian   Swann
1985   Arnold   Krupat

REFERENCES

Bevis, William. 1975. American Indian Verse Translations. In *Literature of the American Indians: Essays and Interpretations,* ed. Abraham Chapman. New York: New American Library, 308–323.

Chapman, Abraham, ed. 1975. *Literature of the American Indians: Essays and Interpretations.* New York: New American Library.

Hallowell, A. I. 1955. *Culture and Experience.* Philadelphia: University of Pennsylvania Press.

Kroeber, Karl, ed. 1981. *Traditional Literatures of the American Indian: Texts and Interpretations.* Lincoln: University of Nebraska Press.

Krupat, Arnold. 1983. Identity and Difference in the Criticism of Native American Literature. *Diacritics* 13 (Summer):2–13.

Ramsey, Jarold. 1983. *Reading the Fire: Essays in the Traditional Indian Literatures of the Far West.* Lincoln: University of Nebraska Press.

Swann, Brian, ed. 1983. *Smoothing the Ground: Essays on Native American Oral Literature,* Berkeley, Los Angeles, London: University of California Press.

Wiget, Andrew, ed. 1985. *Critical Essays on Native American Literature.* Boston: G. K. Hall.

———. 1985. *Native American Literature.* Boston: Twayne Publishers.

Mythographic Presentation:
Theory and Practice

THEORY

When Artifacts Speak,
What Can They Tell Us?

PAUL G. ZOLBROD

I

The first artifacts I wish to consider here include a set of Navajo tapestries on display at the Wheelwright Museum in Santa Fe. Replicas of ceremonial sandpaintings (which, curiously enough, are created to be destroyed), the woven duplicates came to my attention shortly after I became interested in and began studying Navajo ceremonial poetry in the late 1960s. I did not pay much attention to them then, since I had never been trained to associate poetry with the plastic or the graphic arts. As I gained research experience in the field, however, where I listened to stories and observed ceremonies, I saw sandpaintings made and watched weavers work on traditional rugs and gradually came to realize that the story-telling art and the two allied graphic arts were closely linked.

Initially the sandpaintings and the weavings seemed very different; the original designs were produced by men to summon supernaturals with special healing powers during the long, elaborate chantway rituals—dramatic productions that reenact mythical accounts of errant and persecuted heroes and heroines thrust into alien situations where they are pursued, abused, or injured, sometimes fatally. Ultimately those protagonists are saved or restored by the gods and eventually return to their kinship groups with valuable information about how others might be cured of the same afflictions (see Wyman, Oakes, Campbell; see also Wyman 1983: 14–32; Zolbrod 1977). After their use in the ceremony, the drypaintings are disposed of; on the other hand, the weavings, produced by women for permanent display, are not used ceremonially, presumably because they lack the power to attract the deities. Even so, the two arts are very closely linked. They combine the Navajo medicine man's knowledge of traditional lore with the female weaver's skill at the loom. More pervasively, just as the basic theme of the Navajo creation story is that solidarity must be maintained between male and female if there is to be harmony in the world, so the weavings represent a fusion of distinctly male and female activities in Navajo culture. And the creation story—or emergence myth, as it is often called—is fundamental to the entire array of three dozen or so known chantway narratives. Moreover, when considered in the context of Navajo tradition, the stories articulate a relationship between poetry and the other arts that is missing in Western tradition, and perhaps yield a broader understanding of Native American cultures than we might otherwise grasp.

Sandpainting weavings are displayed in a number of museums and exist in private collections (see Wyman 1983: 268, 278). Many have been reproduced in various publications, some of which describe the ceremonials at length (see, for example, Newcomb and Reichard 1975; Reichard 1977; Wyman 1957, 1983). But like the sandpaintings they are modeled after, the weavings are all too often isolated from the poetic context which elucidates them. The artistry of both forms has been widely acknowledged; yet even among those who recognize it, the paintings and the tapestries arouse a much too narrow awareness of artistic achievement, as do other Native American artifacts. Because our culture conditions us to separate one art from another, we are often inclined to apply a more restrictive, specialized set of criteria than those works require.

Poetry differs from the plastic and graphic arts and from the performing arts by being the least accessible to the combined five senses, appearing almost exclusively in print in literate societies such as ours. In preliterate settings, which linger among the Navajos and various Pueblo communities in the Southwest, it is even less materially durable, since it is not even written down. Except for the way it fills a page, poetry occupies no space; it is ephemeral and nontactile. To assert itself physically it must be accompanied by gesture, music, dance, or drawings. Since it is primarily a function of human speech, it can be as fleeting as an unrecorded remark, whose only trace lingers in the memory.

But poetry compensates for its intangibility by being the most articulate of the arts. No other medium can qualify and quantify in the way language can; no other can delineate so precisely. No work of art—not a piece of music, not a pot or a mask or a painting—can so fully bespeak a tradition with its aggregate of values and its nuances of meaning. The other arts require poetry to supplement what they express, or else they communicate less adequately.

Imagine looking at the ceiling of the Sistine Chapel without knowing the Bible. Imagine being unfamiliar with the Gospels and seeing a madonna by Raphael. Visual splendor is incomplete without the use of language, whether spoken, sung, or written. We take that principle so much for granted that we neglect to apply it in trying to understand cultures alien to our own. We profess to admire Native American art by placing it in museums or cataloging it in books. But we persist in knowing too little about Native American artifacts and the poetry that supplements them, with the result that they tell us too little about themselves.

The Wheelwright sandpainting tapestries are a case in point, even though they have been exceptionally well treated there. In the fall of 1982, the Museum published a catalog of the weavings which contained a comprehensive description of the cultural context of their prototypes including a description of the deities and mythological events each depicts (Halpern, McGreevy, Parezo & Parrish 1982). But that publication leaves too much unsaid. A Navajo healing ceremony is no more easily explained to a stranger to Navajo culture than the Roman Catholic mass would be to a non-Christian or a Broadway musical to someone who has never heard a single show tune. It includes music, dance, recitation, participation from its spectators, and the careful application of traditional procedures. Furthermore, it is the closest thing there is to formal worship in the Navajo religious system (see Kluckhohn and Leighton 1974:200–223).

Even those who have written about the healing ceremony in depth have failed to recognize the importance to it of poetry. Essentially a story, a ceremony merges the identity of the patient with that of a mythical character who undertakes a journey-quest for an ancient cure. Members of the patient's family or clan are asked to sing and play various roles, while a medicine man orchestrates the whole production. It differs from our own dramatic works by being

15

primarily functional, which is true of virtually all Navajo art whatever the medium, to say nothing of the art of other Native American
tribes.

While much of this information is acknowledged in the Wheelwright catalog, the weavings manifest a vast tradition not easily
summarized in a single publication. The stories and the way they
are told speak best for the tapestries, and these artifacts—beautiful
in and of themselves—take on additional beauty when integrated
fully with the narratives, chants, lyrics, and prayers that combine
to form the massive poetic corpus of the Navajo ceremonial system.

II

While the poetic material which predicates Navajo sandpaintings
is part of a diminishing oral tradition, much of it has found its way
into print. The Wheelwright Museum has copies of several dozen
manuscripts of chantway narratives closely associated with the
weavings, many as yet unpublished, assembled by Father Berard
Haile and Gladys Reichard, both of whom learned Navajo and won
the trust of medicine men earlier in this century. Duplicate copies
of that material can also be found at the Museum of Northern
Arizona in Flagstaff and in the Special Collections Library at the
University of Arizona. Some of it has been published in the American Tribal Religions Series, and some has been printed by various
academic presses (see Zolbrod 1984:345nn. 5, 16). Earlier, Washington Matthews translated an extensive body of Navajo material,
as did a handful of other ethnographers and linguists. The Navajo
emergence myth, which he included in his monumental volume,
Navajo Legends, forms the basis for my own translation of the Navajo
creation story, *Diné bahane'.* Much of what had been published
earlier was treated as folklore and anthropological data, not as
poetry. When considered poetically, though, it adds perspective to
the sandpaintings. The creation story alone underlies Navajo culture the way the Bible permeates Western culture, and the more
carefully it is examined the more it reveals, not only about Navajo
sandpainting weavings but also about the symbols and aesthetics
of other kinds of artifacts.

One weaving, for instance (fig. A), depicts Naayéé' neizghání the Monster Slayer, the more aggressive of two war gods who rid the earth of ravaging giants. According to the creation story and such chantway narratives as the *Enemyway* and the *Shootingway*, Navajo tradition bears him in high regard. He is shown dressed in black flint sparkling with lightning bolts, a symbol of power and control. The zigzag lightning crossing his body represents the weapons given to him by his father, Jóhanaa'éí the Sun, who also gives both war twins their flint armor, as the narrative explains (Zolbrod 1984:205–212). The story also describes how they were nurtured (pp. 179–187), and how together they managed to climb to the Sun's sky dwelling to seek his help.

Figure A. *Naayeé' neizghání* the Monster Slayer, from *Shootingway*. Wheelwright Museum Collection, catalog no.. 44/12. Photo courtesy of Laura Gilpin, Herb Lotz Photography, Santa Fe, New Mexico.

Thus, as it progresses the narrative gives the illustration added meaning. One incident puts it in characteristically sharp perspective not only for what it relates but also for the style it displays. That passage describes how the brothers destroy Yé'iitsoh the Big Giant, chief of the monsters who must be slain before any of the others (pp. 215–221). He spies them and threatens them four times, and with each threat they add to his anger by mocking him until he hurls four lightning bolts at them. They dodge the first by ducking, the second by rising above it, the third by maneuvering to the right, and the fourth by leaping to their left. In turn the brothers fire four lightning arrows at him. First Naayéé' neizghání fires one and Yé'iitsoh reels dizzily but remains standing. Then the brother, Tó bájísh chíní, or Born For Water, throws one and Big Giant's knees buckle. Monster Slayer fires a third and the creature falls momentarily. When he gets up, Born For Water hurls a fourth and the giant falls again and dies.

This symmetrically styled battle parallels the stylized sandpainting portrait. The overall episode contains four clearly marked parts in which the brothers first seek Yé'iitsoh, then exchange remarks with him, then trade blows and destroy him, and finally follow the bidding of their tutelary god Níłch'i the Wind to make sure he cannot come back to life. Each part, in fact, is told in series of fours, as my brief summary indicates, and the four-part battle reflects the four clearly defined directions in the illustration and its four distinctly marked corners. The narrative does not describe the fight; rather, it shows the twins striking a series of poses, just as in the illustration Naayéé' neizghání assumes a static pose which is integrated into the overall balance of the entire design. In the story the movement is likewise expressed more in terms of balance and design than in terms of conflict as it would be narrated in, say, the *Odyssey* or *Beowulf,* where readers can more easily envision characters actually struggling. One critic of Navajo art, Evelyn Hatcher, observes that "illustrations in the European tradition would center on the battles of Monster Slayer with much use of conflicting movement in the form of opposed diagonals and active lines full of wiggly curves as can be seen in the numerous representations of St. George and the Dragon. But the drypaintings, both in content and in form, glorify not the conflict but the order achieved as a result of it" (1974:171). The monsters and the twins do not actually fight; they trade blows formally in what resembles choreographed movement until the alien god falls. Similarly, this illustration presents Naayéé' neizgháni poised not so much for battle as to maintain the fragile harmony suggested by the nearly symmetrical design. Indeed, in the Navajo cosmic view which the creation story and the various chantway narratives project, gods and mortals must stand ready to protect that harmony, which has been hard won to begin with.

This episode represents just a fraction of what the poetry tells us about Naayéé' neizgháni. His exploits take up a good part of the creation story and are the subject of several other traditional narratives. The more we read about him, the more readily we can relate to the way he is portrayed graphically. On the other hand, merely seeing one sandpainting portrait of him is like seeing a single photograph of a total stranger. The narratives convey meaning that does not come across explicitly in any number of illustrations. The stories articulate a growing wisdom and a depth of experience that language expresses best.

In one of my favorite passages from *Diné bahane'*, Naayéé' neizgháni insists on slaying more creatures after he has destroyed the evil monsters, in spite of his mother's advice to remove his armor and cease his fighting. Ignoring her, he sets out to kill Są'ah, the One Who Brings Old Age; Hak'az asdzą́ą́ the Cold Woman, who freezes the earth each year; Té'é'í dine'é the Poverty Creatures, who gradually wear out goods and utensils; and Dichin hastiin the Hunger Man, who depletes food supplies. As he is about to strike each one, he learns respectively that Są'ah makes room for the unborn, Hak'az asdzą́ą́ gives the earth an annual winter's rest, the Té'é'í dine'é keep people busy fashioning new tools and making new clothes, and Dichin hastiin compels them to plant and harvest instead of idly doing nothing. Thus, Monster Slayer comes to realize that a dynamic balance of ebb and flow is necessary in a world where death terminates life and season follows season in an ongoing cyclical rhythm.

In one way or another, all Navajo art reflects the importance of balance and proportion, as the nearly symmetrical sandpaintings exemplify, but the poetry articulates it most fully. Illustrations convey visually the tenuous set of relationships that Naayéé' neizgháni apprehends when he learns why death, winter, poverty, and

hunger must exist; but they express it abstractly and implicitly—
and only to those intimately acquainted with the culture and its
traditions. The poetry offers a more explicit explanation. Even its
style and syntax reflect the ways in which orderly design pervades
Navajo vision. Consider this short passage, for example, from one
surviving version of the *Beadway* ceremonial narrative:

Ha'a'aahjígo kin łigaigo háagi shį́į́ dah sitą́ą́ lá djín,
Shádi'ááhjigo kin dootl'izhgo háagi shį́į́ dah sitą́ą́ lá djín,
E'e'aahjí kin łitsogo háagi shį́į́ dah sitą́ą́ lá djín
Náhookǫsjí kin diłhiłgo háagi shį́į́ dah sitą́ą́ lá djín,

Binaagóó kin t'óó ahayóí haal'áá lá djín,
Daalkizhgo ła' ałheedadeez'áago ha'al'á djín.

Ha'a'aahjí kin ligai dah sitánę́ę́ji atsałgai kééhat'į́į́ lá djín,
Shádi'ááhjí kin dootl'izh dah sitánę́ę́jí ginítsoh din'é keehat'į́į́ lá djín,
E'e'aahjí kin łitsogo dah sitánę́ę́jí atseełtsoi din'é kééhat'į́į́ la djín,
Nahookosji kin diłhiłgo dah sitánę́ę́jí atsázhin dine'é kééhat'į́į́ lá djín.

On the east side a white house had long been standing, so the story
goes.
On the south side a blue house had long been standing, so the story
goes.
On the west side a yellow house had long been standing, so the story
goes.
And on the north side a black house long had stood, so the story goes.

In each direction the houses stood, the storytellers say.
So that the four colors intersected where the four straight rows con-
verged.

To the east where the white house stood the white eagles dwelled, they
say.
To the south where the blue house stood dwelled the sparrow hawks,
they say.
To the west where the yellow house stood lived the yellowtailed hawks,
they say.
And to the north where the black house stood the black eagles lived,
they say.

20

The measured verbal patterns here reinforce the symmetrical arrangement of houses, colors, and occupants explicitly oriented to the four directions. Furthermore, the nearly identical first four lines and incrementally repetitive last four duplicate the carefully balanced design found in most sandpaintings, while the medial two-line stanza identifies the central point where the four colors converge in the form of a cross. Such a configuration occurs often in Navajo sacred stories, and such patterned syntax occurs often as well. Although I worked out the linear arrangement of this passage myself, the entire story was recited to Father Berard Haile (1931) by a medicine man known as Curly Tó aheedlíinii—River Junction Curly—whose deliberately archaic diction and highly formal language combine to represent what can be called classical Navajo poetic style. Conservative and meticulous in the way he tells a story, Curly maintains the most majestic idiom we are likely to recover from what remains of Navajo oral tradition. The steadily repeated storyteller's term *djín,* which here is a contracted form of the old fourth person distributive plural of the verb *jiní,* he says, in the continuitive tense and imperfective mood, indicates that these lines have been recited continuously by one generation of storytellers after another. The Navajo informant who helped me translate the passage said it was typical of sacred storytelling down to its very rhythm, which had "been very carefully maintained." That, he added, "is why the old storyteller's distributive plural *dajiní* comes out *djín.*" An expert grammarian with a thorough knowledge of ceremonial lore, he called this segment a "sandpainting with words," and he was eager to have me recognize how the elements in it were grouped in pairs and fours, and how much careful balance it displayed.

The more closely traditional stories are examined, the more clearly patterns of rhythm and syntax underscore content and define basic motifs. The cross of houses in rows emanating from a central point in this passage is fundamental to Navajo storytelling and graphic design alike. Such a cross appears frequently in such chantway narratives as *Beadway,* and it is replicated in the ritual sandpaintings. Its fullest description, however, occurs in the opening of the creation story, where, at a place called Tó bił dahisk'id or Place Where the Waters Crossed, an inner world is described:

21

> At *Tó bił dahisk'id* where the streams came together water
> flowed in all directions. One stream flowed to the east. One
> stream flowed to the south. One stream flowed to the west. One
> stream flowed to the north.
>
> Along three of those streams there were dwelling places.
> There were dwelling places along the stream that flowed east.
> There were dwelling places along the stream that flowed south.
> There were dwelling places along the stream that flowed west.
> But along the stream that flowed north there were no dwellings.
> (Zolbrod 1984:35)

After identifying that central world's inhabitants as twelve groups
of primal insect people, the story mentions a sexual transgression
which angers its four gods who preside over the four directions:

> It is also said that the . . . People fought among themselves.
> And this is how it happened. They committed adultery, one with
> another. Many of the men were to blame, but so were many of
> the women.
>
> They tried to stop, but they could not help themselves.
> *Tééhooltsódii* the One That Grabs Things In the Water, who
> was chief in the east, complained, saying this:
> "They must not like it here," he said.
> And *Táłtł'ááh álééh* the Blue Heron, who was chief in the
> south, also complained:
> "What they do is wrong," he complained.
> *Ch'ał* the Frog, who was chief in the west, also complained.
> But he took his complaint directly to the . . . People, having this
> to say to them:
> "You shall no longer be welcome here where I am chief," is
> what he said.
> "That is what I think of you."
> And from his home in the north where he was chief, *I'ni'
> jiłgaii* the Winter Thunder spoke to them also.
> "Nor are you welcome here!" he, too, said to them. (p. 37)

Accordingly the four gods create a flood to drive the insect people
away. The latter flee into the sky, which they must dig through to
escape into a second world. There they compound their sexual
misbehavior and are driven upward into yet another world. The
pattern of their disorder is repeated twice more, so that their
emergence does not stop until the exiles reach this the fifth, outer-

most world, which they shape as the largest and most complex of the five concentric spheres. They start by creating four sacred mountains at the four cardinal points of their realm along with three central mountains—one to mark the sky's zenith, one for the nadir within, and one to designate the central point on the surface. Thus, they recognize the need for orderly conduct in terms of spatial design, and the whole story relates how that order is to be established and maintained, especially in male-female relationships.

Navajo poetry, above all, expresses a sense of orderly design, sometimes by spelling it out in explicit detail, sometimes by alluding to it obliquely, and sometimes by evoking it implicitly in the way a storyteller organizes his syntax or imposes rhythm as he speaks. For those who know the poetry, the sandpaintings thus take on a contextual richness that might otherwise go unnoticed, as three additional illustrations from the Wheelwright collection of sandpainting weavings demonstrate.

The first, reproduced in figure B, is called "The Skies," and belongs with the *Shootingway* narrative, which recounts the exploits of Monster Slayer and his brother in greater detail than the creation story provides. It marks the point when, after they have made their journey to the sky dwelling of Jóhanaa'éí, they must pass a series of tests to prove that they really are his sons. In the painting the white of dawn is represented to the east. To the south is shown the blue of the moon; to the west, the yellow of the sunset; and to the north, the black of night along with the zigzag Milky Way. In the center are the blue and white faces of the Sun and the Moon along with the faces of Black Wind and Yellow Wind looking respectively to the east, the west, the south, and the north. The four sacred plants—corn, beans, squash, and tobacco—are also shown growing toward the four corners in anticipation of crops that will be domesticated once the brothers have made the world safe by slaying the monsters. Notice, too, how the four distinct segments of sky form a near-enclosure around all the objects pictured, complete with a "guardian rainbow" connecting the moon, sunset, and night skies, with only the eastern dawn left open. In one form or another, that image of a broken perimeter appears in most of the sandpaintings.

The second illustration, reproduced in figure C, comes from the *Night Chant*, and is called "Black Sweatlodge." This narrative describes the ordeal of two crippled twins who, in seeking to be cured

23

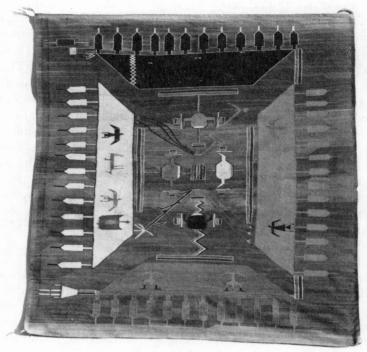

Figure B. "The Skies," from *Shootingway*. Wheelwright Museum Collection, catalog no. 44/8. Photo courtesy of Laura Gilpin, Herb Lotz Photography, Santa Fe, New Mexico.

of their condition, have a sweatlodge built for them by the gods, where they are to be healed. Seated around the circular lodge are male and female deities, while across the center from north to south is the gentle female rain, and from east to west the noisy, destructive male lightning. The circular design here conforms to both the domed roof of the sky overhead and the curved roof of the traditional Navajo sweatlodge with its entrance facing east. Here the enclosure which borders the picture is not broken as it is in "The Skies," but it is interrupted by the recess which symbolizes the entrance.

Also from the *Night Chant* is the illustration in figure D, titled "The Whirling Logs." It refers to an episode in which the protagonist seals himself in a hollow log and makes his way down the San Juan River into the centralmost world. There two logs spin

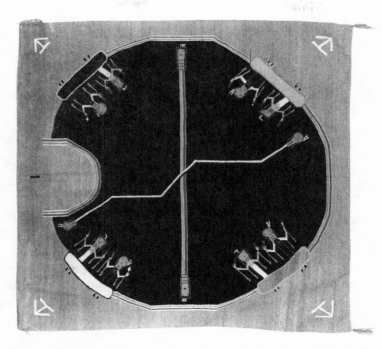

Figure C. "Black Sweatlodge," from *Night Chant*. Wheelwright Museum Collection, catalog no. 44/13. Photo courtesy of Laura Gilpin, Herb Lotz Photography, Santa Fe, New Mexico.

around the swirling surface of the lake from which the four original rivers flow in the four directions. At that place he acquires valuable knowledge about curing and planting, which he takes back to his people. The black cross in the middle symbolizes the spruce logs crisscrossing each other; and from the central lake, symbolized by the blue square in the exact middle, grow the four sacred plants whose cultivation will prevent hunger and whose origins are thus associated with life-giving subterranean water. Positioned around the cross are four pairs of gods or Holy People, each couple consisting of a male and a female dressed in black and white respectively. Two mountain sheep gods carrying black cloud sacks on their backs stand toward the north and south edges of the illustration, and two major deities in the Navajo pantheon, Talking God and Growling God, stand to the east and west. Guardian symbols such as lightning

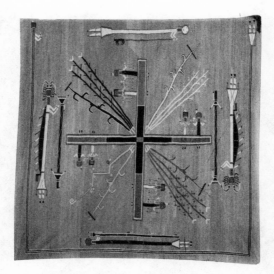

Figure D. "The Whirling Logs," from *Night Chant*. Wheelwright Museum Collection, catalog no. 44/6. Photo courtesy of Laura Gilpin, Herb Lotz Photography, Santa Fe, New Mexico.

arrows, sunflowers, and snakes frequently surround the interior design of a sandpainting, as they do here. Notice, too, how a female rainbow guardian borders the illustration on three sides, leaving an eastern opening to allow evil to escape and good to enter (Wyman 1983:67). Once again we see a broken enclosure around the outer edge.

I have not mentioned numerous smaller details, which are also abundant in most sandpaintings and which refer to minor deities and subordinate plot elements. Familiarity with the stories makes these details easier to recognize, as Wyman demonstrates in his chapter on what the sandpaintings signify (pp. 179–188). While the arrangement of such details may vary from sandpainting to sandpainting, all four shown here share certain broad features common to many. Each conveys a strong image of centrality, for example; the eye is drawn to the middle, yet the design is composed so that at the same time other details radiate outward until the periphery hangs in uneasy balance against the center. The familiar border with its characteristic break surrounds everything else the way four spheres surround a central world in the Navajo cosmos, with each one providing egress to a higher, safer world. Since the potential for disorder is always present, in fact, Navajos compulsively avoid unbroken circles. There must always be an outlet for evil and a place of entry for potentially helpful outside forces (see Zolbrod 1984:374 n. 37).

The radial design occurs in well over half of all sandpaintings. By opposing a perimeter against a central locus, it suggests a tense duality that sets inside against outside, containment against release, upward against downward movement. In the full context of Navajo storytelling, it also stands abstractly for the familiar theme of order versus disorder—a theme expressed in a variety of ways including descriptions of men and women struggling to learn to get along (see, for example, Haile 1981; Zolbrod 1984:55–70). In a key passage of the creation story, when the Navajo goddess Asdzáá nadleehé the Changing Woman tells Jóhonaa'éí the Sun how he must treat her if there is to be stability in the world, she begins by asserting, "You are male and I am female. You are of the sky and I am of the earth. You are constant in your brightness, but I must change with the seasons. You move constantly at the very edge of heaven, while I must remain fixed in one place." She goes on to insist that as unalike as the two of them are, "there can be no harmony in the universe as long as there is no harmony between us" (Zolbrod 1984:274–275).

This important scene of reconciliation between male and female thus helps verbalize the importance of the radial composition of sandpaintings such as the woven ones reproduced here. It also serves as an interesting adjunct to the relationship between the ephemeral sandpaintings that men traditionally make during ceremonies and the permanent likenesses women weave. Everywhere in Navajo culture, in fact, opposites are somewhat tensely matched, analogous to the way Changing Woman insists that the Sun is to be matched with her, and as the creation story frequently demonstrates by employing continuous opposition of centrifugal movement against centripetal force. The narrative scarcely opens before the insect people are compelled to leave the first world, although they struggle to stay. Later, as they begin to fashion the fifth world to make it livable, they learn that death will inevitably draw them back within. And in a still later passage, when the monster-slaying twins are lifted by their father the Sun to the sky's very zenith, they topple dizzily and nearly fall, saved only when a guardian wind holds them up momentarily until they can regain their balance and descend more gently (Zolbrod 1984:213).

The common radial design demonstrates with its visual tension that Navajo sandpainting is an art of extremes positioned as if symmetrically in pairs, or in pairs of pairs, which vary the theme of duality in some interesting ways. It is not too far afield to add that Pueblo traditions suggest a similar dualism. One Keresian myth tells of two sisters, one rich and tall, the other poor and short, who are matched in an uneasy competition for the affections of a male. Another identifies the two "War Twins" as an aggressive, belligerent "outside" chief and a gentler, peaceful "town" chief. Still another tells of the clown god Paiyatemu who leads two opposing lives, as it were, sometimes serving as the sun's companion and sometimes as his foil. In their stories, various Pueblo groups show a penchant for having "everything both ways," constantly defining alternatives that are eventually reconciled, often with the use of humor (Tyler 1964:142). In Navajo tradition, however, tension is likely to be sustained, not resolved; or else resolution is more tentative so that one force remains uneasily balanced against another with disorder constantly threatening. After they are reconciled, Asdzą́ą́ nadleehé the Changing Woman and Jóhanaa'éí the Sun continue to quarrel occasionally. When that happens, "the wind blows and the sky is black with overcast clouds." Lightning then fills the heavens and "the whole world suffers" with the lapse in their "conjugal solidarity" (Zolbrod 1984:277).

III

As the poetry helps to explain, then, looking at sandpaintings is a dynamic process. Tension exists in all of them, as it exists in the world that Navajos perceive and describe in their traditional stories. At first the illustrations seem balanced and static, but they really are tense and dynamic. In "The Whirling Logs" (fig. D), for example, the faces of the mountain sheep are not the same color; nor are those of Talking God and Growling God. There are only three stalks of one plant growing from the center toward the northeast corner and four of the one growing toward the southwest corner. Meanwhile, in "The Skies" (fig. B), the Black Sky borders the sandpainting to the north, while Black Wind occupies the southerly portion of the central area and faces the south, just as the White Sky lies to the east while White Moon sits west of center and faces that direction, all gazing away from the center. Thus, in the context of what looks like repetition and symmetry, there is an implicit suggestion of impending interruption and disarray.

The narratives also seem to lumber along with little sense of action, especially as their language is often stylized and repetitive. Events usually occur in series of four or sometimes five, and just as it seems that nothing is happening a significant progression takes place that has been anticipated right along. In one passage of the creation story, for example, the trickster Coyote asks a maiden what he must do to win her (Zolbrod 1984:131–133). As she repeats her determination not to tell him, he poses the question four times until she finally answers that he must kill one of the monsters. But their exchange seems to lead nowhere, for he then merely walks away without responding. Later she is surprised when Coyote returns with the giant's scalp and demands to know what she will have him do for her next. Thus the relationship between them grows in a quiet, understated buildup of tension until it explodes in a sexual orgy during which he transmits the power of his witchcraft to her. The climax of this passage may seem surprising, since each seemingly emotionless exchange between them is heavily styled with repetition. Balanced between what looks like carefully measured statements and repeated gestures, their behavior moves almost imperceptibly toward its outcome.

The key to understanding what ultimately takes place is that the details are amplified with each repetition while the syntax shifts to a different pattern. Every time the maiden kills Coyote she does so with what looks like an added determination to be rid of him, possibly resisting a repressed hope that he will survive and return. One informant expressed his belief to me that she really wanted him to come back. Why else did she tell him what he had to do to win her in the first place? And later on, when he ultimately succeeds in copulating with her, why will she at first agree to share her blanket with him? The effect of such a passage is similar to that of a series of widening concentric circles. Implicit in what the maiden does is an ambivalence not at first evident, wherein her replies contradict what she really wants. She denies him but she hopes he will continue questioning her; she kills him but she wants him to live; she takes him farther away to do him in but she desires his return. As she continues to rebuke him, he gradually succeeds in winning her over in an almost surrealistic progression of events. A striking feature of Navajo ceremonial narrative, in fact, is that as incredible as they are, the stories display a dimension of psychological and emotional credibility in a stylized, patterned context.

So it is with the seemingly balanced, contained sandpaintings, where a recognizable figure is juxtaposed, so to speak, with an abstract design so that a subtly dynamic undercurrent destabilizes the pattern. The more conspicuous elements appear in pairs and sets of four placed evenly around a central focal point; but on closer examination, smaller, less obvious elements offset each other. A fixed center is merely an optical illusion which must be restored to the vision once it is denied. It is an ideal that is never fully grasped but always begging to be apprehended; an ideal that can be recovered only with the help of external forces summoned from beyond the perimeter to a central place where healing is needed. Only then can order be restored so that familiar cycles of thought and action may resume, for the family and the clan as well as for the patient, since the social group suffers disorder as long as any one individual in it is unwell.

IV

The image of a center counterposed against a perimeter applies broadly to Navajo culture and not just to poetry and design. It is seen in the continued use of hogans and sweatlodges; in the Navajo conception of geography, where four sacred mountains continue to mark the limits of the Navajo world; in the practiced tradition of carrying pollen when leaving the reservation; and in the desire of even the most modernized Navajos to return home, especially to die. Furthermore, this image may also lead to a fuller, more unified appraisal of other Native American cultures. It is well to remember that each tribe has its own distinct identity. But it is also worth discovering how those tribes may be linked, particularly if such associations help define the same kind of coherence which the Navajo ceremonial narratives give to other Navajo artifacts.

Consider again the emergence of the insect people from an inner world where four rivers flow in the four cardinal directions through surrounding spheres. With some minor variations that figure is common elsewhere in the Southwest and in Mesoamerica. It occurs uniformly among the Uto-Aztecan peoples who had settled in both regions long before the Navajos migrated from the north. Athabascan forerunners arrived sometime after the tenth century and established a distinct Navajo identity in the San Juan valley on the Colorado Plateau by the time of Columbus (Van Valkenburgh 1938). They represent an entirely different linguistic stock, and while they brought a distinctly different hunting and gathering culture with them, they were then, as they are today, an adaptive people who assimilated ideas readily. From the Pueblos they learned how to cultivate, possibly as late as the period following the Spanish counterinsurgency ten years after an uprising in the late 1600s, when many of the natives of the Rio Grande valley fled from the returning Spaniards to the San Juan region west of the Divide. With the agriculture they acquired, the Navajos seem to have adapted the accompanying emergence mythology to their own indigenous storytelling and ceremonial practice.

Apparently the image of crossing streams deep within the earth had long prevailed in the high desert country of the American Southwest before the arrival of the Navajos. Tyler, for example, writes that in the Western Keresian Pueblo of Laguna, "there are several fragmentary versions" of cosmic creation "which include the common fourfold underworld, whose lowest level is white, and the succeeding ones red, blue, and yellow" (1964:105). Gunn repeats a Laguna account of a hole in the lowermost world "into which flowed four mighty rivers from the four cardinal points" (1917:110–111). Even though small details may vary, the large theme of emergence from a watery inner world through successive worlds is constant from one Pueblo group to another, and the image of a cross extending beyond one or more circles occurs often. Beyond that, the notion of one world encircling an earlier, more elemental world can be traced through Mesoamerica to the ancient homeland of the Mayas. Intertribal commerce ranging from the Yucatán peninsula and the area now known as Guatemala and Honduras to a point as far north as Mesa Verde in southwestern Colorado may have been common for so long during the pre-Columbian period that the notion was thoroughly diffused in one or another direction well before any Europeans arrived (see Tyler 1964:184).

The figure of the enclosed cross is likely to have spread with the diffusion of agriculture. It is a widely and deeply pervasive image that presents many puzzles, but I believe that the poetry of that vast area could shed light on it. The pattern had evidently become so common by the time of Columbus that it prevailed not only in myth, ritual, and storytelling, but in illustrations and designs of all sorts. It became an omnibus symbol of a fully developed world view that incorporated agriculture, tribal histories, social and political systems, traditions of art, methods of technology, and even science—all of which were conveyed by way of stories told and retold across the span of generations. Architecturally it is reflected in the ceremonial kivas used not only by all Pueblo groups but by the pre-Puebloan Anasazi who once populated the entire San Juan basin, where they had obviously settled and begun to farm as early as the time of Christ.

Still used ritually by the Pueblos today, the kiva is a subterranean or partially submerged circular structure containing in the center of its floor a *sipapu* or symbolic emergence place. Hence, each is a circle embracing a smaller circle, not to mention the circular bench placed against the inner wall where spectators and participants may sit as they watch or become involved in the various rites practiced there, or where they may listen to elders recite traditional stories. Chaco Canyon's Casa Rinconada, the largest kiva known, actually resembles a quartered circle. Two entryways—one to the north and one to the south—duplicate a north-south axis defined by Pueblo Alto on the northern rim of the Canyon one mile off, and Tsin Kletsin one mile to the south on the opposite rim. Furthermore, as figure E illustrates, niches in the east and west walls catch the light of the rising and setting sun on the morning and evening respectively of the summer and winter solstices, marking the northern and southern extremes of its position each year as it moves daily from east to west (Aveni 1984:29; Zeilik 1984). The kiva might very well serve not only as a calendrical and ceremonial center but also as a dynamic model of a mythic world fully integrated with the movement of the sun and passing of the seasons.

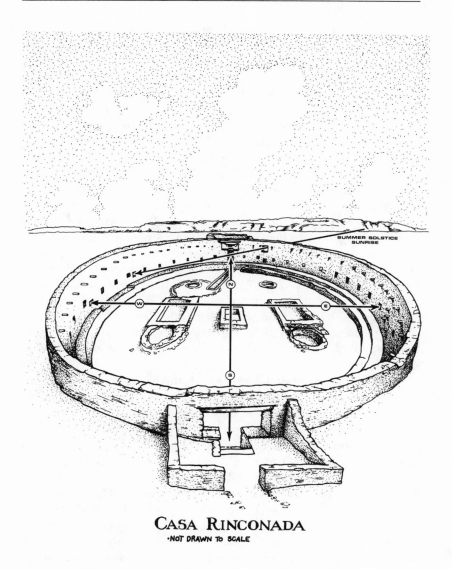

CASA RINCONADA
·NOT DRAWN TO SCALE·

Figure E. The kiva at Casa Rinconada, Chaco Canyon, New Mexico. Drawing by Snowden Hodges, courtesy of Ray Williamson. Reprinted in Aveni (1984), p. 31. Duplicated with permission.

I find it hard to imagine that such ingenious engineering could have existed without a well-defined tradition of emergence and a highly developed pattern of storytelling to give meaning to the whole configuration complete with its seasonal rituals and a sophisticated conception of time and space. Tyler writes that "a sense of the importance of directions is so ingrained in the Pueblos that it has become almost instinctive; the whole community orients itself around a center with a rigidity which would be compulsive if it were a question of individual behavior" (1964:170). To the four cardinal directions on the horizontal plane add the two vertical directions extending from nadir to zenith and a three-dimensional universe obtains. Elsewhere, Tyler says that "the six directions permeate every phase of Pueblo thinking and activity. The directions give meaning to the concept that one's pueblo is the center of the universe, around which point days, seasons, life, and crops, and even the dead revolve" (p. 169). In fact, as the village of Zuni has expanded, the tendency has been for new homes to be placed in an axis extending from the center of town in the four cardinal directions (Kroeber 1917:122). Thus, as Tyler adds, "this deep rooted tendency to orient the house in a quarterly manner must have been ancient," and it must have prevailed among the other Pueblo villages (1964:171).

The alignment of architecture with the heavens is by no means limited to the Pueblos and their Anasazi precursors. In a similarly abstracted form, the image of quartered concentric circles appears adjacent to many of what Anthony Aveni calls naked eye observatories—sites where ancient peoples throughout Mesoamerica kept track of the seasons by watching celestial bodies, marking in particular the position of the rising and setting sun each day. In a seminal article on Native American archaeoastronomy (1978), Aveni describes some of the resulting calendrical systems of the early Indians of that region based on those solar observations. Those who plotted the exact point on the eastern horizon where the sun rose each day were also expert stargazers who oriented their temples carefully so that they could tell with absolute precision what day it was and when each solstice and equinox would occur. And as with the Navajos and the Pueblos, their sun was an effigy of a major character in what the Zuni call a *chimiky'ana'kowa*—an ancient story about how in the *inoote* or long ago, the world was shaped and the surrounding cosmos acquired its manifest form (Tedlock 1972:222). Other celestial bodies including the moon and the stars were also figureheads of characters, especially among the Mayans and the Aztecs, who associated them with temporal units in the process of deifying time at all levels, from individual days to cycles of years running into the millions (León-Portilla 1973).

Less extravagantly, but more readily grasped, the sun priests of the various Pueblos to this day announce when to plant, when to harvest, when to conduct the important ceremonies by observing the sun through various man-made apertures, as Zeilik writes (1984). He presents strong evidence that those shamans associate the seasonal cycle with traditional stories about the creation of their respective villages and about the origin of agriculture. Even corn is "personified"—or deified anthropomorphically—as one Zuni ritual narrative exemplifies (Cushing 1896). Zeilik argues that priestly experts who presided over their respective calendrical sites among such Anasazi population centers as Chaco Canyon and Mesa Verde knew the traditional stories as well as they knew how to read the skies, which represented a vast stage upon which those narratives were reenacted. Just as man-made items replicate things that the stories tell, so does the whole cosmos. The movement of celestial objects; a germinating seed; the passing of the seasons; the well-being of individuals, clans, entire villages, and whole tribes—all are part of an overriding unity, an organic model of a cosmos which humans are obliged to preserve by duplicating it in their thoughts, their behavior, their implements and utensils, their works of art, and especially in how they tell their most sacred stories.

V

Aveni calls the circular image that appears nearby the spectacular temple-observatories scattered across Mesoamerica the "pecked cross symbol" (1978:66). Since Aveni first wrote about this image, it has become the object of careful attention as additional likenesses of it have been discovered (see Aveni, Hartung, and Buckingham 1978; Aveni and Hartung 1982; Iwaniszewski 1982). Embossed in stone, it varies little from site to site, but never beyond easy recognition, as figure F suggests. Its features have been observed in detail and carefully analyzed to match calendrical and astronomical data. Yet, "the full meaning" of its symbolism "still eludes us," as Aveni has written (1978:68). When matched with some of the principal

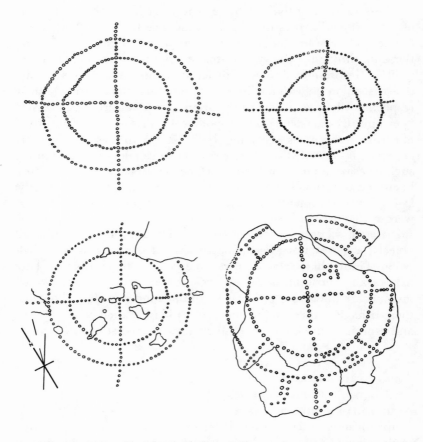

Figure F. Examples of Pecked Cross Petroglyphs found throughout Mesoamerica. Top two diagrams appear in Aveni (1978), p. 66. Reprinted with permission from *Technology Review*. Bottom two facsimiles reprinted with permission from *Archaeoastronomy*, vol. 5, no. 3 (1982): Anthony Aveni and Horst Hartung, "Discovery of Two New Pecked Cross Petroglyphs," p. 21.

surviving pre-Columbian narratives of Mesoamerica and the American Southwest, however, the pecked circle may not be quite so mysterious. Although the individual dots reflect the integrated cycle of solar and ceremonial years among the Mayans by virtue of their quantity and the way they are arranged (Aveni 1978; Edmonson 1971:xv), the overall pattern bears a striking resemblance to the pattern described in the opening of the Navajo creation story and its cognate Pueblo narratives. It is also reflected in the *Popul Vuh* of the Quiche Maya, which likewise tells of the creation of four successive worlds, and which includes a description of four rivers forming a crossroads deep in an enclosed world below (see Edmonson 1971, especially pp. 68–69). The notion of earlier worlds created prior to the building of this world is also familiar among the narratives of other Central American cultures (see León-Portilla 1969:30–59). Usually the earlier domains are associated directly or indirectly with the underworld and are presided over by "innumerable gods of the four directions" (p. 31). In what is perhaps the oldest such story, "four suns or ages have existed before the present era," during which time "there has been an evolution in spiral form, and each successive age has brought better elements, plants and human beings" (p. 34).

Given the evidence at hand, then, could the figure of the pecked cross or the quartered circle be—among other things—a pan-Indian reference to the theme of emergence and the allied theme of balanced opposites as they are articulated in the Navajo creation story and given shape in the way many sandpaintings are composed? Whatever else the symbol means, does it incorporate into a unified scheme conceptions of time, space, ceremonial life, agricultural practice, male and female identity, life and death, and ideal behavior—all synthesized in a communally shared narrative transmitted carefully from generation to generation? And does that narrative have various counterparts among other tribes? I suspect so, although as yet the evidence is incomplete. But the Navajo creation story, which is the most comprehensive Native American chimiky'ana'kowa I know of to have found its way into printed English, may offer some clues; especially as the Navajos appear to have acquired their ideas about emergence from the ancient Anasazi by way of the Pueblos in a long-populated region where early contact with ancient Mesoamerican tribes might have stimulated an exchange of stories as far back as two thousand years ago.

Perhaps the meaning of the ubiquitous quartered circle may not be so elusive after all, even though it remains to be determined how closely the emergence motif of the Pueblos and the Navajos matches what is known about creation legends of Central America. If we examine the poetry of that whole region from a broad perspective, however, such a design might take on the added coherence that the Navajo creation story gives to the sandpaintings. Like the ceremonial narratives I have studied, that poetry is apt to give voice to material objects that silently beg for added interpretation, thereby speaking in behalf of people who wondered intelligently about the origin of life, about the relationship between cosmic energy and germinating seeds, or about other large questions that alert minds have confronted in all great civilizations.

When life and time are predicated upon each other, as in Navajo culture, we do not have mere storytelling in any quaint or superstitious sense. We have poetic activity at its richest, which is asserting a philosophy, defining a way of life, providing a world view, and establishing a traditional identity to be handed down from one generation to another and to be recognized and preserved by all who care for poetry. When poetry is seen to function with other works of art the way classical Navajo stories work in conjunction with sandpaintings, it gives all artistic achievement its full measure. More than that, it assumes its proper place as the highest human function because it enunciates the distinctive ability of humankind to envision and conceptualize in any medium.

REFERENCES

Aveni, Anthony F. 1978. Old and New World Naked-Eye Astronomy. *Technology Review* 81 (2):60–72.
———. 1984. Native American Astronomy. *Physics Today* (June):24–32.
Aveni, Anthony F., and Horst Hartung. 1982. Discovery of Two New Pecked Cross Petroglyphs. *Archaeoastronomy* 5 (3):21–23.
Aveni, Anthony F., Horst Hartung, and Beth Buckingham. 1978. The Pecked Cross Symbol in Ancient Mesoamerica. *Science* 202:267–279.
Cushing, Frank. 1896. The Generation of the Seed of Seeds, or the Origin of Corn. *Outline of Zuni Creation Myths*. Washington, D.C.: Bureau of American Ethnology, Thirteenth Annual Report: 391–398.

Edmonson, Monro S. 1971. *The Book of Counsel: The Popol Vuh of the Quiche Maya of Guatemala*. New Orleans: Middle American Research Institute, Tulane University, Publication 35.

Forbes, Jack. 1960. *Apache, Navaho, and Spaniard*. Norman: University of Oklahoma Press.

Grant, Campbell. 1978. *Canyon de Chelly: Its People and Rock Art*. Tucson: The University of Arizona Press.

Gunn, John M. 1917. *Schat-Chen: History, Traditions and Narratives of the Queres Indians of Laguna and Acoma*. Albuquerque: Albright and Anderson.

Haile, Father Berard. 1932. *The Story of Beadway Told By Curly Txoaxedlini of Chinle, Arizona*. Manuscript Collection, Museum of Northern Arizona, Ms: 12–8–1,2.

———. 1981. *Women Versus Men: A Conflict of Navajo Emergence*. Lincoln: University of Nebraska Press. American Tribal Religions, vol. 6.

Halpern, Katherine, Susan Brown McGreevy, Nancy Parezo, and Rain Parrish. 1982. *Woven Holy People: Navajo Sandpainting Textiles From the Permanent Collection, Forty-Fifth Anniversary Exhibition*. Santa Fe: Wheelwright Museum of the American Indian.

Hatcher, Evelyn Payne. 1974. *Visual Metaphors: A Formal Analysis of Navajo Art*. St. Paul: West Publishing Co.

Iwaniszewski, Stanislaw. 1982. New Pecked Cross Designs Discovered at Teotihuacan. *Archaeoastronomy* 5 (4):22–23.

Kluckhohn, Clyde, and Dorothea Leighton. 1974. *The Navajo*. Cambridge: Harvard University Press.

Kroeber, Alfred L. 1917. *Zuni Kin and Clan*. New York: Anthropological Papers of the American Museum of Natural History, Vol. 16, Part 2.

León-Portilla, Miguel. 1969. *Pre-Columbian Literatures of Mexico*. Norman: University of Oklahoma Press.

———. 1973. *Time and Reality in the Thought of the Maya*. Boston: Beacon Press.

Matthews, Washington. 1887. *The Mountain Chant: A Navajo Ceremony*. Washington, D.C.: Bureau of American Ethnology, Fifth Annual Report. Reprinted by the Rio Grande Press, Glorieta, New Mexico, 1970.

———. 1897. *Navajo Legends*. Boston: Houghton Mifflin and Co.

Newcomb, Franc J., and Gladys A. Reichard. 1975. *Sandpaintings of the Navajo Shooting Chant*. New York: Dover Publications.

Reichard, Gladys. 1950. *Navajo Religion: A Study of Symbolism*. Princeton: Princeton University Press.

———. 1977. *Navajo Medicine Man Sandpaintings*. New York: Dover Publications. Originally published by J. J. Augustin under the title *Navajo Medicine Man*.

Spencer, Katherine. 1957. *Mythology and Values: An Analysis of Navajo Chantway Myths*. Philadelphia: American Folklore Society.

Tedlock, Dennis. 1972*a*. *Finding the Center: Narrative Poetry of the Zuni Indians*. New York: Dial Press.

————. 1972*b*. Pueblo Literature: Style and Verisimilitude. In *New Perspectives On the Pueblos,* ed. Alfonso Ortiz. Albuquerque: University of New Mexico Press.

Tyler, Hamilton A. 1964. *Pueblo Gods and Myths*. Norman: University of Oklahoma Press.

Van Valkenburgh, Richard F. 1938. *A Short History of the Navajo People*. Window Rock, Arizona: U.S. Department of the Interior, Navajo Service. Reprinted in *Navajo Indians III*. Garland Series in American Indian Ethnohistory. New York: Garland Publishing Co.

Wyman, Leland, C., Maude Oaks, and Joseph Campbell. 1957. *Beautyway: A Navajo Ceremonial*. New York: Pantheon Books.

————. 1983. *Southwest Indian Drypainting*. Albuquerque: The University of New Mexico Press.

Zeilik, Michael. 1984. The Ethnoastronomy of the Historic Pueblos: I. Calendrical Sun Watching. Unpublished Manuscript Submitted to the Archaeoastronomy Supplement, *Journal for the History of Astronomy*.

Zolbrod, Paul G. 1979. Big Giant and the Monster Slayers: An Introductory Look at Navajo Ceremonial Poetry. In *Proceedings of the Seventh Congress of the International Comparative Literature Association,* eds. Milan V. Cimic, Juan Ferrate, and Eva Kushner. Montreal: Kunst and Wissen Erich Bieber.

————. 1984. *Diné bahane': The Navajo Creation Story*. Albuquerque: The University of New Mexico Press.

Anthologies and Narrators

DELL HYMES

I

I want to address the relation between anthologies and ethnopoetics. I want to argue that ethnopoetics provides a foundation on which anthologies should as much as possible be based, and to say that this is not for the sake of those who practice ethnopoetics, but for the sake of those who first performed the stories which anthologies and ethnopoetics address. Whatever else ethnopoetics may be taken to be, it is first of all a matter of taking seriously the ways in which narrators select and group words. It is through attention to such choices that individuality of attitude and style can be recognized.

This relation came forcibly to my attention recently because I was asked to review a new anthology.[1] I will discuss that anthology as an indication of the current situation. While criticizing it, I will also provide an index that makes its original material more accessible. Then I will discuss the difference that ethnopoetics makes to two of the texts, and narrators, in the anthology. By doing so, I hope to reveal the interest and value of a body of material from Oregon—texts in Kalapuya—that has hitherto been little noticed.

II

The anthology in question is *American Indian Myths and Legends,* selected and edited by Richard Erdoes and Alfonso Ortiz. The collaboration itself is significant and admirable. Erdoes, born in

Frankfurt, Germany, and educated in Europe, has lived in the United States for some time, and published a number of books on the American West, including *Lame Deer, Seeker of Visions*. Alfonso Ortiz is a Tewa from San Juan, New Mexico, holder of a doctorate in anthropology from Chicago, and, since 1982, a MacArthur Fellowship. He is a professor of anthropology at the University of New Mexico, and a leader of the Association on American Indian Affairs, a man for whom I have the greatest respect. In what follows I take Erdoes, the senior author, to be primarily responsible for the characteristics of the anthology.

The collaboration is admirable, because one point of view would be that only persons of Indian descent should use such materials. (Let us set aside the fact that some who claim Indian identity are only partly Indian in descent, or even discovered not to be so at all.) The fact is that the underlying patterns revealed by ethnopoetics are not available in consciousness, even to those who enjoy an uninterrupted heritage. Like the beautiful and complex patterns of the languages themselves, the patterns that make so many Indian narratives a kind of poetry are acquired and employed without awareness. They are not topics of analytic discussion. The languages lack terms for them. Where continuity in the ancestral language has been broken, for Indian and non-Indian alike, the patterning has to be brought to awareness by the discovery of an appropriate method. Even where continuity has not been broken, transformation of an oral artistry to what is seen on a page requires conscious choices of the same kind. For the present, most work of this kind is done by persons trained in the kind of attention and discovery required by descriptive linguistics. One must hope that the proportion of Indian participants will grow, but the contribution that such work can make to proper appreciation of Indian tradition, and to educational efforts, must depend for the time being to a great extent on persons not of Indian descent. Even when the present imbalance is righted, it will always be desirable to have both "insiders" and "outsiders" share the work. Accuracy and depth of insight require a dialectic between both groups. A world in which knowledge of each people was owned exclusively by that people itself would be culturally totalitarian. Just as it is indefensible to have an anthropology in which only outsiders know, and insiders are only known, so it is simply to reverse that inequity. None of us is able to stand outside ourselves sufficiently to know ourselves comprehensively. The European-derived cultures of the United States need an ever-increasing amount of analysis by Indian people. Conversely, the disciplines which contribute to ethnopoetics are in principle not the prisoners of any one ethnicity.

Another point of view might be that anyone can do anything at all with Indian materials. To a great extent, this is the case: A great deal is in the public domain. Nor is such total openness ultimately a bad thing. Certainly one does not want to treat each original text as a perfection from which every other use is a falling off. That was not the nature of the original tradition itself, and many contemporary Indian authors themselves demonstrate the vitality in transformation of the original traditions in their stories, novels, poems, plays, films. And various of the retellings make the material available to those who might not otherwise encounter it.

Still, if a distinction between Indian and scholar is to be made, here a worthwhile division of labor might be maintained. Let scholars of whatever ancestry contribute what they can to the analysis and understanding of traditional materials. Let those who are not Indian leave the continuing reworking of traditional materials to Indian people. They can be used as inspiration for poems of one's own, yes; but let those of us who are not of Indian descent not act as if the texts of Indians themselves are ours to change. Modern equivalents of the Brothers Grimm, presenting as authentic tradition what they have rewritten, perform a disservice (see Ellis 1983). A century from now, perhaps, it would not matter; but probably it will be a century before the basic work of making available original texts in accurate editions is even halfway complete, resources and scholars being so few. Once it is possible to consult an original that has been verified against the original field recording; whose translation has been reconsidered for consistency and in the light of all that is known about the language; and whose lines and alignments are visible on the page; then other handlings of the text will not be confused with the original, as now they may be. (Such is the case with some stories in the anthology discussed here.) No one mistakes Robert Lowell's imitations for the poems in other languages from which they derive, but we have yet to reach that stage for much American Indian tradition.

In suggesting a division of labor, I do not imply a divorce. The anthology in question here tacitly assumes that the enjoyment of Indian stories has nothing to do with scholarship or literature. None

of the Indian writers making fresh use of tradition is mentioned—
Peter Blue Cloud, James "Gogisgo" Arnett, Ed Edmo, N. Scott
Momaday, Duane Niatum, Simon Ortiz, Leslie Marmon Silko,
James Welch, and others. None of the attention to the traditions
and modern writings by literary scholars is mentioned—nothing of
the Association for the Study of American Indian Literature, or the
work of Karl Kroeber, Jarold Ramsey, Andrew Wiget, and others
that is represented in this volume and its predecessor, *Smoothing the
Ground*. And nothing is said of the comparative and analytical literature, from the essays of Franz Boas and the works of Stith
Thompson to the more recent studies by Alan Dundes, Melville
Jacobs, Claude Lévi-Strauss, and others.

Let us infer that theories, methods, studies, have been set aside
as of no relevance to the life of the stories themselves, or to the
living sources. That kind of "populism" is a form of segregation.
The public, including the Indian public, is kept at the back of the
bus of the mind; allowed to enjoy stories, but prohibited from
entering the conversation about them which is going on at the front
of the bus. Even if it is a question of enjoyment only, the public,
including the Indian public, may enjoy knowing how other versions
go, and having the chance to reflect on the differences. A sympathetic public may welcome the knowledge that some of the best
scholars of the century have devoted themselves to such stories. One
may judge Lévi-Strauss's interpretations, in terms of structural
transformation, to overshoot the mark at times; but if one wants to
show the worth of such stories, why not mention that the world's
most famous anthropologist has devoted years of his life to them?

Neither scholars nor Indian people who wish to use an anthology such as this to gain further access to the traditions are well
served. On the whole I want to stress that it is the public, including
the Indian public, that is the worst served. A scholar may be
annoyed by a citation such as "Based on a tale from 1901" (Erdoes
and Ortiz 1984:385) for an Alsea story, but will know that the only
possible sources for such a story are Frachtenberg's 1920 monograph and four texts published separately in 1917. Finding the story
in question to be absent from the former, he or she will know it must
be in the latter; but an Indian at Siletz or Grand Ronde—recently
reinstituted reservations of western Oregon—aware of some Alsea
ancestry and wishing to trace some content for it, would be stopped.
And everyone will be frustrated by a citation such as "Based on

four fragments dating from 1883 to 1910" (p. 45), or "Based on fragments recorded in the 1880s" (p. 47).

Scholarship serves the public as well as scholars. People of Indian descent, deprived through history of fluency in an ancestral language or tradition, often seek to regain something of it. Much of the scholarly literature, to be sure, is not as accessible to non-scholars as it might be, and that includes writings of my own. If wanted as more than a symbol of a heritage, it may not serve; but many are lay scholars themselves, and others can make use of scholarship, and go on beyond one book.

Being able to go on matters because a good many of the stories in this book are said to be "retold," "based on," "from," "reported by." I have not been able to infer consistent meanings for the various phrases, but "retold" seems to go with the integration of more than one original, while "from" and "reported by" seem to go with the close following of a single source. Even in the latter cases, there appears to have been some reworking. The issue is not that the original translations are sacrosanct. Of course they are not (see Hymes 1981a, chapter 1, and the retranslation of Kalapuya texts below). The issue is whether or not the changed version does justice to the principle recognized in the introduction, that the stories "are embedded in the ancient languages" (p. xi). Sometimes yes, often no.

Some of the reworking is advantageous, in that it liberates separate turns at talk into separate units on the page (e.g., the Cochiti "Crow and Hawk," given here as "The neglectful mother" [pp. 417–418]. Even here some lines of the original are omitted. There appears to be a parallelism, a doubling, at the end of the story that the omission of lines destroys. The content is present, but not the shape. The same is true of the beginning of the Cochiti "Salt Woman is refused food" (p. 61). While introducing conjunctions not present in the original, the telling here omits the second time that Old Salt Woman is refused food, a time that includes direct speech from her. Direct speech, and the pointing up of significance by repetition, are vital features of American Indian narrative. To omit them suggests an insensitivity to the traditional style (see Benedict 1931).

Even stranger is the inclusion in this anthology of versions from other anthologies in which the stories have been freely rewritten. The Alsea story included here is taken from its retelling by Lopez

(1977). The actual story does not begin, as it does here, with the mention of Coyote by name. Its narrator, Thomas Walker (not named here), tells such stories from the standpoint of women Coyote is trying to deceive. He brings such a story around at the end to a question on their part, who was that? Must have been Coyote. Only then does Coyote's name, dramatically, occur.

Every North American Indian people has a trickster figure, but not every one has Coyote. Some have Rabbit, some the Stellar Jay, some Raven, some Mink. And just as Christians have struggled and disagreed as to the relationships between the major powers of their tradition, especially with regard to the attributes of omnipotence and goodness, so Indian people have resolved in various ways the ambiguity of figures who can be both benevolent and buffoons. The Kwakiutl of British Columbia assign one series of adventures to the trickster, Mink, and another to a separate Transformer who has no animal form and whose name, "born to be q'ani," is not further interpretable. The anthology reprints a Transformer story (pp. 362–365), but from Lopez who substitutes "Coyote"—a trickster, and not even the Kwakiutl trickster (1977). If I were a Kwakiutl, I'd be angry.

III

The great virtue of the anthology is that it demonstrates the vitality of the narrative traditions. For any who may think of such traditions as extinct, it will be surprising to find that so many of the stories were collected in recent years, and not only at reservations. Of the 166 narratives, a good third are published here for the first time. Ortiz contributes seven from his native Tewa (the tellers' identities are properly kept confidential). Erdoes recorded one Cheyenne story at the Crow intertribal fair (p. 392), and a Bruel Sioux story around a pow-wow campfire in Pine Ridge, South Dakota (p. 374). One Zuni story was told in several versions during a sacred clown dance and pantomime at Zuni in 1964 (p. 280), and a Cherokee story at a Cherokee treaty council meeting in New York City (p. 107). Leonard Crow Dog told Erdoes stories both in New York City (p. 496) and on Rosebud reservation (p. 499). David Red Bird, identified as a young Green Bay Indian (p. 151), is the source of new Ojibway tellings (pp. 151, 161), as well as of a Winnebago telling (p. 166).

Sometimes we are told that a Cheyenne story was interpreted by someone (pp. 37, 485; see reference to translation on p. 247). Otherwise we are perhaps to assume that the stories were told in English. Certainly it is important to recognize that the traditions may be maintained in English and in diverse localities. The Coos traditions of Annie Miner Petersen that Melville Jacobs recorded in Coos (1940, 1941) were also transmitted in English to a descendant such as George Wasson, later a dean at the University of Oregon, who maintains this knowledge.

There are some 57 new tellings, then, scattered among some 109 others. There is no index, however, to lead one to them, or that would lead one to stories from a particular people. The one index is of titles, and not necessarily the titles that the stories had in the original. Indeed, the editors indicate that they set no store by titles (p. xiii). Yet titles can be scholarly aids, as in the case of the standard catch-phrase "Bear and Deer" for what is represented here in a Miwok version as "The coming of thunder" (p. 216). And when recorded in the native language, titles can express native orientations toward the narrative (see Hymes 1981a, ch. 7). Thus one of the series of Chinook myths that is natively entitled "Bluejay and Ioi" (the name of his elder sister) here becomes "Bluejay visits ghost town" (Erdoes and Ortiz 1984:457). That is not a bad way to differentiate the one story from two others of the same title, but it eliminates the frame that the Chinook title provides. Naming and order of naming in titles covary with outcomes, and the type, "X and elder sibling," is central to a part of Chinookan tradition.

To facilitate access to the new material, I have prepared an index of the names of tribal groups, which gives the initial page of the story. (I have also compiled an index of tribal groups that gives the number of the story in the sequence of the volume as a whole, and will provide a copy on request.) In certain cases, I have provided additional information as to linguistic affiliation (e.g., Chinookan, Iroquois, Salish). The affiliation of the story on page 385 is uncertain, as the heading says "Cheyenne," but the postscript says "Retold from several North Californian fragments." The new material is in italics. To take the Tewa material as an illustration, one might refer to the new material as EO (Erdoes and Ortiz): 175, EO: 285, EO: 295, and so on. (The index may be found at the end of this chapter.)

IV

The great virtue of the Erdoes/Ortiz anthology is also part of a contradiction: The fifty-seven tellings are identified as coming from persons; the stories that come from other books are identified only as coming from tribes. We learn the names (with one shy exception) of the tellers visited by Erdoes, and something interesting about them. Not so with the rest. With them the only names are the names of tribes, or occasionally of someone who is not an original source or Indian at all. A Kalapuya myth is said to be "told by Barry Lopez in 1977" (p. 356). Lopez, of course, is the editor and rewrite-man of another anthology (1977). The myth was told in Santiam Kalapuya (there are three Kalapuya languages) by a man I once had the privilege of meeting in his home, John B. Hudson. In this particular case one could not get back to Hudson even by finding the reference for the story in the back of the book. One has to know to look under Jacobs for *Kalapuya Texts*, and the page numbers given there are to a myth in another language, Tualatin Kalapuya, recorded in the nineteenth century by A. S. Gatschet, probably from Wapato Dave. A scholar, again, can find such things out and trace down the location of the actual original and its source; but why should an anthology preserve a rewriting by a white and let the name of the Indian be lost? Someone aware of some Kalapuya ancestry, perhaps through Hudson, would like to find his name here.

Should one care about the identities of Indians now dead, even if one is not descended from them? Yes. The stories told long ago, just as those told today, came from individuals. Creative personal use of tradition did not begin in our lifetime; it is as old as the narrative art itself. True, collectors in the past often obscured the fact. Usually they gave credit to their sources by name and thanked them, but typically they published stories from a single person as though they represented an entire community. Thus, the myths we have in the language of the Clackamas Chinook, who lived near Oregon City, Oregon, and whose survivors were removed to the Grande Ronde reservation to the west, come from a single woman: Victoria Howard, who dictated them near the end of her life in 1929 and 1930. Her narratives reflect the line of women from whom she learned them, and their experience of a shattered culture. Plots of male adventure are told from the standpoint of their effect on women and children. But the collector published and discussed them all as expressive simply of "the Clackamas" (Jacobs 1958, 1959a, 1959b, 1960).

The narrators, then, create as well as preserve. When what they have said is adequately recorded, and the devices and designs they have employed are understood, we can recognize both a tribal art and a personal voice. It is this exact art which must be the foundation of our attention and interpretation.

V

Three universal principles inform this art. The first is that the narratives consist not of sentences, but of lines. Typically, though not always, a line is a phrase. The second principle, formulated by Jakobson, is that of equivalence (1960): A variety of means is employed to establish formal equivalence between particular lines and groups of lines. The third principle is that formulated by Burke (1925), the arousal and satisfaction of expectation. In other words, the stories are to be heard, or seen, in lines, and thus are a form of poetry. There is a grouping, or segmentation, internal to the tradition not only of lines but also of groups of lines, sometimes at a series of levels. In addition to a segmentation and an architecture, there is also an arc, or series of arcs, to the story, governed by conventional understandings as to the logic or rhetorical form of enacted action.

These principles appear to be universal in that indications of them can be found in oral narrative, even where it survives surrounded by other modes of verbal presentation, some inimical to them, such as those of the prose of schools. Where there is no competitor, where oral narrative is the central art—as among American Indians—the principles can inform accomplishments that deserve a place in any account of literature.

The three principles can be seen to apply to the Kalapuya text included in the Erdoes/Ortiz anthology.[2] First I will present a retranslation and realignment of the story. Retranslation is necessary because published translations typically do not preserve the repetitions and parallelisms that establish equivalence. Thus, the recurrent marker of a line or group of lines as a unit ("verse"), the compound particle *lau'mde,* is variously translated in the source as "and," "and then," "now," "now then," "then," and "and when." Here it is translated invariably as "now then," which fits the independent occurrence of *lau* as "now." The notes, keyed to the retranslation by line numbers, indicate other points of revision.

The realignment recognizes the recurrence of "now then" as the marker of significant units. In the Pacific Northwest initial particles of this kind are frequently the central marker of units, together with turns at talk (but other features can be involved or replace them, such as the quotative suffix in Bella Coola). The logic of grouping involves series of three or five, in keeping with other peoples of the same area, the Chehalis and Cowlitz Salish on the Washington side of the lower Columbia River; the Chinookans along the river from its mouth to past the present city of The Dalles; and the Sahaptins, also along the Columbia, overlapping the Chinookans and east of them. I have found such grouping in all sources of Kalapuya tradition: in what probably is the earliest text transmitted in Kalapuya, a war talk delivered by a Tualatin headman, Xiupa, circa 1844; in a text about Yonkalla Kalapuya shamans changing into grizzlies to eat Tualatins, dictated by Dave Yechgawa (both of these were recorded by Gatschet and are published in Jacobs 1945:185–186); in the myth of the four ages of the world, probably also dictated by Wapato Dave Yechgawa (pp. 173–178); in the fine narratives in Mary's River collected from William Hartless in 1914 by L. J. Frachtenberg; and in texts in Santiam collected from John B. Hudson by Jacobs over a decade in the late 1920s and the 1930s (all these in Jacobs 1945).

The architecture implicit in the grouping provides a framework for recognizing elaboration, emphasis, proportion, pace. Yet two things must be said:

First, the grouping is not mechanical. On one hand, the narrator always has options within the principles of patterning. He or she must be understood as mapping sequences of incident, event, and image into sequences of line and verse. On the other hand, the underlying patterning is a grounding, a matrix, but not the exclusive kind of pattern available. Where the matrix is one of three or five, as in Kalapuya, the alternative of pairing may be used for intensity. (Conversely, where the matrix is one of two or four, as in Tonkawa of Texas, the alternative of three-part grouping may be used for intensity [Hymes 1980].) Such intensity is employed by Mr. Hudson in this text, when the action reaches the climax in which Coyote is using his hand to break the dam.

Second, the grouping is a matter not only of structure but also of process. The formal relationships have a semantic sense. In a matrix of pairing there is a sense of this, then that, of initiation and outcome, initiation and outcome. It pervades the architecture, so that one pair of initiation and outcome stands as initiation to the outcome of a succeeding pair. (See the Tonkawa study just cited [Hymes 1980], and the Zuni narrative in Hymes 1982.) Where the matrix is three or five, there is a sense of premise or onset, ongoing, outcome, for a three-unit sequence. For a five-unit sequence, the third unit is pivotal. It stands as outcome to the first three, and as onset to a second sequence of three. Thus in the first scene of this Kalapuya myth, the first three verses have Coyote find a small deer, set aside a small rib, make a money bead.

The making of the money bead stands as onset to a sequence that describes the Frogs' monopoly of water as ongoing information, and Coyote's intention to drink their water as outcome, both of the sequence and the whole scene. The five verses together express an intention and preparation on Coyote's part that is already introduced with the setting aside of a small rib in the second verse. Similarly, the five verses of the third scene consist of a three-part sequence in which Coyote drinks and uses his hand, interlocking with a three-part sequence in which the outcome of the first triad is onset to the water going through and Coyote's culminating pronouncement.

Since the narrator has options, the interpreter does also. More than one formal segmentation is usually possible. One's sense that the right alignment has been discovered is dependent on being able to read the story consistently in terms of the logic of action, the arousal and satisfying of expectation locally as one goes along. Where formal markers are few, the implicit logic may itself be the decisive factor. A further test of an alignment is that other features cohere. It is rewarding to note that the colloquy with the Frogs stands as a distinct ongoing scene (lines 13–21), and that the other turns at talk, by Coyote alone, each culminate the other two scenes, that of preparation (*i*) and that of outcome (*ii*).

Segmentation, in other words, is inseparable from meaning and interpretation. It is rewarding to press a principle of segmentation as far as it will go; one discovers new possibilities. The result, however, must be controlled by a sense of the narrator's intentions and of the coherence of the whole.

The present narrative provides an example. If one were to count instances of the initial marker "now then" as always forming groups of three and five, one would be led to consider the five lines of Coyote's drinking (22, 23, 24, 25, 26) as constituting a stanza. The remaining three verses (27–29, 30, 31–32) would evidently form a stanza as well. The three verses of the colloquy with the Frogs (13, 14–17, 18–21) are clearly a distinct stanza. The material preceding the colloquy (1–12) would then have to have two stanzas as well, if the narrative as a whole is to have a total that conforms to a pattern number (here, five). Yet there are just five instances of verse-marking "now then." That would constitute just one stanza, giving the narrative a total of four. One could reason that the chiasmus of lines 8–9 ("all the time . . . all the time") is striking; perhaps such a device could be taken to constitute a verse. Then there would be six verses, assignable three each to the required two stanzas (1–3, 4–5, 6; 7, 8–9, 10–12).

This is not an implausible conclusion, and it is indeed the one to which I was led in 1981 when I first analyzed the text. By dividing the parts preceding and following the colloquy each into two, however, this analysis interrupts the unity of setting and topic in each. It lessens the symmetry by which each as a whole ends with Coyote's direct speech, and all scenes with someone's speech. It lacks the integration that comes from recognizing in each an interlocking five-part relationship, in which the third unit is simultaneously outcome of one triad and onset of another. These considerations are preferences, to be sure; the text does not quite require them. Two things, however, can be said to be required: (1) not to promote stylistic devices to the status of markers of verse units, unless overall patterning makes such status clear; (2) not to overlook parallelism of form and content (form/meaning covariation). This first analysis does both those things. It promotes a stylistic device (chiasmus in lines 8–9) to the status of marking a verse ad hoc, departing from the otherwise consistent marking of verses by Hudson always with "now then." It overlooks the parallelism of form and content that runs beyond lines 22–26 to include lines 27–29.

There is an incremental repetition of content in the six verses of these lines. After the colloquy with the frogs, two actions by Coyote are paired and repeated: drinking, use of the hand. Lines 27–29 are the third and concluding instance of the use of the hand. Two tracks of onset, ongoing, outcome of action run in tandem here: he drank, he drank, he stopped drinking (22, 24, 26); he put one hand down in, he put his hand down in the water where it was dammed up, he got up, scooped the dirt aside, scooped it out (23, 25, 27–29). (The elaboration of the third use of the hand gives use of the hand a five-line sequence overall.) The drinking and handiwork that to Coyote are satisfaction and service, to the Frogs deception and dirty work, go together for two pairs of verses, then the deception is ended (26) and the work completed (27–29). The threefold pairing is an intensification of the climax of the action (see Hymes 1985c).

Here is the retranslation and realignment, together with the Kalapuya text, also realigned (the orthography has been slightly revised):

COYOTE RELEASES WATER DAMMED UP BY THE FROGS

i.   *[He prepares]*

    (a)   Coyote was going along.   1

            A small deer had died.   2

                Now then Coyote found it.   3

    (b)   Now then he ate it all.   4

            He set aside one small rib.   5

    (c)   Now then he made a money bead out of the small rib

                                     of the deer.   6

    (d)   Now then together the frogs had the water.   7

          All the time they stood guard over the water.   8

             The people bought it all the time.   9

    (e)   Now then Coyote said: 10
            "I am going to drink water,   11
            "The frogs' water."   12

ii.   *[He buys water from the frogs]*
    (a)   Now then he arrived.   13
    (b)   Now he told the frogs: 14
            "I want to drink water.   15
            "I have a large money bead.   16
            "I want to drink a lot of water."   17
    (c)   Now then they told him: 18
            "Do that!   19
            "Drink!   20
            "We will hold your head."   21

iii.   *[He releases the water]*
    (a)   Now then indeed he drank, Coyote.   22
    (b)   Now then he put one hand down in.   23
    (c)   Now then he drank.   24
    (d)   Now then he put his hand down in the water
                        where it was dammed up.   25
    (e)   Now then he stopped drinking water.   26
    (f)   Now then he got up,   27
               he scooped the dirt aside,   28
               he scooped it out.   29
    (g)   Now then the water went through.   30
    (h)   Now then Coyote said: 31
            "All the time water will be everywhere."   32

COYOTE RELEASES WATER DAMMED UP BY THE FROGS

i.   *[He prepares]*
        Asní gum'í·did.   1
        í·sdu-amú·ki' gum'ála'.   2
            Láu'mdé Ašní gumdá'ts.   3
        Láu'mdé gumhú·k má·dfan,   4
        táu'ne i·-sdu-di'na gump'í·.   5
        Láu'mdé giŋge'ts angawetsad guš-í·sdu-di'ná amú·ki'.   6
        Láu'mdé Antg̣ʷág̣ʷa gʷiník ginip'í·ne ambgé'.   7
            Din'á·wi gini'lé·dgʷane ambgé'.   8
               Amím' giniyándan din'é·wi.   9

	Láu'mdé Ašní gum'nag:	10
	"Cǔm'í-čumkʷít ambgé',	11
	"Gus-Antgʷágʷa-dinibgé'."	12
ii.	*[He buys water from the frogs]*	
	Láu'mdé ginthʷúq.	13
	Láu gum'níšdini Antgʷagʷa:	14
	"Čumhuli-dumikʷí'd ambgé'.	15
	"Tsump'í·ne ubéla' aŋgáwetsed.	16
	"Tsumhúli-dumikʷí't lúi-ambgé'."	17
	Láu'mdé gidi·ni'níšdini':	18
	"Gé'ts!	19
	"Dekʷí'd!	20
	"Čindugʷíndubu bugʷa."	21
iii.	*[He releases the water]*	
	Láu'mde wí·neš-wí gindikʷí'd Ašní.	22
	Láu'mdé gint'múi táu'ne-dilágʷa.	23
	Láu'mdé gidikʷí'd.	24
	Láu'mdé gint'múi dilágʷa guš-ambgé' gidehefúgeče·.	
		25
	Láu'mdé gidi·péslau' duŋkʷítye-bgé'.	26
	Láu'mdé gidi·gódga,	27
	giŋgáwi guš-amp'lú' qʷáčefan,	28
	giŋgáwi.	29
	Láu'mdé ambgé' giŋdengán.	30
	Láu'mdé Ašní gum'nág:	31
	"Din'é·wi ambgé' gamtí mátfanču."	32

Notes on Text and Translation.

Line 1 A conventional opening that marks Coyote stories in many groups.

2, 5, 6 Notice the threefold recurrence of "small."

3 The line initial particle pair, "now then" (*lau'–mde*) is withheld until the third line, at which point the narrative action properly begins. Lines 1–2 set the stage. Each verse throughout the story will begin with this pair, except for line 14, which has only *lau*.

8 "all the time" usually has *e·* as its stressed, middle vowel,

as in lines 9 and 32 of this text. Thus *a·* seems marked,
and the translation is underlined (italicized) to show this.

9   Notice the chiasmus begun and ended by "all the time."

7   The original publication shows no translation in this text
for *gʷinik*.Other occurrences show a sense of collectivity,
"together." Thus there are at least two frogs here (as in
an Alsea myth of Coyote and two frog women). Mr.
Hudson has Coyote encounter five frog women in another
story (the Kalapuya counterpart to the Alsea story just
mentioned [pp. 96–97]), and William Hartless has five
frogs in his version of the present story (pp. 236–237);
thus the number here probably is also five.

11–12   The first instance of direct speech culminates the first
scene.

13   Travel with change of location commonly marks a new
scene.

14   The marker now is simply "now."

14–21   First Coyote, then the Frogs, have three lines of direct
speech. Note the eagerness of the Frogs. This excited colloquy in midpassage is the Frogs' only turn at talk. The
first and third scenes, the preparation and outcome, have
each one, final turn at talk, reserved for Coyote.

22   The initial particle pair lacks a second stress in this one
line, most likely accidentally.

23   The line is indented, as are 25 and 27–29, because of the
threefold binary grouping. The action proceeds by incremental repetition in three steps. He drank, put one hand
down in; he drank, put one hand down where it was
dammed; he stopped drinking, scooped out (by hand) the
dirt damming the water. The pairing in the context of an
organization in terms of three and five unit patterns is an
intensification. To be sure, the sequence has three parts,
and the last member of the last pair is elaborated in three
lines, though containing a pairing (he scooped).

28–29   It is not possible to translate *giŋgawi* identically in both
lines idiomatically; the "out" that seems required in line 29
is omitted in line 28 because of the presence of "aside"
(*qʷacefan*). Notice that there is no "aside" in the Kalapuya
in line 29, though Jacobs has it there, and that the two
verbs are identical, though translated differently by Jacobs.

30   The third pair of actions (drink, use hand) is the pivot of
        the third scene. It is outcome to the sequence (22, 23) (24,
        25) (26, 27–29), and is onset to the concluding sequence
        (26, 27–29) (30) (31–32): the dam is broken, the water goes
        through, Coyote pronounces its universal presence hence-
        forth.

32   It is not beyond the subtlety of such narratives that "all the
        time" in this line completes a trio begun in 8, 9.

VI

Let us compare this analysis of ethnopoetic form with the version
of the story published in the anthology under discussion. Here is
the initial portion, corresponding to the first thirteen lines:

> "Coyote takes water from the frog people"
> Coyote was out hunting and he found a dead deer. One of the
> deer's rib bones looked just like a big dentalia shell and Coyote
> picked it up and took it with him. He went up to see the Frog
> People. The Frog People had all the water. When anyone wanted
> any water to drink or cook with or to wash, they had to go and
> get it from the Frog People (Erdoes and Ortiz 1984:355; Lopez
> 1977:177).

As we have seen, John Hudson had in mind a somewhat different story. He began by framing it as a Coyote story with the
widespread convention of "Coyote was going along" (missing here).
His Coyote was *not* out hunting. He did not just *pick up* a *big* dentalia
shell, but ate all of a deer he found, setting aside one *small* rib. Both
deer and rib are appropriately small ("small" is repeated three
times). It is out of chance and his own appetites, as so often happens—here, through his eating the whole deer and at once—that
Coyote has a chance to benefit humanity. The rib did not *look* like
a dentalium (money-bead) shell; Coyote *made* it so. Mr. Hudson's
Coyote does not immediately go to the frogs; he announces his
intention. Nor do the frogs simply *have* all the water; they *sell*,
making the people *buy* what should be available freely. (This point
is elaborated partly in relation to this myth by Lévi-Strauss
[1981:255–284].)

The retelling loses the *purposefulness* of Coyote's behavior. Hudson has Coyote reserve the deer rib, make the rib, announce his intention. Not so in the retelling. And Mr. Hudson reserves the force of direct speech for just three points: the colloquy of the middle scene, and the two statements by Coyote which end each of the other scenes, stating his intention and pronouncing the future. The retelling turns most of the story into a dialogue as Coyote drinks, some nine additional turns at talk in all, four for Coyote, five for the Frogs. Here is an excerpt:

> Coyote began drinking. He drank for a long time. Finally one of the Frog People said, "Hey, Coyote, you sure are drinking a lot of water there. What are you doing that for?"
> Coyote brought his head up out of the water. "I'm thirsty."
> "Oh."
> After a while one of the Frog People said, "Coyote, you sure are drinking a lot of water. Maybe you better give us another shell."
> "Just let me finish this drink," said Coyote, putting his head back underwater.

This elaboration of dialogue reads well enough; it just is not Kalapuya tradition. In the other version known to us, William Hartless elaborates the striking of a bargain between Coyote and the Frogs, but once it is struck, he, like Hudson, has no more talk, only action. It is accurate, then, for the anthology to say "Told by Barry Lopez in 1977" (p. 356). But we were promised Kalapuya, and should have been given, I argue, what was told by John B. Hudson.

VII

All this is not to say that an anthology can safely stick to whatever translation appears in the original source. As has been shown above, the original translation fails to translate one word (line 7), and does not consistently render the structure-marking particles or the repetition of a climactic verb (lines 28–29). And the arrangement on the page of any translation is an implicit analytical claim, an implicit theory of underlying organization. Jacobs in fact proposes such a claim by dividing the text into five parts, marked by (1), (2), (3), (4), and what precedes (1). Here is the text as presented in the original publication:

1. Coyote releases water dammed up by the frogs

Coyote was going along. A small deer had died, and coyote found it, and then he ate it all. He set aside one small rib, and he made a money bead (dentalium) of the little rib of the deer. (1) Now the frogs (at that time) kept the water. They stood guard over the water all the time. The people always bought it (from them). Now then coyote said, "I am going to drink water, the frogs' water." (2) Now then he arrived, and he said to the frogs, "I want to drink water. I have a large money bead (a valuable dentalium). I want to drink a lot of water." Then they said to him, "Do that! drink! We will hold your head." (3) Then indeed coyote drank. And he put one hand down in, and then he drank. Now he put his hand in the water where it was dammed off. (4) And when he ceased drinking water, and when he arose, he scooped the dirt away to one side (he channeled an egress for the dammed up water), he cast it aside. Now then the water went on through and out. And coyote said, "There will be water everywhere for all time."

The organization corresponds to the text as analyzed ethnopoetically as follows:

Jacobs	Hymes
1–6	1–12, (1, 4, 6/6,7,10)
7–12	
13–21	13–21
22–25	22–32 (22–23, 24–25, 26–27/26–27, 30, 31)
26–32	

This is not far from the earlier ethnopoetic analysis discussed above, and reflects the components of the story fairly well. However, it implies that the culminating point of the culminating action (lines 26, 27–29) is disjunct from the two steps which lead up to it. And it suggests no consistent principle for the grouping of verses in larger units. The five units demarcated in the text consist of 3, 2, 3, 4, and 4 verses, respectively. Such divisions of the story are ad hoc, reflecting a certain sense of the story; but they are either merely conveniences for reading and reference, or invitations to attribute openings, closings, and sequences on the basis of one's own un-examined impressions. Ethnopoetic analysis that liberates the lines of a story on the page and allows their disposition to have aesthetic effect also opens up the sources of effect to cumulative scientific study.

VIII

An anthology must almost inevitably conceal the qualities of a narrator. This is because an anthology typically presents only one telling of a story. The reader cannot discover what is due to the tradition of the community and what is due to the particular performance. The depths of the art, the interplay of convention and option, are thus hidden from sight.

The Kalapuya story of Coyote and the water dammed by frogs permits a deeper view, because we are fortunate enough to have more than one telling. William Hartless told the story to L. J. Frachtenberg in 1914 in Mary's River, a dialect entirely mutually intelligible with John B. Hudson's Santiam—Jacobs indeed checked Mr. Hartless's dictations with Hudson in 1936 (Jacobs 1945:204; the text of this story is in Jacobs 1945:236–244).

Mr. Hartless told the story as the first act of a five-act sequence, and I will take up the implications of that later. Here let us compare the first act to Mr. Hudson's account of the same tradition.

The alignment of the narrative in verses, stanzas, and scenes is for the most part readily apparent. In the first scene Coyote decides to travel (lines 1–8), does travel (9–14), and becomes thirsty (15–20). The first stanza (1–8) uniquely pairs Coyote and his wife. The second stanza (9–14) uniquely reports the travel in a three-part arc: he goes, goes on, camps; morning, he goes again, he camps again; he goes five days (the five indicating a summative statement). The third stanza (15–20) uniquely recounts his thirst and a colloquy about satisfying it.

The next three stanzas establish the bargain with the Frogs. Each begins with travel by Coyote (21–22, 31, 37–38). In the first and third (D, F) the travel frames a four-part colloquy with the Frogs, five verses in all. In between comes the report of Coyote's going off to make himself appear wealthy. Thus, both these first two scenes make reported travel intermediate to initial and closing turns at talk. So, in a sense, does the third and last. It begins with Coyote's beginning to drink, including further dialogue with the Frogs (G). Then there is a report of the action of drinking, tearing the earth, being hit, releasing the water and the fish (H). The third and final stanza again has speech, but now only Coyote speaks, pronouncing to the Frogs. (This pattern suggests a style distinct from Mr. Hudson's reserving direct speech for the end of the first and last scenes.)

All verses begin with a time expression (one day, in the morning, five days) or an initial particle marker (now then, to be sure) or consist of a distinct turn at talk. The exception is at the beginning. As with Mr. Hudson's telling, the narrative action proper does not start the story. First the story is framed. Here there is a parallelism: Coyote stayed there / There stayed his wife. It matches the parallelism which follows in what he says, first by himself, then to his wife. Such initial framing seems part of a general practice of bracketing the action off from the immediate setting and everyday life (see the discussion of closings as a renewal of that relationship in Hymes 1981a:322–327). Indeed, openings and closings together seem the devices for making narration of myth participate in what Marcuse considers the power of art to contradict and transform reality (1978). Such power requires the autonomy of aesthetic form. In these initial lines of myths, lacking narrative tense or narrative particle, often formulaic ("Coyote was going along"), we have signals of such autonomy. To omit or revise them is an aesthetic blunder, or even crime.

"Buy it" is italicized for emphasis in line 26 because the form (*da'yanda*) contrasts with later *de'yanda* (42) in the same way as the form in line 8 does with the forms in lines 9 and 32 of Mr. Hudson's story. Notice that the particle in line 47 stands as a line and verse itself and seems to be a placeholder in the pattern. The pairing of lines 1,2; 3–4, 5–6; 12, 13; 33, 34; 64, 65, 68–69 within the three- and five-part patterning remains always subordinate to that patterning. Thus lines 55–63 (H abc) correspond in purport and length to lines 22–29 of Mr. Hudson's telling (*iii* abcdef), but do not have the intensity of pairing raised to the level of verses. Something like that intensity does occur at the end, where the final pronouncement interweaves two topics—you are not to keep the water (71–73, 74,

78); you will be frogs (75–77, 79)—with three occurrences of the main, first topic formulaicly (71, 74, 78), but only two turns for the second topic. The formulaic lines suggest three sets of pairs (ababab), but the content suggests a five-part sequence (aabab). Note finally that H(e) unites three dispersions: Coyote, water, fish.

Here is Mr. Hartless's narrative:

COYOTE RELEASES WATER AND SALMON DAMMED BY THE FROGS

(i) (He travels and become thirsty)

(A)

(a)	Coyote stayed there.	1
(b)	There stayed his wife.	2
(c)	One day he said,	3
	"I'm going to take a look around the country."	4
(d)	Now then he told his wife.	5
	"I'm going to take a look around the country."	6
(e)	His wife said,	7
	"All right. Go."	8

(B)

(a)	To be sure, Coyote went,	9
	he went on and on,	10
	he camped overnight.	11
(b)	In the morning he went off again indeed,	12
	he camped overnight again indeed.	13
(c)	Five days he went.	14

(C)

(a)	Now then he got thirsty for water.	15
(b)	Now then he was told,	16
	"Over there is water.	17
	"Oh there's a big price for the water."	18
(c)	(——),	
	"Oh, I am thirsty for water.	19
	"I will just have to drink."	20

(ii) (He deceives the Frogs into selling him water)

(D)

(a)	To be sure, he went,	21
	he got there.	22

(b)	"I want water,"	23
	he said.	24
(c)	Frog said,	25
	"No. *Buy* it."	26
(d)	"Oh I am thirsty for water,"	27
	Coyote said.	28
(e)	Frog said,	29
	"You cannot drink it now!"	30

(E)

(a)	Now then Coyote went off.	31
(b)	Now then he dug camas,	32
	he took the camas' tails,	33
	he took a lot.	34
	He made them (appear to be) money dentalia.	35
(c)	Now then he changed himself (to appear rich).	36

(F)

(a)	Now then he went back again indeed,	37
	he got to where the water was.	38
(b)	"I want water,"	39
	said Coyote.	40
(c)	Frog said,	41
	"Buy it.	42
	"How much now do you want?"	43
(d)	Coyote said,	44
	"Give me that much now."	45
(e)	(——)	
	"All right. I will give it to you."	46

(*iii*) (He frees the water and the fish)

(G)

(a)	To be sure.	47
(b)	Now then Coyote put on five hats.	48
(c)	Now then Coyote kneeled down to drink.	49
(d)	Frog said,	50
	"Swallow five times,	51
	"Then stop."	52
(e)	Coyote said,	53
	"All right."	54

(H)

(a)	To be sure, Coyote drank.	55

	He put his hand down into the earth,	56
	he wanted to tear it open.	57
(b)	To be sure, now then Coyote was hit.	58
	Another came again indeed,	59
	she hit Coyote.	60
	There were five indeed of the frogs,	61
	they hit and hit Coyote.	62
(c)	Now then Coyote tore open the water.	63
(d)	To be sure it broke through,	64
	the water broke through.	65
(e)	Now then Coyote ran in flight.	66
	The water went,	67
	all the salmon went out,	68
	all sorts of things.	69

(I)

(a)	Now then Coyote said,	70
	"You are not to be keeping the water!	71
	"Everyone will drink,	72
	"They will not buy it.	73
	"You must not be keeping the water.:	74
	"You will be bull frogs,	75
	"You will live on the river bank,	76
	"That is to be your place.	77
	"But you must never keep the water.	78
	"You are to inhabit the river bank."	79

Let us note that the implicit alignment in the original publication (Jacobs 1945:236–237) scarcely approximates Mr. Hartless's organization of the story. Plain Arabic numerals are used to divide the story into two main parts: *1.* (lines 1–14) and *2.* (lines 15–80). The division corresponds to the first two stanzas of the first scene, and then all the rest. Within the rest the alignment is as follows:

(—)	15–22	(overrides travel in 21–22)
(2)	23–34	(overrides travel in 31)
(3)	35–43	(interrupts colloquy)
(4)	44–52	(interrupts one colloquy, does not reach end of other)
(5)	53–60	(interrupts sequence of Frogs' hitting Coyote)

(6)   61–66   (interrupts triple dispersion)
(7)   67–74   (interrupts pronouncement)
(8)   75–79

Now let us compare the actual alignments of the two tellings. Both have three scenes with analogous roles: Coyote intends to drink; he strikes a bargain with the Frogs; he frees the water. Within this common frame of what appears to be Kalapuya tradition, the two further share as incident that Coyote is going along; that he deceives the Frogs by substituting something else for dentalia; that while he drinks he tears open the dam with his hand; that he pronounces the general availability of water. A common strand, or matrix, of incident can be inferred, granted a certain degree of abstraction: (A) appetite; (B) deception as to identity or possession; (C) trade; (D) deception in action; (E) detection and bodily punishment; situation is righted (F) by freeing the water, and (G) by establishing that it will stay free. The two tellings can be summarized as follows (Hudson above Hartless):

(A)	(B)	(C)	(D)	(E)	(F)–(G)
hungry	deer rib	trade	drink, dig		free water, pronounce
thirsty	camas, rich	trade	drink, dig	head hit	free water, fish, pronounce

In terms of alignment of line and verse and other basic dimensions of narrative comparison, however, the profiles of the two tellings are quite distinct. There are two standard beginning frames for a Coyote story: He was going along, he was staying somewhere. Mr. Hudson uses the first, Mr. Hartless the second. Coyote and Frogs are the core of the actor matrix in both, but Mr. Hartless parallels Coyote at the outset with a wife (and at the end of his five-part sequence, refers to Coyote's children). Thus, Mr. Hartless devotes a first stanza to Coyote's decision to leave a domestic setting to look around (iA) and a second stanza (B) to travel itself, which Mr. Hudson simply announces at the outset with a conventional line. Mr. Hudson proceeds at once to the provision of false dentalia, by way of an accidental encounter conjoined with Coyote's appetite. Mr. Hartless holds the provision of false dentalia to be a response to unnatural monopoly in the second scene. Mr. Hudson reports here that the Frogs make people buy water, but Mr. Hartless withholds identification of them until the next scene. He does have someone tell a now thirsty Coyote that there is a high price for water. The two tellings converge at the end of the first scene, in that both have Coyote say he will drink.

In the middle scene, for Mr. Hudson, Coyote arrives, offers, and the deal is struck. His Frogs are eager at once. Mr. Hartless has the Frogs enact their turning of the communal resource into private property by refusing Coyote at first, since at first he has no money. Then comes a stanza of the making of false dentalia (from camas) and of his own appearance as being someone rich. A second colloquy (I want water : Buy it) leads to an agreement, couched in quite specific terms (that much). All told, there are two colloquies, and three stanzas, instead of one.

In the final scene, Mr. Hudson's Coyote proceeds immediately to drink and dig, and the outcome is immediate as well. Mr. Hartless has Coyote prepare for attack when he digs (a full, fivefold round), and the Frogs display further their pennypinching, before the action starts. Where Mr. Hudson intensifies the climax by poetic form, pairing verses, Mr. Hartless does it by having Coyote persevere while being attacked five times. (We are to infer that each Frog, hitting Coyote, broke one of the five hats—this device is elaborated that way in Columbia river versions.) When the water breaks through, this Coyote runs in flight, perhaps having no remaining defenses, or perhaps to get out of the way of the water, or both. Flight in parallel circumstances in the fourth myth of Mr. Hartless's sequence is to escape community outrage, and so that is presumably an element here. Where Mr. Hudson's Coyote proceeds directly to pronouncement, Mr. Hartless's Coyote must perhaps return to speak from a distance, but in any case takes not one, but nine lines, both remonstrating against the Frogs in establishing freedom of water, and assigning them their place in the world to come. Again, two colloquies, and three stanzas, instead of one.

What unites all this difference most of all, formally, is doubling. Mr. Hartless doubles the common ingredients some seven times. His initial frame has both a domestic setting, and then travel, not travel alone. His Coyote has an appetite of the mind (curiosity), not just of the body (thirst, hunger). When deception as to wealth is called for, his Coyote dissembles both dentalia and personal appearance, not the bead alone. The colloquy negotiating for water is doubled: a no to the moneyless Coyote, a yes to the seemingly rich one. The deception involved in digging with the hand while drinking is extended, and in a sense doubled, by the detection and reprisal of the Frogs, beating Coyote on the head one by one. (To be sure, Mr. Hudson here doubles poetic form.) When the situation is righted, there is doubling at three levels. When the water breaks through, it does so in two parallel lines (64–65); Coyote goes as well as the water; and the going of water is also the going of fish. Finally, the establishment of what is to be speaks not only of water but also of Frogs.

What unites and motivates these differences in terms of theme and attitude is clarified by the rest of Mr. Hartless's myth; but one element is clear in these two tellings themselves, and connects with the display of the differences in alignment and elaboration. The conceptions of Coyote are linked to the use of turns at talk. In the outer scenes, Mr. Hudson's Coyote speaks only at the end, alone. He is a transformer at his task, stating his purpose and his conclusion. In between he and the frogs do use a transitive verb (*-niSdini* "told him") with each other in their one exchange. But that suggestion of reciprocity only serves to heighten the immediate downfall. This is a foresighted Coyote, but not one much for talk.

Mr. Hartless's Coyote is quite different. One aspect of the elaboration of his telling is the elaboration of turns at talk. His Coyote speaks alone at beginning and end, announcing his curiosity (4) and pronouncing, but the first is immediately repeated to his wife (6), with the one occurrence in the telling of the transitive verb (*-niSni* "told"), and the last has the frogs as audience, even if they are given no turn at talk. In between come two exchanges in *i* (Coyote and wife, someone and Coyote); two pairs of exchanges (Coyote and Frog) in *ii;* and one exchange in *iii*. The relations among the exchanges express the point of the story. The two in the first scene show Coyote in relations of freely given advice and concurrence. The remaining scenes each show an initial pair in which Coyote is rejected (*ii*), or told what to do (*iii*), and a final pair in which Coyote, having dissembled, gains the day: water to purchase (*ii*), water for all (*iii*). And this pattern of outer stanzas with talk, an inner stanza without talk, in each scene is characteristic of Mr. Hartless's first act, as against Mr. Hudson's reserving of speech for the end of each of the outer scenes, which are essentially reported action, the only colloquy being in the middle scene. All in all, Mr. Hartless's Coyote is embedded in a social world of frequent talk, both in this first act and in the rest of the myth.

Here is a display of the differences in alignment and elaboration, with Mr. Hudson's telling to the left and Mr. Hartless's to the right. Verses containing direct speech have their line numbers underlined. The order in the Hartless telling is broken in order to show the parallelism of the double colloquy in the first and last stanzas of scene *ii:*

i

		A abcde	(1, 2, 3–4, 5–6, 7–8)
a	(line 1)	B abc	(9–11, 12–13, 14)
a	(2–3), bc (4–5, 6)		
d	(7–9)	C b	(16–18)
e	(10–12)	Cac	(15, 19–20)

ii

a	(13)	Da/Fa	(21–22)/(37–38)
b	(14–17)	Db/Fb	(23–24)/(39–40)
c	(18–21)	Dc/Fc	(25–26)/(41–43)
		Dd/Fd	(27–28)/(44–45)
		De/Fe	(29–30)/(46)
		E abc	(31, 32–35, 36)
		(F: see D	above)

iii

		G abcde	(47, 48, 49, 50–52, 53–54)
ab	(22, 23)	H a	(55–57)
cd	(24, 25)	b	(58–62)
ef	(26, 27–29)	c	(63)
g	(30)	de	(64–65, 66–69)
h	(31)	I	(70–80)

IX

Perhaps the doubling by Mr. Hartless stems from the dual outcome, release of both water and fish, pointing toward it. Certainly the doubling establishes a narrative framework for the rest of his five-part myth and, I think, has the purpose of doing so. The doubling seems to underscore a frame of reference, in terms of which otherwise disjunct Coyote adventures will be connected in order to explore, through narrative, a common theme from a certain point of view or attitude. Four well-known and widespread adventures are so organized: loss of eyes, trading anuses, trading penises, making a fish-trap.

This integration is unique to Mr. Hartless, so far as our knowledge of the region permits us to judge. Of course the knowledge which we have is no more than the scattered tips of what was once an ever-renewing armada of icebergs. Within Kalapuya itself we have only one other principal source, Mr. Hudson, who "heard Santiam and other Kalapuya dialect myths frequently when he was a youngster . . . but . . . the few that he remembers are the ones he heard with especial frequency" (Jacobs 1945:85). In any case, no sequence or cycle of Coyote stories is attested to. Besides the story of the release of water from the frogs, Mr. Hudson did know another story in which Coyote encounters Frog women, and then loses his eyes (96–103); so did Mr. Hartless (231–235). The encounter with Frog women involves salmon, but is distinct: they ask the passing Coyote for some; he deceives them with hornets (as in the Alsea story rewritten in the Erdoes/Ortiz anthology [384–385]). The women revive and cause snow that leads Coyote to enclose himself in a tree. Unable to get a woodpecker to release him, he throws out his body parts, and one eye is taken in the process, which people use to play shinny or gamble; Coyote retrieves it and escapes by disguising himself. The versions by Mr. Hudson and Mr. Hartless are distinct in a variety of details. Together with the first two parts of Mr. Hartless's cycle, they do show a broad Kalapuya tradition of an encounter with Frog women followed by loss of eyes.

Mr. Hudson also told a story of Coyote trading anuses (113–115), but with a man. The motive, to stand out at dances, is the same, and the consequence, inability to catch game, is the same, but the game here is not birds, but gophers; after the trade back, Coyote is shown successful in catching a gopher and saying that that is what he will always do when hungry. Catching gophers indeed is associated with Coyote in the myths of the Takelma and the Maidu as well. No story of trading penises, or making a fish trap, is attested from Mr. Hudson, although probably he heard such things as a youth, as both are popular in the region. Also, as I have said, there is no sequence.

The Coyote cycles that we do know from the region nonetheless suggest that Mr. Hartless's integration is unique. The sequence dictated to Franz Boas by Charles Cultee in both Shoalwater and Kathlamet Chinook has integration, but an integration of repetition. In one after another place Coyote discovers through failure the customs for successful fishing which are part of the locality's nature. He is constant while the customs change. A geographical framework also prevails in the Clackamas and Wishram-Wasco Chinook Coyote cycles. The adventures Mr. Hartless organizes are known in Clackamas, indeed. The release of salmon, kept by two women (Grizzly Bears), is the second half of a myth of Raccoon and Coyote. The other four elements of the Hartless sequence are present, and rather adjacent (8th, 9th, 7th, 11th in the series), but the only framework is that Coyote is going along, twice explicitly upriver. The cycle known to the Wasco and Wishram does start with the release of salmon kept by two women (Swallows); trading penises with subsequent curing of a girl, and making a fish-trap, are included. But again, there is no apparent linkage other than travel upriver from west to east.

Deliberate selection and grouping on Mr. Hartless's part seems all the more likely because he is the source of another Coyote sequence that emphasizes traveling along (222–226). Its frame is similar: Coyote tells his wife he wants to go look around the country, but his curiosity is elaborated in speech:

> Now then one day he said,
> "I am lonesome."
> Now then he said,
> "I will go away,
> "I will look around the country.
> "I wonder what the people are doing.
> "Maybe some person is living up that way.
> "I will go look at the people.
> "I do rather want to see the country."
> Now then he told his wife,
> "I am going to leave you.
> "I am going to look around the country."

The frame is doubled: he stays a year where people are playing shinny and gambling, again marries, and again goes along, saying, "I will really get back again." Three incidents follow; two double

70

the situation of people lacking water because they are ignorantly afraid of something in the water. The same theme is part of the Clackamas and Wishram cycles involving white salmon, which Coyote shows the people how to catch and eat. Here the white salmon is preceded by crawfish. There follows an adventure with mouthless people, for whom Coyote cuts mouths. They ask him to remain and offer him a wife, but he replies, "Oh no. I will be going along first. If when I do get back again, then I may do that. But I will rather still be going along now." Mr. Hartless provides as a formal close (226):

> Now then to be sure Coyote went along.
> Maybe indeed he is still coming.

The third decision not to stay for a woman, the rounding out again with the desire to go along (twice said), and the epilogue itself certainly highlight the traveling Coyote of other sequences. It is as if Hartless kept the traveling aspect of Coyote for this one sequence; in the other, which concerns us here, Coyote goes along only to connect actions, ending, indeed, at a place where he gets children.

Mr. Hartless uses the canonical pattern of five parts and a common narrative framework to do more than link picaresque and explanatory adventures in a geographical sequence. He explores the nature of Coyote as trickster-transformer; the adventures are selected and ordered to this purpose. The sequence of adventures is woven together in several ways. From one standpoint, there are an inner and an outer layer. The outer pair of acts involves provision of food (fish, fishtrap) and domestic setting (wife, children). The inner trio involves exchange of body parts (eyes, anuses, penises). But this is only one of four ways in which the stories form an interwoven set. A second way groups the first three against the rest. Each of the first three involves trade with women who are creatures in the world to come (Frogs, Snail, Nightingale). The rest can be taken as a second, complementary triad, since the fourth part has two internal parts: attempted intercourse and successful copulation. The fifth mentions children, and while the copulation and the children are not causally connected, the post hoc placement suggests a narrative propter hoc. All the other actors in this second triad are simply people, as if the world to come, that of the people, were now near, brought near by casting alone.

From a third vantage point, the sequence constitutes a three-part structure, pairing the first two acts, then the third and fourth, before the fifth. The first two acts show Coyote as a normative trickster-transformer, as in Mr. Hudson's story: his own bodily appetites, and capacity to deceive, serve authentic need. We have seen communal need for water and fish served in the first act. In the second, Coyote, having fallen asleep in a warm sun, wakes to find that Bluejay has stolen his eyes. Making imitation eyes out of rose hips, he persuades an old woman that he can see a louse crawling along a hair in the sky; to trade eyes; and to give him her eyes first. Leaving, despite her protest on discovery, he says:

> You are not to have eyes!
> You will be a snail!
> You will barely go along.

In the third act, going along, Coyote finds a woman sewing and breaking wind. He prevails upon her to trade anuses, thinking of the laughter and attention he will get with hers in an assemblage. But envy and desire for attention prove his undoing. Whenever he tries to catch a bird, the anus makes its noise and the bird escapes. Hunger forces him to trade back.

In the fourth act, going along, Coyote finds an old man with a gigantic penis that must be fed wood chips, and then sees five girls swimming in the river. He prevails upon the old man to trade, and puts his new penis in the river, raising it under the girl he wants so that when she jumps it fits inside her. Her companions come to her aid and pull her back, thus pulling Coyote in. He has to call to them to cut it off, and then has to trade back with the old man.

The second part of this fourth act—a fifth unit in some respects—begins with Coyote again in need of a body part—the tip of his penis. Notice especially that the widespread sequel of Coyote pretending to be an old shaman (medicine-man, doctor) unfolds here with a structure that closely parallels the first act. There, Coyote was told that there was water; here, he tells an old woman that there is a capable shaman (himself). There, Coyote dissembled as a wealthy man; here, as the old shaman. There, the Frogs refused to deal when first asked; here, invited by the headman of the village of the sick girl (who lies abed with the penis tip still in her), Coyote first declines, then says tomorrow, then agrees to come today. And, extraordinarily, and it would seem intentionally, the deception in action at the end has the same five elements in almost the same order. There, Coyote dug while drinking; here, he inserts his penis while singing. In both he reaches and removes the obstruction (the dirt of the dam, the tip of his severed penis); in both the result is the release of stopped up water. In both Coyote is detected. There, it was while digging before the release; here, it is when he arrives. Another coyote warns that he also is one; the attempted detection is rebuked, but then undertaken by the people themselves, after the water's release, when Coyote inside is copulating, while the birds he called upon conceal the girl's screams with loud singing. A louse, a flea, and finally, successfully, a water spider are sent across the flowing water to find out what is happening. Here, as there, Coyote goes in flight. The angry people kill the birds which had helped Coyote sing, including ducks and geese, two of the kind which had escaped him when he had Nightingale's anus—perhaps implying that he now can compass their deaths, even if indirectly.

The fifth part is just three lines:

> Now then Coyote came on downstream.
> He fixed a fish basket trap;
>   at that place there he got his children.

All four full acts end with the establishment of the nature of one or more actors: the Frogs, who are to live on the river bank; Snail, who is to go slowly; Nightingale and Coyote, restored to anus equilibrium; the girl and Coyote, restored to equilibrium with re- gard to the tip of his penis. (The fourth act doubles the incident of penis restoration, first with the trade back with the old man.) Notice that the Frogs and Snail bespeak the world to come, when their natures will be different. The actions with Nightingale and the girl—the two motivated by needs neither necessary nor authentic— do not. Each restores an equilibrium. In each Coyote must trade back to regain that equilibrium, motivated in the second trade by a self-inflicted, authentic need (hunger, injured penis).

It is as though the successful joining of need and ability to deceive in the first two acts has inspired hubris in the second two. A pair of pronouncements for the world to come is succeeded by a pair of lessons leading simply to restoration of a previous balance— though the successful copulation which rounds off the fourth act is a bonus. Perhaps it is a bonus because Coyote is now in a state of actual bodily need, and his ability to deceive serves not only himself but also the sick girl and her community and headman. Restored to an action with an ingredient of common good, Coyote is ready to proceed with other necessary acts of setting the world right for the people to come. The well-known incident of making the first fish trap is briefly mentioned as an indication. But the real story— the exploration of Coyote's own nature in the context of the natures of others—is over.

The third act is pivotal in such a sequence, serving equally as outcome of the first series of three acts, and as onset of the last three. This pivotal act is of course that with Nightingale, the one which first enacts the lesson of equilibrium restored. The third act equally has this pivotal role when the sequence is regarded from the standpoint of the fourth act having two parts, the second completing a five-part sequence within the four full acts. (The fifth act epilogue, functionally completing the fourth as an establishment for the future [fish trap], in this way also completes a trio with the first and second acts.) The explicit parallelism between the first act and the second part of the fourth act, including the detailed elaboration of release of water and flight, suggests this aspect of five within four, plus epilogue. The second part of the fourth act seems to be a rounding out of a cycle of exploration, through narrative, of Coyote's nature.

We are shown, then, a Coyote who has to "return to the place to know it for the first time" (to adapt T. S. Eliot's *Four Quartets*). He can use deception to trade for a body-part when he truly needs it (eyes); when he trades for the sake of popularity or sex, he is thwarted and has to trade back. The underlying, organizing attitude seems to be this: Coyote's nature, just as much of the natures of those he transforms, is already written in the scheme of things. However, being Coyote, he can explore the truths of this nature through experience. (The presence of a second coyote, warning about the deceiving Coyote, seems further to build into the narrative the polarity of Coyote-nature.)

The architecture of the five-part sequence weaves the actions together, as we have seen, in four ways:

    (1) 1 (*2–3–4*) (5) (outer, inner) (*exchange body parts*)
    (2) (*1–2–3*) (4a–4b–5) (*trade with women*)
    (3) (*1–2*) (*3–4*) (5) (+ / – *normative coyote*)
    (4) (*1–2–3–4a–4b*) (5) (*motives established*)

This multiplicity of relationships seems to strengthen the integration of the whole.

The utilization of the framework of incidents can be summarized as follows. The elements are: (A) appetite or need; (B) deception as to identity, body part, or possession; (C) a trade; (D) a deception in action; (E) sometimes a detection and bodily punishment; (F) a righting of the situation; (G) an establishing of what should be.

Act I shows ABCDEFG: thirst; deception with false dentalia and as rich man; trade for water; digging while drinking; detection and hitting on head; freeing of water and salmon; establishment of principle as to water, location of frogs.

Act II shows ABDCFG: blind; deception as to eyesight; deception in trade (you first); trade for eyes; restore own eyesight; eyesight and pace of snails.

Act III shows ABCDEACF: envy; self-deception in expectation of control; trade anus; self-deception in action (hunting); self-punishment (slaps anus); hunger; trade back; restoration of own anus.

Act IV(a) shows ABCDEC: lust; deceives self as to expectation (control); trade penis; deceives girls under water; tip cut off (directed by self); trade back.

Act IV(b) shows ABCDF: tip lacking; deceives as old shaman; negotiates to come as shaman (involving payment in the culture); deceives underneath cover of singing to cure; girl and Coyote restored by recovery of tip.

Act V shows G: establishment of fish trap.

X

If an anthology may, by absence of comparison, conceal the qualities of a narrator, at times an analysis dedicated to comparison may also do so. Such is the case with this myth in the fourth volume of *Mythologiques* by Claude Lévi-Strauss (1981). Structural analysis, of which Lévi-Strauss is the preeminent representative, takes its inspiration in important part from the linguistic principle that structure can be validated *internally*. That is, relationships within the object of analysis show its proper structure. This "emic" perspective developed in contrast to a perspective that could find organization in cultural materials only from the outside, "etically." In the first part of his *Mythologiques*, Lévi-Strauss shows very detailed analysis of myths. The close covariation of details gives the analyses credibility; certainly, transformational relationships do obtain between myths. It is Lévi-Strauss's historical accomplishment to have discovered this.

As he nears the end of his analytical journey, however, Lévi-Strauss often approaches new myths too readily in the light of the old, and without the concern for close covariation of detail which informed his initial work. The respect for the integrity of the object of analysis, which must be the first concern of structural analysis, seems to disappear. Myths are selectively cited, retitled, conflated. In the present case the two tellings by Mr. Hudson and Mr. Hartless are thrown together as "Kalapuya."

Lévi-Strauss correctly says of the Kalapuya tradition, "It is clear that this version stresses the release of *drinking water* rather than that of *edible fish*." However, this statement fails to note that Mr. Hudson's telling mentions *only* water, while Mr. Hartless's telling mentions *fish* as well; and that the place of fish in Mr. Hartless's telling is shown to have significance by its framing of the longer myth (fish in the first act, fish trap in the last).

By omitting the connection of Mr. Hartless's telling to the further acts of which it is a part, Lévi-Strauss contradicts the very point he uses the story partly to make! In these pages he criticizes Sapir for failing to recognize that parts of a myth, even if found elsewhere as separate entities, together constitute a coherent whole (pp. 255, 261). Yet, he ignores the coherent whole of the Hartless myth, attending to just the first of the five acts, and conflating it with Mr. Hudson's separate version.

The difficulty is compounded when Lévi-Strauss relates the first part, not to the rest of its own myth (in Mr. Hartless's telling), but to another Kalapuya myth, which is said to make it possible to suggest why there is stress on release of drinking water. He turns to Mr. Hudson's telling in Santiam Kalapuya of "Panther, coyote, whale's daughter, the flood, obtaining the fire" (Jacobs 1945:103–113; the myth has a Clackamas Chinook analogue [Jacobs 1958:52–67 not cited by Lévi-Strauss]; see also "Flint and his son's son [Panther]" [166–179]). The point of the comparison is that the preceding myth "is concerned with the *obtaining* of drinking *water* by the *demolition* of a dam, and that the Kalapuya have an exactly symmetrical myth explaining the *loss* of cooking *fire* resulting from the *erection* of another dam" (Lévi-Strauss 1981:256). But this latter myth, retitled by Lévi-Strauss "The fire which was lost and found again" (which is not the main point of the story), has no dam in it at all. To be sure, there is a dam that causes loss of fire (cooking is not mentioned) in the Mary's River version told by Hartless (Jacobs 1945:215–221; see p. 221). Lévi-Strauss notices it in these words:

> [It] adds the detail that he [Coyote] built a dam downstream in the hope of recovering his children, who were being swept along by the current. This created the flood which is also mentioned in [the preceding myth], although its precise cause is not stated there (1981:258).

The preceding myth, Mr. Hudson's telling in Santiam, is in fact explicit. The cause is not a dam, but hair. Water pursues the people up a mountain (all this is after the main action involving the matrix of Panther and Coyote as alternate spouses of the same woman). Fire is carried along by Copperhead Snake. Here are the relevant lines from Mr. Hudson's text:

> Now then the people said to Panther,
> "What have you taken?
> "This water does not want to go back."
> Now then he said,
> "I took nothing.
> "I took only my child,
> "and I took that woman's hair."
> "Oh,"
> the people said,
> "Throw away that hair of hers.
> "Maybe it is that which it is pursuing."

Panther tells small Chicken-Hawk to throw the hair into the water, and to be sure, the water goes down. When the people then say that there is no fire, Copperhead Snake explains that he has it in his mouth, and trades it to Panther for a deer-hide blanket.

In short, no dam, and no loss of fire. Mr. Hudson and Mr. Hartless here, as before, do not tell the same story, at least not at the level of precise detail assumed by such analysis.

The problem of conflation of tellings is compounded when Lévi-Strauss goes on to contrast the myth with the withholding of water: "Conversely, one individual is able to deprive the community of fire and to appropriate it, because a newly built dam prevents water from flowing, holds it back and creates a flood." Earlier, he speaks of "a myth which conjures up an era when even indispensable possessions like fire could be monopolized by a selfish minority, and enjoyment of them had to be negotiated" (1981:258). Now, the dam occurs only in one of the two tellings (Mr. Hartless's) and it is built by Coyote *to try to save his children.* In the story with the dam there is neither monopoly nor negotiation. After the flood, first Hummingbird is sent to get fire from where the sun rises, then, successfully, Copperhead Snake. He simply brings it to Panther and again they have fire.

The negotiation for fire with Copperhead Snake is in Mr. Hudson's version, which has no dam. And the trading is amicable; no deception is required. Copperhead is delighted, once he gets a skin dry enough to make the sound (*xaxaxaxxx····*) he will make as he goes along. To be sure, the lower-class people are left out. They have to capture fire by dancing with pitchwood in their regalia around the fire that the upper-class people want to keep as their own. But that is class struggle, not individual appropriation or subsequent negotiation.

Throughout his work, Lévi-Strauss tends to focus on the origin of culture out of nature—fire, cooked food, water as a resource. No doubt that is why the elements of fire and water in these myths attract him. Now, Mr. Hartless's story could be said to end with an explanatory incident that has to do with nature versus culture. Coyote's dam causes a flood that causes a general loss of fire, which is restored, as we have seen, from a natural source (where the sun rises). But Mr. Hudson's story ends with an epilogue that concerns social structure. It follows the in-law conflict of the main plot (Panther versus his wife's people). Trade with the one who has preserved fire benefits only the upper class, so that the lower-class people (Coyote among them) have to dance for their tinder, deceive, and flee. The identification of Coyote with a lower class, scorned by an upper class that identifies with chiefs like Panther, is explicit. It fits Coyote's getting the better of a headman's daughter in the fourth act of Mr. Hartless's cycle. It suggests a use of myth as social criticism, as a contested territory in cultural hegemony. But to pursue such questions, one would have to treat Mr. Hartless's Mary's River myths, and Mr. Hudson's Santiam myths, each as distinct traditions and performances, having each an expressive, and therefore verbal integrity of its own. Before speaking of what the "Kalapuya tradition" is, one would therefore have to speak of William Hartless and John B. Hudson.

To sum up, two tellings are conflated to present a picture in which the following is true of Kalapuya tradition:

dam causes flood
flood causes loss of fire
fire is regained through trade

The facts of the matter are these:

	Hudson	Hartless
flood caused by	hair	dam
fire is	saved	lost
fire regained by	trade	quest

As to the dam, it seems no accident that all the stories in the region of Coyote releasing fish, or water, or both, have him releasing it or them from monopoly by *women*. Fish, and the mythical figure of Salmon, indeed, are connected with ambivalence and tension between the genders, the necessary mutual dependence and reciprocity going together with a projected struggle for dominance or even elimination of the other (see Hymes 1985*b*). It also seems no accident that Coyote twice releases water by deceiving women in Mr. Hartless's myth, both times to the discomfiture of the women, but both times to the general good and, the second time, the good of the woman herself. There within Mr. Hartless's own myth is a second obstruction that illuminates the first.

Structural analysis ought generally to be based on ethnopoetic analysis, for meaning may depend upon shape (Hymes 1985*b*), and the careful attention to verbal detail required in ethnopoetic analysis is also a requisite of convincing structural analysis. Without respect for the specific text, and the individual narrator, apparent precision casts forth an imprecise blur.

The one lesson that seems difficult to learn is that myths are performed and thereby shaped, both in performance and in reflection between performances, by individuals. Even the heroic collector and preserver of what we reliably know about Kalapuya tradition,

Melville Jacobs, succumbed to the ethnological habit of dissolving individual lives into processes labeled with group names. In his monograph, Jacobs comments on the French-Canadian stories of Petit Jean known by Mr. Hartless in terms of a general French-Canadian influence in the region. His original notes disclose that Hartless had a specific French-Canadian family connection (Zenk 1984). Perhaps the unreflecting practices of anthologies, structural analyses, and ethnology can at last be overcome by the simple fact that ethnopoetics requires one to start with language, and starting with language will at last make clear that the first literature of the continent is known to us through shaping minds that bear names such as Hudson and Hartless.

INDEX OF TRIBAL GROUPS IN ERDOES AND ORTIZ

NOTES

1. This essay arose out of a review of Erdoes and Ortiz (1984) invited by *The Nation* (see Hymes 1985*a*). I would like to thank Elizabeth Pochoda for the invitation. Let me also thank Judith Berman for information in connection with the Kwakiutl myth mentioned at the end of section II.

2. I have indicated the presence of these principles in the language in a review of the Lopez anthology (Hymes 1979) and in a comment on another paper (Hymes 1981*b*). The review simply shows the presence of parallelism and repetition in accord with a Kalapuya logic of organizing actions in groups of three and five for a page of travel by Coyote that Lopez had omitted in his retelling of William Hartless's telling in Mary's River Kalapuya (a dialect related to Santiam) of "Coyote gambles playing the hand game" (Jacobs 1945:205–215; Lopez 1977:165–166). The comment shows that John B. Hudson's Santiam version of the "News about Coyote" is the same in shape, despite difference in the language, as that told in Clackamas Chinook by Victoria Howard (see Hymes 1981*a:*235–237). This is the first full published account in ethnopoetic terms of a Kalapuya text.

REFERENCES

Benedict, Ruth. 1931. *Tales of the Cochiti Indians*. Washington, D.C.: Bureau of American Ethnology, Bulletin 98. Reprinted by the University of New Mexico Press (Albuquerque, 1981), with introduction by Alfonso Ortiz.

Ellis, John M. 1983. *One Fairy Story Too Many: The Brothers Grimm and their Tales*. Chicago: University of Chicago Press.

Erdoes, Richard, and Alfonso Ortiz, eds. 1984. *American Indian Myths and Legends*. New York: Pantheon.

Frachtenberg, Leo J. 1917. Myths of the Alsea Indians of Northwestern Oregon. *International Journal of American Linguistics* 1:64–75.

———. 1920. *Alsea texts and myths*. Washington, D.C.: Bureau of American Ethnology, Bulletin 67.

Handler, Richard. 1984. Review of Ellis (1983). *Journal of American Folklore* 97:485–487.

Hymes, Dell. 1979. Review of Lopez (1977). *The Western Humanities Review* 33(1):91–94.

———. 1980a. Tonkawa poetics: John Rush Buffalo's Coyote and Eagle's daughter. In *On Linguistic Anthropology: Essays in Honor of Harry Hoijer 1979. By Joseph Breenberg, Dell Hymes, Paul Friedrich*, ed. Jacques Maquet. Malibu, California: Undena Publications. Pp. 33–87. (To appear, revised, in a volume edited by Joel Sherzer and Anthony Woodbury [Cambridge University Press].)

———. 1980b. Particle, Pause and Pattern in American Indian Narrative Verse. *American Indian Culture and Research Journal* 4(4):7–51.

———. 1981a. *"In Vain I Tried to Tell You." Essays in Native American Ethnopoetics*. Philadelphia: University of Pennsylvania Press.

———. 1981b. Comments. *Journal of the Folklore Institute* 18(2–3):144–150.

———. 1982. Narrative Form as a "Grammar" of Experience: Native American and a Glimpse of English. *Journal of Education* (Boston) 164 (2):121–142.

———. 1985a. Review of Erdoes and Ortiz (1984). *The Nation* 240 (3) (January 26), 85–86.

———. 1985b. Language, Memory and Selective Performance: Cultee's Kathlamet Sun's Myth as Twice-Told to Boas. *Journal of American Folklore* 98 (390):391–434.

———. 1985c. Some Subtleties of Measured Verse. *Proceedings, Niagara Linguistic Society*, 15th Spring Conference 1985, ed. June Hesch. Pp. 13–57. Buffalo, New York.

Jacobs, Melville. 1939. *Coos Narrative and Ethnologic Texts*. Seattle: University of Washington Publications in Anthropology 8(1).

———. 1940. *Coos Myth Texts*. Seattle: University of Washington Publications in Anthropology 8(2).

———. 1945. *Kalapuya Texts*. Seattle: University of Washington Publications in Anthropology 11.

———. 1958, 1959a. *Clackamas Chinook Texts*, parts I and II. Bloomington: Indiana University. Research Center in Anthropology, Folklore and Linguistics, Publications 8 and 11.

————. 1959*b*. *Content and style of an oral literature*. Chicago: University of Chicago Press; New York: Wenner-Gren.

————. 1960. *The People are Coming Soon. Analyses of Clackamas Chinook Myths and Tales*. Seattle: University of Washington Press.

Jackobson, Roman. 1960. Closing Statement: Linguistics and Poetics. In *Style in Language*, ed. T. A. Sebeok. Pp. 350–377. Cambridge: The Technology Press.

Lévi-Strauss, Claude. 1981. *The Naked Man*. (Introduction to a Science of Mythology: 4). New York: Harper & Row. (Translated by John and Doreen Weightman from *L'homme nu* [Paris, 1971]).

Lopez, Barry Holstun. 1977. *Giving Birth to Thunder, Sleeping with His Daughter: Coyote builds North America*. New York: Avon.

Marcuse, Herbert. 1978. *The Aesthetic Dimension. Toward a Critique of Marxist Aesthetics*. Boston: Beacon Press. (Translated and revised by Marcuse and E. Sherover from *Die Permamenz der Kunst: Wider eine bestimmte Marxistische Aesthetik* [Munich, 1977]).

Sapir, Edward. 1909. *Wishram Texts*. Leiden: E. J. Brill. Publications of the American Ethnological Society, 2.

Swann, Brian, ed. 1983. *Smoothing the Ground. Essays on Native American Oral Literature*. Berkeley, Los Angeles, London: University of California Press.

Zenk, Henry. 1984. Chinook Jargon and Native Cultural Persistence in the Grand Ronde Indian Community, 1856–1907: A Special Case of Creolization. Ph. D. diss. Eugene: University of Oregon.

Heidegger and the Aztecs:
The Poetics of Knowing In
Pre-Hispanic Nahuatl Poetry

WILLARD GINGERICH

For the poet the anguishing question—and it is indeed
the subject of the poem—is: how can one not only speak
of Being, but say Being itself. Poetry is the experience of
this question. (De Man 1980:256)

There is much in being that man cannot master. There
is but little that comes to be known. What is known
remains inexact, what is mastered insecure. What is, is
never of our making or even merely the product of our
minds, as it might too easily seem. (Martin Heidegger)

O You by Whom we Live and Move, nothing we say here
is real. What we say on this earth is like a dream;
We only mutter like one waking from sleep.
Here, none of us
says anything real. (Bierhorst 1985:170)

Look; I have the fire in my hands. I understand and work
with it perfectly, but cannot speak of it without creating
it. (García Lorca 1966:403)

It was Father A. M. Garibay, whose indefatigable publications
did so much to make Mexico and all the Spanish-speaking world
aware of the extensive body of literature contained within sixteenth-
century Nahuatl language texts, who first pointed out the epistemological faith expressed in that literature: a conviction that poetry is

one of the most, if not the only, reliable modes of human knowledge about reality.[1] It remained, however, for Garibay's student, Dr. Miguel León-Portilla, clearly to set forth the claims for poetry as the primal language of meaning and human knowledge in the fifteenth century, pre-Hispanic Nahua tradition of thought and expression. The Nahua poets, León-Portilla asserts, universally assumed that "the only truths on earth"—*azo tle nelli in tlalticpac*—are accomplished through the language of poetry, whose Nahuatl name was the metonymic diphrase, *in xochitl in cuicatl* or "the flower, the song." In the conclusion to his book *Aztec Thought and Culture* (*La filosofía náhuatl estudiada en sus fuentes,* first published in 1956) he first posited for the Nahuas something he called "an aesthetic vision of the world" founded on the apparent Nahua conviction that only beauty was ultimately real:

> To know the truth was for the Nahua wise men *[tlamatinime]* to express with flowers and songs the hidden meaning of things, as their own sanctified hearts permitted them to intuit.[2] The philosophy of metaphors did not pretend to explain the mystery completely, but it did lead men to feel that beauty was perhaps the only reality (1963:322).

He calls further attention to this respect for intuition in Nahua thought, a respect essential to the modes of knowing and expressing which constitute poetic perception.

> There appeared finally and consciously what became the characteristic response of the *tlamatinime* to the problem of metaphysical knowledge: it has to do with a sort of salvational intuition. There is only one means to stutter from day to day "the truth" in this world—the road of poetic inspiration, "flower and song." On a foundation of metaphors, conceived in the deepest reaches of his being, or perhaps "proceeding from the interior of the heavens," with flowers and songs, man is able to sketch out in some fashion the truth (1963:319).

Then in a later work, *Los antiguos mexicanos através de sus crónicas y cantares,* León-Portilla begins to speak of an epistemology inherent in the Nahua poetry, still emphasizing the role of imaginative intuition, while tempering somewhat its claim for access to "truth":

> The *tlamatinime* did not believe it was possible to achieve an understanding rationally clear and precise, beyond all objection. As one of their poems suggests, "it may be that no one finally

speaks truth on the earth." Nevertheless, they implicitly approached the formulation of something which, anachronistically, we could call "a sort of theory of knowledge." Making use of a metaphor, one of the many in the rich Nahuatl tongue, they affirmed on countless occasions that perhaps the only possible way to speak words of truth on earth was the way of poetry and art, which are "flower and song." . . . Poetry, and art in general, are for the *tlamatinime* a veiled and occult expression which nevertheless is able, with the wings of the symbol and the metaphor, to raise man in a stuttering power, projecting him beyond himself, which in a mysterious way brings him perhaps near to his own roots of being. They seem to affirm that genuine poetry implies a unique mode of knowledge, fruit of an authentic inner experience or, if you prefer, product of an intuition (1961:128).

These theories of León-Portilla concerning the self-conscious respect of the late fifteenth-century Nahuas for poetic, metaphoric, intuitional techniques of thought and knowledge remain substantially unexplored and unevaluated to date. With the exception of a brief study by Domingo Miliani, "Notas para una poética entre los nahuas," which does little more than systematize the observations of León-Portilla; a short book by Rafael Osuña Ruiz, *Introducción a la lírica prehispánica,* which repeats Miliani; and a brief article by Rafael González, "Symbol and Metaphor in Nahuatl Poetry," which does not address León-Portilla's claims directly but provides a useful statement about the relation between linguistic metaphor and truth in Nahua tradition, there has been no evaluation or development of this claim for Nahua poetics. The question then remains: How valid are these observations of León-Portilla as an approach to the poetry and/or philosophy of Nahua oral tradition? What is their basis in the texts of the poems themselves? And if they do appear to have substance, in what terms are we, tlamatinime far removed from fifteenth-century Anahuac, Central Mexico, to understand these Nahua notions of authentic inner experience, intuition, the divinization of things, and finally, truth, poetry, and knowledge themselves?

León-Portilla founds his observations on several poetic texts from the Cantares mexicanos (Mexican Cantos) manuscript. The first fragment is taken from a lengthy poem of folios 12 and 13. It reads (Bierhorst 1985:170):

Ye antle nel o tic ytohua nican ypalnemohua
can iuhqui temictli can toncochitlehua in tiquittoa tl[alticpac].
Ayac nellin tiquilhuilya nican.

O You by Whom we live and move, nothing we say here
is real. What we say on this earth is like a dream;
We only mutter like one waking from sleep.
Here, none of us says anything real.[3]

His primary evidence rests in a sequence of texts from the region
of Huexotzinco, particularly a section in folios 9–12 of the manuscript entitled "*xochicuicatl*," or "Songs of Spring." It has been suggested, mostly based on internal evidence, that these folios are the
record of a sort of "poets' conference" held about 1490 at the court
of Tecayehuatzin, ruler of Huexotzinco. At least nine passages of
the "Songs of Spring" seem attributed to him, and several appear
to cast him in the role of host to numerous other singers. León-Portilla believes this convocation was called for the specific purpose of
clarifying these questions of poetry and reality. So what clarification
is offered?

The entire text of 160 undivided lines in manuscript (which
Garibay breaks into twenty-four separate, short poems, León-Portilla into eleven distinct statements by diverse poets, and Bierhorst
renders as a single song) is too long to quote in its entirety, but the
key passages for our consideration are the following. For those
unfamiliar with this poetry, I would call attention to the pervasive
imagery of flowers and singing.

11. 13–18
The jade, the plumes of quetzal
rain down; they are your words
and so also spoke Ayocuan
and Cuetzpaltzin, who knew in truth
the God by Whom we live and move.
To do likewise the grand lord
comes now, with handfuls of perfumes and plumes
to delight the One God.
How else could he accept, the One by Whom we live and move?
How else could there be any true thing on the earth?

ll. 28–31

> From within the heavens come
> these measured songs, these measured flowers.
> They ravage our bitterness, ravage our melancholy
> especially those of Tecayehuatzin, Chichimec Lord:
> with those take your pleasure!

ll. 42–47

> Reach, O Heart, for flowers of the shield,
> the flowers of the God by Whom we live.
> What should the heart do?
> Have we come, have we sprouted for nothing
> on this earth? I'll go off
> abolished like a flower.
> Will my fame be nothing one day
> my name without meaning in the earth?
> At least flowers! At least songs!
> What should the heart do?
> Have we come, have we sprouted for nothing
> on this earth?

ll. 51–55

> No one here can extinguish the flower and the song,
> spread abroad in the house of Him by Whom we live.
> This earth is the place of brevity;
> Is Quenonamican, Place of Mystery, the same?
> Perhaps there we dance and grow in friendship?
> No, only here do we come to know
> one another's faces.

ll. 60–64

> Where do you exist, My God
> by Whom I live and move?
> Continually I search you out;
> for you, I am the suffering singer
> wishing only to give you joy.
> Here, in the House of Spring, the House
> of the Painted Word, it rains
> white flowers, white quetzal flowers;
> I wish only to bring you joy.

l. 68

> In flowers is the word
> of the One God held secure

11. 69–70

> So, your House is everywhere,
> God by Whom we live; there
> on the mats woven and surrounded
> with flowers, where the princes
> call upon you.

11. 82–86

> I was in despair, I, Cuauhtencoz,
> and decorated my flowering drum in pain;
> Is man true? Is anything true
> in our songs? Will anything remain standing?
> What will come out in the end?
> Where do we live? Where are we?
> O my friend, we are miserable creatures.

11. 134–137

> Who am I? I live on the wing,
> I compose things, I sing flowers,
> butterflies of song.
> Let them come out, let my heart be known.
> I come down out of the sky,
> a flamingo of spring, I touch the earth.
> I spread out my wings beside the flowering drums;
> My song rises, goes out over the earth.

11. 156–159

> O friends, please listen
> to the word of a dream:
> Every spring the golden corn
> brings us again to life,
> the red-plumed ears refresh;
> we wear a jeweled chain
> in knowing the hearts of friends
> continue true.

We might say, that's all very nice, but where are the statements about truth and reality and knowledge and poetry and all that? A few lines are, of course, obvious reflections on these matters, but there is precious little we could feel comfortable calling a "statement" in this continual panorama of birds, flowers, drums, singing, and lamenting. Are there perhaps other manuscripts where the poetics of reality are addressed more directly? There are a few other relevant passages in the Cantares manuscript beyond the Huexot-zinco cycle. On folio 24r, among the *icnocuicatl* or "songs of anguish" of the Triple Alliance cities, we read:

> Is it true that we have come here
> to live?
>
> . . . .
> We have come to the earth
> only to make songs, to learn
> one another's faces, there by the drums.

On folio 34r, from Chalco, we find an oft-repeated inquiry about the origin of poetry:

> Priests, I ask you:
> from where do the intoxicating flowers
> the intoxicating songs fall?
> They fall from within the heavens,
> from his house; the One God,
> He by Whom we live, sends them down.[4]

The fullest treatment of the origin of poetry, however, comes in a long passage supposedly of Otomí origin, near the beginning of the manuscript. The anonymous poet interrupts a gathering of birds to ask where he can go to find the fragrant flowers of song. The birds, who are said to be like nobles and princes, conduct him "within the mountains," to "Tonacatlalpan, xochitlalpan" or "The Land of Our Sustenance, the Land of Flowers," a place where the "the dew is not dried by radiant sun":

> There I saw at last the flowers
> varied and precious, flowers
> of delightful scents, wrapped in dew
> under the fog of a brilliant rainbow.
> There I was told, "cut whatever you want
> poet, as you desire, and carry them
> to our friends, the princes, those who
> provide the pleasure of the Lord of the World."

Numerous lines in the same manuscript insist, however, that poetry comes equally from within the poet himself. From folio 33:

> From within you the flowers of song
> emerge; you scatter them
> and cast them out over us.
> You are the singer!

Some of the most intriguing lines referring to truth and poetry occur in the one other major Nahuatl lyrical manuscript, entitled Romances of the Lords of New Spain; especially among the texts attributed to the fifteenth-century poet-king Nezahualcoyotl of Tetzcoco. From folio 18 of that manuscript:

> Only our flowers leave us contented
> only with our songs is our melancholy
> dissipated, O princes. Before them
> your ennui flees away.
> They are the work of Him by Whom we live,
> the creation of Him Who invents Himself.

Or folios 19 and 20—and this appears to be a single, complete poem, addressed to supreme deity:

> Is there any truth in you?
> You whose speech is law,
> O Lord by Whom we live.
> Is this true?
> Is this not true?
> Whatever way it is decreed
> Would that our hearts
> were not left in desolation.
>
> Whatever is true
> He says is no longer true.
> The Lord by Whom we live
> is nothing but capricious.
> If only our hearts
> were not left in desolation.

In addition to the Nezahualcoyotl passages, the Romances manuscript offers these comments:

f. 41

> It is a true thing, our song;
> it is a true thing, our flowers,
> the well-measured song.

f. 27

> When we will have gone
> into His house, our words
> will live on in the earth.

f. 28

> Flowers are not carried
> there to His house;
> songs are not carried
> but they live on here
> in the earth.

Again, a number of passages suggest that the inspiring, creative divinity occurs within man the poet.

f. 34

> Within you he lives, he paints
> he creates all things,
> The Lord by Whom we live.

Others assert that he lives beyond human reality as a sort of Coleridgean super-poet who creates and maintains the world, with all its warriors and poets, only as a figment of his primary imagination:

f. 35

> Through flowers you paint all things,
> O Lord by Whom we live;
> through song you trace and shade
> all that will on earth come to be.
> Even the Orders of Jaguar and Eagle Knights
> will someday dissolve.
> Only in your painted book
> do we live here on the earth.

Those are the highlights of the texts which provide the foundation for the poetic and aesthetic doctrines León-Portilla claims to find. Certainly we find here ample evidence of a questing, questioning vision of human reality and human expression, and a solid tradition of literary modes, symbols, and poetic stance; but a "theory of knowledge"? It might appear to be an exercise of considerable interpretation to find something that most of us could feel comfortable calling an epistemology in these passages, though an aesthetic vision of the world is clearly implied, especially in that last passage.

Perhaps, we may suggest, there are native commentators who explicate in prose the nature of poetry and reality? The answer is no, there are no Aristotles or Horaces anywhere in indigenous Mesoamerican traditions. The best we might find are a few scant passages comparing the true and the inauthentic artist. However, in spite of this small body of direct evidence, every reader who becomes at all exposed to the Nahuatl language and acquainted with even small sections of the Florentine or Madrid manuscripts will come to feel that Dr. Léon-Portilla's statements about the primacy of art and the foundation of truth in poetry are somehow unerringly right. But if the evidence put forward is as scant as I have demonstrated, then where are we to look for the origins of this general conviction? I would propose that León-Portilla's claims for the Nahuatl poetic are, in fact, substantially correct and do inform the poetry, but their real evidence is to be found, beyond the statements of the poetry, in the modes and style of the literary idiom itself, in the *tecpillatolli* or "speech of noblemen," a language whose "poetic" qualities have been the bane of translators since 1520.

All natural languages, Heidegger has said, echoing Hölderlin, Shelley, and Emerson, are decayed poetry. Everyday speech he called "a forgotten and therefore used-up poem" (1971:208).[5] Ernest Fenollosa or Ezra Pound, in that brilliant but misguided little essay on "The Chinese Written Character as a Medium for Poetry"—a treatise, by the way, that curiously prefigures a number of Heidegger's notions on language and poetry—writes that "a late stage of the decay [from the original metaphoric language of the ancients to modern speech] is arrested and embalmed in the dictionary" (Fenollosa 1936:24). Of the few languages with which I am acquainted, none more obviously justifies this conception of language as a vastly evolving but degenerated poem than does the elaborate, stylized idiom of the Nahuatl tecpillatolli. Few languages have evoked so insistently their poetic, metaphorical foundations as does this Nahuatl of the sixteenth-century texts. Mastery of this highly baroque style was the mark of civilized men throughout pre-Columbian Mexico. So highly metaphoric and associative is this language that in 1966 a strange little grammar was published with the title

Los mil elementes del mexicano clásico (The 1000 Elements of Classical Mexican). It was based on the premise that the entire linguistic system of Nahuatl could be reduced to some 1,000 primitive roots and inflections from which the language's entire complexity could then be generated. Since earliest times grammarians have spent much effort attempting to explain these imagistic and tropological phenomena of Nahuatl tecpillatolli. In 1547 Andrés de Olmos took the entire eighth chapter in Part III of his *Arte para aprender la lengua mexicana* to record what he called "Manners of Speech Which the Old Ones Used in Their Ancient Discourses" (1885:114–125). Fr. Juan Mijangos added a translation of 195 "Elegant and Metaphoric phrases and modes of speech of the ancient Mexicans" to his 1621 book of sermons ([1623] 1966). Most valuable of all, however, are Chapters 41–43 at the end of Book VI in Sahagún's Florentine Codex, entitled respectively "Proverbs," "Riddles," and "Metaphors" (Anderson and Dibble, VI, 219–260; Sullivan 1963: 93–177). Under the latter heading we find ninety-two different image clusters with elaborate explanation. Almost without exception these are cast in some form of that binary style so characteristic of Nahuatl expression at all levels, a process dubbed the *difrasismo* or "diphrase" by Fr. Garibay. He defined it as "a procedure which consists of expressing a single idea by means of two words which complement one another somehow in meaning, either as synonyms or by association. . . . Almost all of these phrases are metaphoric and their application must be understood, since to take them literally would often be to twist the sense, or find it ill-fitting to the case" (1961:115). The following are a few examples, with literal translation, from the Sahagún manuscript:

> poctli, ayauitl: tenyotl, mauizyotl
> Smoke and mist, fame and glory
>
> teoatl, tlachinolli
> divine liquid, fire
>
> cuitlapilli, atlapalli
> the tail, the wing
>
> tzopelic, ahuiyac
> sweet and fragrant

toptli, petlacalli
a basket, a coffer

in popocatiuh, in chichinauhtiuh
He is smoking, he is sizzling

pollocotli, zacaqualli
chaff and straw

And, of course, there is *xochitl, cuicatl,* "flower and song," which we have seen repeated endlessly in the poetry fragments above. The expression "smoke and mist," Sahagún's explanation tells us, "was said about a king not long dead whose smoke and mist, meaning his fame and glory, had not yet vanished; or, about someone who had gone far away and whose fame and glory had not faded," an image of added poignancy in an oral tradition (Sullivan 1963:145). "Divine liquid, fire" "was said when a great war or a great pestilence occurred. They said: Divine liquid and fire have overcome us, have swept over us. This means pestilence or war itself." The "divine liquid," of course, is blood, that endlessly symbolic commodity of Aztec theology and politics. "Tail and wing," we are told, "means the common people. For this reason the subjects are called tails and wings, and the King, lord of the tails and wings" (Sullivan 1963: 147). Another passage elsewhere in the Florentine Codex notes that the full statement of this image is "tail and wing of the sun," thereby filling out the idea of a general populace whose transcendent mission is to feed and support the cosmos itself. And we could go on and on for all the formulaic diphrases so essential to this literary language, each one generated as either metaphor, metonym, or synecdoche. But the diphrase is only the most basic form of the stylistic dualism which permeates all levels of Nahuatl expression, a function, it has been suggested, of the essential dualism and balance figured in Nahuatl cosmology. Garibay said it almost seems "as if the Nahuatl language could not conceive of things except in binary form" (1971:117). It has more recently been pointed out, however, that the implications of Nahuatl stylistics are considerably more complex than this:

It is becoming clear that the poetic features of Nahuatl style are even more complex than Garibay believed, including not only couplet parallelism as a general feature and Garibay's binominal *difrasismo* as an embellishment, but also a polynominal repetition with both semantic and poetic force (Edmonson 1974:12).

The binominal style of the diphrase often blossoms out into quartets, quadruplets, and necklaces of multiple images, all hovering luminously about the neck of a concept or thing. Close to the diphrase we find a repetition like

> Uel chalchiuhtic, uel teuxiuhtic,
> uel acatic, uel ololiuhqui

> like fine jade, like fine turquoise
> like fine green reeds, like a fine, round sphere

The commentator notes that this was "said of a royal orator who counselled the people very well. They said: 'He spoke magnificently—like jades, like turquoises—and his words sounded like precious stones, long as reeds and very round'" (Sullivan 1963:154). More elaborately we find

> atitlanonotzalli, atitlazcaltili,
> atitlauapaoalli, atimuzcalia,
> atitlachia.

> You are undisciplined, you are coarse and uncouth,
> you are unseemly, you are senseless.

The commentator tells us that this was "said of the person who had no upbringing and no sense. He was stupid and understood nothing. They said to him, 'Assuredly your mother and father did not instruct you and teach you how to live'" (Sullivan 1963:167).

Almost any passage from any longer manuscript would serve to illustrate the totality of these stylistic qualities. The following is excerpted from one of the "Discourses of Admonition" in Book VI of the Florentine Codex and will, I hope, give a clearer holistic impression of the textual realities I am trying to identify in the tecpillatolli speech.

Vncan mjtoa in tlatolli: in qujtoaia tlatoanj, in jquac omotlatoca-tlali ynic qujtlatlauhtiaia Tezcatlipuca: in jpampa in oqujtlatoca-tlalli, ioan injc qujtlanjliaia in jtepaleviliz ioan in jtetlanextiliz injc vel qujchioaz in jtequjuh: cenca miec in jnecnomachiliztlatol

Tlacatle totecoe, tloquee, naoaquee iooalle ehecatle: otla-cauhquj in moiollo, aço tinechmotlanevilia in njmaceoalli in njtlapalivi: in cujtlatitlan in tlaçultitlan nonemja, in anjcemelle in njteuhio, in njtlaçullo. Auh in anommati in njxco, in nocpac: tleica, tle ipampa: cujx nolujl, cujx nomaceoal in cujtlatitlan, in tlaçultitlan in tinechmanjlia? in petlapan, in jcpalpan tinechmotlalilia?

ac nehoatl, ac njnomati in jntlan tinechmjquanjlia in jntech tinechmaxitilia, in jntech tinechmopovilia in motlaiximachoan, in mocnjoan, in motlapepenalhoan in jlvileque, in maceoaleque: in çan njman juh iulque, in juh tlacatque in petlatizque in jcpaltizque, in tiqujmjxcoionj, in tiqujnnacaztlapo: auh in tiqujxox, in tiqujmjpitz: in çan njman iuh iocoloque, iuh oalivaloque: in jpan tlacatque, in jpan maltique: in juhcan ca intonal in tecutizque, in tlatocatizque, in mjtoa, in monetlaxonjoa, in motlatlapitzalhoan muchioazque, in tiqujnmoujtiz, in tiqujnmopatillotiz, in tiqujnmonaoaltiz in jmjtic titlatoz, in mjtztlatenqujxtilizque, in qujnanamjqujzque, in copuchtizque, in qujtzcactizque: auh in qujtlatenqujxtilizque in motechiuhcauh in teteu inna, in teteu inta, in veueteutl in tlexicco, in xiuhtetzaqualco maqujtoc in xiuhtecutli in teahaltia, in tepapaca: auh in qujcotonjlia, in qujcavilia in jpolivia in jacoqujçaia in cujtlapilli, in atlapalli in maceoalli.

Tlacatle, tloquee, naoaquee: otlacauhquj in moiollo otinechmocnelili: aço inchoqujz, aço intlaocul: aço invitz, aço imjeuh vecatlan contlazteoaque in vevetque, in jlamatque in ie nachca ommantiuj:

ma çan nê njnotta ma njcnolviltoca, ma njcnomactoca in njctemjquj, in njccochitleoa: in tlatconj, in tlamamalonj, in etic, in aeoaliztli in aixnamjqujliztli: in vey qujmjlli, in vei cacaxtli, in aqujiecotivi in ie nachca ommantivi, in omjtzmotlapialilico in opetlatico, yn oicpaltico.

Here are told the words which the ruler spoke when he had been installed as ruler, to entreat Tezcatlipoca because of having installed him as ruler, and to ask his help and his revelation, that [the ruler] might fulfill his mission. Very many are his words of humility.

"O master, O our lord, O lord of the near, of the nigh, O night, O wind, thou hast inclined thy heart. Perhaps thou hast mistaken me for another, I who am a commoner; I who am a laborer. In excrement, in filth hath my lifetime been—I who am unreliable; I who am of filth, of vice. And I am an imbecile. Why? For what reason? It is perhaps my desert, my merit that thou takest me from the excrement, from the filth, that thou placest me on the reed mat, on the reed seat?

"Who am I? Who do I think I am that thou movest me among, thou bringest me among, thou countest me with thy acquaintances, thy friends, thy chosen ones, those who have desert, those who have merit? Just so were they by nature; so were they born to rule; thou hast opened their eyes, thou hast opened their ears. And thou hast taken possession of them, thou hast inspired them. Just so were they created, so were they sent here. They were born at a time, they were bathed at a time, their day signs were such that they would become lords, would become rulers. It is said that they will become thy backrests, thy flutes. Thou wilt have them replace thee, thou wilt have them substitute for thee, thou wilt hide thyself in them; from within them thou wilt speak; they will pronounce for thee—those who will help, those who will place on the left, who will place in obsidian sandals, and who will pronounce for thy progenitor, the mother of the gods, the father of the gods, Ueueteotl, who is set in the center of the hearth, in the turquoise enclosure, Xiuhtecutli, who batheth the people, washeth the people, and who determineth, who concedeth the destruction, the exaltation of the vassals, of the common folk.

"O master, O lord of the near, of the nigh, thou hast inclined thy heart, thou hast shown me mercy. Perhaps it is [because of] the weeping, the sorrowing, of the old men, the old women, those who have gone beyond to reside; perhaps it is [because of] their spines, their maguey which they left planted deep.

"May I not regard myself. May I not consider myself worthy of the favor, may I not consider myself deserving of that of which I dream, which I see in dreams. It is the load, the burden on the back, heavy, intolerable, insupportable; the large bundle, the large carrying frame which those who already have gone to reside beyond went assuming when they came to guard for thee, when they came to reign" (Anderson and Dibble 1969: 41–42)

In light of this intensely self-conscious, metaphorical, dualistic, and repetitious style of the tecpillatolli it would not, I think, be an exaggeration to speak of an inherent theory of human knowing, a poetics of epistemology which Nahuatl lyrical poetry assumes and enacts, but only indirectly states. This intrinsic style, which I have so fleetingly danced, so hastily herded and driven, so lightly skimmed, so inadequately brushed and blown and breathed before your eyes, has clear implications for certain notions of semantic and epistemological force.

How are we to describe this force which we now identify in the very character of the tecpillatolli style itself? What is the relationship between human speech and reality which this language and its poetry—or the poetry of this language—enact? In approaching an answer it is first necessary, I think, to emphasize the obvious in order to set our minds in the proper frame, to pass over to the other side of translation, as it were.

The diphrase so typical of Nahuatl does not "mean" one thing or another. The tecpillatolli speaker did not translate *xochitl cuicatl* into some single-word equivalent of the word "poetry"; there was no concept called "poetry." There is instead an ambiance of stylized reference that clustered about the twin images of flowers and singing, offering a fluidity of signification within the clear visual and sensory boundaries of the images themselves. Nor does *atl, tepetl*— "water, mountain"—"mean" city, though that is how it must be translated. These diphrases are not ornamental figures elaborately pirouetting about the real thing or the thing itself. We must put ourselves into a linguistic ambiance where the single signifiers "city" and "poetry" simply do not exist. We must enter the non-referential assumption behind the diphrase, which is that no linguistic act can have the power to obtain directly the reality which it indicates, to capture absolutely the very being of that thing we call its reference. Instead, tecpillatolli Nahuatl assumes that a language act, and therefore the human knowledge which can only emerge through such acts, approaches, encircles, or triangulates reality, but may never actually touch or obtain it.

The Nahuas, it would seem, never believed in the myth of primordial referentiality of linguistic signs, the "common sense" faith that words bear an originating, primal, and ostensive one-to-one relation to reality—this word is that object—or some part of their tradition, at least, was acutely aware of the illusory and simplified quality of this everyday view of language as signifier/signified. Tecpillatolli Nahuatl assumes there will always be an ironic or metaphoric distance between reality and what man knows of it. What you know, the language reminds its speakers continually, for you is always *like* something or *associated with* something or *part of* something and never actually something itself; or, as the poet said, *ayac nelli in tiquilhuia nican,* "No one among us truly and finally speaks here."

A Western literary scholar might be at first inclined to discount these special claims for a Nahua epistemology founded on aesthetics by invoking the Vician paradigm, suggesting that the poems and fragments quoted above are simply fine specimens of a preliterate tradition caught in its prerational adolescence. Vico, after all, had pointed out already in the eighteenth century how the intellectual life of the "gentile" nations had grown from an infancy of poetic credulity, literalism, and fable to a philosophical maturity of abstract reasoning and "science," the history of human thought as a progress "from sense to intellect":

> Hence poetic wisdom, the first wisdom of the gentile world, must have begun with a metaphysic not rational and abstract like that of learned men now, but felt and imagined as that of these first men must have been, who, without power of raciocination, were all robust sense and vigorous imagination. This metaphysics was their poetry, a faculty born with them . . . ; born of their ignorance of causes, for ignorance, the mother of wonder, made everything wonderful to men who were ignorant of everything. Their poetry was at first divine, because . . . they imagined the causes of the things they felt and wondered at to be gods. (This is now confirmed by the American Indians, who call gods all the things that surpass their small understanding.) (1971 [1725]:296)

The implicit conclusion in reference to the Nahuatl texts is that here we find the expression of a people arrested by historical circumstance at a pre-Socratic stage; nothing could be more obvious. This conclusion, however, is not only unfair to Nahua tradition but also simply wrong, if seen from the perspective provided by Heidegger. Heidegger's persistent effort to think back in the history of Western philosophy beyond the origins of reason and "representational thinking," to think of Being as presence itself, not as a series of propositional statements about Being, to think back to the pre-Socratics and begin again from there, gives his work a special utility for students of Native American literatures. Beyond his concern to teach a "shepherding" approach to man's existence (the "poetic dwelling" of man) against the utilitarian arrogance of technology and the obvious relation of this approach to the stewardship philosophies of various indigenous peoples, his specific concepts of *das*

Geviert "the four-fold" (earth, heavens, the mortal, the divine); say-ing versus speaking; truth as *aletheia* "unconcealedness" or "dis-clo-sure"; Being as *Anwesen* "presence"; language as *das Ereignis* "appro-priation" or "en-ownment"; reflective versus propositional think-ing—all contribute to the revelation of an alternative history within Native American traditions where the old positivist and Vician terms could only see underdevelopment.

I take it as axiomatic that we—Western, neo-Platonic, Judeo-Christian rationalists—cannot simply by an act of will and intention "open our minds" to the *weltanschauung* of the Nahua traditions, or of any genuinely indigenous American tradition. The very signif-icance of the word "Native" delineates a radical difference from just those things which make us "other" in the traditional American context. I also, however, assume that communication, understand-ing, valid hermeneutical activity are possible, once we have found within ourselves and our own traditions the sets of terms or instru-mentalities needed to enact the self-revelations which are the pre-condition for discovering vital correspondences between our own history, our own ontology, and those of the Nahuas. My thesis here is that Heidegger serves as such an instrumentality, opening our minds toward the modalities of Nahua aesthetics and thought. Our goal is not to explicate Heidegger but to see more clearly through his terms the poetics and epistemology of the Nahuatl texts. Of course, a concerted respectful effort to enter the language itself—given Heidegger's theory that a language already, or still, contains all the potential saying of its speakers—is fundamental. Heidegger turns the Vician paradigm against itself by asserting that human wisdom, right thinking about Being, not only begins but also ends in poetry, because poetry already encompasses all the epistemolog-ical resources of which language is capable. We cannot, therefore, assume that the Nahua poets are blind, ignorant, superstitious, unsophisticated, or philosophically naive simply because their an-cestors never passed through the great rationalist circle of represen-tational thought.

The Nahuatl substantive commonly translated as "truth" is *neltiliztli*, more often found in its adverbial form *nelli*, "truly" or "with truth." The stem *nel-* connotes, León-Portilla demonstrates, firm rootedness. Truth for the Nahuas, he says, was therefore "the quality of being firm, well founded or rooted" (1961:124). A specific verification of this etymology is found among the "elegant sentences" collected by Fr. Mijangos, who tells us that *nitlanelhuayotocac uel ynelhuayocan onacic* is translated as "I discovered the truth of something," and is taken from the image of a tree whose roots have been dug up and revealed. (Literally, the sentence says, "I sought out the root of the matter; I reached completely down to the place where the roots were" [Mijangos 1966 (1623):18].) The tecpillatolli assumes and the poetry insists that statements of absolute validity, of permanent rootedness, are intrinsically impossible within the flux of the human condition. There is, therefore, simply no foundation on which to base a logical dialectic, since no statement may be admitted as a syllogistic premise. It is poetry, however, as the essence of the activity of language, that comes closest to such rootedness, precisely because the speaker of "flower and song" never loses sight of the impassable and tragic distance between his own mind and reality; an ironic distance into which language echoes but from which it never returns.

> It is a true thing, our song;
> it is a true thing, our flowers,
> the well-measured song.
> (Romances, f. 41)

> In flowers is the word
> of the One God held secure.
> (Cantares mexicanos, f. 10)

> Is man true? Is anything true
> in our songs? Will anything remain standing?
> (Cantares mexicanos, f. 11)

The intuitional leap of association which creates the metaphor invalidates any claim to pure rootedness language might make. The only deep-rooted truth, the Nahua said, is that everything moves, and at the root of the word "heart," *yollo*, is *ollin*, "motion," the name of this present cosmos *nahui ollin*, "4 Motion."

If we are convinced of the validity of Heidegger's "poetic view of being" as set forth in *Aus der Erfahrung des Denkens* "The Thinker as Poet," *Der Ursprung des Kunstwerkes* "The Origin of the Work of Art," "Das Ding" "The Thing," "Die Sprache" "Language," " . . . dichterisch wohnt der Mensch" " . . . Poetically Man

Dwells," and other late essays, and if our translations from the Nahuatl are responsibly accurate, we find that several Heideggerian concepts work well to elucidate the epistemic choices implicit in the assumptions and modalities of the tecpillatolli style. Particularly I have in mind truth as non-referential *aletheia*—"disclosure," "clearing and lighting"; language as appropriation; ontic "nearness" versus ontological "remoteness"; Being as lingering presence; speaking as the coming-forth of silent saying; and poetic language as the modality of original and originating speech.

To think of all language as poetry, as Heidegger suggests, to privilege poetic discourse as the prototype of language itself, is to examine the ways in which language itself, not man, speaks. And "language speaks as the peal of stillness," as the evocation of absence. Ernst Cassirer, in *Language and Myth,* maintains that the origins of language and myth are historically and ontologically simultaneous. The work of naming, which he calls a primordial linguistic concept, is the "process which transforms the world of sense impression, which animals also possess, into a mental world, a world of ideas and meanings" (1946:28). This process, he says, is one of emotional intensification and condensation of some datum of experience that is marked off from all other experience by a verbal symbol, a name, which discharges the emotional energy of the concentrated attention, the "noticing" (34). Heidegger, decidedly not a "symbolist," calls attention to the evocative quality of this naming. The naming which speech enacts, says Heidegger, is not ostensive or referential in its originating nature, because what is named need not ever be physically "here"; naming "does not hand out titles, it does not apply terms, but it calls into the word. The naming calls. Calling brings closer what it calls." But where does the call go? "Into the distance in which what is called remains, still absent" (1971:198). If I say, "The woman sitting in the pale blue Toyota with her bare arm hanging languidly out the window," I invoke "a presence sheltered in absence" (since you cannot "see" the woman), which the naming language—and please note that the whole phrase including its syntax is a name, not simply the nouns within it—calls an image forth from your mind to create. How consciously evocative of that simultaneous absence and imaginary presence it is to say "woman" as tecpillatolli Nahuatl says it in the metonymic diphrase *in cueitl in huipil*, "the shirt, the blouse"; or even better to say "centipede" with the metaphor *petlazolcoatl*, "worn-out mat snake," which factors out to "snake like a frayed-edged mat."

"The sheer naming of things," says Hannah Arendt, one of Heidegger's finest interpreters, "the creation of words, is the human way of *appropriating* and, as it were, disalienating the world into which, after all, each of us is born as a newcomer and a stranger" (1978:100). This appropriating, Heidegger's *das Ereignis*, which Hofstadter also translates as "enownment," occurs only through the instrumentality of language and is the consequence or activity of truth understood as aletheia, that "thing that is unthought in the whole history of [Western] thought" since Heraclitus and Parmenides (Spanos 1976:421).

> Unhiddenness is called *aletheia*—truth, as we translate it, is primordial, and this means that it is essentially not a character of human knowledge and statement. Truth, also is not mere value or an "idea" toward whose realization man—the reason is not very clear—ought to strive. Truth, rather, as self-deconcealing, belongs to Being itself: *physis* [Being] is *aletheia*, deconcealment (Spanos 1976:373).

The self-deconcealment of any thing or being within the universal household of Being is dependent upon the invention of its name, or its image, a cognitive act which opens "a clearing, a lighting" in which the thing stands forth unconcealed (Heidegger 1971:53). But this unconcealing is simultaneously a concealing:

> The open place in the midst of beings, the clearing, is never a rigid stage with a permanently raised curtain on which the play of beings runs its course. Rather, the clearing happens only as this double concealment. The unconcealedness of beings—this is never a merely existent state, but a happening. Unconcealedness (truth) is neither an attribute of factual things in the sense of beings, nor one of propositions.
>
> We believe we are at home in the immediate circle of beings. That which is, is familiar, reliable, ordinary. Nevertheless, the clearing is pervaded by a constant concealment in the double form of refusal and dissembling. . . . The nature of truth, that is, of unconcealedness, is dominated throughout by a denial (Heidegger 1971:54).

It is the function of art, then, as Heidegger explains in "The Origin of the Work of Art," from which this definition of aletheia also comes, to provide the "becoming and happening of truth" which "happens in being composed, as the poet composes a poem" (1971:72). "All art," Heidegger finally asserts, "as the letting happen of the advent of the truth of what is, is, as such, essentially poetry," whether it is naming the daisy ("day's eye"), painting the old shoes of a French peasant, or designing a shopping mall (1971:71–72). The concealment within "daisy" is the actual flowerness of the flower which is ignored, hidden, yet startlingly revealed, in its metaphoric association with an eye in the imaginary face of a personified day, a truth further lost in the collapsed tension of our everyday speech, in which "daisy" has become a used-up, strictly referential non-metaphor.

The "becoming or happening of truth" then depends ultimately on processes that are essentially poetic because "language itself is poetry in the essential sense," and it is language that, "by naming beings for the first time, first brings beings to word and to appearance. Only this naming nominates beings *to* their being *from out of* their being. Such saying is a projecting of the clearing, in which announcement is made of what it is that beings come into the Open as" (1971:74). This "projective saying," which is the act of language discovery, Heidegger calls "poetry." The sum total of this projective saying in any given historical culture, Heidegger calls "the world," meaning the relative collective consciousness of Self and Being which any given language has composed for its speakers throughout its history. All the remaining unknown-ness of simple presence, the unapprehended Being which that culture's "projective saying" does not, cannot, include, Heidegger calls "the earth," the dark foundation of the unknown upon which the world of knowing must stand. Poetry, and therefore all art, is the primal saying of the unconcealedness of what is, and "actual language at any given moment is the happening of this saying, in which a people's world historically rises for it and the earth is preserved as that which remains closed" (Heidegger 1971:74).

Truth as aletheia, then, is the erection of a continuing tension, Heidegger calls it a "rift," by means of language in a process that is by definition poetry, between beings and Being, between consciousness and unconsciousness, between the perceivable and the invisible, a tension by which being reaches into Being, consciousness into unconsciousness, and perception into the invisible. What Heidegger offers is an image of all art and of knowledge itself as metaphor, if we inflate that term to include synecdoche and metonym (Jakobson notwithstanding). Pound/Fenollosa point out that metaphor is the process by which the unseen passes over into the seen, "the use of material images to suggest immaterial relations." Metaphor is claimed to be "the revealer of nature," the very substance of both poetry and language. "The whole delicate substance of speech is built upon substrata of metaphor" (Fenollosa 1936:22). Arendt, citing Kant, points out the utter dependence of thought on the image-making faculty of mind and the metaphysical language of poetry:

> No language has a ready-made vocabulary for the needs of mental activity; they all borrow their vocabulary from words meant to correspond either to sense experience or to other experiences of ordinary life. . . . Speaking in analogies, in metaphorical language, according to Kant, is the only way through which speculative reason, which we here call thinking, can manifest itself. . . . All philosophical terms are metaphors, frozen analogies (1978:102–104).

"Poetry," Pound or Fenollosa continues, "does consciously what the primitive races did unconsciously," and the chief work of poets "lies in feeling back along the ancient lines of advance" (1936:23). Back, we might add in Heidegger's terms, to the place where the metaphor, now a deadened lump of everyday speech, first encircled a space of being and gave some truth a place in which to occur. And Arendt demonstrates that the true meaning of a philosophical term is disclosed only when it is dissolved into the original context of its metaphoric origins, into the world of sensory experience which was vivid to the mind of the thinker who coined it. In its inception, metaphor is a sort of triangulation process by which two images strike a line of relation between each other, and in so doing drop lines of indication to a third previously unseen object or mental quality, which then stands out between those images for apprehension. In other words the speaker, who in this act of primal "projective saying" becomes "poet," says something along the lines of, "This reality which I am coming to perceive about X is somewhat like Y." Take King Lear's "When we are born, we cry that we are come / to this great stage of fools" (4.6). We have long since learned from I. A. Richards a binary terminology of the metaphor, to call the stage in this example the "vehicle," and human life—Shakespeare's primary reference according to Richards—the "tenor." But Heidegger's concepts make it inevitable to see a third term of the metaphoric process, beyond this binary terminology, in the words "something like," in the "rift" of mental tension itself between the X and the Y, between tenor and vehicle, and in the darker rift between life-as-a-stage and the necessary back-ground (earth) of life-as-not-a-stage-but-as-life. There is after all the "meaning," as we say, of the whole thing, the great luminous field of force which the apprehension of "all the world's a stage" awakens in the mind, and which Shakespeare did so much to plant in the deeper soil of Anglo knowledge and convictions about society. In lines like "the woman in the ambulance / whose red heart blooms through her coat so astoundingly" from Sylvia Plath's "Poppies in October," we feel the calling of the images "flower" and "blood," feel them call off from each other to a third thing, a new emotional complex concerning terror, death, and beauty (1965:19).

Notice, however, that the complex of terror, death, and beauty which comes to us so clearly in the Plath metaphor is never, for all its clarity and immediacy, actually touched or named in itself. We as readers, speakers, critics, must each experience these lines as the "name" for that complex. In this way, to return to Heidegger's terms, truth "becomes" or "happens" in the rift of the true metaphor. Truth occurs, as it were, in the interstices of the terms of the metaphor, and the "naming" of which Heidegger speaks is never a one-to-one reference process but a "projecting of the clearing," a clearing set off, defined, encircled by the terms of the metaphor.

It should now be evident that I mean to say that the Nahuatl tecpillatolli style throughout its history maintained an unusually intense awareness of just these evocative and metaphoric processes on which thinking itself and the appropriation of language seem to depend, according to Heidegger and Arendt. The endlessly incremental and densely tropological style which I described briefly is, I suggest, a direct consequence of this awareness and its implications for the finite and movable character of truth accessible through human speech.

The Nahuas had their burdens to bear, but a rationalist dialectic of logical truth was not among them. They never lost touch with the poetic foundation of all human statements about reality and never fell into the delusion that those statements could actually touch the final, indivisible presence of Being itself.[6] Of course, they made no treatises like Heidegger's because they began by believing what Heidegger's densely rationalistic prose strove more and more to enact: poetic ambiguity is already the most rigorous of statements, and "the metaphoric sign records a mode of thinking more rigorous than the conceptual" (Spanos 1976:624). In a tradition of thought that begins with such an assumption rather than coming to it after two thousand years of faith in syllogistic logos and the primordial referentiality of names, there is no incentive to ground a tradition of rationalistic description. Why should anyone undertake to describe representationally what language or poetry is or does if poetry itself, the best vehicle of being and knowing, is flawed and uncertain? The Nahuas are simply "silent about silence," which Heidegger claims is the only "authentic saying." They seem aware of the immanent and unspeakable presence of the unspoken in their traditional, formulaic utterances; their elaborate, convoluted, encircling stylistic devices can be seen as an enactment of this awareness.

The Nahuas were not pursuing a unique and arcane stance toward reality. I would cite the novelistic vision and style of Faulkner as outgrowth of a very similar poetics of Being. Consider Addie's speech about words in *As I Lay Dying;* the telling in *The Sound and the Fury* of the same story from four points of view; and most luminous of all, consider that supreme exercise in the sheer relativity of historical documentation, *Absalom, Absalom,* at whose center stands the simultaneous presence and absence of Thomas Sutpen himself. The Nahuas were unique, however, in their passionate and centuries-long devotion to the awareness of the poetic act as the foundation of human knowing. Before the mystery of this intuitional power they stood in continual awe and celebration, never faltering in their recognition of the limited and derivative nature of rational discourse. They preferred, with García Lorca, to remain in touch with the source of the fire, and would have applauded Lorca's response when asked to describe his poetics: "Here it is," he said, "Look: I have the fire in my hands. I understand and work with it perfectly, but I cannot speak of it without creating it" (1966:403).[7]

NOTES

1. Of course, there is no recorded "pre-Hispanic" poetry in America, as it was entirely contained within performance traditions without benefit of phonetic transcription. Except for the few surviving pictographic codices, of which none contains a visual text corresponding directly to the written songs which are the matter of my discussion, all extant Nahuatl literature comes to us in post-Conquest, colonial redactions. Since only Christian priests operated schools in early New Spain, the p-factor (priestly interpolation) must be assumed to be pervasive throughout all the written documents. I follow, nevertheless, the time-honored if somewhat suspect practice of Nahuatl students in treating certain manuscripts, including the Cantares mexicanos and Romances manuscripts from which the poems under discussion are taken, as substantially representative of the actual pre-Conquest, orally transmitted stylistic and philosophical traditions. Bierhorst's introductory essay (1985) to his edition of the Cantares manuscript adds a new reservation concerning this practice.

2. León-Portilla's description of an intuited truth dependent on a "sanctified heart," *corazón endiosado*, is curiously reminiscent of Jonathan Edwards's appeal to aesthetics for verification of the truth of revealed scripture by means of a "due sense of the heart." We know the Bible is true, Edwards said in "A Divine and Supernatural Light," because we feel its statements to be so overwhelmingly beautiful.

3. The translations of all Cantares and Romances excerpts, while often reminiscent of León-Portilla's Spanish readings, are my own. Unless otherwise noted, paleographs of the Nahuatl are taken from Bierhorst 1985; some of my phrases are also taken directly from Bierhorst's English versions. The Bierhorst volumes, the most authoritative transcription and translation of the Cantares manuscript now available, came into print only as I was completing the present discussion, too late for me to make full use of its detailed language notes.

4. Remember Aristotle's point that the gift for metaphor is "the mark of genius" in poetic composition, and that no one can teach it to another.

5. "Poetry proper is never merely a higher mode (*melos*) of everyday language. It is rather the reverse: everyday language is a forgotten and therefore used-up poem from which there hardly resounds a call any longer" (Heidegger 1971:208).

6. Even Heidegger seems to have succumbed to this delusion in his reverence for the poetry of Hölderlin, who he felt was a pure witness to Being, one poet who had stated the *parousia*, the absolute presence of Being itself. No Nahua poet—nor any other authentic poet—could ever presume so greatly. The experience of the question which de Man identifies as how

to "say Being itself" remains unanswered, as by Heidegger's own distinction between saying and speaking (the latter never adequate to the former) it must (De Man 1983).

7. An earlier version of this essay, in Spanish, was published in *Semana de Bellas Artes* 70 (April 4, 1979).

REFERENCES

Anderson, A., and C. Dibble, trans. 1969. *Florentine Codex*, Book 6. Salt Lake City: University of Utah Press.

Andrews, J. Richard. 1975. *Introduction to Classical Nahuatl*. Austin: University of Texas Press.

Arendt, Hannah. 1978. *The Life of the Mind*. New York: Harcourt Brace Jovanovich.

Bierhorst, John, trans. 1985. *Cantares mexicanos*. Stanford: Stanford University Press.

Bové, Paul. 1980. *Destructive Poetics: Heidegger and Modern American Poetry*. New York: Columbia University Press.

Cassirer, Ernst. 1946. *Language and Myth*, trans. Susan Langer. New York: Dover Publications.

De Man, Paul. 1983. *Blindness and Insight: Essays in the Rhetoric of Contemporary Criticism*. Minneapolis: University of Minnesota Press.

De Olmos, Andrés. 1885 [1547]. *Arte para aprender la lengua mexicana*, ed. Rémi Siméon. México, D.F.: Imprenta de Ignacio Escalante.

Edmonson, Munro. 1974. *Sixteenth Century Mexico*. Santa Fe: School of American Research.

Fenollosa, Ernest. 1936. *The Chinese Written Character as a Medium for Poetry*, trans. Ezra Pound. San Francisco: City Lights Books.

García Lorca, Federico. 1979. *Poesía española contemporánea (1901–1934)*. 9th ed., ed. G. Diego. Madrid: Taurus.

Garibay, Angel María. 1961. *Llave del náhuatl*. México, D.F.: Editorial Porrúa.

———. 1963–1969. *Poesía náhuatl*. 3 vols. México, D.F.: Universidad Nacional Autónoma de México.

———. 1971. *Historia de la literatura náhuatl*. 2 vols., 2d ed. México, D.F.: Editorial Porrúa.

González, Rafael Jesús. 1968. Symbol and Metaphor in Nahuatl Poetry. *E.T.C.* 24 (December): 437–444.

Halliburton, David. 1981. *Poetic Thinking: An Approach to Heidegger*. Chicago: The University of Chicago Press.

Heidegger, Martin. 1962. *Being and Time*, trans. J. Macquarrie and E. Robinson. New York: Harper & Row.

———. 1966. *Discourse on Thinking*, trans. J. M. Anderson and E. H. Freund. New York: Harper & Row.

———. 1971. *Poetry, Language, Thought*, trans. Albert Hofstadter. New York: Harper & Row.

Launey, Michel. 1979. *Introduction a la langue et a la litterature azteques: tome l grammaire*. Paris: L'Harmattan.

León-Portilla, Miguel. 1963. *Aztec Thought and Culture,* trans. Jack E. Davis. Norman: University of Oklahoma Press.

———. 1961. *Los antiguos mexicanos através de sus crónicas y cantares*. México, D.F.: Fondo de cultura económica.

———. 1974. *La filosofía náhuatl estudiada en sus fuentes*. 4th ed. México, D.F.: Universidad Nacional Autónoma de México.

Mijangos, Juan. 1966 [1623]. Frases, y modos de hablar elegantes y metafóricos, de los Indios mexicanos, ed. A. M. Garibay. *Estúdios de cultura náhuatl* 6:11–27. (Taken from *Primera parte del sermonio dominical*. Mexico, 1623.)

Miliani, Domingo. 1963. Notas para una poética entre los nahuas. *Estudios de cultura náhuatl* 4:263–280.

Murray, Michael, ed. 1978. *Heidegger and Modern Philosophy: Critical Essays*. New Haven: Yale University Press.

Osuña Ruiz, Rafael. 1968. *Introducción a la lírica prehispánica*. Maracaibo: Editorial Universitaria de la Universidad de Zulia.

Plath, Sylvia. 1965. *Ariel*. New York: Harper & Row.

Spanos, William, ed. 1976. Martin Heidegger and Literature. *Boundary* 2 (4):337–669.

Sullivan, Thelma. 1963. Nahuatl Proverbs, Conundrums, and Metaphors. Collected by Sahagun. *Estudios de cultura náhuatl* 4:93–177.

Swadesh, Mauricio, and Madelena Sancho. 1966. *Los mil elementos del mexicano clásico*. México, D.F.: Universidad Nacional Autónoma de México.

Vico, Giambattista. 1971 [1725]. In *Critical Theory Since Plato*, ed. Hazard Adams. New York: Harcourt Brace Jovanovitch. Pp. 294–301.

White, David. 1978. *Heidegger and the Language of Poetry*. Lincoln: University of Nebraska Press.

Wooten, Anthony. 1976. *The Dilemmas of Discourse*. New York: Holmes, Meier Publishers.

Post-Structuralism and Oral Literature

ARNOLD KRUPAT

I

To speak of post-structuralist theory in conjunction with Native American literatures may seem as odd as serving dog stew with *sauce béarnaise*. It is an unfortunate fact that until very recently critical theorists, whatever their particular perspective, have been quite thoroughly Eurocentric, while those interested in Indian literatures have treated current theory as if it were indeed the French disease. The latest work of Tzvetan Todorov in France, and that of a number of scholars in this country added to the earlier efforts of Dell Hymes, Karl Kroeber, Joel Sherzer, Dennis Tedlock, and Andrew Wiget may signal a change in the situation I have described. To the extent that this is so, it is a change to be welcomed. Until now the theorists have missed out on all sorts of opportunities to refine and test their concepts by application to literary production generally or globally, while the Native Americanists have ensconced themselves in what amounts to a position of critical Luddism, carrying on their analyses, as it were, at a virtually pretechnological level of sophistication.

The reasons for this situation are beyond the scope of the present essay, but it is worth at least mentioning the hundred-fifty-year-old antagonism in this country between "east" and "west," and "high" and "low" culture, where these terms are not merely descriptive but evaluative. Historically, the first term of each pair asserts its priority and superiority by not deigning to notice or comment upon the second, and the second gets its own back by heaping scorn upon the first. It might also be noted here that "east" and "west," "high" and "low" are also regularly employed as virtual synonyms for the terms textuality and orality, which I shall momentarily examine. For all of this, there are also matters of true principle as well as false pride, of philosophy as well as history, keeping post-structuralists, my special concern here, and Native Americanists apart. Foremost among these is the different commitment of each group to the values it subsumes under the name of writing and of speech, and so its different attachment to the text and to the voice.

II

Central to post-structuralist thought (which rejects such a notion as centrality) is the concept of the text.[1] Ferdinand de Saussure, the Swiss linguist generally acknowledged as the founder of structuralism, began from the proposition that in language there are no positive quantities but only differential relations. *Cat*, Saussure claimed, was not a meaningful sound in itself; rather, it becomes meaningful in differential relation to *bat* and *mat*, or *cab* and *car*. We recognize and commence to understand a speaker's utterances, thus, as a result of our recognition of a relatively few differences among sounds, the differences we are to take as meaningful simply being given by the conventions of the language in question. (The differences any one particular language takes as significant, it should be said, are not necessarily significant in other languages.)

The situation grows more complicated, however, as we move from the phonetic and lexical levels of language (sound units and individual "words") to the levels of semantics and discourse (sentence- and meaning-units, and genres). There, the meaningful differences of the system are less clearly determined by convention and so more nearly open to what may amount to the necessity for infinite interpretation. Every discourse is a system of signifiers, each of which signifies by means of its differential relation—a highly problematic relation, now, as I have said—to other signifiers. At the level of discourse, therefore, the "signified," as Terry Eagleton puts it, or "meaning is not immediately *present* in a sign. Since the meaning of a sign is a matter of what the sign is *not*, its meaning is always in some sense absent from it too" (1983:128); dependent upon the traces in and through it of all the other significant signs it is not. In Jacques Derrida's own statement,

114

Whether in written or in spoken discourse, no element can function as a sign without relating to another element which itself is
not simply present. This linkage means that each "element"—
phoneme or grapheme—is constituted with reference to the trace
in it of other elements of the sequence or system. This linkage,
this weaving, is the *text*, which is produced only through the
transformation of another text. Nothing, either in the elements or
in the system, is anywhere simply present or absent. There are
only, everywhere, differences and traces of traces (Culler
1982:99).[2]

Instead of specifiable signifieds or determinate meanings (however plural), one has instead a series of infinite regress, of constant
difference, and so the deferral of fixed, ultimate, or, as Derrida calls
it, "transcendental" meaning, the very desire for which is stig-
matized as ideological and logocentric, as metaphysical and onto-
theological nostalgia, a kind of *mauvaise foi*. One is freed or constrained—and hence the politics of post-structuralism—to the infinite play of signification. This is the post-structuralist universe of
textuality where the term *text* refers to *all systems of signification,
properly understood,* in the world as well as on the page, spoken as
well as written, as in Derrida's linkage of "written" and "spoken
discourse," of "phoneme" and "grapheme."

From even such a rough sketch of this complex subject, it
should be apparent how post-structuralists can claim that writing
precedes speaking. The precedence meant is logical rather than historical (post-structuralist preference for logic over history is notorious); it may refer to no more than the fact that, as the philosopher
Richard Rorty puts it, Derrida believes "certain universal features
of all discourse are more clearly seen in the case of writing than in
the case of speech" (1984:23). In this sense, "speech" is only a
special—one might say a derivative—form of "writing." Although
it is sounded in time rather than inscribed in space, the actually
spoken is taken to be marked by the problematic of textuality quite
as much as the actually written. For all the physical presence of
any given speaker, the meaning of her words are as much dependent
on other words (unspoken, absent) as the words of any text. Speech
and writing, thus, are only different forms of the same thing.

And yet, in a great deal of post-structuralist theorizing, what
is meant by "speech" is not at all what I have just described. In
this usage, "speech" is treated not as a parallel to "writing," or as

its subsidiary, but rather as its antagonist. Here, "speech" becomes the name given to that understanding of discourse which insists—of course, quite mistakenly!—that specific signifieds and delimited meanings *can* indeed be communicated. Any assertion that spoken discourse—all models of which posit actual material relations between speakers and auditors present to one another (writer/reader models are marked by generalization, abstraction, and absence)—can indeed achieve bounded communication as an effective result of that material presence are taken as manifestations either of ignorance or of that logocentric bad faith to which I have referred. In this regard, as Barbara Johnson, a Yale critic (who now teaches at Harvard) writes, post-structuralism represents a

> reversal . . . of everything that in a signified-based theory of meaning, would constitute "noise." Jacques Derrida has chosen to speak of the values involved in this reversal in terms of "speech" and "writing" in which "speech" stands for the privilege accorded to meaning as immediacy, unity, identity, truth, and presence, while "writing" stands for the devalued functions of distance, difference, dissimulation, and deferment (1984:279).

That is, "writing" stands for exactly those "functions" which, in actual practice, are said to govern all discourse. From this perspective, there is really no such thing—nor was there ever such a thing—as that which "speech" pretends to be; any appeal to speech or to the voice as sources of univocal (or even plural-but-bounded) signification is disingenuous or deceptive. All discourse is textual or scriptive, and it is precisely the nature of script that it can never be scripture, fixed in its meaning as the spoken word is—erroneously, of course—claimed to be.

III

This is all well and good, the student of Native American literatures may say, but it stinks of abstraction, of the archive and the ivory tower. Isn't it all so absurdly *eastern*! Native Americanists, along with most scientists, critics, and scholars generally, have decidedly held (whether they have been aware of it or not) to what Johnson calls "a signified-based theory of meaning," one for which truth, let alone fixed meaning, in statement has always been at least possible. As students of oral cultures and traditions, Native Americanists have in particular referred this possibility to speech and the voice. The implications of traditional Native American narratives for a general theory of meaning remain to be studied. Here I want to quote a comment about meaning that is ascribed to an Indian traditionalist—that is to say, someone from a predominantly oral culture—although the quotation comes from a contemporary written work by a Native American, from Leslie Silko's *Ceremony*. I think it may help us with some of these matters.

Early in *Ceremony*, the old singer Ku'oosh comes to attempt a cure for Tayo, the troubled central character of the novel. Ku'oosh remarks, "But you know, grandson, this world is fragile." The narrator then comments as follows:

> The word he chose to express "fragile" was filled with the intricacies of a continuing process, and with a strength inherent in spider webs woven across paths through sand hills where early in the morning the sun becomes entangled in each filament of web. It took a long time to explain the fragility and intricacy because no word exists alone, and the reason for choosing each word had to be explained with a story about why it must be said this certain way (1978:36–37).

So far, such an account of how language means might easily be squared with the account I have given above of post-structuralist textual theory. We have the web of words and the "linkage" of any single spoken word with other words not then spoken; the necessity of a story for each word, the words of which stories themselves necessitate further stories, with no end to storytelling. Thus, with the infinite deferral of some ultimate signification, this nearly enough recalls Derrida's dialectic of absence/presence, and the trace. Silko's narrator, however, does not end here, but continues, "That was the responsibility that went with being human, old Ku'oosh said, the story behind each word must be told *so there could be no mistake in the meaning of what had been said;* and this demanded great patience and love" (1978:36–37, italics added).

To use language in such a way that "there could be no mistake in the meaning of what had been said" has been the dream of Western social science and philosophy, which have traditionally been dependent upon a "signified-based theory of meaning." Here, Silko attributes such a dream to a representative of a non-Western tradition. (This dream, let me say all too quickly here, may not be Silko's, for her novel shows that there may be more to efficacious storytelling than what Ku'oosh can imagine.)

What is curious to note is that from an historical point of view, such concern for fixed meanings seems not to have been typical of oral cultures at all; rather, it appears to arise only with the shift to literacy and to chirographic means of information storage, only to become emphasized later with the further shift from chirography to typography, from manuscripts to printed texts. So far as research has been able to determine, the audiences for oral performances—Native American or Yugoslav, a hundred years ago or today—are very little concerned with interpretative uniformity or agreement of any exactitude as to what a word or passage *meant*. These are the worries of manuscript and book cultures, pretty exclusively. Thus, it is probably not accidental, as Walter Ong has pointed out, that the post-structuralist insistence on interpretative openness and undecidable meaning coincides with the first moments of—this is Ong's phrase—"secondary orality" in the West, with a technological shift away from print to electronic information retrieval systems that are not exclusively or inviolably text based (1982:3, passim). That post-structuralists in fact call this openness textuality rather than orality is a confusion bred of their relative lack of interest in historical detail.

IV

For the recorder of Native American oral performances, the decision between the "oral" or "textual" theory of meaning—between "speech" and "writing" (as Ku'oosh and post-structuralism rather than historical practice define these), between unmistakable or undecidable meanings—has immediate and practical mythographic consequences: a decision in favor of orality or textuality appears to imply correlative choices between performative effectivity or linguistic/referential accuracy, and (so it would seem) between a disciplinary commitment to science or to literature. The work of Franz

Boas, Edward Sapir, and Melville Jacobs, for example, seems to have equated a commitment to science with the "oral" theory of meaning. Their prose translations tend to slight the dynamics of performances—no doubt unfortunately, although as they seemed to think, perhaps inevitably—so that the goal of strict referential accuracy might be achieved. To write the Native story so that it could be clearly understood (or at least so that it might be stable enough for perpetual analysis); so that the text might stand as the voice of Ku'oosh would speak, volume and pitch and duration would have to be sacrificed—as would the whole contextual dimension of Native performances, which was hardly even recognized as an aspect of narrative. In the recent work of Jerome Rothenberg, by contrast, privilege is accorded more nearly to the "textual" theory of meaning. Rothenberg produces very free verse translations acknowledged in some quarters to be effective from a performative perspective, although highly suspect linguistically and referentially.[3] Rothenberg's commitment, of course, is to literature. His sometime-colleague, Dennis Tedlock, perhaps more than anyone has tried to turn a commitment to the "textual" theory of meaning and to the dynamics of performance into translations both referentially accurate and poetically powerful. It is Tedlock's desire to "provide a performable text," to produce "a performable translation," one which will permit a "reading . . . back from [the] eye to [the] voice" (1983:6, 13, 12). It has been claimed, however, that Tedlock's method, dependent as it is on metalinguistic features, is somewhat inattentive to the (probable) linguistic patterns of the texts he records. Attention to such patterns is, of course, precisely central to the important work of Dell Hymes with Northwest coast narratives. Hymes equates a commitment to exact meanings with verse-drama translations in an attempt also to reconcile science and literature. Hymes's line, act, and scene divisions often provide effectively poetic *texts,* which also give a strong sense of linguistic patterning in the original; they do nothing at all, however, to suggest the dynamics of performance. Anthony Mattina's fascinating "Red English" translations are loosely committed to the "oral" theory of meaning, to prose, to linguistic accuracy, and to science. Mattina has forthrightly acknowledged the inability of his method (and, indeed, the difficulty for one of his specifically linguistic interests) to convey much sense of the actual performance. Mattina's route

to the accurate text, privileging the nonstandard English of his tran-
scriber/translator, has not yet found wide acceptance, although it
seems to have important claims upon our interest and attention.
Other mythographers—most notably Joel Sherzer and William
Bright—have tried to combine some of these various possibilities.
What we have here are attempts to establish the primacy of the
voice or the text; to work for unmistakable meanings or to allow
undecidability its free play; to privilege the performative or the
linguistic dimension of Native American song and story, and thus
to contribute to Western scientific or literary understanding.

Choices between "science" and "literature," "performance" and
"linguistics," "voice" and "text," and other categories perceived to
stand in oppositional relation have up until now structured this
field. But this may be mistaken; perhaps we would do better to say
here at least this much of what Saussure said of language, that these
terms name no positive quantities we can stabilize as oppositions
available for choice, but only systems of differential relations. I
mean to affirm that line of thought (we may trace it roughly in
recent decades from Thomas Kuhn, on the constitution of "science,"
to the late Paul De Man and to Terry Eagleton—different as the
latter two critics are from one another—on the constitution of "literature") which asserts that there is no fixed thing that can count
once and for all as "science," or "literature"; instead there is only
a series of shifting paradigms and practices that have come to define
what Western culture has meant by "science" or "literature" at
different times in history. Even such terms as "speech" and "writing," as I have tried to show, need not refer to what they do in
common parlance. Ku'oosh—or Leslie Silko—may really be thinking of the closure of the printed text while trying to define some
quality of oral storytelling, while Jacques Derrida may actually be
responding to the condition of postliterate, electronic "secondary
orality" when he insists upon the openness of the textual grapheme,
to which he then assimilates the phoneme as well. In science—most
particularly in the *sciences humaines* or social sciences—and literary
analysis it is as Nietszche said of philosophy, that the assertion of
fixed oppositional relations is simply a projection onto the world of
our own mental categories;[4] or, to return to Nietszche's contemporary, de Saussure, what we have most surely to work with are only
systems of difference.

V

The value of these considerations lies in their insistence that the most sophisticated mythographers today must display a considerably greater methodological modesty than they have done (at times) so far. This is not simply a call to pluralism or fairmindedness, as if one actually could establish the superiority of one method to all others on "scientific" grounds but, on moral or political grounds, chose not to. Rather, I am trying to point to what post-structural theory has shown to be in the nature of the case, something over which the individual mythographer's talent and will have no control. Before developing these remarks, I want first to say why such methodological modesty, as I have called it, seems particularly important just at present.

Indian literatures are currently passing through a period of canonization in which a number of different versions of Native materials, produced by methods which frequently seem to be directly opposed to one another, vie for authority and dominance in the eyes of an established and institutionally defined clerisy—the academic establishment—and an ad hoc prophetic class—interested Native American people—which is for the most part only tangentially, adversarially, or not at all affiliated with the Temple of Academe. Those texts (accompanied or supplemented by videotapes or recordings on occasion) which achieve acceptance will define what most people, Native and non-Native alike, understand to be Native American literature.[5] Those texts which are rejected— for their stiffness, on the one hand, or their inauthenticity, on the other, for example—will be marginalized and thus little known or valued.

The current sorting of canonical from apocryphal texts may or may not be strictly comparable to the process of canonization best known to the West, that which took place in the years from 400 B.C. to A.D. 100 when various Hebrew manuscripts achieved the status of scripture. That Native American literary expression has been and continues to be recorded, transcribed, translated, examined, and evaluated for the most part by non-Native people surely constitutes a difference from the biblical situation, as does the equally or more important fact that even Native students of this literature, with deep roots in oral culture, are much farther from that primary orality which knows no writing (and from which traditional narratives derive) than were the earliest compilers of the Bible. In Western culture, shifts from orality to types of literacy and to our present postliteracy occurred slowly over a span of some twenty-five hundred years. Native American shifts from oral "literary" modes to written or mixed modes, however, have occurred in only some three hundred fifty years; nor is the relationship between the oral and the literate in different Native cultures and among different Native individuals at all clear. In these regards, we might well study not only the institutionalization of the biblical, but also of the literary canon—those established works of literature which Northrop Frye calls secular scripture—as a route to some perspective on the current moment in Native American studies. What does it mean, for example, that for Native American cultures and especially for Euramerican culture just now "literature," which once had an important status in the economy of cultural maintenance is functionally quite marginal? At worst, "literature" may be said predominantly to exist in the West as no more than an object of academic study; the literary canon today, so far as it exists at all, is almost strictly a pedagogical canon.[6] For all of this, the historical movement of Native American literatures from voice to text, and the current competition among various textual forms and formats for authority, involve a process that is in considerable degree familiar, and whose consequences, so far as past experience is any guide, can be readily predicted. Should any particular mythographic method successfully assert its authority and attain ascendancy as canonical, it will determine our understanding and evaluation of Native American literatures for a long time to come.[7]

I should like to urge, therefore, an openness based on the rather modern post-structuralist theory of the trace,[8] with some small supplementation from ancient wisdom. From these perspectives, no single mythographic method, however powerful and effective its achievements, could claim full authority as sole representative of— as alone capable of providing the accurate and also effective texts which univocally signify and mean—"Indian literature," for the simple reason that what each method in itself is and can offer is always a function of what it is not and what it can never produce. What the very best mythographers make present to us can only fully be understood in relation to what they have left out, to the absences whose traces we must somehow take into account if we are to understand anything at all. To the extent, for example, that Dell Hymes and Dennis Tedlock, surely the two most influential contemporary mythographers, have presented their work as not merely different from the work of others but as the standard for others to follow, as a model of the right way to proceed, we must be wary. In regard to such claims, we do well to heed the experience of the biblical period of canonization, when the wise were indeed suspicious of an insistence that any given writing—however fixed and unalterable and beyond appeal it might seem—was scripture, or even that scripture was sufficient unto itself. Even scripture, it was reasoned, might be mistakenly comprehended, inaccurately copied, or falsified, as a result of the ignorance or ignominy of men, and so transmitted in ways that could set one "authoritative" text against another. Thus, it came to be recognized that whatever the fixed text found before one—in time this became a printed rather than a manuscript text—it was of the utmost importance for a proper understanding to seek to amplify or alter it on the basis of any and all information available, and in this way to recall that even printed texts derive from manuscript versions, as manuscripts themselves are only the partial record of oral performance. As Gerald Bruns writes of the central Hebrew text, "Torah . . . is fixed, but it is permissible and, indeed necessary to unfix it orally, for otherwise who will understand it" (1982:29)—or, as we might ask, who can be sure it means only what it says and says only what it means, when both saying and meaning are functions of what is absent as well as what is present?

Stated this way, it seems to me that the ancient sense of these matters is really not so far at all from the contemporary post-structuralist sense, particularly from the theory of the trace when it asserts that no single element of a system—no written word alone—can be presumed to function meaningfully in and of itself, to mean only by itself. Phoneme or grapheme, sign, sentence, discourse, or even authorized canonical series, each depends for its meaning on something it is not, or which it excludes. One's situation here is rather like that of the very young Stephen Dedalus, in James Joyce's *Portrait of the Artist,* trying to list clearly on the page nothing more than "himself, his name and where he was" (1958:15). Stephen writes in his notebook:

Stephen Dedalus
Class of Elements
Clongowes Wood College
Sallins
County Kildare
Ireland
Europe
The World
The Universe

But then, he must wonder, "What was after the universe? Nothing. But was there anything round the universe to show where it stopped before the nothing place began?" (1958:16). Stephen's "nothing place," what we might otherwise call infinity, is meaningful only as an endless extension of other terms it is not—except that the very notion of an endless or "nothing place" seems to depend upon our capacity to determine where other terms—the terms *it* is not—"stop," something we cannot do. To make words mean in isolation, as when they are set off in a list, is an impossible task; as Stephen found, the effort "made him very tired . . . made his head feel very big" (1958:16).

What all this implies for Native American literatures is that we must read the texts we have, from Henry Schoolcraft to the present moment, as in need of unfixing, a process by which we acknowledge that any meanings which appear to be present are never fully present; meaning, to return to Eagleton's phrase, "is a matter of what the sign is *not*," as well as of what the sign seems to be. And, of course, the texts of Native American literatures are not only theoretically but also in practice what we may call *oral texts*, an oxymoronic rather than self-contradictory appellation. Tedlock's performance-oriented texts, for instance, have achieved their particular kind of excellence precisely at the cost of some other kind; what is present to them and what they present exists only in relation to what is absent from them and what they cannot present. To note that something is missing from Tedlock's pages is to confirm the coherence of his method rather than its failure. The same is true of what Hymes and Mattina have given us. We must try to imagine the performative dynamics which their approaches cannot provide, recognizing all the while that this absence may be inevitable, the necessary consequence of what is present. Mythographers must choose and limit and specify in order to write their texts at all. This is, however, the very reason why those who read and study those texts must unfix them as a necessity of the impossibility of transferring the qualities of oral performance to writing; of the impossibility of any "writing" standing alone and fully present, able to use words "so there could be no mistake in the meaning of what had been said." That this unfixing must be one of the tasks the future holds should not at all disarm or depress the growing numbers of those interested in Native American literatures.

NOTES

1. It should be said from the outset that there is no more a single post-structuralism whose outlines may be traced than there is a single structuralism, Marxism, or New Criticism. The best short introduction to the subject, I believe, is Terry Eagleton's in his *Literary Theory: An Introduction* (1983), which may be followed with Frank Lentricchia's "History or the Abyss: Poststructuralism," chapter 5 of his *After the New Criticism* (1980). Neither Eagleton nor Lentricchia could strictly be called a post-structuralist—which is not the case with Jonathan Culler, whose *On Deconstruction: Theory and Criticism after Structuralism* is probably the most complete and sympathetic account to be found (1982). Josué Harari's collection, *Textual Strategies: Perspectives in Post-Structuralist Criticism* (1979), contains a range of essays that in the broadest sense define the field—although it is extremely difficult, sometimes to the point of futility, to specify a clear line where structuralism leaves off and post-structuralism begins. Both Culler and Harari provide excellent and detailed bibliographies for those who wish further references.

2. I have given Jonathan Culler's translation of this passage from Derrida's *Positions*, the English translation of which, by Alan Bass, is slightly different, and, I think, slightly more awkward.

3. For example, Jeffrey Huntsman, in "Traditional Native American Literature: The Translation Dilemma," writes, "However little they sound like the Navajo originals, Rothenberg's poems are engrossing and there is much to be gained from the excitement they generate when they are *performed*" (1983:93, italics added). But there is also William Bevis, in "American Indian Verse Translations," who has commented on Rothenberg's "blind attention to content, and total insensitivity to style and aesthetic form" (1975:319). As I understand Bevis, he is referring to the fact that Rothenberg tends to work from some *idea* of the meaning, from

his own highly subjective *feel* for what the poem is about, rather than from close attention to the words themselves and their actual linguistic and referential "content." If this is correct, Bevis and I are in agreement, although we make the point in different language. What is a poem and what is a narrative, of course, is even less clear to us in Native American expressive practice than in our own (although it is quite possible to take secure if not sophisticated refuge in the distinction between sung or chanted materials and spoken materials—more or less). Except for Rothenberg, I speak pretty exclusively of those who try to put Indian story, not song, on the page.

4. See, "There are no opposites: only from those of logic do we derive the concept of opposites and falsely transfer it to things" (in Spivak 1974:xxviii).

5. This may be as good a place as any to acknowledge fully and try to explain, if not justify, my obviously text-based treatment of Native American literatures, which are, of course, oral modes of expression. I agree with Andrew Wiget for example, when he suggests in this volume, that Larry Evers's videotapes of Native performances may be the nearest any of us not privileged to attend actual performances of traditional materials is likely to come to what those performances are really like. In the same way, I am fascinated by Dennis Tedlock's auditory- and performance-oriented attempts at translation; and so, too, even sympathetic to Rothenberg's efforts, in spite of his notorious liberties. These seem clearly the directions to follow where the mythographer seeks to render as closely as possible the *experience* of traditional performance. For purposes of analysis and study, however, for work that predominantly seeks *understanding*, it seems that all phenomena, natural as well as cultural, must be wrenched out of context—purified, magnified, slowed down, speeded up, run backwards and/or repeated, and so on—however we may regret this fact. ("Experience" and "understanding" as I have used them above are, as one might readily guess, conceived as differentially rather than oppositionally related terms.) There appears to be an inevitable Heisenbergianism involved here such that a gain in one aspect of concern is obtained at the cost of a loss in another. Although I believe some deep *experience* of the performed power of Native American poetry or narrative must underlie any powerful *understanding* of it, it does not seem to me that understanding can come from experience alone, and for this understanding one needs texts—to such an extent I am indeed a creature of that print-oriented phase of Western literacy presently coming to an end. My own work to date has attempted to understand the place of Native American history and culture in relation to Euramerican culture. While that work has at every moment tried to keep in mind that Indian literatures were not traditionally written,

it has inevitably had to proceed by studying textualizations of oral perfor-mance, by an attention to texts and what the dominant culture—along with Native Americans, inevitably influenced by (impinged upon, one might say) that dominant culture—has made of those texts.

6. I have developed this point in "Defusing the Canon; or, Opening to the Indians," a paper presented to the New York College English Associ-ation Conference in 1983. See also my "Native American Literature and the Canon."

7. See, for example, Anthony Mattina's essay in the present volume.

8. And thus to base the claim for pluralism not only on vague empirical claims as to "the way things really are," or on a presumptively apolitical appeal to respect for cultural diversity (this has been Wayne Charles Miller's approach in "Toward a New Literary History of the United States" [1984], an essay which I find admirable although naive), but also on a theory of discourse and a reading of history, both of which are shot through with political implications.

REFERENCES

Bevis, William. 1975. American Indian Verse Translations. In *Literature of the American Indians: Views and Interpretations,* ed. Abraham Chapman. Pp. 308–323. New York: New American Library.

Bruns, Gerald N. 1982. *Inventions: Writing, Textuality, and Understanding in Literary History.* New Haven: Yale University Press.

Culler, Jonathan. 1982. *On Deconstruction: Theory and Criticism after Structural-ism.* Ithaca: Cornell University Press.

Derrida, Jacques. 1981. *Positions.* Trans. Alan Bass. Chicago: University of Chicago Press.

Eagleton, Terry. 1983. *Literary Theory: An Introduction.* Minneapolis: Uni-versity of Minnesota Press.

Harari, Josué, ed. 1979. *Textual Strategies: Perspectives in Post-Structuralist Criticism.* Ithaca: Cornell University Press.

Huntsman, Jeffrey. 1983. Traditional Native American Literature: The Translation Dilemma. In *Smoothing the Ground: Essays on Native Amer-ican Oral Literature,* ed. Brian Swann. Pp. 87–97. Berkeley, Los Angeles, London: University of California Press.

Johnson, Barbara. 1984. Rigorous Unreliability. *Critical Inquiry* 11 (Decem-ber):278–285.

Joyce, James. 1958. *A Portrait of the Artist as a Young Man.* New York: The Viking Press.

Krupat, Arnold. 1983. Defusing the Canon; or, Opening to the Indians. Paper presented at the New York College English Association Conference, May 19.

———. 1984. Native American Literature and the Canon. In *Canons*, ed. Robert von Hallberg. Pp. 309–336. Chicago: University of Chicago Press.

Lentricchia, Frank. 1980. *After the New Criticism*. Chicago: University of Chicago Press.

Miller, Wayne Charles. 1984. Toward a New Literary History of the United States. *MELUS* 11 (Spring):5–25.

Ong, Walter S. J. 1982. *Orality and Literacy: The Technologizing of the Word*. London: Methuen.

Rorty, Richard. 1984. Deconstruction and Circumvention. *Critical Inquiry* 11 (September):1–23.

Silko, Leslie Marmon. 1978. *Ceremony*. New York: Signet Books.

Spivak, Gayatri Chakravorty. 1974. Translator's Preface to Jacques Derrida, *Of Grammatology*. Baltimore: The Johns Hopkins University Press.

Tedlock, Dennis. 1983. *The Spoken Word and the Work of Interpretation*. Philadelphia: University of Pennsylvania Press.

North American Indian Mythography: Editing Texts for the Printed Page

ANTHONY MATTINA

I

Those who study American Indian texts are aware of the recent charges made by Dennis Tedlock and Dell Hymes that the traditional prose paragraph is an inadequate means of written representation for Indian texts. While both scholars insist that Indian texts should be transcribed in verse, each argues different points: For Tedlock, verse in ragged-right format reflects the delivery of the text (voice quality, pauses, intonation, and other prosodic features), while for Hymes the verse format is dictated by what he perceives as the rhetorical organization of the text.[1]

Were these scholars expressing only their preferences for text writing, other mythographers would then have their examples to follow, disregard, or experiment with. But Tedlock and Hymes do not stop at expressing preferences; each explains at length the reasons for his preference. Having asked himself how to record narrative performances, Tedlock decides to write faithful scores of actual performances; having asked himself what it is a mythographer commits to print, Hymes decides to produce text reconstructions that mirror some intuited underlying structure. They go beyond explanation of their practice, each asserting a contribution to mythological theory. Tedlock claims to have taken us closer to (an understanding of American Indian) oral poetics, and Hymes to have shown us the grammar of American Indian narrative. While these explanations of the choices for text transcription are helpful guides to the transcripts, I consider these two scholars' ventures from the methodological into the theoretical to have yielded outlandish claims. Let me review the progress of their positions, and then raise again the question of what a mythographer's task is.

II

At first, Tedlock was interested in doing a good English translation of Zuni texts. Unhappy with the paragraph format of earlier recorders, he began by experimenting with two forms: a dramatic one, as suggested by Jacobs (1959), and a couplet form, à la Edmonson (1971). Eventually he settled on a format of his own devising, one akin to free verse. Listening to his Zuni tapes, he discovered that pauses—silences of varying duration—recur throughout a performance and thus, he concluded, they mark lines of oral narrative.[2] Each pause he matched with a carriage return of his typewriter, or, if the pause was extra long, with a proportionately larger number of carriage returns. Keep in mind that Tedlock was inserting these line-marking carriage returns in his English translations, not just in the Zuni transcriptions.

Although Tedlock considered pauses to be the most important of all paralinguistic features of Zuni, he felt that other lesser features also needed to be represented. He decided to print loud utterances in capitals, soft utterances in extra small letters, and to leave the normal ones in intermediate size print; he represented pitch movements graphically by moving the print on the page, above or below the base line, and even in slanting (rising or falling) diagonals.

What Tedlock presented was an English translation reminiscent of the record of an actual performance of a musical score. The intent was to match the voice quality of a particular Zuni in the act of myth-telling.[3] Following the score, readers could do interpretive readings, aloud, of the text, and approximate, *mutatis mutandis*, the Zuni intonations of the original in the English translation.

Tedlock was not inflexible in how exactly the English translations should match the rhythm of the Zuni. He did not require, for example, that the number of syllables in the English line should match precisely the number of Zuni syllables, and he allowed changes in word order. In fact he even advised against too mechanical a reading that would interfere with the flow of the performance. In sum, as Tedlock acknowledged, his translations were experiments, guided by his own "sense of the matter" (1978:xxi). While he saw his early practice as innovative, he was making neither a theoretical nor even a general methodological statement—he was but translating Zuni into English with a performance-based, quasi-"transcriptional" component.[4]

While devising his system for a Zuni-English narrative score, Tedlock was making two corollary points. First, agreeing with other scholars that extant dictated North American Indian texts were of poor literary quality, Tedlock attributed that poor quality partially to bad editing and partially to the use of the paragraph format, a format reminiscent of Western (European) short stories or plot summaries of drama. Because oral narrative is not the equivalent of written prose (the latter being an invention that postdates literacy), Tedlock felt that records of oral narrative should not be printed as written prose.[5]

At the same time that he was displaying his results with Zuni-English "transtypography," Tedlock was making a second point: expecting other North American Indian narratives to be amenable to his style of transcription, he insisted that all such narratives should be scored in his way, and furthermore, read aloud with the prosodic features of the original performance. He wanted to focus on the powers of the voice and retrain our ears to listen, not just let our eyes read.[6] Tedlock was aiming for either an authoritative definition of oral poetics, or an authoritative representational method for the study of oral poetics, or both. By the time he published "Toward an Oral Poetics" (1977), he had gone pan-American and was waxing hermeneutic. That is, he was talking well beyond Zuni, about other oral literatures, and was addressing questions of interpretation.

In the piece just mentioned, after stating that we need a fresh start in the study of oral literature (section I), Tedlock depicted North American Indian narratives as inextricable from the "world," from their context of symbolic reference and (pragmatic) performance (section II). He then proposed that the narrator, the audience, and even critical discourse belong inside the traditional story (section III).[7] As Tedlock broadened his horizons, zooming away from the story to include more and more of the surroundings, geographic and historical, the story per se was becoming less and less significant, engulfed by its universe. Just as it was aesthetic judgment (common sense) that guided Tedlock's decisions on how to translate, it was later a similarly artistic epistemological sense that told him how far to back away from the narrative percept in order to encompass as much as was feasible of the pertinent, attendant, related context.[8] If you stand too close to the tree, Tedlock seemed to warn, you won't be able to see the forest.

Tedlock again addressed the question of the "text" raised in "Toward an Oral Poetics" in a presentation of March 29, 1978, on the third floor of the School of Theology Building, Boston University, when he endeavored to explain his notion of "authoritative text." Starting with the observation that an authoritative or fixed text can be "re-told" by a narrator-interpreter, Tedlock expanded on his views by referring to a specific text, the Word of Kyaklo, a Zuni text about beginnings. This text can be retold by wearers of Kyaklo's mask, and each such retelling becomes "something new *and* a comment, . . . both a restoration and a further possibility" (1981:48). The authoritative text is not a "visible or tangible object," but an "object nevertheless."[9] Tedlock's explanation left the authoritative text undefined. I find it impossible to know which of the two possible interpretations of a "fixed text" he would choose— either a prototext (the earliest text), or a systematic abstract text, a texteme.[10] This ambiguity notwithstanding, to the arguments which purport to explain what an authoritative text is, Tedlock appends a stinging accusation: while narrator-interpreters retell an authoritative text because they "must keep the story going," phenomenologists and structuralists, including Hymes, merely hanker after the text, the "sacred object." What, then, in light of Tedlock's claims, is a mythographer to do? Is Tedlock proposing that the sacred text is an untouchable object, only to be venerated from afar with shut ears and eyes?

We can see that Tedlock has moved from concerns of translation to the broader question: What is it that a mythographer is interested in achieving through recording? Wherever he may fit within the long string of texturalists, textualists, contextualists, structuralists, and deconstructionists, we know that he has voiced disapproval of those who neglect the language of the myth, but he himself has seemed more interested in Zuni diction than in Zuni meanings.[11] Remember, Tedlock gave us English translations with Zuni intonations—English texts with a Zuni accent. In 1978, in the preface to the second edition of *Finding the Center,* Tedlock lamented that his was still the only book done à la Tedlock.

III

While the task Hymes set out to accomplish is, broadly speaking, the same as Tedlock's—to record myths so as to maximize interpretive transparency—his procedures differ substantially. Hymes does not transfer Chinookan performances from tape to paper, but recasts paper transcriptions from a paragraph format into a verse format. What are verses? Formally, Chinookan verses are undefined narrative units. They normally consist of more than one sentence, and often are marked by initial particles. Attendant mythographic details include units larger and smaller than the basic verse. Mythographers must decide whether verses group into stanzas, and if so, how many of them do; how stanzas group into scenes, scenes into acts, acts into parts; they must also decide whether to divide verses into versicles and lines, the latter being, at least in Chinookan languages, most commonly one-verb sentences. Each text so formatted consists of *parts,* which are labeled fully (PART ONE, PART TWO), and to which a title may be given; *acts,* each labeled with a Roman numeral and also titled; *scenes* (if an act contains more than one such), each labeled with a small Roman numeral and usually assigned a title; *stanzas,* not titled, but labeled with capital letters; *verses,* similarly without titles, but preceded by parenthesized small letters; and *versicles* and *lines,* neither titled nor labeled, but both requiring indentations, numbered as in poetry. This format does not intend to re-create or evoke the paralinguistic features of the original narrative performance, but rather wants to make explicit the rhetorical design, including the symbolic organization, of the original. Before we return to the notion of rhetorical design, we should review how one proceeds in the formatting or blocking out of the text, and discuss Hymes's notion of verse.

Given a text, instructs Hymes, the mythographer should propose a pattern—a series of boundaries of narrative units—justified by and supported with syntactic and philological arguments. Having identified some points of the text as prominent, pivotal, or demarcatory, the mythographer confers a shape to the surrounding text; not by transposing any of its parts, but by drawing connections between these points and inserting spaces there. With the points (or dots) connected, the text is blocked out, and a constellation of verse, scenes, and acts appears on the page. An essential question is how such a proposed pattern is arrived at. Hymes tells us that with practice "it becomes easy to block out the rhetorical-poetic form of a passage (1981:353).[12] At the heart of the rhetorical-poetic form of a passage is the measured verse, the basic unit of Chinookan narrative description. We know that Hymes's blocked-out, measured verse is bounded by carriage returns, sometimes begins with a particle sequence, and may consist of one or more lines. But, we again ask, how was it determined or defined? Neither by prosodic nor by grammatical features, and not mechanically, Hymes tells us. One discovers patterns, and these patterns define verses. The process of discovery is not arbitrary, because "it is governed by the coherence and articulation of the particular narrative, and in addition, by a rhetorical pattern . . . *onset, ongoing, outcome*" (1981:320). Also, "Verses are recognized, not by counting parts, but by recognizing repetition within a frame, the relation of putative units to each other within a whole. Covariation between form and meaning, between units and a recurrent Chinookan pattern of narrative organization, is the key" (1981:318). First of all, let us note that if there is no consistent formal marking, then how is there "covariation"? Then, let us go on to see how Hymes explains that the definition of verse is not mechanical.

To begin with, the choice of verse-marking by initial particles is narrator-specific. We are told that Louis Simpson marked all his verses with a special particle sequence, but that Victoria Howard did not. Where Simpson used particles, Howard used functionally equivalent devices that Hymes describes as "indications of change of scene in either location or lapse of time, and indication of change among participants in the action" (1981:319). To paraphrase, in Howard's narratives we know we have a new verse when either the action, or the scene of the action, broadly interpreted, changes.[13] To make matters trickier, discretion is needed because, as Hymes explains, a given particle sometimes signals a verse, and at other times does not. Further, "a verb may recur at intervals and so show that there are units, marked and linked by it," while at other times "a verb or a noun may recur within a short span and so show that there is one unit containing it"; that is, sometimes two occurrences of X mark two verses, and at other times two occurrences of X (or Y) mark one verse (1981:319). The length of the short span is not specified, and we remain without formal criteria for defining verses.[14] In Hymes's words, "once such [verse] patterning has been discovered in cases with such markers [particles], it can be discovered in cases without them" (1981:319).

Note that Hymes's concern with the description of rhetorical design overrides grammatical considerations. Note further that in "Discovering Oral Performance and Measured Verse in American Indian Narrative" (1977), Hymes discussed Chinookan narrative. In "Particle, Pause and Pattern in American Indian Narrative Verse" (1980),[15] however, Hymes proposed that probably all American Indian narratives can and should be transcribed in this format, and that this format promotes the appreciation of these narratives as artistic productions.

Because of the difficulty of a formal definition of verse, the explanatory value of the blocking-out technique is weak in direct proportion to the looseness of the definition of its basic unit of description. Hymes has invoked covariation of form and meaning, but such covariation is not interpretable. Sure enough, some syntactic device can signal a new verse—but so can a change in reference, topic, place, and so forth. How, then, ought one interpret such changes in reference, topic, place, etcetera?

Constellation mythography, because it has not provided rules that define any of the formal poetic units of a text, can only be considered to be an appeal for a transcription that reflects graphically the rhetorical organization of the text. Syntactic correlates of rhetorical organization, sometimes obvious, at other times not obvious, are a bonus, a confirmation of the correctness of the analysis of rhetorical organization.[16] Every new blocking-out is not the discovery of a hitherto unrecognized poetic device/form, but of rhetorical salience.[17]

Hymes says as much himself, having spelled out in 1980 what he had implied in 1977:

> The nature of narrative verse in American Indian languages goes deeper than either pause or particles. It depends upon a conception of narrative action as fulfilling a recurrent formal pattern. All

American Indian narratives, I believe, will prove to be organized in terms of lines and verses, and sets of verses. Where syntactic patterns are present, they will play a role, often a major role . . . ; but the fundamental consideration will not be the presence of the particular linguistic device. The fundamental consideration will be the presence of a certain conception of narrative action. That conception, which can be called a rhetorical conception, will have it that sequences of action will satisfy one or another of two basic types of formal pattern . . . built up of pairs and fours . . . [or] of threes and fives (1980:8–9).

While Hymes earlier had attempted to describe Chinookan narrative by discovering syntactic correlates to rhetorical structure, he later degraded the importance of syntactic markers and focused on the rhetorical patterns of "pairs and fours," and of "threes and fives." Once Hymes relaxed his expectation that syntactic markers signal rhetorical structure, he was able to discover rhetorical pattern easily. Yet nothing in Hymes's "grammar" helps us to see how narrative differs from others kinds of talk. Hymes reduces all talk, including oratory and song, to blockable linguistic matter. All prose is retermed "poetry" or "verse." Rather than sorting out narrative into explicitly defined types, this "grammar" keeps them lumped together.[18]

If we study Hymes's writings we see that he regularly voices concerns with the visually and numerically effective and appropriate; with how to present texts attractively and symmetrically on paper. Consider the high number of charts included in his collection *"In Vain I Tried To Tell You,"* and the concern Hymes voices about the appropriate number of chapters: "I could have the total number of chapters in the book be ten. . . . Ten, of course, is a multiple of the Chinookan pattern number five, a multiple that Chinookans themselves use. . . . And to make a separate chapter of the new text . . . would break the pattern number, ten" (1981:201). Having started, like Tedlock, from a feeling that paragraphs roll on without respite, Hymes attributed the putative dullness and opacity of American Indian texts to their unimaginative mode of prose presentation, or, more precisely, to the unimaginative representation of their rhetorical devices. He felt that, allowed to breathe on the printed page, with spaces appropriately sprinkled, enriched with numbers, letters, and bracketed titles, these texts would open up, lose their impenetrability, and stand alone as artistic forms.

IV

Tedlock starts from a tape-recorded text and writes "verse"; Hymes starts from a transcript (of any kind) and rewrites "verse." If Tedlock and Hymes did not enjoy high prestige in their fields, I would keep to myself that I view their respective conceptions of "verse" as typographic remedies born of the frustration of taming unfamiliar stories. But I do not like to see versification *instead* of contextual, linguistic, and cultural annotation, and though I am no more annoyed by the publication of unannotated versified texts than I am by the publication of unversified and unannotated texts, I am disturbed when, owing to the influence of either or both of these scholars' mythographies, annotated but not versified texts are denied publication. I admit that I might not ever have become allergic to their verses if I hadn't been forced either to "versify" or explain why I do not.

In my mythography I do not want to go beyond any definition of verse based on prosodic features, nor do I assume that all North American Indian narratives are best recorded, for the printed page, in verse. Not all of North American Indian narrative is verse, any more than all of English literature is dialogue. And while some of the shorter narratives, especially myths, may lend themselves to transcription in verse form—because there are linguistic clues to a tightly knit structure (pauses, particles, parallel constructions, and so on)—and while I can leave blanks where the voice is silent, I cannot fool myself into thinking that by following these practices I am a grammarian of narrative or a critic of oral literature.

What is my task as a mythographer? To make texts understandable. In the case of Colville texts, it is to explain what I know about the discourse of Colville narrative, and to translate Colville texts into an appropriate form of English. But let me begin by reporting how I stumbled upon this mythographic business.

All my early text recording was done in the service of syntax. In July 1968, I became acquainted with Peter J. Seymour, a Colville Indian who agreed to teach me some Colville. He did not enjoy paradigmatic elicitation and soon offered to tell me a story in Colville titled Black Pig—a Colville version of Cinderella. Seymour enjoyed telling stories, and so we arranged for more storytelling sessions. During these sessions, with me as his only audience, he would talk into a tape recorder, "take a five" at the end of each tape, roll and smoke a cigarette, chat in English, and then pick up the story where he remembered having left off. I did not understand the language, I did not videotape the sessions, and I can't begin to reconstruct the movements of his hands, head, eyes, and body, of which I remember few. The recordings show an even tone without obvious dramatic pauses, loud peaks, whispers, and other theatrical devices. The rest of that summer and for the next two, I recorded more stories from Seymour (and a few from other Colvilles). In 1969, 1970, and the years following, I began transcribing them and only then discovered how good they were.

Seymour did not have the patience or interest to help me with the transcriptions, but he introduced me to his cousin, Mary Madeline DeSautel, who eventually became my most helpful consultant and the principal translator of the texts. She was at first reluctant to work with me, but in the summer of 1970, a full year after I had met her, she agreed to help me and we worked together, off and on, for six years.

As I was transcribing texts, I began thinking about how much understanding of Colville culture is necessary to appreciate Colville literature. John Updike articulated the problem as follows:

> The shift from spoken to written narrative is nowhere complete; there is always a voice, and in the case of exemplary novelists there is *only* the voice, coaxing us on to another page. . . . When we turn, however, to works markedly nearer the beginnings of writing . . . we experience a dismay, a disorientation, for which the lucid epics of Homer and the oft-retold chronicles of the Bible have not quite prepared us. We do not know the language, the code of mythology and tradition, and feel oppressively confused, as when we look at the Tibetan pantheon arrayed on a *thank-ka,* while an equally populous mural of, say, the Last Judgment or the Battle of Waterloo quickly sorts itself out. There is always a code, and oral narrative disconcertingly assumes that we know it (1984:119).

To what extent can an American from Peoria understand and appreciate Danilo Dolci's *Racconti siciliani?* Not enough, a Sicilian would say, and less without appropriate explanations. And the problems would grow exponentially with Colville texts. I felt that the best way to prepare Colville texts for publication is to give whatever information I can about the narrator and his culture and tradition, and start from texts borrowed from sources with which I am familiar. It was in this spirit that I prepared the introduction and accompanying notes to Seymour's *The Golden Woman* (Mattina 1985), and it is in the same spirit that I will prepare more notes to other Colville texts. The more I can communicate about Colville narrative discourse, the more transparent I can make the texts.

The second part of my task is to translate texts as well as I can. The way Madeline and I transcribed and translated them, is, I suppose, the usual—stretches of tape were played over and over, and each sentence or fragment repeated until correctly transcribed. Then, Madeline would translate each stretch phrase by phrase, but with frequent interruptions when I could beat her to the translation. The thrill of understanding what is said in Colville has never palled for me. It was an exciting game to transcribe and translate, to discern the various syntactic constructions and the morphological make-up of words, and to test new forms and constructions. Madeline's translations were loose—certainly not morpheme by morpheme, and not even word by word. She translated Colville into the English she spoke normally, and I wrote it the way she spoke. This choice of translation style does not meet with everyone's approval, and is subject to controversy, the arguments of which I summarize here.

For convenience, let us call the English dialect spoken by Madeline DeSautel "Red English." I don't think it would be an overgeneralization to state that Red English, with various dialects of course, is a pan-Indian phenomenon, roughly analogous to Black English. Some scholars object to printing this Red English because they think that many lay readers see such a dialect as an impoverished and inferior English that perpetuates the misperception of the American Indian as a backward sort. One anonymous reviewer of our texts put it this way:

> I feel strongly (indeed violently) that common oral English should
> be preferred to what looks like incompetence at language. This is
> not to argue that Indian-English itself is an "impoverished" lan-
> guage; at least, I need to make clear that I make no value judg-
> ment about grammar, propriety, usage, and so on in and of
> themselves. But much of the reading audience will already believe
> in that old stereotype of the semi-articulate (or primitive, or
> "backward") Indian, and I see no reason to strengthen that idea.

I find the objection unconvincing, however, for the problem of perpetuating a stereotype of backward Indians is inherent neither in the Indians nor in the way they talk; the problem, rather, resides in those who judge Indians by their speech habits.

There is another two-pronged argument in favor of a translation into "careful" English. The first prong of this argument, assuming that the Colville of a text is elegant and formal, insists that the language of translation be equally elegant and formal. The other demands that the language of translation reflect the subtleties and complexities of the Colville original, even at the risk of stilting the English. My choice of Madeline DeSautel's Red English as the language of translation has its justification neither in the reviewer's polemic (don't judge people by how you think they should talk), nor in the second argument (translate formal texts only into formal language), but in the slowly emerging tradition of artistic (hence respectable and appropriate) published Red English.

How do Indians speak English? Dissertations, collections of articles and essays on the subject have appeared and even more are coming out; conferences have been and are being held, and research on the topic is encouraged. Much of the discussion is about form, and some is about function. Bruce Rigsby, who has made claims about aboriginal Australians that apply equally well to Native Americans (namely, that the Australian aborigines have made English into an aboriginal language) has written to me, "The parallels between Aboriginal English and Indian English(es) are obvious. For us linguistic anthropologists, the crucial thing is to avoid bogging down on the description of linguistic form (which is intellectually and aesthetically pleasing) and to examine the functions of speech in daily social life." Now, while I don't intend to "bog down" in the description of Red English form, I feel I should give some idea of what this form is, and suggest that this form is—as it should be—gaining respectability in print.

A document that is witness to the legitimacy of Red English as a perfectly beautiful poetic language is Dorothea Kaschube's *Crow Texts*. Recorded in 1953 and published in 1978, the texts include such gems as

> Right now the push-dance song.
> It's a different kind of dance,
> the words in the song,

lots of these songs,
I was lonesome for you.
Was you lonesome for me when you went away (1978:70–71).

Kaschube tells us only that the English of Pretty-On-Top (the Crow Indian who volunteered the Red English translation of her own text) is "more vivid than would be the English translation of Crow by a linguist."

Other works flaunt, not just report, Red English, as well they should. I'll give three examples that attest to the adequacy of Red English as a vehicle for both poetic and journalistic language. In all these cases the authors make no apologies and give no explanations for their use of Red English. The first example—lack of subject-verb agreement and all—is an excerpt from Mary Augusta Tappage, a Shuswap woman born three weeks before Madeline DeSautel:

> I used to help at times of birth, yes,
> I used to help all the women around here.
> I learned it from my book, my blue doctor's book.
> I used to read it all the time.
>
> I made up my mind that if she needs help,
> I will help her.
> I'm not scared.
> You've got to be awfully quick.
> There's two lives there.
> The baby and the mother.
>
> (Speare 1973:28)

This piece was recorded by Jean E. Speare, who does not tell us how and to what extent she edited these lines. Another, an excerpt from a 1980 newspaper article by the Colville William M. Charley, Sr., entitled "Traditional Values," which appeared in the *Tribal Tribune* of October 30, goes as follows:

Today what I have on paper is my life and have learn this the true Indian-way years ago as the child my parents my Father the Chief from the Methow-band and my dear Mother she is from the Wenatchee-band my language the native the two bands mention above and did not know English, the self-taught and feel the true self-made Indian and my knowledge is gain word by mouth from my elders, as did not read about the fine Indian culture from the book-store.

Such as life we do not live this day by day, here we learn for our selves from the past to make mistakes and as this old world turns the same picture shall come before us to let our mind wander back to the past yesterdays as we did this before and why, would this work the second time around, when the first time we fail.

And finally here is an example from Leslie Marmon Silko's *Storyteller*. This book, an Indian writer's telling of Indian story-telling, fits my purpose because it shows us how an educated and widely published Indian artist repeats and reports (in poetry-like verses and prose-like lines) stories that Indians tell—and these are not just Indian mythologies, but all kinds of stories.[19] One excerpt, substandard expressions, ungrammatical conjunctions, elliptical sentences and all, goes:

> Seems like
> it's always happening to me.
> Outside the dance hall door
> late Friday night
> in the summer time,
> and those brown-eyed men from Cubero,
> smiling
> They usually ask me
> "Have you seen the way stars shine
> up there in the sand hills?"
> And I usually say "No. Will you show me?" (1981:9997).

Even as I give these examples and summarize arguments, all I can say is that in the final analysis the reason I translate Colville texts in Red English is that Madeline liked it, and I like it; a matter of taste no more susceptible to legislation than versification.

V

Mythography is the work of collecting and transcribing once-oral texts. Narratives on the printed page are museum artifacts, just as arrowheads in a museum case are spent projectiles. A transcript of a narrative has no more sound than a musical score. The understanding which readers gain from the script is in direct proportion to what they know about the tradition and the context of the text, and mythographers should facilitate the reading of texts by providing whatever they can toward that goal. Over the years, scholars have struggled with how to transcribe texts, and different backgrounds, interests, and personalities have produced different forms and styles of transcriptions and translations. Tedlock and Hymes are two in a string of mythographers, their mythographic practices firmly grounded in their respective personal tastes. Let each sing the panaceaic virtues of his verses, but object when either appoints himself guardian of the texts. Let the texts come forth, in whatever typographic arrangement the editor deems appropriate. Given an understanding of the tradition and context of the text, I expect that the worthiest texts will require the least architectural support. And because it is a good narrator who tells good texts, let him be foregrounded.

NOTES

1. This essay is a reworking of an earlier paper on mythography (Mattina 1983), and of sections of my commentary to a Colville text (Mattina 1985). I wish to thank all those who offered insightful criticism and comments, especially Franchot Ballinger, LaVonne Brown Ruoff, Wallace Chafe, Larry Evers, Arnold Krupat, Nancy Kryder, Ralph Maud, Timothy Montler, Douglas Purl, Robert Rankin, and Michael Silverstein. I owe the term "mythography" to Ralph Maud, who employs it in an excellent survey that extends beyond its title (Maud 1982).

2. Wallace L. Chafe has pointed out to me that "production in terms of brief, prosodically defined spurts which are usually single clauses . . . is a property of *all* spoken language. Such units seem to reflect the focuses of consciousness with which we necessarily proceed while we speak. There is nothing poetic about them, unless for some reason one wants to say that all spoken language is poetic" (personal communication). Chafe calls such spurts "idea units" (Chafe 1980).

3. Tedlock retains in the translation occasional stutters and "errors," but he does change some grammatical tenses (1978:xxvi, xxvii).

4. Note, again, the hybrid nature of Tedlock's view of the matter: *translation* of referential content, but *transliteration* of (para)linguistic material otherwise.

5. What Tedlock calls "analytical advantages" of treating oral narrative as dramatic poetry are really justifications or rationalizations in support of his typographic choices. He implies that something which, written in prose, was considered primitive, will, as soon as it is transcribed as poetry, be considered poetic. He is manufacturing an opposition *primitive : poetic,* which is hardly tenable. See also Chafe (1981), who argues that Seneca ritual language contrasts with conversational discourse in some of the same ways that written English contrasts with oral English. See also Sherzer, who comments on the dichotomies oral/written, ordinary/literary language (1982:372).

6. Note that while Tedlock inveighed against those who record North American Indian narratives as written prose, insisting that it is madness to think of oral narratives in that fashion, he published a book of English translations and paradoxically decided not to include a tape of Zuni originals. Larry Evers, producer of the videotape series *Words and Place,* keeps our feet on the ground with his remarks: "we should constantly remind ourselves that [an anthology of translations] contains printed approximations of vital oral performances of another literary tradition—no more, no less" (1978*b*:269). Printed transcriptions of narrative, he says, are "in the best instances, a transcription and translation of dogged scientific accuracy" (1978*a*:133). We should also remind ourselves that videotapes are visual and audile records of performances, with camera commentary and no footnotes. Tedlock, incidentally, views sound films as inadequate records because they "do not invite participation: the viewer is as silent as if he were silently reading a book" (1977:517).

7. This would make of every work its own analysis.

8. Or, to allude to Geertz, how thick to make the frame of the objet d'art.

9. While surely we must all countenance abstract objects, instantiated through parts in specific modalities, Tedlock's discussions, in this article and in *Finding the Center* (1978), contain the implicit and explicit denial that any one version (picture) is the correct one, an underlying abstract master story: "There is no single, 'correct' picture of a given story even from one Zuni to another" (1978:xxxi).

10. A prototype can be either a synchronic ideal, an underlying abstraction, or an historical reconstruction.

11. Tedlock's more recent concerns include the typology of style. In *Verbal Art* (n.d., forthcoming) he paints a picture of North American Indians who regard the word as a precious or sacred tool, a commodity not to be wasted, and of Whites for whom words are cheap. In American Indian cultures, says Tedlock, the uses of the word range from "relatively artless ordinary conversation" to increasingly more formal (*a*) accounts of secular/recent events; (*b*) narratives of sacred truths (such as migration stories with human and animal characters—these tend toward oratory);

and (*c*) (sacred) mythic stories about the gods (with all-animal casts of actors). This classification of North American Indian verbal art is very similar to Tedlock's earlier one of Zuni. Tedlock discusses how storytellers show personal stylistic preferences, but also belong in a particular artistic tradition. They all make use of certain stock pan-American rhetorical tricks, but "restricted though [they] may be in the use of the most powerful figures of speech, [they do] have all the direct powers of the human voice at [their] command" (n.d.:23).

12. Note, however, that much labor lies ahead: "blocking out is not the same as final version" (1981:353). We know from published pieces that the work of analysis is not finished until the latest version, and we are told in the personal vein Hymes, like Tedlock, seems fond of, how, for example, on a plane between somewhere and Los Angeles, he "went through the text once more, observing a hypothesis as to rhetorical cohesion, and almost every uncertainty vanished. . . . The difficulty had been, as always in such analysis, that the principle of grouping of verses allows for more than one grouping" (1980:71). And so Hymes continues confidently in his reformatting efforts, as "confidence comes from the experience of it being there to find, and of coming to experience pattern without conscious analysis" (1981:354).

13. Note also that Hymes's explanation refers to content (referential) units, not form.

14. As we have seen, Hymes knows and says that blockings are always susceptible to revision, and he insists that it is experience as much as anything else that teaches good and proper blocking. His failure to come up with mechanical means of (rules for) blocking out text has raised questions about the validity of the blocks arrived at. He meets such questions with the observation that "the idea of verse organization is heuristic. . . . What organization is there, verse or syntactic, depends on the relationships that appear within the text" (personal communication).

15. In this title and occasionally elsewhere, for example when he discusses "vocal realizations" (1981:321), Hymes answers Tedlock's calls for accounts of paralinguistic features; but this is not Hymes's central concern.

16. The rhetorical-poetic form of a passage is arrived at by deciding what piece of the story is a rhetorical unit, and matching that unit with one of the poetic units (line, verse, scene, and so on). Let us remember that what led Hymes to re-analyze the myth of Seal and her younger brother was its meaning, "the glaring discrepancy between the published interpretation of its meaning and evident dramatic form of the story itself" (1981:317).

17. This is what punctuation and the paragraph format aim to do, however haphazardly. The question is, to what extent does one need to reflect rhetorical organization on paper? If a character in a story says: "I

need two things, a horse, and some money," are "horse" and "money" allowed to share the same line, or should they be kept poetically separate? Note, incidentally, that for Tedlock the decision would depend on how the line is delivered. Note also that for Hymes the interpretation of a myth follows the blocking out of the rhetorical structure. He "does not discover an import for the myth until a series of lines of evidence as to its structure has been assembled" (1981:275). Note, finally, that this last statement is contradicted by Hymes's admitted practice with reference to the Seal myth referred to in note 16.

18. On this matter, Tedlock's position resembles Hymes's. In an article written in ragged-right verse, he says that much (most?) of what is spoken is poetry: oral history is; narrative is. The crucial difference is that between modern written texts—that is, texts composed for the printed page—and oral texts. He says:

> Tape recordings are infinitely preferable
> to texts taken down in dictation.
>
> . . .
> The finished transcription shows at a glance
> the structure
> of the narrative
> and its delivery (1975:724).

While it cannot be argued that such transcriptions show at least something about the delivery of the text, some would and do argue that such transcriptions needn't show the structure of a text. The question of the difference between a particular performance and narrative performance remains unaddressed.

19. In Silko's narrative the circumstances of the story become part of the story. It's a nice way of putting footnotes, analysis, and commentary all in the text. These narratives become performances and explications at the same time—probably one of the best ways of presenting Indian narratives in print. Note, for example, the following:

> This is the way Aunt Susie told the story.
> She had certain phrases, certain distinctive words
> she used in her telling.
> I write when I still hear
> her voice as she tells the story.
> People are sometimes surprised
> at her vocabulary, but she was
> a brilliant woman, a scholar
> of her own making
> who has cherished the Laguna stories
> all her life.
> This is the way I remember
> she told this one story

about the little girl who ran away.
The scene is laid partly in old Acoma, and Laguna.
Waithea was a little girl living in Acoma and
one day she said
    "Mother, I would like to have
    some *yashtoah* to eat."
"Yashtoah" is the hardened crust on corn meal mush
that curls up.
The very name "yashtoah" means
It's sort of curled-up, you know, dried,
just as mush tried on top.
She said
    "I would like to have some *yashtoah*."
(Silko 1981:7–8)

REFERENCES

Chafe, Wallace L., ed. 1980. *The Pear Stories: Cognitive, Cultural and Linguistic Aspects of Narrative Production.* Norwood, N.J.: Ablex Pub. Corp.

———. 1981. Differences between Colloquial and Ritual Seneca or How Oral Literature is Literary. In *Reports from the survey of California and Other Indian Languages,* no. 1. Alice Schlicter, Wallace Chafe and Leanne Hinton, eds. Berkeley: Dept. of Linguistics, University of California.

Edmonson, Munro S. 1971. *Lore: An Introduction to the Science of Folklore and Literature.* New York: Holt, Rinehart & Winston.

Evers, Larry. 1978a. Review of Ekkehart Malotki, *Hopotuwutsl: Hopi Tales* (1978). *American Indian Culture and Research Journal* 2:132–134.

———. 1978b. Review of J. Ramsey, *Coyote Was Going There. American Indian Quarterly* 4:268–269.

Hymes, Dell H. 1975. Folklore's Nature and the Sun's Myth. *Journal of American Folklore* 88:345–369.

———. 1977. Discovering Oral Performance and Measured Verse in American Indian Narrative. *New Literary History* 8:431–457.

———. 1980. Particle, Pause and Pattern in American Indian Narrative Verse. *American Indian Culture and Research Journal* 4:7–51.

———. 1981. *"In Vain I Tried to Tell You." Essays in Native American Ethnopoetics.* Philadelphia: University of Pennsylvania Press.

Jacobs, Melville. 1959. *The Content and Style of an Oral Literature.* Chicago: University of Chicago Press.

Kaschube, Dorothea V. 1978. Crow Texts. *International Journal of American Linguistics.* Native American Texts Series Monograph No. 2. Chicago: The University of Chicago Press.

Mattina, Anthony. 1983. North American Indian Mythography. Paper presented at the XVIII International Conference on Salishan Languages, Seattle, August 8–10.

———. 1985. *The Golden Woman. The Colville Narrative of Peter J. Seymour.* Tucson: University of Arizona Press.

Maud, Ralph. 1982. *A Guide to B. C. Indian Myth and Legend.* Vancouver: Talonbooks.

Sherzer, Joel. 1982. Poetic Structuring of Kuna Discourse: The Line. *Language and Society* 2:371–390.

Silko, Leslie Marmon. 1981. *Storyteller.* New York: Seaver Books.

Speare, Jean E., ed. 1973. *The Days of Augusta.* Vancouver: J. J. Douglas Ltd.

Tedlock, Dennis. 1971. On the Translation of Style in Oral Narrative. In *Toward New Perspectives in Folklore.* A. Paredes and R. Bauman, eds. Austin: University of Texas Press.

———. 1972. Pueblo Literature: Style and Verisimilitude. In *New Perspectives on the Pueblos,* A. Ortis, ed. Albuquerque: University of New Mexico Press.

———. 1975. Learning to Listen: Oral History as Poetry. *Boundary* 2 (3): 707–726.

———. 1977. Toward an Oral Poetics. *New Literary History* 8:507–519.

———. 1978. *Finding the Center: Narrative Poetry of the Zuni Indians,* 2d ed. Lincoln: University of Nebraska Press.

———. 1981. The Spoken Word and the Work of Interpretation in American Indian Religion. In *Traditional Literatures of the American Indians.* Karl Kroeber, ed. Lincoln: University of Nebraska Press.

———. 1983. *The Spoken Word and the Work of Interpretation.* Philadelphia: University of Pennsylvania Press.

———. n.d. *Verbal Art.* Vol. I of the *Handbook of North American Indians.* Washington, D.C.: Smithsonian Institute (forthcoming).

Updike, John. 1984. Book review column, "Three Tales from Nigeria." *The New Yorker.* April 23. Pp. 119–129.

PRACTICE

Strategies in Text and Context: The Hot Pepper Story

JOEL SHERZER

Kaa kwento (the hot pepper story) is one of many stories told among the Kuna of Panama. Some of these stories are humorous, but while the hot pepper story contains elements of humor, it deals with quite serious matters. My analysis of the hot pepper story begins with one telling, or performance of the story. This telling is discussed in some detail and compared with other performances. Both the story and the events of which the telling of the story is the central part are analyzed in order to demonstrate the interplay between the significance of the hot pepper story and the contexts in which it is performed. An important feature of the structure of the hot pepper story is that it lends itself to multiple interpretations; this feature can be understood as functional in Kuna social and cultural life when situated in the actual contexts in which it is exploited.

The version of the hot pepper story reproduced here was recorded on February 18, 1971, in the gathering house of the island village of Mulatuppu, San Blas. It is told by Mastayans, one of the chiefs of Mulatuppu, to a group of men. More particularly, it is told to an elderly, well-known chief from the village of Achutuppu, who is visiting Mulatuppu for several days in order to chant Kuna tradition in the gathering house. Mastayans, together with a group of Mulatuppu men, is keeping the visiting chief company and entertaining him in the gathering house on this morning, as is required by Kuna custom. Were there no visitor, the gathering house would be locked closed and most of the men of the village, including the chiefs, would be off working in the jungle mainland or fishing.

Mastayans announces that he will tell the hot pepper story if the visiting chief will serve as his *apinsuet* (responder). The visiting chief agrees and does so, participating in the performance by ratifying each line with an affirmative grunt, a *teki* (so it is), a repeated word or phrase, a comment or laugh, or a question. The structure of the telling of the hot pepper story is thus Mastayans as teller, the visiting chief as addressee-responder, and the group of men in the gathering house as audience. This communicative structure (sender—receiver-responder—audience) is a very common Kuna one, characteristic of events ranging from the most ritual and ceremonial to the most informal and everyday (see J. Sherzer 1983:196–200).

THE TEXT

In my representation, the hot pepper story consists of 171 lines. Lines are determined by pauses coupled with falling pitch. This line structure is reinforced by the constant ratifying responses and comments by the visiting chief. Part of the poetics of performance is created by the interplay of relatively longer and relatively shorter lines. Rhythm is also created by means of long pauses, without falling pitch, within lines and by the extensive use of certain words and phrases, such as *teki, kepe, takkarku, emite,* and *takken soke.* These words and phrases, which serve as line-framing elements, typically occur line initially and line finally. At times they occur in the middle of lines, however, playing off contrapuntally against the pause patterning.

The translation mirrors the original Kuna with regard to line structure. As in the Kuna version, pauses within lines are represented by long spaces. The line-framing words are translated with a set of equivalent English expressions—well, then, thus, indeed, now, see, say, it is said, and so on. Readers are thus provided with a sense of their functioning in the poetics of performance.

The translation is relatively literal. Again, this is in order to capture as much as possible the Kuna poetics of performance, which I feel would become lost in freer translations. This is particularly important in that this text repeats and permutes a small number of words and thematic elements, as I will discuss below.

The Kuna tense-aspect system, especially as it is used in the performance of narratives, such as the hot pepper story, is strikingly different from that of Western European languages, notably English. This, of course, poses problems for translation. Given my aim of being as literal as possible in my translation, while still having it be accessible to English readers, I have retained the aspectual details (such as specifying whether an action is beginning or in progress, or where it occurs) and the seeming temporal disjunctions which are characteristic of Kuna cultural logic. In lines 92 and 111, the narrator jumps back and forth from past to present, from the boy alive with his family to buried underground and presumed dead. In line 148 the boy who has just come out of the ground is already a man and the grandmother has already died. These quite consistent temporal disjunctions in Kuna narration, like the moving in and out of quotes, may prove difficult for English readers. They are there in Kuna, however, and are characteristic of Kuna cultural logic and especially the verbal art of narration; thus, I have not tampered with them in my translation.[1] Here then is the text of the hot pepper story, as told by Mastayans, in Kuna and in English translation.

kaa kwento, performed by Chief Mastayans, February 18, 1971

1. ka kwentoki peka an sunmaymarsunno tekir.
2. peka sunmaynayop samosunnoet.
3. peee, weti an apinsuoetit.
4. peka sunmaynayop sasunno.
   (visiting chief: aaa.)
5. peka sunmaynayop sasunnoettene.
   (visiting chief: eye.)
   (comments from gathered audience and brief conversation with Mastayans)
6. takkarku   we kwento sunna   we Mammimullukine saila Mantipaytikinya.
   (comments from gathered audience)
   (laughter)
7. a wis anka irkwen, wis an oturtaynaikusto we, ka kwento kin.
8. wis napir salasik.

153

9. tey 'napir' soke.
   (comments from gathered audience)
10. 'teee, takkarkute, mu warkwen mai' soysunto.
11. muu.
12. 'mute takkarku sirwel ipet mu ma' takken soke, mu sirwel ipet.
13. mu sirwel ipette mai takkarku ipakwena   sirwer, turpamaytakokua   yer kepeunti sirwer turpamaytakoku kwane.
14. silekwa pakkekwace kwantii.
15. teki silekwa pakke kwantii, ipakwenki sirwer iskuarto ipe.
16. 'sirwer takkarku, e turpa patterpakuar' takken soke.
17. sirwer turpa taynae e ipet taynaoku, sirwer turpa pattemai perkwaple.
18. 'key sirwer nue kwankusa.'
19. 'aki mu sokkar' takken soke weteka   'ipikala   an sirwer iskustipa?' soke.
20. 'e turpa   key nue anka nakukusa.
21. tekisokku turpati key nue anka nakukucokku   toa an ipe sirwer turpa eputipaye?'
22. mu pinsatisunto.
    (visiting chief: etto.)
23. 'tek ipakwenkine   emite muteka   kep macikwa amis' takken soke.
24. sirwerki nakkulekeka.
    (visiting chief: e.)
25. mu sokku macikwaka sokku   'maciwakwaye pe anka sirwerki nakkuleko' kar soysun.
26. 'pe anka sirwer etarpoye.
27. wekine   pe anka sirwer etarpetakokua   pitti, ani sirwer turpa epu pe taytako' sokeye.
    (visiting chief: etto so.)
28. maciwakwa sokku 'napir' soke.
29. tek inso   sikwicunna, sirwer, tukkuki.
    (visiting chief: e.)
    taysikucunna. (pitch rises at end of line)
    (visiting chief: e.
                comments
                arkasikwicunna.)

30. arkasikwicunna sirwer turpa taysikwicunto.
    (visiting chief: aa.)
31. mute kar soysat.
    (visiting chief: ipi e turpa eputipaye?)
32. eye ipi e turpa eputipaye?
33. tey wepali   inso ipa oipoarkua   mu taynatsunto.
    (visiting chief: ee.)
34. wepa mu taytapkua   takkampa sirwer pattepukkwa, e
    turpa.
    (visiting chief: ampa pattepa.)
35. wepa mute sokku, wakwaka sokku, weteka   'pe taysa'
    sokeye 'an sirwer turpa tule opattisat pe taysa' sokeye.
    (visiting chief: ee.)
36. wepa sokku, 'sur' soke 'an taysasur takken tule an kwen
    tacur' soke.
    (visiting chief: comments)
37. 'an kwen taysasur' takken soke.
38. 'napir' soke.
39. teysokku 'napir' takken soke.
40. 'tekirtina   emi pe anka seto nakkulepalo' kar soysunto a.
    (visiting chief: etto.)
41. 'seto pe anka nakkulepaloye.
    (visiting chief: comments)
42. nuekwa pe anka taysunnoye a.
43. toa nue sirwer turpa ani eputitipaye.'
    (visiting chief: macikwa.)
44. macikwa macikwa macikwa kar   sikwicunto.
    (visiting chief: etto.)
45. muti nattasunnat neyse.
    (visiting chief: neyse.)
46. eye sirwer ipetti nekki kammatasunto.
    (visiting chief: ee.)
47. 'kepe   pane oipospar' takken soke.
48. ekisnapali.
49. 'ekiciarparkuaa   par takkarkuu   sul ampa sirwer turpa
    na key pattispar' soke.
    (visiting chief: ampa sula.)
50. tey ekispali wakwase   'pe taysa' sokeye a   'an sirwer
    turpa   toa epus pe taysaye?'

51. 'sur' soke 'an kwen tacur' soke.
    (visiting chief: etto.)
52. 'inso' soke.
53. mu istar mu sanpakusku, 'eka nue nakkulesuli,' takkarkua
        mu, urwe a.
    (visiting chief: urwe.
                    'pe arkatisuli.')
54. 'eye arkatisur an pe tayye' kar soysunto a.
    (visiting chief: comment)
55. napir.
56. kep mu pinsaarsunto 'macikwa ilakwen opelokoye uaya
        akku an itto' sokku, 'ilakwen   opelokoye a.'
57. kep mu nappa kwicarsunto.
    (visiting chief: nappa.)
58. nappa kwicatti   talipakke wirkue wilup nappa tiysasunto.
59. nappa kwicasunto muu.
    (visiting chief: comments)
60. kepe muteka   kep arkan yoet ekwacasunto nappa yapa.
    (visiting chief: comments)
61. tey wakwaka sokku 'an arkan yoet arkwas takkenye a.
    (visiting chief: aa.)
62. pe anka sunaye.'
    (visiting chief: aa.)
63. aa   teki wepa   maci kep arsan kal okwicicunto, nappa
    yapa.
    (visiting chief: mm.)
64. kep maciwakwa aitecunto nek urpa.
    (visiting chief: mm.)
65. kep aiteskua, olarkan amiarkua   arsan ikkir susa.
    (visiting chief: aa.)
66. arsan onakkwicunna.
    (visiting chief: key parnakkwe.)
67. key parnakkue iy pe parnakkosunna?
    (comments from gathered audience)·
68. were.
69. kep a emurucunto emur emur emur nappa taska.
    (visiting chief: wakwa wios.)
70. wakwa purkwis.
    (visiting chief: purkwis.)

71. purkwicunna.

72. yapa meretisunna.

73. tey wepa mai   kepe wakwate nan nikkat a, pap nik-
    kapalit.

74. kep amiarsunto.

75. 'pia an maci nattipa?' soke.
    (visiting chief: aaa.)

76. nan imaytikucunna 'pia ani wakwa nattipa?
    macikwa pia ani nattipaye?'
    (visiting chief: comment)

77. tek imaytisuli muse ekiciarsunto, 'pe an macikwa pe taysa?'
    sokeye.

78. 'sul an pe ipe kwen tacur' kar soysunto, 'an taysasurye.

79. napir' soke.

80. tey nanpa potisunto mimmipa.

81. pap potisunna mimmipa.

82. tey pinna pinna pinna iet   iete a.
    (visiting chief: iete.)

83. tikkasurkucunnat iearsunto.
    (visiting chief: mu ietsun?)

84. e nan ietsunna.
    (comments from gathered audience)

85. muti wisi na nappa tiysat.
    (visiting chief: ati wisi.)

86. atina wisi.
    (comments from gathered audience)

87. e nan potisunnat mimmipa.
    (visiting chief: etto.)

88. tek a potii   sanpakus pinna pinna iealir pini ieter pini.
    (visiting chief: ee.)

89. pasur ittokus.
    (visiting chief: ee.)

90. 'tek ipakwen kaarmaytii, punolo nikkapar' soke a.
    (visiting chief: ee.)

91. kwenti susukwa ipe purkwisatteta.

92. tek ipakwen maskuttasunnoe.

93. 'maskunnar' sokele   punorka sokkartasunto sus kepe
    'muuu   ney tikkarpa kep ainiarsun' soke a.
    (visiting chief: etto so.)

94. 'ainiarto tiylesat nappa askin   ainiarto immar mattutikki
ainiar' soke.
(visiting chief: eee.)

95. tey tunkutanisun mu taytisunna i-pi-wa.
(visiting chief: ipi ainiali?)

96. eye.

97. tey pinna nakkwe ainitani ainitani ainitani tey
turpamakkarsunto.
(visiting chief: ee.)

98. tey turpamakkarku e san nakuar takkarku kaa.
(visiting chief: kaa.)

99. mm, 'ka' takken soke.
(visiting chief: ee.)

100. tey muuu   ka, akkwemasunna mukatka kusparsunto
kate a.
(visiting chief: aa.)

101. ka ai ok-kin-no-te (voice vibrates) ka kuarku.

102. weparte e macikwa purkwisatteka, maskunnalile,
sokkartasunto mimmi punorka.
(visiting chief: ee.)

103. 'punorye we mu maitse pe anka ka wis ekisna takkenye
kapa maskunpiye a.'
(visiting chief: ee.)

104. kal ekisnattasunto.
(visiting chief: ee.)

105. tey wepa muka soytapsunnoe   'pe ka wis apeye.'
(visiting chief: ee.)

106. mu 'napir' soke mu kar ka kwanattasunna
(visiting chief: ee.)
ka, kwane   tek mu kuti.

107. tek ipakwenkine, maskunnetkinpali, ekisnatparsunna.
(visiting chief: ee.)

108. wep punoloka soysunna 'ka pe kwanna takkenye.'
(visiting chief: comment)

109. 'teki ka kwannapsun' soke.
(visiting chief: eee muse, comment)

110. teki, muse kwannattasunto, mu ka ipetka kusparsunna.

111. tek e punoloka na kaa kwannai   tule sunmakkarsun
nappa yapa.
(visiting chief: aaa.)

112. aa, '"PU-NO-LO-PI-PI-YE"   soy' takken soke.
    (visiting chief: ee.)
113. '"punolo pipiye" kaa sunmay' soke.
    (visiting chief: aa, nek urpa sunmak?)
114. 'nek urpa tule sunmay' soke.
115. 'pu-no-lo-pi-pi-ye' soke.
116. wepa 'punolo pipiye,' sokkua, ittocunna a
    (visiting chief: aa.)
    tule ese kole.
117. kwakkiali kaki mellet nanse natparsunto.
118. nanka sokku 'ka kwannai tule anse korar takkenye.
119. ka urpa anse korar takken   "PU-NO-LO-PI-PI-YE"
    anka soyye a.
120. an kwakkit' takken soke.
    (visiting chief: kwakkite.)
121. e nan ittosuli a.
    (visiting chief: ittosuli.)
122. kar soysunna 'pe   namar takkenye, pe ittonaoenye a.'
123. kep e nan sunnat ittonatmosunto.
    (visiting chief: comment)
124. 'kep e nan inso punolo ka kwatteku inso korarpar' soke.
    (visiting chief: aa.)
125. '"pu-no-lo-pi-pi-ye   pu-no-lo-pi-pi-ye"   korma' soke.
    (visiting chief: ukak tek korma.)
126. aa, tek korma.
127. pap yoy pinsaale nan yoy pinsaale 'tena sus   tule an
    opurkwisat weki manap ittokusye a.'
    (comments from gathered audience)
128. kep a, eye, ka ipetka kucunto kep ati   kep kwicarsunto.
    (visiting chief: ee.)
129. takke nappa yapa ipi mai.
    (visiting chief: ee.)
130. tey yapa mai   wepa   korarsunna kep kwicarsunna
    eskorokine a
    (visiting chief: ee.)
    mastiketki.
    (visiting chief: ee.)
131. 'wepa korar' takken soke a   'wesikki an nono maiye.'
    (visiting chief: 'wesikki.')
132. 'wesikki an naytukku maiye.'

(visiting chief: ee.)
133. itto tule sunmak.
(visiting chief: ee.)
134. kep pinna pinna pinna kep akkwiar.
(visiting chief: nan akkwinasun.)
135. nan akkwinasun macikwa.
(visiting chief: etto.)
136. takkar inso takkarku macikwa mai, tule keppe   sirwerki
nakkulemaikusat tule mu tiysaku   a   turkucun kannar.
(visiting chief: aa.
                          muu nue imas palamiletsunto.)
137. mu kep amilearsunto.
(visiting chief: comments)
138. kep wepa   suste nononisunto a.
(visiting chief: comment, muu parsoylekoe.)
139. kep ekiciarparsunto   'pia ipika, wey pe kusye?'
140. teki, sokkarsunto.
141. 'sailaki muu, wek an kaarmaytii   mu sirwel akkweka an
siarta' takken soke a.
(visiting chief: ee.)
142. 'teki mu eka sirwerki nue nakkulesur an takketpa, muu
          an itu nappa kwicaye.
(visiting chief: ee.)
143. aa mu an ekwaca takken nappa yaparye.'
(visiting chief: olarkan ekwacaye.)
144. a, olarkan ekwacaye.
145. 'emite a muu   emite nappa yapa an tiysakua   emite
anpa mai, we ka ainiar   an pese koca' takken kar
soysunto.
(visiting chief: etto.)
146. AA.
147. 'napir' soke.
148. tekirtin   macikwa   patto macikwatina   unni
          serkukucokku   kep 'mu annik' soke 'mu anse perkuo
takkenye.'
(visiting chief: aa.)
149. kep macikwa nekkunatse natku kep macikwa nacunna
          nipa nacunto.
(visiting chief: ee.)

150. patteki nakkwis nipa nate.
151. kep immar nue olo acuer suapsunto.
    (visiting chief: ee.)
152. papse suap ittolesunto.
    (visiting chief: mm.)
153. kep a noniku   kep muse natparsunna.
154. mu takkarku soke 'wis-ku-sa-tte.'
    (visiting chief: aa.)
155. mute sokaypa wawanmakkesi topkusikicunna.
    (visiting chief: etto.)
156. kep a acuer nukarki kep kacun mu imasku kep MOK.
157. kep selearparsunto.
    (visiting chief: ee.)
158. mu selearmosunto, tule acuer nukarki   kep aakar
    nakkwicun nakkaaate mmm.
    (visiting chief: ee.)
159. patte epippilet naa naaate.
160. sappi pirkwen sikki emi
    (comment from gathered audience: sotoma nek.)
    sotoma sik.
    (visiting chief: ee.)
161. 'sotoma sik ney pulet so sailakan ney' takken soke.
    (visiting chief: ee.)
162. ikwa walakan kunanamakkekwikwisnae.
    (visiting chief: ee.)
163. paila walakan kunamakkwikwisnae.
    (visiting chief: ee.)
164. tese kep mu takken so aparse.
    (visiting chief: ee.)
165. mu per tippilet.
    (visiting chief: comment)
166. aa.
167. aula we papkan soyte takken soke 'yoo we napnekkine
    mukana   sikkwi tiysamalatti   tese pattema takkenye.
    (visiting chief: ee.)
168. pursipu neysik pur saila kepe tar sappi walakan per
    kwapunyekwikwis   mukan parmilema mukan ase
    oturtaylema.
    (visiting chief: mm.)

169. wey yarkine   wicur sikkwi akkwismalat sikkwi tiysimalat.
(visiting chief: mm.)

170. tese pattemaye'   we papkan ki namay takkenye   anka
soyto.
(visiting chief: ee.)

171. ase peka wis kiar soke.
(visiting chief: yer pe an imasa.)

*The Hot Pepper Story, Performed by Mastayans: Translation by
Joel Sherzer*

1. I will tell you the hot pepper story indeed.
2. I will do so as if speaking to you directly.
3. You, will be my responder.
4. I will do so as if speaking to you directly.
(visiting chief: aaah.)
5. I will really do so as if speaking to you directly.
(visiting chief: Yes.)
(Comments from gathered audience and brief conversation
with Mastayans.)
6. So   this story indeed   the chief of Mammimullu
Mantipaytikinya.
(Comments from gathered audience.)
(Laughter)
7. He was once, teaching me some, some of this hot pepper
story.
8. It seems to have some truth.
9. Well "it is true" it is said.
(Comments from gathered audience.)
10. "Well, in fact, there was once a grandmother"[2] it is said.
11. A grandmother.
12. "This grandmother in fact was the owner of a plum tree
there was a grandmother" see it is said, the grandmother
was the owner of a plum tree.
13. There was a grandmother who was owner of a plum tree in
fact once   the plum tree, when it produced fruit
before when the plum tree produced fruit well it used to be
possible to gather a lot.

14. It was possible to gather up to four baskets.
15. Well one day this plum tree, from which it used to be possible to gather four baskets went bad.
16. "The fruit in fact, of the plum tree began falling down" it is said.
17. The owner went to see the fruit of the plum tree and when she went to see, the plum fruit had fallen   all of it.
18. "It is impossible to gather plums."
19. "That is what the grandmother said" see she says   "why ever   did my plum tree go bad?" she says.
20. "Its fruit   does not get ripe for me.
21. Therefore since the fruit does not get ripe for me   who might it be   that is touching my plum fruit?"
22. The grandmother was thinking.
    (visiting chief: So it is.)
23. "Well one day   now this grandmother   then got   a boy" see it is said.
24. To take care of the plum tree.
    (visiting chief: Yes.)
25. The grandmother said to the boy she said   "grandson[3] you will take care of my plum tree for me" she said to him.
26. "You will guard my plum tree for me.
27. Here   you will come guard my plum tree for me   you, will come see who is touching my plum fruit" she says.
    (visiting chief: So it is.)
28. The grandson said "alright" he says.
29. Well thus   he sat, on top, of the plum tree
    (visiting chief: Yes.)
    He sat looking. (pitch rises at end of line)
    (visiting chief: Yes.
            Comments.
            He sat watching.)
30. He sat watching the plum fruit he sat looking.
    (visiting chief: aah.)
31. As the grandmother had told him.
    (visiting chief: What might be touching her fruit?)
32. Yes what might be touching her fruit?
33. Well when she   thus awoke   the grandmother went there to see.
    (visiting chief: Yes.)

34. When the grandmother got there to see   she saw again
    that her plum fruit, had fallen all over.
    (visiting chief: It had still fallen again.)

35. And this grandmother said, she said to the grandchild, here
    then   "did you see" she says "did you see the person who
    caused my plum fruit to fall" she says.
    (visiting chief: Yes.)

36. And he said, "no" he says "I didn't see I didn't see anyone"
    he says.
    (visiting chief: Comments.)

37. "I didn't see anyone" see he says.

38. "Alright" she says.

39. Therefore "alright" see she says.

40. "Well   now tonight you will take care of it for me again"
    she said to him ah.
    (visiting chief: So it is.)

41. "Tonight you will take care of it again.
    (visiting chief: Comments.)

42. You will look very carefully for me ah.

43. Who might well be touching my plum fruit."
    (visiting chief: The boy.)

44. The boy the boy the boy remained seated   for her.

45. And the grandmother went back home.
    (visiting chief: Home.)

46. Yes the owner of the plum tree is sleeping soundly in her
    house.
    (visiting chief: Yes.)

47. "Then   next day she awoke again" see it is said.

48. She goes to ask again.

49. "When she asked again   when again she saw   the
    plum fruit had fallen again" it is said.
    (visiting chief: Again.)

50. Well she asked the grandson again   "did you see" she
    says ah   "did you see who touched   my plum fruit?"

51. "No" he says "I didn't see anyone" he says.
    (visiting chief: So it is.)

52. "Thus" it is said.

53. The grandmother got very furious at this point, "he doesn't

take good care of it for me," so in fact   the grandmother
gets angry ah.
(visiting chief: Angry.
                   "You were not watching.")
54. "Yes I see that you were not watching" she said to him ah.
(visiting chief: Comment.)
55. It is true.
56. Then the grandmother thought "I will put an end to[4] the
boy right away he doesn't pay   attention to me" she said,
"right away   I will put an end to him ah."
57. Then the grandmother dug the ground.
(visiting chief: The ground.)
58. She dug the ground   four arm lengths deep in the ground
she dug.
59. She dug the ground the grandmother did.
(visiting chief: Comments.)
60. Then this grandmother   then she threw a ring inside the
ground.
(visiting chief: Comments.)
61. Well she said to the grandchild "my ring fell, see ah.
(visiting chief: aah.)
62. You will go get it for me."
(visiting chief: aah.)
63. Aah   well this   boy then stood a ladder up for her,
inside the ground.
(visiting chief: mm.)
64. Then the grandson went down under the earth.
(visiting chief: mm.)
65. Then when he had gone down, when he began to look for
the ring   she grabbed the ladder away.
(visiting chief: aah.)
66. She raises up the ladder.
(visiting chief: Impossible to climb up again.)
67. Impossible to climb up again how can you climb up again?
(Comments from gathered audience.)
68. It's steep.
69. Then she covered over the ground cover cover cover closed.
(visiting chief: Poor grandchild.)

70. The grandchild died.
    (visiting chief: Died.)
71. He truly dies.
72. He was there inside.
73. Well he was there   then this grandchild has a mother ah,
    he also has a father.
74. Then they looked for him.
75. "Where might my boy have gone" they say.
    (visiting chief: aaah.)
76. The mother was searching "where might my grandchild
    have gone? My son where might he have gone?"
    (visiting chief: Comment.)
77. Well he would not appear and she went to the
    grandmother's place to ask, "did you see my son?" she asks.
78. "No I did not see yours" she said to her, "I did not see
    him.
79. It's true" she says.
80. Well the mother was crying for her baby.
81. The father was crying for his baby.
82. Well slowly slowly slowly they forgot   they forgot ah.
    (visiting chief: Forgot.)
83. After a lot of time had gone by they really forgot.
    (visiting chief: The grandmother forgot?)
84. His mother forgot.
    (Comments from gathered audience.)
85. But the grandmother of course knew since she had buried
    the ground.
    (visiting chief: But she of course knows.)
86. As for her she knows.
    (Comments from gathered audience.)
87. The mother was crying for her baby.
    (visiting chief: So it is.)
88. Well she was crying   after a while slowly slowly she
    forgot again she forgot again.
    (visiting chief: Yes.)
89. She did not feel anything anymore.
    (visiting chief: Yes.)
90. "Well one day as it happens, she has a daughter also" it is
    said.
    (visiting chief: Yes.)

91. In fact it was her brother who died.
92. Well one day always as they were going to eat.
93. "While they were beginning to eat" it is said   the boy always said to his sister "near the grandmother's   house then there is something growing" he says ah.
    (visiting chief: So it is.)
94. "It was growing on top of the ground   something very small was growing" he says.
    (visiting chief: Yes.)
95. Well the grandmother saw that it was getting bigger what-was-it?
    (visiting chief: What was growing?)
96. Yes.
97. Well slowly it rises it keeps growing up keeps growing up keeps growing up indeed it produced fruit.
    (visiting chief: Yes.)
98. Well when it produced fruit its flesh got ripe in fact it was pepper.
    (visiting chief: Pepper.)
99. Mm, "pepper," see it is said.
    (visiting chief: Yes.)
100. Well the grandmother   is taking care of, a pepper plant and the pepper plant belonged to the grandmother ah.
    (visiting chief: aah.)
101. The pepper my friend got-ripe (voice vibrates) that is what happened to the pepper.
102. And as for the boy who had died, while he was beginning to eat, he always said to his baby sister.
    (visiting chief: Yes.)
103. "Sister go to that grandmother who is there and ask for some pepper for me see I want to eat with pepper ah."
    (visiting chief: Yes.)
104. She would always go to ask her.
    (visiting chief: Yes.)
105. Well she went there and said to the grandmother   "I want some of your pepper."
    (visiting chief: Yes.)
106. The grandmother says "alright" and the grandmother would always go to gather pepper for her
    (visiting chief: Yes.)

pepper, gather   well the grandmother was there.

107. Well one day, while eating again, she went to ask again.
(visiting chief: Yes.)

108. And she (the grandmother) says to the girl "you go and gather the pepper see."
(visiting chief: Comment.)

109. "Well she went to gather the pepper" it is said.
(visiting chief: Yes to the grandmother's place.
Comment.)

110. Well, she always went to the grandmother's place to gather it, the grandmother is the owner of the pepper plant.

111. Well a person began to speak from inside the ground   to the girl who was gathering pepper.
(visiting chief: aaah.)

112. Aah, "'LIT-TLE-GIRL'   it says" see it is said.
(visiting chief: Yes.)

113. "'Little girl,' the pepper speaks" it is said.
(visiting chief: From under the earth it speaks?)

114. "From under the earth a person speaks" it is said.

115. "Lit-tle-girl" it says.

116. She heard, that it said, "little girl" ah
(visiting chief: aah.)
a person is calling her.

117. She got frightened chased away by the pepper and she went back to her mother's place.

118. She said to her mother "while I was gathering pepper a person called me see.

119. From under the pepper it called me see 'LIT-TLE-GIRL' it says to me ah.

120. I got frightened" see she says.
(visiting chief: Frightened.)

121. Her mother did not believe it.
(visiting chief: Did not believe it.)

122. She (the girl) says to her "you   and me let's go see, so that you can go hear ah."

123. Then her mother herself also went to hear.
(visiting chief: Comment.)

124. "Then with her mother thus when the girl gathered pepper thus it called again" it is said.
(visiting chief: aah.)

125. "'Little girl   little girl'   it is calling" it is said.
     (visiting chief: Only indeed calling.)
126. Aah, indeed calling.
127. The father at once thought the mother at once thought "it is our son the one who the person killed who was heard here ah."
     (Comments from gathered audience.)
128. Then ah, yes, it was the owner of the pepper plant then that one   then they began to dig.
     (visiting chief: Yes.)
129. To see what was inside the ground.
     (visiting chief: Yes.)
130. Well from inside   he   called then they dug with a shovel ah
     (visiting chief: Yes.)
     with a digging stick.
     (visiting chief: Yes.)
131. "And he called" see he says ah   "over here is my head."
     (visiting chief: "Over here.")
132. "Over here are my feet."
     (visiting chief: Yes.)
133. One could hear the person speaking.
     (visiting chief: Yes.)
134. Then slowly slowly slowly slowly then they dug.
     (visiting chief: The mother is digging.)
135. The mother is digging up her son.
     (visiting chief: So it is.)
136. So thus so the boy is there, the person who then   took care of the plum tree the person whom the grandmother buried   he   came back to life again.
     (visiting chief: aah.
               The grandmother really did well she was
               caught.)
137. The grandmother then got caught.
138. Then he   the brother came out ah.
     (visiting chief: Comment, the grandmother will be talked
               about.)
139. They then asked him   "where why, did this happen to you?"
140. Well, he told.

141. "There used to be a grandmother, I was going about
    here   the grandmother always placed me here in order to
    care for her plum tree" see he says ah.
    (visiting chief: Yes.)

142. "Well seeing that I did not take good care of her plum tree,
    the grandmother dug the ground for me.
    (visiting chief: Yes.)

143. This grandmother threw me see inside the ground."
    (visiting chief: She threw the ring.)

144. Ah, she threw the ring.

145. "Now this grandmother   now after she buried me inside
    the ground now while I was still here, this pepper plant
    began to grow   I called you" see he said to them.
    (visiting chief: So it is.)

146. AAH.

147. "It is true" he says.

148. Well as for   the boy   already he was a young man
    since   he had grown up   then "as for the
    grandmother" he says "I'll finish the grandmother off[5] see."
    (visiting chief: aah.)

149. Then this boy who had gone up to the surface of the earth
    then this boy left   he went up to heaven.
    (visiting chief: Yes.)

150. He rose up on a plate and he went up to heaven.

151. Then he surely took a golden hook there.
    (visiting chief: Yes.)

152. He took it from his father's place it seems.
    (visiting chief: mm.)

153. Then having returned here   then he went to the
    grandmother's place.

154. The grandmother indeed it is said "she-al-ready-knew."
    (visiting chief: aah.)

155. The grandmother is sitting trembling with fear by the
    fireplace she is seated there afraid.
    (visiting chief: So it is.)

156. Then he grabbed her then with the teeth of the hook he did
    it to the grandmother then MOK.[6]

157. Then she was carried away again.
    (visiting chief: Yes.)

158. The grandmother was carried away also, with the teeth of the *tule* (Kuna) hook   then she rose off she went mmm.
(visiting chief: Yes.)

159. She is pulled along in the plate she goes she went.

160. To *sappi pirkwen* now
(Comment from gathered audience: the place of Sodom.)
to Sodom.
(visiting chief: Yes.)

161. "Sodom is a very dangerous place the place of the chiefs of fire (there is much fire)" see it is said.
(visiting chief: Yes.)

162. There are many burning *ikwa* trees standing everywhere.
(visiting chief: Yes.)

163. There are many burning *paila* trees standing everywhere.
(visiting chief: Yes.)

164. There then is the grandmother see in the middle of the fire.
(visiting chief: Yes.)

165. The grandmother is all toasted.
(visiting chief: Comment.)

166. Aah.

167. For this reason the ancestors said see it is said "If on this earth the grandmothers   bury birds   they are thrown there see.
(visiting chief: Yes.)

168. The grandmothers will be carried to a place called *pursipu* (white ash)   the place of the chiefs of ashes where then there are many flaming trees all standing everywhere the grandmothers are punished there.
(visiting chief: mm.)

169. Those who do not know how to take care of birds those who bury birds
        in this world.
(visiting chief: mm.)

170. They are thrown there"   the ancestors chant this see he (Mantipaytikinya) said to me.
(visiting chief: Yes.)

171. Up to this I have told you a little.
(visiting chief: You did it well for me.)

TRANSLATION BY BRIAN SWANN

1. I will tell you this story. Well, now.
2. I will tell it as if speaking to you directly.
3. You will respond.
            I will.
4. I will tell it as if talking directly to you.
            Uh huh.
5. That is how I will tell it.
            Yes.
6. Right. This story. Really. It comes from the sakla of
            Mammimullu, Mantipaytikinya.
7. He once taught me a little of this story.
8. It seems to have some truth in it.
9. I believe you'll say "it's true."
10. Right. "There was once an old woman," they say.
11. An old woman.
12. So, this old woman owned a plum-tree. There was
            an old woman, you see, and she was the owner
            of a plum-tree.
13. There was an old woman who owned a plum-tree. Right.
            The tree used to produce fruit. Yes. There were
            a lot of plums to gather.
14. She could fill about four baskets with them.
15. Well. One day this plum-tree, which used to yield
            four baskets of fruit, turned bad.
16. The fruit. That's so. Of the plum-tree. It dropped
            to the ground. You see.
17. When the old woman went to see her tree, she saw the plums
            had fallen, all of them.
18. "I can't gather these plums,"
19. that's what the old woman said. You see. "What could
            have made my tree go bad?
20. The plums are not ripening for me.
21. And since the plums are not ripening for me, who could be
            harming my plum-tree?"
22. The old woman thought hard.
            That's right.

23. Well. One day, this old woman got a boy,
      you see,

24. To guard the plum-tree.
      Yes.

25. She said to him, "I want you to take care of my plum-tree."
      That's what she told him.

26. "You will guard my plum-tree for me.

27. You will watch my tree and find out who is touching it."

28. "Alright," the boy said.

29. Well. He climbed up, and sat in the top branches.
      Yes.

      He sat and kept watch.
      Yes. He sat watching.

30. He sat and watched over the plum-tree. He sat and watched.
      Yes.

31. Just like the old woman told him.
      What could be getting at her fruit?

32. Yes. What could be getting at her fruit?

33. Now. Next day, soon as she woke, the old woman
      went to see her tree.
      Yes.

34. When she arrived, she saw again all her plums had fallen.
      They'd all fallen again.

35. And the old woman says to the boy, "Well, did you see,
      did you see what made my fruit fall?"

36. And "no," he says, "no I didn't see. I didn't see anyone.

37. No. No one at all."

38. "Alright," she says.

39. Now. "Alright," she says.

40. Well. "Tonight you'll keep watch again.

41. I want you to watch again carefully, tonight.

42. You will keep a sharp lookout for me.

43. Find out who's getting at my plum-tree."
      The boy.

44. And this boy, this same boy, sat back up in the tree
      for her.

45. The old woman returned home.

46. Yes. The owner of the plum-tree is fast asleep
      in her house.

47. Next day, soon as she woke, you see,
48. she goes to ask the boy what he's found out.
49. When she saw the plums had fallen again, she asked him
    again. You see.
        Again.
50. Well. She asked the boy again. "Did you see," she asks him
    "who did this to my plum tree?"
51. "No," he replies, "I didn't see anyone."
        That's what happened.
52. Well, then.
53. Now the old woman got very angry. "He's not taking good
    care of it for me." She gets real angry.
        Angry. You weren't watching.
54. "Yes. I see you didn't keep watch," she said to him.
55. And it was true.
56. Then the old woman thought, "I'll take care of him
    right now. He pays no attention to me.
    I'll do him in."
57. She started to dig in the ground.
        The ground.
58. She dug the ground. Four arm-lengths deep she dug
    in the ground.
59. The old woman dug in the ground.
60. Then she tossed a ring down the hole.
61. Well. "My ring has fallen in," she told the boy. "You see.
62. Go down and get it for me."
        Yes.
63. Yes. Well. The boy got a ladder and stood it in the hole.
        Mm.
64. He climbed down, into the earth.
        Mm.
65. When he got to the bottom, and began looking for the ring,
    she grabbed the ladder.
66. She pulled it up.
        Yes.
        He couldn't climb up again.
67. He couldn't climb up again. How can you climb up again?
68. It's steep.

69. Then she filled in the hole. Covered it over, covered it over, closed it up.
       Poor boy.
70. The boy died.
       Died.
71. He really died.
72. He was there, under the earth.
73. Well. The boy who lay buried had a mother. A father too.
74. They set out to look for him.
75. "Where could my son have gone?" they say.
       Yes.
76. The mother looked everywhere. "Where could he have gone? Where could my son have gone?" she asks.
77. Well. He didn't show up, so she went to the old woman's. "Have you seen my son?" she asks.
78. "No," the old woman replied. "I haven't seen him.
79. I'm telling the truth."
80. The mother wept for her lost son.
81. The father wept for his lost son.
82. Then day by day, slowly, slowly, they forgot. They forgot.
       Forgot.
83. After a long time had passed, they forgot all about him.
       The old woman forgot?
84. His mother forgot.
85. But the old woman remembered because she was the one who had buried the boy.
       Of course she remembered.
86. She remembered of course.
87. The mother cried for her son.
       That's how it is.
88. Well. She kept crying. But as time went by, slowly she forgot again. She forgot again.
       Yes.
89. And then she felt nothing.
       Yes.
90. Now it happens that she has a daughter too. See.
       Yes.
91. It was her brother who died.

92. Well. One day the family was sitting down to eat, as usual.
93. While they were eating, the boy said to his sister,
   "There is something starting to grow beside
   the old woman's house." That's what he says.
       That's right.
94. It was starting to grow on top of the ground. Something
   very small was starting to grow. You see.
       Yes.
95. Well. The old woman saw it was getting bigger. What could
   it be?
       What was growing?
96. Yes.
97. Well. Slowly it grows taller. It keeps growing, it keeps
   on growing, keeps on growing, until it produces fruit.
       Yes.
98. Well. The flesh of this fruit became ripe. It was pepper.
       Pepper.
99. Uh-huh. Pepper. You see.
       Yes.
100. Well. The old woman took care of the pepper plant. The
   pepper plant belonged to the old woman.
       Uh-huh.
101. And, my friend, the pepper ripened. That's what happened
   to the pepper.
102. As for the boy who had died, as he began eating, he always
   used to say to his little sister—
       Yes.
103. "Go to the old woman who lives over there and ask her for
   a few peppers. I want to eat some with my food."
       Yes.
104. And she would always go and ask the old woman.
       Yes.
105. She'd go and say to the old woman, "I want a few of
   your peppers."
       Yes.
106. The old woman would say "alright," and go and pick some
   peppers for her.
       Sure.
   Peppers. She'd pick some. The old woman was there.

107. Well. One day they were eating again, and the girl went
    to ask for some peppers.
        Yes.
108. This time, the old woman told the girl, "You can go and
    get the peppers." You see.
109. Well. She went to pick the peppers. That's right.
110. Yes. She always went to pick them at the old woman's.
111. This time someone started to speak from under the earth.
    He spoke to the girl as she gathered the peppers.
        Uh-huh.
112. Uh-huh. "LITTLE GIRL," says the voice. You see.
        Yes.
113. "Little girl," the pepper plant is speaking.
        From under the earth?
114. Someone is speaking from under the earth.
115. "Lit-tle-girl," it says.
116. She heard it, she heard it say "little girl."
        Oh.
        Someone is calling her.
117. She got frightened. The pepper plant scared her away.
    She went back to her mother's.
118. "I was gathering peppers," she told her mother, "and a voice
    began calling me.
119. It called me from under the plant. 'LIT-TLE GIRL,' it said
    to me.
120. I got scared."
        Scared.
121. Her mother didn't believe her.
        Didn't believe her.
122. So the girl said, "Let's go together and see. Come hear
    for yourself."
123. The mother went with her, to hear for herself.
124. And then, you see, when the girl began to pick the peppers,
    the voice called out again:
125. "Little girl, little girl." That's what it said.
        Yes, calling.
126. Ah, calling. Well.
127. At once father and mother thought the same thing: "It is our
    son we heard here. Our son the old woman killed."

128. Yes. That's the one. The owner of the pepper plant.
     They began digging,
129. to see what was inside the ground.
     Yes.
130. Well. The voice started to call from inside. So then
     they dug faster with the shovel.
     Yes.
     And with a digging stick.
131. And the voice said, "My head is over here."
     Over here.
132. "My feet are over here."
     Yes.
133. You could hear the boy speaking.
     Yes.
134. Then they dug slowly, slowly, with care.
     His mother is digging.
135. The mother is digging up her son.
     She is.
136. So well, there in front of them is the boy who took care
     of the plum-tree; the boy the old woman buried.
     He came back to life again.
     *Uh-huh. Well done, old woman! She got
     caught. She got caught.*
137. The old woman got caught then.
138. The boy emerged.
     Everybody will talk about the old woman.
139. Then they asked him, "Where did this happen to you? Why?"
140. Well. He told them.
141. "There used to be an old woman. I was walking here. The old
     woman asked me to take care of her plum tree." You see.
     Yes.
142. Well. Because I didn't take care of her plum-tree, the old
     woman dug a hole in the ground."
     Yes.
143. "This old woman pushed me into the hole."
     She threw the ring in.
144. "Yes, she threw the ring in.
145. This old woman buried me in the ground. and while I was

there, this pepper plant started to grow. I called
out to you," he told them.
That's right.
146. Ah . . .
147. "I'm telling the truth," he says.
148. Well. This boy had grown up into a young man. "As for the
old woman," he said, "I'll do her in."
Aha.
149. The boy had come up to the surface of the earth. After,
he rose up to heaven.
Yes.
150. He rose up on a plate. He went up to heaven.
151. He took a golden hook.
Yes.
152. It seems he got it from his father's place.
Mm.
153. Then he returned here and went to the old woman's.
154. The old woman, you see, she already knew why he'd come.
Aha.
155. She is sitting by the fireplace, quivering with fear.
She is.
156. The young man stuck the hook in her. Thwack!
157. He carried her away.
Yes.
158. The old woman was carried away, impaled on the hook. She
rose into the air, she went away. Whoosh!
Yes.
159. She is towed along on the plate. Off she goes! Off she went!
160. The young man went to *sappi pirkwen.*
The place is Sodom.*
To Sodom.
Yes.
161. Sodom's a very dangerous place. There is fire everywhere. It is
the place of the chiefs of fire. You see.

---

*This comment is from the audience.

162. Burning *ikwa* trees are everywhere.
     Yes.
163. Burning *paila* trees are everywhere.
164. See. In the middle of the fires: the old woman.
     Yes.
165. She is being roasted.
166.   *Aha.*
167. And this is the reason our ancestors say: If on this earth,
     old women bury birds they are thrown in that place.
     You see.
     Yes.
168. The old woman will be carried to a place called *pursipu,*
     white ash; the place of the chiefs of fire. There
     are many trees in flames everywhere. The old women
     are punished there.
     Mm.
169. Those who do not know how to take care of birds, those
     who bury birds,
     Mm.
170. are thrown there. Our ancestors chanted this,
     Mantipaytikinya told me.
     Yes.
171. I have told you a little of what he told me.
     You have done it well, on my behalf.

POSSIBLE CONTEXTS FOR PERFORMANCE OF THE
HOT PEPPER STORY

It is necessary to begin this exploration and explanation of the hot
pepper story by contrasting the performance reported on here with
other possible performances and by viewing the ethnography of this
event in relation to a more total Kuna ethnography of speaking.

The hot pepper story, like other Kuna stories, can be performed
in two different ways in two different contexts for two different
purposes: A story can be spoken by chiefs or other knowers of
stories, typically in the Kuna gathering house but also in one's own

home, for example, to young children. In such performances, there is a focus on entertainment, amusement, play, and humor.

A story can also be chanted by Kuna chiefs in the gathering house, usually in the evening, to an audience of men and women. The chanting of stories is practiced in the eastern portion of San Blas, which includes Mulatuppu. Inhabitants of the western portion of San Blas do not feel that it is appropriate to chant stories, and criticize those who do so. While a chanted story may be pleasing, amusing, or humorous to the listeners, the ultimate purpose of all chanting is to illustrate proper and improper modes of behavior and to call on the community to follow the former.

Further examination of these two ways of performing stories is necessary for an understanding of the problem posed in this chapter. Stories, when performed in spoken form for amusement in the gathering house, are told on days when people do not work (holidays, or days when there is an interdiction on work because of an eclipse, and so forth); when there is a chief visiting from another village and men sit around the gathering house with him; or just before the evening chanting of chiefs. The stories are a diversion for the pleasure and amusement of those present—a small group of men during the daytime or the gradually gathering group of men and women at night. Stories are told in colloquial Kuna, in the style appropriate for gathering-house narration. This linguistic variety and style are easily understood by all Kuna. The focus is on the play and humor of narration. The narrator alternates fast and slow, loud and soft speech, imitates voices and sounds, and tries to make his audience laugh. The audience, especially a single person in it at whom the story is directed, asks questions and makes humorous comments. There is much laughter.

Stories are one of a number of genres, topics, or themes that can be chanted in the gathering house by chiefs. Others are tribal myths, legends, and history; reports of personal experiences, including dreams; and counsel directed at particular individuals, groups of individuals, or the community at large. There are regional and individual differences in practice and attitude in San Blas with regard to what topics are appropriate for chiefs' chanting. (Inhabitants of the western portion of San Blas also criticize those of the east for chanting biblical themes, non-Kuna history [for example, about Christopher Columbus and Simon Bolivar], and personal dreams.)

Chanting is a most serious affair. The subject matter is drawn on by the chief for the purpose of his moral instruction to the audience. The performance is in the form of a ritual dialogue between two chiefs in which one chants verse by verse, with the other responding teki after each verse. The linguistic variety is phonologically, syntactically, and semantically distinct from colloquial Kuna. In this style, metaphors abound. It is the mark of a good chief not only to use conventional, traditional metaphors but also to elaborate and develop them in personal and appropriate ways. The chief states and stresses his moral as he chants. After the chant, there is an interpretation in colloquial Kuna by an *arkar* (chief's spokesman). This interpretation explains the message of the chant. The interpretation of the chant by both chief and spokesman is thus part of the structure and strategy of its performance.

The performance of the hot pepper story presented here is an interesting case with regard to these two Kuna ways of performing stories. The hot pepper story is spoken and told primarily for amusement, on the occasion of a visit of a well-known chief from another village; but the visiting chief takes on the role of apinsuet, as he might in a chanted version of the story. While there is no spokesman's interpretation, Mastayans does provides a short moral using a metaphor, or at least an allusive term, as part of the end of the story. The special properties of this particular performance of the hot pepper story are important to the analysis of its strategic structure and are discussed below.

It is useful to place the distinction between two ways of performing stories (spoken and chanted) within the larger system of Kuna discourse. The three principal Kuna ritual-ceremonial discourse types are the chanting of chiefs, the chants of curing and magical control, and the shouting of puberty festivals, each in a particular linguistic variety and style quite distinct from colloquial Kuna and, especially in the case of the latter two, not intelligible to nonspecialists. The addressees of curing and magical and puberty festival discourse are spirits, which are believed to understand the linguistic variety involved. The efficacy of these texts resides in convincing the object to perform an act or acts, either after having heard the text or concurrently with the hearing of the text. There is no interpretation and none is necessary, since the spirit-address-ees understand the language of the text.

The chanting of chiefs is addressed to humans—the audience which is present and expected to listen to the performance. The spokesman's interpretation is for them and is needed, both because of the metaphorical language of the chants and because of the belief that reformulation and repetition are needed in order to drive home the message. Spoken stories, like reports and personal narratives recounted in the gathering house, are told in colloquial Kuna. There is no formal interpretation as part of the performance. None is needed since the message is clear and easily understood by all those present and no allusive message is involved.

THE STORY AND INTERPRETATIONS

The hot pepper story, as told by Mastayans, has a deceptively simple narrative structure. The telling consists of six parts, with subparts within them.

1. The opening, which consists of metacommunicative commentary about the storytelling event itself (lines 1–9).
2. The grandmother's problem with her plum tree and the actions she takes concerning it (10–89). These include asking the boy to guard the tree (23–28); the boy's failure to catch a culprit (29–55); and the grandmother's burying the boy in the ground as a punishment (56–72). This part ends with the boy's parents looking for him and mourning his death (73–89).
3. The growing of the pepper plant and the discovery and saving of the boy (90–147). This part includes the pepper plant growing at the grandmother's house (90–101); the boy's sister going to pick pepper at the grandmother's house (102–108); the boy speaking to his sister and mother (109–127); the boy being dug out of the ground (128–138); and the boy reporting on his experience (139–147). As discussed above, there is some temporal jumping and dis-continuity involved here, especially when the text is approached from the perspective of western European cultural logic.
4. The punishment of the grandmother (148–166).
5. The moral (167–170).
6. The coda, which like the opening, is metacommunicative (170–171).

The textuality of Mastayans's performance of the hot pepper story involves a series of repeated and permuted thematic elements and words, all of which contribute to its denseness and complexity. Repeated thematic elements include the boy dying and the grandmother dying; the growing of a plum tree and the growing of a pepper plant; the boy twice sitting and watching but not discovering a culprit; the girl and then her mother hearing the calling of the boy; and the girl going several times to gather hot pepper at the grandmother's house.

Repeated and permuted words are grouped within certain semantic fields crucial to the narrative. These include the semantic field of watching, *nakkuleke* (take care of), *etarpe* (guard), *arkae* (watch), *takke* (see, look), and *akkwe* (care for); of rising and growing up, *ainie* (grow), *nakkwe* (rise), *tunkue* (get big), and *serkue* (grow up); of throwing and falling down, *arkwane* (fall), *ekwane* (throw), and *patte* (fall down); of dying, *purkwe* (die), *perkue* (finish off), and *opeloe* (put an end to); of digging and burying, *tike* (plant, dig, bury), *kwie* (dig), and *akkwie* (dig); and of producing and getting ripe, *turpamakke* (produce fruit), *nakue* (get ripe), and *okkinnoe* (get red, ripe).

There are also repetitions in form created by the repeated use of the same or similar sounding words. Examples are *pinna pinna* (slowly); *purkwe* (die)/*perkue* (finish off)/*opeloe* (put an end to); *kwane* (gather)/*arkwane* (fall)/*ekwane* (throw); and *kwie* (dig)/*akkwie* (dig).

The constant shifting of point of view (caused by temporal disjunctions and moving in and out of quotations) coupled with the repetition and permutation of a small number of thematic elements and words characterize the hot pepper story's textuality. While these textual processes might be thought of as reflections of an underlying Kuna cultural logic, it is only by investigating actual discourse, actual verbal performances, that we can uncover this logic and see it in action.[7]

The hot pepper story shares features with other stories and myths found in South America as well as all over the world. It contains good deeds and evil deeds, punishments and rewards, deaths and a rebirth, and a moral. In terms of diffusion, the probable source is the singing bone, or speaking hair motif of European folktales, now widespread in Latin America.[8] It is most interesting that this motif has reached a tropical forest Amerindian society and become well integrated into its social and cultural life and its ethnography of speaking. As rich as the hot pepper story is with regard to narrative development and symbolic oppositions—features that no doubt add to its role as a story told for amusement and entertainment—it does not provide an internal interpretation of the narrative development or symbolic oppositions. This makes it most useful for Kuna chiefs, in that they can develop an interpretation of their own choosing as part of the structure of the telling.

When chanted in the Kuna gathering house, the hot pepper story can be given various interpretations by the chief and the spokesman. These interpretations can be both general and particular, and they can be opposed or in contradiction to one another. At the most general level the text can have to do with proper behavior and ways of treating other people. At a more particular level, it can have to do with the raising and care of young children. At a still more particular level, it can have to do with the care of babies, especially at birth, by midwives. And at the most particular level, it can have to do with what to do with babies who are socially inappropriate in one way or another, twins, albinos, those with birth defects, or the products of an illegitimate relationship. Contradictory interpretations result from differing points of view regarding the issues involved in the care and treatment of babies, children, or people in general.

A clue to the possible interpretations of the hot pepper story and its role in a Kuna ethnography of speaking is provided by the moral offered by Mastayans at the end of his narration on this particular morning in 1971:

167. For this reason the ancestors said see it is said "If on this earth the grandmothers bury birds they are thrown there see.
168. The grandmothers will be carried to a place called *pursipu* (white ash) the place of the chiefs of ashes where then there are many flaming trees all standing everywhere the grandmothers are punished there.
169. Those who do not know how to take care of birds those who bury birds in this world.
170. They are thrown there" the ancestors chant this see

The word *sikkwi* (bird) had not appeared in the story, and what the grandmother had buried was a boy. But sikkwi is a euphemism for baby, and when Kuna babies die they are buried in their house in the village, by the midwives if the death is at birth. Adults are buried in the cemetery outside the village.

This useful hint enables us to examine the hot pepper story in greater detail, starting with the ways in which the text is open to multiple interpretations. First there is the question of whether there is a need or purpose for interpretation at all, and what the nature of interpretation might be. Put another way, can the story be taken point by point for what it is, with no meanings other than the actual characters and actions described, or are these to be viewed as somehow symbolic of or representative of something else?

Among the possible interpretations there are the most general, such as, what are the reasons for or the meanings of the punishments and rewards, of both the grandmother and the boy? That is, what is the significance of the story, taken as a whole? Then there are particular, local interpretations—details in the narrative whose significance is not overtly explained in the text itself. These may also be viewed as features of the text where there is a choice such that the overall general structure of the text (not its interpretation) would not change if another choice had been made. Examples are: Why the title the hot pepper story and not the plum tree story or the grandmother story? Why does the grandmother have a plum tree and not a coconut tree, banana tree, or *ikwa* (wild fruit) tree? Why does a pepper plant grow up where the boy is buried and not a coconut, banana, orange, or plum tree? Why does the tree belong to a grandmother and not a father, mother, or grandfather? Why a boy and not a girl?

Understanding of some aspects and details of the story depends on explaining certain Kuna linguistic, social, and cultural presuppositions, which are not explicitly and overtly stated in the text but are essential to it. Discussion of these presuppositions shows the necessity of placing the text in the context of the language, society, and culture of which it forms a part. At the most general level of the plot, there are the punishments and rewards. The boy is punished for not properly caring for the plum tree, but later comes back to life. The grandmother is punished for having buried the boy. The boy is punished in this world, and the grandmother is punished in the afterworld. The Kuna believe that individuals are rewarded and punished in the afterworld for their good deeds and misdeeds in this world. The rewards and punishments are often appropriate to the individual's role in society.

It is interesting to consider just what the boy is punished for. He was asked by the grandmother to watch over the plum tree—it is common Kuna practice to hire someone to take care of a possession. A plum tree, however, is very unimportant in the Kuna tree-plant ranking system; it is owned, but its fruit is free for anyone to take, in any quantity, at any time (see Howe and Sherzer 1975). So the grandmother had no right to try to protect her fruit. Furthermore, it is never made clear what happens to the fruit, if the tree is merely old and no longer productive, if someone actually comes and takes the fruit, or if the boy is somehow responsible. Nor is it clear exactly who the boy is and what his relationship is to the old woman, the *muu*.

The word *muu* has three meanings in Kuna and all are potentially relevant to an understanding of the story—grandmother, old woman, midwife. I have somewhat arbitrarily chosen grandmother in my translation. The grandmother kills the boy by burying him. Although it is appropriate to bury dead infants on the spot, the boy in question was neither dead nor an infant; so burying him was a misdeed. The pepper plant that grows up on the spot where the boy was buried gives the story its title. The pepper is hot and is used as a condiment in food. According to the Kuna system of ranking plants and trees, pepper is owned, but the owner must give an asker permission to pick some if needed for a meal. This is why the boy's sister asks for and obtains permission from the grandmother. It is important to note that in this case the grandmother is behaving perfectly appropriately. She *akkwe* (takes care of, line 100) the pepper plant and makes it available for others to use, a moral act for which individuals are positively rewarded in the afterworld. Yet this is precisely what does her in. The plate and golden hook used by the boy are part of a complex of objects believed by the Kuna to exist in the afterworld for their use. The grandmother's eternal place of punishment, Sodom, is clearly borrowed from Christian tradition, but it is given a Kuna name as well—*sappi pirkwen,* or *pursipu*—and it is full of trees from the Kuna environment.

The complexity and richness of the text are further elucidated by examining it in terms of the symbolic oppositions found by

Claude Lévi-Strauss to be pervasive in tropical-forest South American mythology.[9] Thus, the drama between the grandmother and the young boy which runs through the story opposes age to youth and female to male. The two plants in the story—the plum tree and the hot pepper—oppose unproductive and unripe to productive and ripe; sticky and sweet to hot and spicy. It might be argued that grandmother is to boy as plum is to pepper; that is, old, unproductive, weak, and falling on the one hand and young, productive, powerful, and rising on the other. Furthermore, according to the Kuna tree-plant ranking system described above, plum/pepper opposes relatively wild (nature) to relatively owned (culture). Since the plum is not eaten as part of a Kuna meal and the pepper is, and since pepper is used almost exclusively with cooked food, plum/pepper also opposes raw to cooked.

The narrative development relates these various oppositions and introduces others, which it also relates to them. The story is essentially about misbehavior and punishment for misbehavior, and life and death. In brief, because the plum lacks life, the grandmother asks the boy to find out who is causing the problem (misbehaving toward it). Because the boy does not properly protect the plum (misbehaves), he is punished with death. The grandmother dies on this earth but comes back to life in heaven. The boy comes back to life on this earth and goes up to heaven to punish the grandmother for her own misbehavior. In the course of this narrative development, the opposition up-above/down-below is introduced. The fruit of the plum tree falls down, the boy is buried underground. The pepper grows up out of the ground, the boy comes out because of it and after it, and the boy goes up to heaven to punish the grandmother.

These textual explanations and explorations enable us to understand the plot of the hot pepper story in general and in detail, including some of its potential symbolism in Kuna life. They do not, however, reduce the text to a single, unambiguous interpretation; rather, they make the various possibilities for interpretation more interesting and intriguing, denser and richer. Thus, we know why the grandmother is punished in the text—for killing the boy. But what does this symbolize? Was the boy not wrong at all, or not seriously wrong, or was he guilty of something? Are there circumstances under which the grandmother would have been justified in killing the boy? More particularly, following the clue provided by

Mastayans's offered moral, was the grandmother punished for killing a baby born with some kind of defect? (That is, should a birth defect be taken as lightly as failure to care for a plum tree?) Or was the grandmother punished for failing to see that there really was no defect, or that it was minor? (That is, is failure to care for a tree that anyone is permitted to pick from not a defect?) The Kuna are a society of more than 30,000 individuals, living in more than fifty villages ranging from traditional and conservative to progressive and acculturation oriented. There is a variety of points of view on how to deal with birth defects, just as there is on other subjects. Flexible texts such as the hot pepper story enable leaders such as chiefs, symbolic moralists who are expected to take public positions in metaphorical language, to exploit a single plot in several ways. The same story can be used to justify and symbolize various and even contradictory points of view.

MASTAYANS'S PERFORMANCE OF THE HOT PEPPER STORY

Let us return to the actual performance of the hot pepper story which I recorded. The strategy and structure of this telling must be understood from several intersecting and interacting perspectives. First, there is a story, told for amusement. Mastayans's telling of the story entertained the assembled group and especially the guest of honor. Second, Mastayans's inclusion of a moral using allusive language and stating explicitly that "the ancestors chant this" (line 170) relates this entertaining telling to the more serious telling which might occur if this story were chanted.

The conversation between Mastayans and the visiting chief which follows the telling of the hot pepper story deals with precisely the fact that this same story can be chanted. Mastayans opens (lines 6, 7) and closes (line 170) his telling by giving credit to his teacher, Mantipaytikinya, a chief from the village of Mammimullu, with whom he has been studying. He points out that "he was teaching me some" (line 7) and "I have told you a little" (line 171). These are formulaic understatements used by ritual leaders which indicate that more is known, by Mastayans himself, by his teacher, Mantipaytikinya of Mammimullu, and by the ancestors. These statements not only give credit to his teacher but also serve to remind the audience that Mastayans himself is a knowledgeable and diligent chief; one who gains prestige for himself and his village by traveling to other villages in order to study with venerable traditional specialists. Mastayans, by combining elements of an entertaining telling (first perspective) with an allusive moral indicating potential for serious chanting and framing devices characteristic of ritual discourse (second perspective), leads us to a third perspective with regard to structure, strategy, and ultimately, interpretation.

The immediate message of Mastayans in performing this story on this day is to announce to a well-known visiting chief and to his own village that "I, Mastayans, am a knowledgeable chief, one who studied with others to learn the traditions of our ancestors and performs them for my own village by chanting in the gathering house." Mastayans utilizes the rich and intricate potential of the hot pepper story to the fullest. He tells it well and it is well appreciated by the audience. Although he provides a moral, he never, any more than the text itself, takes a stand on the crucial issues raised in the story. Grandmothers should treat babies well, but what does this mean? What does treating well or not treating well entail? His moral is just as open to multiple interpretations as the story which led to it. Mastayans is indeed a knowledgeable chief, a clever political leader.

FURTHER CONSIDERATIONS

Understanding of the structure and significance of the hot pepper story depends on placing it in its Kuna context in two senses: an explanation of the linguistic, cultural, and social presuppositions necessary for an appreciation of the laconicity of the narrative and of the potential for alternative interpretations inherent in it;[10] a focus on the performance of the story, in actual Kuna settings, in which various analyses and interpretations are offered by the performers themselves as part of the strategy and structure of the performance.

From the point of view of Kuna ethnography of speaking, it is possible to view *kaa kwento* in terms of a particular constellation of components of speech (Hymes 1974). Thus:

Setting: gathering house; morning, afternoon, or evening
Participants: chief, chief's spokesmen, audience of gathered men
              or men and women
Ends: amusement, social control, demonstration of personal know-
        ledge
Act sequence: story, responses, interpretation
Key: playfully, humorously, seriously
Instrumentalities: spoken colloquial Kuna, chanted gathering-house
                    Kuna
Norm of interaction: verse and then response, audience comment
                      line and laughter
Genre: story

This constellation of components is a set of resources exploited by Kuna individuals as part of the dynamic, emergent structures and strategies of everyday communicative life. Thus, in the performance focused on here, Mastayans utilizes this particular constellation of components of speech in a unique way for his own personal reasons of the moment. The dynamic structure of the event relates the backdrop and ground rules of Kuna ethnography of speaking to the details of interactional life on that particular day. In a sense, Mastayans's clever exploitation of the hot pepper story can be compared to such small, strategic bits of verbal behavior in our own society as namedropping (for example, "You'll never guess who I saw at the club today?"), in which social interactional moves are achieved by reference to a prestigious person or place. But the Kuna way to be clever with language, to gain prestige and acquire recognition, is typically through long verbal performances, whether these are memorized texts or verbal structures developed during performance.

The approach I have taken to the hot pepper story is structuralist in that it is concerned with the structural properties of the story. But these structural properties are not viewed as static organizational features or underlying abstract logic. Rather, the dynamic structure of the text is focused on by analyzing the story in relationship to the contexts in which it is performed, in terms of the potential for openness of interpretation, and in terms of the ways in which this potential is exploited during performance. This approach is consistent with trends in recent or poststructuralism, which are concerned with dynamic, rhetorical aspects of texts and text-context interrelationships.

Lévi-Strauss, as we have seen, has investigated myths that share such features with the hot pepper story as relations between young and old and men and women, the interplay between life and death, and the origin of plants. But this story, as recorded here, has a narrative development and especially a moral that is completely different from the interpretations given by Lévi-Strauss. The story has to do essentially not with the raw and the cooked and nature and culture, but rather with how to treat people, especially babies, at birth. No doubt, on a more abstract level, the occurrence in the story of such basic oppositions as male/female, young/old, productive/unproductive, and life/death is related to the significance and interpretation the Kuna themselves provide. These are the elements which set the stage and weave the intrigue which lead to the moral. They contribute to the potential of the text for openness and multiplicity of interpretation.

Since his primary interest is in abstract, logical structures of myths, independent of particular cultures or societies, Lévi-Strauss's method is to look at similar myths in many societies; the increasing breadth of comparison and contrast leads to the positing of more and more abstract structures. There is no doubt about the validity of searching for underlying or abstract structures of myths or stories. This is in part what analysis is all about. At the same time, however, it is important to insist on principled ways of relating posited underlying constructs to actually performed events. We are in a privileged position with regard to the Kuna, in that they themselves posit underlying structures or meanings in the form of interpretations of the symbolism of the text and its message. Most important, they do so as part of its very performance for an audience to hear, learn from, and criticize. This is not to say that an outside analyst should simply record and repeat Kuna-performed interpretations; but further and deeper analysis should relate in principled ways to Kuna performers who themselves are involved in the analytical process.

Many of the myths which Lévi-Strauss studies are etiological, their significance or point being reported as an explanation of the origin of fire, cooking, plants, or death. The hot pepper story, as I recorded it and as interpreted by the Kuna in their performance of it, is not etiological, but either entertaining, rhetorical, or both. Lévi-Strauss's etiological myths look to the past in order to explain the origin of and reason for the present. The hot pepper story looks to the past—not mythical in the Kuna sense—in order to call for a particular mode of behavior in the future. Thus, in spite of its possible etiological origin (in diffusional terms), the Kuna hot pepper story is now at its core thoroughly rhetorical and political. As has been shown here, in the particular performance I recorded, the teller, Mastayans, uses the story for two rhetorical-political aims: to argue for a particular mode of behavior, by means of an entertaining telling; to convince his immediate audience, especially the visiting chief, that he, Mastayans, is a good chief; that is, a knower and performer of Kuna tradition.

Since the hot pepper story was recorded and analyzed in the context of performance, it is difficult if not impossible to compare it with the myths which form the basis of Lévi-Strauss's study, or with similar myths reported by other collectors or analysts of South American Indian mythology. The latter are reported essentially as summaries of referential content, outside their performance context, and rhetorical purpose is rarely mentioned. However, comparison with similar stories in other American Indian societies does support the notion—already pointed out by T. T. Waterman in a careful study of many North American Indian folktales (1914)—that referential content is independent of the point or explanation provided by particular societies, groups, or occasions. Although Waterman did not study actual performances of tales, his insistence on the separability of content and explanatory element or moral points to a potential for the use of tales in the rhetoric of performance, in which morals are developed and stressed independently of particular referential contents. The concept of potential for rhetorical use, inherent in a text, is similar to Kenneth Burke's notion of "literature as equipment for living" (1957). Thus the same or similar story can have quite different interpretations or purposes in different societies. Even within a single society it is possible for the same story to be structured differently by different groups. The Hopi are a well-documented American Indian case of this. Fred Eggan reports that "it soon became apparent that the origin legends of the same clan from different villages showed major contradictions and that even within the same village the stories of associate clans did not always correspond" (1957). As Nancy Parrott Hickerson has reviewed the Hopi situation:

There is, in fact, no body of Hopi tribal mythology—there is simply the mythology of the several Hopi clans. These clan traditions are related to one another—there is a common geographical setting, and a basic similarity as major events of creation and important supernatural figures recur. However, the mythology tells, especially, of events and places which bear on the properties, prerogatives, ceremonial responsibilities, and political claims of the individual clans (1978:39).

Lévi-Strauss has the Hopi case, among others, in mind when he writes, "La même population, ou des populations voisines par le territoire, la langue ou la culture, élaborent parfois des mythes qui s'attaquent systématiquement à tel ou tel problème en envisageant, variante après variante, plusieurs manières concevables de la résoudre" (1964:338).[11] Notice, however, that the hot pepper story resolves its problems in various ways within the same text; rather, it leaves open to interpretation possible solutions to the problem, and, ultimately, leaves open just what the problem is.

With regard to the hot pepper story, no studies of this singing bones motif exist that provide contextual information about societal interpretation, function, and purpose as I do here. We can speculate, however, in the Waterman and Burkean sense, on the basis of the way similar stories are reported and classified in collections of Amerindian folktales. Relatively similar stories are found among the Umotina of the northern Mato Grosso and among the Zuni of the North American Southwest. The Umotina have a myth in which a couple buries a boy and afterward from his corpse grow various crops, including pepper (Oberg 1953:108–109). In a Zuni myth, two brothers bury their grandmother, and on the spot where they bury her, a hot pepper plant grows up (Cushing 1901). Both of these stories are reported as if explaining the origin of hot pepper. It is quite the contrary, of course, in the Kuna story in spite of its title,[12] which is perhaps evidence of diffusion from groups in which it is used etiologically.

I do not find it strange that the same story or myth can be open to various interpretations as a strategic, structured part of its performance. This seems a natural feature of a nonliterate, American Indian society, in which discourse is central to social and political life. The openness of structure of the hot pepper story is particularly well suited to the Kuna gathering in which individuals, especially chiefs and other political leaders, gain prestige, jockey for position, and convince others on the basis of creative, adaptive, strategic use of speech.

It seems useful, by way of summary, to place this study within a paradigm of possible ways of going about the analysis of literature in nonliterate societies:

(1) Literature is studied in and for itself, abstracted from its use or sociocultural context, perhaps becoming grist for various textual mills—linguistic, structuralist, and so forth.

(2) Literature is seen as a reflection of some other aspect of the life of the people who produce and perform it, an aspect claimed to be more basic—social organizational, economic, psychological, and so forth.

(3) Literature is viewed in relationship to contexts provided by the society and culture in which it is found, and attention is paid to the functions and situations of performance.

While the approach developed here falls most clearly within the third way, it also moves along a continuum that ranges from structuralist to ethnomethodological. The former approach is oriented toward abstract structures and tends not to be interested in concrete contexts. For the latter, context is the focus of analysis and the text is secondary. Careful attention to both text and context, their intersection and interaction, is crucial to an understanding of the Kuna hot pepper story.

NOTES

1. In the preparation of the translation I have benefited in various ways from correspondence with Brian Swann. While he was in the process of preparing his own translation of the story, based on an earlier version of mine, I saw new possibilities for translations of words and phrases. I drew on some of these possibilities from his freer translation while at the same time maintaining a literal adherence to the actual Kuna performance. His version and his questions about mine also made me formulate more explicitly certain aspects of the nature of Kuna cultural logic which are present in this story and which I discuss in my text. It is a tribute to the richness of this Kuna story that it can be fruitfully translated in various ways.

2. As will be discussed below, the Kuna word *muu* has three meanings— grandmother, old woman, and midwife. I have chosen grandmother in the

translation. Even though the ambiguity present in Kuna is thus lost, I feel that grandmother is the most basic of the three meanings.

3. The boy is sometimes referred to and addressed as "boy," sometimes as "grandson." Since Kuna kin terms are frequently used to address non-kin, usage of these terms in the text should not be understood as necessarily implying kin relationships.

4. This translates the Kuna verb *opeloe,* literally, "to cause to end."

5. This translates the Kuna verb *perkue,* to finish.

6. *Mok* is an onomatopoeic particle, used in narration.

7. It is interesting that similar textual patterns are characteristic of certain works within the French new and new new novel, a most avant-garde and self-consciously experimental contemporary enterprise (see Sherzer 1986). Of course a quite different cultural logic is involved in the French works, in which texts are considered experimental and breaking with tradition. In the Kuna case they are quite in keeping with tradition.

8. I am grateful to Roger Abrahams for pointing this out to me. See Mackensen 1923 and Thompson 1961: Type 780 *The Singing Bone,* and Type 780B *The Speaking Hair.*

9. See *Mythologiques* (1964–1971).

10. Careful examination of the text in relation to Kuna language, culture, and society suggests still other analyses and interpretations. One interesting one, which has not been discussed because it is not offered by the Kuna as part of their performance of the story, has to do with Kuna social organization and residence rules. The Kuna are matrilocal; after marriage, a man goes to live in the house of his wife. The grandmother in *kaa kwento* does not live in the same house as the boy; that is, she might be the mother of the father of the boy, but not of the mother. It might be argued that she is punishing her son, lost according to Kuna residence rules, by killing his son. According to such an interpretation, the grandmother would be reacting against the rules of Kuna social organization; the story would be a reminder not to do so.

11. See Lévi-Strauss 1964:339 for a discussion.

12. For the significance of titles, see Hymes 1959.

REFERENCES

Burke, Kenneth. 1957. Literature as Equipment for Living. In *The Philosophy of Literary Form, idem,* ed. Rev. ed. Pp. 253–262. New York: Vintage Books.

Cushing, Frank Hamilton. 1901. *Zuni Folk Tales.* New York: Putnam.

Eggan, Fred. 1950. *Social Organization of the Western Pueblos.* Chicago: University of Chicago Press.

Hickerson, Nancy Parrott. 1978. The "natural environment" as object and sign. *The Journal of the Linguistic Association of the Southwest* 3:33–44.

Howe, James, and Joel Sherzer. 1975. Take and Tell: A Practical Classification from the San Blas Cuna. *American Ethnologist* 2:435–460.

Hymes, Dell. 1959. Myth and Tale Titles of the Lower Chinook. *Journal of American Folklore* 72:139–145.

———. 1974. Studying the Interpretation of Language and Social Life. In *Foundations in Sociolinguistics, idem*, ed. Pp. 29–66. Philadelphia: University of Pennsylvania.

Lévi-Strauss, Claude. 1964. *Le cru et le cuit*. Paris: Plon.

———. 1964–1971. *Mythologiques*. Paris: Plon.

Mackensen, Lutz. 1923. *Der Singende Knochen*. Helsinki: Folklore Fellows Communication No. 49.

Oberg, Kalervo. 1953. *Indian Tribes of Northern Mato Grosso, Brazil*. Washington, D.C.: Smithsonian Institution, Institute of Social Anthropology. Publication No. 15.

Sherzer, Dina. 1986. *Modes of Representation in Contemporary French Fiction*. Lincoln: University of Nebraska Press.

Sherzer, Joel. 1983. *Kuna Ways of Speaking: An Ethnographic Perspective*. Austin: University of Texas Press.

Thompson, Stith. 1961. *The Types of the Folktale*. Helsinki: Folklore Fellows Communication No. 184.

Waterman, T. T. 1914. The Explanatory Element in the Folk-Tales of the North American Indians. *Journal of American Folklore* 27:1–54.

Pima Heaven Songs

DONALD BAHR

Around 1900, twenty years after the first churches were built on Pima land and about the same time as the Ghost Dance and Peyote religions spread through the American West to the north of the tribe, a Pima named Hummingbird dreamt he went to heaven and learned a large number of songs from Jesus, and a smaller number from Mary. Fourteen of the former and two of the latter, collectively called "Heaven songs" (*da:m ka:cim ñe'i,* literally "on top laying songs"), are the subject of this chapter.

Like all Pima songs, Heaven songs are highly narrative. Every syllable (about fifty per song) is part of a word, and each word (about twenty per song) is part of a sentence (about four per song) that is part of a short, vivid narrative, which is part of a multisong set or series. There are no nonsense syllables. Also characteristic of Pima song, however, a song's linguistic content is not immediately apparent to a hearer fluent in the spoken language. There are changes in phonology (Jakobson 1960:374) and in grammar, for example, in syllable reduplication, which is a grammatical process in Pima. In short, Heaven songs are undeniable, but not readily accessible, stories.

All songs sung by living Pimas are thought by them to have been learned from someone else. Songs are either learned while awake from other singers or they are learned in dreams from animals, gods, spirits, and the like. Those learned from other singers are normally traced to an original dream perhaps several singers previous. The only exceptions appear to be some Pima language songs used in telling myths and possibly considered to be statements originally sung and heard in a waking state (and passed on verbatim

198

ever since); and songs learned from Anglo-Americans and considered to be the waking inventions of that race. In short, most native language songs are felt to begin as revelations. Heaven songs are not unusual in that respect.

We can be sure the Pimas learned the story of Jesus from foreign sources prior to Hummingbird's dreaming of the Heaven songs. There is also little doubt that Hummingbird knew of that story before his dream or dreams.[1] Thus he did not introduce Christianity to the Pimas but rather, being transported to Heaven as a kind of representative, introduced the Pimas to Jesus and Mary. He was the first Pima of record to go to and return from Heaven.

Dreamed journeys to mythic personages to obtain songs are well attested from a number of Yuman-speaking tribes immediately west of the Pimas (Kroeber 1925; Herzog 1928a, 1928b). I consider the Heaven songs an instance of this pattern; in fact, the only expression of it not borrowed from Yumans among the uto-Aztecan-speaking Pima and their close cultural and linguistic relatives the Papago. Most Pima-Papago song sets, while dreamt (like the Yumans'), did not derive from individual characters with a place in the tribes' mythology; that is, in their more or less organized and widely told tales about persons and events of long ago. They came instead from what were conceived as recent encounters with ghosts, animals, Christian devils, and the like.[2] While foreign in origin, Jesus was a mythic character to the Pimas. Hence Hummingbird was not only the first Pima dreamer to journey to Heaven but the first to present his tribe with a Yuman-style "mythic dreamt song series" as Herzog named the distinctive literary pattern of the Pimas' neighbors in 1928.

An important element in the pattern is its use for what I will call generalized celebrating. Mythic dreamt song series were not confined to a single purpose, such as only to cure the sick or only to make it rain. Rather, as Kroeber put it, "any song [or set] is intrinsically about equally suitable for any occasion. A singer evidently does not think about the reference or lack of reference of his song to the funeral or the celebration which is going on at the moment" (1925:756).

It is understandable that they weren't used for single purposes because the sets and their myths were extremely long and, as it seemed to Kroeber, rather pointlessly elaborated:

[Yuman song myths are] as frankly decorative as a patterned textile. The pattern is far from random; but it is its color and intricacy, its fineness and splendor, that have meaning, not the action told by its figures [i.e., the plot?]; and as a simple but religious people don the same garment for festivity or worship, . . . or interment, providing only it is gorgeously pleasing enough, so [do] the Mojave [a Yuman tribe] (1925:757).

In other words, rather than having ten different plain ceremonial designs for ten different purposes, the Mojaves had one gorgeous design and each time produced it (not donned it) in one of its several manifestations (different song myths).

Behind Kroeber's statement may be the idea of a possible social economy of ceremonialism in which ceremonies are both elaborated (true of Yumans) and differentiated (untrue of them). Yuman ceremonies are less differentiated than those of the Pueblos, for example, because the latter have different song, dance, and costume combinations for a host of activities: bean song and dance for beans, corn for corn, and so on. Speculating further, we may ask whether ceremonial differentiation is not expected primarily in regard to subsistence, broadly conceived, for example, guaranteeing rain, ensuring the growth of plants and animals, keeping enemy tribesmen at bay, or curing the sick. This exercise at least lets us specify what Yuman ceremonialism was not, in Kroeber's judgment (and I agree): it was not differentiated and not adjusted to particular subsistence concerns.[3]

Contrasting Pima-Papago and Yuman song, Herzog reached the judgment, consistent with the above exercise, that Pima-Papago song had the stronger connection to ceremonialism (1928b:200). I am sure that he had in mind the many Pima-Papago song sets and ritual scenarios devoted to distinct subsistence activities: forty-odd ceremonies to cure the sick, rainmaking ceremonies, salt purification ceremonies, songs to purify warriors after battle, to help shamans find deer, and so on. While counterparts to these ceremonializations were not wholly lacking among the Yumans, I think it fair to say the Pima-Papago (especially the Papago) placed heavier investment in them, to judge from published song collections. It is also fair to oppose these subsistence-oriented ceremonies against generalized ceremonies. We will name the opposition *specialized subsistence* versus *generalized display,* keeping in mind that different peoples may invest differently in them and that both have a potential for elaboration. The fact is that Pimas and Papagos also had generalized display celebrations (Pimas more than Papagos), and Heaven songs were used for them.

Pointless gorgeousness, that is, not having an immediate subsistence purpose, defines these ceremonies. They were of voluntary sponsorship and were open to all people of a few neighboring villages among the Pima-Papago, or to the entire tribe among the more densely settled and politically more segmented Yumans. Any event deemed worthy of celebration, but not necessarily guaranteed a celebration (at least, not a suitably gorgeous one), was fair game. In the mid- to late nineteenth century the stock events were war victories and good harvests. As the twentieth century wore on, when Heaven songs came into use, Memorial Day, Fourth of July, and Labor Day, plus weddings and anniversaries, eclipsed those older occasions. The ceremonies were held where the sponsor dictated, often at his house, and were supplied with songs by singers whom he contracted. They lasted a full night (daytime was irrelevant) and almost always included a form of dancing, whose steps varied, that permitted flirting by any of the adults who attended. Whether or not there was a cadre of costumed "ceremonial" dancers (usually not), there was almost always the opportunity for any man or women present to enter the dance with an eye on a specific partner. The closest physical contact was touching hands, and this was a Pima-Papago, not Yuman, specialty.

Yumans, unlike Pimas or Papagos, also used this form for funerals and post-funeral collective memorial ceremonies, held within the year. This was a point of contention between the two peoples: Yumans cremated, and wailed excessively, and sang and danced at funerals, burning the deceased's house and destroying quantities of donated property in the process; Pimas and Papagos interred, controlled their grief, and either conducted no ceremony at all (Pimas; at least, no strictly native one is remembered or recorded in the documents studied by Ezell [1961]), or followed Christian ritual (Papagos more than Pimas; until the late nineteenth century the ritual was Spanish Catholic).

All these peoples' exposure to Christianity began before 1700. At that time the Pima and Papago ancestors may already have begun interring their dead. In any case, they readily embraced

Christian mortuary customs while retaining the rest of their native ceremonialism, supplemented by churchgoing, until well into the twentieth century.[4] The Yumans, possibly cremating aboriginally, entered the twentieth century with their cremation rituals moved from the realm of subsistence (if they ever were that for them—funerals great or small confined to a specific liturgy of funeralness) into the area of generalized display.

The songs used in these events, whether mythic or not and regardless of the occasion, were deliberately overabundant. The good singer knew too many to count (possibly any amount greater than fifty), and too many to sing completely in one night. Kroeber found this to be true of Yuman song sets (1925:757), and I underscore it for the sets used in Pima generalized celebrations. It was part of their gorgeousness, even pointless gorgeousness; it distinguishes these sets, which I term superlong variable sequence sets, from those used in specialized subsistence ceremonies. The chronic problem with the latter is that the singer does not know enough songs of just the right type (Gila Monster curing songs, Corn Growing songs, Enemy Finding songs, etc.), while the problem with the former is that he knows too many.

SONG AND PROSE, FIXED AND VARIABLE SEQUENCING

This section treats song as literature, specifically as myth. As noted above, dreamt Yuman songs generally, and dreamt Pima Heaven songs uniquely, derive from mythic personages. This is a fact about the songs' alleged source. It says nothing about their content, or qualities, or structure as literature. A moment's reflection will show that myths (as we conventionally think of them) tend to be long stories that are told or at least tellable in prose. Songs are short and are sung in a poetic, elliptical style at some remove from ordinary language. Our general impression is that songs may stem from myths, or may suggest or decorate myths, but they can hardly tell whole myths in and of themselves.

That impression is born out in both the Yuman and Pima-Papago record. Let us start with the Yumans. According to Kroeber, these peoples' "song myths" existed not only in the singers' and audiences' minds as more or less fixed story plots, but were also occasionally performed in informal prose and song sessions where the singer told the story in prose while inserting songs at appropriate spots (called "stations" in the story by Kroeber). Such sessions were distinct from but supportive of the public ceremonial performances described above. Both were under individual sponsorship and both might take place at the sponsor's house, but the informal prose and song performances were always private, typically for family members only, while what I term the formal ceremonies were in some degree public (planned in advance, guests were expected, etc.).[5] Such formal public performances were normally pure song with no prose interpretation or amplification, and they normally featured dancing.

Pima-Papagos knew of the Yuman song myths, occasionally attended both kinds of Yuman performance, and even told one Yuman song myth among themselves. This was the one called "Satukhota" by Kroeber, who traced its manifestations among the Mojave, Diegeño, and Maricopa (1972:109–116). They knew it as a Maricopa song myth, telling it in Pima-Papago prose but singing its songs in what they took to be Maricopa. These tellings/singings were of the informal, private sort described above. The songs, being in Maricopa and hence foreign, were not performed by them in formal, public occasions.

I assume that the Satukhota song myth was given in formal public performance by Yumans.[6] That the Pima-Papago did not treat it this way does not mean they withheld public performance from all foreign myths, because the story of Jesus was just such a myth. Apparently, it was the native-language songs which made the difference. The Christian myth came to them as foreign, but the receipt of native songs for it made it theirs and thus usable for generalized display ceremonies. Such ceremonies had a strong nationalistic component.

Heaven songs are unusual in Pima ceremonial practice, not only because their myth is foreign but also because they refer to any myth at all. In general the songs used in Pima-Papago public ceremony neither derived from mythic persons nor from narrated events set in mythic times. These people had ample myths, which they told in prose at home, like Yumans. If the myths had songs associated with them, as they sometimes did, then the songs were incorporated in private myth tellings, as with Yumans. Unlike Yumans, the myth-telling songs were not dreamt afresh but were considered to be ancient documents, "quotes from the gods" passed down verbatim from ancient times; also unlike Yumans, the myth-telling songs were not sung and danced to in public.

Two important additional facts concern the songs Pima-Papagos did sing and dance to in public. These songs were neither prose *told* nor, in some instances, prose *tellable*. By "not prose told" I mean that singers were not in the habit of telling a prose story in amplification of the episodes narrated in songs. By "not prose tell-able" I mean that the sequencing of at least some sets changed so radically from one singing to the next that there was literally no fixed story line to the set. Other studies will deal with each of those points. One will illustrate a singer's ability to hold a set of forty-four Oriole songs in fixed sequence, his ability to speak the words of those songs in ordinary language (as opposed to "song language," see below), and his unwillingness or lack of interest in supplying prose "filler" between the recited song episodes. The other treats virtuoso variable sequencing (no two performances alike) in a set of over two hundred Swallow songs (Bahr 1986). I consider these to be examples typical of Pima-Papago generalized ceremonial song sets. Heaven songs are exceptional because of their mythic basis.

HISTORY AND USE OF THE SONGS

I first encountered Heaven songs in 1979 on a commercial phono-graph record owned by a Pima singer (Canyon Records, C-8011, 1978). He received it from a Catholic priest who had organized the recording session. The Heaven songs (not so called) were on two discontinuous bands of a side otherwise devoted to Oriole songs. The singing group, identified as the Oriole Singers (locally called The Box Tops, I learned), consisted of Blaine Pablo, Frank Kisto, and Eunice Antone. The first Heaven song on the record, number 1 below, was entitled Salvation Song; the second, number 9 below, was called Mary at the Cross.

In 1980 the man who had received the record, a second Pima singer, and I began to visit Blaine Pablo to practice and record Oriole songs. Pablo lived at the east end of the fifty-mile-long Gila

River Indian Community while the other two, Vincent Joseph and Joe Giff, lived at the center and the west end, respectively. The three men knew each other but had not sung together. As Oriole songs were Pablo's specialty and only I seemed interested in Heaven songs, I decided to visit him alone to satisfy that interest. He sang them as a kindness during four visits in 1981 and 1982, sixteen different songs in all, as against about fifty different Oriole songs. He said there were more, but he had forgotten them.

As he sang, he commented on where the songs belong in the life stories of Jesus and Mary. He never told the story in full or sang the songs in full, but would only sing a song and then briefly comment on the events it made reference to. We spoke in Pima. I sometimes tape-recorded the speech and always recorded the songs. Copies of the tapes were given to Vincent Joseph and Joe Giff.

Pablo's fullest explanation of the history of the songs was the following:

Da:m ka:cimc eḍ ñe'i.

I: o ha'icug hegai geli o'odham.

Wipismal an we:pig u'ahim,
matp an i ñe'iya, do:da'ag oidc u'ahim.

C am hebai ju:, t i hascu atp wuḍ i:dam, s wuḍ ka:ckc eḍ ñe'i,
gn hu wa'i ka:ck oidc ñe'e.

K i:d hia ep bei i:da,
atp am kosc eḍ,
k am i bei, gm hu uapa gn hu—
da:m ka:cimc eḍ.

Heaven songs.

Here there was an old man.

[A] hummingbird took him for the first time,
when they [Hummingbird songs] came out, along mountains it took him.

Then sometime later, there was something, it was Ocean songs,
there along the ocean it sang.

Then he also got this [Heaven songs],
it was in his sleep,
and it took him, took him away—
to heaven.

It is seen that Heaven songs were not the first songs Hummingbird learned. He first learned Hummingbird songs and acquired his name from that experience. Next he acquired Ocean songs. It is unclear from the statement whether the Ocean and Heaven songs might have been varieties of Hummingbird songs, that is, whether such a bird took the man to the ocean and then to heaven, and perhaps even sang to him there. Pablo partly clarified this later by stating (not on tape) that no bird took Hummingbird (the man) to heaven, but Pablo didn't state, and wasn't asked, who took him. On the subject of singing, Pablo said (also not on tape) that song 3 was not sung by Mary to Joseph (as I had asked), but by Mary to Hummingbird. Specifically, she sang about her relationship to Joseph, but the singing was directed to Hummingbird who, knowing Pima, was obviously able to understand it.

Pablo said that as a young man he frequented Hummingbird's house along with other people interested in the songs (not on tape). He spoke neither of public ceremonies with dancing nor of prose myth telling in association with the songs. Another Pima told me in 1984 (Pablo died in 1983) of a man from his village in the center of the reservation who had learned the songs from Hummingbird and sang them for dancing at all-night harvest celebrations. Crops were displayed, the singer wore a rosary or crucifix, and the neighborhood attended. All but one of the above individuals were men and all probably attended Catholic rather than Protestant churches. Protestantism is numerically dominant on the reservation, but it is generally Catholics who still sing Indian songs. In fact, singing was discouraged by both sects during the first half of the twentieth century and has only come to be accepted by both since the liberal 1970s.[7]

Singing was not strong in the mid-1980s. Nightlong (or past-midnight) dances to Indian songs of the generalized category were still held, although to my knowledge the Heaven songs were not used. Typically, the Indian singing and dancing were in combination with Polka-style (instrumental) music for couples dancing, the two forms taking turns at different locations in the same general area (a person's house, a "Community Building," or even a church). The occasions for these dances were no longer war victories or good harvests, but Labor Day, Fourth of July, birthdays, and anniversaries. Singers also continued to sing for each others' private benefit, either to entertain or to learn each others' songs. As I have indicated, these sessions have a minimum of prose story elaboration.

In addition, a new, public use of songs has arisen since the 1970s. This is the "fifteen-minute sing" held for demonstration purposes at tribally sponsored (not church or individual) events. These performances often include child dancers, often in costume. The Canyon Records recording mentioned above represents the kind of song sequence used for such occasions, a short medley of favorites rather than a long series. While effective as spectacles or pageantry, and while it is a form of tribal identity–building generalized celebration, such performances are poorer than those of old times in three respects: the songs are too few, the adult audience sits rather than dances, and the audience tends not to understand the words.

In 1980 there may have been as few as twenty Pimas, even less, who knew more than a hundred songs each. Although an impressive ratio of master singers by Anglo-American standards (there were about 10,000 Pimas), there may have been ten times more singers in Hummingbird's time. The surviving songs were practically all of the generalized celebrating category.[8] Songs were still dreamt in the mid-1980s, but it is doubtful whether whole new series were still coming into existence; there was too little call for them.

CHRISTIAN SONGS

Heaven songs are not the only songs with Christian content; three other types exist:

1. English language-based hymn, folk mass, and country gospel songs. Sometimes translated into the Indian language, these varieties still sound like their non-Indian originals when performed. Since the 1970s many local, church-based singing groups have sung such songs at day- and night-time occasions in

Indian homes and churches, usually with several performing groups
per occasion. They are not danced to. The occasions include weddings, baptisms, wakes, revivals (Protestant), and fiestas (Catholic).

    2. Spanish hymns. These are sung primarily and possibly exclusively by Papagos, variously in homes, small chapels, and regular Catholic churches for fiestas, wakes, death anniversaries, birthdays, weddings, baptisms, and to cure the sick. Pimas sometimes sponsor such events and invite such singers. There is no dancing to these songs.

Papagos have both of these types because they began to sing church songs sooner than Pimas, and those songs were in Spanish. Their Spanish songs are generally led by old women and are without instrumental accompaniment. The English songs, like Heaven songs, are led by men and have instrumental accompaniment (piano, guitar, etc.). Heaven songs are accompanied by percussion only, formerly sticks beat on an overturned basket, more recently sticks beat on a cardboard box.

Heaven songs were not and are not sung in church, like the above types. It is suggested that the church songs came to the Pima-Papago as part of an implanted institutional complex. Although adapted for Indian use (the Spanish hymns in particular are not readily interpretable into their original language, so long have they been molded by Indian pronunciation), duplicates for them exist on the outside. Not so with Heaven songs. They stood apart from the implanted complex as native ceremonial grounds stood apart from churches. I have not heard it said that Heaven songs are forbidden in church, only that there is a "feeling" that "something [bad] might be felt about it." Why is this? I will state two possible doctrinal reasons: The narrative voice in church songs is that of the worshiper (singer of hymns, prayer of prayers), while the voices in these songs are the godly objects of Christian worship, Jesus and Mary. In churches, the clergy dominates the respeaking or repronouncing of Jesus' and Mary's "actual" words—the reading of the Gospels. The songs Hummingbird heard are not Gospel, and he was not an approved cleric. We should not, however, think that the songs languished from inadmissability in church. The singers went to church and were perhaps happy to reserve Heaven songs for use when the audience would be other Indians, not the clergy.

> 3. Devil songs. Devils are said to live in mountains and have dominion over mines, ranches, and money-making activities in general. Roughly, their dominion extends over the frontier type of economy introduced by the Spanish to the Pimas and Papagos in the early 1700s. Like Heaven songs they are an instance of native form embracing Christian content. In this case, the native use is for curing (literally "blowing," *wusota*) rather than generalized celebration. Devils (plural, not singular) are among the forty-odd kinds of "dangerous objects" which are the focus of the native medical system, whose main verbal activity (in diagnosis and curing) is the singing of songs learned in dreams (Bahr et al. 1974). Among the most commonly performed curing songs in the 1980s,[9] Devil songs now seem to reflect an archaic economy, a fact which reminds us of the time depth of Christian knowledge among these peoples.

Confronted with Devil songs, the question about Heaven songs is not why they came to be, but why they came relatively late in Pima-Papago–Yuman history to just one Pima. Assuming that this is correct, I attribute the absence of Heaven songs among Papagos to that people's infrequent use of generalized ceremonies (they were materially the poorest of the three peoples); the absence among Yumans to that people's monopoly over *native* hero (mythic) generalized celebration song sets. Why it was just one Pima, I cannot say—perhaps one was enough (and they did spread).

THE TEXTS

Sixteen different songs—all that Pablo sang (Hummingbird probably received more)—are ordered below according to their possible placement in Jesus' and Mary's lives. Pablo did not sing them in this order and did not sing them all on any one occasion. The numbers in parentheses, which I call "ID [for "identification"] numbers," indicate the order in which Pablo introduced them in the four sequences he sang. The ID sequence of each session is given below. It can be seen that previously introduced songs were sung

the last three times, and that there was variation in the sequencing
of previously sung songs.

Session	ID Sequence
1.	1, 2, 3, 4, 5, 6, 7, 8, 9
2.	6, 10, 2, 3, 11, 7, 4, 12, 8
3.	12, 13, 14
4.	1, 2, 3, 6, 15, 16, 12, 7, 5

Because Pablo sang without planning to do so, on widely scattered days, we should not make much of the variation. It is the
method of representation which is important (ID numbers by order
of introduction as new songs, sessions represented by strings of ID
numbers), and acceptance of the principle that even a practiced or
habitual singer might not sing duplicate or fixed sequences.

Each song is given here six times, twice in Pima and four times
in English. Two English free translations are given immediately
below, one by me and one by Brian Swann. The other four versions,
all mine, are given and discussed, along with some comments on
the free translations, in a note.[10]

Free Translations (Bahr).

1 (1). Jesus descends to bad earth.

> Here I descend.
> Here I descend,
> On this bad earth descend.
> My poor heart,
> I don't know.

2 (10). Jesus descends to moving earth.

> World surface I don't know.
> World surface I don't know,
> But on it I descend
> And the earth moves.

3 (12).   Mary sings of Joseph.

> You are my husband, you think?
> You are my husband, you think, because I go with you?
> You are my husband, you think, here a flower between
> stretches.

4 (6).   Jesus warns about devil.

> Seems the devil ran through here.
> Seems the devil ran through here,
> Now much talk [is here],
> So you join the devil and go.

5 (15).   Jesus warns about devil.

> Do you truly,
> Do you truly,
> Good truth try to follow?
> Much talk goes around,
> So you join it and go.

6 (2).   Jesus foretells his capture.

> Many people follow me
> And I wander.
> What do they say?
> What will I answer?
> Ah, soon you will get me.

7 (7).   Jesus lays blame for his being sent to heaven.

> To heaven send me,
> Whose fault is it you send me there?
> It's not my fault I'm going there.

8 (3).   Jesus speaks during mistreatment on way to cross.

> People cruelly treated me
> And you variously do to me.
> I won't reply,
> My father will call me.

9 (8).   Mary seeks Jesus' disciples after the crucifixion.

> My poor children, where will you flee?
> My poor children, where will you flee? and I so cry and try
> to follow.
> My poor children, all day [I] follow you.

10 (5).   Jesus speaks from cross.

> Just hear me.
> Just hear me,
> In front of a tree they lay me.
> Shining tree
> Is my cross
> And earth will try to cover me.

11 (13).   After Easter, resurrected Jesus speaks to his disciples.

> Here I descend.
> Here I descend,
> Try to see me!
> I'm not special,
> Try to see me!

12 (11).   Jesus bids disciples to become the first Christian priests.

> Already I told you something.
> Already I told you something,
> And here you'll wander,
> Whole world wander.

13 (14).   Jesus tells disciples they will be alone.

> You'll nowhere ever see me.
> You'll nowhere ever see me,
> Even going on far ground
> You'll nowhere ever see me.

14 (9).   Jesus sings as angels descend.

> Angels everywhere above flying.
> Angels everywhere above flying,
> I put myself below them.
> All light crowns
> Fasten on me.

15 (4).   Jesus sees Heaven.

> Many rainhouses stretch.
> Many rainhouses stretch
> And I arrive at them.
> There beside me rainhouses
> Forever duplicated are.

16 (16).   Goodbye song.

> Ah, ah, ah
> Nowhere something to call.
> One world wandering,
> Nowhere to stretch your heart.

Free Translations (Swann).

1 (1)   Jesus descends to this vile earth.

> Here I descend,
> here I descend,

Descend to this vile earth.
My poor heart,
I don't know what will happen.

2 (10)   Jesus descends to the earth that moves.

I don't know the earth's surface,
I don't know the earth's surface.
But I descend to it,
and it moves.

3 (12)   Mary sings of Joseph.

Do you think you're my husband?
Do you think you're my husband because I go with you?
Do you think you are my husband?
A flower extends between us.

4 (6)   Jesus warns about the Devil.

It seems the Devil ran through here.
It seems the Devil ran through here.
Now there's a lot of talk,
so you join the Devil and leave.

5 (15)   Jesus warns about the Devil.

Do you really,
do you really
try to follow the Truth?
There's a lot of talk,
so you join it and leave.

6 (2)   Jesus foretells his capture.

Many people follow me
and I go from place to place.
What do they say?
What will I answer?
Ah, you'll soon take me.

7 (7) Jesus places the blame for his being sent to heaven.

> Send me to heaven.
> What have I done to make you send me there?
> It's not my fault that I'm going there.

8 (3) Jesus speaks while being mistreated on his way to his
crucifixion.

> People treated me cruelly,
> and you do many bad things to me.
> I won't respond.
> My father will call me.

9 (8) Mary looks for the disciples after the crucifixion.

> My poor children, where will you run to?
> My poor children, where will you run to?
> And so I weep, and try to follow.
> My poor children, all day I follow you.

10 (5) Jesus speaks from the cross.

> Just hear me,
> just hear me.
> They lay me in front of a tree.
> The shining tree
> is my cross.
> Earth will try to cover me.

11 (13) After Easter, the resurrected Jesus speaks to his disciples.

> Here I descend,
> here I descend.
> I'm not unnatural.
> Try to see me.

12 (11) Jesus tells his disciples to become the first Christian
priests.

I have told you something already.
I have told you something already.
And here you'll
wander the whole world.

13 (14)   Jesus tells his disciples they'll be alone.

You'll never see me anywhere again.
You'll never see me anywhere again.
Even if you travel far
you'll never see me anywhere again.

14 (9)   Jesus sings as angels descend.

Angels are everywhere,
flying, above.
Angels are everywhere,
flying, above.
I stand below them.
Their crown-light
fastens on me.

15 (4)   Jesus sees heaven.

Many rain-houses stretch into the distance.
Many rain-houses stretch into the distance.
And I reach them.
Here besides me rain-houses
repeat themselves forever.

16 (16)   Song of farewell.

Ah, ah, ah,
Nowhere will you find me to call to,
wandering on this world with
nowhere to stretch your heart.

THE SEQUENCE

I have thus far attempted to place these songs in an intertribal framework. Two issues bearing on the songs as myth will now be considered: how the sequence in which I have ordered the songs (granting that this order was not realized by Mr. Pablo) conforms to Pima-Papago song set norms; and how the myth suggested by the songs alone—for public performances were proseless—might change if the sequence changed. (The second discussion takes us from the conservative Pima use of Christianity into a more revolutionary use associated with the Ghost Dance prophecy.)

The following classification of length is felt to be suitable for all Pima-Papago song sets: short, long, and superlong. Short sets, from three to five songs, play a single episode through a series of variations. Each song is like a facet on a gem; the story doesn't "progress," it "rotates." (Examples of this are analyzed in Bahr and Haefer 1978, and Bahr 1980, 1983.) All the examples known to me are curing (*wusota*) songs. Long sets, ranging from about six to about thirty-six songs, ideally are sung in fixed sequence, like short sets, but they tell a progressive story. Each song tells an episode different from the last. Some songs, especially at the beginning and end, make references to time, the first temporal references normally being to sunset and the last normally being to sunrise. Sometimes the entire narrated span is confined to a night (which is the ideal time span of actual Pima-Papago ceremonial singings, from dusk to dawn); sometimes it includes a few night/day/night/day cycles (e.g., the last two sets in Bahr et al. 1979).

Superlong sets have a variable sequence of different episodes. Such sets contain more songs than the singer can use on any one occasion (e.g., a night); hence, the singer must pick and choose. He not only decides which songs to include and which to leave out, but he may place song ID 61 after ID 93 (as I would say it), even if he had never sung 61 in that order before. He can "free associate," or work "word magic." Nonetheless, within his total inventory of songs are some that deal with sunset, the direction west, and the starting of songs; some deal with sunrise, the direction east, and the stopping of songs. Thus, a superlong set includes the same temporal framing materials as a long set. The number of such framing songs is far greater (as many as forty possible sunset-west-starting songs and another forty at the other end of a superlong set, against a mere two to five invariably at each end in a given long set). Also the overall number of songs is far greater, upwards of two hundred in a single superlong set. Above all, there is no guarantee that any song, possibly even any "framing" song whatsoever, will appear in a given singing. No superlong set has yet been published. Their size and sequential variability pose special problems for publication. Another study treats such a set (Bahr 1986).

The Heaven songs, as I recorded them, fall into the size range of a long set, but they qualify as superlong because the singer did not give them all at any one singing. I feel that they represent a diminished superlong set; that is, they were meant to be variably sung but were originally more numerous. We will consider the possible effects of changing their order below, after first noting how the sequence as I have given it conforms to the rule for long sets in having proper framing references at each end.

My sequence conforms, but with the following departure. Whereas the rule states that the sun sets ("descends," in Pima-Papago, *huḍuñ*) at the start and rises at the end, it is the man-god Jesus who does this in the Heaven songs. This is not the only Pima-Papago set to have an animate (animal or human) hero—Jesus, in the present case—but it is unusual for replacing the normal solar references with that hero. There are no solar references in the set. Having replaced them, the set does something else that is unusual. Its temporal span is a man-god's earthly life, thirty-two years, as the Bible tells us. I know of no other set, Pima, Papago, or Yuman, with this full biographical compass.

Finally, there is the issue of the possible narrative effect of variation in sequence. To show this we will move from the Pima-Papago–Yuman territory to the Great Basin and consider the Christian message given by Wovoka, the Paiute founder of the Ghost Dance. (Wovoka's lifespan overlapped Hummingbird's but it is very doubtful that either knew of the other.) As is well known, some Indian visitors to Wovoka heard him as claiming to be Jesus Christ the Messiah. One such visitor was a Cheyenne named Porcupine, who left an account from which the following excerpt is taken. I have placed this chapter's sequential (not ID) numbers for certain Heaven songs at relevant places in the account to draw attention to the fact that Wovoka's "myth" contains some of the same episodes as Hummingbird's songs, although those episodes come in different sequence.

> The next morning when we went to eat breakfast, the Christ was with us. After breakfast four heralds went around and called out that the Christ was back with us and wanted to talk with us. The circle was prepared again. The people assembled, and Christ came among us and sat down. He said he wanted to talk with us again and for us to listen. He said: "I am the man who made everything you see around you. I am not lying to you, my children. I made this earth and everything on it. I have been to heaven [15] and seen your dead friends and have seen my own father and mother [3]. In the beginning, after God made the earth, they sent me back to teach the people [5], and when I came back to earth the people were afraid of me and treated me badly [8]. This is what they did to me (showing his scars). I did not try to defend myself. I found my children were so bad, so went back to heaven and left them [16]. I told them that in so many years I would come back to see my children. At the end of this time I was sent back to try to teach them. My father told me the earth was getting old and worn out [2], the people were getting bad [1], and that I was to renew everything as it used to be, to make it better" (Mooney 1896:793–796).

I do not claim that Wovoka or Ghost Dance singers sang Heaven songs, that Hummingbird partook in the Ghost Dance, or that Heaven songs were ever sung in the sequence just given. This is only an experiment to show that changing the sequence can change the narrative effect. The essence of the change is a switch between the standard beginning and ending songs, the new sequence beginning with an ascent (of the crucified Christ to Heaven) and ending with the descent of the Messiah. Could a Pima do that? Formally, it would be an additional departure: man-god replaces sun; descent and ascent are inverted. Politically, it could have involved Hummingbird and his followers in a challenge to established authority equal to Wovoka's.

CONCLUSION

Heaven songs are Christian, if we take that to mean "centered on the thoughts and actions of Jesus." Every reader will have some knowledge of Christianity with which to interpret the songs. The concern in this study has been with something the reader cannot do, namely to put the songs in a regional, cultural context. The Heaven songs are Indian as well as Christian; the study of context tells where in the human world they came from, or rather, what they came into.

Pima-Papago and Yuman interactions have been emphasized in giving that Indian context. One knows in advance that Europeans were important foreigners to the Pimas—foreigners who came to civilize them. To the Pima-Papago, Yumans were important foreigners in a different sense—foreigners who came to the ceremonies in which Heaven songs were used. I doubt that Hummingbird had much interest in presenting his songs to the local white clergy; but I suspect he had a considerable interest in such Yumans as might hear them or hear of them. He was part of an Indian early–twentieth-century intellectual community, an Indian renaissance we might say, that was nourished, not awed, by the receipt of Christianity.[11]

NOTES

1. The jacket of a record, discussed below, states that Hummingbird dreamt the songs on the eve of his baptism. This may be legendary. What is certain is that he lived in a village that became strongly Catholic.

2. Southwest Indians have distinct views of time between the ancient, or mythological, and the recent past (see Bahr 1981). The recent past extends from the present for as far as geneologies are remembered and years are counted; that is, for about four preceding generations and 100 to 200 years. Beyond that is the era of myth. This establishes the shallowness of the recent, or what one might call the historical past in the regional cultures and the closeness of the era of myth. When I say the story of Jesus was myth, I mean that it falls into Indian-conceived mythological time. Of course, it is mythic for other reasons. Both Pima-Papago and Yuman mythologies have as their opening and main text the story of a man-god whose birth was miraculous, who didn't marry or reproduce in the normal way, and who was murdered by his followers before attaining old age. The tellers of those native myths must have noted a similarity with the story of Jesus. It is highly doubtful that the native myths were "borrowed" from Christianity, however. Let us simply call them convergent, or parallel with Christianity.

3. Behind this typification of what Yumans were not is, I am sure, a questionable conception of what Pueblos were—the region's greatest subsistence ceremonializers. Neither accepting nor rejecting that view of the Pueblos, I find the idea of subsistence ceremonialization (hence preoccupation) useful for drawing distinctions among the peoples considered in this paper. Thus, one might rank the ceremonial subsistence preoccupation among the Pimas, Papagos, and Yumans as follows: Most highly preoccupied were the Papagos, who had the highest investment in specialized subsistence ceremonies; next were the Pimas. The least preoccupied were the Yumans, specifically the riverine Yumans (Yuma, Cocopa, Maricopa, and Mojave in the twentieth century). Hence, the desert-living Papagos are the most Pueblo-like. If that classificatory shoe fits, which I think it might, then the obvious explanatory correlate would be ownership of riverine land—not in the abstract, but in the changing economic and political circumstances of 1700–1850, which included a great deal of war, slave trading, and so on (see Dobyns et al. 1957 and Ezell 1961).

4. Papagos have been remarked on by all observers for retaining more native ceremonialism than Pimas. This has been explained by greater acculturative pressures on the Pimas, including harsher Protestant as opposed to laxer Catholic missionary pressure. While that is true, the present paper points to an historically prior factor. Most of the ceremonies Papagos kept were specialized subsistence ceremonies, which are the category I believe the Pimas had far fewer of to begin with (e.g., in 1800 or 1850). We should not speak of acculturative pressure as removing something that didn't exist. In the category of generalized display ceremonies it appears the Pimas held fairly firm. They had more of these than the Papagos in 1900, in the 1920s (Hummingbird's heyday), and in 1980. I suspect that observers discounted them because they didn't seem to be properly Indian ceremonies, such as ceremonies for rain making or healing.

5. A simple further expression of this difference is that the singer/teller in an informal event tends to perform in his own home; that is, he is his own sponsor, while the singer (no longer teller) in a formal event has been invited by the sponsor, either to the sponsor's house or to a public place. More simply put, formal occasions require guest singers.

6. No source says it was danced to. Kroeber groups it with three other Mojave song myths. One was danced to, two were not, and Satukhota is not specified (1925:763–764). Being sung and told (no dancing) at a host's house may have been its maximal "public" use, in which case the difference between private and informal versus public and formal reduces to nearly nothing, and the alleged different handling of this myth by Yumans and Pima-Papagos is also reduced.

7. It is possible that the survival of singing among Catholics stems from the official Catholic acceptance of fiestas (among whites and Mexicans, if

not Indians), with smoking, drinking, and dancing, and the denunciation of the same by Protestants. Pimas may have felt that their traditional generalized celebrations were similar to Catholic fiestas and hence were appropriate for Catholics but not for Protestants. The traditional songs and dances, while preserved, were kept away from Catholic churches until the 1970s and hence stood apart from the "church complex" described in the next section.

8. Papagos retained large numbers of curing and rainmaking songs as well, that is, songs for specialized subsistence ceremonies.

9. More commonly among Papagos than Pimas, however.

10. The Heaven songs were put through the several stages of transcription and translation recommended in Bahr (1983). A *native song language* version transcribed directly from the tapes shows how each song apportions syllables to a steady underlying pulsation of beats (musical notes are not transcribed). It is paired with a *syllable-matching English translation:* the syllabic and rhythmic configuration of each native song language word (or word unit) is matched with an English word or phrase of equivalent meaning, equal syllable count, and identical rhythmic configuration. Sound value, of course, is not the same, except coincidentally. Line divisions and vertical alignment are determined by recurrent metered segments called "key metric configurations" in Bahr (1983). There is one such segment per line with varying amounts of unversified material either to the right or left of it. When written in this manner, a song resembles a column (the recurrent metric configuration) with random cantilevered extensions. Syllable-matching English translations are difficult to read. They give the authentic "feel" of native versification by molding English to it unnaturally. They enable a reader to say a Pima poem, syllable by syllable, in English.

SONG 1 (1)

| i / he | ne | pi / ere | ba |
| a / s |
pe / a	ka / a	me / ad	ñe / ea
ku / and	ña / I	si / he	ya / ere	hu / de	nu / e	ki / e	me / scend
ku / and	ña / I	si / he	ya / ere	hu / de	nu / e	ki / e	me / scend
we / earth	na / u	ma / po	ne / on	hu / de	nu / e	ki / e	me / scend
soi / po	ga / o	le / o	nag / heart	boi / y
wa / that	ñi / I	pi	ma / don'tkno	ma / o	ce / ow

ha — su
na — ur
me ne je̱ — face of ea
we de wa̱ — a
pi — not
ma — kno
ci — o
m — w

na — sur
me ne je̱ — face of ea
we de wa̱ — a
pi — not
ma — kno
ci — o
me — ow

ku — and
ñe̱ — I
ga̱ — the
ye — sur
da — face
mo — on
hu — des
nu — ce
ki — ce
me — end

ke ne̱ — ye
et ea
we̱ — a
da — arth
i — he
na — ere
cu ju — ju
mo yoi — ust mo
me — o
da — oves

na̱ — a
po wa ñe̱ ku̱ — are you my hus
na — band
wa — ju
cu̱ — u
me ye̱ — ust wi
li — i
na̱ — shing
he — i
ma̱ — i
ci yoi — ith tra
mel — a
hi — a
me — vel

na̱ — a
po wa ñe̱ ku̱ — are you my hus
na — band
ye̱ — wi
li — i
na̱ — shing
si — ow
me ka — ow er
mo ya — ba ack
hai — forth stre
be wa̱ — a
wa — e
ñe̱ — etch

na̱ — a
po wa ñe̱ ku̱ — are you my hus
na — band
ye̱ — wi
li — i
na̱ — shing
i — he
no yo — ere flo
and' — and'

SONG 4 (6)

na ne si — he kyu — he wu — li no me me da
se e ems — be fore — the e vil — he ere run a round

na ne si — he kyu — he wu — li no me me da
se e ems — be fore — the e vil — he ere run a around

na — si mu mui — wa cu — mo hi no nyo ke
now — so mu u — uch ju — ust he ere ta alk

ke
and

me ga — ye ga ci — ne nya wu — li no we me he da
you ac — cor ding ly — the de vil — he ere joi na runa round

ku
and

SONG 5 (15)

na mi wo ho ñi
do yo tru ly ou

na mi wo ho ñi
do yo tru ly ou

sa pe ka me wo ho cu me yoi da
go o o od tru uth try to fol lo

mu mui we nio ka hi no su li gai m
mu u uch ta alk he ere throowna w

ku me ga ye ga cin ca mo mo
and you ac cor ding ly he e bout

ci na hi me da m hi no we m
and herego a roun d e ere joi n

SONG 6 (2)

mu mu wi yo na me ñoi dai me
ma a ny pe e eople me fol low

ku ñi no yoi me na
and I here tra a vel

sa i mo we ñyo ke na
wha a at they ta a alk

sa ñi ñi kai da me ñyo ke na
wha at I cle ear ly ta a alk

a hi no we ya sa ku me to ñe mei hi me
ah soo o o o on you ou will me ge e et

SONG 7 (7)

da   mai   we   ka   ci   me   wui   ko   ñe   hi me cu   ne
he   e   e   e   ea   ven   to   o   me   se e e   end

do   wa   me   cui   ji   n   ku me se   ga   ye   ka   ci
who   o   ose   fa   aul   t   and youac   co   or   ding   ly

ya   mo   ho we ñi mi cu
the   e   e   e ere me se end

pio   wu   de ñe cui ji   ne   ku ñe se   ga   ye   ka
not   i   is my fa a   ault   and I ac   co   or   ding   ci
                                                              ly

ya   mo   ho   wa   ha   cu mo hi me da
the   e   ere   ve   ry   ju ust go o o

SONG 8 (3)

i / the   no / e   ge / ere   me / eople   soi / po   a / ha / e e   na / eat   mo / ly   ñi / me

na / e   yo / pe   na / ri   ne wua / me tre   ge / orly   ha / e   ya / ong

mi / o   ku / yo   na / va   ya / ou   ko / ous   wa / stro   a / o   ha / o

ñi / o   ñu / do   me / o   hi / o   me / o

ñi / wo   ñi / wo   pya / I   gi / on't   ya / a   sai / ny   wai / thing   ma / you   ha / sa   na / ay

nai / e   ya / the   ge / ther   ce / e   ne / ere   wa / wi   ñe wai / me ca   to / ill   dai / a   me / all

ke / a   ge / as   ño / my   o / fa

SONG 9 (8)

hai ya ñe ma he ma ñe ba to wa ñe ñe ku ñe si soa ke na
a las my chi i il dren where wi ill fly y and I so cry y y

hai ya ñe ma he ma ne ba to wa ñe e ñe
a las my chi i il dren where wi ill fly y y

wa cu me yoi me na
try to youfo ol low

hai ya ñe ma ma we si ta sai yoi kai co moi na hi me
a las my chil dren ev ry da ay thro o oughyou fo ol low

SONG 10 (5)

yu
tre

ke   na ñe
ye   et ea

we   da   i   cu   mo   hi no mai
a   arth he   ju   ust   he ere bu

na
ere

he   na   mo ñe ko   we na   si
tha   at   is my cro   o o   o

to   na   no me yu   si
shi   i   i ning tre   o

ma   cu   ma ust   to ñe wo
o   ju   ma   will me la

ma   so   cu   me   ge ñe ka   po   na
fro   ont   ju   u   ust me hear ay   on

si   cu   me   ge ñe ka   si   sa   pa
ee   ju   u   ust me hear ee   o   ver

to
oss

SONG 11 (13)

```
ku   ñi            ya    hu    nu              ki              ne
and  I             here  de    sce             end             am

ku   ñi            ya    hu    hu    ki        me
and  I             here  de    e     sce       end

cu   me            ko    wa    ha              ha   ñe   ñei   da
ju   u             ust   ve    e               ry   me   lo    ok

pi   ya   ñi       ki    ya    sai             wa   me   cui   ga
not  I    I        so    ome   how             spec ial  a     a

cu   me            ko    wa    ha              ha   ñe   ñei   da
ju   u             ust   ve    e               ry   me   lo    ok
```

SONG 12 (11)

Line 1: ku (I) · ña (the) · ma (ere) · he (be) · kyu (fore) · nai (some) · cu (thing) · wo (will) · ma (you) · ki (tell) · ha (e) · mo ma– · ry you–

Line 2: ku (I) · ña (the) · ma (ere) · he (be) · kyu (fore) · we (ev) · sai (ery) · cu (thing) · wa (ve) · ha (e) · e

Line 3: ki (tell)

Line 4: ku (you) · mi (he) · na (ere) · he (a) · je (a) · le (lone) · i (he) · no (e) · wa (ere) · yoi me da (go o a) · wa (ere) · he (round)

Line 5: je (e) · we (ea) · da (arth) · we (ev) · si (ry) · ko (where) · wa (the) · ha (en) · cu mo (ju) · mo yoi me da (ust go a roun) · n (d)

SONG 13 (14)

ku me to   pi   ye   bai   hi   ya me to   ho ñe ñei   na
yo ou will no   pla   ace   e   ver youwi   ill me se   ee

ku me to   pi   ye   bai   hi   ya me to   ho ñe ñei   na
yo ou will no   pla   ace   e   ver youwi   ill me se   ee

ga   mu   si   me   ko   him je we da   ba mo hi   me ta
a   way   so   fa   a   ar   la a and   to will go o o

ku me to   pi   ye   bai   hi   ya me t   hu   he ñe ñe   wa   hi   ta
yo ou will no   pla   ace   e   ver yo ou   the ere me se   e   e   ee

SONG 14 (9)

do ki ya na me yo na me hi ne we si ko ñe ñe hi me
mustbe fea ea ther pe eo ple he ere ev rywhere fly y y y

do ki ya na me yo na me hi ne we si ko ñe ñe hi me
mustbe fea ea ther pe eo ple he ere ev rywhere fly y y y

ku ñe ne we co wa cu me nu li na cu ne
and I them be e low ju ust my self po si tion

we se ne to nol hin hi ya ñi ñi k ca
ev rywhere li i ight he ere cro o ownsand

ñi ya hi hi na
here me fast ens on

SONG 15 (4)

wa ki mui pa ye wa wa ne
rain house ma a ny stre e etch

wa ki mui pa ye wa wa ne
rain house ma a ny stre e etch

ku ne ge ye da mo ji ni wya
a and I ju ust then a ri ive

i no we nu gi da ne wa a ki
the e ere me be e side rai ain house

he ne na me kui no ne si i me cu hi ga
se e e elf re e pla a a cing i i is

SONG 16 (16)

ke
a

pya   mi   ki   ye   we   yai   a   a   a   he
no   o   o   pl   ace   some   ah   a   ah   a

he   ma   ko   je   we   na   mai   cu   dai   me   n
o   o   one   wo   o   o   on   thing al   lin   g

wa   a   pi   he   bai   wa   wañ   cu   dai   me
a   and   no   o   place e   e   ju   der   ing

                         ba   wa   wañ   me   boi   na   n
                         stre e   e   yoi   hea   ar   t
                                            wan

                         ba   na   i
                         stre o   e
                                            ne   mi
                                            etch your

In the second pair of versions, a *native ordinary language* interpretation of each native song language text is paired with an *English ordinary language* translation of the interpretation. The native version establishes the meaning of a song that is difficult to understand as sung because of syllable reduplication and sound changes. Pima singers constantly make such interpretations for each other as they practice songs. The English version simply carries the native meaning over into English, word unit per word unit. This version is the basis both of the syllable-matching translation (where English words are distorted to match native versification), and of all subsequent free translations (where English words are changed for clarity, euphony, etc.). The slashes in these pairs represent the amount of text per line included in the recurrent key metric configuration; vertical alignment is accomplished by stacking the slashed segments.

ORDINARY LANGUAGE TRANSLATIONS

1 (1).   Jesus descends to bad earth.

                    kuñ s /iːya i huḍ   /
                    And I/here descend, /

                    kuñ s /iːya i huḍ   /
                    And I/here descend. /

        iːda pi ap'ekam jeweḍ /daːm huḍ   /
            Here bad earth   /upon descend: /

                    /ṣo'ig ñ-iːbdag /
                    /Poor my heart/

                    wa /ñ pi maːc   /
                    That /I don't know. /

2 (10).   Jesus descends to moving earth.

            daː /m g jeweḍ pi maː: /c
            Sur /face of earth not kno /w,

            daː /m g jeweḍ pi maː: /c
            Sur /face of earth not kno w.

ku/ñ g da:m huḍu   /n
And/I the surface-on desce   /nd,

/k eḍa jewed in cum ho   /'i
/Yet earth here just move/s.

3 (12).   Mary sings of Joseph.

/nap wa ñ-kuñ   / wa cum elid
/Are you my husband/ just wishing?

/nap wa ñ-kuñ   / elid, kuñ we:maj oimmed
/Are you my husband/ wishing, and I with-travel?

/nap wa ñ-kuñ   / elid, in o hiosig am a'ai wawan
/Are you my husband/ wishing, here flower back-and-forth
                         stretch.

4 (6).   Jesus warns about devil.

na'ags heki hu g /jiawul in mem/da
Seems before the /devil here run/around,

na'ags heki hu g /jiawul in mem/da
Seems before the /devil here run/around.

k eḍa si mu'i /cum in ñio   /k
And now so much /just here tal   /k,

kum g hekaj g/jiawul we: /m c an himad
And you accordingly the/devil joi   /n and here go around.

5 (15).   Jesus concludes warning about devil.

/nam hi woho   /
/Do you truly,   /

/nam hi woho   /
Do you truly,   /

/s-ap'ekam woho   / cem oid
/Good truth   / try to follow?

/mu'i ñiok   / in ṣulig
/Much talk   / here thrown-about,

/kum g heka   /j am we:m c in him
/And you according/ly here join and here go around.

6 (2).   Jesus foretells his capture.

> mu'i /o'odham ñ-oi   /
> Many /people me-follow, /

> > /kuñ in oimmed   /
> > /And I here travel./

> ṣa: /im hu ñiok   /
> Wha /t they talk?

> ṣa: ñ /kaidam ñiok   /
> What I /clearly talk?   /

> a hig o ha'a/s i kumt o ñ-bei /
> Ah, soo/n you will me-get./

7 (7).   Jesus lays blame for his being sent to heaven.

/da:m ka:cim   / wui ñ-himcud
/Heaven   / -to me-send.

/do: am cu'ijig   / kums g hekaj am hu o ñ-himcud
/Whose fault   / and you accordingly there me-send?

/pi o wuḍ ñ-cu'ijig/ kuñs g hekaj am hu o wa cum him.
/Not is my fault   / and I accordingly there very just go.

8 (3).   Jesus speaks during his mistreatment on way to cross.

in hu g /o'odham ṣo'i/g ñ-wua
There /people poor /ly me-treat,

> /kum nan   /ko wa:m ñ-juñhim
> /You vari   /ous strongly me-do.

/pi an ge ha /s ṣa'i m-a:g
/I won't any /thing you-say,

k g ñ-o:g /anai wat   / o ñ-waid
As my father /there wil   /l me-call.

9 (8).   Mary seeks Jesus' disciples after the crucifixion.

/haiya ñ-ma: /mad, ba:t o wa ñe:ñ
/Alas my child/ren, where will fly?

/haiya n-ma: /mad, ba:t o wa ñe:ñ, kuñ si soak, wa cem em-oid
/Alas my child/ren, where will fly? And I so cry, try to you-
                    follow,

/haiya ñ-m: /mad, we:ṣ taṣ oidc em-oid
/Alas my child/ren, every day through, you-follow.

10 (5).   Jesus speaks from cross.

                /cum ñ-ka: /
                /Just me hear, /

                /cum ñ-ka: /
                /Just me-hear. /

        u:s baṣo /cum at o ñ-wod /wa
        Tree front /Just will me-la /y.

                /tondam u: /s
                /Shining tre   /e

        he/g am o ñ-kot /s
        Th/at is my cros /s

k eḑa jeweḑ i:na /cum o ñ-ma'i /ṣa
Yet earth here /just here co   /ver.

11 (13).   After Easter, the resurrected Jesus reappears to his disciples.

/kuñ i:ya i huḑ   /
/And I here descend, /

241

/kuñ i:ya i huḍ   /
/And I here descend: /

/cum g o wa   / ñ-ñeid
/Just very   / me-look.

/pi añ ki has ṣa'i wa: /m cu'ig
/Not I somehow spe /cial am.

/c m g o wa   / ñ-ñeid
/Just very   / me-look.

12 (11). Jesus bids his disciples to become the first Christian priests.

/kuñ am heki hu/ ha'icu o em-a:g
/I there before   / something will you-tell,

/kuñ am heki hu/ ha'icu o em-a:g
/I there before   / something will you-tell.

/kum i:na heje   /l in o wa oimmeḍ
/You here alon   /e here go around,

/jeweḍ we:s   /ko wa cum oimmeḍ
/Earth every   /where then just go around.

13 (14). Jesus tells his disciples they will be alone.

kumpt o /pi hebai hi ampt o   / ñ-ñeid
You will /no place ever you wil/l me-see.

kumpt o /pi hebai hi ampt o   / ñ-ñeid
You will /no place ever you wil/l me-see.

gam hu /si me:k jeweḍ   /ab am o him
  Away /so far land   /-to will go,

kumpt o /pi hebai hi ampt   / hu wa ñ-ñeid
You will /no place every you   /there me-see.

14 (9).   Jesus sings as angels descend to him.

ḍ o ki a'anam o'o/dham in we: /sko ñe:ñ
Must be feathered peo/ple here eve   /rywhere fly,

ḍ o ki a'anam o'o/dham in we: /sko ñe:ñ
Must be feathered peo/ple here eve   /rywhere fly.

kuñ g weco wa /cum ñ-uli   /n
And I them below /just myself posi   /tion.

we:s g tonlig /i:ya gigiwua   /c
Everywhere light /here crown   /s and
/ñ-iaj   /
/here me fastens on./

15 (4).   Jesus sees heaven.

/wa'aki mu'i p a wawañ   /
/Rainhouse many stretch,   /

/wa'aki mu'i p a wawañ   /
/Rainhouse many stretch,   /

/kuñ g eḍa am ji:wia   /
/And I just then arrive.   /

/in hu ñ-hugid an wa'aki   /
/There me-beside rainhouse,/

/hejel am kuinogs i   /m cu'ig
/self replacing i   /s.

16 (16).   Goodbye song.

/a:, a, a: /
/Ah, a, ah,   /

pi am ki hebai ha'icu   /waidahim   /
Noplace something   /calling.   /

hemako jeweḍ da:m cum   /oidahim   /
One world-on just   /wandering,/

ka wa pi hebai ab wawañ   /m-i:bdag   /
And noplace stretch   /your heart./

A fairly conservative free translation was made by Bahr and then a more liberal one by Swann. Both versions follow the European method of vertical alignment ("New lines flush left"). It was understood that Swann's word or part of speech order internal to lines would be closer than Bahr's to standard English. What especially interested Bahr, and what the two corresponded about, were Swann's efforts to clarify the poems' meanings, taking meaning to include the gamut of Jakobson's speech functions. It is felt that such efforts should be consistent with the meanings detectable in the native ordinary language versions of and commentary about songs. The following are among the more interesting exchanges between Swann and Bahr on such matters.

In song 1 (published number, not ID number) Swann proposed "wicked" or "evil" as stronger alternatives to Bahr's "bad" (said by Jesus while descending to earth). The Pima is *pi ap'ekam,* literally "not good." To Bahr, Swann's choices suggested that Jesus knew more about the earth than the song actually says—that it's not merely bad, but *wicked*—and this is a dangerous suggestion considering that in the last line of the song Jesus says, "I don't know." Swann assented and chose "vile" to replace "bad," which he still thought was too petty.

The importance of words of motion in Indian languages is well known, even overestimated, if it is also assumed that English lacks such subtleties. There were two exchanges over spatial words. First, Swann wanted to change the word "descend" in songs 1 and 2 to "come down." Bahr resisted on the grounds that English "descend," like the original Pima-Papago *huḍuñ,* applies equally to solar and to human or godly travels. The significance of Jesus traveling like the sun is stressed in the body of this chapter. Note that "come down" is not said in English about the sun. We say "go down," presumably because "come down" would mean to come to (and burn) us while "go down" means to set beyond the horizon. Recalling that huḍuñ was used in the first person by Jesus in a song addressed to Hummingbird during the latter's visit to heaven, the proper English choice between "come down" and "go down" would probably be "go down." Swann considered the points well taken; "descend" stood.

The second problem on spatial imagery centered on the word *wawañ,* "to stretch." It is in the last, and in effect, punch lines of songs 3 and 16. In song 3 Mary is the singer and "stretching" refers to a flower between her and her addressee. In song 16 Jesus is the singer and the reference is to his addressees' hearts. Swann felt "stretch" makes no sense in reference to a flower in 3; he couldn't visualize the scene. Bahr was of the opinion that the scene isn't meant to be seen clearly. He searched his mind and two Pima-Papago dictionaries and found confirmation that wawañ basically means "stretch," both transitively and intransitively. The word is commonly used of ropes, wires, fibers, animals (in lines), and mountain ridges. Here it is deliberately and poetically used of flowers and hearts. Bahr felt that the use was intentional, and that translation should preserve it in both songs (Swann had proposed changing it to "is held" in 3, but letting it stand as "stretch" in 16). Swann agreed.

Song 3 from Mary also shows the importance of addresseeship in Pima songs. As stated in the body of this chapter, Mr. Pablo considered that the song was sung by Mary to Hummingbird, not to Joseph. It echoes her relationship to Joseph, but this echoing is limited to what Mary chose to express as common to her, Joseph, and Hummingbird. Accordingly Bahr resisted Swann's proposal to translate *we:m oimmed* as "live with" instead of "go with." As Swann pointed out, the former English expression implies cohabitation out of wedlock. Bahr believes Hummingbird understood that Mary and Joseph cohabited *within* wedlock, which situation would be expressed in Pima as *we:m Ki:* (literally "live with," but in Pima this has the connotation of being married or at least permanently bound to each other), and not as we:m oimmed, literally "go with," which might mean as little as "to take a walk with one time, to meet and sing songs to once." Mary "went with" Hummingbird in that sense, but she didn't "live with" him. Swann conceded.

Those were not the only points of discussion, and the reader will see many instances where Swann changed wording as well as word order. Basically, they are instances where Bahr felt the change did not depart from the Pima meanings. Obviously, another reader versed in Pima, or armed with the excellent dictionaries and grammars now available for the language, might find other objections either to Bahr's to Swann's translations, and Pima literary studies will have come more of age.

11. It is noted, however, that most of the songs, like most of the Gospels, are devoted to the forty-day period of Jesus' "Passion."

REFERENCES

Bahr, D. 1980. Four Papago Rattlesnake Songs. *Anthropological Research Papers* 20:118–126.

———. 1981. The Whole Past in a Yavapai Mythology. *American Indian Culture and Research Journal* 5(2):1–35.

———. 1983. A Method and Format for Translating Songs. *Journal of American Folklore* 96(380):170–182.

———. 1986. Pima Swallow Songs. *Cultural Anthropology* 1(2):171–1871.

Bahr, D., J. Giff, and M. Havier. 1979. Piman Songs of Hunting. *Ethnomusicology* 23(2):245–296.

Bahr, D., J. Gregorio, D. Lopez, and A. Alvarez. 1974. *Piman Shamanism and Staying Sickness*. Tucson: University of Arizona Press.

Bahr, D., and J. Haefer. 1978. Song in Piman Curing. *Ethnomusicology* 22(1): 89–122.

Dobyns, H., P. Ezell, A. Jones, and G. Ezell. 1957. Thematic Changes in Yuman Warfare. In *Proceedings of the 1957 Annual Spring Meeting of the American Ethnological Society*. Pp. 46–71. Seattle: University of Washington Press.

Ezell, P. 1961. The Hispanic Acculturation of the Gila River Pima. *Memoirs of the American Anthropological Association* 90.

Herzog, G. 1928a. Musical Styles in North America. *Proceedings of the Twenty-third Conference of Americanists*. Pp. 455–458.

———. 1928b. The Yuman Musical Style. *Journal of American Folklore* 41 (160):183–231.

Jakobson, R. 1960. Closing Statement: Linguistics and Poetics. In *Style in Language*, T. Sebeok, ed. Pp. 350–377. Cambridge: MIT Press.

Kroeber, A. 1925. *Handbook of the Indians of California*. Bureau of American Ethnology Bulletin 78.

———. 1972. *More Mojave Myths*. University of California Anthropological Records 27.

Mooney, J. 1896. The Ghost-Dance Religion and the Sioux Outbreak of 1890. *Bureau of American Ethnology Annual Report* 14:645–1136.

A Note On Translation, and Remarks On Collaboration

BRIAN SWANN

I

There are special problems when translating from Native American languages. We have all manner of bilingual scholars and poets for European, African, or Asian languages, but only a handful of Anglo- or Native American people capable of operating equally well in both English and an Indian language. I think most of us would agree that the best translations are made by translators thoroughly at home in both of the languages being worked on, and that literary expression is best translated by translators who are themselves writers. The translation of Native American literature, however, is still very young—even if it is maturing fast.

Dell Hymes expanded on this theme when he called for poets to enter the field; but in addition to language skills, he says they should be well versed in anthropological philology and be able to utilize "the perspectives and tools of linguistics"! (1981:335). As for Native American poets, only a few know their native language. Ray Young Bear is one who does. Franchot Ballinger and I conducted an interview with Paula Gunn Allen. She is more typical of Native American writers when she says, "I don't speak Laguna, and I find myself in trouble continually." She adds, however, that she "thinks like a Laguna," a statement that might be interesting to explore further, especially in light of Whorf's suggestion that language structures "reality." Of course, we do have luminaries such as Paul Zolbrod, Alfonso Ortiz, Dennis Tedlock, and Dell Hymes; Tedlock has shown just how inadequate are our translations of older material by, for example, Frank Cushing. We need more qualified translators to reevaluate the old "texts," and until that happens their value will retain a hint of the dubious. This isn't just a question of the constant necessity for the retranslation of works; it is also a question of sorting out what forces—frequently unconscious, the result of cultural osmosis—have shaped those translations. We need to be made conscious of just what went into them so we can begin to sort them out again.

Clearly, there are not enough scholar/poet/translators to take on this massive task. Scholars do their own job well; but if we are to get these "tales" and "texts" accepted as literature of a high order, as "story," and "poem," or "play," and then expand the canon taught in schools to include indigenous American word-works, we will have to have works that exist at the cutting edge of language—whether "Red English" or "straight" or whatever—where all literature exists at some time or other, and where great literature exists longest. But a special problem exists here, too. Linguists and anthropologists publish "translations" that seem more nearly a private code, the result of a passion for reproducing the grammatical or linguistic shapes of the original. There is, with good reason, a genuine fear of "versions" and extrapolations, but there is also something else, pinpointed by Dennis Tedlock in *The Spoken Word:*

> From the point of view of the linguist who seeks to crack the code of the unwritten language, translation from this language into his own will seem like a violation of the integrity of the discovered code, unless it takes the modest form of a series of labels or tags running alongside the words of the original language (1984:12).

The result is the creation of a language that is all too frequently incomprehensible, vague, and, at worst, unreadable. We are given something like "interlinear" translations, in Goethe's phrase, somewhere between source and target languages. The reverence is praiseworthy, but I believe that rather than leaning back into the original, one should tread the delicate line between absorbing the "other" and keeping it other. I believe that translations of Native American literature should balance accessibility with distance, "identity" with "difference," to use Arnold Krupat's dichotomy (1983:3).

In an earlier version of this brief essay, given as a talk at the MLA Annual Convention in 1984, I stated that "the translator should disappear. The translation should aim at transparency." I no longer believe this, as the result of reading Krupat's essay in *Diacritics* (1983), and discussion with and a letter from Andrew Wiget, who wrote me:

> My remarks will probably not be helpful, may perhaps seem reactionary, but I would argue that translations should not aim at "transparency." While such a goal may ease the reader's difficulties, it is the formal equivalent of making the Other accessible (or pretending to) in our terms, rather than demanding that we attempt to accommodate ourselves to the language and categories of the Other. Ultimately, of course, my position must preclude translation entirely, but in the attempt to prevent throwing out the baby with the bath water, I would argue that we need to leave clues to our compromises, signs of our unwillingness to compromise, even if it means calling the reader's attention to alternatives available through notes, etc., all in the interest of "coming clean" with the posture of translation, which pretends, by adopting the aesthetic conventions and graphological model of our cultural tradition, to be something that it isn't: *the* text, not simply *a* text, and a radically disputable one at that. Translators may argue discursively that they know they are always "lying," betraying the original, but in practice they aim at perfecting their deception not disclosing it. So I argue for disclosure, for the rough edges, the un"finished" piece that communicates through its own scars the trauma of its posture which would lead to texts whose very appearance and contour would announce "I am not what you think I am. That for which you seek is not here. I but point the way."

The other side to this, of course, is that such texts are not without their own perils. Their very otherness would attract a small body of gnostic devotees, secure in their antiquarian knowledge that they have access to *the* significance of this obscure reality before them. They would constitute a new "Myths & Texts" school and themselves the privileged arbiters of meaning. Such a position is diametrically opposed to that which you advocate by valorizing Opacity over Transparency, but it shares with your point of view an unwillingness, perhaps even an incapacity, to disengage itself from an allegiance to an iconic notion of text as object, and so devalues the tradition of Performance from which it has been transcribed and appropriated for purposes alien to that for which it was created in performance.

I don't know where all this leads, but I'm beginning to think we must imagine Native American oral literature as a plural—it is only translation that provides rationale for a discussion of "literature," not "literatures," though that would be suicidal perhaps for those of us with vested interests in it professionally, but intellectually more honest and certainly politically so (he who controls the academy controls the definitions and by the academy's definition we *are* foreign). Ultimately, it must lead to the privileging of those few who have not only learned a native language with some degree of competence but who have understood the tribal literature associated with that language, for really what we are talking about are the equivalent of 350 poorly collected and transcribed national literatures.

So where does this leave us? I think that until Dell Hymes's super-poet/translator/linguist/anthropologist comes along, we're doing pretty well with Hymes himself, Tedlock, McAllester,[1] and those represented in the present collection of essays. But what about an alliance between poets and linguists/anthropologists? I have worked on a number of collaborative translations from a number of languages over the years; in fact, collaborations between native speakers and poets are something of a contemporary fad, with results depending on the willingness of the poet not to fly off into his own empyrean, and on the willingness of the scholar or native speaker to allow a certain freedom to the poet, and not to pin him or her down to "literal" meanings—assuming there is such a thing as "literal." (Generally, in this context, the word comes to stand for minimal meaning. One should translate the whole context, and not just the words.) William Arrowsmith's Oxford University Press Greek plays have been built around Arrowsmith's premise that poets and dramatists such as Aeschylus, Sophocles, and Euripides can only be properly rendered by translators who are themselves poets. Scholars may, it is true, produce useful and perceptive versions, but our most urgent task is collaborative re-creation by poets and scholars, says Arrowsmith. Since poets seldom possess enough Greek to transplant it without "colonizing" it, or "stripping it of its deep cultural difference," scholars remind us of the work's "otherness" (Arrowsmith 1970:vii).

Recently, however, Richard Howard has spoken out against "the tendency toward versions, towards collaborative translations" (as if the two were the same). But he goes on to give a strange idea of what collaboration is:

> The notion that you can get this archeologist to do a literal Nahuatl or Navajo or something, and then you come along with your expensive poetical equipment and you versify and you fix up and you smooth out or shellac or in some way lubricate this crummy thing, this *literal,* and turn it into a poem,

he finds obnoxious. Howard exempts W. S. Merwin from these strictures, but "maybe he's the only one" (Mann 1982:5). It may be that Howard has Rothenberg in mind as a target (though he mentions no names). But since William Bevis, in a well-known essay, has said most of what needs to be said on that subject, I'll pass it by—except to note that some teachers, such as Jeffrey Huntsman, report that Rothenberg's total translations "can be very useful in the classrooms of the white middle class," to give them a sense, in chanting, "of what it means to be part of a small, coherent, esoteric group, participating in a meaningful community event" (Huntsman 1983:92).

II

Which brings me to the collaboration of Joel Sherzer and myself. Joel made clear in his letters to me that he intended his version to be "fanatically literal," and I know what he means, even though there is a sense in which his version is a selection, and not a reproduction. For example, there are parts, especially near the beginning of the working version he sent me, where what I'll call the stage directions indicate "comments from gathered audience and brief conversation with Mastayans," but these don't get translated. Perhaps they should, if we are talking about a collaborative event of storyteller, responder, and audience. It would certainly enlarge the context. In my version, I have also selected—this time for "feel" rather than transcription—when it comes to those line-ending and repetitive rhythm-words such as those Joel translates as "well," "indeed," "therefore," "thus," "so," and the like. The result is a translation more like drama than poetry (though not a performance, in Tedlock's sense); something close, perhaps, to a Black church service with call and response. Translation into the written word, of course, stabilizes a labile event; but if we remember that the aim is to suggest rather than create definiteness, I think the translation works. We might also note that this story benefits from having context and meaning aided by essay and notes, which can act as another extending voice. In addition, publication of the two versions, Joel's own, and then the collaboration, also moves in this direction. I regard my part in the venture as just another element in that collaboration which created the piece in the first place, from the mouth of the storyteller, who was told it by a prior storyteller, and who then adapts it and responds to his own audience. And we should not forget that the link extends to the probable European original of the speaking bone or speaking hair motif.

I have tried to retain the original style, "somewhere between formal and colloquial," as Joel wrote me. "It is not as formal as formal political speech-making and surely not as ritual as chanting, but not as informal and colloquial as everyday conversation either" (personal communication). In earlier versions, I misread the tone of the piece. Tiring of the limited vocabulary, I tried studding the story with synonyms. But it didn't work. Gradually I realized that I had to use the restricted vocabulary of the original, because I saw that using the same words created a rhythm, set up a beat, a formal sense of expectation and balance. And there were parts where I had to take the original on its own terms, not trying too hard to acclimatize or naturalize. For example, I was baffled (and am still puzzled) by the part where the sister is sitting at dinner, and we're told she heard the voice of her brother telling her to go get peppers for him. Is this habitual action, or is it the voice of the dead brother's spirit? Joel explained that I should try and think in terms of move jump-cuts, or even the manipulation of time and space of a Robbe-Grillet. So, I did what I could, and have left in the possibility that the girl *does* hear a spirit-voice. I can fall back on Joel's statement that we have here a difference of cultural logic, as well as an example of the fascinating ambiguity of the piece, which he has discussed in his chapter.

III

This brings me, by way of closure, to an attempt to outline some of the qualities needed for collaborative translations from the oral tradition:

Never be rigid. Each person learns from the other. But where there is a conflict, the scholar is more often closer to the truth than the poet. The poet can add insight and intuition—and he should never cease to question any part he finds unsatisfactory. But the scholar's knowledge has to be the bedrock on which the poet builds.

The poet's ego should be left at the door, and the scholar should not be pedantic! He or she is simply the latest in a long line of collaborators.

Works translated should be culturally significant to the group whose expression is being translated. Notes, introductions, and the like indicate uniqueness and acknowledge cultural differences. Clearly, we probably will not use that which is totally culturebound; but if we take the easily assimilable, we run the risk of simply taking something because it is, or can easily be made to be, familiar.

We should try to create a similar response in the second audience as in the first (though it is clearly impossible). In the present case, as in many others, this means that a "text" doesn't come alive fully on the page, but in the acting out, even if the acting is done in the mind's eye or with the mind's mouth. The page should talk.

This is where, in my MLA talk, I said: "The translators should disappear. The translation should aim at transparency." As noted earlier, I have seen the error of my ways. While saying that a translator should aim at a balance between identity and difference, I would also like to say that there is no one way of doing this. There is still much room for responsible experimentation and varieties of collaborative, even communal work.

NOTES

1. David P. McAllester has said of his translations that "the aim has been to convey to the reader what the Navajo themselves are saying rather than to create translations which are comfortable to the ears of non-Navajos, and thus to extend to the reader the privilege of participating further than is usually possible in the beauty and vitality of the Navajo poetic world" (1980:16). Accordingly, he retains repetitions and nonlexical syllables, and even tries to retain Navajo word order, "because word order is one of the linguistic clues to Navajo thinking." He also notes that "In written English we have been trained to avoid uncertain referents. 'He is thinking about it' does not tell who is thinking about what. The Navajos, on the other hand, have been trained to a meticulous respect for privacy. Introductions and naming are felt by them to be intrusive, impolite, and even dangerous" (1980:17). Therefore, McAllester retained Navajo ambiguity in his translation, and he tries to satisfy our need to know by using footnotes.

REFERENCES

Arrowsmith, William. 1970–. *The Greek Tragedy in New Translations*. New York: Oxford University Press.

Ballinger, Franchot, and Brian Swann. 1983. Paula Gunn Allen. *MELUS*. 10 (3):3–25.

Bevis, William. 1975. American Indian Verse and Translations. In *Literature of the American Indians: Views and Interpretations*, ed. Abraham Chapman. New York: New American Library.

Huntsman, Jeffrey. 1983. Traditional Native American Literature: The Translation Dilemma. In *Smoothing the Ground: Essays on Native American Oral Literature*, ed. Brian Swann. Berkeley, Los Angeles, London: University of California Press.

Hymes, Dell. 1981. *"In Vain I Tried to Tell You": Essays in Native American Poetics*. Philadelphia: University of Pennsylvania Press.

Krupat, Arnold. 1983. Identity and Difference in the Criticism of Native American Literature. *Diacritics* (Summer):2–13.

Mann, Paul. 1982. The Translator's Voice: An Interview With Richard Howard. *Translation Review* 9:5–15.

McAllester, David P. 1980. *Hogans: Navajo Houses and House Songs*. Middletown: Wesleyan University Press.

Tedlock, Dennis. 1984. *The Spoken Word and the Work of Interpretation*. Philadelphia: University of Pennsylvania Press.

Bluejay and His Sister

M. DALE KINKADE

One of the most popular stories among the Indians of southwestern Washington tells of various adventures of Bluejay.[1] Although some components of this story occur elsewhere and with other protagonists, there is a pattern that is unique to this area. Bluejay is the main character of this minicycle in stories recorded in Quinault (Farrand 1902:85–102), Lower Chehalis (Humptulips dialect; Adamson 1934:293–304), all three dialects of Upper Chehalis (Satsop in Adamson 1934:349–350; Oakville Chehalis in Adamson 1934:27–29 and my field notes; Tenino Chehalis in Adamson 1934:20–27 and Boas 1927), Cowlitz (one episode only, in Adamson 1934:184–185), and Lower Chinook (Boas 1894:149–182).

The last is the only one of these languages that is not Salish; the other four constitute all of one branch of the Salishan language family, located along the Washington coast from Willapa Bay to north of the Queets River, and along nearly the entire drainage of the Chehalis River and the lower reaches of the Cowlitz River. The Lower Chinook lived in the southwestern corner of Washington and northwestern Oregon, just to the south of the Lower Chehalis. But even though a single story (or set of stories) can be recognized, the extant versions vary to a considerable degree. This variance is partly due to the fact that some versions are rather short, but primarily because the selection of episodes emphasized can be quite different. Of the two versions available in Upper Chehalis, one stresses Bluejay's encounters while visiting the Land of the Dead (Boas 1927); the other emphasizes his attempted return from there to his homeland. Largely because of this story, Bluejay is one of the most popular myth characters in the area.

I was fortunate, while studying the Upper Chehalis language in the early sixties, to work with the late Silas Heck. He was one of the last speakers of the language, and probably the last who could tell any of the old stories. His repertoire was small, because as a child he had been sent off to boarding school and told by his parents to forget his language and culture. He did not do so, but still knew only a few stories; given its popularity, it is not surprising that the Bluejay story was one he remembered. Although he had told these stories many times, he would never tell one spontaneously, insisting on rehearsing it to himself the night before he allowed it to be tape-recorded. This would suggest that the episodes of any story he told were carefully selected.

Mr. Heck was quite eager to have these stories recorded, since he knew it could never be done again.[2] He told them even though the setting was all wrong: it was summer, when stories were not originally told, and he had no audience to provide the culturally expected responses. Aboriginally, the storyteller and his listeners would have lain flat on their backs while the story was being told, and the listeners were permitted to utter only a specifically pre-scribed encouraging word (for this and further details on the narra-tive setting, see Adamson 1934:xii–xiii). He had little else to do, however, and wanted the stories preserved. He was in his eighties by this time, and his vision and hearing were limited, so he could engage in few other activities. Internal evidence suggests that he told the stories very well, although he did not usually include all the details and episodes which others might have.

In his version of the Bluejay story, Silas Heck places greatest emphasis on Bluejay's attempted return from his visit to his sister in the Land of the Dead. The center third of his narration consists of this one episode, and this is framed by relatively short sections telling of his encounters with dead people. The story ends with an (apparently expected) explanation of what then happened to Bluejay in terms of where a person goes when he dies, depending on the manner of death. Heck tells of the attempted return with great drama, carefully keeping track of the prairies and Bluejay's water—and making sure that his listeners keep track too. He builds suspense with this counting, and increases tension when the count goes off, culminating in Bluejay's death. This is the high point of this telling, but not the end; Bluejay's final destination must also be reached.

In this presentation of the story, I follow the lead of Dell Hymes in treating it as dramatic verse, dividing it into acts, scenes, stanzas, verses, and lines (1981). If taken as verse, it is more analogous to epic than to lyric poetry, though certainly not everyone would even agree to call it verse. Nevertheless, this seems to be an appropriate structure for Upper Chehalis stories because of their clearly episodic nature and because of the rhythmic recurrence of events, emphasized throughout by mention of the number five and fivefold repetitions. Elsewhere I have shown that this is not just a style used by Silas Heck. Two other stories that I have analyzed were told to Franz Boas in 1927 by Jonas Secena, who appears to have been a master storyteller. One of these, "Daughters of Fire," is an exciting story of the flight of the culture hero from pursuing Fire and his rescue by lowly Trail (Kinkade 1983a); the other is a ritualized conflict between Bear and a team of Ant and Bee to determine the length of days and seasons (Kinkade 1984). Other stories by other narrators also appear to fall into this sort of verse structure. Both semantic and linguistic structure suggest and emphasize divisions at various levels. Changes in protagonists, shifting events or actions, concentration on one event or the other all suggest these divisions. In purely linguistic terms, it is useful to know that Upper Chehalis sentences (and clauses) are generally short, consisting minimally of a single predicate. What passes as a predicate in Upper Chehalis often does not correspond to a predicate in English; virtually anything can be a predicate, whether the English translation suggests verb, noun, adjective, or adverb. Thus, the English temporal expressions in lines 4, 13, and 22; the exhortative in line 26; the noun in line 33; the demonstrative adverb in line 18 are all expressed by predicates in Upper Chehalis. This provides a simple guiding principle for determining line divisions in a story: one main predicate per line. Since the main predicate, apart from a few common particles, is the first word in a sentence, division into lines is usually easy. Furthermore, it turns out that intonation contours and pauses correspond quite well to the line divisions made in this presentation; that the correspondences are not absolute speaks to the narrator's freedom to vary these features too for artistic effect. This sentence structure does not always make it easy to translate the lines into idiomatic English. This may have to be done by translating a single word as a phrase incorporating a predicate, or by forgoing a predicate in the English.

Five, as a pattern number in this area, contrasts with the usual pattern number in other Salishan languages to the north, where it is four. Indeed, five seems to be a relatively uncommon pattern number; three (as in European languages) and four are much more common. But five is a characteristic of this region, and is found in Salish in the four Tsamosan languages mentioned at the beginning of this chapter; Twana and Southern Lushootseed just to the north;[3] Tillamook on the Oregon coast just south of the Columbia River; and Columbian on the Columbia River in central Washington. It is also the pattern number in Sahaptin in central Washington and Oregon, and in Chinookan along the Columbia River.

These languages form one large contiguous block; the fact that most Salishan languages have four as a pattern number, while only these on the southern fringe of the family have five, suggests that this feature has spread north from Chinook and Sahaptin. If this is so, it has been taken over emphatically in Upper Chehalis, where almost nothing can happen in a story unless it is expressed in fives. Thus, in the Bluejay story, there must be five wedges, five prairies to cross, five baskets of water, and five attempts at getting to the forbidden house. In "Daughters of Fire," there are five daughters, Moon makes five attempts to find refuge, and then bathes for five days to purify himself after he has been saved. In "Bear and Bee," the ritual singing and dancing go on for five days and nights, and there are twenty one-line songs sung, each with precisely five repetitions. The overall division of this drama into three acts of five scenes each, and groupings of verses and lines into sets of three or five, seem to be correlated with this pattern number. Indeed, this corresponds to the patterning of threes and fives in Chinookan and Sahaptin.

As a contrast to this dominant three/five structure, the division of each scene into two stanzas is striking. This is characteristic of many Upper Chehalis stories, but not of those in nearby Chinookan. Pairing is a common technique found in many parts of North America, however; it may even be a relic in Upper Chehalis of an ancestral Salishan two/four structure. The principle seems to be to present an episode in one stanza, then repeat or elaborate or complement it in a second stanza. Each pair of stanzas can thus be seen to be more closely related to each other than to preceding or following pairs (scenes).

Since stories such as this originally were strictly oral narratives, their structure could remain much more fluid than that of a written story. This fluidity probably accounts for much of the indeterminacy of division into verses and lines and the specific points of division. Some of these may reflect the temperament of the person making the divisions, and another investigator would likely make other choices. Furthermore, as one grows into the story, one sees different interconnections and divisions, and ideas of organization will change.[4] Thus, the version presented here need not be considered definitive, and an alternative suggested to me by Dell Hymes is given below.

GRAMMAR

Before turning to the story itself, a brief characterization of the Upper Chehalis language might help readers working through the original text to understand and appreciate some of its nuances.[5] The language is rich in consonants, and has great tolerance for clusters of them far beyond what is normal for English—up to ten have been noted, and six is not unusual. The consonants are typical of what is found in this area, with a large number of consonants produced in the back of the mouth. There are far fewer vowels, and underlying unstressed vowels are often deleted, depending on the location of word-stress and how the word ends.

Predicates tend to be highly inflected, primarily by the use of suffixes, although certain basic categories are marked by prefixes. Pronominal objects, subjects, and possessors are indicated by affixes or clitics, and there is a special (extra) third-person suffix to distinguish between multiple referents. One of the most important grammatical categories used is aspect, indicating the nature of the action; actual time is relatively unimportant and often unmarked (future is often indicated, although this might better be considered as unrealized aspect). Many affixes and roots appear in two different forms (mostly depending on presence or absence of vowels), one for continuative (imperfective) and unrealized aspects, the other for completive (perfective) and stative aspects. Passives are encountered frequently in texts. There are several types of plurals, but these are often optional when the plurality is obvious from the context. Diminutive forms are frequent, and indicated mostly by vowel length.[6] Reduplication is less common in Upper Chehalis than in most Salishan languages, and serves different functions (repetitive action, superlatives, and slow action). Word compounding, including that of prepositions to each other and to other items, is relatively common. A feature shared with all other Salishan languages is the frequent use of lexical suffixes, a category of suffixes with fairly specific semantic content.

Parts of speech are not distinguished in the English sense, and apart from various prepositional, conjunctival, and adverbial particles, anything can serve as the main predicate of a sentence and may take any of the possible varieties of inflection. For example, sqᵂə́t'wn may mean "it is burning" or (with a preceding article) "fire"; the special lexical suffix for "fire" is, however, completely different, -staqi-/-stq. The most important syntactic concept is predicate, with a subject or object (better, agent or patient) optionally added as an adjunct. These subjects and objects are themselves underlying predicates; both rarely occur together in one sentence. The usual word order is predicate, then subject and object (if both are present); various personal, adverbial, aspectual, or deictic particles accrete to these basic units. The minimal sentence may be very short, since it can consist of a single predicate (e.g., lines 56 and 150 of the text). Subordinate or dependent clauses have this same structure, except that possessive affixes are used instead of subject affixes; they mostly follow modal particles or various temporal predicates and negatives. When both possessor and possessed are present, the former precedes the latter. Particles contribute a great deal of subtlety, and are often not easily translated. There are few prepositions, and those which occur tend to have broad ranges of meaning. Articles are very important, and have several functions. The simplest ones, t and c are indefinite, while the others are definite. Articles with c are mainly feminine gender; the others are more general.

THE TEXT

[I. Bluejay visits the Land of the Dead.]

i/A	(a)	ʔał tat x̌'áqłnł -	1
		ʔacx̣áłšm - t p'ayə́kᵂ - ča c yá·yn's,	2
		ʔackʷácł náw..	3

B　(a)　q'ačá·　　　　　　　　　　　　　　　　　　　4

　　　　t swins ʔacwéˑx̣ yamš　　　　　　　　　5

　　　　　ʔitu t'úwn - tu ʔał t mák'ʷat.　　　6

　　　　　　slaqálčuwł. .　　　　　　　　　　7

　　(b)　kʷáw'aqn c náw'.　　　　　　　　　　8

　　　　"nałʔíns,　　　　　　　　　　　　　9

　　　　　ʔit sšanám šał t ʔáliss t mák'ʷat. ."　10

　　(c)　tu ta ʔasúln.　　　　　　　　　　　　11

　　　　šóˑk'ʷm' ł t wíntns t mák'ʷt. .　　　12

C　(a)　qax̣álax̣ʷ　　　　　　　　　　　　　　13

　　　　swénsx̣, t p'ayɔ́k'ʷ. .　　　　　　　　14

　　　　　ʔitu x̣ʷimínuwtšitn tac yáˑyn's.　　15

　　(b)　wi ʔéˑnm ʔit q'ał skʷáx̣ʷs. .[7]　　　16

　　　　míłta ʔéˑnm t q'ał kʷáx̣ʷs[8]　　　　17

　　　　　šínx̣,　　　　　　　　　　　　　18

　　　　　　t kʷáx̣ʷkʷx̣ʷ,　　　　　　　　19

　　(c)　ʔamu ʔátmn　　　　　　　　　　　　20

　　　　t q'ał mɔ́y kʷáx̣ʷ šał tamíšs tat mák'ʷat. .[9]　21

ii/D　(a)　q'ačá·　　　　　　　　　　　　　　　22

　　　　t swénsx̣　　　　　　　　　　　　　23

　　　　　ʔitu cúnstš ł t sɔ́x̣tkʷlal's. .　　　24

　　(b)　"ʔóˑ ,　　　　　　　　　　　　　　25

　　　　　λ'áq'ʷ ʔit x̣ʷúqʷn č cílačs t x̣ʷálq'm'łn'. .　26

　　(c)　n sq'ʷáλ'atš,　　　　　　　　　　　27

　　　　šóˑk'ʷals ł tit sq'isč'íss t łukʷáł. .　　28

　　(d)　q'ačá·　　　　　　　　　　　　　　29

　　　　λ'ala swí ʔacwéˑx̣,　　　　　　　　　30

　　(e)　húy n λ'a ʔasúmin. . tit x̣ʷálq'm'łn'.　　31

　　　　šóˑk'ʷm' ł t wíntns, c náw,　　　　　32

　　　　　ʔax̣ʷáł. ."　　　　　　　　　　　33

E　(a)　húy sáʔatn t q'íc'x̣　　　　　　　　　34

　　(b)　ʔitu q'ílicš tat x̣ʷálq'm'łn'　　　　　35

　　(c)　n ʔasúln　　　　　　　　　　　　　36

　　　　šíˑ ·n' ł yalácči ł t qáˑʔ. .　　　　　37

　　(d)　wi čtšán' ł tat qáˑʔ　　　　　　　　38

　　　　t wíntns, tat mák'ʷat　　　　　　　39

　　(e)　wi šán'x̣ tac yáˑyn's. .　　　　　　　40

iii/F (a) húy tálaqapn. . 41
   (b) q'ačá· 42
     ʔitu č'ísn. t wíɬ. 43
      pə́nwn tat wíɬ 44
       míɬta t sʔax̣ə́ts t wá·, 45
        šán'x̣ č'ə́c'ɬ. 46
   (c) spə́nɬ tat wíɬ 47
     wi ʔitu st'áq'awicišs tat sqəʔúqʷls. 48
     ʔaɬ t sč'ə́c'ɬ ʔaɬ tit wíɬ. . 49
   (d) wi stálaqapits tat yá·yn's tu ʔáɬčtšn' 50
     scúnt 51
   (e) "č'ə́c'ɬaʔ ʔaɬ tit wíɬ. 52
     t ʔasyáxʷtč mátwilicinn. ." 53

  G (a) huy č'ə́c'wn 54
   (b) tíwatn čtšán', 55
   (c) c'awáwn. . 56

iv/H (a) húy ƛ'a sx̣ʷúqʷmisn ɬ tat k'é·ci t sqəʔúqʷls. 57
     syə́l'kʷwn. 58
     šʔáɬcni šaɬ t cúliss. 59
   (b) wi č'úsus q'isɬə́cq'ʷiyqmts. .[10] 60
   (c) wi n ʔit nkʷs pə́kʷɬšitm ɬ tac yá·yn's 61
     cúntwali, 62
      "ta· sí·txʷ ukʷa tit ʔanššawácɬtn, 63
       tu sɬə́cq'ʷiyqmistš. 64
        t ʔaɬ nsšawácɬtn tit ʔašúq'ʷ." 65
   (d) "ʔé·nm t q'aɬ swítxʷs nsšawácɬtn t sqəʔúqʷls. 66
     yálš sqəʔúqʷls 67
     ʔit syə́l'kʷwn taš p'ə́nn'ca. 68
     mák'ʷat." 69
   (e) "wi húy, ʔanššawácɬtn." 70

  I (a) ʔitu yə́l'kʷwn tat táw'ɬ sqəʔúqʷls. 71
     šʔáɬcni 72
   (b) wi č'úsus ɬə́cq'ʷiyqm's. . 73
   (c) húy cúnstš ɬ tac yá·yn's, 74
     "ʔac'í ukʷa na tu sɬə́cq'ʷiyqmiss, t ʔasyáxʷtč." 75
   (d) "ʔé·nm tu nswi swi syáxʷtč, t sqəʔúqʷls 76

		mák'ʷt	77
		q'aɬ qʷánn'ɬ.	78
		míɬta nuɬtámš	79
		ʔáliss t snéʔxamš."	80

v/J (a) "có· č'ísaʔ sčá· t nwíntn." 81

   (b) wáksiɬt š ʔéX'nm' 82

      šín skʷáxʷs yamš ʔaɬ t xáš. . 83

      máyawn 84

      ʔé· · ·yu lə́č' tat xáš, ɬ t sqəʔúqʷls. 85

   (c) cwé·x t yə́l'kʷwn xʷàqʷ sčá·nm, 86

      st'ayə́c's yamš máy'aqa. 87

      cwé·x t k'é·ci, 88

      cwé·x t tá·waɬti. 89

      t mák'ʷt. . 90

K (a) húy cúnstš ɬ tac yá·yn's, 91

      "sá·wn t wácšn 92

      ʔaɬ titxtí tit kʷé·swn. ." 93

   (b) húy, kʷxʷáwn šʔaɬ kʷə́ss, 94

   (c) húy n xʷuqʷúwn tat qə́xɬ sqəʔúqʷls. . 95

      tuláp 96

      ʔiyu t ʔacwé·x 97

   (d) húy n ɬə́xʷɬxʷqʷwn tat mák'ʷat—. 98

      sqəʔúqʷls—. 99

      yalə́m'stq. 100

      k'ʷa swətšə́nm ɬ tat mák'ʷat.[11] 101

      mátns ɬə́xʷɬxʷqʷn. 102

   (e) X'áqɬnɬ ʔétq'itači 103

      n námawiɬt. . 104

[II. The attempt to return home.]

i/A (a) qə́xɬ t sq'ítači 105

      cwé·nsx, t p'ayə́k'ʷ. 106

   (b) xʷàqʷ sčá·nm t swákss, 107

   (c) wi, yál'š mák'ʷat t st'úqʷitn. . 108

B   (a)   q'ačá·   109

n t'ayəƛ'úl'nwatn, t p'ayə́k'ʷ.   110

(b)   cúntn tac yá·yn's,   111

"có cútčn t q'ał t'it yáƛ'ł čn tanin.   112

míłta t nq'ał swé·x né'x̣.   113

nač'x̣ʷúqʷł. tit smák'ʷat   114

yál'š sqə'úqʷls. .   115

(c)   có· · · nał'íns   116

'it yáƛ'ł čn. ."   117

C   (a)   ƛ'áqłnł   118

swins sá'at. . .[12]   119

táynut tac yá·yn's   120

ii/D   (a)   húy n cúnstš.   121

"wi nał'íns   122

su'ut 'it yáƛ'ł č.   123

t'it wáks č š'áłtm'šm'. . ."[13]   124

(b)   húy cúnstš tanin ł tac yá·yn's. .   125

"'ala ł tíwt,   126

wi łit yə́q'ʷpataqm š'áłtm'šm'   127

ƛ'ala syə́q'ʷpataqm,   128

'asyə́p.   129

wi ł 'aƛ'aqə́m š'ał t máqʷm.   130

wi ƛ'a sq'ʷə́t'wn. .   131

(c)   cílačs t máqʷm   132

ƛ'ala spanáqʷm,   133

n ł míy t'akʷxʷáws,   134

š'ał tat 'atə́mš. .   135

(d)   wi té'x̣ tit cílačs, qʷasúqʷa',   136

lə́č' ł t qá·'.   137

'ala ł t kʷáxʷmn t 'ó·c's t máqʷm,[14] 138

wi łit łúnaqim'ł č, ł t 'asə́x̣tkʷlš. 139

n łícšitš, tat tə́mš, ł tit qá·'   140

wi łit łə́pł tat sq'ʷə́t'wn.   141

tu ł sitáqʷm č. .   142

(e)   cilčstálmaqʷm   143

ƛ'ala sitáqʷm,   144

	n ɬ t'akʷxʷáws	145
	čá· tala wíntn."	146

E (a) húy tíw'stus t p'aýk'ʷ,   147
  (b) šán', ɬ tat sqəʔúqʷls.   148
       syáxʷtčs.   149
  (c) pə́nwn   150

iii/F (a) húy wáksn.   151
       yə́pwn, t p'aýk'ʷ   152
         ʔitu ƛ'ə́qmitn šʔaɬ t máqʷm.   153
  (b) ʔó· ·· tat sqé· ·lxmaʔs tat máqʷm   154
       ʔacnéʔɬuʔ tit sq'ʷə́t'wn.   155
  (c) wi č'úsus ɬúnaqs tat sə́xtkʷlals.   156
       t'ix t ɬícšitn tat tə́mš ɬ tat qá·ʔ.   157
         c'é· ·č ɬ ʔó·c's t qʷasúqʷaʔ   158
         lə́č' ɬ t qá·ʔ. .   159
           n kʷxʷáwn ɬakʷáqʷ. .[15]   160

G (a) húy t'ayə́q'ʷpataqm hm· ···   161
       ƛ'áqɬnɬ syə́q'ʷpatqms,   162
         n t'aƛ'ə́qmitn šʔaɬ t'aʔó·c's t máqʷm.   163
  (b) húy t'aɬúnaqn t sə́xtkʷlals   164
       t'ix t ɬícšitn tat tə́mš ɬ t qá·ʔ. .   165
         c'é· ·čyaʔqn tat qʷasúqʷaʔ,   166
         wi č'úsus panaqʷáms. .   167

[Interlude.]

H   húy t'ayə́q'ʷpatqmitn t có·tnus,   168
       sálins t máqʷm   169
       spanaqʷáms.[16]   170
         wi có·tus čá·ɬi tanin,   171
           n ɬ, t'aɬačáytm'štn. .[17]   172

iv/I (a) húy wáksn. .   173
       húy panaqʷámitn ʔaɬ t máqʷm.   174

265

		slámstaqn.	175
		sqʼʷúx̣ʷmitn.	176
	(b)	míɬtaws qʼícʼx̣ ɬ tat máqʷm	177
		tat sitáqʷmisn.	178
	(c)	wi čʼúsus wáks,	179
		n ʔit ɬícšn tat qʷasúqʷaʔ	180
		šíˑ ·nʼ ɬ panaqʷáms,	181
		n cʼə́čyaʔqn.	182
		sɬə́pwn tat sqʼʷə́tʼwn. .	183
		panaqʷámitn	184

J	(a)	tʼawáksn ɬ x̌ʼáqɬnɬ,	185
		ʔitu tʼapanaqʷámitn, šʔaɬ tʼaʔóˑcʼs t máqʷm.	186
		lámstaqn.	187
		sqʼʷúx̣ʷmitn. .	188
	(b)	sáli tanin t qʷasúqʷaʔ . t qáˑʔ.	189
	(c)	čʼúsus swáks wétqʷm[18]	190
		sitáqʷmitn	191
		ʔit ɬícšn tat tə́mš	192
		ɬunáqitn t sə́x̣tkʷlals.[19]	193
		panaqʷámitn–	194

K	(a)	húy tʼayə́qʼʷpatqmitn	195
		t qʼačaˑ t x̌ʼáqɬnɬ	196
		n tʼax̌ʼə́qmitn.	197
	(b)	ʔiyu tanin ʔóˑcʼs, t qʷasúqʷaʔ t qáʔs.	198
	(c)	húy wáksn,	199
		n ɬícšitn tat sqʼʷə́tʼwn ɬ tat qáˑʔ[20]	200
		wi čʼúsus qʼisɬə́ps.	201
		panaqʷámitn. .	202
		míɬta tanin t qáˑʔs. .	203

L	(a)	húy wáksn	204
		ʔitu tʼax̌ʼə́qmitn. šʔaɬ t sqʼʷə́tʼwn.	205
	(b)	ʔénm tanin t qʼaɬ síts. .	206
	(c)	x̣ʷàqʷ ʔénm sə́pʼsapʼn tat támʼči ɬ tat. . .[21]	207
		wi sɬə́pwn. .	208
		šíˑ ·n ɬ tat spanaqʷáms	209
		ʔaɬ t cʼə́čɬ tanin tat qʷasúqʷaʔ[22]	210
		ɬit cʼə́čstq. .	211

v/M	(a)	húy t'awáksn	212
		t q'ačá· t x̌'áqɬnɬ t p'ayɘ́k'ʷ,	213
		ʔitu t'ax̌'ɘ́qmitn šaɬ t máqʷm	214
		slámstaqn.	215
	(b)	ʔé·nm tanin x̌'a spɘ́ns.	216
		x̌'a sitáqʷms.	217
		míɬta tanin t qʷasúqʷaʔs–[23]	218
		míɬta tanin t qá·ʔs.	219
	(c)	xʷàqʷ ʔé·nm t sáʔatisc.	220
		tɘx̌ʷsčitn tat qá·ʔ,	221
		wi k'éʔcu t q'istxʷɬɘ́ps	222
		nkʷs t'aq'ʷɘ́t'wn.	223
N	(a)	húy có·tn	224
		"x̌'áq'ʷ ʔit cɘ́qyn' čn."	225
	(b)	húy wáksn šínx̣	226
		cɘ́qiytn	227
		scɘ́qiytn	228
		tuláp t'asɬɘ́pwn tat sq'ʷɘ́t'wn t k'écu	229
		n p'át'staqn caníyaɬ cúlaʔis.	230
	(c)	húy wɘ́tqwn	231
		sátwn	232
		sɬɘ́x̣wn tat náwc'is. .	233
		c'ɘ́cstaqn	234
		ʔátminn t p'ayɘ́k'ʷ. .	235

[III. Death and Second Death.]

i/A	(a)	wi ʔàčə míɬta x̌'i t síns t tá·m	236
		míɬta t stxʷk'ʷɘ́ns k'ʷí t sq'ítači,	237
		ʔít ʔaɬ tat qá·ʔ. .	238
	(b)	stálaqapitn tac yá·yn's	239
		x̌'a swins ʔit mátwali. .	240
	(c)	ʔitu č'ísn tat wíɬ,	241
		ʔacč'ɘ́c'ɬ t nuɬtámš.	242
		ʔəyálwn nuɬtámš.	243
		pɘ́nwn	244
		ʔit scúnt,	245
		"tit'úlɬ č x̌'i."	246

267

(d) "ʔé·· tit'úlɬ čn   247

cútčn ƛ'a t'asč'ismn tit manó·mš. ."   248

(e) wi spə́ns u t p'ayə́k'ʷ,   249

B (a) wi č'ó··su t sšəʔúms tac yá·yn's.   250

cúcutn,   251

"tit cúnci čn   252

ƛ'ala swi ʔacʔə́xnn tat ʔaqá·ʔ.   253

(b) cutčn míɬta   254

cutčn miló·k'ʷm t ʔaspə́q'ʷpaqʷn   255

tuláp   256

n ʔit ʔaskʷáxʷmn tat sq'ʷə́t'wn   257

tu c'ə́čiyq t ʔaqá·ʔ.   258

(c) míɬta ixʷu t ʔaʔacɬačáytm'š.   259

tu q'ʷə́t'ɬ č   260

tu mák'ʷt č tanin."   261

ii/C (a) cútn t p'ayə́k'ʷ   262

"ʔénm t q'aɬ smíyu mák'ʷt.   263

nuɬtámš ntiws né·x.   264

xé··sti uk'ʷa tit ʔanšmə́ntn."   265

(b) "tám tuɬ swíns t'acəniáwmš   266

ʔit ʔastó·k'ʷmis   267

yál'š sqəʔúqʷls.   268

tit ʔašúq'ʷ."   269

(c) "ʔénm tuɬ swins sqəʔúqʷls t manó·mš.   270

ʔéyti tit ʔatmanó·mš."   271

D (a) ʔitu kʷáxʷmsmaln tat nuɬtámš   272

k'ʷpúsnuɬtamš. .   273

(b) cúntn   274

"xéʔs uk'ʷa t'íx na t ʔaššə́n."   275

(c) "ʔé· t'íx nsšə́n   276

t'at'íx ʔit ʔaɬə́cq'ʷiyqmis t sqəʔúqʷls,   277

tiwstéʔx. ."   278

(d) "wi ʔénm t q'aɬ swins sqəʔúqʷls   279

t k'ʷpúsnuɬtamš—."   280

(e) "wi húy cə́ni."   281

iii/E	(a)	húy t'awáksiɬt tanin šaɬ tat x̣áš.	282
		máyawn qə́x̣ɬ tat sšam'álaxʷ	283
		ʔəyáliwan t sšam'álaxʷ.	284
		ʔáctš ɬ tat x̣áš.	285
F	(a)	húy sá·wn t wácšn ʔaɬ tat skʷə́ss tanin.[24]	286
	(b)	húy sá·wn sq'ʷúls yamš	287
		ʔétq'itači. .	288
iv/G	(a)	q'ačá·	289
		cwénsx̣ šánx̣ t p'ayə́k'ʷ	290
		ʔitu cúnstš ɬ tac yá·yn's,	291
		"ʔayúɬuʔ míɬta	292
		t ʔasp'at'álm šó·k'ʷm'."	293
	(b)	qas ʔacwé·x̣ ʔana t šə́wɬ,	294
		ʔacp'at'álm tu ʔaɬ tat wíntns tac yá·yn's.	295
	(c)	"t'íx̣ wi tá·w'ɬ x̣ax̣á·ʔ.	296
		ʔə́y t ʔacwé·x̣ néʔx̣."	297
H	(a)	húy wénnax̣n t p'ayə́k'ʷ	298
		t míɬtaws x̌'áqɩnɬ–	299
		ʔitu có·tn.	300
	(b)	"tám uk'ʷa,	301
		tu ʔaccúntm čn	302
		míɬta nq'aɬ swáks,	303
		míɬta nq'aɬ sp'at'álm.	304
		x̌'áq'ʷs panáxʷs pútitanš."	305
v/I	(a)	húy wáksn,	306
		míɬtaws lé·	307
		nkʷs yáčapits ɬ tac yá·yn's	308
		ɬ t'ayác'tn.	309
		músaɬšn t syác'tut ɬ tac yá·yn's,[25]	
			310
	(b)	wi ʔaɬ t cílčstašn–	311
		n kʷxʷáwn šaɬ t x̣áš. .	312
		šánx̣ t syáčapit, t p'ayə́k'ʷ ɬ tac yá·yn's.	313
	(c)	wi míɬta tan ʔé·nm t q'aɬ t'asyác'stš.[26]	314

269

J   (a)   qas hú·y ʔit kʷáxʷɫ   315
              čá· t wíntns, t q'íc'x̣ ɫ cə́ni.   316
                 ʔit q'ʷə́t'ɫ tat náwc'is   317
                     tu yál'š c'ax̣áy'stq tanin   318
                        t swins nuɫtámš.   319
  (b)   wi šánx̣ ʔaɫ tat x̣áš–   320
              tat sšam'álaxʷ,   321
                 wi q'ʷácyaq'als t wətšə́nm's. .   322
  (c)   wi tat swətšə́nmitn tanin, t p'ayə́k'ʷ   323
           q'ʷácyaq'als   324
           n tat ɫawálstš, ɫ tac yá·yn's. .   325

K   tu st'íx̣ʷuʔ. .   326
          snámuʔss. .   327

[I. Bluejay visits the Land of the Dead.]

i/A   (a)   A long time ago   1
              Bluejay and his elder sister lived there;   2
              Bluebird was her name   3

B   (a)   A long time   4
              they were there,   5
                 when one arrives from the dead people   6
                     to buy a wife.   7
  (b)   Bluebird gives her consent: 8
              "It's all right   9
                 to marry the chief of the dead."   10
  (c)   Then he took her   11
              there to the home of the dead.   12

C   (a)   Many years   13
              Bluejay stays there,   14
                 when he gets lonesome for his sister.   15
  (b)   But how can he get there?   16
              No way to get there,   17

		there,	18
		alive—	19
(c)	if he were dead	20
		he could just get there to the land of the dead	
		people.	21

ii/D	(a)	A long time	22
		he stays there,	23
		when his spirit power tells him,	24
	(b)	"Oh,	25
		you'd better gather five wedges.	26
	(c)	And put them down	27
		towards the rising of the sun.	28
	(d)	A long time	29
		you will stay there,	30
	(e)	and so the wedges will take you	31
		there to the home of Naw,	32
		your elder sister."	33

E	(a)	And so he does this,	34
	(b)	when the wedges rise up	35
	(c)	and take him	36
		there to the edge of a river.	37
	(d)	And on the other side of that river	38
		is the home of the dead,	39
	(e)	and there is his sister.	40

iii/F	(a)	And so he calls	41
	(b)	A long time,	42
		when a canoe comes.	43
		The canoe gets across,	44
		he sees no one	45
		there inside it.	46
	(c)	The canoe got across,	47
		and then the skull moves,	48
		in the bottom of the canoe.	49
	(d)	And his sister calls to him from the other side,	50
		saying,	51

	(e)	"Get into the canoe!	52
		Your brother-in-law will bring you across."	53
G	(a)	And so he gets in,	54
	(b)	he crosses to the other side,	55
	(c)	he gets out.	56
iv/H	(a)	And so the little skulls gather,	57
		rolling around,	58
		toward him, to his feet.	59
	(b)	And he keeps pushing them away with his foot.	60
	(c)	And he was spoken roughly to by his sister,	61
		she told him,	62
		"What are you doing with your nephews?	63
		Then you are pushing them away with your foot.	64
		Those are your nephews there."	65
	(d)	"How can my nephews be skulls?	66
		They are nothing but skulls	67
		rolling around beside me.	68
		They are dead."	69
	(e)	"And so then, they are your nephews."	70
I	(a)	Then the big skull rolls	71
		to him,	72
	(b)	and he keeps pushing it away with his foot.	73
	(c)	And so his sister tells him,	74
		"Why are you kicking away your brother-in-law?"	75
	(d)	"How can my brother-in-law be a skull?	76
		He's dead.	77
		I'm afraid of him.	78
		He's not a person,	79
		this chief of the people here."	80
v/J	(a)	"Well, come to where I live!"	81
	(b)	They go inland,	82
		they get there to a house,	83

		they go in,	84
		the house is just full of skulls.	85
(c)		There is rolling everywhere.	86
		that's the way they travel,	87
		there are little ones,	88
		there are big ones,	89
		dead people.	90

K (a)   And so his sister tells him,   91
         "A dance will take place   92
            on this evening."   93
  (b)   And so they arrive in the evening,   94
  (c)   and so many skulls gather.   95
         At first   96
            they are just there,   97
  (d)   and so then the dead people bob up and down—   98
         skulls—   99
            around the fire.   100
            Because the dead people danced,   101
               their heads bobbing up and down.
                                                              102
  (e)   After a while it becomes daylight   103
         and they finish.   104

[II. The attempt to return home.]

i/A (a)   Many days   105
           Bluejay stays there.   106
    (b)   He goes everywhere   107
    (c)   and he finds nothing but dead people.   108

 B (a)   A long time   109
           and Bluejay gets homesick.   110
    (b)   He tells his sister,   111
           "Well, maybe I can go back home now.   112
             I cannot stay here   113

			together with the dead people,	114
			nothing but skulls.	115
	(c)	So, it's all right	116
		for me to go home."	117

C	(a)	A long time	118
		he's doing . . .	119
		His sister refuses.	120

ii/D (a)   And so then she tells him,   121
             "And it is all right   122
                 for you to go home,   123
                     to go to your homeland."   124
     (b)   And so his sister tells him now,   125
             "When you cross,   126
                 and will walk to your homeland, 127
                     you will walk,   128
                         you will travel,   129
                             and you will come out onto a prairie   130
                                 and it will be burning.   131
     (c)   Five prairies   132
             for you to cross,   133
                 and you will just get back   134
                     to your homeland.   135
     (d)   And here are five baskets   136
             full of water.   137
                 When you get to the first prairie,   138
                     you will sing for your spirit power,   139
                         and sprinkle the ground with water,   140
                             and the fire will go out,   141
                                 then you will cross the prairie.   142
     (e)   Five prairies   143
             for you to cross,   144
                 and you will get back   145
                     where you live."   146

E (a) And so Bluejay was taken across,   147
      (b) to there by that skull,   148
            his brother-in-law.   149
      (c) He crosses,   150

iii/F (a) And so he goes,   151
            Bluejay walks,   152
                when he comes out onto a prairie.   153
      (b) Oh, the prairie is bright,   154
            it looks like a fire.   155
      (c) And he keeps singing his spirit song.   156
               There he sprinkles the ground with the water.   157
                Used up is one basket   158
                  full of water,   159
                    and he gets across the prairie.   160

G (a) And so he walked again a long time,   161
            a long time he walks,   162
                and he comes out onto another prairie.   163
      (b) And so again he sings his spirit song,   164
            there he sprinkles the ground with water.   165
                He uses up the basket,   166
                and he crosses the prairie.   167

[Interlude.]

H   And so he thinks he has walked,   168
          two prairies   169
            he has crossed,   170
                and he thinks there are three now   171
                and he will reach his homeland.
                172

iv/I (a) And so he goes,   173
            and so he gets to a prairie.   174
                It's blazing.   175
                  It's smoking.   176
      (b) It's not like those prairies   177

		that he has crossed.	178
	(c)	And he keeps going,	179
		and he sprinkles from the basket,	180
		he gets across there,	181
		and uses it up.	182
		The fire goes out.	183
		He crosses the prairie.	184

J	(a)	He goes on for a while,	185
		when he comes out again on another prairie.	186
		It's blazing.	187
		It's smoking.	188
	(b)	Two now are his baskets of water.	189
	(c)	He keeps going to the middle of the prairie,	190
		he crosses the prairie,	191
		he sprinkles the ground,	192
		he sings his spirit song.	193
		He crosses the prairie.	194

K	(a)	And so he walks again	195
		for a long time	196
		and comes out on a prairie.	197
	(b)	Just one basket of water now.	198
	(c)	And so he goes,	199
		and sprinkles the fire with water,	200
		and it goes out.	201
		He crosses the prairie,	202
		now he has no more water.	203

L	(a)	And so he goes,	204
		when he comes out onto a fire.	205
	(b)	Now how can he cross?	206
	(c)	He pounds on it every way with that (basket),	207
		and it goes out.	208
		He just gets across there,	209
		but now his baskets are used up,	210
		they're burned up.	211

v/M	(a)	And so he goes on	212
		a long time, does Bluejay,	213
		when he comes out again on a prairie,	214
		it's blazing.	215
	(b)	Now how will he cross,	216
		will he get to the other side?	217
		He has no more baskets now,	218
		no more water now.	219
	(c)	He tries everything.	220
		He spits water on it,	221
		and it goes out a little bit,	222
		then it begins burning again.	223
N	(a)	And so he thinks,	224
		"I'd better kick it."	225
	(b)	And so he goes there,	226
		he kicks it,	227
		he kicks it,	228
		at first the fire goes out a little,	229
		and his feet catch fire.	230
	(c)	And so he falls on his back,	231
		he falls,	232
		his body burns.	233
		He burns up,	234
		Bluejay dies.	235

[III. Death and Second Death.]

i/A	(a)	And it seems as though nothing,	236
		the number of days weren't counted,	237
		he came to the river.	238
	(b)	He calls his sister	239
		to come fetch him.	240
	(c)	Then the canoe comes,	241
		a person is inside,	242
		a good-looking person.	243
		He lands	244

		and says,	245
		"I guess you came back."	246
(d)	"Yes, I came back,	247
	maybe the children will come for me."	248
(e)	And Bluejay crosses.	249

B (a) And his sister keeps crying.   250

          She is saying,   251

             "I told you   252

               to look out for your water.   253

  (b) I guess you didn't,   254

          I guess you wasted it splashing it around   255

             at first   256

               and when you got to the fire   257

                  then your water was used up.   258

  (c) You can't get to your homeland any more.   259

          Then you burned up,   260

             then you're dead now.   261

ii/C (a) Bluejay says,   262

          "How can I just be dead,   263

             when there are people here?   264

               Are these nice ones your children?"   265

  (b) "Those are the ones   266

          that you didn't want—   267

             nothing but skulls.   268

             Those there."   269

  (c) "How can skulls be children?   270

          Your children are nice."   271

D (a) Then a person arrived,   272

          a high-class person.   273

  (b) He says,   274

          "Is this nice one your husband?"   275

  (c) "Yes, this is my husband,   276

          the same skull you pushed away with your foot,   277

             not long ago."   278

  (d) "And how can a skull   279

| | | be a high-class person?" | 280 |
| (e) | "And so then he is." | 281 |

iii/E	(a)	And so they go back now to the house.	282
		Many people go in,	283
		nice-looking people,	284
		inside the house.	285

F	(a)	And so a dance takes place now in the evening.	286
	(b)	And so they have a good time	287
		until daylight.	288

iv/G	(a)	A long time	289
		Bluejay stays there,	290
		when his sister tells him,	291
		"Under no circumstances	292
		are you to continue in that	
		direction."	293
	(b)	Because there was a road	294
		continuing from the home of his sister.	295
	(c)	"This is very powerful.	296
		It's best to stay here."	297

H	(a)	And so Bluejay stays,	298
		and it isn't long,	299
		when he thinks,	300
	(b)	"What is it	301
		when I am told,	302
		that I shouldn't go,	303
		that I shouldn't continue (there).	304
		I guess I must find out."	305

v/I	(a)	And so he goes,	306
		not far	307
		and his sister catches up with him	308
		and takes him back.	309
		Four times his sister takes him back.	
			310
	(b)	And on the fifth time,	311

		he arrives at a house.	312
		There his sister catches up to Bluejay.	313
	(c)	And there is no way now he can be taken back.	314

J	(a)	Because he had arrived	315
		where those like him stay.	316
		His body had burned,	317
		then nothing but coals now	318
		his being a person.	319
	(b)	And there in that house,	320
		they are the people	321
		who dance upside down.	322
	(c)	And now Bluejay is dancing	323
		upside down,	324
		and he was abandoned by his sister.	325

K		Then that's all.	326
		That's its end.	327

COMMENTS ON THE TEXT

A number of points of explanation should help in understanding and appreciating the text; these points are both cultural and linguistic. The prairies of the story are not an artificial device; rather, prairies are an important feature of the Chehalis River valley and were of great importance to the Indians. These prairies vary greatly in size, from a few acres to several square miles, and were kept burned off so that important root crops (particularly camas and bracken fern) and berries would be readily available. The prairies were also the sites of the major villages in Upper Chehalis and Cowlitz territory. Their importance is reflected in the language by the presence of a special lexical suffix for prairie (-aqʷ) and a large number of words referring to them (such as "cross a prairie," "come out on a prairie," "be in the middle of a prairie," "the river edge of a prairie," "go from the center to the edge of a prairie," and the like).

Most modern-day towns are located on these old prairies, and even though much forest has been cleared in the area, many of the original prairies are still recognizable. One important feature of the prairies in the story that is not made explicit is that the first two Bluejay reached were merely covered with bright flowers, and were not burning at all; this did not have to be specified because native listeners would have known this from other tellings of the story. In some versions, there are ten prairies to cross—five with flowers, five burning—and Bluejay and the wedges may have to cross them both in going to the Land of the Dead and in returning (with the flower prairies coming first in both cases).

Only part of the Upper Chehalis beliefs about where one goes after death are expressed in this story. The full reason why Bluejay could not stay with his sister is only hinted at by stating that he had to stay in the house down the road because he had burned to death. In his field notes, Boas says that this is also where a person goes when he dies by falling from something. Adamson notes that a person in the first Land of the Dead (where Bluejay's sister lives) can sometimes be brought back to life by a shaman, but those in the second cannot (1934:24). From this one might infer that those in the first land have died of illness, while those in the second have died by accident. It is not clear where a person who dies of old age or a person who is killed would end up. There is also a third land specifically for very young children (Adamson 1934:27). The location of these lands relative to the real world and relative to each other is not particularly clear, and varies somewhat from informant to informant.

Bluejay's character is not sketched fully in Silas Heck's version of the story, but much of it comes through. He is a know-it-all, and persistently refuses to believe his sister, always getting into trouble as a result. Bluejay's sister is named Náw in this and one other version of the story. In the one other Upper Chehalis version where she is named (told by an older brother of Silas Heck), she is called Yúy; this is also her name in all the downriver and coast versions of the story. There seems to be no pattern to this distribution, and it is probably not significant. The name was translated as "bluebird."

The opening and closing lines of the story are at least partly formulaic, but not unique. Many stories begin with a line that means roughly "a long time ago" ("once upon a time"), but the exact words may vary. Such beginnings, with the line or two that follow them, often serve as a kind of title for the story. But other stories have no such beginning; the narrator plunges right into the story. The penultimate line, "that's all," is one of the most common ways to end a story, but one also often encounters the meaningless kʷalalí (and this may be expanded with another phrase). This last is about the only special vocabulary item encountered in Upper Chehalis stories. There may be peculiar vocabulary items for unusual creatures or phenomena, but their literal meaning is usually transparent; such words, and many novel words, can be readily created by adding lexical suffixes in new patterns. Much modern vocabulary was created in just this way. Lexical suffixes can also be added inappropriately for comic effect.

THE STRUCTURE OF THE TEXT

The story divides easily into three acts: the first takes Bluejay to the Land of the Dead, the second is his attempt to get back home, and the third is the consequences of his death. Each act has five scenes of two stanzas each; the members of each pair of stanzas treat roughly the same or closely related material. There are three exceptions to this pairing: the first scene of each of the first two acts, and Act II, Scene *iv*, where the pairing is doubled in the repetitions of Bluejay's frantic attempts to cross the burning prairies.

The use of three stanzas to begin both Act I and Act II, instead of the usual pairing of stanzas, draws important parallels in these two acts. Each stanza begins with an expression indicating a lengthy period of time. It was probably not deliberate, but the same morphemes are used in both acts, but in opposite orders: in Act I ƛ'áqɬnɬ, q'ačá·, qaxálaxʷ, then in Act II qə́xɬ (which is the base of qaxálaxʷ), q'ačá·, ƛ' áqɬnɬ. It is this striking sequencing which leads me to turn these two scenes into three-stanza sections, although two-stanza alternatives are possible. For this to work out, lines 1–3 can be taken as a combination title and introduction to the drama as a whole; this would be a reasonable device for an untitled story to alert the listener to what is coming. In Act II, lines 118–120 might belong to the following stanza; the plot development would not be disturbed, and in the actual telling there is a significant intonation drop and a pause at the end of line 117, but neither occurs at the end of line 120. As will be seen, however, regular intonation and pause patterns can be overridden for dramatic purposes in the actual performance/telling of the story, and the *húy* at the beginning of line 121 suggests that a stanza is likely to begin there.

The use of húy can easily be seen to have major structural significance. A glance down the left edge of the text will show that the most common word to begin a stanza (indicated by capital letters; all verse and stanza beginnings are at the left margin) is húy; of thirty-five stanzas (counting the Interlude), nineteen begin with húy and another (III.*v*.J) with qas húy. Eight others begin with a time expression (I.*ii*.D and III.*iv*.G, besides the six stanzas of I.*i* and II.*i*), leaving only seven less specifically marked stanza beginnings (even some of these are widely used in other texts: cútn, ?ítu, có·). There are indeed other lines beginning with húy—fourteen of them. All but one of these begin verses, often the last verse of a stanza. The one that does not begin a verse is the second line of a stanza, and both these lines begin with húy. In I.*v*.K, the first four verses (of five) begin with húy, suggesting dramatic emphasis on this stanza, although it is not clear just why this stanza should be emphasized (unless it is simply that it is the last stanza of the act). The last stanza of the second act is similarly emphasized with húy at the beginning of each of its three verses, but here the reason is clear: This is the true climax of the drama. (Another linguistic indication of the significance of this stanza comes through powerfully in listening to a recording of the story, where one can hear the suppression of intonation falls and pauses; this is discussed below in the section on performance.)

Line beginnings are the most varied, but even here there are certain particles which recur frequently (although less in this text than in some others). The most common of these is wi, which is here usually translated as "and," although its meaning is much less specific. Other common line-beginning particles are ?itu/tu (and then), n (and), ?amu (if), có (an exhortative particle), and X̱'áq'ᵂ (well!), but none of these shows significant patterning in this particular text. The best criterion for line divisions is the principle of one main predicate per line.

Besides the three-stanza and time-specification parallels in Scene *i* of Acts I and II, there are other important parallels in these two acts at least through the first stanza of Scene *ii*. In Scene *i*,

Bluejay gets lonesome (Act I) or homesick (Act II) and wants to go somewhere else. Then, in the first stanza of each Scene *ii*, Bluejay is given advice on how to get where he wants to go—by his guardian spirit in Act I and by his sister in Act II. The second of these is done with a long speech by Náw which has some unusual and interesting linguistic features. The two four-line sequences that are here set off as verses (c) and (e) (lines 132–135 and 143–146) are in fact exactly parallel to each other, and mean precisely the same thing. In the first, "five prairies" is expressed in an ordinary way as a phrase; in the second, the words for "five" and "prairie" are combined into a compound word connected by a ligature morpheme. In lines 133 and 144, "cross a prairie" is expressed by two different lexical items with the same meaning. Lines 134 and 145 differ only by the presence of míy (just) in the former. Finally, line 146 is simply a paraphrase of line 135.

The heart of this particular Bluejay story must be the trip back through the burning prairies. It is certainly dramatic, and the narrator uses some very forceful devices to build to the climax of Bluejay's death. Here fives are crucial—so crucial that the narrator repeatedly reminds the listener to keep track of prairies and baskets of water. The first two prairies are not burning at all, but Bluejay mistakes the bright flowers for fire, and wastes two baskets of water. In fact, they are not really said to be burning; the first is described as "it looked like a fire," and fire is not mentioned specifically in regard to the second. But the rest are described as burning, even "blazing," "smoking."

The Interlude functions to remind the listener to count. It specifies that Bluejay "thought" he had crossed two prairies, and "thought" he had two to go. Since he has in fact just crossed two prairies, the listener would surely not have lost count. But he is also implicitly being warned that things are not as they seem, and that the count is not going to come out right. Then, just to make sure that the listener is counting, we are reminded in line 189 that there are two baskets of water left; then, in line 198 that there is one. Following the Interlude is the four-stanza scene, each stanza representing one burning prairie. The fourth is already too many, however, because Bluejay has used up his five baskets of water, and should by now have arrived back home. He manages to beat this fire out and gets across. The next fire is too much for him, however, and here, at the climax of the drama, Bluejay dies, and just because this is the climax, both stanzas of a scene are given over to it.

This central episode of the drama, consisting of the entire second act, is framed by three-scene sequences that again portray exactly parallel events. I.*iii* and III.*i* are roughly equivalent as Bluejay's arrival at the river; I.*iv*.H and III.*ii*.C tell of Bluejay's encountering his nephews and nieces: I.*iv*.I and III.*ii*.D tell of his encountering his brother-in-law; I.*v*.J and III.*iii*.E take him to his sister's house and the people there; and I.*v*.K and III.*iii*.F tell of a dance. Thus, we find the following overall structure:

I.*i*.A	II.*i*.A	III.*i*.A
B	B	B
C	C	
ii.D	*ii*.D	*ii*.C
E	E	D
iii.F	*iii*.F	*iii*.E
G	G	F
iv.H	*iv*.I	*iv*.G
I	J	H
v.J	K	*v*.I
K	L	J
	v.M	
	N	

Boxes are drawn around the parallel three-scene sequences just discussed which constitute the frame around Act II.[27] Within these frames, note how line 66 is inverted into line 270 ("how can my nephews be skulls?" "how can skulls be children?"); and line 76 is inverted into lines 279–280 ("how can my brother-in-law be a skull?," "how can a skull be a high-class person?").

ALTERNATIVE ANALYSIS

Hymes, following the same principles adopted here from him, but with his own intuitions and aesthetic interpretations, has proposed an alternative analysis of this story of Bluejay. While not rejecting the analysis given here, he perceives a somewhat different structure, guided by the occurrence of the introductory particle húy. It is clear that this particle is used in Upper Chehalis narratives as a marker of major divisions within a story. Hymes would see it as regularly setting off stanzas (marked in the text by capital letters); I see it as setting off either stanzas or verses (marked by parenthesized lower-case letters). Taking húy as a stanza marker, Hymes then tries to make sense of the blocks of narrative thus established. His resultant overall structure has three scenes in Act I instead of my five, and his scene divisions within the other two acts are different from mine. By and large, however, our stanza divisions coincide. Hymes's general organization, then, is as follows, giving act, scene, and stanza divisions, and the line numbers which correspond to these divisions (it should be emphasized that this is a tentative, not a definitive, proposal):

I.*i*.A 1–3	II.*i*.A 105–108	III.*i*.A 236–240
B 4–12	B 109–117	B 241–246
C 13–21	C 118–120	C 247–248
D 22–33	D 121–124	*ii*.D 249
E 34–40	E 125–146	E 250–261
ii.F 41–53	*ii*.F 147–150	F 262–265
G 54–56	G 151–160	G 266–269

H 57–69	H 161–163	H 270–271
I 70–73	I 164–167	*iii*.I 272–273
J 74–90	J 168–172	J 274–275
iii.K 91–93	*iii*.K 173	K 276–278
L 94	L 174–184	L 279–280
M 95–97	M 185–194	M 281
N 98–102	N 195–198	*iv*.N 282–285
O 103–104	O 199–203	O 286
	iv.P 204–211	P 287–288
	v.Q 212–223	*v*.Q 289–297
	R 224–225	R 298–305
	S 226–230	S 306–314
	T 231–235	T 315–325
		U 326–327

Hymes recognizes, of course, that the mere occurrence of húy is not enough to justify these divisions, and he makes a number of suggestions to support his proposals. He observes that his Act I, Scene *i* is unified by beginning with the separation of Bluejay and his sister and ending with their reunion. The five stanzas reflect the interlocking onset-continuation-outcome triad which so often occurs in stories of this kind: A is the preface or frame; B is the initiation of the action, the separation; C is the outcome of that and the initiation of a new triad starting as yearning; D is ongoing continuation of C, and E is its outcome. Another such triad occurs in stanza G: Bluejay gets in, crosses, gets out. Other triads occur in stanzas H, I, and J (in these with change of actors in each part of the triad), and one can see other such triads elsewhere in the text. Scene *iii* he sees as a set piece, with its own five-part unity. In Act II, Hymes's divisions put the Interlude at the end of a scene, and conclude the prairies that are not really burning, leaving the actual fires to the next three, fast-moving scenes. And so on.

This brief recapitulation of Hymes's proffered alternative analysis does not do justice to his argumentation, of course, and is presented here in the spirit in which he suggested it—as another way of looking at it. The point is important: different readers react to different features of the presentation, and hence can see different groupings and divisions. Presumably, however, these different approaches will have much in common, and will not detract from the concept of verse structure. In the long run, one analysis should be preferable, and I prefer the one I present here because of the parallels it emphasizes between Bluejay's adventures in the Land of the Dead before and after his death. Comparative evidence presented below suggests further justification for my analysis.

PERFORMANCE

The way the Bluejay story is presented here demonstrates the dramatic structure of the text, following various presentations by Hymes. It differs considerably, then, from the Zuni presentations of Tedlock (1972), which are also designed to show the poetic nature of texts. The difference is one of performance versus competence (to adapt some familiar linguistic terms). Tedlock's format displays a specific performance of stories, and does so admirably. Hymes's format shows how the narrator organizes the stories, and how various parts can interrelate. Both approaches are useful, but it is difficult to combine them into a single presentation. Since Hymes's approach was chosen here, it was necessary to slight the actual performance. So as not to lose touch with this entirely, a few simple orthographic conventions have been adopted to give some indication of how the performance sounded. For this purpose, it is useful to recognize four types of pitch-pause combinations, and use the punctuation in the Upper Chehalis rendition to indicate these (conventional punctuation is retained in the English version, since there is no attempt to indicate performance there).

Only two types of pause are distinguished here: a short one and a longer one, regardless of its actual length (these have not been measured, so the indications are impressionistic). Three final intonations are distinguished: a level one, a rising one, and a falling one. Not all combinations are used, and only four seem significant enough to mark. A pause with no intonation change is indicated with a comma; two commas could indicate a longer pause, but the combination does not occur here. Rising intonation with pause is infrequent, occurring mostly at the beginning of the story (where the pace is generally slower), and only with a short pause; this rising intonation is indicated with a hyphen. Falling intonations with pause are indicated with a period, one period for a short pause, two for a longer pause. By default, lack of marking indicates no intonation change and no pause.

Nearly all stanzas end with falling intonation and a long pause, except in the third act, where most pauses are short (only two are long). There are only two short pauses at stanza ends in each of the first two acts, and Act II also has three stanzas with no pause at all. Although one might argue for different stanza divisions on the basis of pauses, I think that these are varied or omitted for dramatic reasons. It moves the story along more urgently when a pause is overridden. Line ends do not always correspond with pauses either, although fully two-thirds of them do. One striking instance where intonation contours and pauses are clearly omitted deliberately is in II.v.N, where eight of the twelve lines lack them (they are present only at the end of lines 225, 230, 233, and 235). The effect is very dramatic to hear, and it is just at this point that Bluejay is burned to death. The general cadence of Upper Chehalis is rather slow, with marked intonation drops at the ends of sentences; speeding up and omitting drops and pauses is very noticeable.

TRANSLATION

The translation provided here is not intended as an artistic performance. It is my own translation; because Mr. Heck could not hear well, it was not feasible to play the recording of the story back to him to get his exact translation. I have tried to give the content of the Upper Chehalis original, but have made certain systematic changes in order to make it more comprehensible. Upper Chehalis word order puts the predicate first in the sentence, while English puts it second; the order is regularly changed here for the English translation. In dependent and subordinate clauses, Upper Chehalis uses a possessive affix as the subject marker, and these are changed to normal English usage (thus avoiding anything as awkward as a more literal translation of line 107, "everywhere his going" or "his going was everywhere").

Passives are not always translated as such because the progressive passive is an awkward construction in English (e.g., "he is being told by his sister"). Most of the Upper Chehalis narrative uses the continuative (imperfective) aspect for main predicates. The most accurate translation of these forms is into English progressives (e.g., line 8 would be "Bluebird is giving her consent"). But translating them all this way would result in rather cumbersome English, so as a compromise they are translated into an English narrative present—certainly a widely used construction in story-telling. The overall tone of the resulting translation is not altogether satisfying, but it has some justification as a more accurate representation of the aspectual contrasts in the Upper Chehalis original.

No attempt was made to keep line lengths in the translation similar to the Upper Chehalis original. There are two major problems in trying to do so (actually, a remarkable number of lines do come out very nearly the same): One is that by using lexical suffixes (and many other kinds of affixes), Upper Chehalis can incorporate something into a single word which English requires two or three to translate. The other is that it is impossible to equate syllable counts in the two languages; what constitutes a syllable in Upper Chehalis may be quite different from ideas about syllables to an English-speaker. Many consonants in consonant clusters would be pronounced as syllabic (at least at the phonetic level) by a native speaker, and nasals and l are clearly so, even to an English speaker.

The translation of recurrent words, especially particles such as húy and wi, is generally kept consistent; but in a few cases this resulted in such an awkward construction that they were changed. ʔitu begins fifteen lines and its reduced variant tu another nine; it is ordinarily translated as "then" or "and then," and frequently as "when" where that seemed to fit the context better; all fit within the range of meaning this particle may have. One important word that raises particular translation problems is X̣'áq⁺n⁺. It literally means "a long time," but is often used where "a long time ago," "long," "after a while," or "for a while" seems more appropriate. I have not come up with a single translation for it that covers all these possibilities. To confuse the matter further, q'ačá· is here best translated as "a long time," although a more usual translation would be "how much," "how far," or "how long." The translation of line 232 is a guess; I cannot identify the Upper Chehalis word here, and it may be a mispronunciation. A few obvious errors in the original and several errors that Mr. Heck himself corrected have been omitted, but all omissions are indicated in footnotes.

OTHER VERSIONS

A comparison of Silas Heck's version of the Bluejay story with versions told by other speakers of Upper Chehalis and with versions in other languages shows which parts of the story seem indispensable to a narrator, and which may be curtailed or omitted. I have compared the following ten versions:

1. Silas Heck, Upper Chehalis (Oakville dialect), told in Upper Chehalis (from my own field notes).
2. Jonas Secena, Upper Chehalis (Oakville dialect), told in English (Adamson 1934:29).
3. Maggie Pete, Upper Chehalis (Oakville dialect), told in English (Adamson 1934:27–28).
4. Peter Heck (Silas Heck's older brother), Upper Chehalis (Tenino dialect), told in English (Adamson 1934:21–24).
5. Marion Davis, Upper Chehalis (Tenino dialect), told in English (Adamson 1934:24–27).
6. Marion Davis, told in Upper Chehalis (from Boas's field notebooks from 1927).
7. Mrs. Simon Charlie, Satsop, told in English (Adamson 1934:349–350).
8. Lucy Heck (Silas Heck's first wife), Lower Chehalis (Humptulips dialect), told in English (Adamson 1934:293–303).
9. Bob Pope, Quinault, told in English (Farrand 1902:100–102).
10. Charles Cultee, Lower Chinook, told in Lower Chinook and English (Boas 1894:161–171).

These versions vary immensely in length, from only 33 lines (in prose form as given by Adamson) by Mrs. Charlie to 441 lines by Lucy Heck. In order to compare these, the number of lines per episode of the story was counted and then the percentage of the whole which these constituted was figured.

Whether compared in absolute number of lines or in percentages, the differences are striking. Each narrator, except Mrs. Charlie and Bob Pope, included episodes not found in any of the other versions; sometimes these additions are quite long. Marion Davis opens both of his versions with a little tale of Bluejay conniving to examine his sister's vagina (25.6 percent of the English version and 13.3 percent of the Upper Chehalis version). Lucy Heck begins with Bluejay's sister complaining about being bothered by some geese (only 3.4 percent of the total, but given the length of her version, this takes up fifteen lines), and she adds a moral at the end (2.7 percent). Peter Heck has the sister send Bluejay home twice, the first time with a basket of bees, which he manages to let escape, then having to return to the Land of the Dead (19.5 percent). Jonas Secena makes the female protagonist Bluejay's daughter instead of his sister; she sends her baby back with Bluejay, and when he burns to death the baby must also return to her (this return lasts 5.1 percent of the story).

Each version, except those of Bob Pope and Mrs. Charlie, adds details to that part of the story which is devoted to Bluejay's adventures in the Land of the Dead, explaining how everything must be done in some way opposite to actions in the real world: a yawn is perceived as a shout; to see, one must close one's eyes; salmon appears as bark; the dead sleep during the day and are active at night. One popular episode that Silas Heck omits entirely (as do Mrs. Charlie and Maggie Pete) is of a whale that has beached itself, and when Bluejay goes to see it, all he sees is a log (the Lower Chinook version spends 13.6 percent of its time on this episode). The Lower Chinook version also spends 25.5 percent of its time on Bluejay going fishing with his relatives (and 9 percent more on a second fishing trip); Bob Pope gives 12.8 percent to this. Jonas Secena gives 17.9 percent to Bluejay gambling with the ghosts, something no one else mentions. Maggie Pete alone mentions a blue bead that Bluejay takes from a small skeleton (12.3 percent). Only Silas Heck has Bluejay go to a dance before his attempted trip home. Both Maggie Pete (at 27.6 percent) and Lucy Heck (at 19.8 percent) include details of the sister's trip to the Land of the Dead, the details of which are the same as Bluejay's subsequent trip (this may reflect greater interest in the female character on the part of female narrators; Mrs. Charlie also devotes 18.1 percent to the sister's marriage).

The result of these comparisons suggests that there are four main sections to this story. These sections may be expanded with preliminary material (Lucy Heck, Marion Davis), or intermediate episodes (Peter Heck). All must include the sister's marriage (which may be done very briefly); Bluejay's various adventures in the Land of the Dead; Bluejay's attempted trip home through the burning prairies; and Bluejay's return to the Land of the Dead, which ends with him in "Second Death" (a detail omitted by Jonas Secena, Maggie Pete, and Mrs. Charlie). It is instructive to compare the space given to each of these four sections by the various narrators (the figures given are percentages of the total):

	SH	JS	MP	PH	MD-E	MD-C	SC	LH	BP	CC
marriage	3.6	7.7	32.2	4.1	11.1	6.4	18.1	22.2	11.4	1.7
Land of Dead	28.2	51.2	33.7	37.5	37.4	45.6	36.2	43.0	36.8	69.0
prairies	39.7	38.3	23.0	25.8	12.7	16.8	27.2	15.7	22.8	13.0
return	27.9	2.5	10.7	12.7	12.3	17.3	18.1	16.5	28.4	15.3

Clearly, Silas Heck enjoyed telling the last half the best, especially the attempted trip home across the burning prairies. For all the others, Bluejay's adventures in the Land of the Dead were more interesting, while Jonas Secena scarcely mentions anything happening after Bluejay burns to death. These varying percentages illustrate clearly how a narrator might select from the material available and express either his own primary interests or what he considered most instructive for his audience. Silas Heck focused on the burning prairies, and balanced that between descriptions of existence in the Land of the Dead that are roughly equal in length (and, in good part, in content). His sister's marriage is treated briefly, and as the background needed to get on to Bluejay himself and his misadventures.

Marion Davis's Chehalis version also has three acts, but they are made up very differently. He begins with the extraneous prurient interest of Bluejay in his sister and then her marriage; then he spends the longest part of his narration on life in the Land of the Dead. His third act combines the attempted trip home, his return to the Land of the Dead, and his going to Second Death; he spends less time on all this together than Silas Heck did on the attempted trip home. Thus, we can begin to see how Chehalis storytellers shaped their performances.

NOTES

1. My Upper Chehalis texts were collected in the summers of 1960 and 1961 from Silas Heck, who lived on the eastern end of the Chehalis Indian Reservation just out of Oakville, Washington. This work was funded by the American Philosophical Society Library and Indiana University. Although Silas Heck's older brothers and mother spoke Upriver, or Tenino Chehalis, he himself spoke Oakville Chehalis, with a few Upriver words. I thank Joel Sherzer and Anthony Woodbury for inviting me to participate in a workshop on Native American discourse in Austin, Texas, in the spring of 1982, thus forcing me to start analyzing Upper Chehalis (and other) texts. I thank especially Dell Hymes for his long encouragement of me to start this work and his generous comments on my analyses.

2. In fact, I know of only four stories recorded by one other speaker, although a large number were transcribed in Upper Chehalis and English by Franz Boas and Thelma Adamson in 1926 and 1927.

3. But not Northern Lushootseed.

4. Thus Hymes has been motivated to revise some of his analyses of Chinookan stories; see in particular Chapters 3 and 6 of his *"In Vain I Tried to Tell You"* (1981) for a reexamination and reinterpretation of a speech and a set of Coyote stories.

5. For more extensive information on the structure of the language, see Boas 1934 (which is sketchy but basically accurate); Kinkade 1963–1964 (more comprehensive, but badly in need of reworking; I now disagree with a number of statements made there); Kinkade 1976 (on the use of negatives); and Kinkade 1983b (for ideas on the nature of Salishan parts of speech).

6. Vowels may also be drawn out to indicate distance or length of time, as in most languages, and several examples occur in the story. This sort of duration is given special expression in line 161; hm···· (with the m drawn out) indicates nothing else.

7. Heck first says "goes": wi ʔé·nm ʔit q'aɬ swáks. . . skʷáxʷs.

8. He starts the same error: míɬta ʔé·nm t q'aɬ swá. . . kʷáxʷs.

9. There is a hesitation between mэ́y and kʷáxʷ.

10. Heck omits the final s of č'úsus.

11. This line has a false start: n tat . . .

12. Here the periods indicate ellipsis; there is no pause.

13. The š is absorbed into the preceding č.

14. Heck first says kʷáxʷn, and immediately corrects it to kʷáxʷmn.

15. Heck actually says: n kʷxʷáwn š ɬakʷáqʷ.

16. Heck actually says: t spanaqʷáms.

17. The pause here is only hesitation, and the ɬ may be an error.

18. Heck again starts to say panaqʷámitn: č'úsus pan . . . swáks wétqʷm.

19. Heck starts a modal construction: q'iɬ . . . ɬunáqitn t sэ́xtkʷlals.

20. Heck makes two corrections in this sentence, still gets the inflection on the predicate wrong, and leaves out the ɬ: n ʔiλ' . . . t ɬícšn tat qá·ʔ . . . tat sq'ʷэ́t'wn tat qá·ʔ.

21. Heck leaves off qʷasúqʷaʔ, "basket."

22. Heck actually says: ʔaɬ t c'э́čɬ tanin t. . . tat qʷasúqʷaʔ.

23. Heck starts the sentence wrong: cwé·x. . . míɬta tanin t qʷasúqʷaʔs.

24. Heck corrects himself in the middle of this sentence: húy sá·wn t wácšn ʔaɬ tatxtá. . . ʔaɬ tat skʷэ́ss tanin.

25. Heck starts to say "five times" here, then corrects himself: cílčstašn. . . músaɬšn t syác'tut ɬ tac yá·yn's.

26. Heck mispronounces this last word as t'asyác's.

27. Harry G. Edinger, a colleague in the University of British Columbia Department of Classics, has pointed out to me that this frame bears a striking resemblance to the "ring composition" of Pindaric odes, in which the central third is framed by adjacent segments of the outer thirds.

REFERENCES

Adamson, Thelma. 1934. *Folk-Tales of the Coast Salish*. American Folk-Lore Society Memoir 27. New York: American Folk-Lore Society.

Boas, Franz. 1894. *Chinook Texts*. Bureau of American Ethnology Bulletin 20. Washington, D.C.: Government Printing Office.

———. 1927. Chehalis Field Notes. Manuscript in American Philosophical Society Library, Philadelphia.

———. 1934. A Chehalis Text. *International Journal of American Linguistics* 8: 103–110.

Farrand, Livingston. 1902. *Traditions of the Quinault Indians*. New York:

American Museum of Natural History Memoir 4, Part 3. (Publications of the Jesup North Pacific Expedition.)

Hymes, Dell. 1981. *"In Vain I Tried to Tell You."* Essays in Native American *Ethnopoetics.* Philadelphia: University of Pennsylvania Press.

Kinkade, M. Dale. 1963–1964. Phonology and Morphology of Upper Chehalis. *International Journal of American Linguistics* 29(3):181–195; 29(4): 345–356; 30(1):32–61; 30(3):251–260.

———. 1976. The Copula and Negatives in Inland Olympic Salish. *International Journal of American Linguistics* 42(1):17–23.

———. 1983*a*. Daughters of Fire: Narrative Verse Analysis of an Upper Chehalis Folktale. In North American Indians: Humanistic Perspectives, ed. James S. Thayer. *Papers in Anthropology* (University of Oklahoma Department of Anthropology) 24(2):267–278.

———. 1983*b*. Salish Evidence against the Universality of "Noun" and "Verb." *Lingua* 60:25–40.

———. 1984. "Bear and Bee": Narrative Verse Analysis of an Upper Chehalis Folktale. In *1983 Mid-America Linguistics Conference Papers,* ed. David S. Rood. Pp. 246–261. Boulder: Department of Linguistics, The University of Colorado.

Tedlock, Dennis. 1972. *Finding the Center.* Lincoln: University of Nebraska Press.

Telling The Tale:
A Performance Analysis of a
Hopi Coyote Story

ANDREW WIGET

A great part of the pleasure found in any literature, oral or written, derives from its ability to transport audiences into an alternate reality, all the while assuring them that they have never left home. The skills of the storyteller are aimed almost exclusively at creating and sustaining the dynamic collaboration between audience and storyteller which results in a satisfying and significant verbal performance. One purpose of this essay is to suggest the severe limitations which we impose upon ourselves by approaching oral literature in "text" form. More important, however, I hope to illustrate, through a close examination of a particular performance, how the use of performance theory to describe a storytelling event can help us achieve a richer understanding of the social and aesthetic values of oral literature.

"I'ISAU AND THE BIRDS"
BY HELEN SEKAQUAPTEWA

The performance from which the transcriptions and illustrations below derive was recorded on videotape by a crew from the University of Arizona under the direction of Larry Evers, and is available from Clearwater Publishing Co. as part of a series of videotapes entitled, *Words & Place: Native Literature from the American Southwest.*[1]

The performance was recorded in the home of Helen Sekaquaptewa in New Oraibi on the evening of December 20, 1976. In addition to grandchildren present on-camera, other relatives were present off-camera, including her son Emory Sekaquaptewa, an anthropologist at the University of Arizona. A printed commentary providing background on the genre and the performance accompanies the videotape, as well as a transcript of the English language subtitles produced for the videotape. The subtitle-transcript is not a word-for-word rendering. However, Larry Evers was kind enough to provide me with a transcript of the Hopi, produced by Emory Sekaquaptewa and Allison Lewis, one of Helen Sekaquaptewa's daughters. Having had sufficient formal training in Hopi to attend to basic elements of lexicon and sentence structure—though certainly not enough to attempt anything like a total translation—I was able to modify the transcript at the level of lines or phrases and to bring it more in harmony with the Hopi-language transcript of the performance.

In the script which follows, I have adopted a method of representation similar to that proposed by Dennis Tedlock, marking volume changes (from an unmarked baseline through a *second,* THIRD and *FOURTH* level), pitch changes ("di^{ic}ed"), and pauses (suggested by spaces between lines; runover lines are idented).[2] The beginnings and endings of distinct gestures were marked by enclosing a number so: 2> and <2. I should emphasize here some points that I will later reiterate: such a script approximates the performance at best; it is designed only as an instrument of analysis; and it is certainly no substitute for the videotape which constitutes the primary text.

DIANE: Do you not have a /tuuwutsi/ for us, our grandmother?

HS: Yes, well, a short one, I will tell you a short /tuwuutsi/,

ummm. . . .

AUD: Aliksa'i (prompting)
HS: ALIKSA'I
AUD: owi

HS: "oo" you must say, louder
ALIKSA'I, you are not answering

AUD: OWI

HS: It is known that the storyteller is touchy. If
you do not answer she may pout and
[10] not tell a story.

AUD: 'wi

(0:24) HS: It is said at ORAIbi there was LIVing.
AUD: 'wi
WS: Well, as a matter of *fact,* people *lived* there, and

over there

well, many *birds,* it is said, were *around* there.
And, then,
well, they would *fly* around there in their usual
way 1>and LIKE SO
they would fly around.<1
well, they would, when it got on towards winter,
prepare
[20] to store FOOD.

Aud: owi . . . 'wi

HS: And that's because all kinds of GRASSes then

WOULD MATURE.

Then they would go about below their vill . . .
vill . . . village,
and also 2>even higher up along where things
GREW in abundance,
there where the mesa has a ledge

and <2
when the grass seeds

299

[30]   *MATURED,* then they would go about
                  like so
                  picking them.
                  Small PLAQUES 3> they had and, it is said,
                    into them
                  they would harvest. Like this

                  the bean,
                  the seeds, I mean, when they gathered them<3

                  4>THEY themselves would then assemble
                  together
(1:27)   there, then, like you,

                  circ . . .

[40]   Aud: in a circle (prompting)
        HS: in a circle

                  they would sit around<4
                  Then with their plaques filled, thus

                  5>they would rub the seeds and CRUSH the
                    husks.   <5

        AUD: owi . . . 'wi
        HS: 6>It is said *then* they would move all their
                    plaques like so.
                  It is said *then* they would SING while
                  WINnowing.

                  So they say.

                  TRUE it is that WORKing at something is
                    TIREsome,
[50]   and so they would always take up SINGing to
                    thus
                  break up the routine.

                  It is for this reason all of them toGEther

                  would settle around, it is said, and SING, they
                    say.

Perhaps you most likely know this *song:*<6

AUD: owi

HS:
6> Pota, pota, po-ta,
pota, pota, po-ta,
yowa'ini,   yowa'ini,
ph', ph', ph', ph'<6

[60]

and, they say, as they DID this, then the
HUSKS there

7>would FLY away<7

AUD: 'wi . . .

HS: This DONE

then they would put the seeds in something

Then again they would GAther more around
there.
They would crush them; *then* they would rePEAT
this.

(2:33)

All day they did that and each time they would
SING:

6>   Pota, pota, po-ta
pota, pota, po-ta
yowa'ini,   yowa'ini,
ph', ph', ph', ph'<6

It is said THAT *is what they were doing*

when I'isau
somewhere from the south side climbed up

AUD: 'wi

HS: And, it is said, that was *ORAI*bi

the big rock. 8>Are you not fa*mili*ar with it,
Oraibi? <8

[audience member shakes head]

That, in fact, is Oraibi, that BIG rock,
STANding so <9>

[80]   Ah, the VILlage, The village, towards its south
side, from there,

it's said, while hidden, he secretly PEERed at
them

(3:08)   AUD: Um . . . hm . . .

         HS: while they were WINnowing.

Well, as we know,

such creatures go around perPETually hungry,
and probably

he went to the TRASHpile LOOKING for
something, perhaps

SOMEthing, bones maybe,

such as people are apt to throw away.

AND that is what he was looking for, and why
he CLIMBED up, and when

he *HAPpened on them, then he THOUGHT: "I wish
that I could*

(3:30)   [90]   *kill some of these and thus*

enJOY a good snack."

So THIS is what he was thinking as he
WATCHED them.

         AUD: 'wi

         HS: And

well, at first, he decided not to SHOW himself to
THEM

but UNABLE TO RE*STRAIN* HIMSELF, HE
AP*PROACH*ED THEM.

WHEN THEY SAW HIM, AT FIRST THEY
WANTED

TO *FLEE. "I wouldn't do ANYthing
to HURT you,"* he said to them. [smiles]

302

[100]   *"For truly,* you are so delightful to watch,
         that is why I've come to you."

(4:02)   Maybe

         maybe I *can JOIN you?"*
         When he had said this to them

         well then, they looked at each other, like this
         <10>
         as though seeking apPROval from one another.

         It's said ALL of them appeared to conSENT,
         so he sat down with them.

         so too a PLAQUE they provided him,
         and so also he DID there what they were doing.

[110]   AUD: um . . . 'wi
       HS: It is said
                once more THEN *they too* FILLED *their* PLAQUES
                    and again THEY SANG
                Well, I'isau, as we might guess, did not yet
                    KNOW THE SONG,
                they say, [smiles]

                And, for this reason, he could not IMITATE
                    them.

(4:36)   Again they sang:

                6>   Pota, pota, po-ta,
                    pota, pota, po-ta,
                    yowa'ini, yowa'ini
[120]   ph', ph', ph', ph'<6
         [giggles]
         so, *they would DO like this,* THEY WOULD
                THEN SET THEIR PLAQUES DOWN.
         Then, it is said, THEY WOULD *FLY*
         11>HIGH UP SOMEWHERE.
(5:00)   For some time, it is said, they would *do* this, and
         then *come* down<11

And I'isau, not being a feathered 12>creature,
well the poor thing looked on longingly>12 being
    *un*able to *fly*.
with them. And they having *GONE* so far away,
    there was no *pos*sibility
that he could catch up with them.

AUD: 'wi
HS: And

[130]   *When* they came down, they did the very same
                thing.
            so *then*:

            'Maybe I *could*' [I'isau to himself]. "Couldn't
                you then give me some of
            your feathers and some of your d*own*, then
                perhaps I might *fly* with you,"
            he said to them.

AUD: 'wi

HS: *Then* they con*sen*ted.

            Then, it is said, since they had done so, they, the
                birds, from
            themselves
(5:30)   13>began *pluck*ing their *fea*thers<13
            and then, it is said, on I'isau

[140]   wherever they had *plucke*d a *feath*er from their
                bodies, in the same
                    place they put it on him.
            14>It is said this is how they placed them
            on I'isau.<14 AFter

            there were enough to *cov*er him

            *t*hen they *started* again,

            *t*hen, it is said,

            they filled them, then they re*peate*d:

304

[150]

6> Pota, pota, po-ta
pota, pota, po-ta
yowa'ini, yowa'ini,
ph', ph', ph', ph'<6

AUD(ES):   I'isau was happy then? . . .
HS: He took *great* delight *with* them,

Then it is said he LEARNED the song quickly,

So, it is said, they *all* set their plaques down
*a*round,
(6:00)   and *then*, it is said,

15> Tsii-
ii
roo-
oot<15

They would say, and *up* they . . .
And it happened that I'isau flew up with them
[giggles]

[160]

And not just ONCE with them did he fly up.
Then, when he flew up.

it is said,

the LAST time

I MEAN <16>

on the *fourth* <17> time it happened,

on the fourth occasion,
THEN, IT IS SAID

the birds among themselves secretly
(6:30)   whispered<18>

[170]   "Now do it. Now's the time," they said.
[she giggles]

Then, once more, for the last time,
again, they flew up,
again, they went even higher:
      15>   Tsii-
               ii-
                    roo-
                          oot<15

As they said this and glided about, I'isau

it is said 19>*gli*ded about *with* them<19
[audience giggles]

And then, the birds gathered *all* together,
saying, "Let's begin! Now's the time!" and so
saying,

[180]   *then* they closed in on him, and that which was
       his own, each
there he PLUCKED off <20>

whichever feather he had given that he
    PLUCKED off<21>

TAIL feathers

DOWNY feathers

(7:00)   *ALL of them* they plucked off

THEN poor I'isau, *down* he *CAME,*
22> TUMbling over and over like so, and
landed somewhere<22

be*low,*
and the poor thing [tensile voice] di^{ie}ed.

[giggles all around]

[190]   When they came down there, it is said, they
      LAUGHED at him, they said,

"*THUS* you see how it is. This is the fault of

your own heart, because
of your doings,"
like,

"Among us you came *think*ing to eat us,"

(7:35)   it is said they said.
"We thought if we killed you first you would not
eat us,"

it is said they said.

Then from that time on they worked and gathered
alone.

So then it seems *MOST likely* that

they gathered much food there *that* day.

[200]   And *so* it ends.

[HS smiles. Audience reacts. She giggles.]

(7:57)   [in English] It was quite long. I thought it was
short.

TEXT AND PERFORMANCE TRADITION

Genre and Form

Most folklorists would identify the preceding narrative as a folktale. The Hopi word for the genre, /tuuwutsi/, is compounded of two elements: /-wutsi/, which signifies something purely imagined or "make believe," and /tuu-/, which denominates a class of "unspecified, nonhuman objects." As Ekkehart Malotki concludes, "the overall content of /tuuwutsi/ thus adds up to something like 'many false or make-believe things.'"[3] This may seem, at least initially, to indicate a congruence between the folklorist's analytical category and the Hopi ethnic genre.[4] In fact, the /tuuwutsi/ can be seen to carry more meaning for the Hopi than "folktale" communicates to

us, especially when we realize that storytelling at Hopi has traditionally been guarded by a number of restrictions—principally that
restricting storytelling to the season of frost—which must be considered as nonverbal components of any definition of /*tuuwutsi*/.
Reasons for these restrictions will be suggested in the performance
analysis below. Since no such restrictions encumber the Western
notion of the folktale, however, we can only conclude that the Hopis
understand stories, even when they are "false" or "make believe,"
to bear a relationship to the world of experience different from that
of Western folktales. Folklorists might further classify this tale as a
particular kind of folktale known as the *cante fable,* a story marked
by a recurring song. Assessing the relative value of the song's
relationship to both plot and performance is central to appreciating
the tale.

Based on those recurrent actions which define the main lines
of the plot,[5] one can identify several previous tales collected from
Hopis, and at least one from a Zuni, as versions of the same basic
story which I here entitle Coyote and the Birds. These previously
recorded versions, especially those recorded prior to World War II,
frequently include elements of a tale that has been titled Forgetting
the Song. Versions of Coyote and the Birds available for this study
include:[6]

1903	Oraibi (Hopi, Third Mesa)	Recorded by H. R. Voth from Qoyawaima.
1912	Shumopovi (Hopi, Second Mesa)	Recorded by Wilson D. Wallis, from a forty-two-year-old Carlisle student in Philadelphia. Two related stories.
1920	Hano, Tewa (Hopi, First Mesa)	Recorded by E. C. Parsons, from a man whose work she judged highly variable.
1920	San Juan (NM) Tewa	Recorded from a well-known story-teller.
1965	Zuni (NM)	Recorded by Dennis Tedlock from Andrew Peynetsa who was known for telling short stories. January 20.

1968   Moencopi (Hopi)   Recorded by Harold Courlander from
                                       Louis Numkena, Sr.

Only the Tedlock version has previously been published in scripted form—twice in fact, in 1972 and 1978.[7] Comparison of the texts enables us to place them in some kind of relationship to each other on the basis of two elements: variations in the content and function of the song, and the degree to which motifs from the Forgotten Song story are included.

The Song

As in all *cantes fables,* nothing is so immediately striking about these stories as the recurrent song. Yet in the second Shumopovi story the song occurs only as part of the Forgotten Song episode and is not associated with Coyote's flight or fall; in the San Juan version of the story there is no song at all. The Hano and Oraibi versions have songs that resemble each other: Both invoke I'isau (Coyote) twice in the opening line; both refer to the dance motions of his flight ("drop down," "up down"); and both imitate the call of the birds, though with different vocables. Despite their resemblance, however, the Hano and Oraibi songs are entirely different from Helen Sekaquaptewa's song, which strangely enough appears to be more closely related to the song recorded by Tedlock as part of his Zuni story:

> HS: Pota, pota, pota
>   Pota, pota, pota
>   Yowa'ini, yowa'ini
>   ph, ph, ph, ph
>
> Zuni: Yuwahina, yuwahina
>   Yuwahina, yuwahina
>   yohina, yohina, ph, ph
>   yohina, yohina, ph, ph

Tedlock asserts that the song is composed of "vocables which have no meaning."[8] One might assume that he or the Zuni storyteller would be able to identify Hopi words since the same storyteller did so in another tale. Evers-Sekaquaptewa-Lewis translate the words:

> Plaque, plaque, plaque
> Plaque, plaque, plaque
> that which is contained, that which is contained
> ph, ph, ph, ph

These are all minor points, however. What is important is that the song doesn't really contribute substantively to the story line— they seldom do in cantes fables—and consequently it is free to vary without altering plot construction. This explains Helen's comment that "other tellers use other songs," one even using a Navajo song.[9] However interesting all these variations may be for the folklorist, then, the song is not diagnostic of this story as a type; nor does it advance the plot or condition the content of the narration in any way. The story which Louis Numkena, Sr., told to Harold Courlander only refers to singing at pivotal moments, but Numkena does not actually sing a song. Such omissions, however much they diminish audience involvement, do not alter plot. The aesthetic value the song has for the narrator and the audience—for it obviously is a focus of interest—must lie in some other sphere, one whose impact is not felt on the page in any particular linguistic form, be it "pota, pota, pota," or "yowahini, yowahini," or "plaque, plaque, plaque."

The Story

Variations in the tale itself are also not significant in terms of plot. The Zuni and Shumopovi stories are very similar because they share the deception surrounding the Forgotten Song story. In this story Coyote accosts either Grasshopper (Shumopovi 1), Tsiro the Horned Lark (Shumopovi 2), or Junco (Zuni), and asks to be taught the song each sings. The other animal complies graciously, but on the way home Coyote forgets the song and returns to ask again. After several repetitions of this sequence, the exasperated instructor leaves the scene, but not after first leaving behind a rock of a form and color like her own. Coyote returns, and when the rock doesn't answer he becomes frustrated, bites the rock in anger, and breaks his teeth.

This episode forms no part of stories gathered in San Juan, Old Oraibi, or New Oraibi. It is incorporated into Shumopovi 2 preceding the Coyote's Flight story in a short cycle of two tales, but the first episode does not precipitate the second—as usual, Coyote simply "goes along" between incidents. Instead they seem linked thematically, both affirming Coyote's own identity by denying him the ability to perform actions reserved by nature to others. There may also be a kind of "image harmony" in which the use of birds as protagonists in one episode suggests a similar strategy in the next. But such processes and themes are so widespread in Trickster tales—witness the Bungling Host stories—that they too are hardly significant. Again, in terms of plot line and theme, Helen Sekaquaptewa's story is not distinctive. Since Shumopovi is a village with strong Zuni affiliation, we might hypothesize on the basis of the variants that the story came to Hopi from Zuni, or vice-versa.[10]

One might look to metanarrative explanations of Coyote's behavior to discover theme, but again one would be frustrated. The Zuni tale adds an explanatory element to make the tale of the crunched teeth "explain" why Coyotes have no molars, but which "explains" nothing folkloristically or anatomically. Like Helen Sekaquaptewa's story, Shumopovi 2 and Old Oraibi suggest "poetic justice" as a plot motivator: Trickster gets tricked because he often goes about trying to hurt others. The San Juan version suggests a plot by the birds to kill Coyote so that they may eat his eyes after he dies of falling from a leap in mid-air. All of these "explanations" only show that, beyond the most general theme, the significance of the tale is whatever the reader or raconteur wants it to be, a point Waterman made in 1914.[11] In this, too, Helen's tale is not distinctive. She does adapt her tale for a more specific focus, illustrating the perils of avoiding work and asserting with all the seriousness of Herbert Hoover, though in a more palatable manner, that "there is no free lunch." Thus, Helen affirms the strong Hopi work ethic. Anyone who has read her autobiography, *Me and Mine*,[12] will no doubt recognize the theme as a congenial one for her. She has raised a family of achievers, including among her children a past tribal chairman, the editor of the tribal newspaper, and a professional anthropologist.

Having said all this what, in fact, have we said? To state that Sekaquaptewa is "typically Hopi" in her concern for the value of work is an observation accurate in essence but reductive, lacking the particulars and context that would make it truly significant. To say that the several versions of the story are "related" is so unhistorical a statement as to be inconsequential; we may suggest but are ultimately unable to explain how they came to be related, why they should be related, and what the significance of these relationships is. A morphology, after all, is neither a historical nor an aesthetic statement. Perhaps most important, however interesting these issues are to Hopis and others on the level of analysis,[13] they do not seem to be the engrossing factor which occupies the attention of the audience, and that is what we must be primarily interested in.

Text and Performance

The impasse is a familiar one. Folklorists who pay special attention to Native American traditions encountered it in Alan Dundes's observation that in Indian oral literatures "myth and folktale are not structurally distinct genres. The distinction between them is wholly dependent upon content criteria and totally external factors such as belief and function."[14] In effect Dundes was asserting that the structural matters which were of central concern to the folklorist in distinguishing genres were not the distinctive features for the people who generated the narratives, who themselves seemed more preoccupied with "incidentals," "details," and "external" or extra-textual matters. It was a conclusion Dundes underscored in distinguishing between Text, which is essentially paraphraseable content capable of structural analysis; Texture, the linguistic and paralinguistic dimensions of the oral performance which are often forfeited in the translation of Text; and Context, the social situation in which the performance takes place.[15] This distinction is valuable precisely because it highlights the almost exclusive dependence of folklorists and other students of oral literature on Text, the paraphraseable verbal component. This dependence is exacerbated by structural analysis which admits no absolute relationship between Text and Texture, and which, in order to effect comparison, further reduces Text from the paraphrase*able* to the paraphras*ed* content. The former, which is the actual textured text of the performance, it accounts at best a version, at worst an idiosyncrasy; the latter, in truth an after-the-fact abstraction, is considered the never-told-but-yet-dimly-perceived "base tale" from which all stories take their point of departure.[16]

As Barbara Herrnstein Smith has pointed out, this problematic interpretive framework, the genesis of which stretches back through Russian Formalism to Saussurian structural linguistics, has spawned a number of paired terms which however differently nuanced are nevertheless close approximations of each other: "'deep structure' and 'surface manifestation,' 'content plaine' and 'expression plaine,' '*histoire* and *recit*,' '*fabula*' and '*szujet*,' and 'signified' and signifier."[17] Each of these pairs derives its explanatory power from its adherents' prior assumptions about the nature of language. In particular, advocates of such terms consistently distinguish between what they call "normal," "merely" referential, "ordinary" language on the one hand (language in which the linguistic sign represents an equivalency between the concept and the object to which it refers) and on the other hand, a "diseased, aberrant, poetic" language in which this equivalency is replaced by either an overdetermined sign, encumbered by prior usages, or by an insufficiently motivated sign, which falls short of fully expressing the object it is meant to represent. Interpretation is then required in order to account for the difference between an overdetermined or impoverished poetic language and the reality to which it is intended to point. Such a critical posture is inevitably reductive. Helen Sekaquaptewa's story would be reduced to the core of incidents which it shares with other "versions" of the hypothesized base tale, establishing differences as residue or excess which requires explanation in terms of what the storyteller *should* have done, and interpreting her motives for deviating.[18]

Smith and other literary critics, like Stanley Fish and Mary Louise Pratt,[19] have found some utility in an alternate view of language, one which asserts that a significant dimension of the value of every linguistic sign is determined by the situation in which it is uttered. Far from being a static, self-explaining system—an object—language is both object and act, or more precisely an object whose nature is action. Apart from being uttered, its existence is "denaturalized," purely imaginary, and our debates merely reflections on an abstraction. In such a speech-act approach to literature, Smith believes, individual narratives would not be described as sets of surface discourse signifiers that represent (actualize, manifest, map or express) sets of underlying story signifieds, but as verbal acts of particular narrators performed in response to—and thus shaped and constrained by—sets of multiple and interacting conditions.[20]

At almost every conceptual moment this perspective must evoke a shock of recognition from folklorists and anthropologists who approach folklore as performance, and who find in the "thick description" of a tale's texture and context, as fostered by the ethnography of speaking, the native grounds of interpretability and aesthetic satisfaction. Performance theory insists on seeing stories as "storytelling events" in which "texts constitute nothing more than a written representation of one aspect of the message of communicative events."[21] Performance, as Erving Goffman and others have asserted, is simply one of many ways in which a communication may be framed. Through markers, not all of which are verbal and capable of typographic representation, a frame signals to the receiver that a message of a particular kind is being sent which must be interpreted in a particular way in order to be intelligible.[22] Richard Bauman, allying himself with speech-act theorists, goes so far as to question whether there is any such thing as unconditioned communication; that is, communication with an entirely referential content which occurs so frequently that it can be called normal, and in light of which all other speech acts are judged abnormal, nonstandard, artistic.[23]

This conclusion expresses in principle what Toelken learned by experience on questioning a Navajo singer's treatment of him:

> I was being treated for red ants in my system which I had no doubt picked up by urinating on an ant-hill. Some time after the ritual, which was quite successful I must point out, I had occasion to discuss the treatment with the singer: had I really had ants in my system did he think? His answer was a hesitant, "no, not ants, but Ants." Finally, he said, "We have a way of thinking strongly about disease."[24]

In this instance the hesitation between the two pronunciations of the word "ants" worked with the stressed second pronunciation (which Toelken indicated with capitalization) to create a metaphor that linked the two concepts linguistically under the same verbal form ("ants") but disassociated them paralinguistically. This metaphorizing, accomplished by a momentary increase in volume and stress, shifted the frame of communication from the referential or "scientific-objective" plane on which the question was asked, to the theological one on which it was answered. The possibility of such a shift was probably suggested by Toelken's asking for the "real" answer.

All communication, then, is framed, and it becomes imperative to understand the signals or "keys" which tell us what frame is being invoked so that we can properly interpret the discourse. Dell Hymes distinguished, for example, between the frames of reporting and performing, and further between performing and performing in a perfunctory key.[25] In its communicative aspect, Bauman argues, performance is not different from other frames in establishing a relationship with a specific audience under specific conditions:

> Fundamentally, performance as a mode of spoken verbal communication consists in the assumption of responsibility for a display of communicative competence. This competence rests on the knowledge and ability to speak in socially appropriate ways. Performance involves on the part of the performer an assumption of accountability to an audience for the way in which communication is carried out, above and beyond its referential content.[26]

Though Goffman offers a definition of performance that differs in its lack of "accountability," both Goffman and Bauman affirm that oral performance exists before an audience in a relationship that has several levels, of which the text, or verbal component, is only one and not necessarily the most important.[27]

Because performance is framed in such a way that it is set apart from "the continua of communication" for the sake of the audience, it is, in spite of Goffman's objections, "subject to evaluation for the way in which it is done, for the relative skill and effectiveness of the performer's display of competence."[28] The necessary role of the audience, both in evaluating and in eliciting displays of competence, is only now being clearly understood. Inadequate texts are not simply the result of poor transcription techniques by pencil-pushing ethnographers who interrupted storytellers after every phrase so that they could transcribe it. There are some things that even high technology cannot diminish. Toelken tells of his experience listening to his tapes of Yellowman's stories:

It is quite obvious from the tapes made of his stories when no children were present that the audience plays a central role in the narrative style; without an audience, his tales are almost entirely lacking in special intonation, changes in speed, pacing, and dramatic pauses. . . . Speaking in solitude to a tape-recorder, Yellowman gives a rather full synopsis of characters and incidents; the narrative drama, far from being memorized, emerges in response to the bona fide storytelling context.[29]

Such situations help us appreciate Hymes's distinction between performance and performance "in a perfunctory key." And when we think of the hesitancy which Regna Darnell's Cree raconteur felt about broaching what were to him obscene matters in the presence of his daughter,[30] we understand how much of a factor the audience can be in influencing not simply the style but even the content of a story.

Of course, in the case of Helen Sekaquaptewa's videotaped performance, the intrusion of cameras, auxiliary light and sound equipment, and the technical crew must be assumed to have had some impact on the setting. Yet, without diminishing that impact, it must also be said that "ideal" or "natural" performance contexts probably are nonexistent, if by "ideal" or "natural" we mean a setting that demands no accommodation from the performer. Performers not only can but they also regularly do accommodate themselves to a variety of settings and audiences; it is how they do so, not whether they appear to be required to, that ought to be the principal concern. Darnell's storyteller, for example, achieves a remarkable innovation in performance in order to accommodate white members of the audience.

Indeed, the performance exists for the audience as much or more than for the performer, who assumes responsibility for a *display* of narrative competence *before them*. Part of the measure of his competence is dependent upon his ability to create certain narrative features (Goffman calls them "engrossables")[31] that involve the audience in the act of narration. Bauman believes that there is a "heightened intensity of communicative interaction which binds the audience to the performer in a way that is specific to performance as a mode of communication." Whether or not engrossment is specific to performance as a mode of communication, it is undoubtedly part of the game: "Through his performance,"

Bauman continues, "the performer elicits the participative attention and energy of his audience, and to the extent that they value his performance, they will allow themselves to be caught up in it."[32] This restructuring of roles is part of the storyteller's power, a power that is certainly at the heart of Helen's success as a storyteller.

These remarks about audience, style, and form suggest something even deeper, what Bauman calls the "emergent quality" of performance.[33] What the story is—an artistic creation that both expresses and defines a genre—is finally only available in performance. In performance several realities come into being; restructured social roles, redefinition of genre, a stylistically unique linguistic creation, all emerge simultaneously. The consequences of such an outlook are profound, as Yellowman made clear to Toelken:

> Among other questions, I asked him how he would recognize the difference between a Coyote story and someone talking about Coyote if he were to hear only part of the total text; I asked if it would be possible, by listening to a tape recording, to detect the difference between a Coyote story told within a myth, during a chant, or to someone's family. To the first question, he replied that conversations about Coyote would not use the "ancient" words one would associate with the tales; at least subject matter is not distinctive. To the second, he replied that Coyote stories would be told about the same way under all circumstances, but that one might detect differing kinds of audience reaction. On these and other topics it became increasingly clear to me that Yellowman sees the Coyote stories not as narratives (in our sense of the term) but as dramatic presentations performed within certain cultural contexts for moral and philosophical reasons. He does not place, therefore, the materials in a separate category excepting only with respect to the way they are performed; that is, his central consideration is not one of structure/genre but of texture/mode, not because he is unaware of genre (for he distinguishes clearly among song, ceremonial chant, story and oratory), but because in the case of the Coyote materials genre distinctions are far less relevant than are those textural keys which allow the listeners to gain access to important levels of meaning.[34]

Inaccessible to the text-oriented scholar in all this are many of the marks of style which signal not only the competence or incompetence of the performer but also the aesthetic value of the perfor-

mance in native eyes. It becomes critical, therefore, to secure videotape records of performances as primary "texts." These enable the
viewer to examine the co-occurrence of verbal and nonverbal dimensions of performance, especially paralinguistic features like changes
in pitch, stress, volume, and tone, and kinesic features like gestures
and facial expressions. By adding these to notations of setting and
social context, a fuller script can be produced for the sake of
analysis. Never to be confused with the primary "text," scripts like
that reproduced in this essay can nevertheless provide a better
instrument for understanding interrelated dimensions of performance than transcriptions modeled on prose narrative.

A PERFORMANCE ANALYSIS

Nonverbal Frames: Environment, Role, and Audience

We can best begin our analysis of Helen Sekaquaptewa's performance by looking at those elements which set it apart from conventional discourse, which frame it and signal to us that a performance
of a special kind of verbal art is taking place. The frame is designed
both to mark and to transport us across a boundary between two
forms of discourse, a boundary that exists in several dimensions.
As a result, the frame itself is multidimensional, involving many
nonverbal features such as specific natural environments and the
assumption of particular social roles.[35] We see both of these in the
present performance.

ENVIRONMENTAL FRAME

It is told in the evening, during the month of /kyaamuya/, the month
of the winter solstice, which is an important moment of transition
in the ritual calendar and a time especially favored for telling
stories, not only at Hopi and other Puebloan communities but also
throughout Native America.[36] Malotki notes that Hopis also refer
to the month as /tuwutsmuyaw/ or "storytelling month," and that in
the past

storytelling happened nearly every evening during /kyaamuya/. Whole households came together for the occasion, and everybody from small children to great grandparents was present. Occasionally every grown-up member in the audience would contribute his own story. The Hopi language provides a special term for this custom—/tuwutsqoniwma/—which says "story turning in a circle."[37]

Of her own childhood, Helen Sekaquaptewa recalls:

This time [December] is set apart for teaching the young. The uncles (mother's brothers) go to the homes of their sisters in the evening to teach her children. An uncle is treated with respect, and the family gathers around to listen as he tells about the advent of the Hopi, recites traditions and prophecies, and gives instruction. One special night in December, the night for the storyteller, I looked forward to. A good storyteller would be invited to come and tell the stories that go with the traditions. There would be special refreshments, and we liked it.[38]

Coyote stories in particular are properly told at night during the season of frost or snow, because "whoever tells a story in summertime will be bitten by a rattlesnake."[39] The injunction against summertime storytelling and the association of storytelling with the winter solstice may stem from a belief that telling a story is a creative activity that has the power to restructure the world being spoken of, and that the safest time to tell stories is when the sun is coming to a standstill in the sky, to be turned back toward spring.

ROLE-SWITCHING

In this performance, Helen Sekaquaptewa appears in several roles.[40] She has a prominent *social role* as matriarch of the Eagle clan gathered together to hear her this evening.[41] In this setting, her role helps to validate Helen as a competent and legitimate communicator of traditions. Yet, in relationship to the traditions themselves she is also, like the members of her audience, an inheritor. Accommodation to her status as communicator is signaled by the formal request for a story and by the deferential posture of those about her, while her neutral storytelling posture diminishes her authoritative presence and stresses her identification with the audience as a means of developing collaboration, then engrossment.

In addition to her social role, Helen plays a *narrative role*. Adoption of this role is marked in the beginning by her assumption of responsibility for performance of a specific kind, /tuwuutsi/, when she responds affirmatively to the request for a story. The role is maintained throughout the story by metanarration—her own comments about the story, which signal self-consciousness of her role as narrator. Finally, she takes a *narrated role*, assuming the identity of characters within the story. This shift from narrative to narrated roles is often simultaneously "keyed" or signaled in two ways: she uses not only quotative keys (/nam kitota/, "then he said") but also paralinguistic keys—specifically, volume changes, such as having the birds whisper or speak quietly and Coyote speak loudly.

AUDIENCE AND FRAME AFFIRMATION

The storytelling frame is firmly established by her invocation of the opening formula, proclaiming "*Aliksai!*" and requiring and receiving the appropriate reply. Later it will be broken formally by the traditional closing formula (/pay yuk polo/, "and so it ends") and informally by code-switching from Hopi to English.

Thus, from the beginning, both narrator and auditors must participate in sustaining the performance situation. The audience is required to respond creatively to her performance in these roles in order to maintain this collaboration with the narrator, and she, for her part, must reach out to them. The narrator does this in several ways, some of which will be noted during a discussion of gestures. In the verbal dimension she addresses them indirectly through proclaiming the formula, which requires a reply, and directly by asking them questions ("Do you know that rock, Oraibi?" "You perhaps know this song?"). By the same token, the audience responds to her, especially early in the narration, with the customary "Owi," sometimes abbreviated to "wi." Malotki notes that "the audience is obliged to answer the narrator in unison. Every complete sentence is confirmed with a short expletive *oh* from the listeners. This tells the storyteller that he is still sustaining the interest of the group."[42] This may indeed be the norm, but as Helen Sekaquaptewa's performance begins to "roll," or, in Goffman's terms, as the audience and narrator become more and more caught up by the "engrossable features," this affirmation is less and less needed and given. Response to both her metanarrative questioning and to the narration reaffirms her narrative role. Both audience and narrator collaborate, then, to maintain the alternate reality of the story-world within the tangible reality of the living room.

Not needed are evaluative comments from the audience that tend to break the frame by indirectly or directly suggesting the insufficiency of the present narration. During the course of Helen's performance her story is interrupted twice, once in the beginning when someone prompts her with the opening formula (3), and later when a comment is made to her side (40). Both have negative effects that signal unsure narration. The prompting elicits a long rejoinder about answering in the correct manner, a meta-narrative comment that may be interpreted as the narrator's reassertion of competence through a demonstration of knowledge. The second effect is more subtle; hesitancy and reduced volume follow an interruption that detracts from the narrative. Not all interruptions are negative, however; the comment about Coyote's delight made by a member of the audience (152) plays right into Helen's narrative line and she eagerly snatches it up, an example of creative collaboration in emergent performance.

Maintaining this collaboration requires all of Helen's skills as a storyteller in three areas: her choice of words (linguistic), how she expresses those words (paralinguistic), and how she augments them with gestures and facial expressions (kinesic).

Kinesic Features

The storyteller starts her story from a neutral body position, sitting erect and a bit forward on the sofa, her hands in her lap, her eyes slightly lowered. The position impresses the viewer as striking a balance between authority and deference. Though she may vary this position many times throughout the course of the narration, she always returns to it, so that it forms a baseline against which each of her gestures, to which I have given a script number, can be defined. From this position Helen initiates two basic kinds of gesture.

Metanarrative gestures are relatively insignificant since they comment on her narrative and do not augment the story line. An example of this is her nod <#16> by which she kinesically reaffirms the correctness of her verbal expression of choice: "The LAST time . . . I mean <16> the fourth time."

The most significant kinds of gestures are *iconic gestures*[43] which enhance our appreciation of the story itself by dramatizing the action. The first kind of iconic gestures are those which occur primarily within the body plane. Typical of these is the winnowing action <6> associated with the song (see fig. 1). The restricted space occupied by these movements focuses our attention on the narrator, who is viewed or watched as if at a distance. A second set of narrative movements enters a shared neutral space outside of the plane of the narrator's body. These broadly drawn movements, especially those like the birds flying overhead <11, 15> involve audience space and incorporate them in a more participatory manner (see fig. 2). The third and most "engrossing" movements are

Figure 1. Gesture 6. "Then they would sing while winnowing . . . "

Figure 2. Gesture 11. "They would fly high up somewhere . . . "

Figure 3. Gesture 14. "This is how they placed them on I'isau . . . "

Figure 4. Gesture 20. "Whichever feather he had given, that he plucked off . . . "

those which reach into what is exclusively audience space, including actually touching the audience. These actions, for example the plucking and placing of the feathers, transform the audience into characters, so that in an undeniable way they become part of the story (see fig. 3). This is extremely dangerous for storytellers. Such a sudden "upkeying" from spectator to participant can collapse the frame and effectively terminate the performance in embarrassed laughter.[44] Helen Sekaquaptewa's intuitive skill here is remarkable in this regard. Observe that she works up to this most dangerous form of gesture by first testing the audience space with less dangerous intrusions. She leans forward to ask a question. This is metanarrative; she is back in her social role and the children never have to leave their social role to answer. She then enters audience space again, this time in her narrated role, playing the birds who look around the group seeking approval. More dangerous than the first, this is nevertheless not as harmful as physical contact with the audience. Only when the audience is fully caught up in the tale, only when the frame is at its strongest, does she risk touching them, transforming them into characters.

Figure 5. Gesture 22. " . . . down he came . . . "

Most important, these gestures are used in several ways to create both suspense and climax. As one approaches the climax of the story, Coyote's great fall, repetitive gestures increase; the winnowing of the tale's first part is now replaced with the birds' flying up into the air. Throughout the tale both of these actions pace the story, restraining the tendency of the narration to rush to conflict, climax, and crash. Near the climax, however, the gestures become more frequent and more dramatic as almost every utterance is accompanied by motions, most often broadly drawn and involving audience space. Whereas the restrained winnowing motion and song formerly counterbalanced these actions, the equally broad Tsi-i-iro-ot motion now reinforces them. The net effect is increased narrative drama and heightened audience engrossment at the moment of Coyote's great fall (see fig. 5), all the more marked by the complete absence of significant motion after the climax.

Paralinguistic Features

The term "paralinguistic" applies to all nonverbal phenomena associated with speaking, including stress, timbre, pitch, volume, length of sound, and pace of narration. Together with kinesic features, these phenomena are the first to be lost when a speech event is transcribed. The writer tries to enliven the narration with adverbs or adverbial phrases to compensate for the loss of these features, but the oral literary artist must look on as the life of his story is chilled into print.

One of the most obvious paralinguistic features associated with storytelling is conscious change in volume. These have various degrees of significance. For instance, in Hopi narration, the reportative phrase (/*puu yaw*/, "it is said") and several other particles (/*pai*/, /*kurs*/, /*niqw*/) often begin utterances. Because the last sound in a Hopi utterance is frequently a down-pitched and/or unstressed verb suffix, the stressed, up-pitched particle that opens the following sentence seems doubly emphatic. The audible contrast creates a clear utterance boundary in sound equivalent to the period in print.[45] This is not a stylistically significant phenomenon, since it marks Hopi narration generally; nevertheless, the iteration of stress, even at irregular intervals, creates pleasing variation.

In a different category are volume changes used to augment gesture. Notice that when Helen describes how the seeds are put in the plaques (33–34), or when the birds flew up in the air (122–123), or when they pluck feathers from Coyote (181–185), she heightens the effect of the gestures by increasing volume. This is especially evident when the expected, insistent volume increase which comes when she corrects herself ("on the *fourth* time") is contrasted with the effect of the preconceived, artful accenting which accompanies the plucking of the feathers.

Characterization is clearly another function of volume change. Coyote stumbles onto the scene in the middle of the tale. This is itself a somewhat unusual dramatic event.[46] Most Trickster tales begin *in media res* with an opening formula something like, "Coyote was going along . . . " so that the Trickster figure is the baseline for establishing norms for interpreting the behavior of characters. In this tale, Coyote appears suddenly and menacingly in the middle of others' action. His inability to contain his excitement is revealed in the increasing volume of his speech. By increasing the volume, Helen also emphasizes the obviousness of Coyote's intention to eat the birds (89–93). This stands in contrast to the Western convention of diminishing the audibility of the inner monologue. The birds, on the other hand, are characterized by even-tempered behavior. If anything, their normalcy throws Coyote's rambunctiousness into high relief. This contrast, which in the Hopi ethic is less a matter of genus than of mores, is further exaggerated by having the birds whisper among themselves.

Helen's skillful manipulation of volume becomes more apparent when we examine how she uses volume changes to create suspense, advance the dramatic structure of the narrative, and indicate the significance of the action for our understanding of theme. Notice, for example, that by accenting both Coyote's second request for feathers (133) and also the birds' agreement (136), she sets up an expectation in the audience that this deliberate flaunting of nature must result in some kind of Icarian demise. Note, too, how this suspense is maintained through accented repetitions later in the story: "*Then, once more* for the last time, / *again,* they went even higher" (171–173) (174). A similar sophistication is shown in this part of the story by the way in which the plucking of the feathers is sequenced: "whichever feather he had given that he *PLUCKED OFF* / *TAIL* feathers / *DOWNY* feathers / ALL *of them* they took off" (181–186).

All of these elements come together in a particularly artful passage in which Helen introduces Coyote to the birds (94–102). Such introductions, whether in a novel or a folktale, are dangerous narrative moments. The storyteller must create a sense of a distinction between the protagonist and the antagonist. The difference, however, must be diminished in some way, or else the conflict would be immediately at hand, all complication would be foreclosed and the possibilities for a tale reduced to a brief anecdote. Diminishing this distance is frequently accomplished through some kind of masking, in which the protagonist is inhibited, by his own innocence or the antagonist's deceit, from seeing the latter's real nature. In the present tale, Coyote's deceit must be communicated in such a way that an ambiguity about his character, otherwise only too well known by audience and characters, is created and maintained.

When Coyote first sees the birds, his appetite exceeds his self-control (if Coyote can be said to have self-control) and he approaches announcing himself in full volume. The birds too are excited and want to flee, and we are in danger here of losing the possibility of a story. Both characters speak at maximum volume to reflect their emotional states. The next lines are critical. Helen reduces her volume in two steps and shifts from quotation to narration, removing us from the conflict by one point of view: "THEY WANTED to *FLEE*. '*I wouldn't do ANYthing to HURT you,*' he said to them." Back to a normal, narrative voice and volume; a slight pause to look at the audience and a knowing smile. She returns to quotation, having admitted her audience, through volume, pause, and smile, into her knowledge that from here on Coyote's speech masks his true intentions. Having successfully established dramatic irony, she reinforces it through verbal irony, emphasizing how Coyote baits the birds with flattery ("*For truly* you are so delightful to watch . . . ") and by a deferential, even submissive posture, which he signals by his hesitant repetition and his only tentatively increasing volume: "Maybe / Maybe I can *JOIN you*?" As a result of this careful characterization through volume, Helen successfully decreases the distance between the birds and Coyote within the story so that they consent to admit him into their company. What is particularly satisfying, however, is that through irony she is at the same time able to increase the distance between the birds and Coyote from the audience's perspective and clarify the moral values associated with each.

Other paralinguistic features are also stylistically significant. Hopi is a three-pitch language, but Helen's "Tsii-roo-oo-ot" is pitched to several levels, and for synesthetic reasons. On the one hand, the word is perhaps onomatopoetic of the call of the horned lark,[47] but of itself the cascading pitch is mimetic of the birds' dance in the sky and their flight back to earth. This is reinforced by Helen's gestures at this point. Similarly, when referring to Coyote's death, Helen tightens her voice and lengthens the /o/ so that the conversational /moki/ becomes /mo°°ki/, the comic effects of which are not lost on the audience. Vowel lengthening also occurs in the opening lines (/naavinta/ > /naavinta/, /yeesiwa/ > /yeeesiwa/), where it is combined with a stabilized high pitch to produce a pattern of speech that approximates chant. This is not peculiar to Hopi tales alone—Tedlock shows something similar at Zuni[48]—so that near-chant may be part of the mechanism of invoking frame.

Linguistic Features

The most obvious linguistic hallmark of Hopi narrative style is the recurrent /*puu yaw*/, or sometimes simply /*yaw*/, which is a reportative feature signifying that the events being narrated were not personally witnessed by the narrator but were reported to him by someone else. Usually translated as "it is said," the phrase lends to things purely imaginative a verisimilitude associated with things actually seen while disclaiming personal responsibility. Its super-abundant use, as in this text, is so frequently a mark of storytelling throughout Native America that many ethnographers simply didn't record it, or if they did record it in the source-language text, they did not bother to translate/transcribe it in the English text.

In terms of structure, Helen uses several devices to create suspense and so to manage the speed at which the story moves toward its climax. One method is her use of metanarration, that is, her comments about what is going on in the story, and the two songs (if the birds' call can be considered a song). The metanarration occurs in two places, both associated with Coyote's first appearance. Again, it is a matter of controlling the degree of audience engagement, for too much will lead to dissatisfaction if the narrative conflicts are resolved more quickly than the narrator had in mind. So, after briefly introducing Coyote, Helen reaches out to ask the audience whether they know the rock, Oraibi, where he appeared (72–82). Only for a moment is our attention turned away, then back to the tale: "and secretly he peered at them." The audience responds, for they know as much as we do of Coyote's appetites and his sole interest in the birds. Helen slows us down by introducing a comment that is acknowledged as redundant ("as we know") but masterfully functional (83–90); thus, she heightens our anticipation that Coyote will reveal himself, which of course he does.

In a similar manner the songs also control the narrative flow. As Helen Sekaquaptewa narrates it, the story can be understood to have two parts, each marked by a song. The first part, which consists of four episodes marked by the winnowing song (A), highlights Coyote's attempts to ingratiate himself with the birds by contrasting the exertion, tediousness, and seriousness of their real work with his playful mimicry. In the second part, marked by four repetitions of the Birds' Flight Song (two overt: B_1, B_4; two implied: B_2, B_3), Coyote tries to imitate the birds' flight and is unmasked as a fraud. An outline of the story as structured around the songs might look like this:

Opening Formula

PART ONE

Songs	Scenes
	1. Introduction of the Birds and Necessity for Work, Socialization.
A1	
	2. Tediousness of Work Reiterated.
A2	
	3. Coyote introduced, but cannot participate well because he cannot sing the song correctly; cannot fly with them.
A3	
	4. Coyote is ludicrously covered with feathers by birds.
A4	

PART TWO

	5. Coyote then learns song, flies up with them.
B1	
	(two more repetitions [6, 7], and B_2 and B_3 implied here)
	6 (8). Birds conspire to unmask Coyote; he falls to his death.
B4	
	Denouement

Closing Formula

Note that focusing on the songs highlights the Hopi preference for the number four as a structuring principle, both episodes being so divided. Note too that because the songs alternate with narration, they can serve several functions in performance. Appearing as they do at the end of the episodes, the songs seem to function like a refrain, but at the end of episode 4 and again at the end of episode 6 (really 8) this conclusive function comes into conflict with expectations created by the climactic value of the number four. In Episode 4 this is resolved by having audience expectations for a climax with regard to mastery of the song displaced suddenly into a concern for mastery of flight. An effective transition to Part Two is thus created, one that carries the momentum forward instead of breaking the story in half.

It is obvious from the audience's response that they are familiar with the winnowing song and perceive it as comical. It is sung the second time to emphasize the sense of routine and growing social bond which comes with working in common and which Coyote intrudes upon. The song is sung a third time to illustrate Coyote's isolation; he is left out because he doesn't know the song. When the song is sung a fourth time, Coyote joins in, but this time ludicrously covered with feathers. Each time the song is sung, however, it not only highlights the theme but also defuses the narrative power by momentarily halting the forward progress of the story. In so doing, the songs also build expectations for what is to come by making us more conscious of what is being held in abeyance. Further, compared to the real drama of Coyote's appetite for the birds, the song is trivial, and that contrast only heightens our awareness. In Part Two of the story, when our attention is no longer with the birds' winnowing but with Coyote's flying, the birds' call (Tsi-ro-o-o-ot) functions as the winnowing song had in the first part of the story, heightening dramatic tension and building expectations.

It is frequently difficult for nonnative persons to discern the important moments in a narrative—the climax, for example—because they do not understand what constitutes "significant action" in the native storytelling tradition. The record of this performance indicates that the climax of this story is not only indicated at the semantic level (specific actions described in specific words, e.g., Coyote's fall) but the climax is also signaled on the rhetorical level ("*Then once more . . . again . . . again . . .* " [172–174] and "the *fourth* time" [165]). In addition to these rhetorical devices, the number of gestures increases as the climax approaches, and they reach deeper into audience space. At the same time, the performer exercises the greatest range of volume and pace, from very loud (186, 188) to whispers (170, 179); from long utterances (172–175, 178–181) to single words (183 ff.). She even tenses her voice and lengthens vowels for effect (189). The cumulative effect of this "stacking" of paralinguistic, linguistic, and kinesic features is the creation of a "stylistic climax" that coincides with the structural one signaled by the narrated actions.[49] This coincidence of narrative form and content so completely engrosses the audience in the storytelling event that they only break out a bit when the narrator alters her voice on the last word of the climax ("he di^{ie}ed," 189). The giggles, the pause, the voice change, all signal a slight "downkeying" or diminishing of frame intensity.[50]

Only the denouement can follow. And indeed, Helen resumes her neutral body posture, significantly restricts her volume to a single level, and eliminates all gestures. When Sekaquaptewa finally breaks the storytelling frame with the closing formula (200), acknowledged by the audience's response and her own to them, her posture changes and her language shifts from Hopi back to English.

We might conclude by indicating the limitations of performance analysis in dealing with this particular performance, if such limitations are not already clear. This method has given us the ability to see the story as act, and more nearly to approximate it as it really exists in its paralinguistic and kinesic dimensions, as well as its more readily observed linguistic one. However, a single example does not contribute much to our understanding of Hopi /tuuwutsi/ as a genre, or even of the subgenre of Hopi /tuuwutsi/ known as I'isau or Coyote stories. Remembering Yellowman's comments on the distinction between talking about Coyote and performing Coyote stories, one is reluctant to make any generalizations, even when they are restricted just to the Hopi. As an ethnography of Hopi speaking comes into focus and genres become more clearly distinguished by their manner of performance than by their matter, it is possible that Coyote may manifest himself in a range of genres from anecdote and episodic cycle to sacred myth. But the method employed in this paper enables us to appreciate the story experience as the culmination of process—story*telling*—where it lives in all its fullness, and makes available to us the aesthetic delights of performance, bright, vital, and communicative, which outshine the second-hand pleasures of the text.

NOTES

The author wishes to thank Larry Evers of the University of Arizona, Department of English, for his assistance in the preparation of this article, while retaining sole responsibility for any errors in fact or interpretation which may appear herein. Note also that throughout the present article, Hopi-language words are set off by slashes, as in /tuwutsi/.

1. There are also other performances in this series, including songs (Navajo and Hopi), myths and tales (White Mountain Apache), and dance drama (Yaqui). Write for further information to Clearwater Publishing Company, Inc., 1995 Broadway, New York, NY 10023.

2. The theoretical foundations for this methodology are outlined in Dennis Tedlock, "The Translation of Style in Oral Literature," and exemplified in his anthology of Zuni texts, *Finding the Center: Narrative Poetry of the Zuni Indians* (New York: Dial, 1972). The essay on translation and Tedlock's other essays are collected in Dennis Tedlock, *The Spoken Word and the Word of Interpretation* (Philadelphia: University of Pennsylvania, 1983). Subsequent references to Tedlock's work are cited from this volume.

3. Ekkehart Malotki, *Hopitutuwutsi/Hopi Tales: A Bilingual Collection of Hopi Indian Stories,* narrated by Hershel Talashoma (Tucson: Sun Tracks and University of Arizona Press, 1983), xiii.

4. Cf. Dan Ben-Amos, "Analytical Categories and Ethnic Genres," in Ben-Amos, ed. *Folklore Genres* (Austin: University of Texas Press, 1976), 214–237.

5. I realize I am begging a number of questions here about what constitutes a "story," some of which I will address below. Such constructs have no legitimacy, I would argue, except to facilitate analysis, and represent the folklorist's but not necessarily the teller's sense of what constitutes the "story."

6. In the order of presentation, the sources for these texts are: H. R. Voth, *Traditions of the Hopi*, Field Columbian Museum Papers, 8 (1906), Text 72; Wilson D. Wallis, "Folktales from Shumopovi, Second Mesa," *Journal of American Folklore* 49 (1936):50–53; Elsie Clews Parsons, *Tewa Tales,* Memoirs of the American Folklore Society, 19 (1926), Text 24; Parsons, *Tewa Tales,* Text 64; Dennis Tedlock, "Coyote and Junco," *Coyote Stories,* IJAL Native American Texts Series, Monograph No. 1, ed. William Bright (1978) 171–177; Harold Courlander, *Hopi Voices* (Albuquerque: University of New Mexico Press, 1982), 229–231.

7. These are publication dates for Tedlock's versions in *Coyote Stories* (1978) and *Finding the Center* (1972).

8. *Finding the Center*, xxx.

9. Larry Evers, "Iisaw: Hopi Coyote Stories, with Helen Sekaquaptewa," (N.Y.: Clearwater Publishing, n.d.) 9, a brochure of commentary accompanying the videotape performance in the series mentioned in n. 1, above. (Hereafter referred to as "Iisaw.")

10. The historical relationship is well documented in the anthropological literature. For the Zuni borrowing of Hopi tunes, see Barbara Tedlock, "Songs of the Zuni Kachina Society: Composition, Rehearsal and Performance," in Charlotte Frisbie, ed. *Southwestern Indian Ritual Drama* (Albuquerque: University of New Mexico Press, 1980), 24.

11. T. T. Waterman, "The Explanatory Element in the Folktales of the North American Indians," *Journal of American Folklore* 27 (1914):1–58.

12. [Helen Sekaquaptewa], *Me and Mine: The Life Story of Helen Sekaquaptewa*, as told to Louise Udall (Tucson: University of Arizona Press, 1969).

13. Larry Evers informs me that such issues are very much of interest to Hopi people (personal communication).

14. Alan Dundes, *The Morphology of North American Indian Folktales*, Folklore Fellows Communications, No. 195 (Helsinki: Suomalainen Tiedeakatemia, 1964):110.

15. Alan Dundes, "Text, Texture and Context," *Southern Folklore Quarterly* 28 (1964):251–265.

16. Cf. Barbara Herrnstein Smith, "Narrative Versions, Narrative Theories," *Critical Inquiry* 7.1 (Autumn 1980):213–236.

17. Smith, 213.

18. For an example of the difficult position such an assumption puts the critic in, and how it is essentially a demonstration through analogy rather than an analysis, see Jarold Ramsey's comment on a Tillamook performer: "Mrs. Pearson's narrative *carries on* at some length . . . but these episodes constitute a sequel to the story per se, which really reaches *its proper closure* with the killing" (119, emphasis mine). I would argue (1) that we are unable to assert legitimately any notion of propriety in this case simply on the basis of prototypes we might find congenial to our literary tradition, and (2) that in any case, the more relevant question is why Mrs. Pearson "carries on," if that's what's happening, i.e., what is the relationship between the individual performance and the immediate context. See Jarold Ramsey, *Reading the Fire: Essays in the Traditional Indian Literatures of the Far West* (Lincoln: University of Nebraska Press, 1983).

19. See Stanley Fish, *Is There a Text for This Class?* (Cambridge, Mass.: Harvard University Press, 1980) and Mary Louise Pratt, *Toward a Speech Act Theory of Literary Discourse* (Bloomington: Indiana University Press,

1977). The roots of this criticism lie in the theorizing of J. L. Austin and John Searle and constitute an application to literary texts analogous to that which emerges in anthropological linguistics as the ethnography of speaking. See Richard Bauman and Joel Sherzer, eds., *Explorations in the Ethnography of Speaking* (London: Cambridge University Press, 1974).

20. Smith, 226.

21. Robert A. Georges, "Towards an Understanding of Storytelling Events," *Journal of American Folklore* 82 (1969):316. See also the seminal essays by Dell Hymes to which much of Georges's work is related: "Toward Ethnographies of Communication," and "Studying the Interaction of Language and Social Life," in Dell Hymes, *Foundations in Sociolinguistics: An Ethnographic Approach* (Philadelphia: University of Pennsylvania, 1974), both originally published under different titles.

22. The idea of Frame is originally Gregory Bateson's (see his "A Theory of Play and Fantasy," in *Steps to an Ecology of Mind* [1955]), but has been elaborated upon significantly by Erving Goffman in *Frame Analysis: An Essay on the Organization of Experience* (Cambridge, Mass.: Harvard University Press, 1974).

23. Richard Bauman, *Verbal Art as Performance* (Rowley, Mass.: Newberry House, 1977), 10. Originally published under the same title in *American Anthropologist* 77 (1975):290–311.

24. J. Barre Toelken, "The 'Pretty Language' of Yellowman: Genre, Mode and Texture in Navajo Coyote Narratives" *Genre* 2 (1969):231.

25. See Hymes's "Breakthrough into Performance" (1975) in his collected essays, *"In Vain I Tried to Tell You": Essays in Native American Ethnopoetics* (Philadelphia: University of Pennsylvania Press, 1981), 79–141.

26. Bauman, *Verbal Art*, 11.

27. Bauman, "The Patterning of Performance," *Verbal Art*, chap. 4.

28. Bauman, *Verbal Art*, 11.

29. Toelken, 221.

30. Regna Darnell, "Correlates of Cree Narrative Performance," in Bauman and Sherzer, *Explorations in the Ethnography of Speaking*, above, n. 19.

31. Goffman, *Frame Analysis*, 346.

32. This quotation and the one immediately preceding it from Bauman, *Verbal Art*, 43.

33. Bauman, "The Emergent Quality of Performance," *Verbal Art*, chap. 5.

34. Toelken, 224.

35. See Bauman, *Verbal Art*, chap. 4, for examples of how the assumption of performance alters roles. See also Judith Irvine, "Formality and Informality in Communicative Events," *American Anthropologist* 81 (1979):773–790.

36. Evers, "I'isaw," 1.

37. Malotki, xiv–xv.

38. Sekaquaptewa, 228–230.

39. Malotki, xiv.

40. The shifting of roles, and the multiplicity of roles, in relationship to performance is suggested in Bauman, chap. 4.

41. According to Evers (personal communication) many of her relatives were present that evening. Evers writes:

> She was jointed by Victor Owtah, a clan nephew/uncle, who later narrated for the kids as well . . . Victor gives a version of an Owl song which Helen sung before the Coyote sequence, then with the full attention of those present launches into a Sparrow Hawk story with a chaplinesque manner. . . . A full account of the performance context of Helen's story would take account of how it is part of a larger and more complex telling event.

42. Malotki, xv.

43. See Harold Scheub, "Body and Image in Oral Narrative Performance," *New Literary History* 8 (1977):345–367.

44. See Goffman, 366.

45. Cf. Joel Sherzer, "Poetic Structuring of Kuna Discourse: The Line," *Language and Society* 11 (1982):371–390.

46. Folklorists like Ruth Benedict (*Zuni Mythology*, Columbia University Contributions to Anthropology 21:1:xxx) find fewer "animal trickster tales" among the Hopi and Zuni than elsewhere in Native America. This is, of course, a highly subjective judgment disguised in statistical terms. The impression remains, however, that in Hopi and Zuni literature interpersonal interactions are more frequent as subjects than incidents involving animal actors, and that the conventions associated with the latter, say among Plains Indians, such as the *in media res* beginning, do not seem commonplace among the Western Pueblos.

47. "Tsiro" is identified as Horned Lark in the Wallis texts, see n. 6.

48. Tedlock, "The Poetics of Verisimilitude," in *the Spoken Word and the Work of Interpetation*, 161.

49. Gary Gossen refers to the "metaphoric stacking" of couplet verses in order to give greater message redundancy in the more formalized genres of Chamula verbal art; see Gossen, *Chamulas in the World of The Sun: Time and Space in Maya Oral Tradition* (Cambridge, Mass.: Harvard University Press, 1974), 155. I have adapted the term to other purposes, comparing a performance model to a musical score, and the experience in simultaneity of linguistic, paralinguistic, and kinesic features to the experience of hearing a musical chord composed of individual notes "stacked" on the two clefs.

50. For "downkeying" and "breaking frame" see Goffman, chap. 10.

Interpreting the Material:
Oral and Written

ORAL

The Natural History of
Old Man Coyote

WILLIAM BRIGHT*

Few protagonists from the oral literature of native North America
have achieved lasting importance in the folklore or the written
literature of Anglo-America. Of course, one thinks of Longfellow's
Hiawatha, based on Algonkian narratives recorded by Henry R.
Schoolcraft and set by the poet to the meter of the Finnish
Kalevala—itself a somewhat synthetic creation; but today's school-
children no longer memorize "By the shores of Gitchie Gumee, /
By the shining big sea water . . . " American Indian trickster tales
are reflected somewhat indirectly in the Bre'r Rabbit stories of Joel
Chandler Harris, adapted from nineteenth-century Black folk-nar-
ratives, which in turn probably owed a great deal to American
Indian tradition of the southeast U.S.; this material, too, seems to
be little read in its original form now, though it has been Disneyfied.
Competing producers of animated films and comic books may also
have drawn on the Harris stories in their creation of Bugs Bunny—
perhaps the most successful approximation to a folkloric trickster
figure that our Anglo-American culture has yet acquired. Yet for
most of us, Bugs has no clear connection with American Indians
or, for that matter, with biology: He is really no more a rabbit than
Mickey Mouse is a mouse. A more important American Indian
contribution to present and future literature may be found in Old
Man Coyote—to use the name which has become familiar from
many English versions of American Indian narratives.

The animal which the Aztecs called *coyotl,* a word borrowed as
coyote by Spanish-speaking Mexicans, was first called the "prairie

wolf" by Anglo-Americans who met him as they moved west across the continent; later the Mexican term coyote was borrowed, pronounced both [kayō'ti] and [ka'yōt]. Biologists gave him the Latin name *Canis latrans*. The genus name, *Canis* ("dog"), reminds us that the coyote is a member of the canid family, and in fact interbreeds with the domestic dog and the wolf; *latrans* ("barking") is a rather inadequate reference to the coyote's unique howling, barking, yodeling, ululating song. During the past century, the animal has become increasingly familiar, first to inhabitants of the western United States and of Mexico but now also to people all over North America, as the coyote's range has expanded to the eastern seaboard and northward into Canada and Alaska. Coyotes have become especially familiar to many urban dwellers in cities like Los Angeles, where they have adapted to a diet that includes household garbage.

Since the days when Mark Twain first published his famous description of the animal,[1] one sees the name of the coyote more and more often in print. Newspapers regularly publish accounts of the alleged menace which coyotes represent in livestock-raising areas, and of the controversies involving ranchers, conservationists, and the government over possibilities of controlling the coyote population. Along with these problems has come a great increase in biological research.[2] At the same time, Coyote has become more familiar every day in fiction, in poetry, in music—witness Joni Mitchell's hit song "Coyote"—and in the cartoons (both in film and comic-book form), which have cast Wile E. Coyote as the perennial antagonist of "Beep Beep the Roadrunner."

In these latter manifestations we begin to meet not simply the biological *Canis latrans* but also a mythic figure, commonly called Old Man Coyote—the demiurge who made the world as it was known to thousands of North American Indians during the centuries before the arrival of Europeans. But Old Man Coyote, even when he brings fire for the benefit of humankind, is far from being a Promethean hero: he is an insatiable glutton, a gross lecher, an inveterate thief, liar, and outlaw, a prankster whose schemes regularly backfire. In short, Coyote is the archetypal Trickster known from literatures all over the world—Renard the Fox of Medieval French legend, Anansi the Spider of West African and modern Afro-Caribbean tradition.

Since the late nineteenth century and down to our own times, Coyote stories have been transcribed and translated by anthropologists and linguists, and have also appeared in collections for the nonspecialist reader. Since the 1950s, Coyote has begun to appear more and more in the poetry and prose of Anglophone writers who have sought inspiration in American Indian tradition: Anglo writers like Gary Snyder, Native Americans like Leslie Silko and Peter Blue Cloud, and Latinos like Enrique LaMadrid. "New" Coyote stories faithful to the trickster nature of their protagonist have been produced by some poets in writing, just as American Indian narrators must have produced such narratives orally in past times. And, since the 1970s, we have seen the development of "ethnopoetics"—an effort by scholars to capture the performance values and the poetic structure of oral literature. Since this work has been carried out principally by researchers with a primary interest in Native American tradition, such as Dennis Tedlock and Dell Hymes, a natural result has been a fresh appreciation of old Coyote stories, leading to new translations that attempt to recognize and maintain the aesthetic values of the originals. It seems that Old Man Coyote can be counted among the important contributions of American Indian cultures to modern civilization, along with potatoes, tomatoes, peanuts, chocolate—and, remembering that Coyote is a trickster, we may add tobacco.

But the question is, why Coyote? There are other mythic tricksters in native North America. In the Pacific Northwest there is Raven, and sometimes Bluejay. In the Northern Plains the trickster is sometimes called Spider; in the Southeast, he is Hare; and in most of the central and eastern continent, he has a name of his own, not identifiable with that of any animal. Yet, in the western U.S.—the main area of *Canis latrans* distribution at the beginning of recorded history—Coyote is the trickster par excellence for the largest number of American Indian cultures; he dominates native oral literatures of California, of Oregon, of the Plateau area inland from the northwest coast, of the Great Basin, of the Southwest, and of the Southern Plains.[3] Is there, perhaps, something about the behavior of the biological coyote that makes him especially fit for the role of mythic trickster? Similarly, we may ask: Of all possible tricksters, why is it that Coyote has captured the imagination of so many English-speaking writers and audiences? One aim of this chapter, then, is to explore relationships between the behavior of the biological coyote and the character of Old Man Coyote as the most important trickster figure of native North America, and by extension to examine the continuing symbolic importance of Coyote for us human beings who share a continent with him. The nature of the data and discussion is such that we will not be able to reach anything like a scientific proof or a predictive statement. Rather, as in a traditional Native American narration, the purpose is to amuse the audience when Coyote plays the fool, to shock it when Coyote commits incest or murder, to edify it when Coyote gets his comeuppance—and beyond all that, through quotation and example more than through analysis, to expand our understanding of what is possible, to perceive connections previously unnoticed, and to see human nature more clearly as reflected in Coyote.

A Note About Terminology

When appropriate, I distinguish the biological *Canis latrans*, or simply (lower-case) coyotes, from the mythic trickster, Old Man Coyote, or simply (upper-case) Coyote. But since these two types tend to merge in human consciousness, the presence or absence of capital "C" should not be taken too seriously. Also, with apologies to all female coyotes, I should note that individuals of unspecified gender will be routinely referred to here as "he" simply for ease of comparison with mythic Coyote, who is always male (see Ramsey 1983:200 n. 1). By contrast, I refer to the species *Homo sapiens* by terms such as "human beings" or "humankind," rather than "Man(kind)"—even though in quotations we are stuck with the generic masculine.

COYOTE IN LITERATURE

As Anglo-Americans spread across North America in the nineteenth century, the first written mentions of Coyote begin to appear. In one of the earliest and best-known of these, by Mark Twain, Coyote already appears not only as an unprepossessing member of the animal kingdom—"a long, slim, sick and sorry-looking skeleton, with a gray wolf-skin stretched over it, with . . . a general slinking expression all over" (1913:32)—but also as a figure of tall tales, indeed as a legendary trickster whom Twain describes with unconcealed sympathy:

> [I]f you start a swift-footed dog after him, you will enjoy it ever so much—especially if it is a dog that has a good opinion of himself. . . . The coyote will go swinging gently off on that deceitful trot of his, and every little while he will smile a fraudful smile over his shoulder that will fill that dog entirely full of encouragement, and make him lay his head still lower to the ground, . . . and move his furious legs with a yet wilder frenzy. . . . And all this time the dog is only a short twenty feet behind the coyote, and to save the soul of him he cannot understand why it is that he cannot get perceptibly closer . . . and it makes him madder and madder to see how the coyote glides along and never pants or sweats or ceases to smile . . . and *then* that town-dog is mad in earnest, and he begins to strain and weep and swear, . . . and reach for the coyote with concentrated and desperate energy. This "spurt" finds him six feet behind the gliding enemy, and two miles from his friends. And then . . . the coyote turns and smiles blandly . . . and with a something about it that seems to say: "Well, I shall have to tear myself away from you, bub . . . "—and forthwith there is a rushing sound, and the sudden splitting of a long crack through the atmosphere, and behold that dog is solitary and alone in the midst of a vast solitude! (1913:33–34)

Subsequent years have produced an increasing amount of Coyoteana in English, including the work of folklorists, natural historians, biologists, anthropologists, linguists—and, in recent decades, a growing number of literary scholars, poets, and other creative writers.

A type of Coyote literature that has become well established in the twentieth century is that kind of popular writing which combines informal and anecdotal natural-history observations on *Canis latrans* with folkloristic accounts of Old Man Coyote (in which both Spanish American and Native American sources are likely to figure).[4] This class of writing overlaps to some extent with the coyote literature produced by biologists, especially those concerned with ecological aspects of coyote behavior.[5] Such works give us a revealing picture of those characteristics of Coyote which have enabled him to fill so well the role of trickster in both oral and written literature. A closely related field of study looks at the ecology of the coyote in urban areas, giving special attention to his abilities to adapt and survive.[6]

A different line of attention, focusing on the transcription, translation, and interpretation of American Indian traditions, has been pursued by Anglo-American anthropologists and linguists since the late nineteenth century. Monuments of this literature, presented by such scholars as Franz Boas, Edward Sapir, and A. L. Kroeber, can be found in serial publications such as the *Annual Report* and the *Bulletin* of the Bureau of American Ethnology (in the Smithsonian Institution); in the *Publications* of the American Ethnological Society; in the *Publications in American Archaeology and Ethnography* of the University of California—and, in more recent years, in the *Publications in Linguistics* of the University of California and in the *Native American Texts Series* published by the University of Chicago as a supplement to the *International Journal of American Linguistics.*[7] In all these sources, as might be expected, tricksters make frequent appearances. And, in materials from California, from the Plateau and Great Basin areas, and from the Southwest, the trickster role is frequently played by Old Man Coyote. The value of these materials lies in their authenticity, especially for readers who are expert enough to follow the native-language texts. Their weakness is that the technical linguistic format and the literal translations have tended to limit readership to an academic audience. There have also been some books intended to present English translations of Coyote stories in nontechnical format and relatively popular style; these, whatever the authenticity of their sources, lose much of the "feel" of the Native American originals. The best such work is clearly that of Jarold Ramsey, who adds the extra dimension of being a gifted scholar in English literature.[8]

A direct outgrowth of the anthropological-linguistic tradition in the presentation of Native American texts is that which can be called "ethnopoetic"; the term and the group of approaches which it covers were first used in the journal *Alcheringa*, inaugurated under the editorship of Jerome Rothenberg and Dennis Tedlock in 1970. The two editors subsequently took separate routes: Rothenberg, more the poet and literary scholar, developed his controversial method of "reinterpreting" American Indian literature—as previously translated by anthropologists and linguists—in terms of contemporary English-language poetry. As might be expected, Coyote as trickster appears again in these materials.[9] Tedlock, more the linguistic anthropologist, has focused rather on translations that will be as faithful as possible to the originals, and on a verse format that will reflect the poetic qualities inherent in traditional performance.[10]

A somewhat different but also linguistically oriented approach has been that of Dell Hymes, who has re-analyzed the structure of published texts from societies in which narrative traditions are now extinct or moribund, and has shown that such texts can best be appreciated not as prose, but as "measured verse." Here, units such as lines and stanzas are defined not by the phonological units of old-world verse, such as rhyme, meter, or syllable-count, but rather by morphosyntactic, lexical, and semantic features.[11] Other scholars have experimented profitably with the approaches of both Tedlock and Hymes. And, of course, Old Man Coyote makes frequent appearances in all this work. In the remainder of this chapter, I will quote from Coyote stories in the several ethnopoetic traditions, but by preference from those which follow Hymes's model. Since my own field experience has been in particular with the Karok (or Karuk) people and language of northwestern California, I will quote especially from Karok myths that I have myself transcribed, translated, and then reworked in ethnopoetic terms.[12]

Parallel with ethnopoetic work on Native American narrative, there has grown up what might be called, by contrast, a "neopoetic" literature in which poets and other creative writers—of Anglo, Latino, and Native American background—have introduced Old Man Coyote and other figures of oral tradition into their own English-language work. There seems to be little doubt that the entrance of Coyote into contemporary poetry was given its major impetus by Gary Snyder in his poem "A Berry Feast," originally published in the historic collection which first drew wide attention to the "beat" poets of the San Francisco area.[13] The work begins:

> Fur the color of mud, the smooth loper
> Crapulous old man, a drifter
> Praises! of Coyote the Nasty, the fat
> Puppy that abused himself, the ugly gambler,
> Bringer of goodies.

Snyder here introduces Coyote as the self-contradictory trickster, an "old man," yet a puppy; "ugly" and self-indulgent, yet the "bringer of goodies." Coyote announces that "The people are coming"—the human species, the Indians for whom provision should be made: "you will grow thick and green, people / will eat you, you berries!" The end of the poem, however, depicts Coyote as outliving humanity, Indian or Anglo; he is the ultimate survivor:

> People gone, death no disaster,
> Clear sun in the scrubbed sky
> > empty and bright . . .
> From cool springs under cedar
> On his haunches, wide grin,
> > long tongue panting, he watches:
> Dead city in dry summer
> Where berries grow.

Not only as poet but also as essayist, Snyder has focused on Coyote. In "The incredible survival of Coyote" he sums up a motif found in dozens of Indian myths: "Coyote never dies, he gets killed plenty of times, but he always comes back to life again, and then he goes right on traveling."[14] The persistence of Coyote is reflected, as Snyder illustrates, in the work of a growing number of contemporary poets.[15] It is also reflected, as biologists like Bekoff and ecologists like Gill have shown us, in the current findings on *Canis latrans*: increasing geographic spread, improving adaptation to urban living, and ineffectiveness of efforts at predator control.

Coyote is, then, many things. Like humanity, he is an omnivorous, ubiquitous inhabitant of the North American biosphere; he is a mythic trickster, responsible for the world as we know it, yet a persistent bungler and dupe; and he is now, for many whites as well as for Indians, a powerful symbol of a viewpoint that looks beyond abstractions and beyond technology to the ultimate value of survival.

THE MYTHIC BACKGROUND

As I have noted, Native American "Coyote stories" occur over a wide geographical area, ranging at least from British Columbia to Guatemala, and from the Pacific Ocean to the Great Plains. However, the role of Coyote as a figure of narrative varies greatly over this area. It is in the Great Basin (eastern Washington and Oregon, Idaho, and adjacent areas) and in California where we are most likely to find Old Man Coyote as prototypical mythic trickster. As we move farther south, we find that Coyote can move from mythic into modern times; thus, the Diegueño of Baja California relate how he baptizes the chickens, and the Comanche of the southern plains tell how he tricks white soldiers and preachers.[16] Southwestern tribes often have stories in which several coyotes appear. In Mesoamerica Coyote is still a shifty trickster but seldom a successful one, and he is never the "bringer of goodies"; he is almost invariably a bungler and dupe.

One must suppose that this picture involves several historical strands (including some from European folktales, especially in Latin America). However, it is perhaps not only my own primary experience in California that leads me to see the prototypical Old Man Coyote as the figure best known from the tribes of California, the Great Basin, and the Plateau region; and it is to this concept of Old Man Coyote that I will generally refer below (though I may not be able to resist quoting some especially effective Coyote stories from other areas).

A basic fact about Old Man Coyote, then, is that he was a unique individual, and was one of the First People—the race of beings who occupied the world in the mythic times before humans came into existence. Sometimes Coyote is spoken of as having a wife and children, but it is not necessarily implied that they are also coyotes; certainly Coyote is known to mate promiscuously with females such as Frog or Mouse. The First People have names that we now associate with animals—or occasionally with plants and other natural phenomena; and Indians sometimes refer to the mythic period as "the time when animals were people." However, the First People do not seem to have been unambiguously either human or nonhuman in form; since they frequently possess great magical powers, they alter their shapes at will. Among some tribes (though not the Karok), a figure identifiable as the Creator or Old God is also identifiable as coeval with the First People but set apart from them; he may be responsible for the world in which the First People live, but he plays little part in the subsequent events which lead to the existence of human beings and of the world which we now know. For some tribes, the First People include a noble, heroic figure, such as Wolf among the Comanche (see Buller 1983) and the Chemehuevi,[17] who foresees the coming of humanity and plans a perfect, ideal world for them—until his brother Coyote enters the scene as marplot. But concurrent with the creation of man is a great change, whereby the First People are transformed into all the species of animals and plants which we know today—as well as heavenly bodies, mountains, and rocks—and, in some cases, disembodied spirits. All these bear the same names as before, and indeed can not be differentiated from the First People; as Barre Toelken says,[18]

> There is no possible distinction [for the Navajo] between Ma'i, the *animal* we recognize as a coyote in the fields, and Ma'i, the *personification* of Coyote power in all coyotes, and Ma'i, the *character* (trickster, creator, and buffoon) in legends and tales, and Ma'i, the symbolic character of *disorder* in the myths. Ma'i is not a composite but a complex; a Navajo would see no reason to distinguish separate aspects.

Among the First People, Coyote stands out in several respects; for one thing, stories in which he figures are especially numerous and popular. In most of these stories, he is the multifaceted North American trickster figure who was discussed at length by Paul Radin with particular reference to psychological interpretation of the Jungian school.[19] Further light has been shed on this trickster role by M. L. Ricketts,[20] writing from the viewpoint of comparative religion; by Toelken, with particular reference to Coyote as a character in Navajo narratives;[21] and, most recently, for Western Native America in general, by J. Ramsey (1972:24–46). It should be understood, however, that "trickster" in this context does not simply refer to some kind of practical joker, but rather to what Ricketts terms the "trickster-transformer-culture hero." The trickster steals fire and salmon for the benefit of humans, lays down cultural roles for men and women, and even ordains death, but is at the same time "a prankster who is grossly erotic, insatiably hungry, inordinately vain, deceitful, and cunning . . . and a blunderer who is often the victim of his own tricks." In most traditions, he does not act as original creator; rather, "he changes things into the forms they have retained ever since"—he is the creator of "the world-as-it-is" (Ricketts 1965:327, 341). To be sure, he is no altruist; he acts out of impulse, or appetite, or for the pure joy of trickery. Yet his most obscene or amoral exploit is, for human beings, something more than material for humor. Toelken quotes his Navajo consultant, Yellowman, as saying: "If he did not do all those things, then those things would not be possible in the world." In Toelken's paraphrase, Coyote is "the exponent of all possibilities" (1976:76, 164).

One cannot read many Coyote stories without being struck by the degree to which his creativity, his adaptability, his unreliability, and his buffoonery are reminiscent of the genus *Homo* (in this context, *sapiens* should perhaps only be added with a "[*sic!*]" after it). Ricketts goes so far as to say that "The trickster is man"—or later, with some qualification, that he is "the personification of all the traits of man raised to the highest degree"; in contrast to the type of religion which conceives of a transcendent god, the trickster "is a symbol of mankind, the race which, according to this mythic vision, is unconquerable and immortal" (1965:336, 347, 349). Similarly, Ramsey refers to the trickster as "all man's epitome," as "an imaginary hyperbolic figure of the human"—or perhaps more precisely as a Lévi-Straussian "mediator" who links the world of humanity, with all of its curiosity, self-awareness, and resultant "cultural" baggage, to the "natural" world of animals. Ramsey emphasizes Coyote's role as the *bricoleur*, the handyman or fixer-upper, who cannot stop himself from tampering with Original Creation and thus produces the world which we humans now know—imperfect, but *ours* (1972:25, 27, 41).

It is, then, an oversimplification to say that Coyote is really *Homo sapiens;* he is also, in many significant ways, *Canis latrans.* As Ramsey notes, some of the most prominent trickster figures, such as Coyote and Raven, are scavengers and omnivores, and thus—like humans!—can be seen as symbolizing an equivocal middle position between herbivores and carnivores (1972:29). Among many tribes, the trickster is called by some form of the epithet "Old Man"; thus, in Karok, coyotes are called *pihnêefich*, which is etymologically "Shitty Old-Man"—probably referring to tales of the trickster's coprophagy. Elsewhere, especially in the Plains area, the trickster has names of ostensibly human type; but Coyote has many nicknames in various languages—for example, in Karok, *tishráam 'ishkuuntíhan,* "He who lurks in the grassy places."[22]

In fact, I wish to propose that, in the areas where coyotes were best known to Native Americans in pre-Columbian times, *Canis latrans* was an especially appropriate actor—biologically, ecologically, and ethnologically—to play the trickster role. From this, I suggest, has followed the widespread significance of Old Man Coyote in Native American mythic traditions. From this mythic role in turn, along with Coyote's biological characteristics—especially his striking talents as a survivor—has arisen his increasing importance as a figure in English-language literature. In the following discussion, I will attempt to show how some of the attributes of Coyote as trickster and survivor are reflected in correlations between zoological observation, Native American myth, and contemporary poetry.[23]

Coyote as Wanderer

Myths from many tribes begin with variants on the words used as the title of Jarold Ramsey's book *Coyote Was Going There* (1977). In Karok myth, Coyote makes at least two trips up the Klamath River to "the upriver end of the world" (sometimes referred to by Indians as "the North Pole," but more likely to be identified as Klamath Falls, Oregon). In one myth he brings back fire to "the center of the world"—the confluence of the Salmon and Klamath Rivers, at Somes Bar, California.[24] In another myth he travels far north to seek money, but falls into the river and winds up at "the downriver end of the world," that is, the ocean.[25] No other mythic character so traverses the entire length of the Karok universe.

A myth from the Keresan pueblos of New Mexico relates that, for his gluttony, Coyote was condemned to be a perpetual wanderer.[26] Snyder paraphrases a type of passage that occurs in many narratives: "And [Coyote] sort of pulls himself back together and goes around and looks for a couple of his ribs that have kind of drifted down the hill, and pulls himself together and says, 'Well, now I'm going to keep on traveling'" (1977:72). The trickster figure in general has been characterized by Radin as having "an uncontrollable urge to wander" (1972:165), and by Ricketts as "a restless wanderer on the face of the earth" (1965:327). Contemporary poets, both Anglo and Native American, have also noted Coyote's nomadism. As Eugene Anderson writes, "The coyote nature is to travel forever."[27] The Pueblo poet Simon Ortiz sees Coyote on Route 66, "just trucking along."[28]

Coyote's mobility seems easily relatable to both his eternal curiosity and his scavenging nature. Biological research is consistent with the mythic and literary traditions: coyotes have their home burrows, but may range widely. In a study by R. D. Andrews and E. K. Boggess,[29] sixty-three coyotes were tagged, then recovered over a four-year period. The straight-line distance from the location where they were originally tagged was 22.2 miles; however, "Male coyote movements ranged from 0 to 110 miles . . . and females ranged from 0 to 202 miles" (1978:261).

Coyote as Bricoleur

Writers such as Radin and Ricketts have emphasized that the North American trickster frequently is also a transformer and culture-hero, whose accomplishments may include the slaying of monsters, the theft of natural resources for the benefit of man, the teaching of cultural skills, and the ordaining of laws. Yet the trickster is not an ideal heroic type: If he slays monsters, it is through guile rather than bravery. He does not create the world of the First People, but rather "fixes it up" so that it becomes the world of humanity. Thus, Ricketts calls him the "trickster-fixer" (1965:327). Ramsey rejects the term "culture-hero" and applies the Lévi-Straussian conception of bricoleur, "a sort of mythic handy-man who 'cobbles' reality in the form of a *bricolage* out of the available material" (1983:35, 41).

In this role, Coyote has so much responsibility for our world that he is sometimes said to be "the Indian God."[30] The Miwok say that Coyote destroyed the models which the other First People suggested for humanity, substituting a model that would have his own "cunning and adaptability" (Leydet 1977:78–79). For the Northern Paiute, Coyote is the inventor of sexual intercourse, as retold by Ramsey:[31]

> In the old time women's cunts had teeth in them.
> It was hard to be a man then . . .
> whenever fucking was invented it died with the inventor . . .

Coyote was the one who fixed things,
he fixed those toothy women!
One night he took Numuzoho's lava pestle
to bed with a mean woman
and hammer hammer crunch crunch ayi ayi
all night long—
"Husband, I am glad," she said
and all the rest is history.
To honor him we wear our necklaces of fangs.

Many stories tell how Coyote tinkers with the Eden of the original creator, or sabotages the noble intentions of a heroic figure, to make a world appropriate for humans who will be as imperfect as Coyote himself: A Karok story explains why men and women were each given their tasks, "so they wouldn't be lazy."[32] Originally the Klamath River flowed north on one side, south on the other; whichever way a boatman traveled, he could go with the current:

But Coyote said, "No! . . .
    let it all flow DOWNstream.
Let the young husbands have to push their way up there,
    when they travel UPstream."

Similarly, burden baskets originally had legs. Women would fill them with firewood or acorns, whereupon the baskets would walk home:

But Coyote said, "No! . . .
    let the young wives CARRY the loads."
So that's how it is,
    now they don't walk any more,
        those basketloads.

Perhaps most momentous of all, Coyote is, for many tribes, the inventor of death. Some California tribes relate that "Earthmaker" wanted to give people eternal life, but Coyote invented death "to make people take life more seriously." Elsewhere, he foresees that death will be necessary to prevent overpopulation. When his own child dies, he wants to revoke the rule, but by then it is too late; Coyote becomes the first to feel the bereavement which is to be the lot of humanity.[33]

Coyote's character as bricoleur seems to be a function of his inquisitiveness and his reckless willingness to give anything a try. According to Leydet, the Hopi assign Coyote a Pandora-like role (1977:84): His curiosity makes him open the jar in which the stars are hoarded up, letting them escape into the sky—but he is too impatient to arrange them systematically (Tyler 1975:164–165).

A theme that has been developed in the creative imagination of some modern Coyote-poets is that, just as the First People were succeeded by humanity, the time may be coming for humanity to be succeeded by another race.[34] Dell Hymes, speaking as poet, sees the need for a "second coming" of Coyote, to take a second try at his bricolage:[35]

> But now its really time—
> Coyote,
> Don of tricksters,
>
> A generation is near now,
> it needs to see the river
> rush cold below the rimrock, . . .
>
> go ahead,
> finger women,
> gobble food, . . .
>
> fall flat—
> your asshole advisors will
> set you straight,
>
> so you set straight
> this world before the world
> this world should be.

What can be said about *Canis latrans* as bricoleur? The biological connection seems to lie in the elements of curiosity and cunning, for which anecdotal evidence is abundant. Thus, Leydet refers to the coyote's "unsleeping desire to investigate anything unusual" (1977:44); Ryden quotes an ex-trapper as saying that coyotes "are the smartest animals in the world" (1979:4). The zoological litera-ture seems to say little about coyote intelligence as such, though the animal's keen and versatile perceptual abilities are noted. P. N. Lehner observes that the design of the coyote eye allows the animal to be active both by night and by day;[36] Marc Bekoff remarks that coyotes are well adapted for hunting by the combined use of sight, hearing, and smell.[37] Leydet cites an Indian saying that "a feather fell from the sky . . . the eagle saw it, the deer heard it, the bear smelled it, the coyote did all three" (1977:56).

A possible biological explanation for the coyote's inquisitiveness and cunning is offered by Ryden in terms of the fact that young coyotes remain dependent on their parents for a relatively long period—a phenomenon called *neoteny,* displayed most strikingly by humans (1979:250–251). As she puts it, "Neoteny is a characteristic of all species that have not inherited a fixed repertory of behavior, but must *learn* how to survive. . . . The neotenal coyote . . . meets change by learning new responses and is therefore capable of developing a whole new life-style" (1979:250–251). The suggestion is that coyotes have gone beyond their canid brothers, the dogs and wolves—as humans have gone beyond their primate kindred—in their motivation and ability to learn, and have thereby increased their adaptability—a signal quality that will be discussed below.[38]

Coyote as Glutton

As a typical trickster, Coyote is widely depicted as voracious, omnivorous; though he may promise to restrain his appetite, he always gives in. The Karok story of his travel upriver to get money contains a whole sequence of episodes regarding Coyote's hunger and thirst (Bright 1980b:25–34). Becoming thirsty, he steals two baskets of gooseberry juice from Lizard, who in revenge contrives a curse. He creates a brushfire, which produces roasted grasshoppers—which Coyote loves to eat. But these, like salted peanuts, only increase thirst. There follows a passage in which Coyote experiences diarrhea. After plugging his anus with pine-pitch, he gorges himself on grasshoppers; but when he sits on the smoldering ground, the pitch in his anus catches fire.

> What could he do?
> He slid all around there,

on the ground, in the sand . . .
So finally his ass stopped burning.
And he thought
   "Now I'll never eat them again,
     those roasted grasshoppers."

But now the rest of Lizard's curse—that Coyote should become thirsty—comes into effect. Because Coyote is on a wealth quest, he is not supposed to drink water at all; furthermore, each time he approaches a creek, it magically dries up. Even when he stands at a distance and throws his blanket in the creek bed, "only dust puffs up, / the water has gone dry." Finally Coyote begins to think about drinking from the Klamath River, although drinking river water is taboo:

So he hurried downslope.
And he thought,
   "What a bad thing I'm doing,
    going to drink water . . . "
And he thought,
   "I won't drink right here,
    by the shore."
And he said,
   "Fall down,
    you fir tree!"—
     and it fell.
And he walked out over the water on it.
And then he got to the middle of the river.

So then he stooped to the water,
   he stooped a long time,
    down to the water,
     he drank a lot.
And when he got up,
   he'd drunk a lot.
There he fell over backwards,
he fell backwards into the river.

According to another Karok version, Coyote "drowned"—which did not keep him from seducing two girls as he floated down river, as well as breaking up a puberty ceremony and creating general havoc before finally arriving at the mouth of the river. Here, he entered a sweathouse and found that all the furniture was made of tallow; naturally, he ate it.

All this is, of course, typical behavior for the trickster, who is described by Ricketts as "insatiably hungry"; he will "do anything to obtain a meal" (1965:327, 347). His greediness can, of course, be seen as one aspect of the "oral behavior" which Abrams and Sutton-Smith include in thir inventory of trickster traits (Coyote is also an inveterate singer, talker, and braggart) (1977:32).

The natural-history literature and scientific writings of course confirm that coyotes are scavengers and omnivores; according to a Western American saying, "A coyote will eat anything that doesn't eat him first." However, *Canis latrans* is apparently capable of much more restraint than his mythic counterpart; thus, Ryden has observed a coyote "freezing" for as long as eleven minutes when stalking a ground squirrel (1979:214). It appears that the impulsive aspect of Old Man Coyote's appetite, like some other features to be discussed below, is derived more from the human than from the quadruped side of his nature.

Coyote as Lecher

The insatiable and indiscriminate horniness of Coyote is well known. He copulates with married women, with virgins at their puberty rites, with his own daughter, and with crones (perhaps, like Don Giovanni, "Old women he seduces / for the pleasure of adding them to his list."). He is exceptionally proficient at getting his partners pregnant: in the Karok myth quoted above, after Coyote has fallen into the river, he turns himself into a "pretty little piece of driftwood" to attract the attention of two girls (Bright 1980*b*:37):

> Oh, how pretty it was,
>   the driftwood,
>   they took a liking to it!
> And then one threw it to another,
>   they played with it . . .
> And then one girl said, "Ugh!",
>   she said, "Ugh! Maybe it's Coyote . . . "

And then they threw it back in the river,
    that driftwood . . .
Sure enough, in a while, they both were pregnant.

Coyote's erotic exploits do not always turn out so well—but he is never discouraged for long. Consider William Brandon's "free" ethnopoetic version of a Cochití myth, "Coyote and Beaver Exchange Wives" (1971:54–56):

Old Man Beaver started putting his penis into
    Old Coyote Woman and
    Old Coyote Woman cried out and cried out at the
    top of her voice
    Old Beaver don't you hurt my wife
    said Old Coyote
        Shut up Old Man Coyote
        said Coyote Woman
        I am crying out because I like it
        You old fool
        said Coyote Woman

    When they were finished Old Man Beaver came out and
    said to Old Man Coyote
        We won't have bad feelings
        You know this was your idea
    So they remained friends
    the same as ever

Coyote is even capable of autofellation, as recounted in Dell Hymes's translation of a Chinookan text (1981a:236–237):

He went,
    he was going along,
        now he thought:
            "I shall suck myself."
He went on,
    off the trail, he covered himself with five rocks,
        now there he stayed.
He sucked himself,
    he finished,
        he came out.

Shortly thereafter, Coyote meets travelers and asks them for news:

> He told them,
>   "Isn't something news?"
>   "Indeed. Come a little this way."
> He went close to the river.
>   "Yesss,"
>   they told him:
>   "Coyote was coming along,
>   now he covered himself with rocks.
>   He sucked himself.
>   Such is the news that's traveling along."

Coyote finally discovers that, even though he had covered himself with rocks to hide his secret, the rocks had burst open to let the news rush out. He concludes that humanity will not be able to keep secrets either:

> "Now the people are near.
>   Whatever they may do,
>   Should they suppose,
>   'No one will ever make me their news,'
>   Out it will come."[39]

Again, this is typical behavior for the trickster, who is "grossly erotic" (Ricketts 1965:327); his promiscuity can also be seen, in a somewhat larger context, as a manifestation of his "sheer vitality" (Ramsey 1983:41)—his "delightful Dadaistic energy," as Snyder says (1977:81). All this has been especially appealing to a number of modern poets. Here is Bruce Bennett's "Coyote in love":[40]

> "Sure I've done it
> with other women
> but you're the one
> I'm always touching . . . "
> So Coyote
> tells his women
> always the same
> to all his women
> who always believe him.
> Or so he tells me.

Peter Blue Cloud, a poet of Iroquois origin, has written some of the best Coyoterotica, with plots taken from Western Indian traditions and his own imagination. In Blue Cloud's "Coyote Man and Saucy Duckfeather," the trickster plays the traditional role of the seducer who achieves his aims by pretending to give shamanistic treatment. Saucy Duckfeather is a flirtatious young married woman whose dream is to have pure white feathers; Coyote is the great doctor who promises to fulfill her wish. To this end he concocts a story about a "male tree" that can grant wishes if it can only find its mate:[41]

"a tree, a male tree, a dead oak
with a protruding red branch near
the bottom which a woman must
mount and ride upon a four night

ride, an all night ride with
no time wasted, just riding and
wishing a four night journey
to bring about the truth of all

your dreams": and there was Coyote
Man standing inside the hollow oak
his pecker sticking way out and
so hard his hide was stretched

toward the root of his manhood
that he couldn't even blink his eyes,
and she, the Saucy Duckfeather riding
and riding the magic branch and even,

it became obvious that she was
enjoying the ride: and Coyote Man
blew white ash through a knothole,
and what with her sweat and imagination

and secret longing, she just knew
she was turning white, and being
ridden four nights steady, Coyote
Man was content to leave and

> left, and she, poor Saucy Duckfeather was·
> left with knowledge of her greed . . .
>
> and old Magpie Woman stirred her
> salmon soup and to the idle or curious
> would only say, "Well, that's the way
> of doctors, especially if they're Coyote."

Like the impetuous gluttony discussed above, the gross eroticism of Old Man Coyote is not so easy to relate to the behavior of *Canis latrans*. According to J. J. Kennelly,[42] the female coyote—unlike her cousin, the domestic bitch—comes into heat once a year and enters into a monogamous couple that remains stable for at least the first year of the pups' lives. According to Ryden, "Coyotewatchers believe that in many cases the pair bond in coyotes persists through life" (1979:67). Perhaps, then, the lechery of Old Man Coyote reflects a projection of human qualities onto the canid species. In any case, biological similarities exist between the sexuality of coyotes and that of humans: protracted courtship and a degree of monogamy are characteristic, at least sometimes, of both species (see Ryden 1979:68).

Coyote as Thief

Although Coyote's thievery is frequently in the ultimate interest of the human race which is to come, it is clear that Coyote enjoys stealing for its own sake, and for the joy of the trickery involved. In Karok mythology, Coyote retrieves fire from "the upriver end of the world" by theft. Taking a relay team with him as he travels upriver, he finds a house at his destination in which only children are playing (Bright 1979:120–121). He lies down, pretending to rest:

> And the children said:
>   "Maybe he's Coyote . . . "
> And he said: "No,
> "I don't even know
>   where that Coyote is . . .
> "But I'm lying down right here,
>   I'm tired."
> In fact, he had stuck fir bark into his toes.

And then he stuck his foot in the fire.
And then finally it caught fire well,
    it became a coal,
        it turned into a coal.
And then he jumped up again.
And he jumped out of the house.
And he ran back downriver.
And when he got tired,
    then he gave the fire to the next person . . .

Thus, fire is brought back to "the center of the world"—just in time for the creation of humans.

Sometimes Coyote's stealing is less successful. Leslie Silko tells how Toe'osh—Coyote, in the language of her Laguna Pueblo—tried to steal the food from a picnic being held at the bottom of a cliff. As often related in the Southwest, Coyote can occur as a multiple of himself:[43]

And Toe'osh and his cousins hung themselves
down over the cliff
holding each other's tail in their mouth making a coyote chain
until someone in the middle farted
and the guy behind him opened his
mouth to say "What stinks?" and they
all went tumbling down, like that.

Coyote is also known, of course, for stealing songs, stories, and names. The Hopi/Miwok writer Wendy Rose sees him as even stealing the poet's thoughts (1980:70–71):[44]

Trickster's time
is not clicked off neatly
on round dials nor shadowed
in shifty digits . . .
        He sees
when the singers are spread and trapped by their songs,
numbed by the sounds of space . . .
Trickster swings walking off
        with your singer's tongue
        left inaudible.
Trickster dashes under cars
        on the highway and leaves
        the crushed coyote,

Trickster bounces off whistling
with his borrowed coat of patches . . .
We see only his grey tail . . .
as he steals all the words
we ever thought
we knew.

As a co-inhabitant with Coyote of a canyon in the mountain range
that runs through Los Angeles, I have had similar thoughts:

When you're trying to write about tricksters
And you go downstairs at 6 A.M.
and see Coyote padding up the road,
don't think it's a good sign.
He's not there to inspire you.
Later that day, someone might steal your hubcaps.
You might not write another line that week.
Then you'll remember:
Coyote the trickster, right?
Coyote, the thief.

From the viewpoint of *Canis latrans,* of course, "theft" is not a
relevant category—except in that coyotes, like other scavengers,
can be observed to sneak scraps of meat from kills made by larger
predators. If the coyote is a "thief," it is only by the application of
human moral standards.

Coyote as Cheat

Deception is of course the essence of Coyote's nature as a
trickster, and has been repeatedly illustrated here. I will only add
a Diegueño story from Mexico, recorded by Leanne Hinton,[45] in
an attempt at "ethnopoetic" re-translation by myself, which shows
how Coyote remains himself even after conquest and hispanization:

An old woman had a
hen and a rooster—
The hen had seven chicks . . .
Coyote came, he wanted to
carry them all off and
eat them, but he couldn't—

He saw the hen at the door,
he said, "Give me a chick, . . .
I'll take and baptize it," said Coyote—
"All right, take it"—
He took the chick and ate it—

The next day he came
and took still another one—
"Comadre, I'm taking another one to baptize,
the first one is sad, all by himself"—
He carried it off and ate it—
The baptizing was a fake!

The next day he came
and took still another one—
He carried them all off,
he ate up every chick.

Then he came: "Comadre,
come see your children, all baptized,
very big and beautiful;
they want to see you"—
"Go ahead" said the rooster—
Coyote carried off the hen,
he carried her off and ate her—

After eating he came back—
"Compadre, now Comadre cries for you to come . . .
"All right," the rooster said, and went—
Coyote carried him off,
Coyote carried him off and ate him—

When he finished eating,
the old farmer's wife came—
"What happened to my chickens?
They're lost, gone—what happened?
Who robbed me?"

She went to look: Aah, a big cave;
under a stone were a lot of feathers—
All the chicks were eaten,
the hen and all, the rooster and all, all, were eaten—

the old woman went there and saw it,
she got furious: what could she do?
They were all gone.

It is not hard to see this story as an allegory of the historical
relationship between the Indians of Mexico and their hispanized
neighbors. It is worth noting that, in the southwest U.S. and in
Mexico, the term coyote is used by many Indian groups to refer to
"half-breeds" or Spanish-speaking mestizos; and that on the border
between the U.S. and Mexico, coyote refers to the "migrant labor
brokers" who guide undocumented immigrants across the border—
sometimes to their death in the desert, if not into the arms of the
U.S. immigration authorities.

"Cheating" is, of course, like theft, a fairly irrelevant concept
from the viewpoint of the biological coyote; again, we can apply
such a term to coyote behavior only by the imposition of human
moral values.

Coyote as Outlaw

It might seem redundant to characterize Coyote as an "outlaw"
when he has already been convicted of so many crimes. But it is
worth emphasizing the active *glee* which Coyote seems to take in
flouting every social rule; he commits outrages that the First People
have apparently not even thought of before—but in so doing he
provides an *Erschreckensbeispiel*—a "horrible example" of how the
human race should *not* behave—as when, in a Karok myth, he eats
his own excrement.[46]

In a Navajo myth told to Toelken by his consultant Yellowman,
Coyote (Ma'i) attempts a double–double-cross when he persuades
Skunk to help him catch some prairie dogs (1976:149–153). Coyote
tells Skunk: "Go back to the village and tell the prairie dogs that
. . . you came across the body of a dead coyote . . . go make some
clubs, four of them, and put them under me. Tell them, 'Since the
coyote is dead, why don't we go over there where he is and celebrate?'" Skunk brings the prairie dogs, and they begin to sing and
dance around the apparent corpse.

Skunk began to get ready to say what Ma'i had told him to
say. . . . Skunk said then, "Look! Way, way up there is a *t'ajilgai*

[bird sp.] far above us." He said it four times, so the prairie dogs all looked up, and Skunk let out his scent into the air, and it came down right into their eyes. . . . Then Ma'i jumped up and said, "How dare you say I'm dead?" He grabbed the clubs under him and began to club the prairie dogs. He clubbed all the prairie dogs to death.

Coyote and Skunk start roasting the prairie dogs in an earth oven; then Coyote insists that he and Skunk should have a race: "Whoever gets back first can have all the fat prairie dogs." Skunk protests that his legs are too short, but finally agrees. Then, however,

Skunk ran behind a hill and hid under a rock. Soon after that, Ma'i passed by, running as fast as he could. . . . Skunk watched until Ma'i had gone completely out of sight and then went back to where the prairie dogs were buried. He dug up all but the four skinniest prairie dogs and took them up onto a nearby ledge. And while he was eating he watched for Ma'i, who soon came running as fast as he could. He wanted to make a good finish to show how fast he was, so he came running very rapidly and jumped right over the fire. "Whew!!" he said.

Of course, Coyote winds up getting nothing to eat except Skunk's leftovers. Toelken, in his subsequent discussion of the tale, calls attention to "the high incidence of broken customs, or traditions ignored and transgressed" (1976:161–162). As he says,

Admission of hunger or tiredness is considered an extreme weakness and is subject to laughter; begging help from someone of lesser talents [as Coyote does from Skunk] is idiotic and subject to ridicule; begging for food is contemptible and brings laughter; any kind of extreme, overinquisitiveness, gluttony, and the like, is considered the sort of weakness which must be cured by ceremony and is often in the meantime subject to laughter . . . ; betrayal is wrong. . . . In the tale above, one is struck by the presence both of humor and of those cultural references against which the morality of Coyote's actions may be judged. . . . Causing children to laugh at an action because it is thought to be weak, stupid, or excessive is to order their moral assessment of it without recourse to open explanation or didacticism.

But Toelken suggests that Coyote stories have a point even beyond their human and moral relevance:

The clown, then, . . . acts as a test, a challenge to order. . . . Yellowman sees Coyote as an important entity in his religious views precisely because he is not ordered. [Coyote,] unlike all others, experiences everything. . . . Coyote functions in the oral literature as a symbol of that chaotic Everything within which man's rituals have created an order for survival. (1976:104)

In "neopoetic" terms, the actor/writer who uses the name Peter Coyote has described Old Man Coyote as follows:[47]

> . . . the hooker
> whose boyfriend comes out of the
> closet while your pants are down.
> He's also the boyfriend.
>
> He eats grasshoppers and Cockerspaniels.
> Drinks out of Bel-Air swimming pools,
> rainwater basins and cut lead-crystal
> tumblers. He brings luck in gambling.
> Inspires others to write about. He
> is jealousy . . .
>
> Is in the Bible as Onan's hand.
> He's the gnawed squash in your garden.
> The critical missing wrench from
> your toolbox . . .

The quintessentially outlaw nature of Coyote is expressed by Ramsey's reference to his "hostility to domesticity, maturity, good citizenship, modesty, and fidelity of any kind" (1983:27). This is in some ways quite the opposite to the nature of the biological coyote—which, as has been observed, is a faithful mate (at least during the one-year breeding cycle). Coyotes are also conscientious parents: Kleiman and Brady note that coyote parents care for their pups for at least the first nine months, and that some coyote families remain intact for much longer (1978:175). Once more, Old Man Coyote seems not to reflect any "wildness" in the wild coyote. Rather, it appears that human beings, perceiving such traits of coyotes as their wandering habits and their appetites, have projected other characteristics onto them—reflecting, above all, the rebellion of humans against their self-imposed domesticity.

Coyote as Spoiler

We have seen how Old Man Coyote is responsible for bequeathing to humankind, not the Eden of original creation but the actual world we know. In the Karok myth quoted above, Coyote ordains that men and women will have to work for a living, "so they won't be lazy." Elsewhere, as we have seen, Coyote is the inventor of death. Yet a purpose may also be seen here: As Ricketts writes, "for the trickster, who has rejected all supernatural aid and has elected for freedom, there is no hope for immortality. Man must accept the fact of his mortal nature, and even choose it, as the trickster did, for the good of himself and the human race as a whole" (1965:349).

Here again, biological analogies seem to be unavailable. The model for Old Man Coyote as spoiler is evidently human beings, who show an ever-expanding talent for turning the Eden of nature into a Purgatory for themselves, and never run short of rationalizations for doing so.

Coyote as Loser

We have seen abundant evidence of how Coyote's tricks frequently backfire; he becomes *der zerspottete Spötter*. This is especially true in myths from the Southwest: In his attempts to trick Badger out of his wife, or to hoodwink Skunk out of his feast of roasted prairie dogs, it is Coyote who loses.

Coyote also frequently winds up as a loser simply because of his own bad judgment and unrealistic optimism. In the Karok myth of his quest for money (Bright 1980:24–25), Coyote sees ten raccoons sitting in a tree, and resolves to make himself a new suit of clothes:

> And he ripped them apart,
>   his clothes.
> And he tore them to bits,
>   little bits.
> And he threw them downslope.
> And he stood there naked.

And so then he said,
  "Now I'll shoot one!"—
    and he missed.
And the raccoon jumped away downslope.
And again he shot at one,
  again it jumped down.
And he missed every one of them.
And he felt BAD.
And he crept away downslope.
And he collected them,
  all of his torn-up clothes.
So he mended his clothes—
and he hurried upstream.

A number of other myths tell how Coyote came to have an unattractive coat. Simon Ortiz tells how Coyote lost all his money gambling, and finally bet his fur (1977:15–16):

Coyote had the prettiest,
the glossiest, the softest fur
that ever was. And he lost that.

        So some mice
finding him shivering in the cold
beside a rock felt sorry for him.
"This poor thing, beloved,"
they said, and they got together
just some old scraps of fur
and glued them on Coyote with piñon pitch.

And he's had that motley fur ever since.
You know, the one that looks like
scraps of an old coat, that one.

The biological evidence indeed refers to the fact that coyotes often have unsightly coats:[48] "Sarcoptic mange occurs with the [mange mite] burrowing into the epidermal layer of the skin, resulting in lymph oozing through the skin and intensive itch which causes much rubbing or biting of the infected area." The Indian's view of Old Man Coyote reflects such facts.

368

Coyote as Clown

We have seen that the appeal of Coyote's adventures is frequently in their humor. In many of the examples cited, our laughter is at Coyote's expense when his tricks backfire on him. But it should be remembered that we laugh not only *at* Coyote but also *with* him—his tricks, whether successful or not, are clearly designed in many cases both to secure some goal (as in the theft of fire) and for the sheer joy of prankishness.

In an Apache trickster tale narrated by Rudolph Kane, L. J. Evers tells how Ba'ts'oosee ("sly fox"), alias Coyote, tricks his cousin Ba'dotlizhe ("grey fox").[49] Some enemies have tied Coyote up and are going to scald him with boiling water. Coyote tricks Grey Fox into taking his place:

> So they shoved him in the boiling water,
> *Ba'dotlizhe,*
> They put him in.
> Heee,
> it all came off,
> his fur.
>
> The one who took off [i.e. Coyote] returned.
> "Why did they do that to you, my cousin?"
> that's what he said.

The two travel onward to a place where they find water. Now Coyote plays another trick, this one simply for its own sake. The trickster says:

> "My cousin,
> there's *ba'dos* [bread] in there.
> It's mine" . . .
> This down here is the reflection of the moon,
> way down under.
> That's why he tells his friend to drink all the water . . .
> they started drinking it.
> *Ba'ts'oosee* [Coyote]
> just had his mouth on the water.
> The other one [Grey Fox] was really drinking it.

Heee,
his stomach was big . . .

The other one [Grey Fox] was just like a ball.
He was full
from water . . .
That's how it was a long time ago.

Bruce Bennett brings the theme up to date in his poem "Coyote and the gypsies."[50] Someone reports that the gypsies are moving in, and townspeople barricade themselves in their homes:

boats hauled up;
back doors bolted;
children walloped;
shades drawn down.
Everyone braced.
Signs disappeared;
gardens were trampled;
phones went dead;
there were nails in the road . . .

Finally the indignant people emerge to "get" the gypsies:

Well, you guessed the rest.
Not a trace of gypsies.
Not a scrap
to show they'd been there.
So somebody asked
"Hey, who was it saw 'em?"
and nobody knew.

Significantly, Coyote remains unnamed in the text of the poem.

Ramsey speaks of Trickster figures in general as "irrepressibly energetic." Again, he notes that Trickster as bricoleur has "something distinctly less transcendent than a divine plan or teleology to guide him—namely, his own impressionable, wayward, *avid* mind"—his "sheer vitality" (1983:27, 41).

Zoological studies report something comparable when they note, for example, that the coyote, unlike many mammals, is "active both at night and during the day."[51] Perhaps even more to the point are the numerous anecdotal reports of playfulness, such as that from Leydet (1977:65): "[I]t is difficult to escape the conclusion that coyotes *do* have a sense of humor. How else to explain, for instance, the well-known propensity of experienced coyotes to dig up traps, turn them over, and urinate or defecate on them"?

Coyote as Pragmatist

It has been noted that the mythic Coyote is often seen as responsible for the real world of "birth, copulation, and death" which he accepts both for himself and for the human species to come. Many myths end with the statement: "And Coyote said, 'The people will do just like that too, like I did'" (see Bright 1957:205).

Coyote's realistic or pragmatic stance and his lack of interest in abstractions have attracted a number of modern Coyote poets. Bennett reports on "Coyote's metaphysics" (1980):

> "He's bigger than me
> and a whole lot smarter,"
> Coyote remarked
> speaking of God.
> "Only thing is
> He isn't around much
> and it's gotta be someone
> lookin' out for the chickens . . . "

Peter Blue Cloud quotes Coyote in a similar vein (1982:49):

> Coyote was making frybread dough
> when young Magpie stopped in
> to offer his own recipe.
>
> An extra handful of flour and
> another dash of salt, he said,
> would assure very fine results.
>
> Coyote chased him away, shouting,
> "I'm not making very fine results,
>   you asshole,
> I'm making frybread!"

Elsewhere, Blue Cloud reports additional statements of Coyote's philosophy (1982:133):

> Coyote, coyote, please tell me
> What is power?
>
> It is said that power
> is the ability to start
> your chainsaw
> with one pull . . .
>
> Coyote, coyote, please tell me
> Why is Creation?
>
> Creation is because I
> went to sleep last night
> with a full stomach,
> and when I woke up
> this morning,
> everything was here.

Since Gary Snyder has been such an important writer in familiarizing the reading public not only with Coyote but also with the practices of Zen Buddhism, it is not surprising, as Peter Coyote writes that "Some prostitutes, poets, Zen students and several varieties of libertine have re-discovered the wit and utility of the Coyote-Trickster archetype" (1982:43–45). But he notes further:

> I am delighted to see hosts of contemporary references to [Coyote] cropping up. . . . I cannot help noticing, however, the singularity with which most of these references herd Coyote into a[n] . . . already overfull pantheon of American iconoclastic personalities.
> Coyote absorbs Chaplin, W. C. Fields, Bogart. . . . His once extensive range of possibilities and adaptation is being reduced to the narrow spectrum of anti-sociability and personal excess. An example is Coyote's (recent) association with Zen eccentrics.
> Although Zen training and traditions stress personal experience and understanding . . . the transmission of Buddhism owes at least as much if not more to those who chose to operate *within* the non-personal, non-eccentric, framework of tradition, as it does to those who have remained without.

As Snyder himself had pointed out earlier (1977:88–89):

> [T]he always-traveling, always lustful, breaker-of-limits side of the Trickster could destroy any human poet who got locked into it . . . [quoting Will Staple]:[52]
>
>> You're the same as Coyote
>> when you forget who you are
>> that's all he ever did!
>
> Which is why, in one of my own poems, I say "Beasts have the Buddha-nature / All but / Coyote." The *Mu*/"No" of the shapeshifter sets us free.

As Snyder says (personal communication):

> This is a rather subtle point. The Buddha can be called a Trickster because he causes us to study, practice, anguish over a truth which is as plain as the nose on your face. That truth is realized by an act of letting go: of the self-image, preconceptions, opinions, concepts & theories that one is always nourishing. The hardest to let go is the idea of "Buddha-nature" and the idea of "having" or "accomplishing" realization, of "having potential" etc.—so that paradoxically the person who has cut loose the ties & pulled out the nails "has" no Buddha-nature. Or has "no" Buddha-nature. That's all Coyote ever did.
>
> So it is not a case of having consciousness and choice that sets Buddha/Coyote apart; quite a many miles beyond that: having no special consciousness; no need to choose; the condition of resting in the fluid totality of things. Thus Dogen: "We study the self to forget the self. When you forget the self you become one with the 10,000 things."
>
> The shapeshifter can keep shifting because he has no fixed ego-notion. I see a bulldozer, "RRRRRR!"; a chicken, "Cluck!"; a cloud, . . . float by . . . ; a paradoxical & knotty intellectual problem, you energetically get all knotted into it until it gets loose by itself.

So, as many Buddhist teachers have done, Coyote reminds us about the dangers of intellectualization. The American Zen Master Robert Aitken presents us with Coyote as guru (1982:47–48):[53]

A student asked, "Can Essential Nature be destroyed."
Coyote said, "Yes, it can."
The student asked, "How can Essential Nature be destroyed?"
Coyote said, "With an eraser."

And again: "A student said, 'I have found that there is no basis for emptiness,' and he and Coyote burst into laughter."

It is perhaps unnecessary to invoke the zoological literature for evidence that coyotes are not metaphysicians. However, the nature of Old Man Coyote as a superior pragmatist is surely related to the great opportunistic skill, adaptability, and flair for survival which are well documented for *Canis latrans,* and which will now be discussed.

Coyote as Old Man

It has been noted that the mythic Coyote is often referred to, directly or otherwise, as "Old Man."[54] However, considerations of chronological age seldom seem to be of importance in Coyote's adventures: He has a grown daughter, but in one Karok myth he is certainly not too old to lust after her—or too feeble to carry his house on his back to a different location, to disguise from the girl that her new "husband" is really her father (Bright 1957:202–205). Indeed, Coyote is always the most lustful and energetic of the First People. Why, then, is he called "Old Man"? Both mythic and biological answers can be suggested.

In terms of myth, although he never mentions Coyote as such, Paul Radin notes that the trickster figure is usually "depicted as a being who has always existed, and as an old man" (1972:124–125). From a viewpoint of cultural evolution, Ricketts proposes a specific explanation: "[T]he more strongly the tribe has been influenced by an agricultural way of life, the less important is the place of the trickster-fixer. . . . This fact alone would seem to indicate that he is an extremely archaic figure, belonging to the culture of primitive hunters and gatherers" (1965:328). In Ricketts's view, this would explain why Coyote is both "trickster" and "fixer" in many areas, but much less of a "fixer" among the corn-growing pueblos of the Southwest U.S.—and even less so in Mexico, where corn-based agriculture seems to have originated.

Radin presents a picture of the trickster as originating in the most psychologically primitive strata of the human mind (1972:164). According to Carl Jung, who contributed a chapter to Radin's book,[55] the trickster is "obviously . . . an archetypal psychic structure of extreme antiquity . . . a faithful copy of an absolutely undifferentiated human consciousness, corresponding to a psyche that has hardly left the animal level" (1972:200). Ricketts expresses skepticism about the specifically Jungian analysis, but agrees with Radin that the trickster "is the most ancient figure in [North American] Indian mythology," and indeed in all mythologies (1965:333). Whatever psychological explanations may be offered, it seems that studies in comparative myth provide some validation for Coyote's credentials as an "Old Man."

It may be significant that zoologists also regard *Canis latrans* as "old." As R. M. Nowak writes,[56]

> The living coyote . . . is the most primitive member of its genus in North America. This is not to say that the species is in any way less intelligent or adaptable than the larger wolves . . . ; indeed the opposite may be true. By the term primitive is meant that . . . the species represents the ancestral, *less specialized* condition [emphasis added].

Features of neural anatomy, skull, and teeth indicate that coyotes have not become as specialized in their adaptation as wolves; for example, they are more omnivorous.[57] To quote Nowak further:

> These various characters should not be considered handicaps, in the evolutionary sense. [The coyote's] smaller size, and ability to utilize small prey and vegetation more efficiently, may help the coyote survive periods of adverse conditions under which the wolf would perish. Indeed, this process may be occurring today as the wolf progressively declines through competition with man, while the coyote continues to thrive and even expand its range.

Nowak also provides some interesting paleontological data: *Canis lepophagus*, a precursor of *Canis latrans*, is known from the "Blancan period" of the late Pliocene and early Pleistocene eras, some three to four million years ago (1978:6–7). The development to *Canis latrans* shows that "the braincase became more inflated, at the expense of the sagittal crest." He goes on to say that "it seems most likely that *Canis latrans* already had developed by the end of the Blancan, and thereafter did not undergo any great changes" (1978:9). The Rancholabrean period of 8,000 to 500,000 years ago—named after the famous Rancho La Brea tar pits in Los Angeles—shows abundant remains of *Canis latrans,* along with those of the now extinct camel, mammoth, sabertooth tiger, lion, and dire wolf (Nowak 1978:9–12). Coyote bones from the same period are reported from all over the western and midwestern U.S., from Maryland and Florida, and in Mexico as far south as Oaxaca.

It is evident, then, that the coyote is indeed *old* in two biological senses: relatively nonspecialized anatomy and paleontological antiquity. It is not to be expected, of course, that North American Indians would have applied the name "Old Man Coyote" because they knew that *Canis latrans* had been a contemporary of the sabertooth. It seems plausible, however, that early Native Americans applied the name in recognition of the coyote's talents for adaptation and survival—precisely the qualities for which *Canis latrans* is labeled "primitive" in biological terms. Coyote has, in brief, been around a long time; he has seen everything and tried everything—and if he has not learned everything, he has surely learned that the key to survival is to *keep* trying.

Coyote as Survivor

In various versions of Coyote's travels as told by the Karok, he "drowns"; but immediately afterwards he is seducing young girls (Bright 1957:173). At a later stage he apparently "drowns" again and is washed ashore, where all the flesh is picked from his bones by birds and insects—until Yellowjacket gets around to taking a bit of the testicles, at which Coyote jumps up, defends himself, and heads off for further adventures, apparently as good as new (Bright 1980*b*:167). Snyder's "Berry Feast" gives poetic expression to a similar mythic incident (1957:112–113):

> . . . and when Magpie
> Revived him, limp rag of fur in the river
> Drowned and drifting, fish-food in the shallows,
> "Up yours!" sang Coyote
>   and ran.

As Ricketts notes, although the mythic trickster may be the inventor of death and his own child is the first to die, he himself never dies,

> or more precisely, whenever he dies he rises up again. This is because he is a symbol of mankind, the race which, according to this mythic vision, is unconquerable and immortal. But individual men must die, and the trickster's child, who represents *us,* dies and does not return. The trickster's only remedy for death is tears, followed by laughter. He cannot save us from our mortal destiny, but he does something better: he gives us a purpose for living this life. He says that this life is good, that it is to be grasped with enthusiasm and enjoyed to the hilt. (1965:349)

The vision of Coyote as survivor has attracted a number of contemporary poets. Thus Will Staple writes (1977:35):

> Hard to enjoy
>   a supper of rocks and sand
> so coyote
> does what his bones say to do
>   "stay alive"

But in Snyder's "Berry Feast"—which, we might say, launched Coyote on his "neopoetic" career—the Old Man is seen as the *ultimate* survivor. Snyder seems to envision the end of civilization (1957:113):

>   . . . grey dawn,
> Drenched with rain. One naked man
> Frying his horsemeat on a stone.

But Coyote survives, even though humanity may be extinct (1957:113–114):

> Coyote yaps, a knife!
> Sunrise on yellow rocks.
> People gone, death no disaster.
> Clear sun in the scrubbed sky
>   empty and bright
> Lizards scurry from darkness
> We lizards sun on yellow rocks . . .
>
> From cool springs under cedar
> On his haunches, white grin,

long tongue panting, he watches:

Dead city in dry summer,
Where berries grow.

There is no shortage of references by naturalists and zoologists to the survival capacities of the coyote. Thus Leydet speaks of "all the white sheepmen and trappers who had said to me . . . 'The coyote will be here long after we are all gone!'" (1977:77). Ryden reminds us of the coyote's adaptability:

> He can hunt either by day or by night, dine on fresh meat or survive off carrion . . . run in packs or operate as a loner. . . . The advantage to an animal of being in an unfinished state can best be demonstrated by noting the fates of those North American animals who were better perfected for existence in their special niches [such as] the bison and the wolf. (1979:xiv)

Don Gill has shown how well coyotes have adapted to urban environments; he estimates that they are more numerous in Los Angeles now than they were in Indian times. In fact, as Nowak states,

> When the white man first arrived in North America, *Canis latrans* was distributed mainly in the western half of the continent [and in Mexico]; apparently it had disappeared from its earlier range east of Illinois. But since then it has been spreading eastward . . . in all likelihood the coyote will again occupy the entire eastern United States just as it did 10,000 years ago. (1978:12–13)

L. D. Mech adds: "the coyote has actually extended its range and filled in where the wolf was exterminated."[58]

In New England there is even evidence that the coyote has taken a new, quick step in evolution by interbreeding with the wolf and/or dog. H. Hilton notes the possibility that the development of such "coy-wolves" may "combine the versatility of the coyote with the greater strength and aggressiveness of the wolf."[59] As Ryden states, the hybrid animals can be seen as "filling a near-vacant predator niche" in the New England ecosphere (1979:63). Thus Native American storytellers seem to have been supported by contemporary poets and biologists in seeing Coyote as the survivor par excellence, in the age of the First People as well as in our own.

Summary

We have met Coyote, and, as Pogo might ask—is he us? Some authors have given a positive answer, such as Ricketts: "The trickster is man, according to an archaic intuition, struggling by himself to become what he feels he must become—master of his universe." Again, the mythical trickster/transformer/culture-hero is said to be "integrated into one character, who, in reality, is none other than Man" (Ricketts 1965:336, 343). But if that were the whole story, then scores of Indian tribes of Western North America might as well have given their mythic trickster a human name and shape, instead of that of Coyote. After all, the simultaneous manifestations of *Homo sapiens* and *Canis latrans* in Coyote can only be isolated by a kind of dangerous intellection, against which we have been warned by mythmakers, poets, and Zen masters. I agree with Ramsey in concluding that Old Man Coyote is an especially apt "mediator" between culture and nature, and one who may be needed more than ever by modern urbanized humanity (Ramsey 1983:28–29). The following haiku by Steve Sanfield, datelined "Modesto, California," is to the point:[60]

> Coyote calling
> & suddenly it's alright
> —this terrible motel.

But to state all this is not to say that we have Old Man Coyote within our grasp, stabilized and taxonomized. As Ramsey reminds us, the mediator is to be understood as "a dynamic interposing of the mind between polar opposites, as if affirming 'either/and' . . . " (1983:29). To quote Radin:

The symbol which Trickster embodies is not a static one. It contains within itself the promise of differentiation, the promise of god and man. For this reason every generation occupies itself with interpreting Trickster anew. No generation understands him fully but no generation can do without him. . . . And so he became and remained everything to every man-god, animal, human being, hero, buffoon, he who was before good and evil, denier, affirmer, destroyer and creator. If we laugh at him, he grins at us. Whatever happens to him happens to us. (1972:158–159)

NOTES

*I became acquainted with Old Man Coyote as a myth character in 1949, during my first field work among the Karok of northwestern California. Thanks to a fellowship from the National Endowment for the Humanities in 1980, I was able to devote considerable time to research on Coyote and on American Indian ethnopoetics.

I am indebted for all time to the great Karok storytellers, no longer living, who introduced me to Coyote—Nettie Reuben, Julia Starritt, Chester Pepper, and Mamie Offield—as well as to the fellow scholars and Coyote-poets who have given me advice and encouragement: Eugene Anderson, Larry Evers, Dell Hymes, José Knighton, Ken Lincoln, Lise Menn, Jarold Ramsey, Wendy Rose, Gary Snyder, and Dennis Tedlock. In 1980, the journal *Alcheringa* kindly published an "announcement" by me to the effect that I was preparing a book on Coyote, and welcomed correspondence. I thank everyone who responded. I apologize for not yet having finished the book; and I say again that I would like to hear from anyone on the subject of Coyote.

Finally I thank Peter Blue Cloud—who, when I wrote him that I was interested in the mythic Coyote, sent back a postcard saying, "You sure Coyote is a myth?"

1. Mark Twain, *Roughing It* (New York: Harper, 1913), chap. 5, pp. 31–36.

2. Marc Bekoff, ed., *Coyotes* (New York: Academic Press, 1978) provides a data-packed volume of papers by coyote scientists, which I will refer to frequently below.

3. See Jarold Ramsey, *Reading the Fire* (Lincoln: University of Nebraska Press, 1983), 25–26.

4. See F. Frank Dobie, ed., *The Voice of the Coyote* (Boston: Little, Brown, 1949); J. Van Wormer, *The World of the Coyote* (Philadelphia: Lippincott, 1964); Hope Ryden, *God's Dog* (New York: Coward McCann & Geohegan, 1975); and F. Leydet, *The Coyote* (San Francisco: Chronicle Books, 1977). Of these works, Ryden's is especially valuable for its many firsthand observations of coyote behavior.

5. See A. Murie, *Ecology of the Coyote in the Yellowstone* (Washington, D.C.: Government Printing Office, 1940); S. P. Young and H. H. T. Jackson, *The Clever Coyote* (Harrisburg, Penn.: Stackpole, 1951); L. Pringle, *The Controversial Coyote* (New York: Harcourt Brace, 1977); and Bekoff, ed., *Coyotes*.

6. See D. Gill, "The Coyote and the Sequential Occupants of the Los

Angeles Basin," *American Anthropologist* 72 (1970):821–826; D. Gill and P. Bonnett, *Nature in the Urban Landscape* (Baltimore: York Press, 1973), 87–108.

7. Two numbers in the last-named series are devoted entirely to Coyoteana: W. Bright, ed., *Coyote Stories* (*IJAL-NATS,* monograph 1, 1978), and M. B. Kendall, ed., *Coyote Stories II* (*IJAL-NATS,* monograph 2, 1980).

8. Apart from his *Reading the Fire,* already cited, see Ramsey, *Coyote Was Going There* (Seattle: University of Washington Press, 1977). Also valuable is R. A. Roessel, Jr., and D. Platero, eds., *Coyote Stories of the Navajo People* (Phoenix: Navajo Curriculum Center Press, 1974). To be avoided is B. H. Lopez, *Giving Birth to Thunder, Sleeping with his Daughter: Coyote Builds America* (Kansas City, Kansas: Sheed, Andrews & McMeel, 1977), in which narratives "lifted" from the anthropological literature, without stated provenance, are "retold" with extreme license. There is also a whole bookshelf of Coyote stories adapted for children (e.g., Reed 1979); in these one misses not only the style of the originals—which were told for audiences of adults and children together—but also, of course, all the "best parts" of Coyote's scatological and erotic adventures.

9. Well-known books in this mode include *Shaking the Pumpkin: Traditional Poetry of the Indian North Americas,* "edited and translated" by Jerome Rothenberg (Garden City: Doubleday, 1972), and William Brandon's *The Magic World* (New York: William Morrow, 1971). Important critiques of such "reinterpretation" include William Bevis, "American Indian Verse Translations," *College English* 35 (1974):693–703, and Jeffrey F. Huntsman, "Traditional Native American Literature: The Translation Dilemma," in *Smoothing the Ground,* ed. by Brian Swann (Berkeley, Los Angeles, London: University of California Press, 1983), pp. 87–97.

10. See Tedlock's book of Zuni narratives, *Finding the Center* (New York: Dial, 1972).

11. See Hymes, *"In Vain I Tried to Tell You": Essays in Native American Ethnopoetics* (Philadelphia: University of Pennsylvania Press, 1981).

12. My original transcriptions and translations are in *The Karok Language* (Berkeley and Los Angeles: University of California Press, 1957). I have discussed problems of ethnopoetic reworking in "A Karok Myth in 'Measured Verse': The Translation of a Performance," *Journal of California and Great Basin Anthropology* 1 (1979):117–123.

13. *Evergreen Review* 2 (1957):110–114.

14. *The Old Ways* (San Francisco: City Lights, 1977).

15. Since 1970, an intermittent journal of new writing has been published under the name *Coyote's Journal.* A recent special issue is devoted entirely to Coyoteana: James Koller et al., eds., *Coyote's Journal* (Berkeley: Wingbow, 1982).

16. Cf. L. Hinton, in Bright, ed., *Coyote Stories*, 117–120; G. Buller, "Comanche and Coyote, the Culture Maker," in Swann, ed., *Smoothing the Ground*, 245–258.

17. Carobeth Laird, *Mirror and Pattern* (Banning: Malki Museum Press, 1984).

18. Barre Toelken, "Ma'i Joldloshi: Legendary Styles and Navajo Myth," in *American Folk Legend*, ed. by W. Hand (Berkeley, Los Angeles, London: University of California Press, 1971), 203–211.

19. Paul Radin, *The Trickster*, 2d ed. (New York: Schocken, 1972).

20. M. L. Ricketts, "The North American Indian Trickster," *History of Religions* 5 (1965):327–350.

21. In addition to Toelken's "Ma'i Joldloshi," cited above, see his "The 'Pretty Languages' of Yellowman," in *Folklore Genres*, ed. by D. Ben-Amos (Austin: University of Texas Press, 1976), 145–170.

22. Cf. Ramsey, *Reading the Fire*, 204 n. 41. Even in families of closely related languages, it is often impossible to reconstruct a common proto-form for "coyote"; e.g., in the Takic group of Southern California, Cahuilla has *'isily* (cf. the corresponding augmentative *'iswet* "wolf"), but Luiseño has *'anó*.

23. Before leaving the general topic of tricksters, I should cite an exceptionally interesting discussion of Trickster stories by D. M. Abrams and B. Sutton-Smith, "The Development of the Trickster in Children's Narrative," *Journal of American Folklore* 90 (1977):29–47. These authors' data consist primarily in Bugs Bunny cartoons and in stories told by Anglo-American children of differing age groups; there is occasional comment on Native American tricksters (but no specific reference to Coyote). As a working tool, these researchers have compiled a trait-list that they call a "Trickster inventory" (32–34); this should have considerable value for cross-cultural research on Trickster literature. However, it includes some features that seem relatively uncharacteristic of Coyote, and fails to highlight such prominent Coyote traits as his wanderlust. Nevertheless, I will occasionally refer to the categories of Abrams and Sutton-Smith in my discussion below.

24. W. Bright, "A Karuk Myth in 'Measured Verse'," 117–123.

25. W. Bright, "Coyote's Journey," *American Indian Culture and Research Journal* 4 (1980) 1/2:21–48.

26. H. Tyler, *Pueblo Animals and Myths* (Norman: University of Oklahoma Press, 1975).

27. Eugene Anderson, "Coyote Song," *Coyote's Journal* 4 (1965):29–35.

28. "Telling About Coyote," in Simon Ortiz, *A Good Journey* (Berkeley: Turtle Island, 1977), 15–18.

29. R. D. Andrews and E. K. Boggess, "Ecology of Coyotes in Iowa," in Bekoff, ed., *Coyotes*, 249–265 (1978).

30. Cf. Jaime de Angulo, *Indian Tales* (New York: Wyn, 1953), 239.

31. "How Her Teeth Were Pulled," in Rothenberg, ed., *Shaking the Pumpkin*, 274 (1972).

32. W. Bright and N. Reuben, "Coyote Lays Down the Law," in Koller et al., eds., *Coyote's Journal*, 68–71 (1982).

33. Ramsey, *Reading the Fire*, 9–10, points out that the bricoleur's motive for inventing death can be that of teaching human beings the meaning of compassion.

34. Cf. David Wagoner's "Song for the First People," in his *Who Shall Be the Sun?* (Bloomington: Indiana University Press, 1978), p. 14.

35. *Spearfish Sequence* (Cambridge, Mass.: Corvine Press, 1981), 4.

36. "Coyote Communication," in Bekoff, ed., *Coyotes*, 128–162 (1978); see p. 129.

37. "The Social Ecology of Coyotes," in his *Coyotes*, 97–126 (1978), p. 118.

38. "Coyote Behaviour in the Context of Recent Canid Research," in Bekoff, ed., *Coyotes*, 163–188 (1978), p. 175: "some young coyotes disperse at about nine months. . . . However, coyote families under stable conditions may remain intact for much longer"—thus continuing the protected environment for learning.

39. Ramsey, *Reading the Fire* (44–45), gives an ethnopoetic translation of a very similar myth from the Santiam Kalapuya.

40. In Koller et al., eds., *Coyote's Journal*, 127 (1982).

41. *Elderberry Flute Song* (Trumansburg, N.Y.: Crossing Press, 1982), 40–49; see pp. 48–49.

42. "Coyote Reproduction," in Bekoff, ed., *Coyotes*, 73–93 (1978).

43. "Toe'osh: A Laguna Coyote Story," in Leslie Silko, *Storyteller* (New York: Seaver, 1981), 236–239; see p. 239.

44. "Trickster," in Wendy Rose, *Lost Copper* (Banning, Calif.: Malki Museum Press), 70–71.

45. L. Hinton, "Coyote Baptizes the Chickens," in Bright, ed., *Coyote Stories*, 117–120 (1983).

46. W. Bright, *The Karok Language*, 200.

47. Peter Coyote, "Muddy Prints on Mohair," in Koller et al., *Coyote's Journal*, 43–46 (1982); see pp. 45–46.

48. H. T. Gier et al., "Parasites and Diseases of Coyote," in Bekoff, ed., *Coyotes*, 37–71 (1978); see p. 39.

49. "Ba'ts'oosee: An Apache Trickster Cycle" (MS, University of Arizona, n.d.).

50. B. Bennett, *Coyote Pays a Call* (Cleveland: Bits Press, Case Western Reserve University, 1980).

51. P. N. Lehner, "Coyote Communication," in Bekoff, ed., *Coyotes*, 128–162 (1978); see p. 129.

52. "Coyote," in W. Staple, *Passes for Human* (Berkeley: Shaman Drum, 1977), 36.

53. R. Aitken, "Excerpts from *Coyote Rōshi Goroku*," in Koller et al., eds., *Coyote's Journal*, 47–49 (1982).

54. The ancient Aztecs, too, recognized a god named Huehuecoyotl, which is quite literally "Old Man Coyote." Although Ryden (xiii) refers to the deity as a trickster, my sources identify him only as god of the dance.

55. C. Jung, "On the Psychology of the Trickster Figure," in Radin, *The Trickster*, 195–211.

56. R. M. Nowak, "Evolution and Taxonomy of Coyotes and Related Canis," in Bekoff, ed., *Coyotes*, 3–16 (1978); see p. 5.

57. D. L. Atkins, "Evolution and Morphology of the Coyote Brain," in Bekoff, ed., *Coyotes*, 17–35 (1978); see p. 21.

58. "Foreword," in Bekoff, ed., *Coyotes*, xii–xiv (1978).

59. H. Hilton, "Systematics and Ecology of the Eastern Coyote," in Bekoff, ed., *Coyotes*, 210–228.

60. S. Sanfield, "A Few for Coyote," in Koller et al., eds., *Coyote's Journal*, 10–11.

REFERENCES

Abrams, David M., and Brian Sutton-Smith. 1977. The Development of the Trickster in Children's Narrative. *Journal of American Folklore* 90: 29–47.

Aitken, Robert. 1982. Excerpts from *Coyote Rōshi Goroku*. *Coyote's Journal*, 47–49.

Anderson, Eugene. 1965. Coyote Song. *Coyote's Journal* 4:29–35.

Andrews, Ronald D., and E. K. Boggess. 1978. Ecology of Coyotes in Iowa. In Bekoff, ed. *Coyotes*, 249–265.

Atkins, David L. 1978. Evolution and Morphology of the Coyote Brain. In Bekoff, ed. *Coyotes*, 17–35.

Bekoff, Marc, ed. 1978. *Coyotes: Biology, Behavior, and Management*. New York: Academic Press.

Bennett, Bruce. 1980. *Coyote Pays a Call*. Cleveland: Bits Press, Dept. of English, Case Western Reserve University.

———. 1982. Coyote in Love. *Coyote's Journal*, 127.

Bevis, William. 1974. American Indian Verse Translations. *College English* 35:693–703.

Blue Cloud, Peter. 1982. *Elderberry Flute Song: Contemporary Coyote Tales.* Trumansburg, N.Y.: Crossing Press.

Brandon, William, ed. 1971. *The Magic World: American Indian Songs and Poems.* New York: William Morrow.

Bright, William. 1957. *The Karok Language.* Berkeley & Los Angeles: University of California Publications in Linguistics 13.

Bright, William, ed. 1978. *Coyote Stories.* (International Journal of American Linguistics, Native American Texts Series, Monograph 1.) Chicago: University of Chicago Press.

————. 1979. A Karok Myth in "Measured Verse": The Translation of a Performance. *Journal of California and Great Basin Anthropology* 1:117–123.

————. 1980*a.* A Coyote Reader [announcement]. *Alcheringa* n.s. 4:196.

————. 1980*b.* Coyote's Journey. *American Indian Culture and Research Journal* (UCLA) 4:1/2:21–48.

Bright, William, and Nettie Reuben. 1982. Coyote Lays Down the Law. *Coyote's Journal:* 68–71.

Buller, Galen. 1983. Comanche and Coyote, the Culture Maker. In Swann, ed., *Smoothing the Ground,* 245–258.

Coyote, Peter. 1982. Muddy Prints on Mohair. *Coyote's Journal,* 43–46.

De Angulo, Jaime. 1953. *Indian Tales.* New York: A. A. Wyn.

Dobie, J. Frank. 1949. *The Voice of the Coyote.* Boston: Little, Brown.

Evers, Lawrence J. n.d. Ba'ts'oosee: An Apache Trickster Cycle. Manuscript, University of Arizona.

Gier, H. T. et al. 1978. Parasites and Diseases of Coyote. In Bekoff, ed., *Coyotes,* 37–71.

Gill, Don. 1970. The Coyote and the Sequential Occupants of the Los Angeles Basin. *American Anthropologist* 72:821–826.

Gill, Don, and Penelope Bonnett. 1973. Los Angeles: A City with Islands of Wild Landscape. In *Nature in the Urban Landscape.* Baltimore: York Press, 87–108.

Hilton, Henry. 1978. Systematics and Ecology of the Eastern Coyote. In Bekoff, ed. *Coyotes,* 210–228.

Hinton, Leanne. 1978. Coyote Baptizes the Chickens. In Bright, ed. *Coyote Stories,* 117–120.

Huntsman, Jeffrey F. 1983. Traditional Native American Literature: The Translation Dilemma. In Swann, ed. *Smoothing the Ground,* 87–97.

Hymes, Dell. 1981*a.* *"In Vain I Tried to Tell You": Essays in Native American Ethnopoetics.* Philadelphia: University of Pennsylvania Press.

————. 1981*b.* *Spearfish Sequence.* Cambridge, Mass.: Corvine Press.

Jung, Carl. 1972. On the Psychology of the Trickster Figure. In Radin, *The Trickster*, 2d ed., 195–211.

Kendall, Martha B., ed. 1980. *Coyote Stories II*. (International Journal of American Linguistics, Native American Texts Series, Monograph 6.) Chicago: University of Chicago Press.

Kennelly, James J. 1978. Coyote Reproduction. In Bekoff, ed. *Coyotes*, 73–93.

Kleiman, D. G., and C. A. Brady. 1978. Coyote Behavior in the Context of Recent Canid Research. In Bekoff, ed. *Coyotes*, 163–188.

Koller, James et al., eds. 1982. *Coyote's Journal*. Berkeley: Wingbow.

Laird, Carobeth. 1984. *Mirror and Pattern: George Laird's World of Chemehuevi Mythology*. Banning, Calif.: Malki Museum Press.

Lamadrid, Enrique R. 1972. *Cantos del coyote*. Albuquerque: Associated Gold Street Olive Press.

Lehner, Philip N. 1978. Coyote Communication. In Bekoff, ed. *Coyotes*, 128–162.

Leydet, François. 1977. *The Coyote: Defiant Songdog of the West*. San Francisco: Chronicle Books.

Lopez, Barry Holstun. 1977. *Giving Birth to Thunder, Sleeping with his Daughter: Coyote Builds North America*. Kansas City: Sheed Andrews & McMeel.

Mech, L. David. 1978. Foreword. In Bekoff, ed. *Coyotes*, xii–xiv.

Murie, Adolph. 1940. *Ecology of the Coyote in the Yellowstone*. U.S. Dept. of the Interior, National Park Service, Fauna Series, 4. Washington, D.C.: Government Printing Office.

Nowak, Ronald M. 1978. Evolution and Taxonomy of Coyotes and Related Canis. In Bekoff, ed. *Coyotes*, 3–16.

Ortiz, Simon. 1977. *A Good Journey*. Berkeley: Turtle Island.

Pringle, Laurence. 1977. *The Controversial Coyote: Predation, Politics, and Ecology*. New York: Harcourt Brace.

Radin, Paul. 1972. *The Trickster: A Study in American Indian Mythology*, 2d ed. New York: Shocken.

Ramsey, Jarold. 1977. *Coyote Was Going There: Indian Literature of the Oregon Country*. Seattle: University of Washington Press.

———. 1972. How her Teeth Were Pulled. In Rothenberg, ed. *Shaking the Pumpkin*, 274.

———. 1983. *Reading the Fire: Essays in the Traditional Indian Literatures of the Far West*. Lincoln: University of Nebraska Press.

Ricketts, Mac Linscott. 1965. The North American Indian Trickster. *History of Religions* 5:327–350.

Roessel, Robert A., Jr., and Dillon Platero, eds. 1974. *Coyote Stories of the Navajo People*, 2d ed. Phoenix: Navajo Curriculum Center Press.

Rose, Wendy. 1980. Trickster. In *Lost Copper*. P. 70. Banning, Calif.: Malki Museum Press.

Rothenberg, Jerome, ed. 1972. *Shaking the Pumpkin: Traditional Poetry of the Indian North Americas*. Garden City: Doubleday.

Ryden, Hope. 1979. *God's Dog*. Harmondsworth & New York: Penguin.

Sanfield, Steve. 1982. A Few for Coyote. *Coyote's Journal*, 10–11.

Silko, Leslie. 1981. Toe'osh: A Laguna Coyote Story. In *Storyteller*. Pp. 236–239. New York: Seaver.

Snyder, Gary. 1957. A Berry Feast. *Evergreen Review* 2:110–114.

———. 1977. The Incredible Survival of Coyote. In *The Old Ways*. San Francisco: City Lights.

Staple, Will. 1977. *Passes for Human*. Berkeley: Shaman Drum.

Swann, Brian, ed. 1983. *Smoothing the Ground: Essays in Native American Oral Literature*. Berkeley, Los Angeles, London: University of California Press.

Tedlock, Dennis. 1972. *Finding the Center: Narrative Poetry of the Zuni Indians*. New York: Dial.

Toelken, Barre. 1971. Ma'i Joldloshi: Legendary Styles and Navajo Myth. In *American Folk Legend*, ed. Wayland Hand. Pp. 203–211. Berkeley, Los Angeles, London: University of California Press.

———. 1976. The "Pretty Languages" of Yellowman: Genre, Mode, and Texture in Navajo Coyote Narratives. In *Folklore Genres*, ed. Dan Ben-Amos. Pp. 145–170. Austin: University of Texas Press.

Twain, Mark. 1913. *Roughing It*. New York: Harper.

Tyler, Hamilton. 1975. *Pueblo Animals and Myths*. Norman: University of Oklahoma Press.

Van Wormer, Joe. 1964. *The World of the Coyote*. Philadelphia: Lippincott.

Wagoner, David. 1978. Plateau Indian Myths and Legends. In *Who Shall Be the Sun?* Pp. 27–50. Bloomington: Indiana University Press.

Young, Stanley Paul, and H. H. T. Jackson. 1951. *The Clever Coyote*. Harrisburg: Stackpole.

Life and Death in the Navajo Coyote Tales

BARRE TOELKEN

Since the mid-1950s I have been studying and trying to understand the meaning of Navajo Coyote stories. Although I have enjoyed the enthusiastic cooperation of the Yellowman family (and other Navajo friends), the complexity of the language and culture, plus the variations in situation and context in which these tales function, have made the task a very slow one. In 1969, I published "The 'Pretty Languages' of Yellowman," in which I set forth all of what I could see as important aspects of meaning and implication in the narration and reception of a single story.[1] That study had taken about thirteen years to work out, and I felt by that time that I knew something about the subject. My argument there was a fairly simple one: The surface level of the stories uses humor, description, and other textural features, not to provide an etiology of the world but rather to set forth a powerful drama that articulates the worldview, the shared attitudes and values, the important but unstated assumptions and anxieties of Navajo culture. I argued that by observing where the audience laughed, and by noting textural features supplied by the narrator, we could come closer to appreciating the meaning of the story than we could by focusing on manifest content or apparent structure. A story about Coyote juggling, then losing, his eyes, which ends, "That's how Coyote got those yellow eyes," is not seen by the Navajos as an explanation of how coyotes got yellow eyes at all; but the story dramatizes the ways in which Coyote's selfishness, lack of sense, and willingness to mistreat his body result in eye diseases.

388

In a culture that avoids calling attention to a particular individual, that dislikes an individual who calls undue attention to himself, group-oriented laughter applied to a guilty person is a very persuasive mechanism. The Coyote tales, I argued, allow Navajos to laugh at Coyote for doing the things which would earn them derisive laughter if *they* were to do them. In laughing at Coyote, Navajos are not only able to enjoy vicarious experience with taboos, disorder, or defective morality but they can also feel for the moment that they are superior to the defects of Coyote: "You wouldn't catch *me* doing something like that!"

More recently, I took the opportunity to retranslate the same tale into lines representing the actual phrases used by Yellowman. In doing this article, "Poetic Retranslation and the Pretty Languages of Yellowman," with the help of Tacheeni Scott, I discovered that a phrase-by-phrase translation revealed several matters that had not emerged in the first study, and "disconfirmed"—I think that's the safe way of describing mistakes—some of my earlier findings.[2] Armed now with the feeling that I had learned what there was to discover, and having done scholarly penance for previous errors, I willingly accepted an invitation from some Navajos who asked me to be the lone non-Navajo speaker in a lecture series on Navajo cultural values. The audience would all be Navajo, and each speaker would be followed by a panel of three medicine men ("singers") and tribal judges. Mine was to be the first lecture in the series. Taking this invitation, somewhat immodestly, as a sign of approval by the Navajos, I went to Sweetwater, Arizona (not far from Red Mesa, Teec Nos Pos, and Tes Neziah), and delivered a one-and-a-half-hour discourse on the meaning and function of Navajo Coyote stories to a large audience of Navajos. I was relieved that my remarks were well-received, and I was satisfied to hear from the singers (as I had already learned from Tacheeni Scott and his father, also a singer) that my interpretations encompassed much of what could be said on the subject in such a relatively sterile language as English.

Then, one of the medicine men, Little John Benally, in formulating the considered opinions of the panel, said, "I think it's now time for us to talk about the really *important* aspects of these stories. Now that you know why we tell them to our families, maybe it would be interesting for you to hear—and for some of our younger people here in this room to hear—why these stories are so important to our religion." We were then treated to an impromptu two-hour lecture on the medicinal uses of Coyote stories in Navajo ritual. I would like to pass on the general content of this conversation (not mentioning topics that I was asked to keep secret), partly because the subject is interesting and in itself important, but mainly because it led to still another discovery that is loaded with danger.

The gist of Little John Benally's comments was this: The stories about Coyote are themselves considered so powerful, their articulation so magical, their recitation in winter so deeply connected to the normal powers of natural cycles, their episodes so reminiscent of central myths, their imagery so tightly connected with reality, that elliptical reference to them in a ritual can invoke all the powers inherent in their original dramatic constellations. In a ritual, an allusion to a well-known line, or speech, or action of Coyote will summon forth the power of the entire tale and apply it to the healing process under way. Thus, when Yellowman and others told me that the tales were a strong way of thinking about things,[3] they were not simply referring to the metaphorical quality of the stories, which do indeed make concrete most of the abstractions of Navajo culture. Much more than that, the stories provide the resource for a way of invoking a stronger reality through a kind of traditional synecdoche: The Navajos believe that language does not merely describe reality; it creates it.[4] The telling of stories and the singing and narrating of rituals are ways of actually creating the world in which the Navajo live. The Coyote stories function, on the one hand, to create the world ahead of the young people—that is, the stories dramatize for the young the key issues, taboos, concerns, mores. The healing rituals, on the other hand, are (mostly) to re-establish reality and order after a break with it has taken place—through disordered living, through bad thoughts, or through witchcraft. In the rituals, allusions of the briefest sort are capable of uniting narrative reality and ritual order into a powerful healing force. Synecdochic references to the tales are used as a kind of medicine.

Level I of the Navajo Coyote tales can be called the *entertainment* level; that is, the surface story with all its descriptions of Coyote's selfish, humorous—and occasionally heroic—behavior. Level II can be called the *moral,* or evaluative level, where each of Coyote's actions will be registered and responded to according to how it reflects or flaunts Navajo values and morality. The function of Level III is, then, *medicinal*: the conscious application of the story and its imagery to specific ailments and their treatments during healing rituals.

The story which I translated in the Yellowman articles, where Coyote wishes for rain so that he can use the flood to kill and eat prairie dogs, appears by brief allusion in the Rainmaking segments of several rituals. The power of the allusion is enhanced by the prairie dog imagery, for prairie dogs are thought to embody the same forces underground as those which are represented above-ground by rain. Prairie dogs are said to "cry for rain." A Navajo belief relating rain to burrowing animals was inadvertently "collected" by government agents in the 1950s when they proposed to get rid of prairie dogs on some parts of the reservation in order to protect the roots of the sparse desert grass and thereby maintain at least marginal grazing for sheep. Navajos objected strongly, insisting, "If you kill off the prairie dogs, there will be no one to cry for rain." Of course they were assured by the amused government men that there was no conceivable connection between rain and prairie dogs, a fact that could be proven easily by a simple scientific experiment: a specific area would be set aside and all burrowing animals there would be exterminated. The experiment was carried out, over the continued objections of the Navajos, and its outcome was surprising only to the white scientists. Today, the area (not far from Chilchinbito, Arizona) has become a virtual wasteland with very little grass. Apparently, without the ground-turning processes of the burrowing animals, the sand in the area has become solidly packed, causing a fierce runoff whenever it rains. What sparse vegetation was once there has been carried off by the flooding waters.

It would be incautious to suggest in this instance that the Navajos were possessed of a clear, conscious, objective theory about water absorption and retention in packed sand. On the other hand, it would certainly be difficult to ignore the fact that the Navajo myth system, which insists on delicate reciprocal responsibilities among elements of nature, dramatized more accurately than our science the results of an imbalance between principals in the rain process. One aspect of Navajo religious thought concerns the continued maintenance of such delicate systems, in large part through the same rituals which continue to revive and maintain the health of the Navajos themselves. Lots of prairie dogs are an indication that there will be lots of grass and lots of rain—both of these considered elemental parts of the fertile and healthy earth. In the story, the prairie dogs seem to function as representatives of those who live in and on the earth, who must move in interaction with the sacred powers which engender fertility, life, and death (Coyote).

In several rituals, one simply hears Coyote speak the line "I am the rain, the male and female rain." This is enough to evoke all the associations of the stories in which these symbolic participants in the constellation of nature interact. In the story under discussion here, the prairie dogs gather around the apparently dead Coyote to dance in celebration of his death. Although this leads to the hilarious (for the Navajo listeners) death of the prairie dogs, it actually depicts something a Navajo would never do, for it suggests witchcraft, a subject that will emerge more clearly later in this essay.

Several stories in which Coyote takes out his eyes and throws them in the air (Yellowman tells two distinctly different ones) are used in rituals dealing with eye ailments. The force here is that of replacement and regeneration. If Coyote can replace his eyesight by the use of pitchballs, then humans, using herbal medicines, words, and rituals can restore their eyesight as well. In one of these stories, Coyote learns from the birds how to take his eyes out and catch them in his sockets, but eventually he tries it too many times, or throws them too high in the air, and can't get them back (inappropriate behavior: *birds* are supposed to see from the sky). His recovery of eyesight by the use of pitch balls and herbal medicine is referred to in several rituals just before dawn. The birds are mentioned by name, and the herbal medicines are revealed as being those of the ritual in progress. The songs which the birds sang in order to bring about Coyote's recuperation in the story are sung as dawn approaches, and the people are warned not to close their eyes during the chanting. They need not be reminded that Coyote is associated with the dawn, a most powerful period of time: Coyote says, "You will hear my voice at dawn."

In one story, Coyote wants to kill Yeitso (Big Spirit, or Monster). To accomplish this, he lures him into the sweatlodge, where Yeitso has never been before, by convincing him that the sweatlodge can cure anything, even broken bones. After they are inside, the Monster demands proof of the sweatlodge's power. Coyote produces a deer's leg, which he has secretly brought inside, holds it where his own leg should be, and asks Yeitso to feel his leg. In the darkened sweatlodge, of course, no one can see anything. Yeitso feels what he takes to be Coyote's leg, after which Coyote smashes it to a pulp with a large rock. When Yeitso now feels the leg, he is amazed to find it virtually destroyed. Coyote now sings some songs, gets rid of the deer's leg, and asks Yeitso to feel again. Of course, Yeitso feels Coyote's own leg, and demands to try the same process on himself. Coyote teaches him the proper chants and cautions him to have patience, then gives him the rock, and on pretext of needing to urinate, departs. When he returns, of course, Yeitso has smashed his legs to bits and in spite of loud and furious singing has been unable to restore his legs to health. Coyote then delivers himself of a long and somewhat pompous oration on the need for patience in healing, the dangers of self-destruction (ironic topic for him, but memorable), and on the efficacies of the sweatlodge for those who use it properly. Yeitso dies in great pain.

This story is alluded to in several rituals, including, of course, those in which bones are set. The story is also related to hunting, partly because hunting deer entails killing, rending flesh from bone, and then later the ritual restoration of the deer in the sweatlodge. When I once asked Yellowman to tell me about the Navajo traditions of hunting, so I could record them on tape, he said: "First you need an introduction to what hunting is all about," whereupon, without further comment or explanation, he narrated a very long version of this Yeitso adventure. In the prayers which are recited before dawn on any day of deer season, the story is alluded to several times.

Another story tells how Coyote intrudes on the cornfields of Old Lady Horned Toad and starts eating all her ears of harvested corn. After failing to chase him away, she jumps on one of the ears and is swallowed, after which she takes a slow tour of Coyote's innards and methodically cuts him to shreds from within. As he dies, she comes up his gullet, slits his throat, and steps out—just barely in time to admonish him about eating too much corn, not sharing, eating inappropriate foods, and so on. Needless to say, this story is alluded to in treatments for stomach ailments. In addition, it is important to note that the horned toad is widely used as a symbol in sandpaintings and in everyday life, for the small lizard is equated with power, longevity, healing properties, and inner stability of the abdomen.

Since Old Lady Horned Toad has come close to death and come back, her story can be alluded to in any ritual in which the chief process has to do with restoring inner health. In addition, since she was impervious to death, she is considered a protective defense against disease and against the projectiles of enemies in war, or of witches. "She is a shield for us," say some Navajos, and they refer to this story in prayers for protection, especially when going to war. Also, when a traditional Navajo finds a horned toad along the way, she will usually pick it up, hold it to her heart, against her forehead, and briefly against the other parts of the body which are normally rubbed with corn pollen during healing cere- monies (inner forearms, inner thighs, top of head, etc.). While horned toads, corn pollen, and coyotes would not normally fit together in the same biological category in Western thought, they form a meaningful constellation for the Navajos: sacred nutrition, protection against outside malevolent forces, and healing of inner ailments stemming from inappropriate behavior—a cluster of sym- bolic reference based on an entirely different logical set.[5]

Other stories feature a variety of lizards. In one, Coyote sees the Lizard people entertaining themselves by sliding down a steep slope on flat stones. He demands (four times) to be allowed to play, and reluctantly the lizards teach Coyote how to slide. He gets overconfident, or chooses too large a stone, or a too-steep section of the slope, and the stone flips over (in some versions repeatedly, to the delight of listeners, who envision him appearing, then disap- pearing, under the wildly flipping stone). When the lizards find him at the bottom of the hill, he is mashed to a pulp, and there is nothing left but some fur and bones. They supply medicine and spirit power, and they dance around him until he revives and goes on his way. On the entertainment level, it is a funny story about Coyote botch- ing up his life again; on the moral level, it dramatizes the results of inappropriate intrusion into the normal lives of others; on the medicinal level, it provides still another source of healing imagery.

In another story, Coyote sees the Beaver people playing a hoop game that involves gambling and taking their skins off. Coyote insists on playing, is dissuaded three times, but is finally allowed to participate (usually, a request made four times cannot be denied). Coyote loses his hide entirely, but unlike the Beavers, his is not restored when he goes swimming in the river. In order to cure him and restore his skin, the Beaver people bury him in the ground until a new skin grows back. This story is referred to in rituals having to do with skin diseases, any ritual where regeneration is needed, any treatment for a disease triggered by intrusion or inappropriate behavior. Not so coincidentally, Navajo witches, when they put on or take off the animal skins they wear, are said to pass the same kind of hoops over their bodies as are used in the game mentioned in this story. Note that Coyote *loses* his hide by playing the hoop game, while witches *put on* hides using hoops. Coyote is *restored* by the Beavers, while people are *harmed* by witches. The protective and restorative functions of the Beavers are also dramatized in the Navajo myth of the Twin heroes: When their father, the Sun, tries to kill them by freezing them in the ocean, the Beaver covers the boys with her hide until morning, thus saving their lives.

The Coyote stories feature a continual round of death and restoration, with ants, horned toads, beavers, lizards (and others) either ensuring their own continued lives by prophylactic means, or resuscitating Coyote through their magic, knowledge of herbs, and symbolic powers. All of these processes seem to be happening within the stories, but the Navajos view them as actualities in the world they live in, in which ritual, symbolism, and language play a central role.

It is only fair to point out that, following the requests of the singers who shared this information with me, I have not provided the actual phrasing for most of the allusions actually made during healing rituals. Although some of this material is already in print in various studies of Navajo Chantways and can be ferreted out by the knowledgeable researcher, singers would rather that I not add more signposts, for reasons that will become more clear.

While I was pursuing some of these questions in the winter of 1982, an elderly singer asked that I stay on after other visitors had left his hoghan. It was late in the evening and we had enjoyed a long story-telling session. When all was quiet, he asked, "Are you ready to lose a member of your family?" When I responded negatively and with surprise, he unveiled to me a fourth level of meaning in the Coyote stories, one which I was totally unaware of, but which can readily be understood, given the nature of the information I have brought forward here. It has to do with witchcraft.

To the Navajos, witches are those who intend to do evil to others, usually by inflicting physical or psychological harm upon them. They are described as independent, competitive, acquisitive. If a Navajo becomes wealthy and does not share the goods, he or she may be suspected of witchcraft. Witches are characterized as having unbridled appetites for sex, and they can inflict psychological damage on others by the use of ointments, herbal magic, and the "shooting" of magical agents through the air. They are thought to be often in contact with death: They dig up graves in order to get old jewelry and body parts to use in their ceremonies. They consort with animals, almost exclusively with predators. They are most often, though not always, men, and the most feared of all are those who in their daily lives are medicine men ("singers"). They are aggressive and they come looking for their victims, doing their reconnaissance at night when most Navajos are at home with their families. They put on animal skins (wolf, coyote, or dog) by passing through ritual hoops (analogous to the hoops used by singers to *rid* people of disease), and since they wander about at night in the form of predators, they are called *yenaaldloshi* (literally "evil walking animal-like," but usually phrased as a noun in English: "skinwalker").

Since words and narratives have power to heal, they may also be used to injure and kill. Thus, when witches wish to damage the health of others, they use selected parts of the same Coyote stories in *their* rituals; the difference is that instead of integrating the story with a model of order and restoration, their idea of deployment is to use images, symbols, and allusions separately, divisively, analytically, in order to attack certain parts of the victim's body, or family, or livestock. One becomes a witch in order to gain personal fortune and power by causing weakness and death in others.

When one becomes a witch, the price of that power to destroy is paid by losing the life of a member of someone in the witch's family. Since my questions had been selective and analytical, since I was clearly trying to find out exactly what was powerful about Coyote stories, since I stood to gain by this knowledge, the old singer wanted to warn me of two possible dangers: If I became a witch, I would lose someone from my family; if others *thought* I was a witch, someone might try to kill someone in my family. In either case, Navajo informants would assume that my detailed knowledge indicated witchcraft, and no one would be willing to tell me stories any more. I later found out from a mutual friend that this singer was himself believed to be a powerful witch.

I now see a fairly complex system of four levels in which there are several pairs of related functions: Levels I and IV both deal with disorder; on Level I it is humorous drama which foregrounds and acts out the serious cultural values which exist unstated on the moral (worldview) plane, Level II; while on Level IV, the disorder is purposeful, focused, and destructive and causes many of the ailments which are treated on the medicinal plane, Level III. Levels I and II are experienced in the everyday life of the Navajos (at least during the winter when the tales are properly told, as well as at the summer equinox), which means that even though the narrations are restricted to certain times of year, they—and the worldview context of values which gives them meaning—are encountered at home under the normal circumstances of home life. Levels III and IV would be encountered only in a ritual setting under the control of a singer (or whatever the witches' equivalent may be). Levels I, II, and III, from the Navajo view, are concerned with integrating the individual spiritually and physically into the ongoing processes of life, while Level IV has to do with death and destruction (see chart 1).

It is tempting to imagine that this model has a mirror image in Navajo culture (much like the patterns on a Navajo rug), and that there is a "Level V" representing what the witches take to be Medicine, a "Level VI" that constitutes the witches' worldview and unstated moral system, and a "Level VII" that would be the stories told by witches to entertain themselves and raise their children. But we have no evidence of a separate set of stories told by witches; apparently, they listen to the same Coyote stories, but it may be they understand them to refer to a different set of values. Chart 2, then, suggests another way of viewing the matter. The question arises, in any case: Why would it be of interest and importance for Navajos to make this distinction, to believe in witches and witchcraft? Is there really such a thing as Navajo witchcraft? Does a non-Navajo researcher need to take heed of such a belief?

To begin with, Navajo witchcraft is a complicated phenomenon,

CHART 1.
LEVELS OF MEANING IN NAVAJO COYOTE NARRATIVES
(NAVAJO PERSPECTIVE)

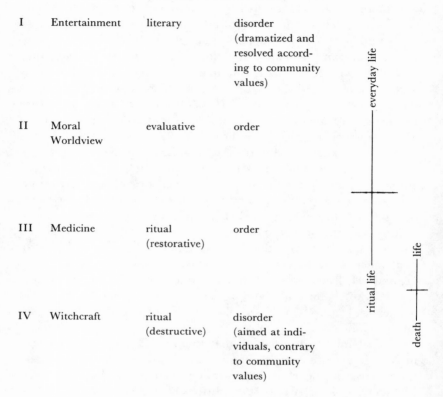

I	Entertainment	literary	disorder (dramatized and resolved according to community values)
II	Moral Worldview	evaluative	order
III	Medicine	ritual (restorative)	order
IV	Witchcraft	ritual (destructive)	disorder (aimed at individuals, contrary to community values)

and has already received a good deal of attention; I need not amplify the fact here that the belief is widespread and quite functional in the culture, for it is a subject of long standing in Navajo ritual belief and practice.[6] The ironic thing is that belief in witchcraft seems to be on the rise, and most heavily in those areas where Navajos have come into greatest and most enduring contact with whites. Another look at the characteristics of witches may indicate why: White culture is competitive and individual-centered. White people pay admission to watch people get killed in the movies. Violence and killing can be shown on their television shows. They

CHART 2.
LEVELS OF MEANING IN NAVAJO COYOTE NARRATIVES
("OBJECTIVE" PERSPECTIVE)

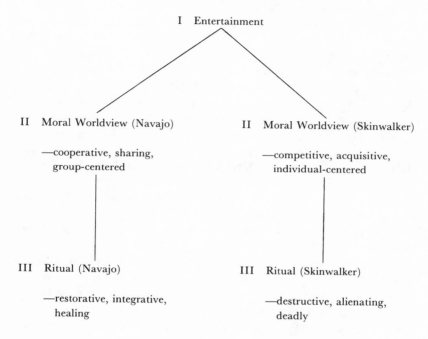

I   Entertainment

II   Moral Worldview (Navajo)

—cooperative, sharing,
  group-centered

II   Moral Worldview (Skinwalker)

—competitive, acquisitive,
  individual-centered

III   Ritual (Navajo)

—restorative, integrative,
  healing

III   Ritual (Skinwalker)

—destructive, alienating,
  deadly

encourage a system in which personal wealth and individual drive are seen as signs of success. In order for a Navajo child to be successful in school, he or she must begin acting like a witch. This must set up a considerable amount of stress among the Navajos, and I believe it shows in a number of the statistics on alcohol and family violence.

What I have stumbled on in my study, then, is nothing new, but it certainly brings up a number of important considerations about Navajo concepts of mental health in a world that seems to be having an erosive effect on their culture and values. But the situation presents a folklorist with a distinctly ethical dilemma and it places someone who has long-standing familial relations with the Navajo in a very delicate personal fix. Even if I reject their warning that there is danger in deeper inquiry into the stories, for me to actually do further work would necessitate a repudiation of Navajo beliefs and values—treasures that I feel ought to be strengthened and nurtured by folklore scholarship, not weakened, denigrated, or given away to curious onlookers.

Just as a folklorist needs to know where to begin, so one needs to recognize where to stop, and I have decided to stop here. My intention is to deal with Level IV of the Navajo stories not at all, beyond acknowledging here that it exists and that it is considered dangerous by those in whose world it functions. Level III, while fascinating, involves such heavy implications for Level IV that I think it should also be left alone by outsiders; the present essay is the fullest statement I anticipate making on it. There is plenty left to be said on Levels I and II, the levels which engage the conversation of several thousand Navajos in their homes in the evenings during the winter months. There is still much to be learned and said about the power of the Navajo language to articulate cultural values and to create the worlds of meaning in which they (and we) live. This strikes me as the appropriate area of inquiry for folklorists studying Navajo Coyote tales.

I do not mean for this to sound like the scholarly game of shut-the-door-so-the-unwashed-will-not-have-access-to-my-unique-information. Rather, as far as discussion of the Coyote tales is concerned, I intend to avoid the information myself, as unscientific and as unscholarly as that may seem. Indeed, in that regard, this is an un-scholarly non-essay, an un-report on what I am not going to be doing with texts recorded over the past twenty-five years. The Navajos have developed and, for the most part, retained an impressive body of oral literature that embodies many key aspects of their worldview on reality and on human health. Their concept of health is largely psychological in nature, thus any psychological intrusion can—and will—have an effect on them and on their sense of stability. The world which now surrounds them provides them with more than enough stress, tension, and dislocation, and I do not care to add our curiosity to their burden. In addition to the ethical, professional, and personal considerations, there is the distinct possibility that—as in the case of the prairie dogs at Chilchinbito—the Navajos may know exactly what they are talking about.[7]

NOTES

1. "The 'Pretty Languages' of Yellowman: Genre, Mode, and Texture in Navajo Coyote Narratives," *Genre* 2 (1969):211–235; repr. in Dan Ben-Amos, ed., *Folklore Genres* (Austin: University of Texas Press, 1976), 145–170.

2. "Poetic Retranslation and the 'Pretty Languages' of Yellowman," in Karl Kroeber, ed., *Traditional Literatures of the American Indian: Texts and Interpretations* (Lincoln: University of Nebraska Press, 1981), 65–116.

3. "Poetic Retranslation," 80, 90.

4. The most penetrating description of this feature in Navajo language is Gary Witherspoon, *Language and Art in the Navajo Universe* (Ann Arbor: University of Michigan Press, 1977).

5. For a full account of a ritual based on this constellation, see Leland C. Wyman, *The Red Antway of the Navajo*, Navaho Religion Series, vol. 5 (Santa Fe: Museum of Navajo Ceremonial Art, 1973).

6. The standard work on this subject, first issued in a limited 1944 monograph by Harvard University, is Clyde Kluckhohn, *Navaho Witchcraft* (Boston: Beacon Press,1967). Gladys Reichard of course notes it throughout *Navaho Religion: A Study of Symbolism*, 2d ed., Bollingen Series no. 18 (Princeton: Princeton University Press, 1974), as does almost every commentator on Navajo religion and culture. More recently, Margaret Brady has published a collection of Navajo children's narratives which focus mainly on the "skinwalker" complex: *Some Kind of Power: Navajo Children's Skinwalker Narratives* (Salt Lake City: University of Utah Press, 1984).

7. Most of the tales I have referred to in this article are available (without their ritual connections) in *Coyote Stories of the Navaho People* (Rough Rock, Arizona: Rough Rock Demonstration School, 1968); the stories are produced there in good translation, but of course they lack the stylistic devices of oral Navajo delivery which would make them meaningful to their normally esoteric audiences. The result is that they appear more or less like children's stories; perhaps, in view of the dimensions discussed in this paper, it is just as well. A more serious ritual aspect of the Coyote rituals is found in Karl W. Luckert, *Coyoteway: A Navajo Holyway Healing Ceremonial* (Tucson: University of Arizona Press, 1979); in this ceremony, instead of appearing in fragmentary allusions, Coyote provides the central generating power for an entire healing ritual. Much of Luckert's commentary provides strong evidence for those tremendous forces in the Coyote corpus which are available for use in affecting numan stability.

Wesucechak Becomes a Deer and Steals Language: An Anecdotal Linguistics Concerning the Swampy Cree Trickster[1]

HOWARD NORMAN

I

Wesucechak is the Omuskakoo, Swampy Cree, Trickster.[2] While there is no set physical description of Wesucechak, the name is evocative. We are offered what he does, what he turns into, or reversal of form (i.e., "Then he became Wesucechak again," or "He was tired of being a moose. He changed back"). Infinitely adapting to metamorphosis—as it must, since Wesucechak at any instant might "turn into" an animal or human—the name is kinetic. Wesucechak's vocation, his fate, is endless wandering; within his wanderings are hundreds of episodes. Today, as throughout past generations, Swampy Cree *tipachimoo* (tellers) delight audiences, children and adults alike, with Wesucechak's foibles and triumphs. In a tale, when Wesucechak enters a village his levity is highly suspect (should a teller say, "Wesucechak was lighthearted," children may shout, "Watch out!"); his earnestness is equally worrisome. His very appearance, in whatever mood, forecasts outlandish, even cataclysmic results—plundering, prestidigitating, other power-plays. He can juggle Time: in one narrative, Wesucechak makes a man walk so slowly that he becomes his own grandfather.

Without grief, morals, or guilt, Wesucechak teaches by negative example, as do many of his tribal counterparts throughout North

America, such as Coyote, Mink, Raven, and several phantasmagoric "human-like" beings (the latter may best describe Wesucechak). His talent for duping and clowning his way into positions of temporary power is inexhaustible. The most intimate of human endeavors, love-making, death, are by no means immune to Wesucechak's invasions. He meanders through personas, exploitations, lies, dramatic disclaimers, until each time a village (or individual) stops him. Then he is exiled. He "sets out again," or "goes walking," *ad infinitum.* He gives the impression of being entirely without memory (*entire* without memory) as we might normally think of it. Having created enormous stress, having wreaked havoc—say he has made a woman give birth to twin pheasants, or placed in a tree a deafening chorus of gray jays who camouflage his loud mating with every woman in a village—eventually he forgets he has done that very thing. One of his favorite, rhetorical exclamations, "Did I do that?" is said by many Cree tellers in a tone of exaggeratedly profound self-congratulation, seldom seeming like a true question, never infused with remorse. Nevertheless, put simply, one of his many traits is heroic: Wesucechak is immortal, insofar as this implies "able to endure as long as this world." Wesucechak is the junction of Time and Language. He has wandered the northern Manitoban forests and icy wetlands since before the Cree language existed. Indeed, it is said that he "brought words over" from animals to people.

Here is an essential vocabulary: *atuyokawin* is the act of relating an *atuyookao*, a legend about an *atuykun*, a hero. Narratives concerning Wesucechak are categorized as atuyookao. They can concern a time before the earth was in its present, definitive state (many Cree refer to this as "before people"), or be contemporaneous with *otawemak*, ancestors. Wesucechak, too, is very much active in today's world; in 1981, I heard a narrative in which he was responsible for the crash of a communications satellite near Great Slave Lake.

In August 1977, while traveling in the Burntwood River, Sipiwesk Lake region of Manitoba, my companion, John Rains, a forty-seven-year-old Cree man, related an atuyookao to an audience of fourteen people. It began: "This is about Wesucechak. He was out thieving things. He was thieving words this time. He'd been doing this for a long time, since long ago. People have to work hard to get the words back."

This essay, I hope, serves as a kind of anecdotal linguistics. I want especially to discuss the narrative "Wesucechak Learns About Double-Shout Lake," including two variants of another tale, one of which is the above-mentioned, told by John Rains. All of these tales illustrate the striking motif of Wesucechak's stalwart attempt to manipulate people by stealing words.

In "Wesucechak Learns About Double-Shout Lake," the word *deer* may be seen to represent what the Cree refer to as the "old agreement." This agreement provides a symbiosis between the Cree and food-animals. It is the basic moral and physical framework of the Cree's subsistence. Animals give themselves up if the Cree attend to them properly. When Wesucechak forces on someone a linguistic amnesia, makes that person forget an animal's name, the animal is insulted. One might say "an insult has been put on the land." The ecological consciousness of a Cree village is shaken. It can upset the overall equilibrium by, more succinctly, causing a break in communication between Cree hunters and their environment. The slighted food-animal may not "come around" for a considerable period of time; in dire, isolating winter months, this could initiate the process of starvation. Or, the animal may delve into *achestowyetumoowin* (roughly, "is holding an active grudge").

Ernst Cassirer's thought applies here: "The original bond between the linguistic and the mytho-religious consciousness is primarily expressed in the fact that all verbal structures appear as also mythical entities, endowed with certain mythical powers, that the Word, in fact, becomes a sort of primary force, in which all being and doing originate" (1946:44). When in a Cree narrative an insult takes place, it is required that the food-animal's name be spoken out loud; a praise-song forceful enough to counteract the insult is sung, or some other reparation made.

II

Wesucechak gave the Cree language, and became a thief of it; the three narratives included here well attest to this. His uncanny repertoire of linguistic intrusions is not, however, limited to theft—he has devised a variety of methods. Wesucechak is a consummate mimic ("he can talk as anyone"), and is equally unsurpassed as a ventriloquist (in one narrative he "throws" from his throat the myriad sounds of a nighttime swamp, making them seem to emanate from a daytime field). Gaston Bachelard has written of metamorphosis as part of the "visual language of fear in myth." More often than not, Wesucechak metamorphoses spontaneously— in one sentence! Sometimes, however, we witness a slower evolution. Here Wesucechak is about to join a flock of crows in flight:

> Wesucechak was very angry, he was hopping sideways and flapping his arms, but he hadn't flown yet. He wasn't a crow yet.
> . . . .
> Wesucechak was flying with crows now. He tried out his crow voices. He thought he'd start up a conversation in the air. But the crows told him, "Those are the voices we use on the ground!"

Wesucechak can make a person stutter, or confuse and frustrate a speaker with obnoxious interruptions, or make a person mute, as in "Wesucechak Steals Who-Crawls-Through-Dusk." In the tale in which Wesucechak makes a man walk so slowly he goes "into" his own grandfather, the lapse is verbal. The young man does not grow wrinkled or hobbled. He simply speaks in the voice and through the memory of his grandfather. Consequently, the elders in his village gather near him. They reminisce. During their conversations, it is revealed that many of them still suffer nightmares about a lightning storm that struck their village when they were children. Wesucechak, ever the eavesdropper, snaps up this useful information. That night, he brings in a storm whose lightning bolts split trees and char a flock of geese huddling among reeds. In all the commotion, Wesucechak easily ransacks the village's supply of fish. He takes a few caribou shoulders as well. Indicted by the elders for such ill-doings, he is insulted. He responds with yet another rhetorical (egomaniacal) recitation that might be called dithyrambic: "WHO DO YOU THINK MADE LIGHTNING? WHO DO YOU THINK MADE GEESE? WHO DO YOU THINK MADE THE WORLD?"

Rarely, but nonetheless effectively, Wesukechak uses *strays*. In "Wesucechak and the Fainting Bird," for example, those seemingly nonsensical phrases spoken by A-Damp-Night are strays (see appendix). In the linguistic sense, strays are vagabond alignments of words that suddenly wedge into an otherwise coherent sentence.

When this occurs, the speaker is bewildered by what he hears himself saying. At his least harmful Wesucechak makes strays merely laughable distractions—at worst, they can torment a person for a long time, as a kind of aphasia.

III. THE TEXT

"Wesucechak Learns About Double-Shout Lake"[3]

Wesucechak hadn't caused trouble in a few days. He went walking. He said, "I'm going to the first village I ever made." He was talking about a time, long ago, when he walked around starting villages. Duck villages. Wolf villages. Crow villages. Animals scattered out from these villages. Then he started human villages, too. Wesucechak started those! Wesucechak knew about the origin of many things. But he also brag-lied. He twisted stories around, if he wanted something. Sometimes his tricks worked, sometimes they didn't. Yet no matter what he did, Wesucechak ended up setting out again alone. Walking. And the time I'm telling about here, Wesucechak said, "I'm going to that village of humans. I'll tell them who made their village I'll tell them who made the world. They'll take good care of me there . . . "

As he neared the village, Wesucechak smelled fish and heard scale-scraping; noises of fish out of water. Then he heard an old woman say, "This pickerel had a bad temper. He bit at reeds. He chased himself," she laughed. Wesucechak walked closer, to watch. The old woman scraped the scales from the fish. Then she cut it open and took out its insides. Up in a tree, a crow asked for the insides of the fish. The crow said, "Give me those insides and I'll tell you what I see from up here . . . " The old woman tossed the fish insides on the ground, and the crow swooped down and ate them. Then the crow said, "From in my tree I saw fish insides being tossed to the ground. Awwwgh, awwwgh!"

Whenever a crow came around, humans got some practice in being tricked. But the old woman tricked back, "Crow—you know what I saw in those fish insides?"

"What?" the crow said.

"No, first you tell me if Wesucechak is around here. Then I'll tell you what I saw in those fish insides."

The crow flew from tree to tree. The crow circled the village, then landed again. "No, Wesucechak isn't around," the crow told the old woman.

"Then who's that standing just at the edge of our village?" she said.

With that, the crow flew. But the crow had to worry what was in those fish insides! The crow worried the whole day about this.

The old woman went on cleaning fish. Wesucechak still hid in the trees. The old woman said, "This pickerel,"—she held it very still, in the air—could hold still in the fastest of currents . . . Then she scraped that fish. She cut it open and tossed its insides on the ground, but the crow didn't take them. Then the old woman held a pickerel away from her. She said, "This one has many scars from fighting. This one liked to fight." She scraped that fish too. She had a good memory, from what she was taught and from what she saw. Many women were cleaning fish, and she was talking about the fish lives. "Pickerel have difficult lives," she said, "but they can have good lives too." She talked about pickerel.

Just then Wesucechak shouted, "WHO DO YOU THINK MADE PICKEREL? WHO DO YOU THINK MADE THE WORLD?"

Nobody looked up. They just went on cleaning fish. The old woman said "The edge of the village is talking again."

"IT'S ME SHOUTING! WESUCECHAK!"

The women just went on cleaning fish.

The old woman said, "There's still a very old pickerel in the lake," she wrinkled her face, "so old, old, old. And so smart about life, it even forgot how to be caught. Doesn't even think about that! So old, it's learned to nab a whole day from the top of the water—just before the day sinks into the lake. Old. Old. I'm thinking this pickerel made the world," she said. She didn't look over at Wesucechak.

Hearing all this, Wesucechak grew angry. He shouted, "I MADE THE WORLD!"

The old woman leaned over to listen, at a fish. "I hear someone shouting. Is it you, fish?"

More angry, Wesucechak stood right in front of the old woman. "I'M HERE!"

Finally the old woman looked up from the fish. She said, "Are *you* Wesucechak? I can't remember."

More angry, Wesucechak said, "Can't you see who it is? CAN'T YOU REMEMBER? I MADE YOUR VILLAGE! I TAUGHT YOU TO CLEAN FISH!"

The old woman looked back to the fish. "I'm sorry, fish," she said, shaking her head, "I planned only to remember things about you fish today. But now it seems I'll have to remember something else . . . "

Then she said to Wesucechak, "Well, I'm still not sure it's really you. I'll have to ask old Two Loons. She'll know. She has the best memory of anyone."

"I HAVE THE BEST MEMORY!"

"Now I remember something else," the woman said. "I remember that Two Loons has a better memory than Wesucechak. A better memory than you, Wesucechak, who has none! If that's who you really are!"

All this made Wesucechak even more angry.

The old woman walked Wesucechak to a lake. Wesucechak just followed her. Whenever an old woman walked to a lake, Wesucechak followed even though he never knew what would happen there. On the lake shore, the old woman shouted, "Two Loons! . . . "

"Two Loons! . . . Two Loons!" the lake shouted back.

This was a lake that doubled every shout.

She dove into the lake. She disappeared under the water. Soon she flew out and stood in front of Wesucechak. She was dripping wet. She said, "I am Two Loons. But I had to dive into this lake to remember that. I have the best memory, after I dive into this lake."

Then Wesucechak felt water dripping from himself, too. "WHO DID THIS TO ME?" he pointed to the water dripping from him. "WHO DID THIS TO ME?"

"That's just the kind of thing this lake does," Two Loons said.

Wesucechak was confused. Wesucechak was puzzled by this, but still he said, "I knew that! WHO DO YOU THINK MADE THIS LAKE?" He bragged.

Wesucechak bragged but Two Loons was already walking away from him, toward the village. Then she flew there. Wesucechak followed her.

When they arrived in the village, Wesucechak gathered everyone together. Everyone was supposed to look at him.

Then Wesucechak turned into a deer.

Wesucechak asked Two Loons, "What is my name?"

Two Loons said, "*Utiwaswun.*" . . . deer horns.

Then worry was on everyone's faces. Two Loons noticed this.

Two Loons tried again, "Your name is *Utiwas-tise* . . . " . . . deer's sinew.

Someone said, "Two Loons can't remember the word!"

Two Loons grew frightened and began calling out, "Deer-eyes, deer voice, deer hooves!" But none of these worked.

Wesucechak then said, "I'm making it so you—Two Loons—are the only one who can call DEER in close. So if you can't remember how to say DEER, all the DEER will be insulted and leave, and there will be no DEER to eat!"

Two Loons flew back to the lake, and Wesucechak followed. She dove in, and swam on the lake awhile. She flew out and landed back in the village. Soon after Wesucechak arrived. There Two Loons began to sing:

> You who stands sideways
> looking at us
> You who flick your tail
> up
> You whose fawn is covered
> with dew

Her song went on, and it had many deer in it, and the things you always see deer doing.

The deer were listening. They heard that Two Loons knew many things about them, and they were pleased with this. The deer walked into the village.

"They're giving themselves up!" someone said.

When this was said, many more deer appeared next to the lake. Some were killed and stored for food and some were eaten right away. Seeing the deer being killed frightened Wesucechak so he changed back to his old self, just in time!

Two Loons said, "Yes, that must be Wesucechak, who remembered to change back in time! Ha!—he's no longer a DEER." There was much laughing.

This laughing sent Wesucechak out of the village. He went walking.

He walked and walked, and he couldn't find anything to eat. "I'll find something in a dream!" he said. Then he fell asleep. It became night. During the night, Wesucechak turned over in his sleep. He turned again. Then he turned another way, all during his sleeping. When he woke, he said, "In which direction was I walking in?" He'd forgotten. His sleep-turning got him lost. He set out again. He walked and walked. He said, "That dream didn't bring me any food!"

After awhile Wesucechak smelled something. Venison! He walked to a village-edge. In the village he saw people preparing a deer to eat. This made him call out, "I'M HUNGRY!"

No one looked up from the deer. Wesucechak shouted, "WHO DO YOU THINK MADE DEER?"

Just then Two Loons landed on Wesucechak's head. He was back in the same village! Two Loons said, "Why should we give you food? You tried not to let us eat deer!"

"Did I do that?" Wesucechak said. "Did I do that?"

Then a villager tossed Wesucechak some antlers. Another tossed him some deer's sinew. Another tossed him some deer hooves. Wesucechak begged for venison . . .

They went on cleaning the deer.

Wesucechak threw himself to the ground. He groaned. He groaned and cried. He tied the antlers to his own head. He tied the deer hooves to his own feet. He begged for venison again.

Finally they gave Wesucechak some venison to eat.

Wesucechak can't change though! He tried to get more. He tried to gobble the whole deer! But the villagers wouldn't let him. They sent him walking. He went walking, but right away his antlers got stuck in some low branches. He tripped and fell over, and the groaning and crying started up for real then. He got up but fell again, because he couldn't walk on those hooves. Finally he took them off, the hooves and antlers.

He went walking.

IV

I suspect that the teller, Samuel Grey Sturgeon, had expanded the first part (first paragraph in my translation) for the benefit of the non-Cree listener, especially the sentences, "Sometimes his tricks worked, sometimes they didn't. Yet no matter what he did, Wesucechak ended up setting out alone again," which would be blatantly redundant to a wholly Cree audience. In the last sentence of the first paragraph, Wesucechak prefaces his trickstering with grandiose etiological declarations ("I'll tell them who made their village," etc.) to exonerate himself beforehand; the implication and presumption are that no matter how awfully he behaves, people will ultimately be beholden to him, as they owe him their very existence. As teller John Rains said, "He thinks something's true just because he's said it."

In the second paragraph, Wesucechak first hears his adversary, the old woman (transformed Two Loons), who represents accumulated Time-Wisdom, therefore *memory*, decidedly a threat to him. This paragraph is peculiarly interesting, too, in that in Cree Trickster narratives—at least in the hundreds I have witnessed—it is only in the three variants included here that this "testing" of a village's resistance to trickery takes place (see appendix), with the principal antagonist being a character other than Wesucechak. Since Wesucechak, in other narratives, on occasion uses owls, weasels, wolverines, and so on, as emissaries of different sorts, it can be assumed that the crow serves a similar function—especially as the otherwise opportunistic crow lies on Wesucechak's behalf, obviously under his influence. That the old woman "tricked back" at the crow, with Wesucechak observing, amplifies her role as adversary. Then it is told that there are "many women" cleaning fish, and that the older woman continues to be the teacher among them. Watching, listening, Wesucechak is put in a child-elder relationship—he's being told about fish, exactly the way a Cree child is educated in this skill. What is more, the information Wesucechak hears whittles away at his pose as originator of all things—his delusion—and therefore at his control over his environment, especially when the old woman speculates on the intuitive wisdom of the old pickerel she is holding: ". . . old, old, old. And so smart about life, it even forgot how to be caught." Unlike Wesucechak, who is always caught by his own greeds, lust, and so forth. "Old, old," the woman continues, "I'm thinking this pickerel made the world" (the coup de grace).

Wesucechak's literal hunger, plus his longing to "belong," to be invited into a village, also reveals him as not being in control of his environment. Under normal circumstances a visitor would be asked to join in with the fish-cleaning, to earn one's meal, and this in turn assumes that one is at least tacitly participating in the "old agreement." Wesucechak, however, is *never* invited in (in fact, sometimes he is pointedly rejected, as in "Wesucechak Steals Who-Crawls-Through-Dusk"). Of course, Wesucechak is further enraged when his bravado and the wild exclamations by which he defines himself ("IT'S ME SHOUTING! WESUCECHAK!") result in: "The women just went on cleaning fish." Initial recognition of who he is would be the springboard of his power; here, though, total disregard for his presence defuses Wesucechak.

As the verbal jousting continues, Wesucechak is almost reduced to begging for recognition, and the old woman builds up to another assault: her own metamorphosis. This is even more of an incitation; she utilizes one of Trickster's primary strategies for gaining power. That is supposed to be *his* domain, his wild card. He will of course use it later when he turns into a deer and steals language, but for the moment the tables are turned.

At this point in the narrative the circuitous argument about *memory* leads to water. The whole Swampy Cree region (the name itself) is riverine, dotted with pothole lakes, a wetland. In his wanderings Wesucechak is always near water. In many Cree narratives water is the repository of memory, of "history." Each day "sinks into water" (note that in "Wesucechak Steals Who-Crawls-Through-Dusk," Trickster gargles in order to recall his future wife's name). Eventually Two Loons dives into Double-Shout Lake, then not only remembers her name but becomes her name incarnate—a loon. In the equation of memory and power, Two Loons (two-water-birds-in-one), joining with Double-Shout Lake multiplies her formidability. She has become her true self, an animal, part of the older order of things, who gave language to people through Wesucechak. Finally, by defeating Wesucechak's oppositional force at the end of the narrative, the "old agreement" is reinstated: that older world and language again woven together.

Before this inevitably occurs, however, we witness the theft of language; Wesucechak has taken the word *deer* (*wawaskasew*, red deer). He has changed it into a false word, in this respect, since he is in the form of a deer but does not act as any deer would. His behavior falsely represents deer. In this he assaults the sacredness of the "old agreement." Two Loons reverses all of this by flattering the deer with the explicit details of her praise-song.

The boomeranging continuum of Wesucechak's attempt to gain power ends with his begging again, under false pretenses, for the very venison of which he would have deprived his hosts. On his way out of their village the first time, Wesucechak assumed that his own subconscious (which he may well be working from night and day anyway)—that is, his dreaming—would provide food for him, or at least "map" food out. In this he wasn't entirely misguided. After tossing and turning, he wanders back to Two Loons's village; fate has puppeteered him there. While receiving a second barrage of ridicule, he is in fact fed, then exiled. Leaving once again, he mocks his own deer-metamorphosis, failing worse than the first time, tripping on his hooves.

I wish to point out here that during Samuel Grey Sturgeon's telling of "Wesucechak Learns about Double-Shout Lake" there was a crescendo of audience response throughout this part:

> Then Wesucechak felt water dripping from himself, too. "WHO DID THIS TO ME?" He pointed to the water dripping from him. "WHO DID THIS TO ME?"
> "That's just the kind of thing this lake does," Two Loons answered.
> Wesucechak was confused. Wesucechak was puzzled by this, but still he said, "I knew that! WHO DO YOU THINK MADE THIS LAKE?" he bragged.

It was clear that at this point Wesucechak was found out. In a later conversation, when I asked Sam Sturgeon why his audience had responded so enthusiastically at that moment, he said, "Wesucechak—they knew he had to think up something fast."

APPENDIX

Variant—1

WESUCECHAK STEALS WHO-CRAWLS-THROUGH-DUSK[4]

Wesucechak was out walking. Not too far from here. It was over by the Burntwood. He hadn't been sleeping. He was staying awake, day and night.

He arrived at a village-edge. It was nearing dusk. There was something going on in the village. Wesucechak drew closer. He saw that a sleepwalking contest was going on. Everyone had gathered for it.

Presently a young woman walked out of her house, into the center of the village. Her name was *Who-Crawls-Through-Dusk*. She was beautiful, a beautiful woman. As a child she earned her name. Whenever dusk arrived she got restless and she crawled around. After dusk her mother would soak her daughter's knees.

Now the beautiful woman was sleepwalking.

Just then, a crow landed on her head. "Awwgh! Invite me to sleepwalk!" the crow said.

"Be quiet," the young woman's mother said. "You'll wake her up."

"Invite me to sleepwalk!" the crow said.

"All right," the old woman said, "Go ahead, sleepwalk."

With this, the crow fell asleep. Then it walked right off Who-Crawls-Through-Dusk's head! The crow fell to the ground. It was knocked out. When it woke up, it said, "Did I win?"

"No, you fell to the ground," said the old woman.

The crow flew to the village-edge.

The contest was about to start up again.

It was then that Wesucechak arrived, and walked into the center of the village. "I'll go first!" he said.

"No! You can watch," said the old woman, "but you can't sleepwalk among us."

"WHO DO YOU THINK MADE SLEEPWALKING?" Wesucechak shouted.

Then Who-Crawls-Through-Dusk began to speak. Her mouth opened, but no words came out.

"Hey—hey," said a man, "what is she saying?"

"I'm the only one who knows," Wesucechak said. "Follow me. A lake has got her voice."

"No—no, don't," the old woman said. "Don't stay with Wesucechak. Just bring a little lake water back for her to drink."

Everyone except the old woman went with Wesucechak to the lake. They guided Who-Crawls-Through-Dusk along with them, too.

"We are here. Here is the lake," said Wesucechak. Then he

took up some water into his mouth. He tilted his head back and gargled. This was loud. He gargled loudly, then spit the water out, along with some fish. He said, "I know her name now. It is Who-Crawls-Through-Dusk. Bring her closer."

Some people brought the beautiful woman over to Wesucechak.

"Now I'll marry her!" Wesucechak said.

Just then a young man cried out, "Oh, oh!" He held up his hands. "The tips of my fingers are frostbitten!"

"But this is summer!" another man said.

"Still, they are frostbitten," he said. Then he showed everyone his fingers. "They'll fall off!"

"Wake her up now!" a man said. "She knows about such things. She knows how to call deer in quickly. She knows how to thaw out fingers in a deer's entrails."

They did that. They woke her up. "Look, this man's fingers are frostbitten," they said.

She opened her mouth. No words came out. But a deer arrived.

But this deer was Wesucechak!

He said, "What is my name?"

She opened her mouth. Again, no words came out.

"I'm making it so that she is the only one who can call deer in," Wesucechak said. "I've made this so. Unless I marry her, this man's fingers will stay frozen."

"I don't care," said the man. "Never—never will she marry Wesucechak." The man was betrothed to Who-Crawls-Through-Dusk. They were going to be married right after the sleepwalking contest.

"Try again," the man said.

She tried again. She opened her mouth. No words came out.

Then it was night. Everyone could hear the man whose fingers were frozen groaning with pain. He was next to his bride-to-be. But in the night he saw some deer entrails steaming on the ground. He went and put his fingers in them—but just then Wesucechak appeared! Wesucechak took up the entrails and put them back into his own stomach!

The next morning she was gone, the beautiful woman was gone.

"He's taken her!" cried the man. "Wesucechak's taken her!"

Everyone went out to search, but they could not find her.

"They've gone far away," the mother said.

Wesucechak took the young woman off to a hiding place far away. There she became pregnant. When the child was born it was a deer. The deer-son grew up there. She weaned him and took care of him. Then, one morning, they ran off—back to the village.

"This is my son," she said there.

Presently the man whose fingers were still frostbitten walked over. "Look, my fingers have remained so," he said. "Give me your entrails," he said to the deer-son.

Then Wesucechak arrived. He was still a deer. "Give her back to me," he said. "Give my deer-son back too."

"We'll have a contest," said the old woman. "A sleepwalking contest. The winner can do as he pleases. The loser must give up his entrails to the frostbitten man."

"All right," said Wesucechak.

"All right," said the deer-son.

The contest began. Both of them fell asleep. They started to walk. They walked and walked, in opposite directions. Then Wesucechak tripped over some rocks. He fell down. He was crawling around. He was a deer crawling as a human would. Then he woke up. He said, "WHO DO YOU THINK MADE SLEEP-WALKING?"

"You woke up," the old woman said. "You woke yourself up. You lost."

The deer-son was still sleepwalking. Some people woke him up.

All right," someone said. "Let's bathe this man's fingers in that deer's entrails." He pointed at Wesucechak.

"NO!" shouted Wesucechak. Then he wasn't a deer any more. He was himself again. Now the man's fingers were warm again.

Who-Crawls-Through-Dusk said, "Now my son, who is a DEER, will be a handsome boy." And this happened.

Then the marriage took place. Wesucechak was sent away beforehand, far away from the marriage. He went walking.

Variant—2

WESUCECHAK AND THE FAINTING BIRD[5]

This is about Wesucechak. He was out thieving things. He was thieving words this time. He'd been doing this since long ago. People have to work hard to get them back.

This time he was very hungry. He said, "I'll go fishing." He fished but he had no luck.

So, he started walking. He happened upon a village. Everyone there was preparing fish. They were going to have a feast.

Presently a crow landed, right on the edge of a cooking pot! "These fish are rotten!" the crow said. "They'll make you toss around the village."

An old woman said, "Okay—thanks for telling us." Then the villagers stood away from the fish. With this, the crow picked up a fish and flung it over to Wesucechak, who was standing just outside the village edge. Wesucechak quickly ate the fish.

Then he walked into the village. But, suddenly, he began tossing around! He tossed up, then swirled upsidedown. He did somersaults. Then he lay on the ground, gasping.

"That's an honest crow!" the old woman said. Everyone laughed at Wesucechak.

This made him angry. He said to the old woman, "Give me your daughter. I'll marry her now."

"No—!" the old woman said. "She's betrothed to A-Damp-Night."

Just then A-Damp-Night said, "Go away."

With this, Wesucechak turned him into a kingfisher.

"Now we'll have a contest," the old woman said. "The winner can marry my daughter. The loser must leave. It will be a fishing contest."

This was agreed on.

The kingfisher flew to a branch. Then he dove and caught a fish. When he got back to his branch everyone saw that he had stabbed right through the fish with his bill! The fish was stuck there. The kingfisher couldn't swallow it!

"He can't swallow the fish!" the old woman said.

Then Wesucechak dove into the lake and came up with many fish.

"I won," he said. "Now I'll marry your daughter."

"No—!" the old woman said, "that was just the first part of the contest. Now both of you must tell about fishing."

The kingfisher flew down. The old woman removed the fish from his bill.

"WHO DO YOU THINK MADE FISH?" Wesucechak said.

The kingfisher said, "I was on my branch. I was looking down at the lake. I saw a fish. Then I *APIWEKIPIWESE* . . . ! What did I just say? I was looking down at the lake. I saw a fish. I dove. Then I OOPIKEMESTIS! What?" The kingfisher stopped talking. He was very confused.

"Wesucechak is making him stray this way!" the old woman said.

Wesucechak turned the kingfisher back into A-Damp-Night.

With this, Wesucechak said, "The contest is over." Then he took the old woman's daughter away. He took her to a far place. There she became pregnant. When the child was born it was a kingfisher! She took care of it. She raised it. Then one day they went back to their village. But what they found was a pond! In the pond were all the villagers! They were fish now.

Presently Wesucechak arrived. He said, "Come back with me— now!"

"No!" they said.

"Okay—" Wesucechak said. Then he was a kingfisher. He dove in and started to fish. He came out with a fish in his mouth. He was about to swallow it, when the young woman said, "No—don't. That is a villager!"

"Then return with me," Wesucechak said.

"All right," she said. "But we'll need some food. Better catch some fish. But don't catch my villagers."

Wesucechak dove back in. But the villager-fish caught him! They held onto Wesucechak. "Let me go!" he shouted. They let him go then.

"I'll ask you this: who won the contest?" the woman said.

Wesucechak changed the fish back to villagers again. "But now I'm starving!" he said.

The villagers gave him some fish. Wesucechak tossed and flung around—out of the village. That's how he left.

Variant—2

WESUCECHAK AND THE FAINTING BIRD[5]

Wesucechak was hungry. He went fishing but he caught nothing. No luck. He went walking. He happened upon a village. In the village they were smoking fish on big racks—fish were everywhere! Wesucechak wanted those fish.

Presently a crow arrived and landed on a fish-smoking rack. "Awgh! Those fish are rotten!" He said. "They look fine but the poison in them will make you toss around the village. You'll toss around the village in different ways, if you eat those fish. Better leave them alone!"

"Thanks for telling us!" an old woman said, whose daughter was about to be married. "Yes, we'll leave the fish alone. My daughter doesn't want to be tossing around the village before she gets married!" Then the people there stood away from the fish. Quickly the crow took up a fish and dropped it in the bush. Wesucechak ate it up right away, but when he walked into the village he began tossing around. Up in the air he tossed, and he fell onto the ground and tossed around there too.

"That's an honest crow!" the old woman said. Everyone laughed.

"WHO DO YOU THINK MADE FISH?" Wesucechak shouted.

The crow flew off.

Then the old woman said to Wesucechak, "Be off too."

But Wesucechak turned her into a kingfisher. She was in a branch over a lake. She flew out and dove into the water, and when she came up she had caught a fish! But—there was this: the kingfisher had stabbed the fish straight through. Its bill was sticking out through the fish. The kingfisher flew back to its branch. But it couldn't swallow the fish because its bill was stuck in it!

"She can't swallow the fish!" a man said.

"No—she can't!" Wesucechak said. "I'm making it so that no one can swallow fish!"

The fish was stuck on the kingfisher's bill. Now the fish was drying. It dried and grew stiff. It was days in a row that the kingfisher couldn't eat. Then she fainted and fell into the lake.

A man from the village took his canoe out and picked her up. He tried to pull the dried fish from her bill but it wouldn't come off. He put her back on her branch.

"Don't bother with her!" Wesucechak said. "I'll take care of that dried fish." Then the dried fish fell away. The starving kingfisher said, "Now I can eat!" Then Wesucechak made all the other villagers turn into fish. They were swimming under the kingfisher, who was very hungry. She dove and stabbed a fish. She flew with it to her branch but when she was about to swallow it she recognized it as her own daughter!

"Wesucechak turn her back!"

"Only if I can marry her," Wesucechak said.

"No—" the kingfisher said. "I'd rather starve." Then she dropped her daughter, who was a fish, toward the lake. But before she landed Wesucechak turned her into a human anyway.

Now the kingfisher saw Wesucechak about to take her daughter away. She flew at Wesucechak's head. Wesucechak threw himself onto the ground.

"Hey—hey," he shouted, "stop that!"

"No," the kingfisher said, "no!"

But Wesucechak took her away anyway. He took her to a far place. When they had a child it was a kingfisher! The young woman raised it up. Then one day they ran back to the village. No one was there! They all were still fish.

Wesucechak arrived then. "Come back with me," he said.

"No," they said. "We'll have a contest. A fishing contest. Whoever wins can decide where we will live. The loser must leave."

The contest began. Wesucechak and the kingfisher-son hovered over the lake. They both dove.

Wesucechak went into the water but he didn't come out! The fish-villagers had caught him! He shouted, "Let me go!" This they did.

The kingfisher-son said, "Look." They saw he had a pile of fish.

"You've lost," the young woman said. "Leave now."

"No, I'm starving," Wesucechak said. "Give me that pile of fish."

"First change the fish back to humans," she said.

This Wesucechak did. The fish in the lake became humans again. Then Wesucechak took up the pile of fish and ate it all. Then he tossed around—he tossed and flung himself out of the village! That's how he left.

NOTES

1. This essay was originally a lecture given at The Center for Northern Studies in Wolcott, Vermont; it was the first in a three-part series on northern Trickster figures.

2. I use the Swampy Cree term *Wesucechak*. However, within the Cree language other names for Trickster exist; *Westokik* is popular in the Sandy Lake region, *Wisahketchahk* is spoken of among the Sweet Grass Cree of Saskatchewan, and so forth. That Trickster has many names seems consistent with the diversity of his character.

3. "Wichikapache [Wesucechak] Learns About Double-Shout Lake," was narrated on July 26, 1976 by Samuel Grey Sturgeon, Kiskito Lake, Manitoba.

4. "Wichikapache [Wesucechak] Steals Who-Crawls-Through-Dusk," was narrated on September 4, 1977 by Michael Autao, Sipiwesk Lake, Manitoba.

5. Narrated by John Rains, Sipiwesk Lake, Manitoba. "Wichikapache [Wesucechak] and The Fainting Birds," was narrated on August 8, 1977 by Tommy Pike, Gods Lake, Manitoba.

REFERENCES

Cassirer, Ernst. 1946. *Language and Myth* (New York: Harper & Brothers).

How the Bird that Speaks Lakota Earned a Name

JULIAN RICE

Acquiring the *śicun*, or spiritual potency, of a Lakota oral narrative depends upon restoring as much of the traditional symbolic context as possible. Selecting a central symbol in a given story can be an effective means of intensifying a merely episodic narrative into a concentrated source of eidetic vision. Like a sacred song or a *wakan* stone, such a story may be "read" many times over without depleting its power to augment *wookaĥniġe* (understanding) in listeners of varying development. But experienced as a written text, a Lakota story recovers much of its vitality when it is recognized as a compressed symbolic sequence, like a ceremony. Only essential characters and actions are manifested to the listener, for whose benefit a temporary depletion of power has been suffered by the teller. Such a story-as-rite wastes little time on diverting description or surprising reversals. Only the youngest listeners are likely to be transported by a suspenseful plot or character conflict; the rest will know what happens, not only at the end of any given story but at the end of each episode. The narrator is supplied by a vast literary *parfléche* from which he draws character relationships and deeds so that the achievements of Blood-Clot Boy in one story may be those of Falling Star in another.

Eugene Buechel, S.J., did not exclude English translations from his *Lakota Tales and Texts* because he was a purist who believed in only one correct version. His experience was reportedly similar to that of the collection's editor, Paul Manhart, S.J., who observed the creative elasticity possessed by a living oral tradition:

> I personally witnessed, in the course of a period of six months, a master Sioux story-teller, Mr. Frank Kills Enemy of Kyle, South Dakota, spontaneously tell the story of the Bat in three unique but different ways and as a spoken interpretation of three distinct but related current life situations. I could only stand and marvel. (Buechel 1978:ix)

The adjustment to a different audience or situation could sometimes be so specific as to be focused upon one individual. In a 1969 interview conducted by Bea Medicine for the American Indian Research Project, Mrs. Rachel Ashley recalls the impact of trickster stories upon her childhood in Fort Thompson, South Dakota:

> Usually, when they told an *Iktomi* story, it was usually if you were a bad little child that day and you did something wrong, then the story would be about you; but it would be the *Unkto* who was the character. . . . So anything you did could be translated into a story so you see a lot of these stories weren't documented because it was on your individual behavior for the day. From day to day to day it changed. If you were good, then it was a good story. If you were naughty, then it was an *Unkto* story. And usually you sorted that out in your mind somehow that you must have been the *Unkto* because you sort of acted like him, you know. (Ashley 1969:18–19)

Like all stories that are good enough to repeat, Lakota oral narratives could further the growth of adults as well as children. An experienced storyteller urges his listeners to *blihe'iciyayo* (take courage) on the basis of the story's example. The theme of encouragement is animated by the continuing presence of benevolent supernatural powers among the Lakota people in the historical past, in the lives of the story's characters, and in the immediate transmission of the story.

Conscientious readers must place themselves within the circle of shared associations if they are to assist in the expression of a story's wakan resonance, its only true value. Critics cannot rely complacently on their personal insights or non-Lakota associations any more than an already developed, spiritual persons can expect to receive additional visions without disciplined effort. Each aspect of *lakol wicoh'an* (Lakota ways) should be patiently studied and imaginatively related to the whole tradition within the circumference of the students' experience as their knowledge grows. And that circumference should remain within the hoop of a specific tradition for a sustained period if the subtleties and details of the literature are to appear to readers, of whom many, perhaps even most, do not understand the language or customs of the *hunka* (ancestors).

In the recently reclaimed territory of traditional oral narratives, inexperienced readers should follow the road of specific cultural knowledge straight past archetypal accommodation, even if its categories offer authoritative definitions of American Indian culture. This dead-end prospecting usually inhibits continued growth. An analogy-gatherer bags his limit of specimens, stashes them as evidence for the existence of a pattern, and eventually publishes. A familiar example may be drawn from Joseph Campbell's *The Hero with a Thousand Faces* (1972:326–330). The collective hero of the human spirit is a foundling, adopted by humble people and often by animals. In most Lakota versions of the "Wicaȟpi Hinȟpaya" (Falling Star) story the animal guardian is a meadowlark, a bird with strong, specific significance in Lakota stories, ceremonies, and everyday life. Noting "meadowlark," the archetypal critic might simply list the bird in the "animal guardian" column and move on.

Still another unproductive response might come from the reader who is already well versed in English nature poetry. Wordsworth and Shelley both addressed poems "To a Skylark." Their responses to the skylark, though somewhat different from each other, are radically different from the traditional Lakota perception of the meadowlark. While both the English Skylark and the American Western Meadowlark nest on the ground, and though both have notably clear and musical voices, Wordsworth and Shelley are moved to emphasize the skylark's soaring flight while the Lakota meadowlark is most often shown defending her nest or perched on a tipi pole speaking humorously and helpfully to human beings. The two British poets derive no such warmth from their ethereal bird, which serves only to remind them of the burden of their humanity. Shelley predictably praises the bird as a "scorner of the ground," but Wordsworth reverses this in the last line of his poem by scorning the ground himself in anticipation of "higher raptures . . . when life's day is done." Until then, Wordsworth expects to "plod on" through this "wilderness dreary," consoled by the thought of eternity, and a secure advantage over the skylark, now perceived as "free of Heaven" (Woods 1950:323). Shelley is not so anthropocentric, though he only hails the bird's blithe spirit in order to devise a rhetorical complaint about the human condition: "We look before and after, / And pine for what is not: Our sincerest laughter / With some pain is fraught; Our sweetest songs are those that tell of saddest thought" (Woods 1950:731).

In the Lakota perception of the meadowlark and of many other animals, envy and scorn are rarely expressed. While, for the Lakota, animals do provoke independent human thought, as in most English-language poetry, they also communicate messages of immediate and long-range benefit, both physical and spiritual, to individuals and to the people through these individuals. The meadowlark's benevolence is so consistent and specific, however, that his presence in a story cannot be fully understood without some knowledge of how the whole culture perceived this bird.

Of all the *śuntalapi* (birds) and *śitoblayapi* (animals) which spoke to human beings, the meadowlarks spoke so often and so helpfully that they were recognized as "the birds that spoke Lakota" and even as "The Sioux Bird" (Vestal 1980:21). They were one of the first birds to return in the spring, and in that sense they always brought new hope. Similarly, when an individual or a band was sick or in danger, a meadowlark sang in such a way as to ensure their survival. The meadowlarks were also noted for courageously defending their young and ingeniously ensuring their perpetuation, so that the Lakota people felt a special identification with their survival abilities. Similarly, *taśiyagnunpa* (the meadowlark) silenced complaint with good-natured teasing and musical celebration in times of peace, although like the people the bird led a dangerous existence. As the guardian of Falling Star, the meadowlark portrays the ideal parent; as the defender of the nest, the meadowlark manifests the warrior spirit; and as a reporter of seemingly trivial matters around the village, the meadowlark articulates experience for the people so that they may continue to live as Lakota. In effect, the meadowlark "spoke Lakota" in order to tell the story of the people's life, to enliven them with joy.

On a tape that was recorded and transcribed by the American Indian Research Project at Eagle Butte, South Dakota, Mrs. Louise Hiett, then eighty-four, recalled how meadowlarks (singing audibly on the tape) might repeat whatever they heard the people say:

. . . sitting up on the tent pole at night, when people are awake you know, the poles are like this. Moonlight nights you can see them. And a meadowlark would be singing, and he would be talking about something they talked about. Somebody said, "We're going to move camp because," they said, "the buffalo are awful thick down so-and-so creek," the meadowlark next was singing, so we listened to them and "we're gonna move down the creek where there's lots of buffalo," in Indian and then he laughs, the bird laughs, chatters like he were laughing. So they're a tattletale . . . they understand what the Indian people say. And one little lark was singing "grandmother's lazy, grandmother's lazy." And then he says, "a calf's liver is rich, a calf's liver is good eating," *"oyu waśte, oyu waśte,"* and bring it out twice. Things like that, they hear and they say. (Hiett 1971:4)

In a much older description, transcribed by John Bruyier for J. O. Dorsey in 1888 and annotated by Ella Deloria in 1937, another aspect of the meadowlark's gossip, only hinted at by Mrs. Hiett, is explicitly reported:

It is said too that they imitate the talk of people, and that they eavesdrop, while they sit in their tipis at night. And the following morning, they mimick their talk. Some say this, (I myself have heard them,) "Dance with little Lefthand!" or "Ce-sake in ye lo" (makes no sense to me. Dorsey writes for *cesake* "Membrane virile" D.) Or they cry, "Ptehicala pi napi," Calf-liver tastes rich and oily." Or, Hi, ho, hi, ho, hi, ho, hi" (no meaning,) or "Kola, tawiye lo." [Dorsey's interlinear: *Friend, cum ea coiit*. And that is approximately the meaning. D.] (Deloria 1937:2–3)

The connection between simple gossip and the widened vision which a more structured story provides has been illuminatingly set down by Leslie Silko:

There's nothing . . . often times idle gossip, the two words are linked . . . it brings everyone closer, and it makes you seem much more like a part of the stories and the next time something happens, your story's going to be right there with all the others. . . . It brings the individual in touch with things and people that happened a hundred years ago. There's sort of a continuity. (1983:4)

The "tattletale" may have been especially loved for putting the people's experience into words, especially when his report banished strife from the *tiyośpaye* (community) by humorously acknowledging their closely shared being.

If the meadowlark is known as a chatterbox, it is also noted for its parental protectiveness. No wonder a conscientious storyteller, instinctively speaking to provide a healthful atmosphere for his listener's growth, would so often choose the meadowlark from among all the closely observed and admired Lakota birds to play a major role in his stories. In effect the meadowlark represents the storyteller, while the story or song he brings into the world embodies the heroism which will teach the listeners to fly on their own. Each reader or listener is a foundling, but a good parent only holds his child's attention long enough to make him independent.

Bruyier explains how the people did not simply appreciate or admire the songs of the birds—they needed them. The same might be said of the Lakota attitude toward the songs and stories which were given by the spirits in order to generate life:

> In this and similar ways these birds are said to sing. . . . As for us, we think we understand the speech of these birds, so we listen for their songs; many of them are very talkative, and of a morning they fill the air with their chatter; and they make the days pleasant—we depend on them to do this. They do their utmost by their singing to try to make the days pleasant thereby. (Deloria 1937:3)[1]

All of the meadowlark's characteristic speech cheers the people in one way or another, from pride-deflating gossip divulged from the tipi pole to directing attention to whatever has true value. A meadowlark is most often reported as celebrating things of essential worth—"ptehincala, pi napin" (a calf's liver is rich); or a meadowlark requests acts of careful and legitimate affection—"Scepan, micakca" (sister-in-law, brush my hair), or "Śic'e, micakce" (brother-in-law, brush my hair). The meadowlark may warn people protectively by announcing an imminent thunderstorm: "Kola, waḱinyan ukiyelo, tiyo napa po" (Friend, the thunder is coming, run inside). A typical conversation between meadowlarks shares good fortune without rivalry: "Taśiyagnunpa, nitakoja wan gli yelo, iwakici yo" (Meadowlark, your grandson has returned, dance in praise of him). The other one then dances and sings conventional syllables of happiness: "Hahe, hihoho" (Buechel 1970:483).

The meadowlarks play a significant part in the Lakota celebra-

427

tion of sharing itself—the *Hunka* (Making of Relatives) ceremony. While the people seat themselves in the ceremonial lodge, a *walowan* (ceremonial singer) sings, "The meadowlark, my cousin / A voice in the air." Walker's gloss explains, "The meadowlark is an *akicita* or servant of *Okaġa,* the South Wind. The meaning of the song is that the messenger of the South Wind promises the *walowan* a fair day and pleasant time" (1980:226).[2] The singer feels related to the meadowlark because both are voices in the air, probably the same voice. Typically, the spirit of the man and the meadowlark are so compatible as to be virtually united, and both celebrate their relationship and its incarnation in song. The relationship between man and meadowlark becomes the model for the relationship between the two individuals whose spirits are to be joined in the spiritual bond of the Hunka ceremony. Since the meadowlark is the *akicita* (messenger) of Okaga, the south wind,[3] his song and that of his hunka, the walowan, generate new life by concentrating the power to live in words and music. In this sense, a storyteller, too, is a hunka of the meadowlark and an akicita of Okaġa.

Like the warm Spring winds, a storyteller's breath becomes the words which seed a larger and more detailed life in the listeners. Both the narrator and the meadowlark derive their powers from the Chief god, the Sun. In order to ensure continuing light and warmth, a sacrifice of personal comfort is always required. It takes intense effort to learn and remember a story and to sharpen one's expressive skills. While the songs of the meadowlark and the rhythms of many stories are delightful, the delight exists only because the narrators and birds have sacrificed to perpetuate themselves in those who are sheltered by their mature expressions. The Sun Dance is the most concentrated expression of this will to continue in wisdom and joy:

> As for the meadow-larks, they follow a certain style of dancing, the sundance style. They are black on the breast in a quartermoon shape. (*wi-kaĥya*) made like a moon . . . and in the very center of the breast they are marked with a yellow spot; and from that it is said they have painted a sunflower on their breast, as it were and when they go into their dance, they do not do so in a group, but singly, they dance somewhere. Long ago, a meadow-lark cried, "He-ya-a-he-ha-e!" and stood on a rock and straight up and down he sent himself, as though he had no wings, so closely held in they were. (Deloria 1937:249:2)

And as the meadowlarks dance separately, so each dancer is essentially alone in the Sun Dance circle and each lamenter stands on the hill alone, although he performs the rite for *kitakuyepi oyàs'in* (all his relatives). The meadowlark's color and disposition augment the striking resemblance of his dance to *wi wanyang wacipi* (the Sun Dance). A meadowlark protects his meadowlark people whether he defends them physically, feeds them, or shares his songs. Of all nonhuman forms of life, he is most likely to join the ceremony which is crucial to the survival of all "peoples"—plant, animal, or human. Frank Fools Crow attests to the eternal kinship between Taśiyagnunpa and the *oyate* (the nation):

> In 1972, when I was leading the Pine Ridge Sun Dance, a meadowlark came and sang and danced with us. The people saw it dancing around and singing, gracefully hopping on one foot and then the other, and stretching out its little wings like arms. Then it danced over toward the east entrance of the enclosure and flew off. The people were very happy about this. They knew it was a good sign, that the spirits were with us. (Mails 1979:184)[4]

The blessing of the spirits on a ceremonial quest is concludingly pronounced by a meadowlark at the end of the *hanbleceya* (rite of praying for a vision) in William Powers's *Yuwipi*. After the Thunder-Beings have passed over, a meadowlark appropriately arrives to bring a comforting end to the ordeal:

> All was quiet except for birds singing: first a meadowlark encouraging him to be brave, then a host of swallows chirping above him in their clipped language, which he could not understand but still rejoiced in. The meadowlark told him to go home. Then it turned and with its characteristic pecking movement sauntered down the hill. As it moved farther away, its footsteps sounded human, as if it were wearing boots and trudging through the tall prairie grass. At this moment Wayne recognized Plenty Wolf coming over the hill. (Powers 1982:93)

The metamorphosis of meadowlark to medicine man indicates the still vital recognition of this bird's role as guide and healer.

This explanation of the specific Lakota relationship to the meadowlark is essential to understanding how extensively the meadowlark influences the meaning of the Lakota stories in which he has a major role. Unlike the animals of Romantic and much twentieth-century British and American poetry, the meadowlark is neither more nor less blessed than man; rather, he exists in the Lakota consciousness as both model and messenger. Claude Lévi-Strauss perceives that the meadowlark is "synthetic" to many western American Indian tribes: "the bird belongs at one and the same time to the sky and the earth" (1978:238). While Wordsworth concluded that ultimately man alone could "belong to the sky," and Shelley saw the bird as being privy to the secrets of the sky which man can never share, Lévi-Strauss also uses the meadowlark to separate distinctly higher and lower orders of being. The meadowlark "is capable of differentiating between what belongs to the world above and what concerns the world below" (Lévi-Strauss 1978:237–238). In Lakota oral narratives, all elements of being, spirit and flesh, sky and earth, can be inhabited simultaneously without active differentiation; but the ability to live in a sacred manner, with both feet securely on the earth, requires maturity.

The growing resourcefulness of a human being is often manifested in oral narratives where imminent danger, especially to one's family or tribe, evokes traditional virtues. "Meadowlark and the Rattlesnake" (E. Deloria 80–82) is a Lakota deception-narrative that has no documented analogues in other tribes. A mother bird has taken all the usual precautions to ensure the survival of her young. Her nest has been placed in protective high grass and her children have grown to near maturity, but they still have not taken their first flight (*kiyapilaśni*). Suddenly, a rattlesnake coils himself around her nest and although her heart is beating frantically (*lila cate iyapa*) she addresses her oldest son in an offhand manner, instructing him to borrow a kettle so that she may cook a meal for their visiting *lekśi* (uncle). The mother meadowlark, like all good parents and storytellers, imparts the power of flight and is prepared to take the necessary risks to ensure that her children may survive on their own. Each of the three children is successively dispatched on his first "solo" flight to fetch the belated kettle-borrower until the way is prepared for her own freedom. As the Lakota *oyate* responded to an enemy attack by carefully providing for the safe retreat of non-combatants, the mother meadowlark transmits the full virtue of *wawacintanka* (patient fortitude) to her children before she can sing of victory: *"Tuwe ca he wo'nicihikta heciha"* (There keep on waiting, whoever you are expecting to cook you a meal).[5]

The meadowlark's intense concentration under stress is a requisite for developing a voice to strengthen others, who can only absorb *wawacintanka* and *woohitike* (courage) empathically. Fulfillment comes when she can celebrate the transmission of these virtues in articulated triumph. Whether the snake is understood as being the voracious *wašicu* (white man) or as a spiritual predator like Iktomi, the person or bird who is the akicita of the generative spirit will make every effort to preserve her children's inner freedom. Stories reflexively trace the transition from passive listening to spiritual travel effected by the mature management of words. In deceiving the snake, the meadowlark-mother hypothetically proposes to the youngest child (*hakela*) that his brother may be lost (*nunipi sece*), knowing all along that in flying independently they will be at home wherever they are. By using the power of speech she delays the spirit-destroying snake and keeps her children safely at home until home is no longer safe. While the stories protect for a long time, when dependence on another's telling or interpretation reaches a critical point, each hearer must practice his imaginative powers before they are suffocated in sluggish passivity.

The meadowlark physically reminds the Lakota to live vigorously through the unflinching joy of songs, bright clothing, and inventive survival techniques. He is at home on the earth and in the sky just as the Lakota people must learn to continually celebrate the multiplicity of an infinitely mysterious world in songs and stories. From the oldest to relatively recent Lakota versions of "Wicaȟpi Hinȟpaya," the meadowlark plays a prominent role as the mediator between spirit and body and as the cultural parent of the ideal human being. This story may be the most extensively diffused North American oral narrative. Thompson lists eighty-six versions from forty-six tribes throughout North America. It has stimulated analysis utilizing many ideologies and methods by such notable scholars as Lévi-Strauss, Reichard, Swanson, and Thompson. In the familiar prologue, two girls, often sisters, unappreciatively long to escape their homes and marry stars. The consequences are similar to the Adam and Eve story. Longing for transcendence results in disappointment and further longing until a new

431

kind of life is miraculously born. The girl who wished to marry the brightest star gets her wish but the star turns out to be a very old man, while the other girl who had wished for a dimmer star discovers her husband to be a handsome young man.[6] Nevertheless, it is from the more intense discontent of the first girl that the greater light ultimately comes.

The still-ambitious girl becomes pregnant and the Lakota term *iglus'aka* (overburdened with herself) in the Buechel version implies that a transition from her immature egotism is about to occur. Although she has been warned against digging *tinpsila,* or prairie turnips (in some versions it is a particular kind, while in others she is directed not to push her belly against the stick), the forbidden fruit is irresistible and she breaks through the ground of the sky. She then falls to earth, as she had earlier "fallen" upward to the sky. Now the dualism of sky and earth which promoted the ambition for transcendence has been encompassed and a larger world can be explored. When she hits the ground her belly bursts open like a seed pod and her baby bounces out unharmed.

The story has moved in a complete circle up to this point and so has cleared the way for the shining lessons of the meadowlark, who can properly teach the child, *"iokel omayani unsimala yo"* (have compassion as you travel). In the Riggs text, which is the oldest extant Sioux telling, the child's true parent in the sense of being a mentor is not identified as a meadowlark until after his actions in adopting the child and raising it, and his words to his wife and to the child, have been expressed. Only then does the storyteller allow the man to earn his name and become a true tasiyagnunpa. An animal or a man is accurately called what his deeds have manifested.[7] In Lakota culture the name tasiyagnunpa has all the connotations of the "old man's" revealed character. When the grandfather sees the baby in Riggs's D-dialect transcription, he immediately picks it up without question or anxiety. But when he arrives home he gently teases and tests his wife before he reveals the child's presence:

> Wakanka, iaku wan wanmdaka unkan cante masice do, eya. Unkan tawicu kin He iaku he, eya. Unkan winohinca wan tezi kamdas ta wanka: unkan hoksiyopa wan nagangata wanke, ahna wicana tuka ce, eya. Wicahinca, tokeca ayakusni he, eya. Unkan, Dee do, eya ca itipi tanhan icu. Unkan tawicu kin heya:

Wicahinca, ito de icahunye ces, eya. ("Old Woman, I saw something to-day that made my heart feel badly." "What was it?" said his wife. And he replied, "A woman lay dead with her belly bursted, and a little boy child lay there kicking." "Why did you not bring it home, old man?" she said. He answered, "Here it is," and took it out of his blanket. His wife said, "Old man, let us raise this child.") (Riggs 1977:90–91).

The old man and the old woman have proper reverence for new life, and the old man, in briefly withholding the news, shows a highly developed self-control as well as the capacity to please others through timed revelation and expression. The old man manifests love as a storyteller, his first story being the gift of learning to love and care for others.

The next task is to hasten the growth of the child and the listeners, to raise them to *icimani* (travel by themselves like Falling Star) throughout the imaginative world. First the old man instructs his wife to roll up the sides of the tipi to allow the child freedom of movement and secure reentry. Opening up the scope of vision and spiritual movement for the listener is also the storyteller's vocation, and he may impart greater resilience to his listeners, who understand as well as experience the old man's treatment of his tender infant as an ideal formula for creating a heroic adult, found in many other stories: "ticeśka kin ohankohoya iyeya. Unkan aḣmiḣmanhiyaye ca hinḣpaya. Unkan śdohanhan tin hiyu" ([he] whirled it up through the smoke hole. It went whirling around and fell down, and then came creeping into the tent.) (Riggs 1977:91). The boy learns the patience which his ambitious mother lacked when the old man initially refuses to make arrows out of the appropriately green sticks the boy offers. Instead the hero must be thrown through the smoke hole once again. After each "flight" into and back through the sky the boy grows in physical independence, but each time the old man has more to teach him.[8]

Finally the old man judges that the boy's "story" is ready for arrows "Hecen wanhinkpe ota kicaġa" (So he made many arrows for him) (Riggs 1977:91). The boy responds by bringing home buffalo to feed those who have cared for him. He has become like them, a member of a meadowlark nation. Human beings grow into an affinity with specific animal natures. After a sufficient demonstration of compassion and purpose the old man is named and becomes tasiyagnunpa; concurrently, after a sufficient definition of value and purpose, the narrator is about to begin the story proper about the deeds of Wicaḣpi Hinḣpaya. But before he does so, the old man fills out his role as parent and storyteller, the instrumental agent of renewal, and the akicita of the Spring wind which will melt the greedy winter-man, *Waziya*, through the improvised deeds of Falling Star. (The Riggs narrator honors his hero with the name Wicaḣpi Hinḣpaya only after he has proved his bravery against Waziya.) Rejoicing over the son he has properly raised, the old man assumes the prominence of an *eyanpaha* (tribal crier) to tell the world from his elevated perspective of the received blessings they may now sing over. Just as the old man briefly withheld the presence of the baby from his wife, so the narrator does not explain how the old man can be delivering his proclamation from the apex of his tipi, but when the words of the old man's celebration are actually pronounced, his blessing turns out to be inseparable from his name:

> Miye tazu waton, tasiyaka sin mdadopa, eya. Unkan he Tasiya kapopo hes keyapi. Zitkana wan tasiyakapopo eciyapi kin hee; maku zi ka cokaya sape cin he anpao zi kin he tatanka he sdusduta e inapin keyapi. ("I, I have abundance laid up. The fat of the big guts I chew." And they say that was the origin of the meadow lark, a bird which is called tasiyakapopo. It has a yellow breast and black in the middle, which is the yellow of the morning, and they say the black stripe is made by a smooth buffalo horn worn for a necklace.) (Riggs 1977:91)

The meadowlark's proclamation sings of the abundant gifts which nature provides. Unlike those Euro-American poets who envy the carefree beast, the spirits of the bird-father and storyteller (often a relatively old person) join in grateful praise. The marrow-filled gut is the emblematic reward bestowed on all who wholeheartedly contribute to healthy growth. A human being with a meadowlark spirit is entitled to inwardly "wear" the yellow of the dawn (*anpao zi*), the generative power of the sun (*cokaya sape*, the sun flower), and the healing power and generosity of the Sun's associate, *tatanka ḣe* (the buffalo horn necklace). Having completed an introductory cycle of demonstrating the nurturing spirit of the meadowlark, similar to the story of the mother meadowlark and her children, Wicaḣpi Hinḣpaya is unsentimentally instructed to *omani* (travel) without further guidance: "Tunkanśina, ito omawanini kta ce eya. Unkan wicahinca kin heya. Ho, takoza, kośka eca oyate ecen wawanyang omani ce, eya keyapi." ("Grandfather, I want to go traveling." "Yes," the old man replied, "when one is young is the time to go and visit other people." (Riggs 1977:91).

In each village that Falling Star rescues from a previously invincible personification of greed, he lives in disguise with an orphaned young man and his grandmother, to whom he behaves generously as brother and grandson. The influence of the meadow-lark is instrumental in determining the future acts of Falling Star who, along with *Inyan Hokśila* (Stone Boy), is the most representative and recreated hero of the Dakota and Lakota. Just before Wicaḣpi Hinḣpaya leaves taśiyagnunpa, the relational terms *Tunkanśina* (grandfather) and *Takoza* (grandson) are used between them for the first time, as if to stress the maturity necessary to really feel their impact; knowing himself to be a relative of a small circle of people directs the hero to take pity upon the neighboring nations which his deeds will liberate. The episodic repetition of living with his grandmother further suggests the introjection of the meadowlark's lessons as śicun in the *naǧi* (sentient soul) of Falling Star. To live with one's grandmother is to have an uninterrupted consciousness of human origins and the obligation of "feeding" one's spiritual ancestors by living the life they have illuminated and offered.

Although a hero is applauded as though he were autonomous, he always returns in private devotion to his grandparents, some of whom he sustains physically in this world, and some of whom he feeds and summons with prayer. After relating the last of Falling Star's major accomplishments, Buechel's narrator reminds the audience that although the people praised him extensively (*lila yaonihanpi*), Falling Star's story has not existed to produce a desire for personal glory but to spread compassion among the people. The story concludes:

> "Hecel oyate iyaza omani na taku econpicaśni econ keyapi. Na tuktel taku wanica nains taku icakijapi ca niwicaya omani keyapi. Na hehan tokel t'in nains tokahan kin tuweni slolye śni, keyapi."
> (Henceforth the people became compassionate as they traveled, and they did whatever was possible to help others, they say. And whenever anyone was in poverty or was suffering, the people assisted them as they traveled, they say. And if someone died and

someone was in mourning, nobody ignored them, they say.)
(Buechel 1978:36, my translation)

A meadowlark is hunka to those human beings who through
stories, songs, and deeds can evoke empathic, spiritual recognition
in the young. In Lakota culture it is felt that such feeling will not
radiate a trickster's web of excessively intricate technique, which
may draw more attention to the *tour de force* than the transformative
essence. The Lakota storyteller omits superfluous description. This
can be observed conveniently by comparing the original Falling Star story, which Black Elk told to John G. Neihardt, with
Neihardt's fairy-tale rendition of the material for his novel *When the
Tree Flowered*. In a style anticipating that of Disney, Neihardt reduces the meadowlark and his wife to tame domesticity. When the
meadowlark goes to obtain food for the infant, he must summon all
his courage to carry off a piece of liver from a buffalo carcass that
other birds and animals are frantically devouring. Neihardt's
meadowlark is plucky but entirely lacking in the supernatural power
which the Lakota relied upon more strongly than physical size or
strength:

> Meadowlark thought it was a good time to sneak out of there. So
> he began pulling the piece of fat liver a little at a time. Nobody
> noticed him. He pulled it a little more. Everybody out there was
> fighting and yelling so hard that nobody knew Meadowlark was
> around. So he got a good hold on the piece of liver, jumped outside
> with it, and began flying. (Neihardt 1970:164)

This whole episode is absent from other written versions of the
story. In Black Elk's original, as with the versions given by Riggs,
Buechel, and Beckwith, Falling Star in his *koškalaka* phase brings
the liver to Meadowlark, who then celebrates his son's growth in a
typically brief Lakota song:

> One day the young man Falling Star brought a young buffalo calf
> in. The liver was good eating. Meadowlark got on top of his tipi
> and announced: "My grandson brought me a good buffalo calf
> liver. The calf liver is rich." To this day you hear the meadowlark
> saying: "pti-hin-chla pinapin [ptehincala pi napin], 'calf liver
> rich!'" They had a lot of papa [dried meat] made, because the
> grandson had provided so well for them. (Black Elk 1984:399)

In every version, Falling Star delivers meat in response to his Tunkašila Tašyagnunpa's gift of a bow and arrows, but Neihardt has Falling Star make his own bow of such Ulyssean strength that "even" Meadowlark could not pull it. This condescending fable shows little evidence of the Lakota respect for their nonhuman relatives. The bodily shape, coloring, and habits of an animal, even a small bird, contained serious meaning for the thorough observer, and the Lakota never personified animal life in Neihardt's cartoon-like style. Without precise study of the associations accorded to specific animals, even a theoretically advanced student like Neihardt could continue to see animals as reductively as in this minor domestic crisis:

> "Our big new baby is gone! Somebody has taken Falling Star!" . . . The mother Meadowlark was crying very hard. Meadowlark was so frightened that he could hardly talk, but he had to make brave, so . . . they began looking around, and all at once they were happy again. For over yonder, not very far away, Falling Star was sitting up among some flowers that were growing there, and he was playing with the flowers and saying "Goo-oo" to them. (Neihardt 1970:162)

In *When the Tree Flowered*, Mr. and Mrs. Meadowlark provide for the baby's physical needs but are incapable of teaching him anything of value. In the story "Iron Hawk," told by the skilled Left Heron to Martha Warren Beckwith in 1926,[9] the foundling hero is comforted by a wise old man (as in the Riggs version) who gradually "becomes" a meadowlark by virtue of his acts. He stills the child's crying and suffusingly coaxes his *ni* (life-breath) into the vigorous rhythm of one who knows his world. The man's ritual acts smoke away fears, orient the child toward endurance on the red road, and instruct his *nagi* (sentient-soul) in spiritual awareness:

> He cried and cried and the old man painted the boy with red paint and grease. They made a smoke out of a weed and smoked him and he stopped crying and went to sleep. The old man said, "This is night-time. That means everybody goes to sleep. In the morning the sun will rise and everything will shine; then we shall arise. The sun sees everyone. He may pick persons out for old age even though they are poor. Perhaps you will be one of those." (Beckwith 1930:379)

The immediate effect of accepting powers greater than the self is to enhance one's own power to see clearly:

> The old man saw that he was looking about at everything in the lodge. He said, "That is right; you should notice all you see. Now there is a man coming from the East. He notices everything. When he sees you he will pick out certain things to help you. Although you are poor these may help you to reach old age." (Beckwith 1930:379)

Like the spirit voice in the *hanbleceya* section of Black Elk's *The Sacred Pipe*, the old man urges Iron Hawk "to be attentive as he walks" (Black Elk 1971:64). The boy is encouraged to observe empathetically a man from the East called "Giver-of-all-life." Simultaneously the old man and the storyteller confer a widened universe on the listeners by repeatedly reminding them of powers beyond their present scope of vision. The boy, now hunting on his own, brings back successively larger game until the fifth morning, when he presents a buffalo calf to the meadowlark. His consistent offerings reveal how the care with which he has been nurtured has shaped his being. This is also the creative work of the storyteller, who can now manifest his meadowlark spirit and disclose the "old man's" name.

Left Heron provides an explanation of Taśiyagnunpa (literally "double-gut"). Iron Hawk takes an intestine out of the calf's stomach just as he himself had been taken out of his untransformed mother. Then he washes it just as the old man had repeatedly purified him with smoke and red paint when he was a baby. Next he fills it with nourishing marrow, as he himself has been filled with the healthiest *woslolye* (knowledge) and presents the gift for cooking in the pot. Left Heron supplements this described power to transform with an unforgettable image of the meadowlark's home. The meadowlark finds his being by changing sound into words and by arranging these words into "nests." Each orally performed story is a temporary circle of attention within which a listener may safely develop:

> After this meal the old man went to the knoll overlooking the village and announced to the people what his grandson had done for him. Now the old man and woman were the Meadowlark and his wife. The lodge spoken of is the nest in which they live. From

that day the meadowlark has the name "Marrow Gut"; *"Tašiyak-nupa,"* an old Indian when he hears the meadowlark says. Many a word the lark utters an Indian can understand. The larks are clever birds. Their nest is made on the ground out of grass, oval like a wigwam, with a hole where they can go inside out of the rain. (Beckwith 1930:381)

In the broader cultural context, the name tašiyagnunpa comes to bear the meaning of "the one who celebrates creation and continuity." Word-nests not only ensure the growth of the healthy but they can also recover the health of those who have become weak. The first story on Vine Deloria, Sr.'s recording, *Stories of the Lakota* (1976), tells of a tribe suffering from a mysterious epidemic that they can neither diagnose nor cure. Told in 1976, "The Little Warrior and the Magic Tree" may be understood to express the spiritual malaise of people who have forgotten the language of the meadowlark. The story has no transcribed analogues, but Deloria has creatively recalled a characteristically Lakota "animal-helper" to dispel an apparently hopeless depression.

Louise Hiett, in the previously cited interview, reveals the alienation from nature which *wašicu* polarities have brought about: "Lots of things I heard the meadowlark, I used to understand them, but I can't understand these meadowlarks, but I do know what they're talking about. I think they're talking Russian. Chatterboxes. Once it was a 'big miracle' to hear an animal talk, you know, that's a great thing, but instead they run from you" (Hiett 1971:4). Deloria describes a tribe's enervation in images of indefiniteness, expressing a need for clear wakan manifestation. Many years ago (*"maybe 200"*) a small band of Dakotas (*"maybe 50 tipis"*) was camped *"somewhere I don't know* but it was towards Spring." The initial time suggests renewal, but the people and the land have not yet reached it. Suddenly they "found themselves" besieged by *"some sort of* epidemic." Again the story places the people in a state of vulnerability, reflecting an identity diffused into spiritual and cultural assimilation.

Although the story occurs *maybe* 200 years ago, maybe it occurs at the time it is told. They are all very ill, very thin, and desperately need to resume the dimensions of people deriving strength from the spirit world. Like the woman overburdened with herself just before she releases the wakan mediator, Falling Star, the people are ready to pass over and back into a life of richer possibility. In the mean-time, however, they do not know which medicines to use and they are dying "rather alarmingly." And so, on a warm night in the month of ripe berries, *Wipazuka* (June), with the tipis rolled up to facilitate inspiration, the narrator opens the story with an image that may well reflect the alienated listener: A man's woman is so exhausted from caring singlehandedly for her husband that she has fallen asleep on the ground because she lacks the strength to crawl to her bed. But while she sleeps the dreamless sleep of one without supernatural experience, her husband is mysteriously chosen to reestablish communication with an ancient guardian of the Lakota.

It all happens as it should, "just as the sun was about to break the horizon." Suddenly, the husband hears a voice and looks in the direction of a once again unspecified being, "a little tree"; but now the narrator foreshadows a return to health by realizing a clearly defined picture of the tree as part of the incarnation of mystery his narrative completes. Previous narrators have not named the species of tree, but "by the way the story's told, I thought of a small lilac tree, no more than four feet high." In the tree, "a little warrior," in yellow buckskin clothes, sings his song and earns by his contri-bution to the people's survival the identity which he assumes at the song's end. The sudden intrusion of music into the heretofore hope-less situation lifts the story's mood until it fades on the delayed last vocable, as Lakota songs do, into the silence which now promises more mysteriously sent sound: "Nitunkaśila wana hinapelo he / Kikta hiheena / Kalyayena / yageyeya yo / Hecunapi kinhan / Mna waheśni / Teya yaunpi kte lo ooo" (Your grandfather the sun is about to rise. Sit right up, brew it up, drink it down, and you will live without diminishing). The song is as condensed as the medicine it prescribes. As enlightenment arrives, the song says, take courage! Use such means of transformation as are available (brew up a story) and you will have many children, as well as an undiminished spiritual understanding within the *oyate* (the nation).

Deloria's voice becomes emphatic only once during the whole story. The man hears the voice as in a dream while his wife and the others sleep; then the story pivots into joy as soon as the restorative formula has been spoken: "And here that little warrior then / *sort-a-shook* [sudden intensity] and it was a meadowlark [understated astonishment], and as he flew away he broke a piece of that branch he was standing on, about six inches long, and it fell to the ground." The story itself is personified at that moment, but it can only offer a cure. The listener must pick it up and may have to overcome a characteristically modern barrier, expressed by the wife's skeptical smile and question, "what do you want it for?" But the primary requisite of love for her husband allows her to heed the voice which speaks through him and to use the "branch" which turns the water red, the color of spiritual vitality, and restores the people.

Health endures as the spiritual being of all "peoples" is remembered. Then, the voices of a vast array of living creatures can reanimate the human spirit. When the people are healthy, Deloria tells us, they understand the words of the meadowlark and they do not forget that the "branches" of the tree have been given miraculous powers to heal each other. Based on this appreciative assumption, Deloria's conclusion has an interesting twist: "My regret is this—why didn't our Indian people in telling these stories tell us also what kind of tree or root, or *whatever it was*, that had a certain healing power. And so that's the end of *one* story."

It is an assumption of Lakota healing practice that restorative power often inheres in the mysterious "whatever it was" rather than the specific physical properties of a plant. Of course, some kinds of medicine, particularly that of a *wicaśa pejuta* (herb-doctor), did depend upon the equivalent of chemical reliability. But the healing practiced by a *wicaśa wakan* (sacred man) is not dependent on physical formulas, and since such healing still exists through a variety of individual and group rites there is nothing to regret at the end of only "one" story. A time of spiritual ripeness (*wipazuka*) will always come round again, just in time to soothe longing for the past. In *lakol wicoh'an*, remembering, prayer, and fulfillment invariably go together.

When Falling Star proceeds from the meadowlark's nest into the world, he repeatedly establishes new homes with several grandmothers, who serve to remind us that wherever our journey takes us we can provide for ourselves and our relatives only if we sustain appreciation of our origins. At the end of Black Elk's "Falling Star," even the hero requires the intervention of his grandmother in order to split a storm of Thunder Beings and save his own life. The Lakota believe that the *wamakaśkan* (animals) are our older relatives and should therefore be addressed as *Tunkaśila* (Grandfather). Like Vine Deloria, Sr., the poet Elizabeth Cook-Lynne (Crow Creek Sioux) narratively evokes one of these ancestors:

> The little meadowlark, *taśiyakapopa*, is the most beautiful of all birds and the most durable. She has a yellow breast like the yellow of morning and she wears a black necklace made from a buffalo horn. To the Sioux, her song speaks of all things in man's consciousnss: desire and love, fidelity and courage, perseverance and labor, and strength. Because she builds her nest on the ground, her young are constantly in danger from predators; thus, many legends tell of her courage as a mother. Significantly, these legends say it is her *song* which she uses to make herself strong. (Cook-Lynne 1983:14)

When her younger brother kills a meadowlark with a slingshot, Cook-Lynne's ability to hear takes a quantum leap: "midsong, the little bird dropped to the earth. The leather reins fell from Old Man's hands, and when I looked into his eyes I knew that there had been another sound in the air. After that, I listened for it" (1983:14). The songs of the old animal messengers return to fill the void in many of Cook-Lynne's poems in *Then Badger Said This*. Contemporary Indian literature allows us to hear spirit-singers who have been silent for a long time, even when we are not specifically aware of their origins and presence. Traditional oral narratives, however, can be heard clearly only when particular symbols and embodiments of their supernatural creation are recognized. For Lakota culture in particular, written and recorded sources are extensive and await our respectful exploration.[10] Without this generous give-away of memory and wisdom, we might not listen carefully when Meadowlark says all this.

NOTES

1. Vestal reports that the meadowlark has at least twenty-six songs and can imitate the songs of other birds; "it always tells the truth, too, and is therefore regarded as an oracle"(1980:21). Ella Deloria emphasizes the universal accessibility of the meadowlark's message: "Anyone, with or without supernatural power, can understand the meadowlark" (1974 [1932]:258).

2. Walker includes a similar description: "To the Lakota the meadow-lark is the symbol of fidelity. . . . By claiming relationship to the lark the Shaman claimed power to influence for fidelity . . . [and] he implied that the influence for fidelity pervaded the camp" (1979:129).

3. In Walker's literary cycle, Okaġa's flute resembles the voice of his *akicita*, Taśiyagnunpa, because the bird has addressed him so pleasingly: "My messenger, I will answer you in your manner of speaking and pray that your voice may always bring pleasure as it has this day" (1983:347). The meadowlark's special ability to soothe anxiety prompts Okaġa to send him to comfort Wohpe and Tate, who wait for Okaġa and his brothers to return from establishing the directions: "Fly to the dear ones and make music that will cheer them" (Walker 1983:354).

4. See also Thomas E. Mails's *Sun Dancing at Rosebud and Pine Ridge* for Fools Crow's account of the same occurrence with slightly different descriptive details (1978:206).

5. A more recent oral version of this story in *Buckskin Tokens* (Theisz, ed. 1975:71) is remarkably close in narrative detail to Ella Deloria's transcription of forty-three years earlier. The mother meadowlark taunts the snake in the story's last line, "There, sit there and wait for whoever is going to cook for you."

6. In *When the Tree Flowered*, Neihardt romantically excludes the first girl's hubris. Although her husband turns out to be old, "he was young too. I think he was much older than the other because he had been young so much longer." The emphasis on transcendence is distinctively Christian, and the Star-men are angels: "I think there are no canes where these men came from, no wrinkled skins, and no uprooted teeth, and no white hairs" (Neihardt 1970:154–155). But in most versions of the story including Black Elk's original, it is simply said that the girl "saw she was with a very old man. He was a star all right, but he was very old," while the girl who wanted to marry the dim star "had a handsome man" (1984:396). Unlike Neihardt, Black Elk expresses the wise counsel that asking for less results in having more.

7. Ella Deloria explains the descriptive nature of a Lakota name: "You do not say, if you are idiomatically correct, 'What is your name?' but, 'In what manner do they say of you?' That means, 'According to what deed are you known?'" (1983:100).

8. In "The Eagle Boy" (Deloria 1974:120–125), a meadowlark provides a home for a young woman whose whole tribe has been annihilated by a tribe of Eagle People. Her son's father is a member of the Eagle tribe. Like Falling Star, the boy is only half human, but he learns compassion and courage from a meadowlark man who throws him outside the tipi four times and imparts to him the spirit of making and protecting relatives. The

meadowlark also exemplifies the value of humbly invoking powers higher than himself so that each time he prays the boy gains new abilities.

9. Biographical notes on Left Heron as well as several of his stories are included in Walker's *Lakota Myth* (1983:101–133).

10. In the bibliographical supplements and in the body of his writings, Raymond J. DeMallie has demonstrated the range and depth of source material on Dakota and Lakota culture. "It is no exaggeration to assert that among the Indian peoples of North America, the Sioux have been foremost in recording their accounts of traditional life" (Black Elk 1984:304).

REFERENCES

Ashley, Rachel. 1969. Interview by Bea Medicine. Tape and Transcript no. 360, American Indian Research Project, South Dakota Oral History Center, University of South Dakota, Vermillion, S.D.

Beckwith, Martha Warren. 1930. Mythology of the Oglala Dakota. *Journal of American Folklore* 43:339–439.

Black Elk. 1971. *The Sacred Pipe*. Ed. Joseph Epes Brown. New York: Penguin.

———. 1984. *The Sixth Grandfather*. Ed. Raymond J. DeMallie. Lincoln: University of Nebraska Press.

Buechel, Eugene, S. J. 1970. *A Dictionary of the Teton Dakota Sioux Language*. Pine Ridge, S.D.: Red Cloud Lakota Language and Cultural Center.

———. 1978. *Lakota Tales and Texts*. Ed. Paul Manhart, S. J. Pine Ridge, S.D.: Red Cloud Lakota Language and Cultural Center.

Campbell, Joseph. 1972. *The Hero with a Thousand Faces*. Princeton: Princeton University Press.

Cook-Lynne, Elizabeth. 1983. *Then Badger Said This*. Fairfield, Wash.: Ye Galleon Press.

Deloria, Ella. *Teton Myths* ca. 1937. [George Bushotter coll.], MS 30 (x8c.3), Boas Coll., American Philosophical Society, Philadelphia.

———. 1974 [1932]. *Dakota Texts*. New York: AMS Press.

———. 1983. *Speaking of Indians*. Vermillion: State.

Deloria, Vine. Sr. 1976. *Stories of the Lakota*. Phoenix: Canyon Records.

Hiett, Louise. 1971. Interview by Steve Plummer. Tape and Transcript no. 0690, American Indian Research Project, South Dakota Oral History Center, University of South Dakota, Vermillion, S.D. July 8.

Lévi-Strauss, Claude. 1978. *The Origin of Table Manners*. New York: Harper & Row.

Mails, Thomas E. 1978. *Sun Dancing at Rosebud and Pine Ridge*. Sioux Falls: Augustana College.

——. 1979. *Fools Crow*. New York: Avon.

Neihardt, John G. 1970. *When the Tree Flowered*. Lincoln: University of Nebraska Press.

Powers, William K. 1982. *Yuwipi*. Lincoln: University of Nebraska Press.

Reichard, Gladys A. 1921. Literary Types and Dissemination of Myths. *Journal of American Folklore* 34:269–307.

Riggs, Stephen Return. 1977 [1893]. *Dakota Grammar, Texts, and Ethnography*, ed. James Owen Dorsey. Marvin, S.D.: Blue Cloud Abbey.

Silko, Leslie Marmon. 1983. *Running on the Edge of the Rainbow: Laguna Stories and Poems*. Videotape transcribed by A. Lavonne Brown Ruoff for NEH Seminar on American Indian literatures. University of Illinois at Chicago.

Swanson, Guy E. 1976. Orpheus and Star Husband: Meaning and Structure of Myths. *Ethnology* 15 (2):115–133.

Theisz, R. D., ed. 1975. *Buckskin Tokens*. Aberdeen, S.D.: North Plains Press.

Thompson, Stith. 1965 [1953]. The Star Husband Tale. In *The Study of Folklore*, ed. Alan Dundes. Pp. 414–474. Englewood Cliffs, N.J.: Prentice-Hall.

Vestal, Stanley. 1980. *Sitting Bull: Champion of the Sioux*. Norman: University of Oklahoma Press.

Walker, James R. 1979 [1917]. *The Sun Dance and Other Ceremonies of the Oglala Division of the Teton Dakota*. New York: AMS Press.

——. 1980. *Lakota Belief and Ritual*, ed. Raymond J. DeMallie and Elaine A. Jahner. Lincoln: University of Nebraska Press.

——. 1983. *Lakota Myth*, ed. Elaine A. Jahner. Lincoln: University of Nebraska Press.

Woods, George Benjamin, ed. 1950. *English Poetry and Prose of the Romantic Movement*. Chicago: Scott.

Traditional Osage Naming Ceremonies: Entering the Circle of Being[1]

CARTER REVARD

In 1928, Francis LaFlesche published *The Osage Tribe: Two Versions of the Child-Naming Rite* as one among a series of volumes recording ceremonies that were still being practiced in the later nineteenth and early twentieth centuries.[2] This essay, by offering some comments on and analysis of the naming ceremonies, is meant to honor the names of the two Osage elders who gave those ceremonies and helped LaFlesche understand them—as well as to honor Francis LaFlesche himself, an Omaha who obtained the doctorate in anthropology, and without whom so much of Osage traditional song and ceremony would never have gained the relative permanence of printed form.[3] The Osage elders, Wa-xthi-zhi and Shon-ge-mon-in, "were typical full-blood Indians, neither of them spoke the English language, and nothing in all that they have given suggests foreign influence."[4] They speak to us today, even through this brief and inadequate essay, in ways that open our minds and spirits to the good thoughts and good hearts of those who have gone before us.

While the naming ceremonies were given to us *through* Wa-xthi-zhi and Shon-ge-mon-in, these men did not individually create them. As LaFlesche puts it, "The thoughts embodied in the symbolic tribal organization and in the formulated rites were gathered by the 'holy men' from the open book of nature, not in a single season or a single lifetime, but through years of patient mental toil."[5] Nor did the naming cermonies exist in a unique, "authorized" form that could never vary and which in that form served the Osage nation. Rather, each of the tribe's clans or gentes had its own special version, reflecting that group's symbolic ties to earth and sky and living creatures therein. Their ceremonies were parallel, but in each the recitations and songs specified the particular "way" of that gens, naming its particular "power-beings" and their attributes: the Puma gens was not the Black Bear, or the Thunder, gens.

Yet when a child was given its name, even though it was brought into one particular gens, many gentes took part in the bringing in, with each reciting its special version of the relevant parts of the naming ceremony. The child thus could count on the strength of each gens, as it entered the tribe's circle of gentile being. But there was a still deeper ordering of the ceremony: At the heart of each name-giving, three gentes would be singing. The first, of course, was the child's own, that of its parent. Of the other two, one had to be from the tribe's Sky moiety, the other from its Earth moiety—and in each, the representative would come from a Peaceful gens within that moiety.

Physical arrangements supported this cosmic symbolism. In the house where the naming ceremony was held, the seating of participants embodied the symbolic organization into which the child, by its name, was being brought. Child and parents were seated at the east, along with representatives of the child's gens and of the Sky and Earth gentes. To the north sat representatives of the Sky moiety; to the south, those of the Earth moiety. In this way the human placements embodied Osage understanding that the orderly movement of the cosmos required participation of the great beings of Heaven and Earth. Sitting at the east, the child looked toward the west, as does the Sun every morning: The child's journey through life was to follow, as does the Sun's, the great path of life and power, the orderly way of the heavens, the unfailing and irresistible life-road of the beings who rise in beauty, who move in brilliance, who go down into peaceful splendor.

Nor was this all. The child's journey was shown to be but one part of the nation's movement through an endless procession of days. At one point the ceremony speaks of the child as praying for the powers of the sun as Male Star, and for those of the moon as Female Star. When the blessings of these great Male and Female Beings are given to the child, then with these powers the child will help carry the nation onward, will beget those future beings who shall keep the Osage nation moving into future time.[6] Perhaps such endlessness, in their journey through time, is what was meant by the placement of the gentes within the house where the child was being named, with the west being left open as the region to which the unending and ordered movement of the child, of the gens, of the nation, was to direct itself, as Sun and Moon and beings of this Earth direct themselves.

But these general assertions must now be shown to apply to the particulars of the naming ceremony. We shall be considering only that version of the ceremony given by Wa-xthi-zhi—the version of the Puma gens. The account will follow LaFlesche's transcription and commentary, with only a few changes meant to clarify points (all page references will be to LaFlesche 1928).[7] The parts of the ceremony are discussed in separate sections for the reader's convenience, but not to imply the occurrence of such actual breaks or segmentations in it.

PRELIMINARY ARRANGEMENTS

The child's father asks the Sho-ka (Chosen Messenger) of his gens (Puma) to call the elders (Non-hon-zhinga) from three gentes to assemble in the evening at the father's house. The three gentes are Puma, Tzi-zhu Wa-shta-ge, and Wa-tse-tsi Wa-shta-ge. The term *wa-shta-ge* means "peaceful" or "gentle"; Tzi-zhu Wa-shta-ge is the Peace gens of the Sky moiety of the tribe, while Wa-tse-tsi Wa-shta-ge is the Peace gens of the Earth moiety. When they have assembled at the house of the child's father, the latter speaks formally, requesting that his child receive a name. The head men of the Tzi-zhu Wa-shta-ge and Wa-tse-tsi Wa-shta-ge then ask the Sho-ka to go and summon the elders of eleven other gentes (named by LaFlesche, p. 33) to assemble the next morning at the house of the child's father.

THE KI-NON (DECORATION OF THE XO-KA)

Next morning, before sunrise, there is an assembly at the house of the man asked by the child's father to serve as Xo-ka. The Xo-ka will take on the attributes which are to be bestowed upon the child with its name; he will receive the blessings and powers and transfer these to the child. The people assembled here are of the Puma gens, and when they have taken their places, the first ritual speech or chant (*wi-gi-e*) is recited by the Master of Ceremonies (*A-ki-hon Xo-ka*). This wi-gi-e specifies the symbolic articles with which, as it is being recited, the Xo-ka is being decorated by an assistant. There are four ceremonial articles, and each is placed upon the Xo-ka as one of the four parts of the wi-gi-e is being recited.

The first part of the wi-gi-e chants of the red dawn before the sun has risen, and accompanies the placing on the Xo-ka's cheeks of red paint. The wi-gi-e is not mere celebration of the dawn's beauty or romantic colors, but makes reference to the creation story of the Osages. This story tells of the time before time, when the Osages were not yet a people, when they existed in the starry heavens, waiting to emerge as the Sun emerges. In that existence, the story tells us, they asked by what means they might be able to take on bodily forms and, descending to the earth, live enduringly. They ask, in the wi-gi-e: *With what shall the little ones decorate their faces, as they travel the path of life?*

While the Master of Ceremonies is reciting this part of the wi-gi-e, the Xo-ka's assistant is preparing the first act of decorating: He spreads his palms toward the dawn, which is now reddening the sky outside the lodge, and puts red paint onto his palms. Just when the Master of Ceremonies is answering his own question (*The little ones shall decorate their faces, as they travel the path of life, with the symbol of the god [wa-kon-da] who never fails to appear at the beginning of day*), the assistant paints the face of the Xo-ka with the red paint, which now symbolizes the Sun's power as he infallibly appears and begins to move through the world each day. The wi-gi-e continues: *When they decorate their faces with this symbol, they shall be difficult to overcome by death, as they travel the path of life.*

This completed, the Master of Ceremonies asks a second question: *What shall they use as a plume?* The answer to this, like that to the first question, is a daring metaphor: They shall use the *plume-like shaft of light* which shoots up from the Sun as it first appears over the horizon. As this answer is chanted, the assistant takes a white, downy eagle-plume and fastens it to the scalp-lock of the Xo-ka. This feather, as LaFlesche says (p. 34), symbolizes one of the two white shafts of light that may be seen at either side of the sun as it rises through the fading color of the dawn. Each of these two shafts symbolizes a never-ending life. The one at the right belongs to the Hon-ga great division and the one at the left to the Tzi-zhu great division.

That is, on the child's head are being placed not merely the Sun's powers, but those assigned to each of the tribe's two great divisions, Earth and Sky moieties.

The third question of the wi-gi-e is now asked: *With what shall the little ones anoint their hair?* The answer is given: *With the fat of the young male buffalo;* simultaneously, the assistant anoints the head of the Xo-ka with this fat, which now symbolizes the abundance of earth's food and sustenance, by which the child, as the wi-gi-e says, *shall live to see old age, as he travels the path of life.*

In the fourth and final part of the Ki-non wi-gi-e, the chanter asks: *What neck ornament shall they put upon him?* and answers: *They shall put upon him the Sun,* as the assistant places around the neck of the Xo-ka a necklace with mussel-shell gorget—a mother-of-pearl Sun, whose life endures forever, in its full noontime brilliance. Now the wi-gi-e is completed: *When they make of the Sun the means by which to reach old age, they shall always live to reach old age, as they travel the path of life.*

What we see in the four parts of the Ki-non, then, is that the Xo-ka is decorated with red paint on his face to symbolize the powers of dawn; with a white plume on his scalp-lock to symbolize the powers of the Sun coming over the horizon; with buffalo fat on his hair to symbolize earth's life-sustaining abundance; and with a shell gorget symbolizing the Sun's full midday powers and brilliance. The Xo-ka is now ready to proceed to the house of the child's father, where all those participating in this naming are gathered.

THE TSI TA-PE (APPROACH TO THE HOUSE)

The Xo-ka, having been ceremonially prepared, goes out of his house, following the Sho-ka. Around himself, the Xo-ka has wrapped a buffalo robe, and he carries a pipe with which to make his offering to Wa-kon-da. As the two men proceed to the house where the naming will be accomplished, they pause four times; at each pause, the Xo-ka sings a song, then recites one of the sequence of four parts of the Footstep wi-gi-e. The song says: *Into a star you have cast yourself, into my star.* Part one of the wi-gi-e asks: *Toward what shall the little ones take their footsteps?* and replies: *Toward the Male Star* (the Sun). Part two asks the same question, but replies: *Toward the Female Star* (the Moon). These questions and answers are repeated in parts three and four of the wi-gi-e, each time preceded, as before, by the song.

We see that in this "Approach to the House," the Xo-ka is asking the question proposed by the Osage elders: To whom shall our prayers be addressed, that we may live a long life? The metaphoric use of "footstep" for "prayer" shows us that the whole "Approach to the House" is being presented as symbolic prayer, as a ceremonial approach to the Eternal Powers made by the Xo-ka as "standing for" the child to be named. We are not surprised, therefore, to find that the house itself, with its assembled gentes, is now conceived of as a figure for the ordered cosmos, and has become the House of Mystery, the House of Wa-kon-da. Within it now are seated the gentes in a ceremonial arrangement that represents the cosmic ordering, with Sky and Earth people on either side of the child's gens (Puma), and the two Peaceful gentes of Sky and Earth being the special representatives of those moieties, so that the child now looks from the east, where Sun and Moon take their beginnings each day, and is here prepared to move unfailingly and recurringly as they do, from the first reddening of dawn to the peaceful close of twilight. As LaFlesche comments, the pairing of Sun and Moon, Male and Female Stars, in this wi-gi-e implies that the prayers are not only for the child's long life but for the continuance of that life by the procreation of the next generation beyond.

THE WA-THE-THE (SENDING)

Now the Xo-ka and his group have joined the assembled gentes in the House of Mystery, which has for this occasion become what we would call a "church," and the next part of the naming begins. This is called the "Sending," because at this time the child's parents send, to each head of a gens participating, some fee—a blanket or something of value. The fee is regarded as request for that head of a gens to recite for the child the wi-gi-e by which that gens relates itself to its life-symbol. For instance, the Hon-ga A-hiu-ton will recite a wi-gi-e of "the mottled eagle . . . that led the people down from the sky to the earth," while the Tho-xe head recites the wi-gi-e which tells "the bringing of the maize to the people by a buffalo bull, and his offer to aid the little ones to reach old age" (LaFlesche, p. 39). In this way, the various gentes, for the fees sent to their heads, offer to the child the life-giving powers of the Sun, the Golden Eagle, the Red Cedar, the Everflowing Waters, the Buffalo, the Elk, Fish, Mussel, Deer, Black Bear, and the other powers which sustain the various gentes.

Since, as LaFlesche points out, all these wi-gi-es are different and all are recited at the same time by the various heads of gentes, the effect must have been of an outpouring of voices, all saying different things at once. Yet, to the initiates, it must have been clear that all the stories and chants were part of one great story and chant; that the origin stories of the various clans were parallel; that they all moved as the tribe's members on a journey moved, not in military order yet in living order, as all moving in the same direction and reaching the same goal—as the stars move, as Sun and Moon and planets move. The child, of course, would not have known all this, any more than most young children at some great symbolic occasion.

THE ZHA-ZHE KI-TON (NAME) WI-GI-E

After the "Sending" chants have been completed, the members of the child's gens (Puma) then recite the "Name" chant which, as LaFlesche says, has three parts (p. 40): The first part is itself called Zha-zhe Ki-ton (Name-taking); in this, the chant tells us of the time before time when the people assemble among the stars and decide to descend to this world to become a people, but are in need of names so that they may become persons. They appeal to the "god of Day" (Wa-kon-da hon-ba) for help in obtaining the names with which they may become persons; this god tells them that their little ones should be named after him, and that if this is done, they will always live to see old age as they travel the path of life (p. 41).

He then gives them certain names for their children: Child-of-the-Sun, Sacred-arrowshaft, Giver-of-clear-speech, Woman-who-travels-over-the-earth, Arrow-maker, Beloved-child-of-the-sun, and Dark Eyes.[8]

This first part of the "Name" wi-gi-e takes up, therefore, where the previous symbolic actions left off. In the latter, the Xo-ka had been decorated with symbols of the life-giving powers and endurance and creativity of the heavenly beings; he had been brought into the House of Mystery, where the assembled gentes had chanted all their versions of the origin story and of their moving into this ordered arrangement by which the nation lives and moves and keeps its being. Now, those around this new member of the nation chant for him or her the story of how they have been given sacred sanction for the taking of names, by which each of them has been able to become a person in this earthly life. (*Wa-zha-zhe*, perhaps, means "those with names.")

Now follows the second part of the Zha-zhe Ki-ton, known as the U-non U-tha-ge. This time the wi-gi-e tells of how the people, having been given names, find means of living into old age by appealing to certain great beings of Earth, the Soft Stone and the Friable Stone. First the people, realizing that although they have reached this earth and received their personal names, they have nothing of which to make their earthly bodies go hurriedly to *in-xe shton-ga* ("the soft stone that sitteth upon the earth"). The Soft Stone answers their appeal: If they make their bodies of him, then when they become ill they may cling to him and receive the heat by which they shall be purified. Reassured, they proceed further, finding "the friable stone," or *in-sho-sho-dse*, from whom they receive also a favorable answer: If they make of him their bodies, "they shall cling to him as one who can produce the heat by which their bodies can be purified."

In this second part of the Zha-zhe Ki-ton, the child is being assured that here in this new realm of being there are powers kindly to the newly taken body, which indeed is made of the same substance as these beings. If one is disordered, diseased, in this realm, there will be the warming, purging, healing powers of these beings to sustain one. (I assume that we have here reference to the "healing rocks," of which one is still known to exist on the Osage Reservation, and to the stones of the Sweat Lodge.)

In the third part of the Zha-zhe Ki-ton, the wi-gi-e tells of the people's finding the life-giving foods that sustain them in their journey (U-non-bthe u-gi-dse is this part's name). They find the root of the American lotus (*Nelumbo lutea*) and that of another water plant, the *do* (*Apios apios*). These are plants that are not part of the people's own sowing and harvesting, but grow in the earth to which, having left the heavens, they have descended.

In sum, the child in the "Name" (Zha-zhe Ki-ton) portion of the ceremony has been symbolically provided with these essentials for becoming a person: a name, given by the Sun; powers of healing, given by the Stones; and food, in the roots of Water Plants. Heavens, and Earth, and Water have been prayed to for sustenance and being, and have blessed the child with their response.

THE WATERS, THE CEDAR, AND THE CORN

The ceremony now enters its semifinal phase, bringing the child into touch with "the everflowing waters, the red cedar, an everlasting tree, and the life-giving corn" (LaFlesche, p. 48). To accomplish this, the Sho-ka "places before the head of the Tzi-zhu Wa-shta-ge gens a bowl of water into which had been put fronds of the red cedar," these being life symbols of the people who had come to earth from the stars. As these are placed before the child, a wi-gi-e is recited in which the Cedar and the Waters promise that when the little one shall make of them its body, it shall live to see old age. At the same time, a bowl of shelled corn, life symbol of the Tho-xe (Buffalo) gens, is set before the head of the Tzi-zhu Wa-shta-ge gens. Thereupon the Sho-ka takes the child and places it in the arms of the Tzi-zhu Wa-shta-ge head man, who then

> passes the tips of the fingers of his right hand over the bowl of water and cedar fronds, and the bowl of the life-giving corn, then touches with the tips of his fingers the lips, head, arms and body of the child. The two bowls and the child are then passed on to the head of the *Wa-tse-tsi* gens, who goes through the same motions with the child. The child and the bowls are then passed on to the heads of each of the other gentes who make the same motions over the child.

By the time these acts have been performed, the child has been made ceremonially suppliant to the powers of the Heavens, the Earth, and the Waters; has been promised by them strength, endurance, and long life, the healing forces of the Stones, an abundance of food, and a life of continuing order and tranquility into old age.

These prayers and promises have been placed in the context of those timeless acts by which the entire tribe, through each of its gentes, has become a nation, and by which its individual members have become persons. The names which have been recited in the wi-gi-es thus far reported are those which link individual persons to this sacred history, and thus carry the stories of how the nation created itself with the sanction and the aid of the great powers of the Heavens, the Waters, and the Earth.

As the culmination of all these rites and ceremonies, the child is at last given its own sacred gentile name—as LaFlesche puts it, "without further ceremony" (p. 48). But even in this there are choices open to the child's family. In some gentes, more than one name is available to the child, in which case the child's mother may choose among them. Her choice will be affirmed ceremonially; the Xo-ka

> offers to the mother two small sticks prepared for this purpose, each of which represents a name mentioned in the origin ritual of the gens naming the child. The mother usually chooses the stick representing the name which to her has the greater religious significance and is the most euphonious.

From this point onward, the subject of Osage name-giving grows much more complicated than I can begin to understand, let alone trace in a brief essay.[9] There were, for instance (as LaFlesche points out), not only Sky names—one of which, I assume, was that given the child in the ceremony as described above—but also Earth names. As LaFlesche tells us, Wa-xthi-zhi (himself of the Puma gens, and the elder who recited the entire naming ceremony for LaFlesche) narrated the story of how the first two Earth Names were obtained: When the people were coming from Sky to Earth, they sent two messengers ahead to find ways of dispersing the Waters so that the Earth would be habitable, and they obtained the help of the Great Elk in doing this. Then the messengers led the people over the dry land, and suddenly the first messenger, Wa-tse-gi-tsi (The One From The Stars), met In-gthon-ga (Puma). Thereupon, the messenger changed his name and became, himself, In-gthon-ga; similarly, his fellow messenger, whose name meant Radiant Star, met the Black Bear and took as his Earth Name Black Bear (Wa-tha-be).

Apparently, this story symbolizes the fact that members of the Puma and Black Bear gentes considered themselves simultaneously Sky and Earth people, and had names pointing to both these natures. Wa-xthi-zhi provided for LaFlesche both the Earth-Names wi-gi-e and lists of the names involved in the change from Sky to Earth names for his gens (Puma) (pp. 49–53).

INSTRUCTIONS TO THE CHILD'S MOTHER

The last aspect to be considered here in discussing the naming ceremony (as presented by Wa-xthi-zhi in LaFlesche's account) is the instructions which are ceremonially given to the child's mother, and the actions which the mother is then expected to carry out in the year following. After the child has been blessed by the heads of the various gentes, the mother is brought to a seat in front of the Xo-ka, who then gives her special instructions. First, he speaks to her concerning the specially decorated buffalo robe which is spread before them. He addresses her as his daughter-in-law, and expresses his gladness that she has acquired and decorated this buffalo robe, which is to be used in the right ceremonious ways and understood in its symbolic meanings. There is to be a four-day observation by the mother, confirming the naming ceremony's accomplishments: The mother is to paint red the parting of her hair as a sign that she appeals to the god of Day, whose path lies over the middle of the Earth, for a long and fruitful life for herself and her child. She has reddened, in like manner, the head and forelegs of the buffalo robe, to symbolize the east at dawn, where the god of Day always rises to begin his journey; at that time of day, she is henceforth to rise and go out to prepare food for her child. She has painted a red line from the robe's head along its back to the tail, again representing the Sun's path; at its midpoint she has placed a round spot, as the middle point of the Sun's daily journey. At this midpoint she is to turn her thoughts once more to feeding her child. She has also reddened the back legs and tail of the robe to symbolize the red glow of sunset—when, once more, she is to put her mind on caring for the child.

The robe, then, epitomizes the naming ceremony, and will be a reminder to the mother every day of the child's dependence upon her and of her promises to nourish it. At night, the mother is to take the child in her arms, draw the robe about them both, and sleep; the robe will thus become the Heavens as source of all life, and the very act of her drawing it about them will affirm the powers of Heaven to sustain and protect mother and child, as well as supplicating them to do so.

The Xo-ka continues his instruction by speaking of the foods the mother is to gather, and the good thoughts and good heart with which she is to gather them. He names the root of the lotus, which had been found by the people when they were descending from the stars and searching for the food which would sustain them, and he tells the mother that as she goes to gather this root she is to paint red the parting of her hair in thanks to the god of Day who gives, on his journey, the life-giving power to the plant and to her and her child. He tells her that in gathering the lotus-root from the lake-bottom's mud she will use a staff, and that she should choose for this staff the willow tree, which clings persistently to life, so that what she leans upon in her search for food will in itself be an appeal to the life-sustaining powers for a long and fruitful life for herself and child. When she brings up the root, she is to take some of the mud around it and touch her body and forehead with it, as an appeal to the life-giving powers of the earth; and she is to return to the earth the first lotus-root she gathers so that the plant may always be abundant.

The Xo-ka then turns to another sacred plant, the maize. He tells the mother that she raises this plant every year, and that now she should use a certain ceremony in planting it, as a sign of her faith that Sky and Earth will yield abundance, returning many ears of corn and many animals to the planters and hunters. She is to plant seven hills of corn: one grain in the first, two in the second, and so on until she plants seven grains in the seventh hill, repeating at each the ritual acts and supplications, and pressing down her foot on each hill when it is planted. (This would produce twenty-eight corn plants, or seven times four: The Osages refer to themselves, in these ceremonies, as "a people of seven fireplaces," and four is the sacred number—and a "moon" is twenty-eight days.)

When the Xo-ka has completed his instructions concerning the buffalo robe, the root-gathering, and the corn-planting, the naming ceremony ends, and each member of the gentes taking part in it makes a point of coming to speak with the child's parents before leaving, wishing the child and them well. But there is one more thing that will complete the occasion, that will confirm the child's having been brought into the tribal circle of being. This is the feast which the mother will prepare after the sacred corn she has planted has matured and been harvested.

THE FEAST AND RECITATION OF ORIGIN
WI-GI-E OF THO-XE GENS

The Xo-ka who had taken part in naming her child is invited to the feast given by the mother. He then invites some of his friends, each of whom at one time or another has served as Xo-ka in a naming ceremony. If among these one is of the Tho-xe (Buffalo Bull) gens, and he is versed in the ceremonies of his gens, this person is asked to recite the Origin wi-gi-e of the Tho-xe gens, who were regarded as those who had found and brought to the people the sacred maize. So the ceremonial feast on the life-giving corn, offered to the circle of men who had presided at name-giving ceremonies, is crowned with a recitation of the tribal history in coming from the stars to Earth and in being given the gift of corn through the mediation of the Buffalo Bull. Red corn, blue corn, white corn, speckled corn, all are named as given. With this feast and recitation, the whole cycle of rituals and actions of the naming ceremony comes to an end: The child, as LaFlesche puts it (p. 58), now "has a right to a place, not only in its gens, but also in the sky and the earth, which the two great tribal divisions, the *Hon-ga* and the *Tsi-zhu,* represent."[10]

Thus far, my contribution to this account has been very slight: Mostly, I have paraphrased or summarized what LaFlesche presented, and in so doing, regrettably, have not quoted much of the actual ceremonial chants and songs which LaFlesche transcribed and translated. If my task has been accomplished the reader will already have gained much of what I hope this essay will provide; it will be clear that the Osage naming ceremony was a sophisticated philosophic and religious ritual, that it offered to the assembled participants a re-affirmation of the tribal history, of the ways in which their gentile organization reflected that history, and of the ways in which the organization and the ceremony were meant to keep the life of their nation moving in peaceful and orderly ways as the people traveled into the future.

It will have become clear that the symbolic dress, paint, feathers, seating arrangements, and gentile life-symbols were all meant to evoke and sustain the sense of history both in sacred and in ordinary time. If a member of the tribe wore red paint, that was not a symbol of the mundane, of the "political" (as we might call it) dimension of war or peace among human groups; it was, rather, a way of evoking the relationship of an individual or tribal member to the great cosmic and natural powers. The eagle feather was not just a symbol, in this instance, of "war honors" (as we are often told when commentators "explain" the Plains Indian "war-bonnets"); it is a reminder of what one sees at dawn when the sun first sends shafts of light up through the clouds. In that way, it relates the person wearing it to the strength, the order, the endurance of the natural beings of heaven and earth, which never fail, which always move in their assigned places.

The most important insight to be derived from the study of this ceremony, however, is the perception of how creative, how figurative, how daring the Osage thinkers were as they put together the parts of the ceremony. Here are two ordinary Osage lodges, for instance, one where the Xo-ka lives, one where the parents of the child to be named live. By the metaphors and ceremonies of this naming ritual, these become sacred; the Osage elders thus created a church—though they did not build one—as symbolically dense with meaning, as carefully arranged so that its orientation expressed the reverence of its "worshipers," as a medieval cathedral was. For the Osage, the church is the people, their seating arrangements, the way these arrangements reflect their tribal and gentile organization, and the way that organization in turn reflects their sacred history.

As they recite that history, we see that the Osage naming ceremony offers the equivalent of a recitation of the Law and the prophets, or of one of the Gospels.

At this point, one should be able to say that the term "nomadic" has been put into its proper place, as a foolish and even despicable word with utterly mistaken connotations. Insofar as such a people as the Osage moved, regularly, from one part of the earth to another in their seasonal rounds, one supposes that they were "nomadic." But the point of a ceremony such as the naming ceremony is to consecrate any given lodge as, for the time being, a "cathedral": Just as a given word may have its literal meaning but when taken in the right ways and contexts may have an allegoric or figurative meaning, so every mundane feature of an Osage encampment might be taken thus allegorically during a ceremony. Footsteps became prayers; feathers became the sun's rays; a shell gorget became the sun. The child became for the moment more than the "infant, mewling and puking in its mother's arms," as Shakespeare described it: It took part in this tribal Epiphany, thus becoming one more being in the endless circle of life, moving out of a sacred past into an eternal future. When the ceremony was over, things could relax into their mundane selves. But the child, once it had come to fuller consciousness, would have this mythic dimension of itself, this enduring awareness of its place in the universe, to keep it in confidence and dignity. One can see here some of what must have allowed Indians of earlier times, when taken on the steam-trains to Washington to be awed, to keep their composure, their sense of their own worth and place; this, despite the overwhelming evidence of power and numbers of people among whom, they surely saw, their own nation's numbers could not prevail.

It is the idea of oneself that a naming ceremony must create, and the idea in the Osage ceremony is of a self within a community of people and of natural beings besides humans, where the great powers and nonhuman beings offer themselves to the human ones as friends who come to support and sustain. Through the ceremony the Osage nation recognizes this new self, and assigns it a proper place within the circle of human and nonhuman beings. The name thereafter affirms, not this person's relationship to real estate and movable property and inheritance—which is what is affirmed by Western European names and the ceremonies which affix them—

but its relationship to the nation, to the nonhuman, in a way that always points to the communal self as well as the individual self, and that understands community as having the sacred allegorical dimension, always implicit and available at any time.[11]

NOTES

1. A version of this paper was given in October 1983 to the symposium "Oklahoma Indians: A Continuing Heritage" at the University of Science and Arts of Oklahoma in Chickasha. I thank Carol Hampton and colleagues for inviting the paper, for the many fine papers presented during the symposium, and for the concluding pow-wow in which I took part as a Gourd Dancer. I record also gratitude to those who taught me over the years the ways of Gourd Dancing and helped me put together my outfit for it: Evalyn Wahkinney Voelker, Phyllis and Paul Calcaterra, and others of the St. Louis Gourd Dancers, and my Ponca aunt and cousins, Mrs. Jewel McDonald Camp Farmer, Casey and Mike, Carter and Craig and Dwain and Darlena.

Crucial to my discussion of the Osage naming ceremony is that in September 1952, thanks to the kindness of my late grandmother Mrs. Josephine Jump, and to Chief Paul Pitts, Mr. and Mrs. Wakon Iron, and many others, I was given my Osage name in what is now Wakon Iron Hall in Pawhuska, Oklahoma. My heart goes out to them, to my stepfather Addison Jump and to Uncle Kenneth and Aunt Arita, for the support and blessing of that occasion, and the fun as well as the seriousness of it, in the handgames and all. To dance in my new blanket over the Palm Beach suit was to feel very strange and yet to have this completely new sense of myself and what "Indian and white mixed" means.

Dr. Carol Hunter, herself a member of the Osage Nation, kindly made available her dissertation (1978), and I thank her for this.

2. See reference list for five of LaFlesche's publications on the Osage.

3. The best recent account of the work of Francis LaFlesche is that by Margot Liberty (1976).

4. It seems likely that LaFlesche stressed the fact that Wa-xthi-zhi and Shon-ge-mon-in knew no English because he knew it might be suggested, otherwise, that any possible sophistication in the ceremonies must derive from European influences. I think that by the 1980s both the sophistication and the genuinely Osage origin of the ceremonies would be granted. The interesting question now is whether a printed text of the Osage naming ceremony may prove acceptable within a "standard" course in American

literature or world literature, in this country. It would seem reasonable, to me, to include such Osage, or Navajo, Iroquois, or Pawnee texts in translation in one of the omnibus anthologies used in such courses, yet there are obstacles, some reasonable and some (I think) chauvinist. For a text to be taken into the "canon," there must be an authoritative text, and to be teachable in the "standard" courses this must be available with notes, background information, sufficient for teachers interested but untutored in such matters to offer a respectable presentation of their contents and significance. Such a scholarly text with sufficient apparatus is not available yet for the naming ceremony. Even if it were, however, my guess is that there would be considerable reluctance to include it in either an American or a world literature course for undergraduates. I find this ironic, and hope my guess will prove wrong. Osages are Americans, and the naming ceremony as published by LaFlesche is an excellent text, composed by Osages in an American language (Osage) and translated by LaFlesche into English as good as that in most anthologies of Greek or Hebrew ceremonial "literature."

5. The communal basis of "literary" or "religious" texts evident in such works as the Osage naming ceremony offers an obvious challenge to the post-Romantic identification of art with artist. If a biography of Wa-xthi-zhi were available (which, thank goodness, it is not), there would certainly be critics swarming to show how the biography accounted for, or at least offered crucial insights into, the naming ceremony. We have a plethora of such work done not only on such texts as Milton's "Comus" or *Paradise Lost*—where at least we can try linking the literary documents with a good many biographical ones—but even on the works of William Shakespeare or Geoffrey Chaucer, where practically no biographical facts are available to link to the literary texts.

Notice, incidentally, the bizarre consequences of our tendency to seek an artist whose life can explain a text, in the case of a modern "art" that is at least semicommunal: a series of movies written to star a particular actor, say, Clint Eastwood. Critical attention, in printed discussion of such movies, seems to me almost never directed toward the scriptwriters but toward either the major star or the director. Reams are published psychoanalyzing the actor, nothing about the person who put the words into the actor's mouth. We seem so hellbent on making every "work of art" the product of an individual that we simply create an artist for the product: even the spaghetti Westerns with Eastwood as star are so discussed, so far as my limited reading has shown me. There is a frantic avoidance of recognizing movies as communally created by many contributors. How long before some sensible critic notices this?

6. See LaFlesche (1928:28) for discussion of this.

7. LaFlesche's work on Osage materials occupied the period 1910–1932, and at times involved him and his Osage informants not just in arduous but in dangerous labors; one of them was killed. Some of the hardships and dangers are clarified by Margot Liberty (1976:47, 49, 51, 53–54). The printed fruits of these labors, as she points out, enrich more than 2000 pages—which were described in a memorial issue of the *American Anthropologist* (1933:328–331; my reference is taken from Liberty's article, cited above)—as "the most complete single record of the ceremonies of any North American people." She stresses the complexity and difficulty of interpreting many of the materials, remarking in particular of the naming ceremony that here "all seems to dissolve under scrutiny like a swirl of smoke." I hope my discussion has brought out some of the solid substance in the ceremony. Her survey of the Osage materials in the cited article, nevertheless, is very valuable.

8. These names were translated by LaFlesche. Only the name Dark Eyes offers a puzzle as to how it might have been connected to the Sun. Child-of-the-Sun, Woman-who-travels-over-the-earth, and Beloved-child-of-the-sun are straightforward enough, and it seems likely that the "arrows" of Sacred-arrowshaft and Arrow-maker are, like the sacred plumes, figurative of the Sun's rays. I would guess also that Giver-of-clear-speech was thought to have a figurative connection with the clarifying light of the Sun. The name in Osage is I-e-thka-wa-the: *i-e*, "to speak, speech"; *thka*, "white, shining, clear"; *wa-the*, apparently a causative suffix. Perhaps Dark Eyes refers to the Moon's ability to "see" at night?

9. For instance, I have not considered the question of which names are appropriate to a child in relation to its status within the family as first-, second-, or third-eldest son or daughter. This is discussed by LaFlesche (1928:31–32).

10. An important recent account of Osage names in relation to the history of villages, bands, and clans is offered by Louis F. Burns (1984), along with an extensive bibliography of printed materials relating to Osages.

Garrick Bailey has provided a somewhat different analysis from LaFlesche's of Osage political and social organization (1973a; 1973b). His work is highly important for study of these matters.

John Joseph Mathews, in *The Osages* (1961:331–337), has given a narrative account of the naming ceremony that is beautifully readable, the more so as he had also provided in previous chapters a coherent version of the Osage creation story and marriage ceremony. Readers may see for themselves where my account of the naming ceremony differs from his. Since I have profound respect and admiration for him and for his work, it hardly needs saying that any such differences imply only that at times it has seemed to me that Mathews did not reflect all of what I find in LaFlesche's text. Mathews knew far more of the Osage people than I can hope to, and his *The Osages,* already a classic, will be the book which anyone wanting to know of our people must read, and will take pleasure in reading, for a long time to come. Yet I take his account as true, but not the whole truth, and have therefore offered such further clarification as I may. For a further (brief) discussion, see my earlier essay (1980).

11. Lack of space (and of qualification on my part) prevents more than brief consideration here of naming as cultural phenomenon. Yet two points may be put forward. The first is that we seem to be encouraged, in the present American culture, to throw away all name-ties to community at large, in favor of links with just our immediate blood parents from whom our property and wealth will be inherited. The form of government (democracy) and form of religion (predominantly Protestant Christianity) may be chief encouragers of this: Those who came here from Europe wanted to destroy the hierarchic social structures of aristocracy and Catholicism; they wanted to view social status as something to be achieved individually, and not by birth-ties; and they wanted to be new persons, not determined by ancestral origins. The surnames were patrilineal and one line therefore would come down alongside another (unless it absorbed or extinguished it), as alike yet separate as lines of rain. Naming was to be an act of free will by parents, a randomizing process creating community by arbitrary choices, preventing any disadvantageous pigeonholing of the person being named. It is a private-property naming. It contrasts considerably with, say, Catholic or Jewish naming. Catholics might, as I understand has been the case in France, be constrained to choose first names from among a list of saints, a constraint that would at least connect the persons named with religious history, with particular days of the year, with godparents as well as blood parents. In this regard their naming is somewhat more like the Osage customs as I perceive them from LaFlesche's work.

For Christians generally, the change from giving Biblical first names (Hezekiah, Abraham, Abigail) to media-popularized names is notable. The change away from Hebrew (Old Testament) names might be linked to the growth of anti-Jewish groups in the United States, though that opens a whole range of questions. The mere shift from saints to movie stars is puzzle enough to account for.

And the second point about names is this: Consider the difference it makes whether we know the name of a skeleton dug out of some "archaeological site." If the skeleton has no name, it is likely (in this country) to be considered "Indian," not "white," and can be displayed in a museum. I know this is an assertion that some readers will think outdated, but the last time I visited Woolaroc, the old Frank Phillips lodge on the Osage

Reservation that is now a museum, there was an unnamed skeleton displayed in a windowcase there, which was said to be that of an Indian who died along the Trail of Tears. If it had a name, it would not be displayed, I believe. Some people may think it is simply racism involved here, that a "white" skeleton would be thought to connect to the community of those still alive, while the "Indian" one would not. But I think *namedness*, or *nonymosity*, is part of the complex of sanctions and permissions here; to have a name is to be a person, and we do not put persons on display in glass cases, for the most part, but substitute waxen images for them. A name, therefore, is not merely some way of "tagging" a body or individual, even in a culture where "individuals" are expected to do all they can to separate themselves from past and future, from communal history, as unique beings unconnected to families and histories left in Europe, so they may be defined by what they do and by the monetary and social status so attained. But the subject is too large and unwieldy to be wrestled with here.

REFERENCES

Bailey, Garrick A. 1973a. Changes in Osage Social Organization 1673–1969. Ph.D. diss., University of Oregon.

———. 1973b. *Changes in Osage Social Organization 1673–1906.* University of Oregon Anthropological Papers No. 5.

Burns, Louis F. 1984. *Osage Indian Bands and Clans.* Fallbrook, Calif.: Ciga Press.

Hunter, Carol. 1978. A Study of Osage Mythology. A Literary Perspective. Ph.D. diss. University of Denver.

LaFlesche, Francis. 1921. *The Osage Tribe: Rites of the Chiefs, Sayings of the Ancient Men.* Washington, D.C.: Bureau of American Ethnology Annual Report No. 36, 1914–1915. Pp. 35–597.

———. 1925. *The Osage Tribe: Rite of Vigil.* Washington, D.C.: Bureau of American Ethnology Annual Report No. 39, 1917–1918, pp. 31–630.

———. 1928. *The Osage Tribe: Two Versions of the Child-Naming Rite.* Washington, D.C.: Bureau of American Ethnology Annual Report No. 43, 1924–1925, pp. 23–264.

———. 1930. *The Osage Tribe: Rite of the Wa-xo-be.* Washington, D.C.: Bureau of American Ethnology Report No. 45, 1927–1928, pp. 529–833.

———. 1932. *A Dictionary of the Osage Language.* Washington, D.C.: Bureau of American Ethnology Bulletin.

———. 1939. *War Ceremony and Peace Ceremony of the Osage Indians.* Washington, D.C.: Bureau of American Ethnology Bulletin.

Liberty, Margot, ed. 1976. *American Indian Intellectuals*. St. Paul: West Publishing Company, 1976.

Mathews, John Joseph. 1961. *The Osages*. Norman: University of Oklahoma Press.

Revard, Carter. 1980. History, Myth and Identity Among Osage and Other Peoples. *Denver Quarterly* 14(4):84–97.

WRITTEN

Walking the World of the
Popol Vuh

DENNIS TEDLOCK

In the city of Chicago, whose name is Algonkian and means "Place of Wild Onions," the Newberry Library houses a manuscript whose Spanish title means "Here begin the stories of the origin of the Indians of this province of Guatemala." The work that follows, written in the letters of the Roman alphabet but in the language of the Quiché Maya, is best known by the title the authors used when they cited the hieroglyphic work that served as their source: Popol Vuh, meaning "Council Paper" or "Council Book." The only person named on the cover page is Francisco Ximénez, a Dominican priest who copied the Quiché text from a previous manuscript and made the first Spanish translation. He gives the town where he worked its Quiché name, Chuuila or "Above the Nettles,"[1] but the outside world knows it better by its Nahua name, Chichicastenango. Ximénez gives no dates, but we know that he served as parish priest there between 1701 and 1703. The text he worked from was already old in his time, having been written between 1554 and 1558, not long after the Spanish arrived in Guatemala (Recinos et al. 1950: 22–23).

The authors of the alphabetic Popol Vuh refer to themselves only as "we" or "we who are the Quiché people," but they drop hints that point to their probable identity as three men who held the lordly title Nim Chocoh or "Great Toastmaster" (D. Tedlock 1985:60–61). There was one lord with this title within each of the three lineages that ruled the ancient Quiché kingdom: the Cauecs, the Greathouses, and the Lord Quichés. We know the name of the

man who was Great Toastmaster for the Cauecs when the Popol
Vuh was written: Cristobal Velasco. He and his counterparts in the
other two lineages were eloquent speakers, serving as masters of
ceremonies at wedding feasts; together, the Popol Vuh tells us, they
were called "Mothers of the Word" and "Fathers of the Word"
(227, 339). The Word in question was the Other Tzih or "Ancient
Word," and its source lay in "the original book and ancient writing"
which preceded the alphabetic Popol Vuh. Sometimes the readers
of this book sought answers to practical divinatory questions, but
when they gave "a long performance and account," it was their aim
to explain everything in the whole *cahuleu* or "skyearth," which is
the Quiché way of saying "world" (71–72).

Even after nearly two centuries of European presence in
Guatemala, the world conjured up by the Popol Vuh had the power
to inspire fear in Ximénez. What troubled him was not so much
the points at which the text seemed utterly foreign as it was the
points at which it combined the near and the distant, the familiar
and the unthinkable. The opening section, for example, has a
strange way of recalling the first chapter of Genesis while at the
same time contradicting it, as when the gods make a monad of mud,
an apparent Adam, but then let it dissolve into nothing (D. Tedlock
1983:261–271). In his prologue, Ximénez sternly warns the readers
of the Popol Vuh that it may sometimes seem "to conform to the
Holy Scripture and Catholic faith, alluding to what we know
through the revelation of the Holy Spirit," but that these allusions
are "wrapped in a thousand lies and tales."[2] Indeed, he writes, the
Popol Vuh "should no more be believed than the Father of Lies,
Satan, who was its author," and who wished to deceive the Indians
with impurities equal to those which "he sent through the mouths
of Arius, Luther, Calvin, Mohammed, and other arch-heretics"
(Ximénez 1857:2–3). On the next two folios after this warning come
greetings that are written in Quiché but invoke the Holy Trinity
and the Holy Church of Rome. These texts are meant to be recited
by a priest when taking up duties in a Quiché-speaking parish. As
an epigram for the Popol Vuh, they have the effect of a magical
charm, providing protection against the dark powers of what
follows.

For his ecclesiastic readership, Ximénez saw the task of taking
up the Popol Vuh as analogous to taking over a Quiché parish,

where even the actions of the Indians that seemed to be in conformity with Christianity would in fact be "wrapped in a thousand lies and tales." But the irony is that by briefly invoking Trinity and Church before entering upon the text of the Popol Vuh, he was following a sequence much like the one followed, to this day, when Quiché priest-shamans visit an outdoor shrine high on a mountain or down in the floor of a canyon. The difference is that for them the line between European and Quiché ways, between celestial and earthly powers, or between wooden saints and stone gods is not to be confused with the line between good and evil. On the mountain called Turcah, barely a kilometer's walk from the church where Ximénez once preached in Chichicastenango, they briefly pay their respects to the Christian gods, perhaps reciting an Our Father and a Hail Mary, before they get down to the business of invoking powers, through the intercession of a sacred stone, that reside not in Rome but in and around the mountains and plains, the lakes and seas, of Guatemala.

The authors of the alphabetic Popol Vuh, like the priest-shamans at Turcah, acknowledge the European presence near the beginning of their work, noting that they are writing "amid the preaching of God, in Christendom now." At the same time they point out that their own gods "accounted for everything—and did it, too—as enlightened beings, in enlightened words." The scene of their writing is "here in this place called Quiché," they tell us in their first sentence; in their last they add the new name that was bestowed on their place in 1539, writing that "everything has been completed here concerning Quiché, which is now named Santa Cruz" (D. Tedlock 1985:71, 227). They are talking about the next town north of Chichicastenango, off the beaten track today, but once the capital of the most powerful kingdom in all the Mayan highlands.

There are two sides to the place called Quiché. On the east side is the part that properly bears the name Santa Cruz Quiché, on the headwaters of the Río Motagua, which runs eastward to the Gulf of Honduras. Here are streets locked in a grid plan, centering on a square plaza, a government palace, and a cathedral, all laid out in the midst of a flat. Much of the stone in the older buildings of this eastern Quiché was taken from the still older buildings of the western Quiché, which lies three kilometers away. The streets which lead in that direction pass through an army compound that seems intended to protect the modern Guatemalan state from the ancient Quiché kingdom. Beyond the walls of the compound are open cornfields, but soon the flats break away into canyons that form part of the headwaters of the Río Chixoy, which eventually becomes the Río Usumacinta and runs northward to the Gulf of Mexico. On three high necks of land cut out by these canyons are raised earthen platforms that once bore lordly palaces, the rocky masses of pyramids that once carried temples, and the footings of fortifications that once guarded all approaches not blocked by canyon walls. The central of the three sites here is often referred to in modern writings as Utatlán, the name by which it was known to the speakers of Nahua languages; this is a translation of its Quiché name, which is 3umarakah or "Rotten Cane," referring to the softened and brittle stalks of a previous season's cane plants.

The ruins of Rotten Cane completely fill their peninsula of level land, centering on a rectangular plaza with much of its original concrete pavement exposed, flanked by the remains of three pyramids, three palaces, and a ball court, each stripped of every single usable piece of its original stone facing. But the most remarkable feature of this site, a feature that links the builders of Rotten Cane with the very foundations of Mesoamerican civilization, lies well beneath the feet of those who walk its surface. In one of the canyon walls which bound the high peninsula is the entrance to a cave, a cave that runs all the way back to a point beneath the center of the ruins. This is not a natural cave but a system of tunnels, all of them cut into solid rock.

There is a clue to the meaning of this cave in the Popol Vuh. At a time when the Quiché ancestors were still living in the Gulf-coast lowlands of Tabasco or Campeche, before their migration to the Guatemalan highlands, they were assigned their patron deities at a great city whose names are given in the Popol Vuh as "Tulan Zuyua, Seven Caves, Seven Canyons" (D. Tedlock 1985:172). Many Mesoamerican cities have borne the mythic Nahua name Tulan, meaning "Place of Cattails," but the additional name Zuyua permits at least the hypothesis that this particular Tulan was located at Puerto Escondido in Campeche (Thompson 1970:23). The ultimate Tulan seems to have been Teotihuacan, northeast of Mexico City. In its day of glory, which ended around A.D. 600, this was one of the largest cities in the world, even as Mexico City is now. It has only recently been discovered that beneath the Pyramid of the Sun at Teotihuacan lies a natural cave whose main shaft and side chambers (as described in Heyden 1975) add up to seven. In opening up an artificial cave beneath Rotten Cane, it seems, the Quichés were memorializing a Tulan that was older and grander than any likely candidate for the site of Tulan Zuyua.

The walls and ceiling of the cave beneath Rotten Cane are black from the smoke and oily from the tars left by the burning of copal, a resinous incense that has been used since the very beginning of Mesoamerican civilization and is still used today. The visitor who ventures to the end of one of these tunnels may be startled by the scent of fresh smoke and a flicker of fire, burning out the last remnants of offerings that were left there less than an hour before. Directly overhead, out in the sunlight, are other active shrines, marked by ashes and soot, by sticks used to stir burning copal, and by the discarded leaves in which the pieces of fresh copal were wrapped before being offered. These shrines are on the two main pyramids, at the ball court, and out in the plaza within the outline in the pavement that traces the foundation of the small round temple that was dedicated to the god named Sovereign Plumed Serpent. Sometimes the government caretaker sweeps away the traces of the plaza shrine, but it has a way of reappearing.

These four shrines, together with the cave, are frequented by the priest-shamans of Quiché and surrounding towns and villages who visit Rotten Cane in the daytime to make offerings, and in their dreams to seek encounters with a diminutive god called Zaki 4oxol or "White Sparkstriker," who is somewhere down in that cave beneath the site. These priest-shamans are called *ah3ih* or "daykeepers" in Quiché; their visits to such shrines are timed not according to the calendar that regulates the ordinary affairs of Santa Cruz Quiché but according to a scheme for reckoning time that is considerably older than the Christian one. There is nothing of spectacle in what they do when they come here by day, one or two at a time; the only act which dramatically sets them apart from people praying in church is that they set their offerings on fire, offerings that rest upon the ground. A subtler touch is that instead of bowing their heads and closing their eyes, they look sometimes down at the earth and sometimes up at the sky. They toss their pieces of copal into the flames one at a time, punctuating the requests they make in their prayers. The blood and lymph they once offered have long since given way to tallow candles and sprinklings of strong liquor. Sometimes a daykeeper will drench a shrine with the blood of a chicken, but the gods of today drink human blood only when it is spilt on the ground by accident or in war.

When the petitioners at Rotten Cane have finished with words and can see that no part of their offerings is likely to remain unburnt, they leave as quietly as they came. Such are the subtle ways of ancient customs, of ancient reverences, in a land where four and a half centuries ago Europeans imposed a monopoly on all public forms of visible expression, whether in writing, painting, sculpture, architecture, or in drama. Here today, in Santa Cruz and in scores of other Indian towns, are paintings and sculptures of saints, plazas dominated by the towers and arches of Spanish colonial churches and palaces, and masked dance dramas in which many of the characters have pink faces and golden hair and in which even the pumas and jaguars look like Old World lions and tigers.

To understand the extent to which the present world of the Quichés exceeds the boundaries of what came with the Europeans requires time for conversation, time for the Quiché language, time to ponder the content of prayers, and time to listen to formal statements of native doctrine that have been developed in response to the rote arguments of Christian catechists and the endless sermonizing of parish priests. Only by this route will we learn that the visible signs of Europeanization constitute a sort of hieroglyphics in which the archangels Michael and Gabriel may be read as the gods Newborn Thunderbolt and Raw Thunderbolt, in which the high altar of the local church may be read as marking a spot sacred to the earth deity, and in which a masked dancer dressed in red is not the devil but the hero of the drama that reenacts the Spanish conquest, a hero who saves the indigenous religion by escaping into the woods with it. That is where it used to be anyway, the Popol Vuh tells us (D. Tedlock 1985:180), back in the era when, instead of building stone monuments for them, the ancestors put the gods in arbors decorated with bromelias and hanging mosses.

To the west of Santa Cruz Quiché is a town called Chuua 4,ak or "Before the Building." The Popol Vuh lists it as one of the citadels that were incorporated in the Quiché kingdom during the reign of Quicab, five generations before Europeans arrived. When the leading Quiché lineages sent "guardians of the land" to occupy newly conquered towns (D. Tedlock 1985:214, 216–218), Before the Building was assigned to a Greathouse lineage segment whose descendants still possess documents that date from the same period as the alphabetic Popol Vuh (Carmack 1977:33–35, 62–63). Among contemporary Guatemalan towns it is without rival in the degree to which its ceremonial life is timed according to the Mayan calendar and mapped according to the relative elevations and directional positions of outdoor shrines. Once each 260 days, on the day named Uahxakib Ba4, or "Eight Monkey," daykeepers converge from all over the Guatemalan highlands for the largest of all present-day Mesoamerican ceremonies which follow the ancient calendar. That Before the Building was a religious center even before the fall of the Quiché kingdom is indicated by its Nahua name: Momostenango, meaning "Citadel of Shrines."

Qualified daykeepers—diviners who know how to interpret illnesses, omens, dreams, messages given by sensations internal to their own bodies, and the workings of the Mayan calendar—are quite numerous in Momostenango. Some male daykeepers, those called *chuchkahauib* or "motherfathers," serve as the heads of their respective patrilineages and look after the shrines that every proper patrilineage has on its lands. At a higher level are motherfathers who serve as the keepers of canton or district shrines, and above them are two motherfathers who look after shrines belonging to the town at large. It was in this town, in the summer of 1975, that I began my search for someone who might be able to read through the Quiché text of the Popol Vuh with me, shedding light on some of the darker passages. I returned there for the whole of 1976, and before that year was over I had become a daykeeper myself.

From the very beginning of our fieldwork in this "Citadel of Shrines," Barbara Tedlock and I went on walks to sacred places, listened to prayers and chants (even before we could understand them), and began to keep track of the progress of the days according to the rhythms of the Mayan calendar. These were dangerous things to be doing but we continued, all unknowing, until we asked a daykeeper and motherfather named Andrés Xiloj Peruch to demonstrate divination for us. It turned out that when it comes to divinatory matters, there is no such thing as a "demonstration." There is no way to divine without getting answers, and there are no answers that do not reflect upon those who ask for a divination. Don Andrés divined that we had not only annoyed people at shrines but had entered the presence of those shrines on days when we had not been sexually continent. Having predicted dire consequences, he suddenly got up to leave. Asked what could be done, he prescribed offerings at the same shrines we had visited, to be made by him on our behalf.

In subsequent meetings, don Andrés took on the task of answering all our inquiries about the shrines, the people who went there, the calendar, and the process by which he had divined the nature of our offense. One day, when we had asked for a detailed description of the way in which daykeepers are trained and initiated, he displayed unusual reticence. What little he did say seemed to imply that just as one cannot describe divination without divining, so one cannot describe the training of diviners without training them. We thought we caught a hint that he might be interested in training us. After debating the meaning of his remarks all night, we asked him the next day whether he had meant that he would in fact be willing to take us on as apprentices, and he said, "Of course." Our training, which had to be timed according to the Mayan calendar, began on Hun Queh or "One Deer," April 21, 1976, and we made our debut as daykeepers on Eight Monkey, August 23, 1976.

Diviners are, by profession, interpreters of difficult texts. They can even start from a nonverbal sign, such as the crossing of a road by a coyote or the hatching of an egg in a dream, and arrive at a "reading," as we would say, or *ubixic*, "its saying" or "its announcement," as is said in Quiché. When they start from a verbal sign, such as the name of a day on the Mayan calendar, they may treat it as if it were a sign from a writing system rather than a word in itself, arriving at "its saying" by finding a different word with similar sounds (B. Tedlock 1982:107–131).

It should therefore come as no surprise that a diviner might be willing to take on the task of reading the Popol Vuh, whose text abounds with intriguing difficulties of interpretation. When don Andrés was given a chance to look at the Popol Vuh, whose authors call it an *ilbal* or "instrument for seeing," he produced his own ilbal in the form of a pair of glasses and began reading aloud. His previous knowledge of alphabetic reading and writing was limited to Spanish, but he quickly grasped the Quiché orthography of the Popol Vuh. When archaic words caused problems I offered glosses drawn from colonial dictionaries. He was seldom content with merely seeking a close reading of the sheer words of a given passage. Every few lines he would remove his glasses, settle back, and abandon his philological mode of discourse in favor of hermeneutics.

When don Andrés read in the Popol Vuh that the appearance of the first mountains was "just like a cloud, like a mist, now forming, unfolding" (D. Tedlock 1985:73), he was able to interpret this in the context of the very day on which we sat there working. He said, "It's just the way it is right now. There are clouds, then the clouds part, piece by piece, and now the sky is clear." Perhaps the mountains were there in the primordial world all along and were revealed, little by little, as the clouds parted. But don Andrés complicated this interpretation by remarking, "Haven't you seen that when the water passes—a strong rain—and then it clears, a vapor comes out from among the trees? The clouds come out from among the mountains, among the trees." This lends a cyclical movement to the picture: The clouds arise from the mountains, then conceal the mountains, then part to reveal the mountains, and so on.

But it is also possible to see the formation of the clouds where there were none before and the parting of those clouds as a simile for the formation and differentiation of the mountains themselves rather than as something happening in the atmosphere around the mountains. Such a simile would give the mountains themselves, and not their mere appearance as confused by clouds and mists, a certain insubstantiality. Don Andrés swung toward such an interpretation when he read that it was the *naual*, the "genius" or "spirit familiar" of the gods that had been at work here (D. Tedlock 1985:73). He concluded that "these mountains are for no other reason than representing that there *are* hills or volcanoes." That is to say, he took the mountains of the text to be mere *retal* or "signs," unfolding themselves "just like a cloud, like a mist," rather than being substantial.

But just as when clouds and mists are taken to be covering real mountains rather than to be similes for mountains, there turns out to be something hard hidden behind the insubstantiality of mountains that are mere signs. When don Andrés read, further on, that the god or gods known as Heart of Sky and Heart of Earth were the first to think of the formation of the earth (D. Tedlock 1985:75), he took this to be an act of self-revelation on their part, comparing them to the present-day *u4ux puuak* or "Heart of Metal" (or Silver, or Money), which reveals itself to the fortunate. As he explained it, "When one has luck, one picks up some kind of rock, but in the form of an animal; this is the Heart of Metal. When the moment comes, suddenly it appears." Such rocks may be volcanic concretions that happen to resemble animals, or they may be ancient stone artifacts. The finder takes them home, and if they are properly cared for they will multiply: "This is where one prays, this is where the fortune, the money, abounds. Here in the Popol Vuh, the Heart of Sky and the Heart of Earth appeared, and this is where the earth was propagated."

The notion of a "Heart of Sky" might seem out of place where something as substantial as earth or stone is concerned, but don Andrés's interpretation is supported by a much later passage in which the names Heart of Sky and Heart of Earth are both addressed to stone gods (D. Tedlock 1985:222). The connection between these gods and the sky lies in the fact that they were petrified when the sun first rose and burned them (182). The objects called "Heart of Metal" today also have their celestial dimensions: Volcanic concretions with animal shapes are said to have been formed at the first sunrise, just as the stone gods of the Popol Vuh were, while ancient stone artifacts are said to have been formed where thunderbolts struck the ground. The Popol Vuh does not mention the latter process, but it does include thunderbolts among the attributes of the Heart of Sky (73). The Book of Chilam Balam of Chumayel, an alphabetic text written in Yucatec Maya, takes the question of celestial stoniness home to the sky itself, declaring that the "Heart of Heaven" is a bead of precious stone (Roys 1967:91).

In the sudden appearance (or self-revelation) of the earth in a world that previously contained only the sky and the sea, we have the first of many events that don Andrés read as portending the establishment of patrilineage shrines, in this case the particular shrine devoted to the Heart of Metal. If objects that have revealed themselves are to multiply properly, their shrine must be looked after by the head of the patrilineage of those who found them, the *chuchkahau* or "motherfather." This composite term is an esoteric way of saying "parent," but without any final reduction of the difference between the sexes; in ritual terms, the motherfather is both mother and father to those who live on the land of his lineage. The Popol Vuh raises this concept to the divine level: The god or gods named Maker and Modeler are also called "motherfather." It may have been the Heart of Sky and Heart of Earth who first thought of the earth, but it did not become a reality until they came to the Maker and Modeler, who at that time resided on or in the sea, and revealed their idea in conversation (D. Tedlock 1985:72–73). It was the Maker and Modeler who actually saw to it that great mountains arose from what was then a calm sea.

The narrative movement from words to action and from the level of the sea to high mountains suggests the arrangement of today's lineage shrines and the order in which they are visited. As don Andrés explained it, each shrine is divided into two parts, with the lower part, called the water-place, near a spring or at the bottom of a canyon, and the higher part, called the mountain-place, on a rise or a mountainside (B. Tedlock 1982:76–80). The human motherfather visits the water-place first, addressing it by its own name but also speaking to it as if it were all the lakes and seas of the world, and he announces his intent to visit the higher part of the shrine, naming it as if it were all the mountains and plains of the world. In effect, the actual visit to the mountain-place trans-forms the earth from something that previously existed only in words into a concrete reality.

It is not only the Maker and Modeler but the first four human males who are called motherfathers in the Popol Vuh, and except for the man named True Jaguar (who had no male children), each of them founds one of the ruling Quiché patrilineages: Jaguar Quitze begins the Cauecs, Jaguar Night begins the Greathouses, and Mahucutah begins the Lord Quichés (D. Tedlock 1985:165, 168). Today's motherfather invokes all his predecessors in his prayers; according to don Andrés, the ideal is to begin either nine or thirteen generations before one's own. This alerts us to the mythistorical nature of the lordly genealogies offered in the Popol Vuh; attempts to use these lists as a measure of the time depth of Quiché history, beginning with the writings of Ximénez (1967:12) and continuing today, are hazardous indeed. In the case of the Lord Quiché lineage segment holding the title of Crier to the People, the Popol Vuh gives exactly nine generations; for the Greathouse line holding the title of Lord Minister it gives thirteen (D. Tedlock 1985:225–226). But the most interesting case is that of the two Cauec lines holding the titles of Keeper of the Mat and Keeper of the Reception House Mat, which are given thirteen generations running from Jaguar Quitze, their common founder, down to Tecum and Tepepul, the first Cauec lords who were "tributary to the Castilian people," as the Popol Vuh puts it (224). In the fourteenth place come Juan de Rojas and Juan Cortés, who were in office when the Popol Vuh was written. If they were serving as motherfathers at this time, then the names leading from Jaguar Quitze to Tecum (in the case of de Rojas) or from Jaguar Quitze to Tepepul (in the case of Cortés) are precisely the names they would have used when making prayers and offerings at their lineage shrines, each of them invoking his thirteen predecessors.

Together, the shrines of the contemporary Quiché patrilineage are called the *uarabalha,* the "sleeping-place of the house" or "foundation." There are four kinds of foundation shrines (each with its lower and upper parts): the foundation of the animals, for the health and increase of the animals on the lands of the patrilineage; the foundation of the people, for the human residents of those lands; the *uinel,* for the crops; and the *mebil,* for wealth in the form of valuable objects. The mebil is the shrine devoted to the Heart of Metal, and its upper part is not on a mountain but on an altar inside the home of the motherfather (B. Tedlock 1982:77–81). Visits to these three shrines are scheduled according to a 260-day cycle that was once common to all Mesoamerica. This cycle is made up of two shorter cycles, one consisting of an endlessly repeating sequence of thirteen day numbers and the other of an endlessly repeating sequence of twenty day names. Since thirteen and twenty have no common factor, the interdigitation of thirteen numbers with twenty names produces a larger cycle consisting of 13 × 20 or 260 days, each with a unique combination of number and name. If we begin with the day that combines the number Hun or "One" with the name Queh or "Deer," the list of successive days proceeds as follows:

Hun Queh	One Deer
Quib 3anil	Two Yellow
Oxib Toh	Three Toh

Cahib 4,ii	Four Dog
Hob Ba4,	Five Monkey
Uakib E	Six Tooth
Uukub Ah	Seven Cane
Uahxakib Ix	Eight Jaguar
Beleheb 4,iquin	Nine Bird
Lahuh Ahmac	Ten Wrongdoer
Hulahuh Naoh	Eleven Thought
Cablahuh Tihax	Twelve Tihax
Oxlahuh Cauuk	Thirteen Cauuk
Hun Hunahpu	One Hunahpu
Quib Imox	Two Imox
Oxib I3	Three Wind
Cahib A3abal	Four Foredawn
Hob 4at	Five Net
Uakib Can	Six Snake
Uukub Came	Seven Death

From Seven Death the count goes on to Eight Deer, Nine Yellow, and so forth, returning to One Deer after 260 days. Andrés Xiloj insists that the period of human pregnancy is the ultimate basis for the length of this cycle. Medically speaking, 260 days is indeed a sound, average figure for the period lasting from the time when a woman first misses her menses to the time when she gives birth.

The Popol Vuh first alludes to the 260-day calendar and to the foundation shrines when it says that the Heart of Sky came to Sovereign Plumed Serpent and the other gods who were in or on the sea "in the darkness, in the early dawn" (D. Tedlock 1985:73). Instead of using the ordinary word for "late night" or "early dawn," which would be *a3abil,* the text has *a3abal,* an archaic form that is also the proper name of a day. Like other day names, A3abal is often given a divinatory interpretation by means of sound play, and one of the words used to play on it today is in fact a3abil, an allusion to the fact that the rituals appropriately scheduled on the day named A3abal (hereafter translated as "Foredawn") are best carried out during the time of day known as a3abil. The rituals in question, appropriately enough, involve the first steps toward the negotiation of new social relationships that will last a lifetime (B. Tedlock 1982:108–109). On One Foredawn, a motherfather will walk to the foundation shrine of the people to discuss (in prayer) the fact that a family in his patrilineage wishes to propose a marriage between one of its young men and a woman from another patrilineage; a later day of the same name may be chosen for the making of the actual proposal at the house of the prospective bride. On One, Eight, and Nine Foredawn a motherfather who has taken on the responsibility of training and installing the successor of his deceased counterpart in a neighboring lineage will go to the shrines of that lineage to discuss the fact that one of its members wishes to become its new motherfather.

In both a marriage and an installation, the negotiation of a new relationship has two levels: It is not only the living who must give their approval to the bond between husband and wife or between the new motherfather and the foundation shrines (which is thought of as a spiritual marriage) but also the ancestors and the gods. In the case of the Heart of Sky's discussion with the Sovereign Plumed Serpent the problem is a more fundamental one. When, by their joint efforts (and those of other gods), they eventually succeed in making four different motherfathers, each of them married to one of four different women, these will be the first human motherfathers and the first human married couples who ever existed.

The Popol Vuh makes a further allusion to the 260-day calendar and the foundation shrines of the patrilineage when it tells of the making of the first *queh* or "deer" and *4,iquin* or "birds," animals that give their names to two of the days used for uarabalha rites, and when it tells how the divine motherfathers gave these animals a *uarabal* or "a place to sleep" (D. Tedlock 1985:76–78). The human motherfather of today uses a low-numbered day bearing the name Queh (Deer) to go to the foundation shrine of the people to announce that a woman married into his patrilineage is pregnant, and to pray for the child she bears (B. Tedlock 1982:113). This ritual is called a "sowing," just as is the long process in which the divine motherfathers of the Popol Vuh speak of making humans and prepare for their coming long before they actually succeed in making them a reality. Deer result from one of their four attempts to make humans; these animals are, in effect, an approximation of real humans, their fault being that they walk on all fours and lack articulate speech. The implication here is that in visiting the two parts of a foundation shrine to announce a child on the day named after the deer, the human motherfather not only commemorates the movement of the Maker and Modeler from the sea to the mountains but the process whereby properly walking and talking humans were spoken of and approximated before they were realized.

The day named Deer is followed by 3anil, meaning "Yellow"; two successive days bearing these names are used for the rites of the uinel shrine (B. Tedlock 1982:80). The motherfather goes to the uinel every Seven Deer and Eight Yellow, regardless of season, but he also goes there on the Deer and Yellow (of whatever number) that fall nearest the beginning of the growing season, in order to announce the sowing of the cornfields. The growth cycle of the variety of corn used in the Guatemalan highlands is such that he will be able to return to the uinel to give thanks for the ripened crop 260 days later on a Deer and Yellow of the same numbers as the Deer and Yellow used for the sowing rite (B. Tedlock n.d.). In other words, the crop in the field and the child in the womb grow and ripen according to cycles of the same length, and they do so not only where they were sown in deed but where they were sown by word.

The most startling link between shrines and deer—deer as animals rather than days named Deer—manifests itself in dreams. On this point I can give firsthand testimony. During the period of my formal apprenticeship as a daykeeper in Momostenango, I told don Andrés of dreaming that I was followed along a path by a series of large deer. After a laugh of immediate recognition he told me that I had been followed by shrines! He explained that outdoor shrines have spirit familiars that frequently take the form of deer— and, these days, of horses and cattle. The path, of course, was that of the days of the calendar, along which each shrine had its proper place in a sequence. The deer were following me in anticipation of the time when I would end my apprenticeship and feed them—that is, make offerings of my own.

When the divine motherfathers of the Popol Vuh make birds, the allusion to the day named 4,iquin (Bird) is more overt than in the case of Deer (D. Tedlock 1985:78). They begin a speech to the birds by saying *ix ix 4,iquin*. The second *ix* might be treated as a scribal error, but it is essential to the full understanding of this phrase. The first *ix* is plainly enough "you," in the familiar and in the plural, but the second one has a double meaning. At one level it is diminutive, making the whole phrase translatable as "You, little (or precious) birds," but at another level it is the day name Ix (archaic for "Jaguar"), which immediately precedes Bird in the sequence of twenty day names. These are the two days devoted to the rites of the patrilineage shrine called the mebil, specifically, Seven Jaguar and Eight Bird (B. Tedlock 1982:81). Indeed, this shrine is often referred to simply by naming these two days.

The Popol Vuh mentions, in passing, that pumas, jaguars, rattlesnakes, and yellowbites (fer-de-lances) were placed on the earth along with the deer and birds (D. Tedlock 1985:76), but it gives no hint as to how these animals might be connected with shrines until much later, after humans have entered the scene. When Jaguar Quitze, the founding ancestor of the Cauecs, enshrines his lineage's patron deity on a mountain, we are told that the surrounding woods were thick with jaguars and serpents (179). In Momostenango today, these are the forms taken by the spirit familiars of shrines visited only by the two motherfathers who serve the entire town, and which are at higher elevations than the shrines of patrilineages (B. Tedlock 1982:82). They are also the forms taken by a shrine located atop a high waterfall, whose visitors are the participants in a dance drama that gives major roles to monkeys but includes a puma and a jaguar. Such shrines show themselves as dangerous animals to intruders, or when their legitimate visitors have failed to abstain from quarrels and sexual contact on the day of a visit, or when they are starved for offerings.

At this point in the Popol Vuh, when animals already inhabit the earth but the making of true human beings will take up three further experiments by the divine motherfathers, the rites of the foundation shrines and the full operation of the 260-day calendar are no more than a portent. Andrés Xiloj states that some of the days, including Foredawn, Deer, and Bird, are "older" than others, by which he does not mean to say that the cycle was once shorter than it is now, but that some of its days received their meanings before others. In the Popol Vuh the full structure of the cycle, if not its full range of meanings, seems to be present by the time the gods are considering a third attempt at making human beings, having just given up on their second attempt, a solitary figure fashioned from mud (D. Tedlock 1985:79). At this point they decide to consult diviners who know how to read the portents of the numbers and names of the 260 days.

The daykeepers of the Popol Vuh, Xpiyacoc and Xmucane, work together as husband and wife. Xpiyacoc is the "master of the coral seeds," which means that he knows how to count the days of the calendar using the hard red seeds of a tree called *4,ite* in Quiché. Xmucane "stands behind others," which means that she knows how to go before the gods to plead the case of a client with a bad prognosis (D. Tedlock 1985:83). The human diviner, whether male or female biologically, is symbolically male on the right side of the body and female on the left (B. Tedlock 1982:139–140), and can therefore count the days (like Xpiyacoc) and pray for the client (like Xmucane). Nevertheless, it is the ideal that both partners in a marriage should be daykeepers, and don Andrés was quite pleased that Barbara Tedlock and myself were able to undertake our apprenticeship simultaneously. He insisted that the clearest answer to a question comes when both members of a couple count the days, each with a separate set of red seeds. Indeed, when calendrical divination is performed in the Popol Vuh, Xpiyacoc and Xmucane do it together. Where the sexes part company in daykeeping is in two of the specialized skills that some of them take up: The woman, like Xmucane, may become a midwife, "standing behind" a mother when she gives birth; the man may become a matchmaker, arranging and conducting a marriage ceremony on behalf of a young man and his family (B. Tedlock 1982:74). The human matchmakers of today, unlike those of the Popol Vuh, do not bear the title of Great Toastmaster, but they do offer toasts and they do have a reputation for eloquence.

The divine daykeepers of the Popol Vuh are an elderly couple, senior even to the gods called Maker and Modeler, who include the Sovereign Plumed Serpent, and to the Heart of Sky and Heart of Earth. The Maker and Modeler are also known as Bearer and Begetter, but they join the other gods in addressing Xmucane as "Bearer twice over" and Xpiyacoc as "Begetter twice over," putting the two of them in the parental generation prior to their own parenthood (D. Tedlock 1985:80). The gods also call Xmucane "midwife," which gives her a role prior to motherhood, and Xpiyacoc "matchmaker," which gives him a role prior to fatherhood. Making the two of them still more senior, they call Xmucane "our grandmother" and Xpiyacoc "our grandfather." But beyond and behind all of this, and despite the fact that Quiché descent is reckoned in the male line, the gods close off the infinite regression of generations by giving the final priority to grandmotherhood. Their ultimate epithet for Xpiyacoc and Xmucane together is "Grandmother of Day, Grandmother of Light" (81). As don Andrés explained it, "day" and "light," when combined, refer to the totality of time; a grandmother of day and light would be a grandmother for as long as there are days and as long as there is light, from the beginning to the end. The notion of "days" predates the appearance of the actual sun in the Popol Vuh; apparently, days were once marked by such phenomena as the rising and setting of Seven Macaw, who claimed to be the sun but was actually the seven stars of the Big Dipper, and the daily or nightly appearances of Venus as the morning or evening star (D. Tedlock n.d.). But for all this there is also a literal level to the divine grandmotherhood of day and of light: Xmucane is the actual grandmother of Hunahpu, the god who eventually becomes the true sun and therefore the greatest of all lights.

When Xpiyacoc and Xmucane are called upon to do a divinatory counting of days in the Popol Vuh, their clients are none other than the Maker and Modeler and Sovereign Plumed Serpent. These gods are hoping to make beings who will be articulate in every way, walking and working with two feet and two hands instead of going on all fours, speaking instead of uttering animal cries, and keeping the days—that is, walking to shrines, handing over offerings, and speaking prayers according to a coherent scheme for reckoning time. The Quiché term for such beings is *uinak,* which is also the term for "twenty," the number of the human toes and fingers, the number of day names in the 260-day cycle, and the basis of the Mayan system of numeration in general. The specific question posed for consideration by Xpiyacoc and Xmucane is whether these twenty-digited beings should be made of wood. The procedure they follow in seeking an answer fits contemporary Quiché divinatory practice in every way.

Having been given their question, Xpiyacoc and Xmucane do something the Popol Vuh calls *ukahic* or "the borrowing" (D. Tedlock 1985:81), a term immediately recognized by don Andrés. When today's daykeeper speaks the opening prayer for a divination, invoking the sheet-lightning, clouds, mists, and damp breezes of the world, he or she is said to be "borrowing" these forces from the days themselves, each of which is ruled by a lord, and from the mountains of the world, each of which has a spirit familiar (B. Tedlock 1982:189–191). The divine daykeepers of the Popol Vuh are not as modest as this human daykeeper in their borrowing of lightning, moisture, and air currents: Xpiyacoc and Xmucane name the Heart of Sky, whose electrical aspect ultimately manifests not as far-off and silently flickering sheet-lightning but as close-up thunderbolts, also known as Hurakan or "Hurricane," the bringer of rains and winds of world-destroying proportions (D. Tedlock 1985:83, 343).

Meteorological forces, large or small, serve to connect the cosmos at large, both temporally and spatially, with the microcosmic scene of the divination, transmitting information about distant places or times through the counting of days and through lightning-like sensations that occur in various parts of the diviner's own body. Having invoked these forces, the contemporary daykeeper asks, for the sake of the client, that they "tell no lies" (B. Tedlock 1982:138–146, 164). Xpiyacoc and Xmucane make a similar request in the Popol Vuh, addressing the ultimate meteorological force and mentioning one of their own clients: "Have shame, you up there, Heart of Sky: attempt no deception before the mouth and face of Sovereign Plumed Serpent" (D. Tedlock 1985:83). This may seem a strange way to address the ultimate celestial deity, but Quiché theology allows no monopolies where the truth is concerned.

During the divination performed in the Popol Vuh, "the hand is moved over the kernels, over the coral seeds, the days, the lots" (D. Tedlock 1985:81). Just as is the case today, the coral seeds are not only called by their own name, 4,ite, but are metaphorically called *ixim*, "corn kernels." At present the daykeeper first pours the seeds out of a small bundle into a pile on a table and mixes them, moving the right hand over them with palm down flat and fingers spread, and then grabs a fistful. The remaining seeds are then set aside; those from the fistful are sorted into lots of four seeds each, arranged in parallel rows so that the days can easily be counted on them, one day for each lot. Like Xpiyacoc and Xmucane, the human practitioner speaks to the seeds while arranging them, asking for a clear outcome. When seeds are left over from the division into fours, a remainder of three seeds is made into two additional lots (with two seeds in one and one seed in the other), while a remainder of one or two seeds counts as one additional lot. Once the clusters are complete the diviner begins counting the days of the 260-day cycle, starting in the present (the day of the divination itself), the past (the day the client's problem began), or the future (the day of an action contemplated by the client). The augury is reckoned from the character or portent of the day that is reached by counting through to the final lot of seeds. The more general outcome of a divination is usually formulated on the basis of several days, arrived at by counting through the same lots a second time, or by starting all over again with a new fistful of seeds. The results given by the days themselves are further modified and refined according to the portents of the lightning signals received in the body of the diviner.

The alphabetic Popol Vuh does not give the actual numbers and names of the days counted by Xpiyacoc and Xmucane in this earliest of all divinations, but its hieroglyphic predecessor may have been like the Book of Chilam Balam of Chumayel, which treats the first counting of days as nothing less than the origin of the 260-day calendar itself and gives not only numbers and names but day-by-day interpretations, running through twenty days (Roys 1967:116–119). In the Popol Vuh text as we know it, Xpiyacoc and Xmucane simply offer their clients a summary of the results of their own counting: "It is well that there be your manikins, woodcarvings, talking, speaking, there on the face of the earth" (D. Tedlock 1985:83). This is an accurate augury as far as it goes, since the wooden people did indeed turn out to be "human in looks and human in speech," but it fails to mention that although they would succeed in populating the earth, they would fall short of being true humans.

As things turned out, the wooden people failed to pray to the gods and keep the days; as the Popol Vuh has it, "They just went and walked wherever they wanted" (D. Tedlock 1985:83). Or, as don Andrés remarked when he read this phrase, "They were like animals." He explained that one of the major differences between animals and humans is that humans must ask permission to go abroad in the world, praying that nothing bad happen to them in the road. In punishment for having forgotten their gods, the wooden people meet with a great disaster. Their houses are invaded by animals; to this day, when a wild animal such as a possum or coyote enters a house or its outbuildings to kill domestic animals, this is taken as a sign of neglected prayers and offerings. In the Popol Vuh even the domestic animals attack, along with household artifacts (84–85). All this occurs under the general cover of a great, world-darkening and world-flooding rainstorm, sent by Hurricane. The survivors are the monkeys of today.

Beyond the episode that deals with the fate of the wooden people lie the sections of the Popol Vuh which deal with the lives of the children and grandchildren of Xpiyacoc and Xmucane. In the course of their adventures they not only initiate astronomical cycles but establish various rituals for the future use of humans, some of which don Andrés readily recognized as the rituals per-formed by present-day motherfathers. It is the grandchildren, Hunahpu and Xbalanque, who establish a custom that corresponds to the patrilineage shrine called the uinel. When they are about to descend into the underworld, where they will be in great danger, they leave their grandmother a sign that will help her keep track of their fate. They plant corn, but it is ears of corn (not grains) they plant, and they plant these ears "neither in the mountains nor where the earth is damp, but where the earth is dry, in the middle of the inside of their house" (D. Tedlock 1985:133–134). And they leave the ears planted not in the earthen floor of the house but up above it (159), in the attic or loft, which is where harvested corn is stored today. They tell Xmucane that when the corn dries up or ripens (which don Andrés took to be the corn in the field rather than the ears stored in the house) it will be a sign of their death, and that when it sprouts again it will be a sign that they are alive.

The corn plants grow after the twins leave, but when they are burned in an oven the plants dry up, and at this point Xmucane burns an offering of copal as a memorial to her grandsons (D. Tedlock 1985:158–159). Then, when the twins come back to life and the corn grows a second time, their grandmother is happy at heart again. Now she gives names to the ears which had been kept in the house, including "Middle of the House" and "Middle of the Harvest." Don Andrés explained all this as follows:

What was "left planted" by Hunahpu and Xbalanque was a custom. They left it "planted" that because of the corn, they would never be forgotten. Now, this is a matter of the uinel. When the corn is ripe one has to give thanks, to burn copal in the uinel. One gives thanks so that the seeds will have to sprout again; one takes ears of corn to the burning place, and when one is finished praying one passes these ears through the smoke of the copal, saying, *Are 4u ua ru4ux,* "This here is the heart." This is what their grandmother must have done in the Popol Vuh. And after the ears are passed through the smoke they are placed in the center of the house, in the middle of our crop.

Don Andrés surmised that when Xmucane burned copal at harvest time, she must have replaced the ears Hunahpu and Xbalanque had left in the house with smoked ears from the new crop, thus following out the custom they themselves had begun when they left for the underworld.

Today the ears of corn that serve as the "heart" of the crop are kept with the rest of the harvested ears but are not eaten until a new crop has ripened a year later. Even though these smoked ears are not used for seed corn they are nevertheless thought of as alive, and it is because "the heart of the corn has not died" that the seed corn is able to sprout in the fields. In this sense the ears which Hunahpu and Xbalanque left planted were not merely a sign of their fate but the very thing that made it possible for them to survive the dry season and "sprout" again. In their own case, however, becoming "dry" meant nothing less than immolation; the return of wetness came when their ground-up remains were thrown in a river. At first they looked like catfish when they grew again (D. Tedlock 1985:149), and here we have a glimpse of what the rituals of the uinel must have been like when the Quichés were still in the Gulf-coast lowlands: If they were using raised fields like those whose traces are now being discovered in various parts of the lowlands, with heaped-up platforms of soil bordered by drainage ditches that are thought to have been well supplied with fish (Hammond 1982:160–163), they may well have paralleled the planting and harvest rites for their corn with other rites in which ground fish bones were "planted" in the drainage ditches and the grown fish were "harvested."

In addition to setting a precedent for one of the rituals of the uinel, Hunahpu and Xbalanque establish at least one aspect of the shrine known as the foundation of the people. At this shrine the motherfather not only marks the pregnancies and births occurring in his patrilineage, as was discussed earlier, but also the deaths. The deaths that concern Hunahpu and Xbalanque are those of their own father, One Hunahpu, and his brother, Seven Hunahpu (also called "father"), who were sacrificed by the lords of the underworld (D. Tedlock 1985:113). The names of the fathers are, of course, the numbers and names of days on the Quiché calendar; as don Andrés pointed out, to attach the numbers one and seven to a given day name is to call up all thirteen days of that name. That is because the numbers which prefix a particular day name fall out in the order 1, 8, 2, 9, 3, 10, 4, 11, 5, 12, 6, 13, and 7 (after which they return to 1). When Hunahpu and Xbalanque follow their fathers into the underworld they end up establishing the ritual meaning for all thirteen days bearing the name Hunahpu, having survived a long series of contests with the lords of that region. Among those lords are One Death and Seven Death, whose names call up all thirteen days bearing the name Came or "Death."

Once Hunahpu and Xbalanque have humbled the lords of the underworld and restricted the future circumstances under which they will be allowed to kill human beings, they go to visit the grave of their fathers at an underworld location, the Place of Ball Game Sacrifice (D. Tedlock 1985:159). One Hunahpu's body is headless, his head having been cut off when he was sacrificed and having long since become one with the fruit of a calabash tree (113), but the body of Seven Hunahpu is complete. Hunahpu and Xbalanque attempt to revive Seven Hunahpu and want him to speak, but he can say very little, given that there is scarcely anything left of his face other than the empty mouth, nose, and eyes of his skull. They leave him (and One Hunahpu's headless body) behind at the burial place, promising that "you will be prayed to here," and "you will be the first to have your day kept by those who will be born in the light, begotten in the light"—that is, by human beings, who will honor days bearing the name Hunahpu (159). That the Place of Ball Game Sacrifice was near or even in a ball court may be guessed from the fact that *hom*, the term for "ball court" in the Popol Vuh, is at present the term for "graveyard."

Don Andrés was more excited by Hunahpu and Xbalanque's visit with Seven Hunahpu than by any other Popol Vuh episode that establishes present-day customs. He explained that when there is a death in the patrilineage, the funeral rites are not complete until the motherfather has gone to the foundation of the people on a Hunahpu day that falls after the actual death. There he prays that the lingering soul of the deceased, which is a spark of light, might pass on into the underworld, from which it may later have the good fortune to rise into the sky like a star. The number of the Hunahpu day is chosen according to the age and importance of the deceased, with a very low number for a small child and a high one for a very old person who occupied important offices (B. Tedlock 1982:124). With or without a recent death, Hunahpu days are appropriate for visiting the graves of relatives, where prayers are said and offerings are burnt in much the same way as at patrilineage shrines, except that the entire family may go along and make a day of it, taking along a picnic lunch and strong drink. This takes us back to the beginning of the section of the Popol Vuh which deals with death and the underworld, where the narrators speak directly to their audience and propose a toast to One Hunahpu:"Let's drink to him, and let's just drink to the telling and accounting of the begetting of Hunahpu and Xbalanque" (D. Tedlock 1985:105). Don Andrés pictured the narrators as seated on the very grave of One Hunahpu, having gone there on a day bearing the name Hunahpu.

The mebil, which is the first of the patrilineage shrines to be portended in the Popol Vuh, is the last to have its story completed, a long time after the appearance of humans. When the true sun first rose, the one that is still with us today, its heat petrified the gods of the ruling Quiché lineages—Tohil, Auilix, and Hacauitz—along with such pumas, jaguars, rattlesnakes, and yellowbites as were alive at that time, making each of them into a kind of stone the Popol Vuh calls *4abauil* (D. Tedlock 1985:182). This term may once have meant something like "open-mouthed," but I have generally translated it as "god," in the sense of that term that includes images of gods (247). Before they were petrified, Tohil, Auilix, and Hacauitz spoke to their worshipers in person, but afterwards it was only the spirit familiars of their stone bodies that appeared and spoke (185). Such an appearance took place whenever a stone was given an offering of blood—the blood of female birds and female deer, or blood let from the ears and elbows of worshipers, or blood from human captives who had their hearts cut out and their heads cut off (186–187). The offered blood was poured directly into the stone's mouth.

As for the animals which were petrified when the sun rose, the diminutive god called White Sparkstriker took these with him into the woods, where he himself escaped petrifaction (D. Tedlock 1985:182). To this day he may be encountered at night, in dark woods or in caves such as the one beneath the ruins of Rotten Cane (B. Tedlock 1983). He is the keeper of the volcanic concretions and ancient artifacts which don Andrés calls the Heart of Metal, and it is he who permits the fortunate to discover these objects and take them home. In Momostenango the common term for an object of this kind is mebil, after the shrine in whose upper part it should be kept, though there are reports of the former existence of a particular stone called 4abauil, which was kept in a cave (Cook 1981:501). In the eastern Quiché area, including Santa Cruz Quiché itself, the present-day term for powerful stones is 4amauil. It is in the eastern area that the treatment of such stones most resembles what is described for the stone gods of the Popol Vuh. A 4amauil must have a mouth, and it is through this mouth that it is given a drink of strong liquor—and, on occasion, the blood of a chicken. According to Lucas Pacheco Benítez, a motherfather from a town east of Santa Cruz, one of the best days to do this is the one named I3 or "Wind," and the stone itself may be addressed by this name. The spirit familiar of the stone may appear in dreams as an animate, speaking being. If the stone itself were to speak in broad daylight, its voice would be a shrill whistle, warning of dire happenings.

For an imagination that has been fed on Christian notions of what idolatry might be, these Wind stones are one of the most unsettling aspects of Quiché religion. For the most part, they bear little outward resemblance to life forms. They do not answer very well to words like "icon" or "idol"—for that, images of saints would serve better. As art, the stones are more in the nature of found objects than fashioned objects. Many of them are changed by the human hand only in being removed from the canyon or mountain where they were discovered and placed in an established outdoor shrine or on the earthen floor beneath a household altar. Such a stone might have a size and shape close to that of a human head, but with a flattening and tapering along the horizontal axis that begins to suggest the head of, say, a reptile. If the tapered end has a concavity or a groove in it, then that is where drinks will be offered. A stone that first came to the notice of the waking eye may then begin to disclose its true shape to the dreamer. If it is immovably embedded in the very landscape, people will go to that spot on camping trips, not to "see the sights" in the usual sense but in the hope of seeing something in their sleep.

The Popol Vuh tells us that Jaguar Quitze once went looking for a place to hide the stone whose spirit familiar was his patron deity, Tohil by name. He found that place on a mountain in a "great forest," and "the mountain is called Patohil today" (D. Tedlock 1985:179). At first, Tohil was set beneath bromelias and hanging mosses, but eventually temples were built for him, one at Patohil itself and another atop the pyramid that stood for Patohil on the plaza at Rotten Cane. No one knows where the original stone (or the fragments of it) may be today, and no one invokes Tohil himself except indirectly, by praying to the lord of the day that was sacred to him, the one named Toh. But in the great forest east of Santa Cruz Quiché, on top of the mountain called Patohil, amid the rubble of a stone temple platform that has been dynamited by European treasure hunters, is a small enclosure open to the sky, and in that enclosure are some stones that have mouths. The stains left by the burning of copal incense and tallow candles mark this as a spot that remains sacred, but an adventurer in search of priceless idols would never know which stones were the ones he was looking for.

NOTES

1. The Quiché orthography used in this essay is that of the Popol Vuh and other native-language documents from colonial Guatemala. Except for a long/short distinction in Quiché vowels, all phonemes are taken into account. For present purposes the five vowels should be pronounced approximately as in Spanish. Doubled vowels indicate a vowel followed by a glottal stop. The voiceless velar stop (like English *k*) is *c* (before *a*, *o*, *u*) or *qu* (before *i*, *e*), while the voiceless uvular stop (like Hebrew *qoph*) is *k*. The glottalized forms of these stops are respectively *4* and *3*. With the following exceptions, the remaining consonants are as in Spanish: *b* is a

glottalized *p*, *l* is dental (like Welsh ll), *tt* is a glottalized *t*, *x* is an alveopalatal fricative (like English *sh*), *4h* is a glottalized *ch*, and *4* is a glottalized *tz*. Stress is nearly always on the final syllable of a word.

2. Translations from the Spanish of Ximénez are by this author.

REFERENCES

Carmack, Robert M. 1977. *Quichean Civilization: The Ethnohistoric, Ethnographic, and Archaeological Sources.* Berkeley, Los Angeles, London: University of California Press.

Cook, Garret W. 1981. Supernaturalism, Cosmos, and Cosmogony in Quichean Expressive Culture. Ph.D. diss. State University of New York at Albany.

Hammond, Norman. 1982. *Ancient Maya Civilization.* New Brunswick: Rutgers University Press.

Heyden, Doris. 1975. An Interpretation of the Cave Underneath the Pyramid of the Sun in Teotihuacan, Mexico. *American Antiquity* 40:131–147.

Recinos, Adrián, Delia Goetz, and Sylvanus G. Morley. 1950. *Popol Vuh: The Sacred Book of theAncient Quiché Maya.* Norman: University of Oklahoma Press.

Roys, Ralph L. 1967. *The Book of Chilam Balam of Chumayel.* Norman: University of Oklahoma Press.

Tedlock, B. 1982. *Time and the Highland Maya.* Albuquerque: University of New Mexico Press.

———. 1983. El C'oxol: un símbolo de la resistencia quiché a la conquista espiritual. In *Nuevas perspectivas sobre el Popol Vuh*, ed. Robert M. Carmack and Francisco Morales Santos. Pp. 343–357. Guatemala: Piedra Santa.

———. n.d. La dialéctica de la agronomía y astronomía maya-quiché. In *Arqueoastronomía y etnoastronomía en Mesoamérica*, ed. Johanna Broda and Stanislaw Iwaniszewski. Mexico, D.F.: Universidad Nacional Autónoma de México (forthcoming).

Tedlock, D. 1985. *Popol Vuh: The Mayan Book of the Dawn of Life and the Glories of Gods and Kings.* New York: Simon and Schuster.

———. n.d. The Sowing and Dawning of All the Sky-Earth: Astronomy in the Popol Vuh. In *Ethnoastronomy: Indigenous Astronomical and Cosmological Traditions of the World*, ed. John B. Carlson, Von Del Chamberlain, and Jane Young. Salt Lake City: University of Utah Press.

———. 1983. *The Spoken Word and the Work of Interpretation.* Philadelphia: University of Pennsylvania Press.

Thompson, J. Eric S. 1970. *Maya History and Religion*. Norman: University of Oklahoma Press.

Ximénez, Francisco. 1857. *Las historias del origen de los indios de esta provincia de Guatemala*. Introduction, paleography, and notes by Carl Scherzer. Vienna: Academia Imperial de las Ciencias.

———. 1967. *Escolios a las historias del origen de los indios*. Sociedad de Geografía e Historia de Guatemala, pub. 13.

Chief Seattle's Speech(es): American Origins and European Reception

RUDOLF KAISER

<hr>

I

All those who have watched the development of ecological thinking in Europe over the last years will realize that, more than any other group of people, American Indians are seen and presented as models of an ecological attitude, sometimes even as born conservationists, or as patron saints of a close relationship between man and his natural environment. One of the reasons for this very special and very topical reputation of American Indians seems to reside in the widespread dissemination of a text that is regarded as a manifesto of ecological feeling and thinking—a speech, sometimes referred to as a letter, by Chief Seattle. While American Indians are seen by some people to be ecologists by birth, Chief Seattle is hailed as the prophet of an ecological sentiment that is said to be lacking in Western industrialized nations. The following are examples of the wide publicity which Chief Seattle's speech has gained in Europe:

In August 1978, a youth organization of Catholic students in the Federal Republic of Germany published a booklet about ecological problems entitled *Seattle*. This booklet contains not only the text of Chief Seattle's speech but also a somewhat similar speech by a Chief Tulavil from an island in the South Pacific. In addition, there are commentaries, notes, songs, and cartoons, all referring to the issue of ecology. The booklet also serves as the guide to a musical, which is also called *Seattle*. Finally, there is a record that goes with the musical and the booklet. The title of this record is—*Seattle*.

At the end of a very committed, informative, and depressing book about the exploitation and destruction of the earth, its author, who is German, wants to leave his readers with a glimpse of hope and a view of the correct attitude of man toward nature: He ends his book with the full text of Chief Seattle's speech (Drewermann 1982).

The interdenominational Women's World Day of Prayer in 1981 had as its theme, "The Earth is the Lord's." The texts and prayers for the service were prepared by American Indian women of the Christian faith, representing Indian tribes from throughout the United States. The reason Indian women had been asked to do this is given in the introduction to the prayers: "Their special reverence for nature and their feeling of kinship with all creatures of the earth, sky and water enable them to teach us how to live justly, respectfully, and in harmony with our world and each other" (Women's World Day of Prayer 1981:2). One of the prayers is taken from the famous speech by Red Jacket; another is from that by Chief Seattle.

Many schools and other educational institutions in Europe teach courses on ecological issues that frequently make use of a film that in German-speaking countries is available under the title of "Söhne der Erde" (Sons of the Earth).[1] As the film was made in the United States, it is probably also available in other languages. The narration of the film consists solely of Chief Seattle's speech. (We shall see that this film played an important part in the genesis of the speech.) The photography attempts to illustrate and underline this narration by showing the white man's destruction of the environment and contrasting it with pictures of a beautifully unpolluted countryside.

During the eighty-seventh Deutscher Katholikentag (Congress of German Catholics) at Düsseldorf in 1982, a short song was repeatedly and enthusiastically sung whose text repeats over and over again just one sentence from Chief Seattle's speech: "Jeder Teil dieser Erde ist meinem Volke heilig" (every part of this earth is sacred to my people).

The periodical of a German missionary order published the full text of Chief Seattle's speech together with photographs of unspoiled nature in its March 1983 edition (Seattle, 1983).

Swiss singer René Bardet has produced a record that is entirely devoted to words and themes from Chief Seattle's speech. The text of the speech is reproduced almost entirely in twelve songs. Moreover, the cover informs one at great length about the singer's ideas on and impressions of Chief Seattle's speech.

Finally, different German publishers have published booklets containing a German translation of Chief Seattle's speech. All of these booklets contain illustrations of polluted and unpolluted nature to accompany the text.[2]

These examples of Chief Seattle's popularity in Europe could give the impression that only Germany or German-speaking countries are at present following the trail of the Indian chief. Although it seems that Seattle's speech is more frequently referred to and utilized for discussions of ecological issues in German-speaking countries than in some other West European countries, the most comprehensive adaptation of Seattle's ideas comes from England.

The United Society for the Propagation of the Gospel, in London, has produced a multimedia teaching aid under the title *Testimony—Chief Seattle*. This comprises a tape, a film, and a script, all devoted to Seattle's speech. Together with these items is a resource pack of no less than some one hundred pages that tries to present all the available information about Chief Seattle, his time, his tribe, and his language. It also attempts to give suggestions to parents, teachers, and leaders of youth groups about ways of utilizing the speech (e.g., using it for games, or theological discussions comparing Seattle's words with texts from the Old Testament or with the Christian prayer "Our Father"). It is also in this resource pack that the speech receives the highest consecration imaginable in a Christian society: It is set on a near-equal footing with the four Gospels of the New Testament and called by Monsignor Bruce Kent, "a fifth Gospel, almost."[3]

A Dutch translation of Seattle's speech in typescript is being circulated and disseminated by, among others, the "Volkenkundige Boekhandel," called "The Trading Post" in Ixialaan/Holland. Moreover, the Dutch text of the speech is included in a booklet that was put together by the "Aktie Stroohalm en de Ecologische Uitgeverij," and which is propagated and sold by the NANAI (Nederlandse Aktiegroep Noord-Amerikaanse Indianen) in Rotterdam.[4]

In Sweden, Seattle's speech was first published in two different Swedish translations in 1976 and 1977, and was used in a third translation by a Swedish pop group in one of its records.[5] It was an Englishman living in Sweden, Carl Ross, who took on the task of putting the authenticity of the text to the test, however. (This will be discussed further below.)

Many more examples of the adaptation and use of Seattle's speech for environmental purposes in other European countries, such as Italy, Portugal, and Denmark, can easily be found. There may be hardly a country in Western Europe where Seattle's speech has not been published in translation and hailed as a document of an exemplary ecological sentiment. It is precisely this great number of publications which makes it impossible to mention them all.

We should not, however, fail to consider whether and how European ecological parties in general and the German Greens in particular have appropriated Seattle's work. West Germany, Holland, and Belgium are those countries in Western Europe in which the development of ecological parties seems to be farthest advanced. In all these parties or groupings, American Indians—and above all Chief Seattle—enjoy the image of being something like model ecologists. This does not mean that in party programs and manifestos the names of Chief Seattle or other American Indians are expressly mentioned. This is not the case as far as the German Greens are concerned; nor is it, to my knowledge, the case in other European countries. But it is agreed by the bulk of the members and the supporters of these parties that more than any other group of people around the world, American Indians have something that Europeans have lost and must learn again for the sake of the future of this planet: an exemplary relationship between man and nature. Neither American Indians nor Chief Seattle are to be found in the public or semipublic statements and declarations of ecological parties in Europe; but most people see and feel them through and find them behind both the philosophies of these parties and the pronouncements of their speakers. Many such groups print the text of Seattle's speech and distribute it among their supporters and other interested people. They also mention or quote Seattle (and, at times, other Indians) frequently, certainly more frequently than any other group of people.

Two further examples indicate that Seattle's speech has not only been influential in books, brochures, records, films, and so on but that it has also had its impact on European radio programs.

These are taken from German programs that concentrate on ecological problems and are intended for young listeners:

In April 1979, the North German Broadcasting Corporation
(Norddeutscher Rundfunk) included a transmission about the destruction of the environment in its programs for schools. In it,
Seattle's speech was quoted in German translation and contrasted
with reports of present-day pollution in German cities, rivers, and
forests.

In October 1982, the West German Broadcasting Corporation
(Westdeutscher Rundfunk) aired a program about a project carried
out by boys and girls in a German school. The pupils had read
Seattle's speech, and on that basis they discussed their own traditional understanding of the environment and their attitudes toward
nature. In the course of this project, they discovered that Seattle's
attitude toward nature had the greatest significance for them in
their current ecological situation. The words of a young Swiss lady
may be taken as being representative of what many young people
in Europe feel: In a letter to me she wrote that, for her, Seattle's
speech has become "the embodiment of all 'environmental ideas.'"[6]

As this essay is primarily concerned with the European response
to Seattle's speech, I will present only a short glimpse of the American scene: Dale Jones, the northwest representative of Friends of
the Earth in the city of Seattle, writes in a letter referring to his
part in disseminating Seattle's speech, which he and some other
publications call a "letter":

> I first saw the letter in September 1972 in a now out of business
> native American tabloid newspaper. . . . I clipped the article and
> mailed it to a few friends. Soon thereafter the letter appeared in
> *Environmental Action* and has subsequently appeared in a number
> of publications around the world.

One of these publications, apparently, was the April 1974 issue of
Passages, the magazine of Northwest Orient Airlines. Many later
publications of the text, which then appeared in a great number of
ways and places in the United States, refer to *Passages* as their
source. The *Seattle Times* and the Sierra Club, a conservation organization, reprint the speech from time to time. Thus, I received a
surprise when I asked students of the Acoma-Laguna High School
on the Laguna Reservation about their associations with the name

"Seattle." These young Pueblo Indians knew Seattle only as the name of an American city, but not as the name of an Indian chief! This experience seems to confirm the view that the situation in America is very similar to that in Europe: while the text of his speech is famous in ecologically oriented circles, Chief Seattle as a historical person does not seem to be as well known as his words, not even among young Indians.

II

When we read or hear or see these numerous European utilizations and applications of Seattle's speech, and if we look and watch and listen carefully, something strikes us: There are obvious differences between some of these texts of the speech (sometimes only in phrasing and wording but sometimes also in content), all of which are ascribed to Chief Seattle. Moreover, these differences cannot be the result only of different translations of one identical text, because in one case the difference amounts to the opposition between "Your god is not our god," and "Our god is the same god." In this way, we find all the shades from identical to downright opposite phrasing and thinking. (We shall take a closer look at these differences further on.) This discovery leads to one of the following conclusions: The different versions of the text refer to different speeches by Seattle; or, different versions of one speech are in existence. These conclusions give rise to such questions as: What is the source material? What does basic research tell us? How authentic are these texts?

There is no doubt that Chief Seattle existed. He lived from about 1786 to 1866 and was a chief of the Suquamish and the Duwamish Indians on the Pacific northwest coast of what is now the United States. His native name, Seeathl, was debased by whites to its present spelling and pronunciation. There is also no doubt that Chief Seattle was present at the Port Elliott Treaty negotiations of 1855, which signed away a good deal of Indian land for white settlement. Seattle was the first Indian chief to sign that treaty and on that occasion gave two short speeches that are now preserved among the documents of the treaty proceedings in the National Archives in Washington, D.C. Seattle was converted to Catholicism around 1830 and never fought in a war against white people. The largest city of the State of Washington has borne his name since approximately 1860.

Unfortunately, we tread on less safe ground when we approach the question of the authenticity of his famous speech. The two short speeches just mentioned bear no resemblance to what is currently being publicized as "Seattle's speech" in America and Europe. The tone and subject matter of both those speeches are definitely at variance with the speech popularized in recent publications.[7] Yet, several searches by the staff of the National Archives have revealed no other record of a speech or letter by Chief Seattle.[8]

The oldest document of the speech which has become so famous in our time dates from the year 1887. On October 29 of that year, the *Seattle Sunday Star,* which went out of print a few years later, published an article by H. A. Smith, under the heading "Early Reminiscences Number 10," entitled, "Scraps from a diary—Chief Seattle—a gentleman by instinct—his native eloquence etc. etc." Its author, a physician who is usually known as Dr. Henry Smith, begins with a very favorable description of the appearance and behavior of Chief Seattle, of his bearing and delivery of the speech, and of his impact on the people around him. Dr. Smith continues: "When Governor Stevens first arrived in Seattle and told the natives he had been appointed commissioner of Indian affairs for Washington Territory, they gave him a demonstrative reception in front of Dr. Maynard's office, near the water front on Main Street" (p. 10). After the governor had been introduced by Dr. Maynard and had given an explanation of his mission there,

> Chief Seattle arose with all the dignity of a senator, who carries the responsibilities of a great nation on his shoulders. Placing one hand on the governor's head and slowly pointing heavenward with the index finger of the other, he commenced his memorable address in solemn and impressive tones. "Yonder sky, that has wept tears of compassion upon our fathers for centuries untold, . . . "

After recording Seattle's speech Dr. Smith concludes his article with the following remarks:

> Other speakers followed, but I took no notes. Governor Stevens' reply was brief. He merely promised to meet them in general

council on some future occasion to discuss the proposed treaty. Chief Seattle's promise to adhere to the treaty, should one be ratified, was observed to the letter, for he was ever the unswerving and faithful friend of the white man. The above is but a fragment of his speech, and lacks all the charm lent by the grace and earnestness of the sable old orator, and the occasion. (p. 10)

I have quoted Dr. Smith's introductory and the concluding remarks at some length, because there are some important points in them which we have to keep in mind if we want to blaze a trail through the thicket of differing opinions and misleading hints:

a. According to Dr. Smith, this address by Seattle was not given on the occasion of the signing of the Point Elliott Treaty, but at a reception for the new commissioner of Indian Affairs for Washington Territory, Governor Stevens, and the location was "in front of Dr. Maynard's office" on Main Street. This means at the same time that this speech was not made in January 1855, when the Treaty of Point Elliott was signed, but in November or December 1853, or in 1854, for it was in November 1853 that Stevens arrived in the new Washington Territory as Governor and Commissioner of Indian Affairs. The most likely date for the address seems to be December 1854, when Stevens returned from a trip to the East.

b. The second point which we ought to remember is Dr. Smith's remark, "The above is but a fragment of his speech, and lacks all the charm," and so on. This means that Dr. Smith does not claim to have recorded Seattle's speech word for word and in full.

c. On the other hand, Dr. Smith obviously took notes of Seattle's speech, which is indicated both by the heading "Scraps from a diary" and by the concluding remark, "Other speakers followed, but I took no notes." By pointing out that he took no notes of the other speakers, Dr. Smith implies that he did take notes of Seattle's speech.

There is, moreover, to be found in John M. Rich's booklet another document confirming that Dr. Smith on his deathbed told a Vivian M. Carkeek "that he had made extended notes of the address at the time it was given and from those notes he reconstructed the entire address" (1970:45). In this declaration, Dr. Smith seems to run counter to his prior statement, made toward the end of his original newspaper article of 1887, that "The above is but a fragment of his speech."

A solution to this seeming contradiction may be that with the phrase "the entire address," Dr. Smith did not refer to Seattle's actual address but to his own rendition of it. However that may be, Dr. Smith's notes have been lost, and unless somebody should happen to find them, we shall never know what Dr. Smith's diary contained and how closely he adhered to his notes when he wrote that newspaper article thirty-three years after the speech was made.

There is also the question of whether Seattle gave the speech in English or in his native language and, if so, whether Dr. Smith understood this native language. William Arrowsmith, who himself made a "translation" of Dr. Smith's Seattle address, says in a letter to Carl Ross (1/20/78), that "Seattle's English was minimal" and that he purportedly delivered his speech "in his native Duwamish." All of the authors who have written about Seattle seem to agree that he did not speak English, let alone write it. Concerning Dr. Smith's mastery of Seattle's language, W. C. Vandenwerth says that Dr. Smith "mastered the Duwamish language in about two years," but that Seattle's speech "was delivered through an interpreter" (1971:119). John M. Rich writes that Seattle "conveyed his thoughts in the dignified, picturesque, Indian language" (1970:48).

Neither Vandenwerth nor Rich gives the source of his information. Nevertheless, we can take it for granted that Seattle did not deliver his speech in English, but that he used his native Indian language, which was not called Duwamish (this was the name of one of Seattle's tribes, not of a language) but Lushotseed. As was the custom on such occasions, the speech was then translated by interpreters, first probably into the so-called Chinook Jargon, which consisted of elements from European and Indian languages and was then used as an interlanguage in the area, and then into English. The question of whether Dr. Smith took his notes from Seattle's native Lushotseed or from the translation must remain open. This point is irrelevant because Dr. Smith does not claim to give a full record of Seattle's speech in its original phrasing.

Putting together our findings so far we can say:

1) Two short speeches by Seattle that are recorded in the National Archives in Washington, D.C. bear no resemblance to the texts of the speech popularized under Seattle's name.

2) The first published version of the now-famous speech was presented

to the public by a Dr. H. A. Smith in 1887, more than thirty years after the chief is said to have delivered it. Although this text is different from most of the publicized versions of today, it is similar enough to indicate a relationship.

3) The selection of the material and the formulation of the text is possibly as much Dr. Smith's as Seattle's. There is no way of determining the degree of authenticity of this text, as Dr. Smith's notebook has not been found.

4) We can, however, take it for granted that there is at least a core, a nucleus of authentic thinking and, possibly, language in the text, as Dr. Smith was able to base his version of the speech on "extended notes" in his diary, taken on the occasion of the delivery of the speech. As Arrowsmith wrote to Carl Ross, "I incline to think that much of Smith's version was authentic," a confirmation of his assertion in the *American Poetry Review* (1975) that "the speech in Smith's version evidently followed the original closely." (p. 26)

It seems that not many people took notice of Dr. Smith's publication of Seattle's speech. Apart from a full reprint of the text in the *History of Seattle* by Frederic James Grant (1891:432 ff), there is hardly a reference to the speech prior to the early thirties. In 1931, Clarence B. Bagley published an article in the *Washington Historical Quarterly* under the title, "Chief Seattle and Angeline," in which he reprints, with some variations, the complete text of Chief Seattle's speech from Dr. Smith's publication in the *Seattle Sunday Star*. The most striking variation is probably that Bagley adds three short sentences to the speech. Dr. Smith ended Seattle's address with the words: "The white man will never be alone. Let him be just and deal kindly with my people, for the dead are not altogether powerless." Bagley adds: "Dead—did I say? There is no death. Only a change of worlds" (1931:255).[9] This handling of the text seems to have had two important effects: The addition was accepted by the public—most later publications of the address have it. It may also have opened up the way for a very free handling of the original text by other editors.

Only one year later, in 1932, John M. Rich published a booklet entitled *Chief Seattle's Unanswered Challenge* (1970). This booklet contains not only Dr. Smith's version of Chief Seattle's speech, again with some variations and Bagley's addition to the text, but also the story of how Rich discovered the text, what the occasion of Seattle's address was, and some very flattering remarks about the impact of the speech on Rich himself. Moreover, the booklet tries to confirm the authenticity of the text by reproducing a letter from a law firm in Seattle. (This letter was quoted above, because it endorses the view that Dr. Smith reconstructed Seattle's address from extended notes, taken while the speech was being given.) Rich's booklet was reprinted several times without attracting too much attention. Occasional excerpts of the speech, mostly adopting Bagley's modifications of the text, appeared in the 1960s.[10]

By the late sixties and early seventies, it seems that a greater awareness had developed for the problems which Seattle touched on in his speech. In 1969, an American poet and writer, William Arrowsmith, published the "Speech of Chief Seattle" (see appendix, version 2). The reader will quickly see that not so much the content as the wording and phrasing of this text are different from that published by Dr. Smith.

Only a few years later, between 1972 and 1974, yet another text appeared under the title, "The Decidedly Unforked Message of Chief Seattle" (see appendix, version 3). In order to make matters even more complicated, at the World Fair of 1974 in Spokane, Washington, a "Speech by Chief Seattle" was displayed in the U.S. pavilion (see appendix, version 4) that, again, seemed different in style and wording.

Had new speeches by Seattle been discovered that had been unknown to the world until then? Not at all. Though all these "speeches," "addresses," "messages," or even "letters" of Chief Seattle differ from each other sometimes more, sometimes less, they are yet similar enough to indicate that they all used one text as their basis. William Arrowsmith expressly states at the end of his *Speech of Chief Seattle* that the text is "Translated from the Victorian English of Dr. Henry Smith of Seattle, published in the *Seattle Star* on October 29, 1877."[11] The anonymous author of "The Decidedly Unforked Message of Chief Seattle" (*Passages* 1974) notes in a preliminary remark that it is "An adaptation of his [Chief Seattle's] remarks, based on an English translation by William Arrowsmith." Finally, the text from the 1974 Expo at Spokane displays, on close reading, a very great similarity to this "Decidedly Unforked Message."

We can see that, although all three of these versions of Chief

Seattle's speech differ to varying degrees in their content and language, none of them claims to have a new or direct line of descent from the Old Chief, a line that might have escaped the public's attention so far. On the contrary, all of them directly or indirectly refer to, and are therefore dependent on, that text of Seattle's speech which was published by Dr. Smith in the *Seattle Sunday Star* in 1887. Dr. Smith's version (which we should therefore call version 1, and which is listed in the appendix as such) is the only true ancestor of all these later—legitimate or illegitimate—generations of the text. It is the source of the version by William Arrowsmith (version 2), of the "Decidedly Unforked Message of Chief Seattle" (version 3), and of the text from the Spokane Expo (version 4).

III

When we compare these four versions with each other and then look at the texts of the speech which roam around Europe and America, a striking realization takes place: In those texts which find highest acclaim and are most widely publicized today there is little of version 1 or version 2. By far, most of the texts now in vogue are either excerpts or relatively complete renderings of version 3. This also applies to a so-called "letter" by Chief Seattle to President Pierce in Washington. This text appeared in America and in Europe in the mid-seventies, along with versions 3 and 4, and is virtually identical to other circulating texts of version 3 (and partly of version 4). This letter by no means represents a new version but is merely a variant of version 3. (By the way, no trace of the original of such a letter could be found in the National Archives in Washington or in the Seattle Public Library.)

Starting with a comparison of versions 1 and 2, we find that throughout the texts the two authors follow the same ideas in the same order, so that the subject matter and the content of the two texts are very much the same, almost identical. One recurring aspect of the texts is the nineteenth-century Manifest Destiny ideology from a seemingly Indian point of view. Both texts display a good number of metaphors and similes, but it is in the use of vocabulary where they differ markedly. Version 1 uses very elevated, literary, and sometimes even archaic language, while the author of version 2 writes simpler sentences and uses more modern and down-to-earth language. A close reading of the two texts shows that the difference between versions 1 and 2 is, above all, one of language, not of ideas. (As its author, William Arrowsmith has stated, version 2 is a translation "from the Victorian English of Dr. Henry Smith.")

We enter into a markedly different kind of relationship if we now take version 3 into consideration and compare it with versions 1 and 2. Whereas the step from 1 to 2 brought a change of language but not of content, the step from 2 to 3 brings not only a change of language but also of subject matter and content. Moreover, this change of content takes several directions: One is the attitude of the speaker toward the white man, for whereas 1 displays a positive and friendly feeling toward whites—it calls the President of the United States "our great and good father," and later adds, "I will not . . . reproach my pale-face brothers"—the text of version 3 shows a much less friendly and sometimes a resentful attitude:

[T]he white man may come with guns and take our land.

We know that the white man does not understand our ways.

Continue to contaminate your bed and you will one night suffocate in your own waste.

This change of attitude toward whites in version 3 is by far outdone by the change of attitude which it shows toward nature. While in versions 1 and 2, considerations of the natural environment play only a secondary role, the text of version 3 concentrates almost entirely on environmental issues. It puts forward the great dangers which arise from the white man's irresponsible dealings with the natural world. Thus, it is only in version 3 that the text adopts a definite ecological slant and that Chief Seattle becomes an ecologist. Here are some of the added environmentalist statements:

How can you buy or sell the sky, the warmth of the land? The idea is strange to us. . . . The rivers are our brothers, they quench our thirst. The rivers carry our canoes, and feed our chil-dren. . . . The air is precious to the red man, for all things share the same breath—the beast, the tree, the man, they all share the same breath.

This we know. The earth does not belong to man. Man belongs to the earth. This we know. All things are connected like the blood which unites one family. All things are connected.

Whatever befalls the earth, befalls the sons of the earth. Man did not weave the web of life; he is merely a strand in it. Whatever he does to the web, he does to himself.

The differences of attitude toward the white man and the natural environment in version 3 extend even to the attitudes expressed toward God. Compare the following quotations:

Version 1	Version 3
"Your God loves your people and hates mine; . . . he has forsaken his red children; . . . The white man's God cannot love his red children."	"Our God is the same God. . . . He is the God of man, and His compassion is equal for the red man and the white."

Finally, we should not fail to mention a number of anachronisms in version 3—remarks that Seattle could not have made in 1854. We read, for example, the following sentence in this text: "I have seen a thousand rotten buffaloes on the prairie, left by the white man who shot them from a passing train." This single sentence contains several errors:

1. When Seattle made his speech in 1854 there were no trains running across the prairie in America. It was more than ten years later that the first transcontinental railway was built.
2. The appalling and senseless killing of buffaloes by white people occurred mainly in the second half of the nineteenth century—especially between 1860 and 1890—and not in the first half, so that Seattle could not have seen it and referred to it in 1854.
3. It is unlikely that, in all his life, Seattle ever left the Pacific Northwest of the United States, where he was born—one more reason why he could not have seen "a thousand rotting buffaloes on the prairie."

The text contains other minor errors, such as references to birds and trees that are not native to the area where Seattle lived. Such discrepancies all constitute additional confirmation that Seattle did not compose the text which we know as version 3 of his speech. It seems that the author of this version mainly adopted from the first and second versions the idea that "the Great Chief in Washington sends word that he wishes to buy our land." This is, therefore, and fittingly, the opening line of 3. After that, the text soon deviates from the thought pattern exhibited in the former versions and develops its own concept of white people, of God, and, above all, of the essential significance of an unspoiled natural environment. In other words, Seattle's speech is used as a peg on which to hang its editor's own story.

Little need be said about version 4, which was exhibited in the U.S. pavilion at the 1974 World Fair in Spokane, Washington. The author of this text obviously used the third version, which he not only shortened and simplified in range but also enlarged by means of style and rhetoric. We find many repetitions, alliterations, enumerations, and even fragmentary sentences in this text. It is wholly ecological and nature-related in its outlook, and has therefore concentrated on the environmental passages of version 3; it is very impressive because of its poetic language. It has, to my knowledge, never been published in a book, however, and its influence should therefore only be considered in close connection with that of version 3.

This comparison of the four versions indicates the following:

1. William Arrowsmith's text, version 2, varies mainly in language from the Smith text, version 1, while in content it clearly follows that version. Arrowsmith himself calls his version a "translation" of the Seattle speech, by which he means "the removal of the dense patina of 19th century literary diction and syntax."
2. Version 3 differs markedly from versions 1 and 2 in language and in content, but at the same time it is obvious that the writer of 3 knew 1 and 2 and used them as a base. What is most strikingly new in version 3 is that its content is profusely ecological. It is only here that Seattle becomes a modern ecologist. Therefore, although some lines of versions 1 and 2 have been transcribed verbatim, the greatest part of this text is new material with a new slant.
3. Version 4 is very close to 3 in content and in language; it is basically a shortened, poetic adaptation of version 3.

IV

In view of the fact that versions 3 and 4 are very similar to each other, but markedly different from versions 1 and 2 in content and form, and in view of the fact that the authors of versions 1 and 2 are known to us, the question arises: Who wrote versions 3 and 4? Whose authorship can they claim? Remembering that 4 is a somewhat modified replica of 3, and keeping in mind that version 3 is the source of most speeches in Europe (and America) that are attributed to Chief Seattle, the problem actually boils down to asking where, when, and above all, by whom was the text of version 3 produced?

In 1975 a journalist in the city of Seattle by the name of Janice Krenmayr delved into the question of the authenticity of version 3 and published an article in the *Seattle Times Magazine* (Jan. 5) entitled "The Earth is Our Mother—Who Really Said That?" In this article, Krenmayr attempts to uncover the origin of the so-called letter by Chief Seattle to President Pierce in Washington. (As we have seen before, this letter is virtually identical to version 3 of Chief Seattle's speech.) Krenmayr writes of her search for the source of the text:

> It [the text] first came to notice as an excerpt in *Wildlife Omnibus*, a newsletter published by the National Wildlife Federation, November 15, 1973. . . . A request was dispatched to the Wildlife Federation for a copy of the entire letter. The editor replied, it had been "picked up" from *Environmental Action Magazine*, November 11, 1972. Environmental Action indicated, its source was the Seattle Office of Friends of the Earth. . . . We queried the latter organization. It disclaimed knowledge of the authenticity and suggested we contact the Seattle Public Library. But that we had done in the beginning. The letter was not on record. (p. 6)

Such experiences of futile efforts and frustration seemed to await all who tried to discover the authorship of version 3.

Here is one of the avenues which I pursued without results: The material which accompanies version 3 (the Bruce Kent interview, entitled "Testimony—Chief Seattle," from the United Society for the Propagation of the Gospel in London), indicates that this text was "discovered by Bruce Kent in the House of the Community for Creative Non-Violence in Washington, D.C." Here seemed to be a new lead, possibly the source of that text. It took me some time to find out that Monsignor Bruce Kent was the National Chaplain of Pax Christi in Britain and that he had discovered the text of Chief Seattle's testimony (version 3) in Washington, D.C. in 1974. This was two years after the first publication of the very same text in the West of the United States! Therefore, it was no real first discovery. One more loop came to its end; no findings could be reported.

In this frustrating situation, help came from Friends of the Earth, from Carl A. Ross in Herrljunga, Sweden, from William Arrowsmith—and from the man who wrote version 3. The Northwest Representative of Friends of the Earth in Seattle, Dale Jones, writes in a letter:

> I first saw the letter [speech version 3] in September 1972 in a now out of business native American tabloid newspaper. . . . I clipped the article and mailed it to a few friends. Soon thereafter, the letter appeared in *Environmental Action* [November 11, 1972] and has subsequently appeared in a number of publications around the world.[12]

William Arrowsmith, author of version 2, in a number of letters, goes further back to the roots of the creation of text 3:

> In the early seventies a colleague at Texas, Ted Perry, . . . asked me if I would let him use the speech in my rendering as the basis of a filmscript. I said yes, provided I could approve the results. Perry wrote a script—largely "ecological" in its emphasis and freely adding new materials *ad libitum*. . . . (. . . he had no intention of redoing Seattle and then claiming the results were historically genuine; he was doing a script "after" Seattle's speech. . . .)
>
> Perry tried to insist to his producer for the film (The Southern Baptist Convention) that the speech was not in any sense a translation. But they overrode his decision. . . . Hence they talked glibly about a "letter" to President Pierce. . . .
>
> In the course of their work, the Baptists added still more "material" to the speech. The bulk of *their* additions is the (Baptist) religiosity of *their* Seattle. . . . Ted Perry broke with his producer and the Baptists over their high-handed procedures. (Arrowsmith 1978).[13]

> I feel quite certain that *all* "ecological" texts and reprints of the Seattle speech derive ultimately from Ted Perry's script . . . the Perry script is profusely "ecological"—unmistakably, Perry's "contribution" to the original. (Arrowsmith 1978)

This seems to be a complete and knowledgeable report of how version 3 came into existence. It is confirmed in Carl Ross's highly informative article, "What did Chief Seattle Say?" and in a letter by Bonita Sparrow of the Radio and Television Commission, Southern Baptist Convention:

> Ted Perry used brief portions of the speech [by Seattle] in his film script for "Home," a film on ecology produced by the Southern Baptist Radio and Television Commission in the early 1970s. . . . [T]he film . . . won several industry awards for excellence. . . . I do not know if Ted Perry's version of the script was altered or modified in any way but I doubt that it was.

Finally, here is Ted Perry's own point of view in this matter in a letter to me:

> Some time in 1969 or 1970 the Southern Baptists proposed to me the making of several films, one of them on the subject of pollution. While I was beginning to work on the script I heard Professor Arrowsmith read the Chief Seattle speech at some kind of rally; Earth Day, I think it was called. In any case, it was a large gathering devoted to environmental issues. Subsequently, I asked Professor Arrowsmith (he and I were both teaching at the University of Texas) if I might use the idea as the basis for the script; he graciously said yes. . . . So I wrote a speech which was a fiction. I would guess that there were several sentences which were paraphrases of sentences in Professor Arrowsmith's translation but the rest was mine. In passing the script along to the Baptists, I always made it clear that the work was mine. And they, of course, knew the script was original; they would surely not have paid me, as they did, for a speech which I merely retyped.
>
> In presenting them with a script, however, I made the mistake of using Chief Seattle's name in the body of the text. I don't remember why this was done; my guess is that it was just a mistake on my part. In writing a fictional speech I should have used a fictional name. In any case, when next I saw the script it was the narration for a film entitled HOME aired on ABC or

NBC-TV in 1972, I believe. I was surprised when the telecast was over, because there was no "written by" credit on the film. I was more than surprised; I was angry. So I called up the producer and he told me that he thought the text might seem more authentic if there were no "written by" credit given. Surprise. I cancelled my contract with the Baptists to do another script for them (November 11, 1983).

In a letter to Carl Ross, Perry asserts: "I . . . certainly would never have allowed anyone to believe that it was anything but a fictitious item written by me" (May 19, 1978).

So here we are. This so-called speech by Seattle, which we called version 3, and which has by now conquered the imagination of millions of people in many countries all over the world, was in its main parts written in the winter of 1970–1971 as a filmscript for the Southern Baptist Convention by Ted Perry, who was at that time teaching at the University of Texas. He used as his opening lines brief portions from Seattle's speech, versions 1 and 2, but then composed his own ecological text. In their film, the Southern Baptists neglected to give credit to Ted Perry for his part in the filmscript, but gave credit to Seattle for what he in fact had never said or written.

The essence of our findings, then, is that of the different versions of Chief Seattle's speech, only version 1 can claim a certain authenticity, as Dr. Smith clearly was present and took "extended" notes when Chief Seattle made his speech in 1854. The later versions of 1969, 1970, and 1974 consist either of translations or adaptations of that first version, or of new creations. Their claim to present a text by Chief Seattle is valid to the same degree to which their texts, in thought and language, are in accordance and in line with the text of 1887, and to the degree to which this first text by Dr. Smith is in accordance with what Chief Seattle really said in 1853 or 1854. The first question of accordance can be answered by any of us after a careful reading of the different versions.

The second question of accordance cannot be answered by any of us, until someone happens to find Dr. Smith's notebooks or some other record of Chief Seattle's speech during what Smith called that "demonstrative reception in front of Dr. Maynard's office near the water front on Main street" in what is now the city of Seattle, in late 1853 or in 1854.

V

This seems to be the end of a detective story. But it cannot be the end of the whole story, for we cannot be content with calling the text a "fake," "spurious," "fictitious," "bogus," "not authentic," "fraudulent," "a pollution of the past"—all of which terms have been used by people who were in the know or who doubted the authenticity of the text—but we must ask ourselves: How could the text of version 3, whose claim to Seattle's authorship must largely be called unjustified, spread as it did, first in America and then in Europe? How could it captivate the imagination of hundreds of thousands of people and strongly influence their thinking, possibly also their actions? How could this text cause Monsignor Bruce Kent to remark: "It's a whole religious concept. . . . I think it's really a fifth gospel, almost"?

We cannot answer these questions fully; nevertheless, I shall venture an attempt:

1. The text seems to give expression to thoughts and feelings which are on many people's minds these days, thoughts and feelings which find nourishment in publications of the Club of Rome about an end to industrial growth, and which have led to social and political groupings with which many young people identify themselves wholeheartedly. It is the complex of ideas which circles round the term "ecology" and which includes sentiments, fears, and hopes expressed in terms like "exploitation of nature," "destruction of the environment," "pollution," "conservation of natural resources," "anti-nuclear movement," "alternative ways of life," and many others. These ideas seem to be on the way to becoming some of the major issues concerning people and nations at the turn of the millennium, at least in the Western world. The text of version 3 seems to have given language and expression to this emotionally charged situation, and in this way to have given it impetus. As J. Lindholm said, "If it wasn't written it should have been" (1975).

2. The imagery, the symbolism, the phrasing, and the wording of version 3 seem to be in perfect unison with its purpose and its message on the one hand, and with the wishes, the concerns, and the expectations of many people on the other hand. I think it would be difficult for all of us to arm ourselves against the impact of phrases like these:

> Every part of this earth is sacred to my people . . . we are part of the earth and it is part of us. The perfumed flowers are our sisters, the deer, the horse, the great eagle, these are our brothers. The rocky crests, the juices in the meadows, the bodyheat of the pony, and men, all belong to the same family. . . . The air shares its spirit with all the life it supports. The wind that gave our grandfather his first breath so receives his last sigh. And the wind must also give our children the spirit of life. . . . All things are connected. . . . Whatever befalls the earth, befalls the sons of the earth. If men spit upon the ground, they spit upon themselves. This we know. The earth does not belong to man; man belongs to the earth. This we know. All things are connected like the blood which unites one family. All things are connected. . . . When the last red man has vanished from this earth and his memory is only the shadow of a cloud moving across the prairie, these shores and forests will still hold the spirits of my people. For they love this earth as a new born loves its mother's heartbeat. So if we sell you our land, love it as we have loved it. Care for it as we have cared for it. . . . We may be brothers after all.

Even if we did not know the name of the person who wrote this, many of us would probably admit that, whoever wrote these words, they constitute an impressive piece of writing. It is easy to see that such words may well function as a mythical or religious statement rather than as a historical document.

3. Lastly, these words seem to touch on an idea and a feeling that have so far largely been banned from our occidental, Christian, Western culture. It is the idea that the worldly and the spiritual, the mundane and the beyond, the profane and the sacred are not wholly separate from each other, as we are used to thinking; but that these seeming opposites are actually very closely connected in this world and that therefore everything in this world without any exception is seen as sacred in its nature and its character. This idea that each and every thing and creature in this world is spiritual and sacred, may well prove to be the salient point of this text, salient for a society which has always neatly separated the temporal and the spiritual and in this way has tried to justify man's claim that all the non-sacred world is at his disposal.

We may well acknowledge these qualities of version 3 and appreciate it as an impressive ecological text in its own right. But we must at the same time repudiate its claim to authorship by Chief Seattle. This text does not represent the mind of the old Chief, but the mind of a sensitive Euro-American, worried about our ecological situation and the general dualism in our culture. The text of the speech is, therefore, valid; but the claim that Chief Seattle was its author certainly is "spurious."

APPENDIX

Chief Seattle's Speech.

VERSION 1—RECORDED BY DR. HENRY SMITH

Yonder sky has wept tears of compassion on our fathers for centuries untold, and which, to us, looks eternal, may change. To-day it is fair, to-morrow it may be overcast with clouds. My words are like the stars that never set. What Seattle says the great chief, Washington, (the Indians in early times thought that Washington was still alive. They knew the name to be that of a president, and when they heard of the president at Washington they mistook the name of the city for the name of the reigning chief. They thought, also, that King George was still England's monarch, because the Hudson Bay traders called themselves "King George men." This innocent deception the company was shrewd enough not to explain away for the Indians had more respect for them than they would have had, had they known England was ruled by a woman. Some of us have learned better.) can rely upon, with as much certainty as our pale-face brothers can rely upon the return of the seasons. The son of the white chief says his father sends us greetings of friendship and good-will. This is kind, for we know he has little need of our friendship in return, because his people are many. They are like the grass that covers the vast prairies, while my people are few, and resemble the scattering trees of a wind-swept plain.

The great, and I presume also good, white chief sends us word that he wants to buy our lands but is willing to allow us to reserve enough to live on comfortably. This indeed appears generous, for the red man no longer has rights that he need respect, and the offer may be wise, also, for we are no longer in need of a great country. There was a time when our people covered the whole land as the waves of a wind-ruffled sea cover its shell-paved floor. But that time has long since passed away with the greatness of tribes almost forgotten. I will not mourn over our untimely decay, nor reproach my pale-face brothers with hastening it, for we, too, may have been somewhat to blame.

When our young men grow angry at some real or imaginary wrong and disfigure their faces with black paint, their hearts, also, are disfigured and turn black, and then their cruelty is relentless and knows no bounds, and our old men are not able to restrain them.

But let us hope that hostilities between the red man and his pale face brothers may never return. We would have everything to lose and nothing to gain.

True it is that revenge, with our young braves, is considered gain, even at the cost of their own lives, but old men who stay at home in times of war, and old women who have sons to lose, know better.

Our great father Washington, for I presume he is now our father as well as yours, since George has moved his boundaries to the north; our great and good father, I say, sends us word by his son, who, no doubt, is a great chief among his people, that if we do as he desires, he will protect us. His brave armies will be to us a bristling wall of strength, and his great ships of war will fill our harbors so that our ancient enemies far to the northward, the Simsiams and Hydas, will no longer frighten our women and old men. Then he will be our father and we will be his children. But can this ever be? Your God loves your people and hates mine; he folds his strong arms lovingly around the white man and leads him as a father leads his infant son, but he has forsaken his red children; he makes your people wax strong every day, and soon they will fill the land; while our people are ebbing away like a fast-receding tide, that will never flow again. The white man's God cannot love his red children or he would protect them. They seem to be orphans and can look nowhere for help. How then can we become brothers? How can your father become our father and bring us prosperity and awaken in us dreams of returning greatness?

Your God seems to be partial. He came to the white man. We never saw Him; never even heard His voice; He gave the white man laws but He had no word for His red children whose teeming millions filled this vast continent as the stars fill the firmament. No, we are two distinct races and must ever remain so. There is little in common between us. The ashes of our ancestors are sacred and their final resting place is hallowed ground, while you wander away from the tombs of your fathers seemingly without regret.

Your religion was written on tables of stone by the iron finger of an angry God, lest you might forget it. The red man could never remember nor comprehend it.

Our religion is the traditions of our ancestors, the dreams of our old men, given them by the great Spirit, and the visions of our sachems, and is written in the hearts of our people.

Your dead cease to love you and the homes of their nativity as soon as they pass the portals of the tomb. They wander off beyond the stars, are soon forgotten and never return. Our dead never forget the beautiful world that gave them being. They still love its winding rivers, its great mountains and its sequestered vales, and they ever yearn in tenderest affection over the lonely hearted living and often return to visit and comfort them.

Day and night cannot dwell together. The red man has ever fled the approach of the white man, as the changing mists on the mountain side flee before the blazing morning sun.

However, your proposition seems a just one, and I think my folks will accept it and will retire to the reservation you offer them, and we will dwell apart and in peace, for the words of the great white chief seem to be the voice of nature speaking to my people out of the thick darkness that is fast gathering around them like a dense fog floating inward from a midnight sea.

It matters but little where we pass the remainder of our days. They are not many. The Indian's night promises to be dark. No bright star hovers about the horizon. Sad-voiced winds moan in the distance. Some grim Nemesis of our race is on the red man's trail, and wherever he goes he will still hear the sure approaching footsteps of the fell destroyer and prepare to meet his doom, as does the wounded doe that hears the approaching footsteps of the hunter. A few more moons, a few more winters and not one of all the mighty hosts that once filled this broad land or that now roam in fragmentary bands through these vast solitudes will remain to weep over the tombs of a people once as powerful and as hopeful as your own.

But why should we repine? Why should I murmur at the fate of my people? Tribes are made up of individuals and are no better than they. Men come and go like the waves of the sea. A tear, a tamanamus, a dirge, and they are gone from our longing eyes forever. Even the white man, whose God walked and talked with him, as friend to friend, is not exempt from the common destiny. We *may* be brothers after all. We shall see.

We will ponder your proposition, and when we have decided we will tell you. But should we accept it, I here and now make this the first condition: That we will not be denied the privilege, without molestation, of visiting at will the graves of our ancestors and friends. Every part of this country is sacred to my people. Every hillside, every valley, every plain and grove has been hallowed by some fond memory or some sad experience of my tribe. Even the rocks that seem to lie dumb as they swelter in the sun along the silent seashore in solemn grandeur thrill with memories of past events connected with the fate of my people, and the very dust under your feet responds more lovingly to our footsteps than to yours, because it is the ashes of our ancestors, and our bare feet are conscious of the sympathetic touch, for the soil is rich with the life of our kindred.

The sable braves, and fond mothers, and glad-hearted maidens, and the little children who lived and rejoiced here, and whose very names are now forgotten, still love these solitudes, and their deep fastnesses at eventide grow shadowy with the presence of dusky spirits. And when the last red man shall have perished from the earth and his memory among white men shall have become a myth, these shores shall swarm with the invisible dead of my tribe, and when your children's children shall think themselves alone in the field, the shop, upon the highway or in the silence of the woods they will not be alone. In all the earth there is no place dedicated to solitude. At night when the streets of your cities and villages shall be silent, and you think them deserted, they will throng with the returning hosts that once filled and still love this beautiful land. The white man will never be alone. Let him be just and deal kindly with my people, for the dead are not altogether powerless.

VERSION 2—REVISED BY WILLIAM ARROWSMITH

Brothers: That sky above us has pitied our fathers for many hundreds of years. To us it looks unchanging, but it may change. Today it is fair. Tomorrow it may be covered with cloud.

My words are like the stars. They do not set. What Seattle says, the great chief Washington[14] can count on as surely as our white brothers can count on the return of the seasons.

The White Chief's son[15] says his father sends us words of friendship and goodwill. This is kind of him, since we know he has little need of our friendship in return. His people are many, like the grass that covers the plains. My people are few, like the trees scattered by the storms on the grasslands.

The great—and good, I believe—White Chief sends us word that he wants to buy our land. But he will reserve us enough so that we can live comfortably. This seems generous, since the red man no longer has rights he need respect. It may also be wise, since we no longer need a large country. Once, my people covered this land like a flood-tide moving with the wind across the shell-littered flats. But that time is gone, and with it the greatness of tribes now almost forgotten.

But I will not mourn the passing of my people. Nor do I blame our white brothers for causing it. We too were perhaps partly to blame. When our young men grow angry at some wrong, real or imagined, they make their faces ugly with black paint. Then their hearts too are ugly and black. They are hard and their cruelty knows no limits. And our old men cannot restrain them.

Let us hope that the wars between the red man and his white brothers will never come again. We would have everything to lose and nothing to gain. Young men view revenge as gain, even when they lose their own lives. But the old men who stay behind in time of war, mothers with sons to lose—they know better.

Our great father Washington—for he must be our father now as well as yours, since George[16] has moved his boundary northward[17]—our great and good father sends us word by his son, who is surely a great chief among his people, that he will protect us if we do what he wants. His brave soldiers will be a strong wall for my people, and his great warships will fill our harbors. Then our ancient enemies to the north—the Haidas and Tsimshians[18]—will no longer frighten our women and old men. Then he will be our father and we will be his children.

But can that ever be? Your God loves your people and hates mine. He puts his strong arm around the white man and leads him by the hand, as a father leads his little boy. He has abandoned his red children. He makes your people stronger every day. Soon they will flood all the land. But my people are an ebb tide, we will never return. No, the white man's God cannot love his red children or he would protect them. Now we are orphans. There is no one to help us.

So how can we be brothers? How can your father be our father, and make us prosper and send us dreams of future greatness? Your God is prejudiced. He came to the white man. We never saw him, never even heard his voice. He gave the white man laws, but he had no word for his red children whose numbers once filled this land as the stars filled the sky.

No, we are two separate races, and we must stay separate. There is little in common between us.

To us the ashes of our fathers are sacred. Their graves are holy ground. But you are wanderers, you leave your fathers' graves behind you, and you do not care.

Your religion was written on tables of stone by the iron finger of an angry God, so you would not forget it. The red man could never understand it or remember it. Our religion is the ways of our forefathers, the dreams of our old men, sent them by the Great Spirit, and the visions of our sachems. And it is written in the hearts of our people.

Your dead forget you and the country of their birth as soon as they go beyond the grave and walk among the stars. They are quickly forgotten and they never return. Our dead never forget this beautiful earth. It is their mother. They always love and remember her rivers, her great mountains, her valleys. They long for the living, who are lonely too and who long for the dead. And their spirits often return to visit and console us.

No, day and night cannot live together.

The red man has always retreated before the advancing white man, as the mist on the mountain slopes runs before the morning sun.

So your offer seems fair, and I think my people will accept it and go to the reservation you offer them. We will live apart, and in peace. For the words of the Great White Chief are like the words of nature speaking to my people out of great darkness—a darkness that gathers around us like the night fog moving inland from the sea.

It matters little where we pass the rest of our days. They are not many. The Indians' night will be dark. No bright star shines on his horizons. The wind is sad. Fate hunts the red man down. Wherever he goes, he will hear the approaching steps of his destroyer, and prepare to die, like the wounded doe who hears the steps of the hunter.

A few more moons, a few more winters, and none of the children of the great tribes that once lived in this wide earth or that roam now in small bands in the woods will be left to mourn the graves of a people once as powerful and as hopeful as yours.

But why should I mourn the passing of my people? Tribes are made of men, nothing more. Men come and go, like the waves of the sea. A tear, a prayer to the Great Spirit, a dirge, and they are gone from our longing eyes forever. Even the white man, whose God walked and talked with him as friend to friend, cannot be exempt from the common destiny.

We may be brothers after all. We shall see.

We will consider your offer. When we have decided, we will let you know. Should we accept, I here and now make this condition: we will never be denied the right to visit, at any time, the graves of our fathers and our friends.

Every part of this earth is sacred to my people. Every hillside, every valley, every clearing and wood, is holy in the memory and experience of my people. Even those unspeaking stones along the shore are loud with events and memories in the life of my people. The ground beneath your feet responds more lovingly to our steps than yours, because it is the ashes of our grandfathers. Our bare feet know the kindred touch. The earth is rich with the lives of our kin.

The young men, the mothers, and girls, the little children who once lived and were happy here, still love these lonely places. And at evening the forests are dark with the presence of the dead. When the last red man has vanished from this earth, and his memory is only a story among the whites, these shores will still swarm with the invisible dead of my people. And when your children's children think they are alone in the fields, the forests, the shops, the highways, or the quiet of the woods, they will not be alone. There is no place in this country where a man can be alone. At night when the streets of your towns and cities are quiet, and you think they are empty, they will throng with the returning spirts that once thronged them, and that still love these places. The white man will never be alone.

So let him be just and deal kindly with my people. The dead have power too.

VERSION 3—WRITTEN BY TED PERRY

The Great Chief in Washington sends word that he wishes to buy our land.

The Great Chief also sends us words of friendship and goodwill. This is kind of him, since we know he has little need of our friendship in return. But we will consider your offer. For we know that if we do not sell, the white man may come with guns and take our land.

How can you buy or sell the sky, the warmth of the land? The idea is strange to us.

If we do not own the freshness of the air and the sparkle of the water, how can you buy them from us.

We will decide in our time.

What Chief Seattle says, the Great Chief in Washington can count on as truly as our white brothers can count on the return of the seasons. My words are like the stars. They do not set.

Every part of this earth is sacred to my people. Every shining pine needle, every sandy shore, every mist in the dark woods, every clearing, and humming insect is holy in the memory and experience of my people. The sap which courses through the trees carries the memories of the red man.

The white man's dead forget the country of their birth when they go to walk among the stars. Our dead never forget this beautiful earth, for it is the mother of the red man.

We are part of the earth and it is part of us. The perfumed flowers are our sisters the deer, the horse, the great eagle, these are our brothers. The rocky crests, the juices in the meadows, the body heat of the pony, and man—all belong to the same family.

So, when the Great Chief in Washington sends word that he wishes to buy our land, he asks much of us.

The Great Chief sends word he will reserve us a place so that we can live comfortable to ourselves. He will be our father and we will be his children.

But can that ever be? God loves your people, but has abandoned his red children. He sends machines to help the white man with his work, and builds great villages for him. He makes your people stronger every day. Soon you will flood the land like the rivers which crash down the canyons after a sudden rain. But my people are an ebbing tide, we will never return.

No, we are separate races. Our children do not play together and our old men tell different stories. God favors you, and we are orphans.

So we will consider your offer to buy our land. But it will not be easy. For this land is sacred to us. We take our pleasure in these woods. I do not know. Our ways are different from your ways.

This shining water that moves in the streams and rivers is not just water but the blood of our ancestors. If we sell you land, you must remember that it is sacred, and that each ghostly reflection in the clear water of the lakes tells of events and memories in the life of my people. The water's murmur is the voice of my father's father.

The rivers are our brothers, they quench our thirst. The rivers carry our canoes, and feed our children. If we sell you our land, you must remember, and teach your children, that the rivers are our brothers, and yours, and you must henceforth give rivers the kindness you would give any brother.

The red man has always retreated before the advancing white man, as the mist of the mountain runs before the morning sun. But the ashes of our fathers are sacred. The graves are holy ground, and so these hills, these trees, this portion of the earth is consecrated to us. We know that the white man does not understand our ways. One portion of land is the same to him as the next, for he is a stranger who comes in the night and takes from the land whatever he needs. The earth is not his brother but his enemy, and when he has conquered it, he moves on. He leaves his father's graves behind, and he does not care. He kidnaps the earth from his children. He does not care. His father's graves and his children's birthright are forgotten. He treats his mother, the earth, and his brother, the sky, as things to be bought, plundered, sold like sheep or bright beads. His appetite will devour the earth and leave behind only a desert.

I do not know. Our ways are different from your ways. The sight of your cities pains the eyes of the red man. But perhaps it is because the red man is a savage and does not understand.

There is no quiet place in the white man's cities. No place to hear the unfurling of leaves in spring or the rustle of insect's wings. But perhaps it is because I am a savage and do not understand. The clatter only seems to insult the ears. And what is there to life if a man cannot hear the lonely cry of the whipporwill or the arguments of the frogs around a pond at night? I am a red man and do not understand. The Indian prefers the soft sound of the wind darting over the face of a pond, and the smell of the wind itself, cleansed by a midday rain, or scented with the pinon pine.

The air is precious to the red man, for all things share the same breath—the beast, the tree, the man, they all share the same breath. The white man does not seem to notice the air he breathes. Like a man dying for many days, he is numb to the stench. But if we sell our land, you must remember that the air is precious to us, that the air shares its spirit with all the life it supports. The wind that gave our grandfather his first breath also receives his last sigh. And the wind must also give our children the spirit of life. And if we sell you our land, you must keep it apart and sacred, as a place where even the white man can go to taste the wind that is sweetened by the meadow's flowers.

So we will consider your offer to buy our land. If we decide to accept, I will make one condition: The white man must treat the beasts of this land as his brothers.

I am a savage and I do not understand any other way. I have seen a thousand rotting buffalos on the prairie, left by the white man who shot them from a passing train. I am a savage and I do not understand how the smoking iron horse can be more important than the buffalo that we kill only to stay alive.

What is man without the beasts? If all the beasts were gone, men would die from a great loneliness of spirit. For whatever happens to the beasts, soon happens to man. All things are connected.

Whatever befalls the earth, befalls the sons of the earth.

You must teach your children that the ground beneath their feet is the ashes of our grandfathers. So that they will respect the land, tell your children that the earth is rich with the lives of our kin. Teach your children what we have taught our children, that the earth is our mother. Whatever befalls the earth, befalls the sons of the earth. If men spit upon the ground, they spit upon themselves.

This we know. The earth does not belong to man; man belongs to the earth. This we know. All things are connected like the blood which unites one family. All things are connected.

Whatever befalls the earth befalls the sons of the earth. Man did not weave the web of life; he is merely a strand in it. Whatever he does to the web, he does to himself.

No, day and night cannot live together.

Our dead go to live in the earth's sweet rivers, they return with the silent footsteps of spring, and it is their spirit, running in the wind, that ripples the surface of the ponds.

We will consider why the white man wishes to buy the land. What is it that the white man wishes to buy, my people ask me. The idea is strange to us. How can you buy or sell the sky, the warmth of the land?—the swiftness of the antelope? How can we sell these things to you and how can you buy them? Is the earth yours to do with as you will, merely because the red man signs a piece of paper and gives it to the white man? If we do not own the freshness of the air and the sparkle of the water, how can you buy them from us.

Can you buy back the buffalo, once the last one has been killed? But we will consider your offer, for we know that if we do not sell, the white man may come with guns and take our land. But we are primitive, and in his passing moment of strength the white man thinks that he is a god who already owns the earth. How can a man own his mother?

But we will consider your offer to buy our land. Day and night cannot live together. We will consider your offer to go to the reservation you have for my people. We will live apart, and in peace. It matters little where we spend the rest of our days. Our children have seen their fathers humbled in defeat. Our warriors have felt shame, and after defeat they turn their days in idleness and contaminate their bodies with sweet foods and strong drink. It matters little where we pass the rest of our days. They are not many. A few more hours, a few more winters, and none of the children of the great tribes that once lived on this earth or that roam now in small bands in the woods will be left to mourn the graves of a people once as powerful and hopeful as yours.

But why should I mourn the passing of my people? Tribes are made of men, nothing more. Men come and go, like the waves of the sea.

Even the white man, whose God walks and talks with him as friend to friend, cannot be exempt from the common destiny. We may be brothers after all; we shall see. One thing we know, which the white man may one day discover—our God is the same God.

You may think now that you own Him as you wish to own our land; but you cannot. He is the God of man, and His compassion is equal for the red man and the white. This earth is precious to Him, and to harm the earth is to heap contempt on its Creator. The whites too shall pass; perhaps sooner than all other tribes. Continue to contaminate your bed, and you will one night suffocate in your own waste.

But in your perishing you will shine brightly, fired by the strength of the God who brought you to this land and for some special purpose gave you dominion over this land and over the red man. That destiny is a mystery to us, for we do not understand when the buffalo are all slaughtered, the wild horses are tamed, the secret corners of the forest heavy with the scent of many men, and the view of the ripe hills blotted by talking wires. Where is the thicket? Gone. Where is the eagle? Gone. And what is it to say goodbye to the swift pony and the hunt? The end of living and the beginning of survival.

God gave you dominion over the beasts, the woods, and the red man, and for some special purpose, but that destiny is a mystery to the red man. We might understand if we knew what it was that the white man dreams—what hopes he describes to his children on long winter nights—what visions he burns onto their minds so that they will wish for tomorrow. But we are savages. The white man's dreams are hidden from us. And because they are hidden, we will go our own way. For above all else, we cherish the right of each man to live as he wishes, however different from his brothers. There is little in common between us.

So we will consider your offer to buy our land. If we agree, it will be to secure the reservation you have promised. There, perhaps, we may live out our brief days as we wish.

When the last red man has vanished from this earth, and his memory is only the shade of a cloud moving across the prairie, these shores and forests will still hold the spirits of my people. For they love this earth as the newborn loves its mother's heartbeat.

If we sell you our land, love it as we've loved it. Care for it as we've cared for it. Hold in your mind the memory of the land as it is when you take it. And with all your strength, with all your mind, with all your heart, preserve it for your children, and love it . . . as God loves us all.

One thing we know. Our God is the same God. This earth is precious to Him. Even the white man cannot be exempt from the common destiny. We may be brothers after all. We shall see.

VERSION 4—FROM THE SPOKANE EXPO OF 1974

The President in Washington sends word that he wishes to buy our land.

Buy our land! But how can you buy or sell the sky? the land? The idea is strange to us. If we do not own the freshness of the air and the sparkle of the water, how can you buy them?

Every part of this earth is sacred to my people. Every shining pine needle, every sandy shore, every mist in the dark woods, every meadow, every humming insect. All are Holy in the memory and experience of my people.

We know the sap which courses through the trees as we know the blood that courses through our veins. We are part of the earth and it is part of us.

The perfumed flowers are our sisters. The bear, the deer, the great eagle, these are our brothers.

The rocky crests, the juices in the meadow, the body heat of the pony—and man, all belong to the same family.

This shining water that moves in the streams and rivers is not just water, but the blood of our ancestors.

If we sell you our land you must remember that it is sacred. Each ghostly reflection in the clear water of the lakes tells of events and memories in the life of my people. The water's murmur is the voice of my father's father.

The rivers—they are our brothers. They quench our thirst. They carry our canoes, they feed our children. So, you must give to the rivers the kindness you would give to any brother.

If we sell you our land, remember that the air is precious to us, that the air shares its spirit with all life it supports. It is the wind that gave our grandfather his first breath. It is the wind that receives his last sigh.

The wind also gives our children the spirit of life. So, if we sell you our land, you must keep it apart as a place where man can go and experience the Sacred.

Keep the land as a place where man can go to taste the wind that is sweetened by the meadow flowers.

Will you teach your children what we have taught our children? That the earth is our mother?

Whatever befalls the earth, befalls all the sons of the earth.

This we know: The earth does not belong to man, man belongs to the earth. All things are connected like the blood which unites us all.

Man did not weave the web of life, he is merely a strand in it. Whatever he does to the web, he does to himself.

One thing we know: Our God is also your God. We both know that the earth is precious to Him and to harm the earth is to heap contempt upon its Creator.

Your destiny is a mystery to us. What will happen when the buffalo are all slaughtered? The wild horses tamed? What will happen when the secret corners of the forest are heavy with the scent of many men?

What will happen when the view of the ripe hills is blotted by talking wires? Where will the thicket be? Gone. Where will the eagle be? Gone. and what is it to say goodbye to the swift pony and the hunt? That would be the end of living and the beginning of surviving.

When the last red man has vanished with his wilderness and his memory is only the shadow of a cloud moving across the prairie, will these shores and forests still be here? Will there be any of the spirit of my people left?

We love this earth as a newborn loves its mother's heartbeat. So, if we sell you our land, love it as we have loved it. Care for it as we have cared for it. Hold it in your mind. Keep forever the memory of the land as it is when you receive it. Preserve the land for all children and love it.

As we are part of the land, you too are part of the land. This earth is precious to us. It is also precious to you.

No man, be he red man or white man can be apart.
One thing we know: There is only one God. We are all brothers.

NOTES

1. The film may be rented or purchased from Zoom-Filmverleih, Saat-wiesenstr. 22, 8600 Dubendorf, Switzerland.

2. Four of these publications are: Rudolf and Michaela Kaiser, *Diese Erde ist uns heilig* (Münster: Edition Blaschzok, 1984); Weigert, Musall, Werth, *Mutter Erde, Bruder Himmel* (Gelnhausen: Burckhardthaus-Laetare, 1980); Seattle, *Wir sind ein Teil der Erde* (Olten und Freiburg: Walter Verlag, 1982); and Karl Pförtner, ed. *Seattles Brief an den weissen Häuptling* (Weissenburg: Kanalpresse, 1976).

3. Monsignor Bruce Kent is quoted as saying about this text of Seattle's address: "I think it is a whole religious concept of the value of people, of animals, of land, of our transitory nature. I think it is really a fifth Gospel, almost—of what life is all about." At a later stage:

> The significance of Seattle is terrific! The response to Seattle . . . I'd no idea when I got it into the Catholic Herald originally. It was reprinted as a piece, and they had hundreds and hundreds of requests for back copies of that edition. Then we got it reprinted in a little red booklet, three or four thousand of these, (I've forgotten how many.) And they have all gone now. From all over the world—from Ocean Islands to Finland and Yugoslavia—from all over the world someone has written, and this message has gone out somehow, and people have accepted it. The World Council of Churches has spread the book too, they reprinted it. And so it has absolutely caught on. (1978:98)

4. In a leaflet, handed out by *NANAI*, Seattle's speech is characterized in the following words:

> In de onvergetelijke toespraak van Chief Seattle die hij in 1854 uitsprak, klinkt de verbondenheid en afhankelijkheid van de Indiaan met de aarde en met alles wat erop leeft, door.
> Seattle's woorden zijn nog steeds aktueel en zeker van toepassing op de "Blanke man" van deze tijd.

5. Carl A. Ross, "What did Chief Seattle Say?" Paper sent by Ross to Dale Jones, Friends of the Earth, Seattle, Washington, dated 23 April 1979. The publication of Seattle's speech of 1976 was in *Miljö och framtid* 1. The publication of 1977 was in *Pax* 6. The pop group Nationalteatern Nynningen used it in its record *Vi kommer att leva igen*.

6. "Die Rede des Häuptlings Seattle ist für mich zum Inbegriff aller 'Umweltgedanken' geworden." Quotation from a letter, written by Beate Weyrich to me, dated 10 March 1983.

7. According to the original manuscript of the record of the Point Elliott Treaty negotiations (National Archives, Washington, D.C.), Governor Stevens made a somewhat lengthy speech at the treaty negotiations on Monday, 22 January 1855, and then added: "Does anyone object to what I have said? Does my venerable friend Seattle object? I want Seattle to give his will to me and to his people."

According to the original manuscript, Seattle answered:

> I look upon you as my father. I and the rest regard you as such. All of the Indians have the same good feeling towards you and will send it on paper to the Great Father. All of them, men, old men, women and children rejoice that he has sent you to take care of them. My mind is like yours. I don't want to say more. My heart is very good towards Dr. Maynard [a physician who was present]. I want always to get medicine from him.

Later in the treaty proceedings—it is 23 January 1855—the document states:

> Seattle then on behalf of himself and the other Chiefs brought a white flag and presented it saying: "Now by this we make friends and put away all bad feelings if we ever had any. We are the friends of the Americans. All the Indians are of the same mind. We look upon you as our father. We will never change our minds, but since you have been to see us we will be always the same. Now, now do you send this paper of our hearts to the Great Chief. That is all I have to say."

Indeed, this is all he *did* say according to the original manuscript of the Point Elliott Treaty proceedings!

Apart from these two short speeches—and apart from the one long speech which is dealt with in this paper—only two other short speeches by Seattle are recorded: a fragment of a speech recorded by the interpreter B. F. Shaw in 1850 and a lament by Seattle in May 1858 that the Treaty of Point Elliott had not been ratified by the U.S. Senate, leaving the Indian tribes in poverty and poor health (Janice Krenmayr, "'The Earth is Our Mother'—Who Really Said That?" *The Seattle Times Magazine* (Seattle, Washington, 5 January 1975).

8. "We have made several searches of the records of the Department of the Interior and of the War Department in the National Archives Building, but have not found the speech or the letter ascribed to Seattle" (from a letter written to me by the General Services Administration, National Archives and Records Service, Washington, D.C., dated 19 August 1983). Nor does the Library of Congress or the Seattle Public Library have any record of such a speech or letter.

9. It must, at this moment, remain open whether Bagley added these sentences on his own or whether he adopted them from some other publication of the address, possibly even from John M. Rich's publication.

Although Rich's booklet was published a year later (1932), Rich and Bagley may have contacted each other about Seattle's speech prior to their respective publications.

10. See, for example, L. T. Jones, *Aboriginal American Oratory* (Los Angeles: Southwest Museum, 1964), p. 99.

11. There are two mistakes in this remark by William Arrowsmith: The first publication was not in the *Seattle Star,* but the *Seattle Sunday Star,* and the year was not 1877 but 1887. These mistakes have been copied over and again in later publications of the text.

12. Quotation from a letter, written by Dale Jones to me, dated 8 July 1983. One of this "number of publications" was the often-quoted April 1974 issue of *Passages,* the in-flight magazine for passengers on Northwest Orient Airlines.

13. There is similar information in a letter written by W. Arrowsmith to me, dated 9 September 1983.

14. The early Indians believed that Washington was still alive, perhaps because they confused the name of the city with the name of the "reigning chief."

15. That is, the governor of Washington Territory, I. I. Stevens.

16. The Indians believed King George III was still on the English throne, perhaps because the Hudson Bay traders referred to themselves as "King George men." In any case, the confusion was encouraged by the Hudson Bay Company in the belief that the Indians would not respect the subjects of a country ruled by a queen.

17. A reference to the Oregon Compromise of 1846, redefining the boundaries between the United States and British Columbia.

18. The Haida Indians lived on Queen Charlotte Island (British Columbia) and the southern part of Prince of Wales island in Alaska. The Tsimshians lived on the adjacent islands and coastal mainland.

REFERENCES

Aktie Stroohalm en de Ecologische Uitgeverij. 1982. (Dutch text of Seattle's speech.) Rotterdam: Nederlandse Aktiegroep Noord-Amerikaanse Indianen, *NANAI-Notes,* December.

Arrowsmith, William. 1969. Speech of Chief Seattle, January 9th, 1855. *Arion* 8:461–464.

———. 1975. Speech of Chief Seattle. *The American Poetry Review.* Pp. 23–26.

———. 1978. Letter to Carl Ross. 20 January.

Bagley, Clarence B. 1931. Chief Seattle and Angeline. *Washington Historical Quarterly* 22:243–275.

Bardet, René. 1982. *"Vielleicht weil ich ein Wilder bin . . . "* Worte des indianischen Häuptlings Seattle an den amerikanischen Präsidenten im Jahre 1855. Zweitausend-eins-Versand Frankfurt (Federal Republic of Germany).

Brenner, Gerd, et al. 1978. *Seattle.* Köln: Katholische Studierende Jugend.

Drewermann, Eugen. 1982. *Der tödliche Fortschritt—von der Zerstörung der Erde und des Menschen im Erbe des Christentums.* Pp. 160–165. Regensburg: Pustet.

Grant, Frederic James. 1891. *History of Seattle.* New York: American Publishing Company.

Jones, L. T. 1964. *Aboriginal American Oratory.* Los Angeles: Southwest Museum.

Kaiser, Rudolf, and Michaela Kaiser. 1984. *Diese Erde ist uns heilig—Die Rede des Indianerhäuptlings Seattle.* Münster: Edition Blaschzok.

Kent, Bruce. 1978. A Fifth Gospel: An Interview with Bruce Kent. *Testimony–Chief Seattle.* Pp. 94–98. London: United Society for the Propagation of the Gospel.

Krenmayr, Janice. 1975. "The Earth is Our Mother"—Who Really Said That? *The Seattle Times Magazine,* January 5. Pp. 4–6.

Lindholm, J. 1975. *Outdoor America.* December.

Norddeutscher Rundfunk. 1979. *Wie die Zerstörung der Umwelt begann—Die Rede des Indianerhäuptlings Seattle.* Schulfunkprogramm, April 23.

Nationalteatern Nynningen. 1977. *Vi kommer att leva igen. Pax.* 1977. Swedish translation of Seattle's speech. June.

Pförtner, Karl, ed. 1976. *Seattles Brief an den weißen Häuptling.* Weissenburg, Federal Republic of Germany: Kanalpresse.

Point Elliott Treaty. National Archives, Washington, D.C.

Rich, John M. 1932/1970. *Seattle's Unanswered Challenge.* Fairfield, Washington: Ye Galleon Press.

Ross, Carl A. 1978. *What did Chief Seattle Say?* Herrljunga (Sweden).

Seattle. 1976. *Miljö och framtid* 1. January. (Swedish translation of Seattle's speech.)

Seattle. 1983. *Michaelskalender.* March. Pp. 33–37. Nettetal 2 (Federal Republic of Germany).

Seattle. 1982. *Wir sind ein Teil der Erde.* Olten und Freiburg: Walter Verlag.

Smith, Henry A. 1887. Scraps from a Diary—Chief Seattle—A Gentleman by Instinct—His Native Eloquence. *The Seattle Sunday Star,* October 29. P. 10.

Söhne der Erde. 1975. Erzählung nach einer Rede des Dwamish-Oberhauptes Seathl. 8022 Grünwald (Federal Republic of Germany): Institut für Film und Bild.

The Decidedly Unforked Message of Chief Seattle. 1974. *Passages.* April.

Vanderwerth, W. C. 1971. *Indian Oratory*. Norman: University of Oklahoma Press.

Weigert, Dedo, Musall, Peter, and Inge Werth. 1980. *Mutter Erde, Bruder Himmel*. Gelnhausen (Federal Republic of Germany): Burckhardthaus-Laetare.

Westdeutscher Rundfunk. 1982. *Die Erde ist unsere Mutter—Indianer wandeln das Naturverständnis deutscher Schüler*. Schulfunkprogramm, October 24.

Women's World Day of Prayer. 1981. *Order of Service*. March 6.

Sam Blowsnake's Confessions: *Crashing Thunder* and the History of American Indian Autobiography

H. DAVID BRUMBLE III

I have elsewhere suggested that the history of American Indian autobiography will be found to recapitulate the history of Western autobiography (1981:1–5). The earliest autobiographical writings in the Western tradition, for example, are what have been called the *res gestae,* stories which the Greeks and Romans wrote about their great deeds;[1] this kind of writing corresponds very closely to the *coup* tales and hunting tales told among the early Indians.[2] Later, some of the ancients began to write memoirs, narratives about great events they had witnessed; we find that the Indians came to produce this sort of narrative as well. Sometimes the Indians themselves wrote memoirs; more often their memoirs were taken down by historians and anthropologists. (There is, for example, a remarkable number of Indian memoirs having to do with the Custer battle.[3]) Then, with Augustine's *Confessions,* we find a very different kind of autobiographical writing, something much closer to what has been called "true" autobiography—that which articulates an individual sense of the self. I would like to argue that here there is also a parallel in the history of American Indian autobiography. A Winnebago Indian, Sam Blowsnake, alias Crashing Thunder, "re-invented" the autobiography.[4]

Since, like so many Indian autobiographies, Blowsnake's comes to us via an intermediary—in this case the anthropologist Paul Radin—it is important first to consider just how much of this book is Blowsnake's and how much of it is Radin's. We must remember, too, that Radin published Blowsnake's autobiography in more than one form. *Crashing Thunder* (1926)[5] was based upon an earlier book, *The Autobiography of a Winnebago Indian* (1920). Radin wrote in his introduction to the 1920 version that it was simply a translation— with very little editing—of a text written in Winnebago by Blowsnake himself. Radin also stated that "No attempt of any kind was made to influence [Blowsnake] in the selection of the particular facts of his life which he chose to present" (p. 2).

Crashing Thunder is a reworking of *Autobiography*. In it, Radin added excerpts from material that he had collected from Blowsnake over the years. Where Blowsnake mentioned in *Autobiography*, for example, that he had prayed at a certain time to the spirits, Radin here interpolated an appropriate prayer that he had at some time taken down from Blowsnake's dictation. As Arnold Krupat has demonstrated, Radin was not above changing wording and style in places, but the pattern of the two versions is the same (Radin 1983:205–212). Radin did no reordering of the narrative sequence.

Given all this, Ruth Underhill's comment on the 1926 version is of considerable interest:

> *Crashing Thunder* is not strictly an autobiography, although every word of it came from the Indian's mouth. Rather it is a drama, centering around a religious experience. From the jumble of reminiscences which anyone pours out when talking about himself, one feels that the ethnologist has selected first, those bearing on religious education and myths, then the fall to drunkenness and murder, and finally, the salvation through peyote. . . . His vision achieved, Crashing Thunder's drama closes. . . . Here Radin was artist rather than ethnologist. (1971 [1966]:ix)

Paradoxically, Underhill errs because she knows a great deal about American Indians and their autobiographies. Underhill is simply assuming that *Crashing Thunder* was the result of the method she herself had employed to produce *The Autobiography of a Papago Woman* (1936)—the same method, that is, which has produced so many of the Indian autobiographies:[6] ethnologist encourages informant to relate life history, asking questions along the way to guide the informant and to ensure adequate detail; ethnologist then edits this great bundle of material (now usually in translation) into something like chronological order, cutting repetitions and making the other changes necessary to transform a collection of transcripts of individual oral performances into a single, more-or-less continuous narrative. But the ethnologist does not add to the words of the Indian—and the ethnologist does not impose a pattern upon the material.[7] According to Underhill, Radin did impose a dramatic pattern upon Blowsnake's material—which is to say that Underhill mistook Blowsnake's structuring of his autobiography for Radin's.

What was it about Blowsnake's narrative that fooled Underhill? She herself says that the narrative's dramatic pattern led her to her conclusion. But by this she could not have meant that no Indian could produce either a dramatic narrative or a patterned narrative. Certainly many of the episodes which Underhill elicited from Maria Chona and then edited into *Papago Woman* were dramatic in the everyday sense which Underhill seems to intend; she must certainly have recognized patterns in many of the stories Chona told her. What Underhill saw in *Crashing Thunder* was that the episodes were tied together to form a larger pattern; *she saw that the episodes worked together to explain just how it was that Blowsnake had come to be the person he was.* This was not at all the sort of thing Underhill would have expected in an Indian autobiography elicited by an anthropologist. Blowsnake had written an *autobiography*—he wrote a narrative that was so like the autobiographies of our own tradition that even so keen a student of the American Indian as Ruth Underhill could mistake the form as being Radin's rather than Blowsnake's.

Indians who had been educated by whites had written integrated life histories, certainly. Charles Alexander Eastman wrote the first of his autobiographical books in 1902 and a second in 1916. Born a Santee Sioux, and trained for hunting and war until he was taken away to school at the age of fifteen, Eastman certainly had a sense of how the peculiar circumstances of his life had made him the person he was: he saw himself as an embodiment of Social Darwinist ideas. His own life recapitulated the course of the development of mankind from "primitive" to "enlightened." But by the time he began writing autobiography, Eastman had graduated from Boston Medical School. Later in his life, Eastman did question the value of "civilization," but he was by then thoroughly acculturated—however ill at ease he may have been—and widely read.

William Apes published his *Son of the Forest* in 1829. He had spent most of his youth with white families. Okah Tubbee, who

wrote his autobiography in 1848, was raised as a town slave in
Natchez. En-me-gah-bowh was educated by missionaries and had
for years served as their interpreter before he wrote his *En-me-gah-
bowh's Story* (1904). The remarkable George Copway had only
twenty months of formal schooling, but he was thoroughly Christ-
ianized and sufficiently familiar with Anglo-American literature to
be able to preface his 1860 autobiography by lamenting that he
could "not wield the pen of a Macaulay or the graceful wand of an
Irving."[8]

Blowsnake, on the other hand, had virtually no white education;[9] indeed, Radin introduced him to the world as a "representative middle-aged [Winnebago] of moderate ability" (1963 [1920]:2),
and as a man who could give us an "inside view" of what a "real
Indian" is, "how he thinks, feels, reacts, adapts himself to the
varying conditions of life" (1983 [1926]:xx). This is a bit disingenuous. Blowsnake was a convert to the Peyote Cult; he had partici-
pated in more than one Wild West show; and he could write, albeit
in a syllabary adapted for the writing of Winnebago (he was not at
all fluent in English). He was a man, as we shall see, of more than
"moderate" ability. A "real Indian" he doubtless was—but he was
a different kind of Indian than his grandfather had been. As we
read Blowsnake's autobiography, however, we find ourselves in the
presence of a man who is very far from being acculturated in the
way that Apes, Eastman, En-ma-gah-bowh, and the rest had been.
Amazed as we may be by the lives these men lived, and moved as
we may be by their accounts of their immense journeys, that they
were able to write autobiography does not surprise us. Autobiography was simply one part of the culture which they had assimilated. But Blowsnake had read no autobiographies, and he was not
eager to undertake the work which Radin had assigned him. It was
only when he found himself badly in need of money that he accepted
the work, for which Radin was willing to pay him.

When he did set to work, he managed—like Augustine before
him—to adapt the confessional forms to the demands of autobiography. In a very real sense, however—and again he is like Augustine
in this—his work was without precedent in his own experience. By
this I mean to say that Blowsnake stands in relation to the history
of American Indian autobiography where Augustine stands in relation to the history of Western autobiography. Just as Augustine's

Confessions represents a new kind of autobiographical narrative in the Western tradition, Blowsnake's autobiography represents a new kind of autobiography among the Indians.

There are five important reasons for Blowsnake's accomplishment. The first was the fact that Radin asked him to do a life history. Obviously, Blowsnake would never have written an autobiography had Radin not nagged him and paid him to do so. But we must also remember that the very suggestion that one could write the story of one's life *whole* could allow an unacculturated Indian to look at himself in a new way. Indians had long told stories about their personal experiences—one thinks, again, of the coup tales and hunting tales—but they did not tell their lives whole. The historian Karl Weintraub discusses this same phenomenon among the early Greeks and Romans. He suggests that they did not write whole autobiography largely because of the importance to them of kinship ties:

> Ask a Homeric hero who he is, and most likely he will answer: I am Telemachus, the son of Odysseus, the son of Laertes. . . . Individuals were imbedded in the social mass of given blood relations. In fundamental ways, often so hard for us who live in a highly differentiated society of individualists and individualities to understand, these earlier lives are enmeshed in and derive their meaning from basic social and kinship relations. (1978:2)

This is very much like what we read about the pre-reservation Indians. There is very little sense that individuals can be thought of—except pejoratively—as apart from the group. Heroes there may be, but they stand out as ideal expressions of their society's values (Weintraub 1978:4); there is no reason for a hero to try to explain how the peculiarities of his life made him what he is. Long hair, abstention from strong drink, and the favor of the Lord are enough to explain even the prowess of a Samson.

Imagine, then, what might have been the effect upon one of the brighter Homeric heroes of an ethnologist's insistent questioning: Well, yes, I understand that you slew your wife's suitors, but how did you *feel* about that? You are a sometimes devious man. What was it, do you think, about your childhood that made you cunning? Yes, I know that you resisted Circe's advances, but why was that? Why were you able to do so when none of your men did? Yes, doubtless you were a better man, but why? Yes, I know your family. I have already done the kinship study. But now I want to know what it was about your family, really, that makes you act the way you do. How were you raised? Was your father much away from home?

Before he wrote his autobiography, Blowsnake had spent a good deal of time with Radin working as an informant, answering Radin's questions about this ceremony and that, about this family and that clan. By the time he finally set to work on his autobiography, he had a good sense of what Radin wanted—the ethnologist wanted to know *why* and he wanted to know in detail. And so Blowsnake wrote not only that he had led a life of sin and that he then joined the Peyote Cult but also what it was about himself and his life in particular that led him to join the Peyote Cult. He described himself as one who had been searching throughout his life for something "holy." He tried the Winnebago fasting and vision quests; he found nothing holy. He tried the Medicine Dance; he found no power there, nothing holy. He tried alcohol. He even took his father's advice and went out upon the warpath; he killed a Pottawattomie blacksmith, but he found that he had won no power from the act. In peyote his life's quest was finally satisfied: he had his vision; he experienced the holy; he gained sacred power.

Ironically, then, the work with an anthropologist, the work of dredging up answers to questions about the shape of the old ways, the old life, provided Blowsnake with training in modern, Euro-American modes of thought.[10] Blowsnake asked "why ?" of his life as a whole. I know of no other life history by an Indian so little acculturated which does this, which self-consciously relates the details of a life to a unified conception of the self.[11] (It is important to mention that this claim is made only with reference to published life histories. There is an immense amount of material in anthropologists' field notes that has never been published. For example, the field notes of John Peabody Harrington, now resting in the Anthropological Archives of the American Museum of Natural History, run to well over a million pages.)

The second reason Blowsnake was able to write as he did was that, like Augustine, Blowsnake had available to him the form of the confession. Both men were able to adapt this form to autobiography. Public confession was a part of Christian ritual in the time

of Augustine; and the confessional forms were well known to
Blowsnake because the Peyote Cult, as it was spread among the
Winnebago by John Rave and Albert Hensley, was heavily influenced by Christianity,[12] and public confession was very much a
part of the ritual. Oliver Lamere, Radin's Winnebago interpreter
and himself a participant in the Winnebago Peyote Cult, has described the Winnebago ritual as it was in Blowsnake's time. He
mentions the public bearing of testimony as being a regular part of
the ritual. Usually this bearing of testimony would include public
confession, because, as Lamere put it, "If a person eats peyote and
does not repent openly, he has a guilty conscience, which leaves
him as soon as the public repentance has been made" (in Radin
1970 [1923]:347). Lamere also mentions that those who try to eat
the peyote without first repenting are likely to "suffer a good deal"
from the effects of the peyote. Radin summarized the Winnebago
Peyote meetings as follows:

> During the early hours of the evening, before the peyote has begun
> to have any appreciable effect . . . [there are] speeches by people
> in the audience and the reading and explanation of parts of the
> Bible. After the peyote has begun to have an appreciable effect,
> however, the ceremony consists exclusively of a repetition of the
> ritualistic unit and confessions. (1970 [1923]:341)

When Blowsnake was asked to write down the story of his life,
then, he wrote in the confessional mode. He and many other devout
Winnebago Peyotists had talked about their lives in just this way
on many occasions at the Peyote meetings. Indeed, John Rave,
whom Blowsnake would have heard speak at many Peyote meetings,
remembered his own life in much the same way: "Throughout all
the years that I had lived on earth, I now realized that I had never
known anything holy. Now, for the first time, I knew it. Would that
some of the Winnebagoes might also know it!" (in Radin 1970
[1923]:343).

When Radin asked Oliver Lamere to tell him about the history
of the Winnebago Peyote Cult, Lamere included, as a matter of
course, an account of the wicked lives Hensley and Rave had led
before their conversion: "the Bible was introduced [into the Winnebago peyote ritual] by a young man named Albert Hensley. He,
too, had been a bad person, although he had been educated at

Carlisle. Like Rave, he was a heavy drinker and fond of wandering" (Radin 1970 [1923]:346).

Lamere was able to say this, of course, because he had heard Rave's and Hensley's stories often in the course of the Peyote meetings.[13] Blowsnake had heard them too, and so, toward the end of his autobiography, his "confessions," Blowsnake, too, can say, "Before (my conversion) I went about in a pitiable condition, but now I am living happily, and my wife has a fine baby" (Radin 1963 [1920]:67). On another occasion Blowsnake expressed this more fully (and Radin included it in *Crashing Thunder*):

> Before I thought that I knew something but really I knew nothing. It is only now that I have real knowledge. In my former life I was like one deaf and blind. My heart ached when I thought of what I had done. Never again will I do it. This medicine alone is holy, has made me good and rid me of evil. (1983 [1926]:184)

The peculiarities of the peyote ritual among the Winnebago, then, provided Blowsnake with the confessional form for his auto-biography—but these same peculiarities also largely determined which of his remembrances Blowsnake was to include in his auto-biography. The Peyotists were very much opposed to drunkenness, and so Blowsnake tells us about his drinking. The Peyotists urged married monogamy, and so Blowsnake tells us about his insatiable womanizing. The Peyotists opposed fighting and killing, and so Blowsnake writes about his fighting and his murder of the Pottawat-tomie. The Peyotists opposed the use of (Indian) medicines and amulets, and so Blowsnake writes about his love potions and his pretended powers. And there was bitter conflict between traditional and Peyotist Winnebagoes in the first decade of this century, and so Blowsnake tells us a good deal about the old ways.

All he writes about the old ways, then, is intended to describe a moral wasteland. His vision quests were fruitless; the old ways were never able to fulfill his better longings. He describes the Medicine Dance, for example. Since the secrets of the Dance were closely guarded, the very detail with which he describes it must be seen as a deliberate act of defiance and iconoclasm, but he is careful to explain not only that the central drama of the Medicine Dance—the shooting and the coming again to life—was a clever fraud; he must also confess that he was himself a willing participant in the fraud:

They showed me how to fall down and lie quivering (on the ground) and how to appear dead. I was very much disappointed for I had had a far more exalted idea of it (the shooting). "Why, it amounts to nothing," I thought. "I have been deceived," I thought. "They only do this to make money," I thought. . . . However, I kept on and did as I was told to do. (Radin 1963 [1920]:20; 1983 [1926]:110–111)

Small wonder, then, that it should occur to Radin, resourceful as he was and knowing the Peyotists as he did, to convince Blowsnake to write his life history by urging that he do so, "so that those who came after [him], would not be deceived" (1963 [1920]:67; 1983 [1926]:203).

A third reason for Blowsnake's accomplishment was that he was literate. He wrote in a syllabary then commonly in use among the Winnebago that they had adapted from one used among the Sauk and the Fox Indians. His literacy, then, came to him from the Indians and not from the schoolroom. Still, one is likelier to question one's past when one sees it written upon a page, where ideas and sequences remain fixed. Ideas in the mind are slippery, plastic things indeed. Jack Goody and Ian Watt, in their work on "The Consequences of Literacy" (1963), provide fascinating examples of the ways in which oral histories have changed to accommodate changing social realities.[14] Certainly Radin, who knew Blowsnake and the Winnebagoes very well indeed, believed that Blowsnake would be able to accomplish things in writing which he could not have done orally:

There is one aspect of the use of the syllabary that deserves special consideration because of its possible bearing on the general subject of the influence of the adoption of writing on oral literature. Not a few syllabary texts were obtained that contain personal reflections of [Blowsnake] and a few contained highly unorthodox composition. One exceedingly long text [by Blowsnake] is quite manifestly composite in origin. There is little question, in my mind, that both are specifically connected with the new opportunities for self-expression and literary individuality which writing introduced. (Radin 1949:4)

Radin goes on to talk about some of the ways in which Blowsnake's written versions of myths and other narratives differ from what Radin would have obtained had Blowsnake been dictating the material to him. He concludes:

What we have here, therefore, is something quite new, something intimately connected with the new medium, more particularly with one feature of it, its elimination of an immediate, visible, and controlling audience and the leisure provided for reflection, selection, and correction. (1949:5)

Radin is certainly not saying that there are necessary consequences of literacy. None of the other Winnebagoes who could write in the syllabary had written anything at all like Blowsnake: "Only to a literary artist of Sam Blowsnake's skill, of course, would this mean anything. For the average man [writing] meant only another method for the perpetuation of the accustomed narratives in the accustomed manner" (1949:5). This is the fourth reason. Blowsnake was, as Radin described him, a "literary artist of unusual gifts and possessed of a style of his own" (1949:5). He had a real sense of what the written word would allow. Certainly Radin gave him the opportunity to practice and develop his talent: Blowsnake wrote 90 percent of the texts Radin collected which were written in the syllabary (1949:4).

The fifth reason for Blowsnake's autobiography, I think, was that he lived in a time of spiritual and cultural turmoil. This was also, of course, the case with Augustine. Augustine's *Confessions* may not be as relentlessly individual as Rousseau's, but they reveal an inwardness and a sense of the writer as an individual which were then without precedent. Weintraub begins his discussion of this phenomenon as follows:

The historian of autobiography often finds a rich harvest in the great periods of crisis when the lives of Western men take decisive turns. In the "classical" ages, possessing the more coherently elaborated cultural configurations . . . individuals less urgently face the need to account for the meaning of their existence. The ages of crisis, in which the firm assumptions about man and his world are being called into question, force upon the individual the task of doubting and reinvestigating the very foundations on which his self-conception traditionally rested. (1978:18)

The parallel with Blowsnake's condition is striking. I hardly need to rehearse the cultural dislocations attendant upon Indian-white contact in general. Blowsnake's autobiography itself provides a vivid sense of the consequences among the Winnebago. His father urges him to go on the warpath; it is a "good" thing to do, but all it amounts to is the pathetic murder of the Pottawattomie and legal entanglements. Blowsnake cannot even tell of his "war" experiences around the campfire—cannot tell his coup tale—for fear that he will be found out by the police. He tells about "chasing the payments," courting women who have just collected their government payment. He assures us that the old ways are without power; the old ways offer no visions. And yet, clear as it seems to Blowsnake that he has cut himself off from his past utterly, we see clearly that he is formed by his past, that his desires are rooted deep in his Winnebago upbringing. Even the visions which peyote granted him, the visions that convinced Blowsnake that *here* at last was something holy, even these visions would not have had so profound an effect upon him had he not been reared with the traditional Winnebago belief in the importance of visions, had he not as a boy been taught to seek them.

One might here expect a conclusion that would speak of Blowsnake as being like the heroes of so many novels by and about American Indians, a man caught between two cultures. But Blowsnake did not think of himself in this way. Augustine's idea of himself—like his *Confessions*—was a work of synthesis, the synthesis of Neo-Platonism and Christianity. Blowsnake's autobiography is also a work of synthesis. His traditional Winnebago yearnings for prestige and transcendental experiences are finally satisfied in the Peyote Cult—in something like the way Augustine's Neo-Platonic yearning for transcendence is finally satisfied by Christianity. Augustine, however, was quite self-conscious about his work of synthesis. He wrote several times that the wisdom to be obtained from the pagans was like the Egyptian gold which the Hebrews, with God's blessing, took with them out of the land of bondage.[15] Blowsnake, on the other hand, seems entirely unaware that he is straddling cultures. Like other Winnebago Peyotists early in this century, he sees himself as entirely apart from the misguided ways of the traditional Winnebagoes. His autobiography is entirely constructed to condemn his evil past. That we can recognize his intention, and yet see so clearly that the work reveals Blowsnake to be his whole history's continuing creation, this is the fascination of Sam Blowsnake's own invention, the autobiography.

NOTES

1. My own sense of the early history of Western autobiography is derived mainly from Karl Weintraub and Georg Misch.

2. Many such tales have been collected by the ethnologists. See, e.g., Kroeber (1908); see also Eagle-rib's coup tales in Goddard.

3. See, e.g., Libby (1973 [1920]).

4. What follows is the working out of an idea I first suggested in "Reasoning Together" (1981:267–268).

5. This book has just been reprinted with an introduction and afterword by Arnold Krupat. Krupat provides a good account of the nature of Radin's work as editor.

6. More than 40 percent of the nearly 600 narratives which I listed in *Bibliography* (1981) were elicited and edited by professional anthropologists, and another 40 percent by amateur historians, poets, journalists, and other Indian enthusiasts—most of whom were influenced by the assumptions and methods of the anthropologists.

7. Of course, it might be noted that the imposition of a chronological order is in itself the imposition of a pattern—a pattern that is basic to most narratives in the Western tradition. Underhill, by the way, would have come by her positivistic conception of facts and objectivity—like Radin—in the course of her Boasian training. See Harris (1968:250–318).

8. See also Copway's *Life, History, and Travels of Kah-ge-ga-gah-bowh* (1847). For the differences among the various versions and editions of Copway's autobiographical writings, see Brumble (1981:44; 1982:252–253).

9. Blowsnake himself said that he had only attended school for one "winter" (Radin 1983 [1926]:89–90).

10. Blowsnake was not alone in being so affected by an anthropologist's questioning. Leo Simmons's years of work with Don Talayesva (Hopi) resulted finally in *Sun Chief: The Autobiography of a Hopi Indian* (1974 [1942]). In the late stages of his work as Simmons's informant, Talayesva was writing out highly detailed accounts of his life and ways—with Simmons prodding all the time for detail that was more and more personal, more and more individual. It is one of the commonplaces of American anthropology that the Hopi were (and are) among the least individualistic of the American Indians. Since Simmons's collaboration with Talayesva covers so many years, we can actually see Talayesva changing during the course of his autobiographical labors. Here we have autobiography shaping autobiographer.

11. A number of autobiographical narratives have been collected from shamans. In many of these narratives the shaman tells how it was that he

came by his special powers, and so these would seem to be doing what Blowsnake is doing. But one soon sees that these narratives are like the coup tales in that the shamans are telling about the acquisition of powers that differ from those of others in the tribe not in quality but in degree. One sees the ways in which these variants are conventional. Joan Halifax reprints many of these narratives (1979), although her insistently credulous commentary is more than a little cloying.

Albert Hensley, Blowsnake's fellow Peyotist, composed not one but two autobiographies at about this same time, but Hensley's narratives are quite brief, just a few pages each; and Hensley had had a Carlisle Indian School education. See Brumble (1985).

12. See, e.g., La Barre (1971 [1959]:163–166). The Russellites (later to be known as Jehovah's Witnesses) and the Mormons were prominent in their influence on the Winnebago Peyote Cult. Both churches were actively proselytizing among the Winnebago in these years. The Russellites, according to La Barre (168), appealed to the Peyotists not least because of their refusal to subject themselves to any "earthly" government at a time when the earthly government of the United States was actively persecuting the Peyotists. John Rave's brother once said (quoting another Peyotist), "'My friend we must organize a church and run it like the Mormon church,'" and one of the eventual founders of the Native American Church, Jonathon Koshiway, was for a time a missionary among the Indians for the Mormons. Both the Mormons and the Russellites incorporated the public bearing of testimonies and of confession into their services.

13. For two autobiographies by Hensley, see Brumble (1985). See also the autobiographical narrative by Sam Blowsnake's elder brother (whose name really was Crashing Thunder), which Radin edited as "Personal Reminiscences of a Winnebago Indian" (1913).

14. See also Goody, *The Domestication of the Savage Mind* (1977). Goody and Watt argue that there are psychological as well as cultural consequences of literacy, and this is controversial. See Scribner and Cole (1981); see also Frake (1983).

15. See, e.g., *On Christian Doctrine*, 2.40.

REFERENCES

Apes, William. 1829. *Son of the Forest*. New York: William Apes.

Brumble, H. David, III. 1981. *An Annotated Bibliography of American Indian and Eskimo Autobiographies*. Lincoln: University of Nebraska Press.

———. 1981. Reasoning Together. *Canadian Review of American Studies* 12: 260–270.

———. 1982. A Supplement to *An Annotated Bibliography of American Indian and Eskimo Autobiographies, Western American Literature* 17:242–260.

———. 1985. Albert Hensley's Two Autobiographies and the History of American Indian Autobiography. *American Quarterly* 37:702–718.

Copway, George. 1847. *Life, History, and Travels of Kah-ge-ga-gah-bowh.* Albany: Weed and Parsons.

———. n.d. (c. 1980 [1860]). *Indian Life and Indian History.* New York: AMS.

Eastman, Charles Alexander. 1922 [1902]. *Indian Boyhood.* Boston: Little Brown.

———. 1977 [1916]. *From the Deep Woods to Civilization: Chapters in the Autobiography of an Indian.* Lincoln: University of Nebraska Press.

En-me-gah-bowh. 1904. *En-me-gah-bowh's Story.* Minneapolis: Women's Auxiliary, St. Barnabas Hospital.

Frake, Charles O. 1983. Did Literacy Cause the Great Divide? *American Ethnologist* 10:368–371.

Goddard, Pliny Earle. 1915. Sarsi Texts. *University of California Publications in American Archaeology and Ethnology* 11:222–223, 232–235, 238–245, 268–272.

Goody, Jack, and Ian Watt. 1963. The Consequences of Literacy. *Comparative Studies in History and Society* 5:304–345.

———. 1977. *The Domestication of the Savage Mind.* Cambridge: Cambridge University Press.

Halifax, Joan. 1979. *Shamanic Voices.* New York: Dutton.

Harris, Marvin. 1968. *The Rise of Anthropological Theory: A History of Theories of Culture.* New York: Crowell.

Kroeber, A. L. 1908. Black Wolf's Narrative. *Ethnology of the Gros Ventre, Anthropological Papers of the American Museum of Natural History* 1:197–204.

La Barre, Weston. 1971 [1959]. *The Peyote Cult.* New York: Schocken.

Libby, O. G., ed. 1973 [1920]. *The Arikara Narrative of the Campaign against the Hostile Dakotas, June 1876.* New York: Sol Lewis.

Misch, Georg. 1949–1950. *Geschichte der Autobiographie,* vol. 1 (in two parts), *Das Altertum.* Bern: Francke.

Radin, Paul. 1913. Personal Reminiscences of a Winnebago Indian. *Journal of American Folklore* 26:293–318.

———. 1963 [1920]. *The Autobiography of a Winnebago Indian.* New York: Dover.

———. 1970 [1923]. *The Winnebago Tribe.* Lincoln: University of Nebraska Press.

———. 1983 [1926]. *Crashing Thunder: The Autobiography of a Winnebago Indian,* with a new introduction and afterword by Arnold Krupat. Lincoln: University of Nebraska Press.

———. 1949. *The Culture of the Winnebago: As Described by Themselves.* Bloomington: Indiana University Publications in Anthropology and Linguistics, Memoir 2.

Scribner, Sylvia, and Michael Cole. 1981. *The Psychology of Literacy*. Cambridge: Cambridge University Press.

Simmons, Leo. 1974 [1942]. *Sun Chief: The Autobiography of a Hopi Indian*. New Haven: Yale University Press.

Tubbee, Okah. 1848. *A Thrilling Sketch of the Life of Okah Tubbee . . .*, ed. L. L. Allen. New York: n.p. (probably Cameron's Steam Power Presses).

———. 1848. *A Sketch of the Life of Okah Tubbee*, ed. Laah Tubbee. Springfield, Mass.: H. S. Taylor. (For an account of the differences between these two versions of Tubbee's autobiography, see Brumble 1981: 141–142.)

Underhill, Ruth. 1936. *The Autobiography of a Papago Woman*. Memoirs of the American Anthropological Association, no. 64; reprinted as part 2 of Underhill, *Papago Woman*. New York: Holt, Rinehart and Winston.

———. 1971 [1966]. Foreword to Nancy O. Lurie, *Mountain Wolf Woman, Sister of Crashing Thunder*. Ann Arbor: University of Michigan Press.

Weintraub, Karl. 1978. *The Value of the Individual: Self and Circumstance in Autobiography*. Chicago: University of Chicago Press.

On Stereotypes

DUANE NIATUM

I approach this subject with a good deal of trepidation, since most of us are well aware how quickly we become our social masks and how for aeons societies around the globe have struggled with the way their neighbors with simple sarcasm have reduced them to things. Let us try to remember, for example, how the Japanese people during the Second World War were reduced to the lowest human terms by cartoonists from American newspapers and the federal government's propaganda centers. As a child of seven by the war's end, the stereotype of the Japanese as prime villain was firmly entrenched in my unconscious. Many years had to pass before I could see a Japanese person as a human being and not as some wild beast hollering, "banzai, banzai!" Besides, these enemies of compassion and pity which we create out of a fear of closeness and lack of confidence in ourselves will hardly be affected by my concern. Nevertheless, it seems important to deal with them, since the Native American must constantly challenge the countless stereotypes people have made of him if he is ever to know a moment when he can see himself as other than a freak of nature, a cigar-store Indian.

To take up the verbal sword and do battle with the cruel jester, I know very well, is to enter the ring of the powerless. But I would like to make at least one feeble effort to counter these grotesques which continue to demoralize and haunt my people, on the reservations or in the towns and cities. Fortunately, my tribal elders encouraged me as a youth to scrupulously avoid making too many public claims that I knew more about a subject than anyone else in the community when I became an adult. They would especially caution one regarding defining artistic goals or standards. But what they would admit in public or private is that society or art is not created in a vacuum, and that standards will have to be found somewhere in the process—preferably at the beginning of things. And we are all aware that there are far too many "Popes" in the United States, advocating the young do this or that, or nothing.

Furthermore, the old ones I paid particular attention to as a boy and young man would acknowledge with an approving nod Anton Chekhov's remark, "the artist must lose himself in obscurity." (It was no doubt easier for Chekhov's generation, now almost a century past. In our age with a predatory mass media and another generation preoccupied with promoting the self as a flickering display-case, it has become almost impossible to live a life apart from consumer culture.) Our tribal elders would still agree with Chekhov, however, because their fathers and their fathers before them may have made a similar statement to their young artists centuries before Chekhov. What I understand this to mean is that there is much to be gained from the traditions of our ancestors and from the people we have come in contact with. But since more than half of all Native Americans now live in the towns and cities off the reservations, they encounter a very thin line of identity between the world of their fathers and mothers and that of the White men. They live in two distinct worlds of shared chaos for better or worse.

This paradox could become fertile land for the imagination of the Native American artist. He or she could use it as a defense against apathy and despair, alcohol and suicide. He or she could transcend this ugly reality of living between two fragmented societies by using the imagination to its fullest potential. We can already see glimpses of this transformation in the work of Native artists in all forms at an increasing rate since the 1960s. Therefore, we ought to watch for what evolves from these forms into new visions with silent but accepting observation and with a revived sense of the need for continuity in our lives and arts; we ought to appreciate the moral and aesthetic rewards of cultivating patience and personal integrity as a means to transformation. In other words, we may not always enjoy seeing ourselves or things from a historical or mythical perspective, but we would be foolish to ignore their important function in the art and society of the past and what hope there is for the present in the future.

Now I will go against the grain of my nature, by discussing the problem of aesthetic standards for "Native Americans." Is there a Native American aesthetic that exists completely separate from all other cultures today? If I have an arrow to chip, it is this: folk heroes, yes; patronizing stereotypes, no. It is my opinion that there is not a Native American aesthetic that we can recognize as having separate principles from the standards of artists from Western European and American cultures. And anyone who claims there is encourages a conventional and prescriptive response from both Native Americans and those from other cultures. The result is that the reader's imagination is actually inhibited. Stereotypic expectations break down the free play between reader and writer.

Besides, if the Native American artist has something to offer us, he or she should be able to offer it to anyone who would be willing to take an active part in the experience. If a Lakota poet, for example, wrote poems *only* in Lakota, he or she would not only exclude the non-Native American from the experience, but the Hopi, the Mohawk, the Klallam, and most other tribal peoples inhabiting other sections of the continent, including Canada and Alaska. Thus, any Native American who takes the written arts seriously—I speak solely of artists possessed by the spirit of the arts—must train himself or herself to become sensitive to the many facets of the English language and the world this language calls a home, with the same devotion a shaman had for the word in his healing songs thousands of years ago. Like the tireless and inquisitive shaman, he or she must gladly spend life becoming more aware of the limitless ways in which one can discover how life shapes language and language, life. Of course, as much as is humanly possible, the world's diverse literatures and arts ought to feed the fire of his or her creations too. (It is not impossible to maintain ethnic pride and values within the sphere of a dominant society— take the Jews, as just one example—while at the same time learning what you can from those around you. There is no longer any choice for the Native American and other minorities in this country when the language of those around you now happens to be the dominant language of the tribe).

This leads me to chip that arrow again. It certainly would not hurt any of us to question just a little the modern artist's infatuation with Ezra Pound's dictum—"Make It New." After all, making it new does not guarantee that the result will be art, good craft, or even worth our attention. For it seems to me this mania reflects too painfully the final erosion of man's faith in the uniqueness of specific things and individuals in stories and poems, and worse, in real life. As Wright Morris has wisely shown, "a sense of the aggregate, whether we like it or not, is displacing our sense of uniqueness" (1975:77). What Morris means by "aggregate," I assume, is the way modern man, whether an artist or a man in the street, has rejected the freedom of making distinctions between a horse and a horse-fly, a computer and "The Holy Grail." In other words, Pop Culture can't seem to consume enough of the new. It doesn't help much to admit that during this tail-spinning century men and women have felt incredibly threatened by the old. Old people, oaks, bridges, buildings, rivers and mountains—you name it—make them nervous and itchy and ready to destroy these things or themselves. So modern artists sniff around for the new and shiny as if it were some kind of opium poppy. These artists and their unfortunate audience—what is left of it—however, are also uncomfortable with the icy fact about this obsession. That is, as Morris further states: "newness—other qualities being absent—identifies the product as an art object." So, "to make it new—rather than make it good, or make it sound, or make it true—makes of the rejection of the past what there is of value in the creative act." And later he states, "In its essence, it is an appeal to action, and generates rejection rather than creation" (1975:80, 81). (Notice how we reject people as fast as we do our cars, TVs, clothes, etc.) Although this proves the vitality of the imagination, Morris goes on to say, "the deliberate pursuit of what is new proves to be a limiting performance, anticipating its own early obsolescence."

Thus, we might develop a healthy skepticism about the ways we have mastered the art of self-indulgence. Then perhaps the young artist will have the chance to contribute to the art that engages him or her. For, as Hayden Carruth wrote: "We speak of the uses of poetry; poetry is what uses us." So it seems to me, the Native American's standards of art are no different from anyone else's. This applies to the other arts too. Naturally, there will be different results, as there is between an artist from Moscow and, say, Chicago. One possible difference between an Anglo artist and a Native American is that the latter may introduce into the work ancestral myths and legends, stories, and jokes. But those people from other cultures should have no problem identifying with the art experience, if the artist has accomplished the job.

To illustrate the absurdity of stereotypes, I will quote briefly three poets whose work I admire: Richard Blessing, an Anglo-American; Simon J. Ortiz, an Acoma Pueblo; and Ted Hughes, an Englishman.

Blessing:
>The raven lands in a book
>of shadows. The ice tree,
>the flower tree, are one
>to him. He feeds on shadow
>and shadow grows back.
>The nest he builds is a nest
>of shadow. It is dark
>and he wants it darker.[1]

Ortiz:
>You come forth
>the color of a stone cliff
>at dawn,
>changing colors,
>blue to red,
>to all the colors of the earth.[2]

Hughes:
>Buttoned from the blowing mist
>Walk the ridges of ruined stone.
>What humbles these hills has raised
>The arrogance of blood and bone,
>And thrown the hawk upon the wind,
>And lit the fox in the dripping ground.[3]

Without too much stretch of the imagination, the context of each of these poems could be considered as Native American in imagery and symbol and theme, but only Ortiz is of tribal heritage. I say, could be, because each poem has elements that are often associated with Native American cultures. Blessing's poem, for example, refers to the most important figure in Northwest Coast Haida mythology, which balances their other central totem animal, the eagle. All other animal figures in Haida mythology are of minor importance in comparison. It is an animal of the spiritual world too, since it is free to fly between the physical world and the other world we dream of. In addition, Raven can appear as a trickster of the greatest skill and cunning. He can transform himself into a rock, a pine cone, a shark, or whatever he wants to become. Regardless, Poe, that very Victorian American writer of the last century, wrote a famous poem on the raven as well. Moreover, the crow and raven are common characters in the art and poetry of China and Japan. (I have no actual proof, but I would guess that they are birds that play an important role in the folklore and mythology of many African cultures as well.)

Within Ortiz's poem we find several images that represent both Anglo and Native American worlds, if not the worlds of most people everywhere; images like "stone cliff," "dawn," "earth," and "spider," in another section of his poem. Yet it is only through how Ortiz uses these images in the particular context of his poem that they become symbols of an Acoma Pueblo chant. Ted Hughes's poem portrays a rather direct confrontation with the awesome forces of Nature, in the form of a blowing mist that even ridges of stone cannot endure forever, let alone the hawk upon the wind, the fox in the dripping ground, or the narrator who acknowledges it, albeit with the arrogance and pride of blood and bone. It could be thought of as rooted in the countless varieties of Native American legends, depending on what tribe or nation you focus your attention on. There is one exception, however. In contrast, a Blackfeet or a Navajo or a Swinomish writing about a similar experience—if well versed in the traditions of his or her ancestors and caring about the values enough to integrate them into his or her art—might respond to this storm, but far more humbly and openly (without Hughes's arrogance), having discovered from the people's songs, ancient sparks, that the way is to be with the turning earth, the blowing mist, the cycle of human as well as earthly changes.

Most Native Americans have spent at least some time living in Anglo communities in the towns bordering their reservations, or in the major cities of the country. Radio, television, film, the newspaper and magazine have all reached the Nisqually and Choctaw, the Chickasaw and Eskimo, no matter how remote the reservation might be from the nearest Anglo community. And because these artists have not been blind, deaf, and dumb to other cultures with which they have come in contact, their artistic expressions have usually been cross-culturally fertilized. A Miwok or Apache could just as easily write a novel about Anchorage, Mexico City, or Denver, as Sacramento Valley or Chinle, Arizona. For instance, what label would you give the Kiowa novelist N. Scott Momaday, whose *House Made of Dawn* tells of the struggles of Abel, a man split in two by blood and selves? Obviously, the models for the right form for his fiction were the works of the highly innovative and sophisticated Anglo writers, Joyce, Woolf, Faulkner, and Hemingway. I don't mean to imply that Abel, the novel's central character, is not Native American, or that his interior or exterior worlds are not. On the contrary, we quickly realize that his story is very much caught up in the struggles of an individual haunted by the nightmare reality of how hard it is to maintain a sense of honor and a sense of self as Kiowa in a society that is doing everything in its power to destroy that shield, shatter the wheel of that identity and vision. In the minds of many, Anglo as well as Native American, Abel's physical and spiritual deterioration and burden are only a sharper, clearer painting of our own trial through our age's sinister labyrinth, whether we live in Seattle, Detroit, Hong Kong, or Amsterdam.

When we look closely at the way Momaday has structured his novel, his unique syntax and imagery and rhythm, we see how one author challenges such labeling. And how many times have we heard this common one? "Harriet, isn't he that Indian novelist?" These people never seem willing to admit that a man can be born on a reservation, be reared by parents and grandparents who follow closely the traditions of their Kiowa ancestors, attend Bureau of Indian Affairs Schools, then later, as he becomes seriously involved in the arts and scholarship, absorb and use for his own art the incredible new directions in which authors have taken the novel in this century.

We can see a parallel to this absurd game we play with one another in terms of stereotypes in James Welch's *Winter in the Blood*, an impressive first novel, masterfully constructed by a gifted poet of Blackfeet and Gros Ventre ancestry. It is no doubt crucial to the development of the story that it opens and closes on a Blackfeet reservation in Montana; but with a few important changes in point of view, the emptiness of the land and the indifference of the narrator to his fate, as sure to winter in his blood as the next blizzard, could *almost* be the fate of his white neighbor's, just off the reservation.

As any Montana cattleman will tell you today, regardless of race, he must deal with a similar war with Nature, must endure a similar routine or be overwhelmed by the country he loves and hates often in the same gasping breath. Welch, like many modern artists, refuses to sentimentalize the destiny of his people. He gives all who enter his fiction the real world, no matter how much that world is eating away his guts or ours. It certainly seems that he is achieving the one goal he considers most important to the Native American writer: "to communicate with Native American people, to encourage them to say 'that's the reality of it, that's the way it really is.'"

When I first read Welch's novel, I could not help but notice how the tone and sparsity of style, tremendously understated, is comparable to the best work of Camus. (The obvious difference being that Camus, like so many other Existentialist writers, seemed devoid of any sense of humor. Bleak and existential as Welch's landscape and the spiritual void of his narrator are, his novel does transcend its bleakness and despair with moments of grand humor.) In fact, I feel that much of the power of the novel is derived from its humorous colors, which illuminate a new side of character and scene.

The light moments give integrity and courage and balance to this austere lyric in prose of the anger and frustration of a thirty-two-year-old individual stumbling toward self-destruction. And we finally realize that the land is just as indifferent to the young man's pain as his own soul is. The clean, simple, yet earthy power of the narrative, always precise and concrete, is a major achievement and a credit to Welch's gift as a writer. The cycle of events seen, heard, tasted, smelled, and touched, all the nuances of sensation and feeling experienced in the story, takes us far beyond the boundaries of the Blackfeet reservation, where the story finds its place in our memory. It is an amazing feat of craftsmanship and art. While remaining uniquely Blackfeet on a personal level, it is much more than that on the symbolic level, being part of the universal thread of human challenge and defeat.

Now this leads me to another reason I decided to write about this bad joke that is as old as Coyote's tail or Raven's mask—my resentment at being categorized, boxed, and sealed: "Indian writer." (I'm sure my reaction would be the same as that of the poet Galway Kinell, if the next time he came to Seattle to read he was introduced as "White poet.") Because of the tyranny of stereotypes, the reluctance by people around the world to give them up, Native American artists would do well to synthesize their bicultural experiences and education and use them to broaden the base of their art as much as possible. The Native American is in an excellent position to add something significant to American art and literature for a number of reasons, not the least being because of the untapped sources of images and symbols that make up the tales, legends, and mythologies just being discovered by the uninitiated. But perhaps of equal importance is that artists, no matter where they come from in the world, use or try to use some images and symbols that show us their particular place and moment in time and that prove to be uniquely their own. What is remarkable and soul-catching about the symbol with a body as well as mind is that it inspires us to joy and wonder, regardless of what part of the earth we sprang from.

Compare Momaday:

> Oh Milly the water birds were beautiful I wish you could have seen them I wanted my brother to see them they were flying high and far away in the night sky and there was a full white moon and a ring around the moon and the clouds were long and bright and moving fast and my brother was alive and the water birds were so far away in the south and I wanted him to see them they were beautiful and please I said please do you see them how they pointed with their heads to the moon and flew through the ring of the moon. (1969:111)

And Faulkner:

> "You snagged on that nail again. Cant you never crawl through here without snagging on that nail"
> Caddy uncaught me and we crawled through Uncle Maury said to not let anybody see us, so we better stoop over, Caddy said. Stoop over, Benjy. Like this, see. We stooped over and crossed the garden, where the flowers rasped and rattled against us. The ground was hard. (1966:2)

You have noticed, I'm sure, that what these two prose excerpts have in common is their subject matter: the pre-consciousness of a single character, which is what most distinguishes the stream-of-consciousness novel. Divorced from censorship, rationality, logic, causality, the trappings of speech and writing, they are free to accent the pre-speech patterns of their characters, the essences of our souls. As the writers since Joyce continued to experiment and develop this new narrative style while adding their personal voices to its form, they discovered instinctively what modern science has confirmed: There are no walls separating inner or outer worlds, beginnings and endings, but a fluid sea of connections; the several worlds of being and doing, feeling and thinking, seeing and dreaming, living and dying, become interconnected aspects of experience. To me, this is the golden path between our worlds, how we may with effort and will and patience not see the other man, woman, child, fish, mountain, or river, as a stranger, a type, or a category.

So it may be possible to one day see the stereotype of the Native American as Indian challenged, if not eliminated from our literature and art, and imagination in general; to see a stronger sense of empathy with regard to Native American life, particularly when it is combined with knowledge of a specific tribal culture. To be the most successful, however, Native Americans when they are described as characters in novels, stories, plays, or poems, should possess the same dignity and fallibility as other human beings. And as Berkhofer, the historian, has clarified in *The White Man's Indian,* for realism to work in challenging the stereotypes of Native Americans, they need to be seen "as individuals rather than as Indians, as human beings and not assemblages of tribal traits." He goes on to suggest that "the motives and behavior of the Native Americans should seem natural to the reader in the situations described. Humanness, *not* race should be the essential criterion" (1979:106). For all concerned feel as he states here, "neither nostalgia nor sympathy per se is a substitute for knowledge . . . ; only an accurate understanding of cultural diversity and tribal detail combined with first-hand experience constitutes a true basis for the realistic depiction of Native American life" (1979:104).

Then even if his Anglo critics are correct—that the Native American's past is lost and buried forever; that nothing remains but his or her songs, legends, and mythologies—I am convinced that this is all he or she needs in order to build from these ruins a new past out of his or her art made as fertile as the sun rising to its zenith.

NOTES

1. A section of "Raven," from *Winter Constellations* (Boise: Ahsahta Press, 1977).

2. First stanza of "To Insure Survival," from *Carriers of the Dream Wheel* (New York: Harper & Row, 1975).

3. A section of "Crow Hill," from *Selected Poems, 1957–1967* (New York: Harper & Row, 1973).

REFERENCES

Berkhofer, Robert F., Jr. 1979. *The White Man's Indian*. New York: Vintage Books.

Blessing, Richard. 1977. *Winter Constellations*. Boise: Ahsahta Press.

Faulkner, William. 1966. *The Sound and the Fury*. London: Chatto & Windus.

Hughes, Ted. 1973. *Selected Poems, 1957–1967*. New York: Harper & Row.

Momaday, N. Scott. 1969. *House Made of Dawn*. New York: Signet Books.

Morris, Wright. 1975. *About Fiction*. New York: Harper & Row.

Ortiz, Simon J. 1975. *Carriers of the Dream Wheel*. New York: Harper & Row.

Bringing Home the Fact: Tradition and Continuity in the Imagination

PAULA GUNN ALLEN

"My grandfather is dead," Abel repeated. His voice was low and even. There was no emotion, nothing.

"Yes, yes. I heard you," said the priest, rubbing his good eye. "Good Lord, what time is it, anyway? Do you know what *time* it is? I can understand how you must feel, but . . . "

But Abel was gone. Father Olguin shivered with cold and peered out into the darkness. "I can understand," he said. "I understand, do you hear?" And he began to shout. "I understand! Oh, God! I understand— I understand!"[1]

I

The way of the Imagination is the way of continuity, circularity, completeness. The way of the intellect is the way of segmentation, discontinuity, linearity. We persist over time; we endure. We forget our origins and lay waste to the claims of the past, simultaneously deeming them to be the only truth, but not overtly. The novel is a construct, an act of the imagination struck in coherence, a whole that signifies something about life and mind. The imaginative construction of personhood is the best, and perhaps the only kind of life, as N. Scott Momaday suggests when he writes that "an Indian is an idea which a given man has of himself."[2]

As much can be said of any person, of any society, of any civilization, and of any work of art. For human beings, life is a continuous act of the imagination. When old Ko-sahn appears before Momaday's amazed eyes, she tells him the truth about the imagination: "You have imagined me well," she says, "and so I am." And, in confusion, he replies that all of this imagining is taking place in his mind—that she is not actually in the room with him.

"Be careful of your pronouncements, grandson," she answers. You imagine that I am here in this room, do you not? That is worth something. You see, I have existence, whole being, in your imagination. It is but one kind of being, to be sure, but it is perhaps the best of all kinds. If I am not here in this room, grandson, then surely neither are you.[3]

Ultimately, perhaps, it would be fair to say that it is the imagination which provides continuity in literature and in life. Yet, while continuity is a necessary process, it is not necessarily recognized when it occurs. The point of this discussion is to examine the phenomenon of continuity as it exists in the study of literature within the university, and as it applies to the study of modern American Indian literature.

There is an impulse toward wholeness that characterizes the act of writing; this impulse is the essential nature of thought and is the primary motivating principle of the imagination. In the university, this impulse is continuously met with a counterimpulse toward fragmentation, toward what, in the terms of William Carlos Williams's poem "Paterson," is divorce, the failure of communication and completion. The terms of the discussion are not whole; the circuit, broken at some point, cannot carry the impulse clearly over from wherever the writer has brought it to the audience. The essential linkage is that of tradition: of the symbols and structures shared in a deeply buried unconsciousness by a community of people.

This impulse toward whole articulation, toward realizing what Ezra Pound defined as an intellectual and emotional complex presented in an instant of time, has led writers again and again toward the source of the imagination in their time, their history, their landscape, and their mythic roots. But in America these roots are confused. The American writer's time is not only that of a technological, industrial, urban present; his or her history is not only that of

Aristotle, Aquinas, Dante, Luther, Milton, Hawthorne, Thoreau, Melville, Whitman, and Hemingway. The American writer's landscape is not that of France, England, Italy, Greece, or Egypt; the myths that embody his or her vision and hold it secure for all peoples in all times and histories is not only that of the Old Testament and the New. Writing is the attempt of the single being to articulate the singleness of that being; it is, then, a primary act of the imagination: to articulate, in an instant of time, what is known and felt; to erase chronology and to present simultaneity. So Ko-sahn tells her grandson when he asks her how old she is:

> "I do not know," she replied. "There are times when I think that I am the oldest woman on earth. You know, the Kiowas came into the world through a hollow log. In my mind's eye I have seen them emerge, one by one, from the mouth of the log. I have seen them so clearly, how they were dressed, how delighted they were to see the world around them. I must have been there. And I must have taken part in that old migration of the Kiowas from the Yellowstone to the Southern Plains, near the Big Horn River, and I have seen the red cliffs of Palo Duro Canyon. I was with those who were camped in the Wichita Mountains when the stars fell."[4]

In her imagination, Ko-sahn can realize what has gone into the making of her own consciousness. It is not significant that she was not personally present when the Kiowas emerged from the hollow log; she is capable of the most profound act of comprehension: She can make real, in her imagination, what would otherwise be an empty, albeit important, occurrence in the history of the Kiowa.

Literature reflects the deepest meanings of a community. It does this by carrying forward archetypes through the agency of familiar symbols arranged within a meaningful structure. It is the sequence in which the archetypes occur which allows the depth we customarily associate with literature, just as it is the accretion of meaning created by this structuring which gives a sense of wholeness and immediacy to the work.

The juxtaposition of certain symbols in particular sequence makes the inner meaning of these charged formulations apparent. This creates an understanding between audience and story that, under certain circumstances, can lead to the sort of act of imagination that Momaday encountered when Ko-sahn appeared before him. Whether this imaginative act be written or spoken is not important; what is important is that it be whole, entire, and in its entirety create a like wholeness in one's connection to another:

> Who is the storyteller? Of whom is the story told? What is there in the darkness to imagine into being? What is there to dream and to relate? What happens when I or anyone exerts the force of language upon the unknown?[5]

Momaday is concerned with the source of reality. For, he implies, it is this source, created through vision within the human mind, which allows for the essential coherence upon which all society and all art depend. I might add that the source of this reality is probably not accessible directly to human consciousness, though it is accessible, to a greater or lesser extent, indirectly. It is through the agency of symbolization that we are able to communicate, outside of time, our total vision of reality. Further, it is the nature of symbols, layered with significance as they are, to convey levels of meaning that are not otherwise conveyable by language. It is also the nature of the symbol to communicate to others those intuitions which seize us. "If there is any absolute assumption in back of my thoughts tonight," he continues, "it is this: We are what we imagine. Our very existence consists in our imagination of ourselves. Our best destiny is to imagine, at least, completely, who and what, and *that* we are. The greatest tragedy that can befall us is to go unimagined."[6]

The primary impulse of the imagination is wholeness. It is, in that sense, the faculty which relates exterior perception to interior impression. It closes the circuit, as it were, between I and other, creating a coherent relationship, a meaningful vision of what is.

Charles Olson, a truly American poet, premised his poetics on this idea. His search into Native American poetics and usages was directed by this conviction. He "saw this break between the spirit [energy] and the immediate object as the major fracture of meaning confronting the modern poet."[7] His thrust as poet and as formulater of a poetic for American writers was in the direction of wholeness, which he found embodied in Mayan glyphs, of which he wrote: "Signs were so clearly and densely chosen that, cut in stone, they retain the power of the objects of which they are the images."[8]

Olson incorporated this notion into "The Kingfishers," where the confusion and bewilderment of modern existence are contrasted with the E on the stone; he saw those glyphs as a measure of the interrelationship of the object with its environment, so that the object was not an object but a significance. It is important to note here that significance is a function of what is known. It arises out of the total context of interrelated elements, allowing the mind to attribute meaning to a single object by virtue of its placement within an entire field. This process is continuity; we may alter singular elements in particular ways, but their meaningfulness will only be apparent because of their connection to one another within a previously known or assumed pattern. In acknowledgment of this, Olson writes, in "The Kingfishers":

> Dead, hung up indoors, the kingfisher
> will not indicate a favoring wind,
> or avert the thunderbolt. Nor, by its nesting
> still the waters, with the new year, for seven days.
> It is true, it does nest with the opening year, but not on the waters.
> It nests at the end of a tunnel bored by itself in a bank. There,
> six or eight white and translucent eggs are laid, on fishbones
> not on bare clay, on bones thrown up in pellets by the birds.
>
> On these rejectamenta
> [as they accumulate they form a cup-shaped structure] the young are
> born.
> And, as they are fed and grow, this nest of excrement and decayed fish
> becomes
> a dripping, fetid mass.[9]

The relationship between the whole and the part is the relationship of the egg to the nest, and the flight to the bird; or, as Olson's credited source for his theory, Alfred North Whitehead, has phrased it, "the notion of existence involves the notion of an environment of existence and of types of existences. Any one existence involves the notion of other existences, connected with it and yet beyond it.[10]

It is significant that much of Olson's poetic is formulated out of a belief in the primal, the relation of person-acting to the space in which the action occurs, the mythological and ritual which some-times results from this interaction, and the consequent integration and reintegration of being into significance as process. While, as

Robert Bertholf observes in his essay "On Olson, His Melville," Olson finally feels that he can move beyond the myth and the ritual and settle for a poetic based on non-Euclidian geometry and quantum physics. This movement is more likely a result of not being able to articulate what he can envision, because he does not come out of a tradition of the whole, because he does not address a community that assumes that holism is valuable and primary to coherence, and because there is no ritual circle to which he undeniably belongs.[11] Rather, Olson speaks from and to a community that is alienistic in its primary perceptions, and whose basic premise is that human beings, particularly civilized, advanced ones, are necessarily isolate individuals, not varying expression-forms of a greater whole. The belief that isolation is fundamental to mature human consciousness makes the integrated perception of unity or of wholeness unacceptable in intellectual discourse.

Yet Olson's original impulse is accurate, whether or not he understood that it is the nature of poetry to unite itself with the highly charged symbols of the ancient, ritual-centered past. By carrying forward those image-constructs which reach beyond our fragmented present, the poem units us to our own meaning. Evidently, Olson did not realize that non-Euclidian geometry and quantum physics are themselves reformulations of ancient understandings, or that they derive their potency from their congruence with universal law and their significance in human terms from their inextricable relationship to ritual. He assumed that the ancients could make glyphs, but that the moderns alone can make sense. But though poet is maker, and the task of the poet is to make us whole, this task is simultaneously the task of shamans and an effect of ritual understandings and perceptions. It cannot be accomplished in the absence of a commonly held belief, a worldview, that incorporates the likelihood of real transformations in its everyday thinking.

In his study of Charles Olsen and Herman Melville, Robert Bertholf comments on the roots of the dichotomizing consciousness implicit in the Western Judeo-Christian worldview, which, he says, enacts separation as a major premise of existence. "In separation," Bertholf comments,

> a hero is one who most successfully asserts his will over reality. . . . The imperative of "the Lordship over nature" widens the estrangement between man and his environment, isolating him

from the roots of his existence, and necessitating the manufactory of catalogues and systems of thought and analysis to replace the natural, multiphasic environment, now neglected.[12]

One can trace this archetypal pattern from Genesis forward. The central motif of the Bible is the distance between God and Man; its primal thrust is reunification of the shattered, alienated psyche.

Nor is the motif confined to the Bible. It is a basic premise of literary criticism: The tragedy is that imaginative construct which chronicles the separation of the hero from the source of his being; his flaw is preeminently that of perceiving himself as more than, or different from, his own being in its godly and/or human components. The comedy, on the other hand, is an imaginative construct that chronicles the reunification of the hero/heroine with society, God, and self. And what is the story of the Fall and the Redemption, if not the tale of separation/fragmentation and its obverse, reunification/integration? Deeply embedded in the consciousness of Western peoples as these primal motifs are, there is an underlying motif implicit in these: an assumption of wholeness as essentially good, and of separation as essentially evil.

If we are familiar with the Bible, we are in a position to understand the greater part of Western lore: Western literature, art, science, and mathematics are all, to some extent, based on the perceptual modes which the Bible embodies. On a conscious level, this is fairly easy to perceive. But there are unspoken assumptions about the nature of truth and, therefore, the nature of meaning, that have also come to us through attitudes toward the Scriptures that are not so apparent. The belief that written works are more worthy of intellectual consideration, are more factual, or more believable, or more respectable, is one of those unspoken ideas which has been transmitted through the generations. This is the structure of the university, at base. Were it not for this belief that worthwhile matters are written, indeed, are printed, because the Bible, the "source of all truth," was the earliest manuscript to find its way into print, there would be no university as we know it today. The impact which symbol structures have on our minds and on our modes of perception and being cannot be minimized. Continuity, that process which gives our individual lives their coherence and significance, is a factor of every facet of those lives. The meanings of the past create the significance of the present. *Scriptural* and *written* mean the same thing. It is no accident that literacy is so highly valued in the West. The fact that an imaginative act is written is as important to a scholar as the fact that a chantway heals is to a Navajo.

II

Life is a mystery play. Its players are cosmic principles wearing the mortal masks of mountain and men. We have only to lift the masks which cloak us to find at last the immortal gods who walk in our image across the stage.[13]

As familiarity with the Bible makes Western culture accessible to the understanding, the basic texts of the Pueblo or the Navajo make their cultures, especially their literature, accessible to scholarly interpretation. It is a nearly hopeless task to explicate *House Made of Dawn* without such a familiarity, though an understanding of historical processes in the Southwest and of Western attitudes and lore is also important to this task. The basic meanings important to these American Indian systems are carried over into the book. To be unaware of the meanings of these symbols and their accompanying structures is to miss the greater part of the significance of the novel.

It is not impossible to read this novel when one is not conversant with the underlying symbolic structure, but the reading will result in confusion and distortion of what the writer was up to. It will also probably result in political distortions that will have an ultimately disastrous effect socially, for such is the power of the imagination over our more conscious activities. The symbols are there; the deep meanings are there. It is necessary to bring these factors into consciousness when studying the novel in order for them to have the ultimate curative or restorative effect which is the basic purpose of that book. For if elements improperly understood are imagined with sufficient care, a distortion will occur in our relationships with those misimagined persons. If *House Made of Dawn* is seen only as the chronicle of a man "fallen between two chairs," the impact on Indian men and women will continue to be that of victimization. For as we perceive, so we behave; and as we behave, so we create.

In order to imagine Abel as he is, the symbol-structure of the novel must be carefully examined. The underlying assumptions about the nature of reality and of the human being's place within it must be imagined truly; for Abel is not so much a man caught between two cultures and two orientations to reality as he is a medicine person who does not understand the nature of his being or of his proper function. The novel, in its structure and in its symbolic content, carefully makes this clear, though the meaning of Abel's experience is not evident unless the beliefs of the Pueblo and Navajo are taken into account. Momaday makes this point through the eyes of Angela St. John, through the eyes of Benally, and through the peculiar character of Tosamah as it contrasts with that of Abel. The identity of the protagonist is drawn through the author's personal history, through the history of the Bahkyush and through the journals of Fray Nicolás; it is apparent in the peculiar interweaving of names and places and, especially, in the sequence of events as they occur in the novel.

House Made of Dawn is an act of the imagination designed to heal; it is about the relationship between good and evil, and the proper place of a certain human being within that relationship. It is not about redemption,[14] for redemption is not a Pueblo (indeed, not an American Indian) notion; it is not about a fall from grace. It is about sickness and disharmony, and about health and harmony. The title is the clue: "House Made of Dawn" is the first line of the chant sung on the third day of the Navajo healing ceremony called the Night Chant. It is the first prayer of the third morning ritual; the third day is designated the Day of the West.[15] The prayer appears in the third chapter of the novel. Narrated by the Navajo friend of Abel, Ben Benally, this chapter is concerned with Abel's sojourn in Los Angeles, the major relocation center for southwestern Indians on the west coast. The prayer is sung in the Night Chant as part of the Purification section of the ceremony, and is accompanied by a rite in which a set of eight prayer offerings "sacred to gods of the shrine known as the House Made of Dawn (in the distant canyon of *Tségihi*)" are used to bless or purify the patient and are then sacrificed or offered to the sun.[16] Tségihi is an ancient Pueblo ruin, and the controlling metaphor of the book can be said to be the relationship of the sun to Abel. The sun forms the central issue of life at Walatowa (Momaday 1969:177). It is the race which is performed each year at spring equinox as an offering of the strength of the people to the sun and as a source of strength and power among them for the coming planting season which frames the book. The peyote ceremony in Los Angeles is a sun rite, and so is one of the purification rituals which Abel must go through (pp. 101–106). It is also significant that a patient participating in a Night Chant offers himself on the last morning of his healing to the rising sun, singing these words:

> Thus will it be beautiful.
> Thus walk in beauty, my grandchild.

As these words are sung, the patient faces east and breathes in the breath of dawn.[17]

In addition to these clues, Momaday has structured his novel in ways that are directly analogous to the major Chantway structure. The events of twelve days are chronicled, and each of these is divided into subsections that consist of flashbacks, events of that day in the past, and events surrounding the main action on that day.

According to Leland C. Wyman, there are ten or twelve more-or-less standard rituals within a major Chantway.[18] These can vary with circumstances and the particular Chantway selected for healing the particular illness troubling the patient.[19] The major variants which appear in *House Made of Dawn* include the consecration of the hogan (which does not appear in the novel until Abel returns home), a short singing, a setting-out of prayer offerings, a purification, an offering ceremony (to attract the Holy People), a cleansing, an all-night singing, a shock rite, blackening and ash-blowing, and the final dawn procedure. A feature of a healing is that various ceremonies may be tried experimentally; it seems that this may be the case with Abel. Another practice of note is the fact that the completion of a ceremonial healing may be delayed for years.[20] Not surprisingly within a Native American framework seven years pass as Abel seeks his appropriate ceremonial and is finally healed.

In addition to the ceremonial structure, there is a layer-structure that is Pueblo at the deepest layer, Christian at the next layer, and modern Anglo at the topmost layer. Or, to phrase it another way, the book at its most superficial layer is about a displaced Indian caught between the old and the new; it is, in that sense, a sociological novel. In its middle layer it is concerned with religious conflict, that conflict which began with the first Franciscan missionaries in the Southwest and continues on to the present in the person of John Big Bluff Tosamah, missionary and Priest of the Sun. Its deepest layer is Indian: the tradition, the knowledge, the deep values of the Indian on a continent whose land and creatures are also Indian, but whose surface has been overlaid with a thin epidermis of European society. In its branching and circularity, the novel operates structurally in a way similar to the Navajo Chantway system, and in its careful divisioning it follows the number structure of 4–7–6 and 12, which are the major ceremonial numbers of the American Indian and are the classic divisions of a major chantway.

III

Ei Yei! A bear and a maiden. And she was a white woman and she thought it up, you know, made it up out of her own mind, and it was like that old grandfather talking to me, telling me about *Esdza shash nadle*, or *Dzil quioi*, yes, just like that. . . . A long time ago it was dark, and you looked in the fire and listened, and he was going on about all he knew, and he knew everything and there was no end to the stories and the songs. (170)

As the mythic structure of *Moby Dick* is the Bible, so the mythic structure of *House Made of Dawn* is Beautyway and Night Chant.[21] As there are departures from the source in the former, so there are departures from the text in the latter. This is the nature of continuity: to bring those structures and symbols which retain their essential meaning forward into a changed context in such a way that the metaphysical point remains true, in spite of apparently changed circumstances. It is, perhaps, a manifestation of that law which demands that literature have a quality that appeals to humankind universally: Surely there is no more universal a theme than that of the play between good and evil, and no more universal a plot than the part humanity plays in the balance between them. There are those laws of our being which are always true; there are those processes common to humankind which always occur. It is this fact of commonality which allows a Kiowa to read and understand *Moby Dick*, given appropriate references, and which allows a New Englander, also appropriately guided, to read and understand *House Made of Dawn*.

The exchange between good and evil is not to be understood in the context of *House Made of Dawn* as it is understood in the context of Christian cosmology. It is the understanding that evil is an unavoidable aspect of the universe which finally allows Abel to begin his return to wholeness and to his proper place in things. It is the way of the Christian to oppose evil, and this Abel attempts to do. But it wounds him, like the arms of the dying witch, "only in proportion as Abel resisted" (Momaday 1969:78).

Abel had thought that he could leave the pueblo and get a job, but he did not reckon with universal processes. Angela St. John was to help him get a job, but then, according to what he'd told Benally, "he got himself in trouble" (Momaday 1969:161). The dream of the modern world was not for Abel, for it was his part to be Monster Slayer and, in his own time, to bring the people to a new world. The story, in its mythic dimension, began with Francisco—perhaps it began before Francisco, with the coming of the Bahkyush to Walatowa. Perhaps it began with the European invasion. But it was Francisco who slept with the daughter of a witch, and who abandoned her after their child was still-born (p. 184). And because of his perfidy and fear, Porcingula's mother (the old Pecos *bruja*) cursed Abel (p. 15). In the pueblo, witches traditionally transform themselves into snakes (or snakes turn themselves into humans for the purpose of witchcraft), and after the little boy is cursed by the Bahkyush bruja known as Nicolás *teah-qhau*, and runs, he hears a certain sound: the wind whistling around a snake hole, "and it filled him with dread. For the rest of his life it would be for him the particular sound of anguish" (p. 16). Indeed, for the rest of his life, as it is known to us through the novel, he would bear that curse; he would kill a snake and in turn be mortally wounded by another, the *culebra* Martinez in Los Angeles (pp. 129, 166). Yet, had it not been for the curse and for his encounters with evil, had it not been that within his own person, perhaps because of that curse, he contained the contrary principles of light and darkness, Abel could not have made that final run and delivered that final blessing to himself and his people. Abel, like his grandfather Francisco, is a *brujo* himself, and so he recognizes evil. He is Snake Man and he is Bear Man (p. 169). At some level, he is also Monster Slayer, prototypical hero of the Navajo. He is, like his grandfather, kin to those spirits who must run forever, keeping evil in its place (pp. 104, 187–

188). In order to do this he must first come to terms with the enormity of the thing; he must, like his grandfather, acknowledge that "evil had long since found him out and knew who he was" (p. 64).

The idea embodied here is perhaps strange to the Westerner. It is presumed that the forces of good are separate from the forces of evil, and the universe is conceived as a dualistic structure forever at war with itself. And so Abel perceives it, or tries to, and Tosamah perceives it so as well. But the point that is being made is that such a concept is not so: The old priest learns this, and through his journals, so does Father Olguin, who considers Fray Nicolás a saint—perhaps because the old priest was more like Francisco than like those with pious fantasies of sanctity being that condition untainted by any form of sin or evil (Momaday 1969:45–52).

The interplay between the dual forces of good and evil in this system must be recognized. It is not for human beings to attempt to annihilate either force; it might be said that it is our destiny to be forever manifesting one or the other, until we can locate the balance between them. This balance is located for Pueblos in the House of the Sun, at the mid-point of the northern and southern poles of its journey. "Just there at the saddle, where the sky is lower and brighter than elsewhere on the high black land" is the position that signals the time to clear the ditches and the "long race of the black men at dawn" (Momaday 1969: 178). The House of the Sun, which is a feature of every pueblo, is the calendar which allows the people to locate their own equilibrium in the continuous interplay of the forces of the universe; it is the ceremonial timepiece which allows a person to know "who and what and *that* they are" (p. 103).

The essential nature of pueblo life is its mysteriousness. The central issue of pueblo belief is growth and transformation; the belief in spirit is strong among them, and their life is a matter of locating the mortal being in spirit. This is not a factor of historicity, nor is it a matter of linear chronology. There is, for each individual, a perfect moment when the balance of mortal and spirit is achieved, though this moment occurs at a different point in the life of each person. Francisco achieved his perfect moment when he was a young man. He played the drum during the clan dance for the first time; he changed drums without missing a beat: "there had been nothing of time lost, no miss in the motion or the mind . . . and it was perfect" (Momaday 1969:187). Afterward, the women came out and distributed food among the assembled people "in celebration of his perfect act. And from then on he had a voice in the clan, and the next year he healed a child who had been sick from birth" (p. 187).

In some sense, all the stories of the pueblo are about the ways in which that perfect act is achieved. The ways are different as the individuals are different; in that sense, *House Made of Dawn* is in the long tradition of the people, for it is a story about how a modern Indian locates his being within the center of all things, and achieves that equilibrium which is beyond words and thought.

But Abel is sick, disequilibrated; in order for him to discover himself balanced in the universe of being, he must be healed. The Navajo elements of the story are the healing elements, and the events which Abel experiences are analogous to those commonly experienced by those who have been wounded or cursed as they make their journey toward wholeness. For wholeness is the essential nature of healing: One who is whole is healed; one who is whole is holy.

Abel's trials are in the nature of the testing which the protagonist of the Chantway undergoes. Abel is subjected to at least eight such tests, and like the protagonists of Beautyway and of Mountaintopway, he disobeys prohibitions established by the Holy People and gets himself into trouble. But, by this disobedience, Abel, like the Chantway protagonists, is taught the ceremonial which will be brought back to the people item by item.[22]

What penetrates Abel's consciousness during those final brutal weeks in Los Angeles is the song Benally sings. For him, thoughts of home, the music, the stories, are the only comfort he finds; not even Milly can reach across the barriers of his isolation after he has been wounded by Tosamah (Momaday 1969:146), and by Martinez (p. 159). Benally narrates his account: "House made of dawn. I used to tell him about those old ways, the stories and the sings, Beautyway and Night Chant. I sang some of those things, and I told him what they meant, what I thought they were about" (p. 133).

The prime feature of Navajo life is the healing.[23] Singers devote many years to learning one Chantway perfectly. The ceremonies are handed down in the traditional way, but must be learned and paid for by the apprentice before he can practice independently.[24] The Navajo may be the finest healers in the world; certainly, their

Chantway system is one of the more complex metaphysical systems, made even more so by its relationship to Pueblo ceremonialism. The two are related, vaguely, as are Abel and Benally, who says "We're related somehow, I think. The Navajos have a clan they call by the name of that place" (Momaday 1969:140). This relationship is an old one. It goes way back in time, beyond the coming of the Spaniards, and is as complicated in its interworkings as the Chantway system itself. The relationship is important, for clansmen have a tighter bond than might be supposed, and this bond is of more Spirit than of earth. For clanspeople derive from the same mythic, the same archetypal source; their power and their consciousness are more closely attuned, because of their common source, than are those of many blood relatives. Then, too, Benally is a deeply traditional person himself; he'd have to be since he is able to sing parts of the Chantways and talk about what they mean. Benally is not a singer, but he is as much of one as Abel is of a priest when they meet—he is as much of one as many modern Indians will ever be, and it is enough. For through the power of his song, Abel survives the worst beating Benally has ever seen (p. 167) and returns to Walatowa to spend the seven days of Francisco's dying with him (p. 177). After preparing the old man for burial, Abel takes up his place; running into the dawn, he performs his own perfect act of pure balance, and learns the true meaning of the songs:

> He was alone and running on. All of his being was concentrated in the sheer motion of running on, and he was past caring about the pain. Pure exhaustion laid hold of his mind, and he could see at last without having to think. . . . He was running, and under his breath he began to sing. There was no sound, and he had no voice; he had only the words of a song. And he went running on the rise of the song. *House made of pollen, house made of dawn.* (p. 191)

So Abel finds himself healed, and in the recovery of his primal completeness he sings the chant to the sun, in the dawn light, which is sung by one who is healed.

The ceremonial is the means of achieving wholeness of being; it is the vehicle of the imagination which allows the human being to imagine himself fully—outside the bounds of social concerns, and beyond the constraints of physical imperatives. It is that part or function of consciousness where the Spirit and the Human meet and merge and become one, and it is beyond history or time as it is far from the narrow confines of pure reason. What happens to Abel is analogous to what happens to the protagonists of Beautyway and Mountaintopway.[25] The narrative concerning his journey toward the center of his being is analogous to the narratives connected to the Chantways and the ceremonial narratives of the Pueblo, in which the significance of events is embodied and transmitted. It is this process of working events into meaning which makes them true—more true, perhaps, than they would have been otherwise.

Literature is that act of the mind which allows significances created by events to become apparent. If the work of literature is imbued with the power which is in the mind of the writer, that meaning will take a form and shape that is real and vital, and that will continue to bear meaning for generations to come.

"You have imagined me well, grandson, and so I am," Ko-sahn tells the writer as she stands, tiny but complete before him. And when she is done, he imagines that he is alone in the room.

NOTES

1. N. Scott Momaday, *House Made of Dawn* (New York: Harper-Signet, 1969), p. 190.

2. Momaday, "The Man Made of Words," in *Literature of the American Indian: Contemporary Views and Perspectives,* ed. Abraham Chapman (New York: New American Library-Meridian, 1975), p. 96.

3. Ibid., p. 99.

4. Ibid., p. 99.

5. Ibid., p. 103.

6. Ibid., p. 103.

7. Robert Bertholf, "On Olson, His Melville," in An *Olson-Melville Source-book, I: The New Found Land, North America,* ed. Richard Grossinger (Vermont: North Atlantic Books, 1976), p. 5.

8. Charles Olson, in Bertholf, p. 6, from *The Human Universe and Other Essays,* ed. Donald Allen (New York, 1975).

9. Charles Olson, "The Kingfishers," in *The Distances* (New York: Grover Press, 1960), p. 6.

10. Alfred North Whitehead, in Bertholf, p. 5, from Whitehead's *Modes of Thought* (1938; New York, The Free Press, 1966), pp. 6–7.

11. Bertholf, p. 28.

12. Ibid., p. 6.

13. Frank Waters, Masked Gods: Navajo and Pueblo Ceremonialism (rpt. 1950, Swallow Press; New York: Ballantine Books, 1970), p. xvii.

14. This interpretation is made by Barbara Strelke in her essay, "N. Scott Momaday: Racial Memory and Individual Imagination," in Chapman, p. 349.

15. The Night Chant, in *Four Masterworks of American Indian Literature: Quetzacoatl / The Ritual of Condolence / Cuceb / The Night Chant*, ed. John Bierhorst (New York: Farrar, Straus and Giroux, 1974), p. 307.

16. Bierhorst, p. 307.

17. Ibid., p. 332.

18. Leland C. Wyman, ed. 1975. *Beautyway: A Navajo Ceremonial*. New York: Bollingen Series LIII–Pantheon Books.

19. Ibid., p. 10.

20. Ibid., pp. 8–10.

21. See Bierhorst's edition of Night Chant and Wyman's edition of Beautyway. Wyman has used the original myth recorded and translated by Father Berard Haile and a variant myth recorded by Maud Oakes in his edition.

22. Wyman, p. 27.

23. Ibid., p. 4.

24. Ibid., p. 13.

25. Wyman's discussion of the stories of Beautyway and its allied chant, Mountaintopway, casts a great deal of light on the symbolic story of *House Made of Dawn*, especially pp. 15–35, which shows a relationship between these sister chants and Night Chant.

Native American Novels:
Homing In

WILLIAM BEVIS

> But you know Crows measure wealth a little differently
> than non-Indians. . . . Wealth is measured by one's
> relatedness, one's family, and one's clan. To be alone,
> that would be abject poverty to a Crow.
> > Janine Windy Boy-Pease,
> > from the film *Contrary*
> > *Warriors: A Story of*
> > *the Crow Tribe,* Rattlesnake
> > Productions, © 1985

How Native American is the Native American novel? And in what
ways? Novels are certainly not traditional Native American arts,
and we have only begun to ask how novels can be significantly
Native American in anything but subject matter and politics.
Should we say that Native Americans write not "Native American
novels" but "novels about Native Americans"? The questions recall
debates over "Black literature" in the 1960s: How deeply has a
minority point of view entered these arts?

In the handling of plot and nature the novels of McNickle,
Momaday, Silko, and Welch are Native American. This sounds
simple, and in some ways it is; however, both "plot" and "nature"
lead to culturally conditioned concepts and to pervasive differences
in white and Native American points of view. As we shall see in
their "homing" plots and their surprisingly "humanized" nature,
these works are drenched in a tribalism most whites neither under-

stand nor expect in the works of contemporary Indians, much less when they are professors (all four novelists have taught at universities). I will present the arguments on plot and on nature referring mainly to the novels of McNickle and Welch. They wrote about northern plains tribes only two mountain ranges apart; I will draw most evidence and comparisons from tribes between the Salish in western Montana and the Crows in eastern Montana, thereby hoping to minimize problems introduced by tribal variety.

This essay is neither proscriptive nor exhaustive. Native American novels *need* not have the characteristics I am proposing; many other possible characterizations—such as Momaday's calling Silko's *Ceremony* a "telling" rather than a novel, or Lincoln's comparison of Welch's surrealism to trickster tales—may well be apposite, yet are not discussed here. What we seek is the special appropriateness of "homing" plots and a humanized nature to Native Americans past and present, an appropriateness that is manifest in their novels.

HOMING

American whites keep leaving home: *Moby Dick, Portrait of a Lady, Huckleberry Finn, Sister Carrie, The Great Gatsby*—a considerable number of American "classics" tell of leaving home to find one's fate farther and farther away. To be sure, Ahab or Gatsby might have been better off staying put, and their narrators might finally be retreating homeward, but the story we tell our children is of lighting out for the territories. A wealth of white tradition lies behind these plots, beginning with four centuries of colonial expansion. The Bildungsroman, or story of a young man's personal growth, became in America, especially, the story of a young man or woman leaving home for better opportunities in a newer land. In *Letters from an American Farmer,* St. Jean de Crevecoeur defined Americans as a people who leave the old to take the new: "*He* is an American, who, leaving behind all his ancient prejudices and manners, takes new ones from the mode of life he has embraced, the new government he obeys, and the new rank he holds" (in Bradley et al. 1974:184). The home we leave, to Crevecoeur, is not only a place; it is a past, a set of values and parents, an "ancien regime."

Such "leaving" plots—not really picaresque because they are directed toward a new mode of life—embody quite clearly the basic premise of success in our mobile society. The individual advances, sometimes at all cost, with little or no regard for family, society, past, or place. The individual is the ultimate reality, hence individual consciousness is the medium, repository, and arbiter of knowledge; "freedom," our primary value, is a matter of distance between oneself and the smoke from another's chimney. Isolation is the poison in this mobile plot, and romantic love seems to be its primary antidote. Movement, isolation, personal and forbidden knowledge, fresh beginnings; the basic ingredients of the American Adam have dominated our art, even if many of our artists are dissenters from mainstream myths of success. The free individual may be a tragic failure, but his is the story we tell and always in our ears is Huck's strange derision: "I been there before."

In marked contrast, most Native American novels are not "eccentric," centrifugal, diverging, expanding, but "incentric," centripetal, converging, contracting. The hero comes home. "Contracting" has negative overtones to us, "expanding" a positive ring. These are the cultural choices we are considering. In Native American novels, coming home, staying put, contracting, even what we call "regressing" to a place, a past where one has been before, is not only the primary story, it is a primary mode of knowledge and a primary good.

Let us begin with the simplest consideration, the plots of the six most prominent Native American novels, and then see how these plots thicken. In D'Arcy McNickle's *The Surrounded,* Archilde comes home from Portland—where he "can always get a job now any time" playing the fiddle in a "show house" (1936:2)—to the Salish and Kootenai ("Flathead") reservation in Western Montana. He has made it in the white world, and has come "to see my mother . . . in a few days I'm going again" (p. 7). From the very beginning, however, family ties, cultural ties, ties to place, and growing ties to a decidedly "reservation" (versus assimilated) girl are spun like webs to bind him down. He does not leave, and finally is jailed by the white man's law. It seems to be a "tar baby" plot; Archilde takes one lick and then another at his own backward people, and suddenly he is stuck. At first, being assimilated into a white world, he had expected to remain mobile, thinking of "wherever he might be in times to come. Yes, wherever he might be!" (p. 5). McNickle's repetition underscores the plot: whites leave, Indians come home.

Although the white point of view would find in such a homing-as-failure plot either personal disaster or moral martyrdom (e.g., Silas Lapham, Isabel Archer), McNickle's point of view toward his home village of St. Ignatius is more complex: that of a Salish Indian turned anthropologist, B.I.A. administrator and a founder of the National Congress of American Indians and the Newberry Library in Chicago. His novel does not present Archilde as simply sucked into a depressing situation, although he certainly is; the novel applauds his return to Indian roots. At first Archilde is "on the outside of their problems. He had grown away from them, and even when he succeeded in approaching them in sympathy, he remained an outsider—only a little better than a professor come to study their curious ways of life" (1936:193). He has, in short, the charm of an anthropologist. When he stays, however, to gratify his mother's wish for a traditional feast and to help his Spanish father harvest the wheat, "It was a way of fulfilling the trust placed in him. He was just learning what that meant, that trust" (p. 177). And as he watches his mother dress her grandson for the feast, he begins to appreciate the old ways, and to enter a different time:

> Watching his mother's experienced hands, he could guess how she had lived, what she had thought about in her childhood. A great deal had happened since those hands were young, but in making them work in this way, in the way she had been taught, it was a little bit as if the intervening happenings had never been. He watched the hands move and thought these things. For a moment, almost, he was not an outsider, so close did he feel to those ministering hands. (pp. 215–216)

We can hardly wish such beauty to be "outmoded," and although Archilde cannot save his mother or with any convenience apply her old "mode of life" to himself, the point of view of the novel offers profound respect for the past, family, and tradition; more troublingly, it asks us to admire Archilde's chosen involvement on the reservation even as it leads to personal doom. At first this plot may seem "Romantic" and "Primitivist," but as we shall see, it is not.

The plot of *The Surrounded* is typical. In McNickle's other novel of contemporary Indians, *Wind from an Enemy Sky* (1978; first published after his death), a young boy on the same reservation is abducted by whites to a Mission school (not uncommon—it happened to McNickle). Four years later he returns, an outsider, to his very traditional grandfather and tribe. The plot hangs on the tribe's attempt to recover from white authorities a lost Feather Boy medicine bundle. In the course of the book, the young boy and the reader gain increasing respect for this futile and regressive effort to "bring back our medicine, our power" (p. 18), a perfect example of an activity whites cannot easily appreciate. Grounds for our respect for such regression would usually be existential or heroic, but again, something different is going on. As in *The Surrounded*, action focuses in concentric circles from the outside world to the few miles between McDonald peak and the Flathead river; just as Archilde had recovered his traditional mother, so young Antoine is initiated by his conservative grandfather into the tribe. The traditional Indians, however, once more win the past only to lose the war.

Three of the other novels also tell of a wanderer in the white world coming home. In Momaday's *House Made of Dawn* (1966), an Indian serviceman comes back to the reservation, drinks and kills, drifts in Los Angeles, and finally returns to the pueblo to give his grandfather a traditional burial and participate in the annual healing race, which his grandfather had once run. In Welch's *Winter in the Blood* (1974), a thirty-ish Indian who has quit his job in an Oregon hospital returns to the ranch in northern Montana, to a desperate round of drunken bar hopping that leads, finally to discovering his grandfather, pulling out of his lethargy, and throwing the traditional tobacco pouch in his grandmother's grave. In Leslie Silkos's *Ceremony* (1977), an Indian serviceman returns from Japan to the Southwest Laguna tribe, and slowly breaks from a pattern of drinking and madness to participating in a healing ceremony guided by an old medicine man, a ceremony that begins with a quest for cattle and ends with an amended story and rain for the desert land. In the last of the six novels, Welch's *The Death of Jim Loney* (1979), an Indian in northern Montana refuses to leave—despite pressure and opportunity—his hopeless town and native land. He shrinks back into the darkest corner of all, as his circle spirals inward to one place, one past, and suicide. In all these books,

Indian "homing" is presented as the opposite of competitive individualism, which is white success:

> But Rocky was funny about those things. He was an A-student and all-state in football and track. He had to win; he said he was always going to win. So he listened to his teachers, and he listened to the coach. They were proud of him. They told him, "Nothing can stop you now except one thing: don't let the people at home hold you back." (Silko 1977:52)

First let us agree on the obvious: In the six novels, an Indian who has been away or could go away comes home and finally finds his identity by staying. In every case except Loney's, a traditional tribal elder who is treated by the novel with great respect precipitates the resolution of the plot. In every case except Loney's that elder is a relative—usually parent or grandparent—with whom the protagonist forms a new personal bond. In every case including Loney's, the ending sought by the protagonist is significantly related to tribal past and place. With or without redemption, these "homing" plots all present tribal past as a gravity field stronger than individual will.

What is interesting is not this simple "structuralist" pattern, but its implications and the attitudes toward it within the novels. Tribalism is respected, even though it is inseparable from a kind of failure. Under examination, that "homing" to tribe is complex: Tribalism is not just an individual's past, his "milieu" or "background." Tribe is not just lineage or kinship; home is not just a place. "Grounded Indian literature is tribal; its fulcrum is a sense of relatedness. To Indians tribe means family, not just bloodlines but extended family, clan, community, ceremonial exchanges with nature, and an animate regard for all creation as sensible and powerful" (Lincoln 1983:8). These books suggest that "identity," for a Native American, is not a matter of finding "one's self," but of finding a "self" that is transpersonal and includes a society, a past, and a place. To be separated from that transpersonal time and space is to lose identity. These novels are important, not only because they depict Indian individuals coming home while white individuals leave but also because they suggest—variously and subtly and by degrees—a tribal rather than an individual definition of "being."

The tribal "being" has three components: society, past, and place. The "society" of the tribe is not just company; it is law. Catherine, Archilde's aging mother in *The Surrounded*, makes clear that what they have lost are the customs, rituals, and practices of law which bind people together into more than a population. In the central feast scene, the Indians lament the banning of dances, ceremonies, and practices by secular and religious authorities, just as conquered white Americans might lament the loss of courts, due process, and private ownership of land. The tone of the discussion is that, under white rule, "mere anarchy is loosed upon the world." *Wind from an Enemy Sky* is filled with discussions of white attempts to break Indian law:

> What kind of law is that? Did we have such a law? When a man hurt somebody in camp, we went to that man and asked him what he was going to do about it. If he did nothing, after we gave him a chance, we threw him away. He never came back. But only a mean man would refuse to do something for the family he hurt. That was a good law, and we still have it. We never threw it away. Who is this white man who comes here and tells us what the law is? Did he make the world? Does the sun come up just to look at him? (McNickle 1978:89)

Just as in American law, these tribal guarantees of rights within the nation are not necessarily extended to foreigners (other tribes). So in *Wind*, the young Indian's murder of the white man tending the white dam is met by the Chief with a shrug, the casual counterpart of colonial invasion: "The man up there was not one of us. He has people to mourn for him. Let his own people be troubled" (p. 65).

In each of these novels, the protagonist seeks a meaningful relation to a meaningful structure: He becomes a healthy man through accepted social ritual (Silko, Momaday) and a self-respecting man through deeds traditional to his people and needed by them (McNickle, and Welch's pouch on the grave in *Winter in the Blood*). Self-realization is not accomplished by the individual or by romantic bonding only; that would be incomprehensible. In *Wind*, Henry Jim tries assimilation, which means individualization, by farming his own land, living in his own frame house (with rooftop widow's walk overlooking the valley—the government had decided to showcase Henry Jim), and by white standards he succeeds as an individual. But:

> The government man said it would be a good thing. He wanted the Indians to see what it is like to have a nice house like that. In those days I had the foolish thought that a man stands by himself, that his kinsmen are no part of him. I did not go first to my uncles and my brothers and talk it over with them. . . . I didn't notice it at first, but one day I could see that I was alone. . . . Brothers, I was lonesome, sitting in my big house. I wanted to put my tepee up in the yard, so people would come to see me, but my son and his wife said it would be foolish, that people would only laugh. . . . Two days ago I told my son to put up this tepee; it is the old one from my father's time. "Put up the tepee," I said, "the stiff-collars can stay away. I want to die in my own house."
>
> Every voice in the circle murmured. Antoine looked up, stealthily scanning each face, and he could feel what was there among them. It shamed them that they had stayed away and had been hard against this old man. It shamed them, and they were in grief. (McNickle 1978:117–118)

So the first assumption of tribalism is that the individual is completed only in relation to others, that man is a political animal (lives through a relationship to a village-state), and the group which must complete his "being" is organized in some meaningful way. That meaning, not just land, is what has been lost: "now in old age she looked upon a chaotic world—so many things dead, so many words for which she knew no meaning; . . . How was it that when one day was like another there should be, at the end of many days, a world of confusion and dread and emptiness?" (McNickle 1936:22).

The second component of tribalism is its respect for the past. The tribe, which makes meaning possible, endures through time and appeals to the past for authority. Tribal reality is profoundly conservative; "progress" and "a fresh start" are not *native* to America: "Modeste was silent for a long time. Then he announced that he too . . . had turned back to that world which was there before the new things came" (McNickle 1936:210). Most of the Western tribes shared a belief in a "distant past": "Back in time immemorial, things were different, the animals could talk to human beings and many magical things still happened" (Silko 1977:99). Old Betonie in *Ceremony*, the grandfather in *House Made of Dawn*, Catherine in *The Surrounded*, Bull in *Wind from an Enemy Sky*, and Grandfather Yellow Calf, who talks to the deer in Welch's more skeptical *Winter in the Blood*—all are in touch with a tradition tracing from the distant past, and all extend this connection to the young protagonists. Only Loney fails to find a connected ancestor, and only Loney fails.

In these novels, whites, mobile in time as well as space, have left their own past behind. The liberal Indian agent in *Wind*, Rafferty, reflects on Henry Jim's request:

> And he asks me to help bring back this old bundle, whatever it is—this old symbol. It's been gone twenty-five or thirty years, but he thinks the people should have it.
>
> Nobody in Marietta, Ohio, would make such a request—in Marietta, if it's like towns I know, they're trying to get away from the past. (McNickle 1978:36)

Most instructive is McNickle's recital of a Christian welcome to Mission school:

> You students, now, you listen to me. I want you to appreciate what we're doing for you. We're taking you out of that filth and ignorance, lice in your heads, all that, the way you lived before you came here. . . . Forget where you came from, what you were before; let all that go out of your minds and listen only to what your teachers tell you. (p. 106)

Quite apart from the tyranny of such hair-scouring and brainwashing is the stupidity of the white demands from an Indian point of view. Indians were understandably startled at white heterogeneity, at the political and religious differences among whites, at their rapid and ill-considered change of all within their grasp. In opposing the past, whites were opposing a fundamental reality and were likely to fail: "They're just like young bears, poking their noses into everything. Leave them alone and they'll go away. . . . Wait until a hard winter comes . . . they would go away and the world would be as it had been from the beginning, when Feather Boy visited the people and showed them how to live" (McNickle 1978:131, 135).

Native Americans had excellent grounds for valuing the past, grounds that do not seem as impractical, quaint, or primitive as faith in Feather Boy. The source of respect for the past in Indian life and novels is respect for authority. Since Socrates and the growth of the ideals of free inquiry and the practices of ingenious manipulation, we have hardly known such stability. At least in the last four hundred years, few Europeans have absorbed the respect for parents, elders, customs, and government, the belief in *the benevolence of power* that Plains Indians knew. The aging Crow Chief Plenty-coups spoke to Frank Linderman in 1930:

> "This talking between our mothers, firing us with determination to distinguish ourselves, made us wish we were men. It was always going on—this talking among our elders, both men and women—and we were ever listening. On the march, in the village, everywhere, there was praise in our ears for skill and daring. Our mothers talked before us of the deeds of other women's sons, and warriors told stories of the bravery and fortitude of other warriors until a listening boy would gladly die to have his name spoken by the chiefs in council, or even by the women in their lodges.

> "More and more we gathered by ourselves to talk and play. . . . We had our leaders just as our fathers had, and they became our chiefs in the same manner that men become chiefs, by distinguishing themselves."

> The pleasure which thoughts of boyhood had brought to his face vanished now. His mind wandered from his story. "My people were wise," he said thoughtfully. "They never neglected the young or failed to keep before them deeds done by illustrious men of the tribe. Our teachers were willing and thorough. They were our grandfathers, fathers, or uncles. All were quick to praise excellence without speaking a word that might break the spirit of a body who might be less capable than others. Those who failed at any lesson got only more lessons, more care, until he was as far as he could go." (Linderman 1974 [1932]:8–9)

That is far from the America which Crevecoeur viewed, and such respect for the old ways necessarily mocks change.

A culture believing that power corrupts, naturally encourages dissent. A culture believing that power is benign, naturally respects its elders. We should not see the regressive plots of these novels as returns only to a "distant past" of Edenic unity, magic, and medicine bundles. Right down to the raising of young and the conduct of tribal councils, Native Americans successfully practiced a system that engendered respect for the immediate as well as distant past. That is, the past, too, was part of tribal authority and culture and therefore part of identity. Each plot of all six novels hinges on the insufferability of individuality in time as well as space: Severed from the past, the present is meaningless, outcast, homeless. The connotations of "regression" are cultural; not all people equate their "civilization" with "discontents," and therefore a return to a previous status quo is not necessarily a romantic "escape" from an unbearable present of cultural or individual maturity and anxiety. Indeed, Native Americans said and still say that Marietta's attempt "to get away from the past" is the escapist fantasy that will not succeed.

I suggested earlier that, to white Americans, the individual is often the ultimate reality, that therefore individual consciousness is the medium, repository, and arbiter of knowledge, and that our "freedom" can be hard to distinguish from isolation. In contrast, I suggested that Native Americans valued a "transpersonal self," and that this "transpersonal self" composed of society, past, and place conferred identity and defined "being." Why not, the skeptic might ask, use a vocabulary of "individual" and "context," and simply explore the differing degrees of emphasis on each by the cultures in question? That might be possible, but such discourse presumes both the separability and independent value of each category, as if the individual is a meaningful category with or without context. That an individual exists is not contested, and Native American life and novels present all the variety of personality expected in our species; but the individual alone has no meaning. In all six novels, the free individual without context is utterly lost, so it would be misleading to apply to him so hallowed an English term as "individual." No "free individual" who achieves white success in these six books is really admired—not Rocky, Henry Jim (the closest case would be Kate in *Loney*)—and certainly the free "mode of life" they have "chosen" is not preferred to tribal context. So, to call Welch's narrator in Minough's bar, or Tayo back from the war, or Abel in Los Angeles, or Loney at the football game an "individual," implying all the weight of dignity, promise, and law which is carried by that term in white culture, is misleading. In every one of these books the protagonist seeks an identity that he can find *only* in his society, past, and place; unlike whites, he feels no meaningful being, alone. Individuality is not even the scene of success or failure; it is nothing.

In a similar way, "knowledge" is formed and validated tribally in Native American life and in these books, although of course the individual cortex does the thinking. Consider the vision quest, the most radically isolated "knowing" an Indian was encouraged to seek. Alone for days, fasting and punishing the body, the young man sought the hallucinatory dream or vision which would help him realize his identity by revealing his spirit helpers and special animal henchmen, and which also would supply information to the tribe. Quite apart from the obvious tribal acculturation involved in even the acquisition of such knowledge (a context often overlooked in American knowledge gained by individual "free inquiry"), its *interpretation,* that is, the conversion of traditionally sought phenomena to knowledge, was usually tribal. Plenty-coups, for instance, had his private dream but depended on the tribal council to determine what it meant: "By articulating his visionary experience so that it can be socially embodied, the dreamer frees himself from a burden of power while enhancing his tribal culture" (Kroeber 1983:330). Tayo's mythic romance and the narrator's visit to Grandfather in *Winter* place their acquisitions of crucial knowledge in a social and family context. Old Two Sleeps in *Wind* dissolves into the natural world (loses individuality) to gain his knowledge, and what is gained is so tribal that the entire encampment spends the winter months watching his furrowed brow, waiting for his vision to come forth.

Not only is knowledge usually sought, interpreted, and applied in a social context in these books, but useful knowledge is also knowledge from and of the past. From Henry Jim's point of view:

> It was not just an old story intended for the passing of an afternoon. As he had announced, he had come to ask for something—and a white man, a government man, might not understand the importance of the thing he asked unless the story was carried back to the beginnings. Today talks in yesterday's voice, the old people said. The white man must hear yesterday's voice. (McNickle 1978:28)

These plots are regressive because Native American knowledge is regressive; the traditional elders of *Ceremony, House, Surrounded, Wind,* and *Winter* (tragically, such lineage fails to develop for Loney) teach the protagonists the only knowledge which proves useful in each book. "I been there before" is a primary virtue. It does not seem too strong to say that in these books both meaningful "being" and meaningful "knowledge" are supra-individual, aspects of tribe.

The third component of tribalism inherent in these novels is place. In all six novels the protagonist ends *where* as well as *when* he began. Even in Welch's works, the most contemporarily realistic of the novels, the reservation is not just a place where people are stuck; it is *the* home. Curiously, all six novels are from inland West reservations and all six come from tribes not drastically displaced from their original territories or ecosystems. Place is not only an aspect of these works; place may have made them possible.

In each book the specific details of that one place are necessary to the protagonist's growth and pride. In *Ceremony*, "All things seemed to converge" on the Enchanted Mesa: "The valley was enclosing this totality, like the mind holding all thoughts together in a single moment" (Silko 1977:248–249). In *House*, that one particular road must be run; in McNickle the Mission Mountains must be the last stand; in Welch, the gate where Mose was killed, the ditch where his father froze, and Loney's Little Rockies, on the reservation, must be the scenes of growth.

Conversely, white disregard and disrespect for place is crucial to these books:

> . . . the cities, the tall buildings, the noise and the lights, the power of their weapons and machines. They were never the same after that: they had seen what the white people had made from the stolen land. (Silko 1977:177)

> These mountains, trees, streams, the earth and the grass, from which his people learned the language of respect—all of it would pass into the hands of strangers, who would dig it up, chop it down, burn it up. (McNickle 1978:130–131)

Fey and McNickle, in their scholarly work, identified the concept of individual, transferable title to the land as the "prime source of misunderstanding" between whites and Indians (1959:26). McNickle thought that Indians understood land payment as a gift and perhaps as a rental fee for land use, but that probably, even late in the nineteenth century out West, Indians could not conceive of private land ownership. The Cherokees, by 1881, had learned and dissented: "the land itself is not a chattel" (p. 27). Fey and McNickle eloquently state the difference between the white transmutation of land to money (does that medicine work?) and the Native American view: "Even today, when Indian tribes may go into court and sue the United States for inadequate compensation or no compensation for lands taken from them, they still are dealing in alien concepts. One cannot grow a tree on a pile of money, or cause water to gush from it; one can only spend it, and then one is homeless" (p. 28).

Thus, all six novels depict Indians coming home and staying home, but "home" is not the "house" of white heaven, as dreamed by Catherine in *The Surrounded:* "everything they wanted, big houses all painted, fine garments . . . rings . . . gold," all out of sight of neighbors. Home to the Indian is a society: "Then I went to the Indian place and I could hear them singing. Their campfires burned and I could smell meat roasting" (McNickle 1936:209). In all of these novels the protagonists succeed largely to the degree in which they reintegrate into the tribe, and fail largely to the degree in which they remain alone. Although such aspirations toward tribal reintegration may be treated by a novelist sentimentally, or romantically, or as fantasy, these aspirations are not *inherently* sentimental or romantic. Rather, they constitute a profound and articulate continuing critique of modern European culture, combined with a persistent refusal to let go of tribal identity; a refusal to regard the past as inferior; a refusal—no matter how futile—of even the wish to assimilate.

Whites may wonder why Indians are still living, as it were, in the past of having a past. It is a reasonable question, and it influences our reading of these novels. Only a little over one hundred years ago, in 1884, Montana Territory was fenced, the railroad came, the cattle market boomed, and the last buffalo was shot. Elders who remembered that winter of '84 ("Starvation Winter") lived into the 1930s; some of their children are now sixty to eighty years old. Indian students right now have relatives who heard from the lips of the living what it was like to ride a horse, belly deep in grass, across unfenced plains dark with buffalo. Several of my Crow students speak English as a second language; many members of all tribes have relatives who tell the old stories.

Even to occasional university professors such as the four authors under consideration, tribalism is not necessarily so distant as many whites think; these authors are not resurrecting archaic rituals for symbolic purposes, but telling of entire communities and drifting individuals still feeling the pull of tribal identity, tribal despair, tribal pride. There were surges of white interest in Indians in the 1880s, at the time of Helen Hunt Jackson and the final massacres; in the thirties, as the last fieldwork recalling pre-White culture faded; in the sixties, as Indians and whites grew politically active. But in between, Native Americans were forgotten, and each surge of interest or neglect has resurrected the same issues: allotment, assimilation, termination of reservations, despair. The "Indian Question" is not an *old* question, beyond living memory, nor is it answered. The major threats of a hundred years ago still threaten, and many Native American tribes are still a people unwilling to buy wholesale the white ways or to abandon their own: "In many areas whites are regarded as a temporary aspect of tribal life and there is unshakable belief that the tribe will survive the domination of the white man and once again rule the continent" (Deloria 1970:13).

If these novels assert a trans-individual tribal identity, it is not surprising that whites should overlook the phenomenon. Whites have long overlooked tribalism, preferring to project onto Indians their own individualistic fantasies. The distinction between Native American "homing" and white "wandering" plots is sharpened by considering white novels about "going native."

There are several good stories of whites marrying Indians in McNickle and Welch country—between the Mission mountains and the Crow range. In *Tough Trip through Paradise* (1967), Andrew Garcia tells his tale, true as the old coot could make it forty years later, of meeting (in 1878) a Nez Perce girl, survivor of the terrible massacre of Chief Joseph's band at Bear Paw in northcentral Montana. The girl is lodged with an alien tribe near the Musselshell; Garcia marries her and they journey back to the Big Hole valley to find and properly bury her father and brother, killed there during the retreat. The quotation excerpted for the back of the book captures Garcia's spirit: "I would become innoculated with the wild life of the Indian and become one of them . . . wild and free like the mustang." Indians, like animals, are to Garcia wild and free in a state of nature. This simplistic Romantic primitivism describes Garcia, who has followed a wandering plot away from his native Rio Grande, away from his hated father who threatened to slit his throat if he consorted with loose women, off to faraway Montana to soldier, trade, and marry an Indian. *He* was "wild and free." But throughout the book his Indian wife is mourning the loss of her kin, wishes only to bury her father according to tribal custom, and indeed is probably using Garcia, diplomatically and strategically, to get out of the Musselshell country and back toward her home. *She* is civilized, not "wild and free." So also the mustang prefers the hierarchical society of its own kind. The primitivist white—in this case a sensitive, observant, loving husband—projects separation from society, past, and place, his own wandering plot, onto Indians, completely overlooking the tribalism manifest in his wife's desires. It would be amusing, had history not pushed the irony too far.

The most egregious example, however, of whites trying and failing to "go native" in Welch country is in Guthrie's *The Big Sky* (1947). In Part Four, set in 1842 among the Blackfeet, the protagonist, Boone, has finally gained the long-sought object of his obsession, Teal Eye, and has settled down in her family's encampment on the banks of the Teton River west of present Choteau, Montana, within a few miles of Guthrie's home. Boone had always wanted to be an Indian, and now the mountain man from Kentucky sits in buckskin in the heart of redskin land:

> A man could sit and let time run on while he smoked or cut on a stick with nothing nagging him and the squaws going about their business . . . and feel his skin drink the sunshine in and watch the breeze skipping in the grass and see the moon like a bright horn in the sky by night. One day and another it was pretty much the same, and it was all good . . . Off a little piece Heavy Runner lay in front of his lodge with his head in his squaw's lap. . . . In other lodges medicine men thumped on drums and shook buffalo-bladder rattles to drive the evil spirits out of the sick. They made a noise that a man got so used to that he hardly took notice of it. (1947:257–258)

Boone "hardly took notice." In the previous two chapters, Boone had ridden into their camp seeking Teal Eye. First we were told by the interpreter that her father, "Heavy Otter dead. Big sickness." The sickness is small pox. Within pages we and Boone learn: "White man bring big medicine, big sickness. Kill Piegan. Piegan heart dead. . . . Goddam dead" (Guthrie 1947:250). But like Gatsby, Boone has only one thought: "Ask him about the squaw." The suspense of the scene hangs on whether Teal Eye is already married. Within minutes of Boone's postcoital streamside revery, Red Horn will be saying, "The white Piegan does not know. He did not see the Piegans when their lodges were many and their warriors strong. We are a few now, and we are weak and tired. . . . We are poor and sick and afraid" (p. 262). Boone certainly *does* know that they are very sick, that Teal Eye has lost her father and many relatives, and that the tribe's "heart is dead . . . we are weak and tired." Red Horn sees the political result of disease and white encroachment: "We are weak. We cannot fight the Long-Knives" (p. 262).

In the midst of this crushing tribal despair Boone not only finds perfect happiness (hardly noticing the sick rattles), but has the audacity to blend his personal contentment with historical revery:

> It was a good life, the Piegan's life was. There were buffalo hunts and sometimes skirmishes with the Crows . . . it was as if time ran into itself and flowed over . . . so that yesterday and today were the same. . . . and it was all he could ask, just to be living like this, with his belly satisfied and himself free and his mind peaceful and in his lodge a woman to suit him. (p. 258)

In some ways, Guthrie seems to share in Boone's primitivism. Never does Boone participate in rituals or councils, nor are they narrated. Never is Teal Eye's point of view offered—is she perfectly happy as her society and past unravel? What is the marital consequence of Boone's blindness to her grief? We only know, "What she cared about most was to please him." "Teal Eye never whined or scolded . . . just took him and did her work and was happy" (pp. 259–260). We are asked to share Boone's happiness, achieved through freedom from constraint.

When the elders crowd Boone, asking him not to show white men the pass through the mountains, Boone stomps off and does it. Nobody tells *him* anything. "Strong Arm is a paleface," says Red Horn, unable to comprehend Boone's loneliness. "He will go back to his brothers . . . " "No! . . . Damn if I ever go back" (p. 262). Boone has gotten away from it all, away from a hated father (who, like Garcia's, physically threatened him), away from kin, race, towns, away even from the red brothers around him and possibly away from his wife. He is free, disconnected from society and past, with no respect for any authority but himself. He does love place, but it is not an Indian's place. In his view the sun is disconnected from any larger reality, the river disconnected, the present time disconnected—or rather, all are connected only in the moment of an individual's sensation, the lone source of meaning.

To this day, the irony of Boone's streamside revery in the Blackfeet camp, as he and apparently Guthrie think he has happily "gone native," has to be pointed out to white Montana students. The Indian students, however, read it differently. "What do you think of this scene?" I once asked. "Treasure Island," shouted a Blackfeet. Boone is nowhere near Indian country; he is living in white heaven: in suburbia, on about as fine a piece of real estate as you could find, with a pretty wife, and a full refrigerator, and utterly alone.

Garcia and Guthrie, while very knowledgeable about Native Americans, still had to believe that to live in nature is to be "wild and free" of civilization. Primitivism thus shapes the extreme "white plot": Boone wanders away from all kin and custom to an untouched paradise. This plot *is* escapist and casts the rogue male, lonely and violent, as the culture hero of a mobile society. Although Huck needs a family, the lone gunslinger needs a town, and Boone needs a wife, the primitivist remains within his culture: The mobile individual is the arbiter of value. Emerson's "Thou art unto thyself a law" is the exact opposite of Native American knowledge. What looks so often to whites like individual regression to some secure Eden may be in Native American novels an enlargement of individuality to society, place, and past: "Archilde sat quietly and felt those people move in his blood. There in his mother's tepee he had found unaccountable security. It was all quite near, quite a part of him; it was his necessity, for the first time" (McNickle 1936:222). Henry David Thoreau, that most pure abstainer from society, from the past and from all outside authority, is said to have died murmuring "Moose. Indian." Indians, however, were never wild and free, nor did they live in Thoreau's beloved wilderness: "We did not think of the great open plains, the beautiful rolling hills, and winding streams with tangled growth as wild. Only to the white man was nature a wilderness. . . . When the very animals of the forest began fleeing from his approach, then it was for us the Wild West began" (Luther Standing Bear 1978 [1933]:26).

The typical Indian plot, then, recoils from a white world in which the mobile Indian individual finds no meaning ("He had lost his place. He had been long ago at the center, had known where he was, had lost his way, had wandered" [Momaday 1966:96]) and as if by instinct, comes home:

> As an adolescent sent off to school for the first time, he waited for the dead of winter to run away from Genoa, Nebraska, a government boarding school, and traveled almost a thousand miles, most of the time on foot, to reach home in the spring. He didn't like to talk about it, how he sheltered, what he ate. By the time he reappeared as part of the Little Elk population he was a grown man. (McNickle 1978:80)

This "homing" cannot be judged by white standards of individuality; it must be read in the tribal context.

THE DEER SAYERS

As soon as Americans hear the words, "nature in Native American novels," we have primitivist expectations of the sacred earth prior to the evils of civilization. First we have assumed, however, that the "natural" is the opposite of the "civilized." The famous "sacred reciprocity" of Indians and nature certainly exists, but the quality of the Indian "sacred" within novels needs elucidation.

The handling of nature is most interesting in the works of James Welch. In *Winter in the Blood*, to me one of the finest Native American novels yet written, nature is unpredictable and various. Indeed, just as there is no real category "Indian," but only various tribes, so in Welch there is no "nature," only various instances—of what? Consider the "function of nature" in this passage:

> Later, as we drove past the corral, I saw the wild-eyed cow and a small calf head between the poles. The cow was licking the head. A meadowlark sang from a post above them. The morning re-

> mained cool, the sun shining from an angle above the horse shed.
> Behind the sliding door of the shed, bats would be hanging from
> the cracks. (1974:14)

The wild-eyed cow reminds us of his brother's death, while the bats
hardly fit the "pastoralism" of nurturing and meadowlarks on a
cool morning. Are bats benign symbols to Native Americans? Is the
narrator revealing his dark mind, imagining evil behind the door
of appearance? No and no. Cows and bats happen to be hanging
around the barnyard; they are not abstracted to a homogeneous
whole; they are not symbols. They "function" to reveal that the
narrator respects what's there.

A similarly disjunct and intriguing image occurs in McNickle's
Wind: "The students came from many miles away and from many
tribes, all snatched up the way coyote pups are grabbed and stuffed
into a sack while mother coyote sits on her haunches and licks her
black nose" (1978:107). The passage presents coyote pups in a
straightforward comparison to human children. Naturally, when
the coyote mother is introduced we expect a parallel to human
mothers; then, as she "sits on her haunches and licks her black
nose" we seek the meaning of that action in human terms. Are
coyotes and Indian mothers whacked on the nose as children are
snatched? No, coyote snatchers in western Montana tell me, the
pups can be taken without a blow. Is this chilling indifference? Not
on the part of humans; in McNickle's novels, several children are
taken and mothers vehemently protest. The parallelism simply
breaks down. The mother coyote takes over the text, licking her nose
for coyote reasons and thinking coyote thoughts. Nature is not subordinate to humans. Animals have their own rights in life and art.

"Mosquitoes swarmed in the evenings outside the kitchen window and redwing blackbirds hid in the ragged cattails of the irriga-
tion ditches" (Welch 1974:104). When Keats mentions the murmur-
ous haunt of flies on a summer's eve, or Emily Dickinson at death
tells of a great blue fly interposed between herself and the light, we
scramble to figure out why. The remarks have an effect on us
because we are accustomed to using nature, abstracting it, confining
it to our purposes. In Welch's work, such interpretive reaction to
each natural phenomenon would engender (and has engendered)
silly misreadings. The natural world in Welch is strangely (to
whites) various, objective, unsymbolic, as if it had not yet been

taken over by the human mind. Indeed, the book as a whole, although it hardly seems a paean to farming, is filled with landscape beautiful as well as harsh, and Welch himself says the book began as a kind of High Line (the route across northern Montana) pastoral (*Dialogues* 1982:165).

What about the deer? It is a bold move by Welch, and an exciting moment in the novel when this most realistic and antisentimental of narrators walks into Yellow Calf's world. We have to wonder how the author will handle the scene, even as the skeptical narrator wonders how he will handle the old man's claims:

> "No man should live alone."
> "Who's alone? The deer come—in the evenings—they come to feed on the other side of the ditch. I can hear them. When they whistle, I whistle back."
> "And do they understand you?" I said this mockingly.
> His eyes were hidden in the darkness.
> "Mostly—I can understand most of them."
> "What do they talk about?"
> "It's difficult . . . About ordinary things, but some of them are hard to understand."
> "But do they talk about the weather?"

The narrator's pressing is ours; surely even talking deer are "primitive." The old man's answer is wonderful:

> "No, no, not that. They leave that to men." He sucked on his lips.
> "No, they seem to talk mostly about . . . " he searched the room with a peculiar alertness—"Well, about the days gone by. They talk a lot about that. They are not happy."
> "Not happy? But surely to a deer one year is as good as the next. How do you mean?"
> "Things change—things have changed. They are not happy."
> "Ah, a matter of seasons! When their bellies are full, they remember when the feed was not so good—and when they are cold, they remember . . . "
> "No!" The sharpness of his own voice startled him. "I mean, it goes deeper than that. They are not happy with the way things are. They know what a bad time it is. They can tell by the moon when the world is cockeyed." (Welch 1974:67–68)

The narrator has tried mockery, humor, and naturalistic reduction, but at every point he is foiled. Leave the silly reductions to men, he is told; deer are more sophisticated.

The scene is cleverly constructed. The narrator has been quickly drawn into a discussion of what the deer say and why, and old Yellow Calf observes, "You don't believe the deer," as if their talking were assumed and only the content could be questioned. The narrator tries to duck the issue of his own belief, and suggests that the deer could be wrong. Yellow Calf says, "no matter. . . . Even the deer can't change anything. They only see the signs" (p. 69). "Even . . . only." The sly old fellow has pulled ahead at every turn, and the final verb of the chapter bows gracefully in his direction: "I started to wave from the top of the bridge. Yellow Calf was facing off towards the river, listening to two magpies argue" (p. 70). The narrator will soon discover that Yellow Calf is his grandfather.

We have finally come to sacred ground, to an Indian listening to animals, to Grandfather, to the language and mind of nature— and the deer grumble like existential philosophers in a Paris cafe.

Native American nature is urban. The connotation to us of "urban," suggesting a dense complex of human variety, is closer to Native American "nature" than is our word "natural." The woods, birds, animals, and humans are all "downtown," meaning at the center of action and power, in complex and unpredictable and various relationships. You never know whom you'll bump into on the street:

> "One day in the moon when leaves are on the ground [November] I was walking with my grandmother near some bushes that were full of chickadees," Pretty-shield continued. "They had been stealing fat from meat that was on the racks in the village, and because they were full they were all laughing. I thought it would be fun to see them all fly, and tossed a dry buffalo-chip into the bushes. I was a very little girl, too little to know any better, and yet my grandmother told me that I had done wrong. She took me into her arms, and walking to another bush, where the frightened chickadees had stopped, she said: "This little girl is my granddaughter. She will never again throw anything at you. Forgive her, little ones. She did not know any better." Then she sat down with me in her lap, and told me that long before this she had lost a close friend because the woman had turned the chickadees against her. (Linderman 1974 [1932]:154–155)

The reasons for the reversible connotations of "urban" and "natural" are not difficult to unravel. Europeans have long assumed a serious split between man and nature, and after 1800, they have often preferred nature to man's works. Lacking respect for their own civilization, when European whites have imagined a beatific union of "man and nature" they have assumed that the union would look not "human" but "natural"; therefore, they perceived the Indians as living in a "primitive" union of man and nature that was the antithesis of civilization. However, respecting civilization as they knew it, when Native Americans imagined man and nature joined, they assumed the combination would be "human," "civilized." Thus, the variety of personality, motivation, purpose, politics, and conversation familiar to human civilization is found throughout Indian nature. "Mother Earth" is not wild. Nature is part of tribe. That is why its characteristics are "urban," and that is why Welch's deer talk like philosophers in a Paris cafe.

They are humanlike beings—apparently semiologists—at the center of the civilized world. Nature is "home," then, to Native Americans in a way exactly opposite to its function for Boone. Nature is not a secure seclusion one has escaped to, but is the tipi walls expanded, with more and more people chatting around the fire. Nature is filled with events, gods, spirits, chickadees, and deer acting as men. Nature is "house": "There was a house made of dawn. It was made of pollen and of rain, and the land was very old and everlasting" (Momaday 1966:7).

What gives this system divinity is the same authority, distant past, and brotherhood which unites the tribe; "sacred reciprocity" does not derive its sacredness only from a transaction with the awesomely distant or alien "other." One's meaningful identity includes society, past, place, and all the natural inhabitants of that place.

Such incorporation of nature into the body of tribe has two major and apparently (to whites) antithetical consequences in these Native American novels. First is the grand attention to place, the *macro* sacredness of earth which has been noted by whites because it can be hammered to fit primitivist expectations. Second is the apparent fragmentation of the natural world into a huge cast of individual, civilized *micro* characters, a fragmentation that has not been properly noticed because it does not fit white formulas. In this second scheme, natural phenomena are not abstracted and therefore behave with individuality and whimsicality: "a rich, flexible imagining of animal beings," as Karl Kroeber writes (1983:329). Cows, bats, mosquitoes, blackbirds, coyotes, magpies act in their individual, peculiar ways. Meaning, to be sure, is still tribal, located in the larger system, but the paradoxical effect of this "micro" brotherhood is to stress the individuality of fellow inhabitants. In *Loney*, when they have driven to the Mission Canyon for a precious moment in the place where Loney will die, Rhea sees a deer "through the rear window. It was a large deer, without antlers. It stood broadside, his head turned directly toward the car. Rhea watched it flick its right ear, then lift a hind hoof to scratch it." The deer's casual individuality helps make the moment sacred: "the best secret ever" (Welch 1979:15).

McNickle deliberately juxtaposed the "micro" sacredness of nature to white symbolism in *The Surrounded*. Archilde is at Mission school, and one afternoon a cloud

> by curious coincidence . . . assumed the form of a cross—in the reflection of the setting sun, a flaming cross. The prefect was the first to observe the curiosity and it put him into a sort of ecstasy . . .
> "The Sign! The Sign!" he shouted. His face was flushed and his eyes gave off flashing lights—Archilde did not forget them.
> "The Sign! Kneel and pray!"
> The boys knelt and prayed, some of them frightened and on the point of crying. They knew what the sign signified . . . The Second coming of Christ, when the world was to perish in flames!

The cloud, of course, melts away, but curiously Archilde does not need this empirical proof to reject Christianity's symbolic use of nature:

> It was not the disappearance of the threatening symbol which freed him from the priests' dark mood, but something else. At the very instant that the cross seemed to burn most brightly, a bird flew across it. . . . It flew past and returned several times before finally disappearing—and what seized Archilde's imagination was the bird's unconcernedness. It recognized no "Sign." His spirit lightened. He felt himself fly with the bird. (McNickle 1936:101–103)

What a marvelous scene: Archilde trusts the bird to know if its world, *their* world, is coming to an end; just as Yellow Calf trusted the deer to have seen true signs, Archilde trusts the bird not to have seen false ones. The bird, like the ear-scratching deer, reassures him through its "unconcernedness," and he feels a symbiosis with this individual, sentient (with the capacity for knowledge and concern) brother in the sky. He is saved not by a "strange" symbol, but by the "familiarity" of what is. Therefore, he rejects the fiery Christian teleology prescribed for this evil earth, estranged from divinity, in favor of immediate brotherhood in a divine familial system.

Delicacy is perhaps the main effect of the individuation of nature in Native American life as well as art. We are charmed when Chief Plenty-coups, after another tale of bloody war, says, "All my life I have tried to learn as the chickadee learns, by listening,—profiting by the mistakes of others, that I might help my people (Linderman 1962 [1930]:307). The effect is to direct our attention to detail, to small habits—chickadees listen? profit by mistakes?—to individual differences, to natural nuance.

The individuation of nature is strongest in Welch, even though of the four authors he seems to pay the least attention to traditional Native American culture. McNickle is straightforwardly and effectively didactic, and Momaday and Silko more taken with the grand themes of sacredness and place. But possibly because he works by the nuance of poetic image and avoids historical generalization, Welch makes the most use of that Native American world which is made up of thousands of unique characters interacting in a wealth of detail.

In such a world, reconsider Indian history. Whites were advancing not only on Indians but on the chickadees listening, the bird unconcerned, the deer scratching. White willingness to wage environmental war was to the Indians shocking, as Pretty-Shield said: " . . . kill *all* the buffalo. Even the Lakota, bad as their hearts were for us, would not do such a thing . . . yet the white man did this, even when he did not want the meat" (Linderman 1962 [1930]:250). Killing a man who could kill you was understandable and honorable; killing our harmless and useful brothers was a senseless attack on the system which makes meaning possible. To this day, white discussions of neutron bombs as immoral because they are "anti-personnel" and nuclear bombs as less immoral because they only obliterate the earth, stun ears on the reservation.

From the Native American point of view, then, whites waged war not only on individual Indians, on tribes, and on the macrocosmic sacred earth but also on the microcosmic individuals of the tribe spread across plains and through the woods. The history of *that* war has never been told, and is one aspect of Welch's novel, *Fools Crow*, perhaps the most radically Native American work yet attempted by a major novelist:

> . . . he pulled his musket from its tanned hide covering. . . . Then he heard the raven call to him. He was sitting on a branch. . . . "You do not need your weapon, young man. There is nothing here to harm you."
>
> White Man's Dog felt his eyes widen and his heart began to beat like a drum in his throat. Raven laughed the throaty laugh of an old man. "It surprises you that I speak the language of the two-leggeds. . . . I speak many languages. . . . I even deign to speak once in a while with the swift silver people who live in the water—but they are dumb and lead lives without interest. I myself am very wise."

Raven has been sent by Sun to help White Man's Dog direct his bullet toward a white intruder; he fulfills that role with the personal insouciance of Raven alone. We are brought into a world that is both one, and myriad. Welch's historical novel about the Blackfeet in the year of 1869–1870, when they were torn by the Baker massacre from a traditional buffalo culture to recognition of white superiority, is meticulously researched and told from the point of view of Native American characters. This design, combined with Welch's talent for stark realism, clear prose, and pure imagery, engenders a unique American novel.

Delicacy and violence are strangely mixed in these Native American documents and novels. Reading a Plains Indian story we are often struck first by the acceptance of violent attack, murder, and maiming as part of life and honor:

> Big-nose intended to count a double coup and jumped from his running horse beside the Pecunie to take his gun. As he sprang toward him the fellow fired, and Big-nose fell with his own thigh broken.

They faced each other, each with a broken thigh, neither able to stand, Big-nose wholly unarmed because he had thrown away his gun when he jumped from his horse so that he might count a fair coup. I saw the Pecunie raise his knife and saw Big-nose back away. (Linderman 1962 [1930]:220)

These are the same men who have "tried to learn as the chickadee learns" (p. 307), and the European liberal's head is left spinning between the poles of disregard for human life and delicate respect for all other life, established in such tales. They seem an inversion of American culture, which demonstrates an unprecedented solicitude for human longevity from fetus to old age, while waging unprecedented war on the rest of the earth. In a parallel opposition, the Indians saw whites as violent in *personality*—"White men are like that, always angry, always shouting" (McNickle 1978:91)—and violent toward nature, while extraordinarily concerned (is it guilt?) for human life. McNickle shows how the warrior Native Americans cherished the delicacy of their world:

He comes from a big world where his power is in a machine. Or maybe he carries it in his pocket and he can take it out and tell you where the sun is. We live here in this small world and we have only ourselves, the ground where we walk, the big and small animals. But the part that is man is not less because our world is small. When I look out in the coming day and see a bluebird—we call it our mother's sister—I see the whole bluebird, the part that is blue and the part that is yellow, just as this man does. I don't have half an eye because I live in this small world. (p. 123)

These points are germane to all the novels at hand. In every book the protagonist is unusually intelligent, sensitive, even delicate, yet in most of the novels he also participates in deliberate murder. Abel drives a knife into a stomach, and Archilde and Elise chuckle over her killing of the sheriff: "'You're just a damn fool.' He kissed her and saw her smile" (McNickle 1936:295). Just a few pages before, that impending murder had been set in a Plains Indian context. The Sheriff was "a kind of last foe—the one who would make the final count on him." In *Wind*, the white man at the dam is casually shot, while at the end Old Bull is honored for killing two unarmed white liberals, well treated and well known to readers throughout the book. In young Antoine's eyes: "Black blood would spill on the ground. His grandfather would feel strong again, and the boy was proud for him" (McNickle 1978:255). Along with honorable murder comes honorable suicide, *at the hands of his own tribe*. The Indian policeman "Boy" must act, and Bull knows it: "'Brother! I have to do this!' Bull turned, knowing it was to come, and received the Boy's bullet point-blank to the heart. He had not tried to lift the rifle" (p. 256). Jim Loney similarly organizes his death at the hands of an Indian policeman, at the time and place of his choice, in Mission Canyon on the reservation. Just like Bull, in receiving the bullet from his brother he seems to have declared an ultimate relation to past and place that cannot be comprehended by the terms "suicide of an individual." Likewise, in white law Loney's accidental shooting of Pretty Weasel is a defensible mistake; but in finding himself guilty for the murder of a tribal brother, Loney is choosing Indian law (Welch 1979:146).

What is particularly interesting about violence in these books is the way it rehearses Plains Indian history. *The* question was whether to fight and die, or cooperate and live. The Crow Plenty-coups is troubled by Crow cooperation with whites, which he had urged, eloquently, as necessary for survival. But longevity was not very important to these people, and McNickle and Welch seem to support the policy and plot recommended by the Sioux Crazy Horse instead of the Crow Plenty-coups; even Loney, in his complicated, modern half-breed mess, seems in some ways to have said, "Here I stand," and "It is a good day to die."

The presentation of violence in both white and Indian novels reflects each culture's view of nature and civilization. The white Boone becomes a mountain man by learning to kill without regret. His regression to the "primitive Indian life" is marked by a decrease of delicacy, sensitivity, and emotion. His violence is directed toward nature as well as tribe (he kills beaver as "things"; he shoots his best friend). But he never enters the Indian's psychic world, for "Visions never come to an angry man" (McNickle 1978:21). Boone's murder of Jim might be partially mitigated in white law as a "crime of passion." But in the Indian novels, murder after murder of humans is political, historical, premeditated, "in cold blood," and therefore benign. Only "crimes of passion" (slapping Marlene?) are inexcusable. To whites, murder and violence are part of uncivilized "nature," while to Native Americans they are part of civilization. There is plenty of room in tribal custom for violence as policy and entertainment, best carried out by the comrades of bluebirds and chickadees. Hence, we find in these novels the remarkable combination—not juxtaposition—of delicacy and violence, brotherhood and murder. Both the natural characters whom American whites think of as "other" and the power and violence which Americans would so like to believe could be alien to their institutions are, in the Native American novel, part of sacredness, part of tribe:

> It was a time of pleasure, to be riding in the early morning air, to feel the drumming earth come upward through the pony's legs and enter his own flesh. Yes, the earth power coming into him as he moved over it. And a thing of the air, like a bird. He breathed deeply of the bird-air, and that was power too. He held his head high, a being in flight. And he sang, as his people sang, of the gray rising sun and the shadows that were only emerging from the night.
>
> To be one among his people, to grow up in their respect, to be his grandfather's kinsman—this was a power in itself, the power that flows between people and makes them one. He could feel it now, a healing warmth that flowed into his center from many-reaching body parts.
>
> Still, he had no shell of hardness around him. He was going into a country where danger would be waiting. (McNickle 1978:106)

THE DEATH OF JIM LONEY

We have seen that even contemporary Native American novels tell the story of a certain kind of homing; that the natural world is part of tribe both as a oneness and as a cast of characters; and that traditional violence still plays an accepted part in these novels. Although we have been using only six major and by now "classic" novels as examples, these points can be applied to other new Native American works such as Erdrich's *Love Medicine* (1984), a beautiful novel of the North Dakota Chippewa. The inland west reservation Indians are generating a remarkable literature, out of all proportion to their numbers or their access to conventional American discourse.

Knowledge of the Native American point of view may change our readings of these works; for instance, the slighting of character and historical didacticism of *Wind* may serve it well as a political novel, and that genre can be seen as profoundly tribal. McNickle shows a Jamesian ability to sketch characters from their own point of view—the absolutely right treatment of Pell at the Boston Harvard Club, followed by old Two Sleep's vision quest in the Mission mountains, prove the range of his portrait ability; yet in *Wind*, McNickle repeatedly drops the line of development of major characters. Is this poor plotting, or is the book saying that individuals, no matter how clearly "personalized," are subordinate to the history and politics of the tribe? In her analysis of Momaday's *House*, Barbara Strelke gives a good reading of Abel: "personal redemption . . . in the context of racial memory and community" (in Chapman 1975:349). The most interesting rereading engendered by these issues, however, occurs in the case of the most troubling book on the list: *The Death of Jim Loney*.

McNickle and Welch could hardly be more opposite—McNickle the scholar of sweeping historical and political perspective, Welch with a poet's chastened truth of the senses—yet all four of their novels pose the same question: Has the protagonist succeeded or failed? McNickle's Archilde seems a failure as he is led away in handcuffs for killing the sheriff, while the Indian agent shouts what sounds like a hostile review of *Loney:* "You had everything, every chance, and this is the best you could do with it! A man gets pretty tired of you and all your kind!" (1936:296). *The Surrounded,* as we have seen, maintains the momentum of a Plains Indian success story—Archilde returns to the tribe—while simultaneously, by white standards, he is going to the usual fates imposed by Europe on his kind—hell and jail. Loney certainly suffers failure; does he also, like Archilde, achieve some kind of success? Welch himself believes that *The Death of Jim Loney,* as well as *Winter in the Blood,* has a positive ending (*Dialogues* 1982:176); but for whites especially, Loney's achievement is hard to perceive. Kenneth Lincoln, writing with considerable awareness of Indian points of view, finds *Loney* "almost too real" (1983:168).

When Welch first published *Winter in the Blood,* in 1973, he was hailed for his spare prose and social realism, and compared to

Hemingway. Certainly his style is in the realistic tradition, although Welch adds the poetic image which gives rhetorical depth while avoiding subordination: "the paring knife grew heavy in the old lady's eyes." Paragraphs and chapters in *Winter* often end with echoing images that stop the reader and force reflection. Welch's surrealism, too, is antinarrative, taking the reader out of the story by exploding it, forcing us to search for connections among the shards. Realism, surrealism, and the shock of poetic imagery may describe Welch's technique, but his voice never shares the decadence and erudition of Hemingway or Pound. His voice in *Winter* is closer to Vittorini's *In Sicily* as translated by Wilfred David (and introduced by Hemingway), which Welch knew and admired. Vittorini used realistic prose to tell of coming home to his native subculture, Sicily, strange to most readers and half-strange to himself, and of finding there no easy location of his own needs. That is the voice of *Winter in the Blood*.

What does the protagonist of *Winter* find when he comes home? Although white readers better off in money, variety, and environment often think the book bleak, there is no denying the positive aspects of its end. The narrator of *Winter* has found his grandfather, learned his grandmother's history, reconciled himself to his brother's death, and in the final sentence, he alone in his family has honored his past by throwing the pouch on grandmother's grave. Those are strong upturns in the Indian "homing" plot.

The narrator also improves his white plot. His futile but wholehearted attempt to drag the cow out of the mud—an unprecedented action adventure ("the rope against my thigh felt right")—his new confidence in his knowledge, his resolve to buy Agnes "a couple of cremes de menthe, maybe offer to marry her on the spot," coupled with his Indian returns suggest an existential hero: He can't really change anything in his absurd universe—the past may be dead and Agnes worthless—but he is creating the slightest new dignity, confidence, and meaning within himself, spinning them out of his guts as well as his past. In *Winter in the Blood,* the white existential plot, the Indian homing plot, and the first-person poetic brilliance coincide. In *Loney,* however, white values are more severely rejected, the third person narration hides Loney's mind, and the "homing" plot is harder to find.

Jim Loney's friends believe he should try "leaving behind all his ancient prejudices and manners." He is bright, has performed well in school, and seems to lack only the motivation to do something with himself. Rhea, his white lover from Texas, like Garcia from the Rio Grande and Boone from Kentucky, has come to the Montana plains for "a complete break with my past" (p. 86). She next wants to go to Seattle: "Don't ask me why I chose Seattle. I guess it just seems a place to escape to" (p. 87). Rhea wants Jim Loney to escape with her. Ironically, she is in competition with another escape artist, Loney's beautiful and upwardly mobile sister, Kate, who works for the government in Washington, D.C. She, also, offers Loney the white way of novelty, mobility, and meaning through individual experience and possession of things. Leave, she says, and "you would have things worthwhile . . . beautiful country, a city, the North, the South, the ocean. . . . You need that. You need things to be different, things that would arouse your curiosity, give you some purpose" (p. 76).

Kate and Rhea are very attractive characters. Unlike Silko, Momaday, and McNickle, Welch does not bring "the enemy" onstage in these two novels; he avoids didactic or dogmatic overtones, and the oppression represented by white culture appears in the gaps between images, between possibilities, between plots. Even the sheriff, Painter, is treated quite sympathetically, as is the successful, ranch-owning Indian, Pretty Weasel, who quit his basketball scholarship at Wyoming to come home in "automatic response, the way a sheepdog returns to camp in the evening" (p. 81). Neither the white world nor white success seems odious in this book; on the other hand, Harlem, Loney's hometown, may not be the end of the world—but you can see it from there. Traditional Indian culture is less evident here than in any other of the six novels: Loney's Indian mother is dead; his white father and Kate are his only kin; he lives off the reservation, in town. The reader easily joins Kate and Rhea and most critics in urging him to leave, to find "purpose" in "things" that are "different."

Twice in the book, Loney analyzes himself. In each case, he draws much of his vocabulary and values, his conscious knowledge, from the white world, but then like a sheepdog keeps trotting back to family, past, and place as the source of identity:

"I can't leave," he said, and he almost knew why. He thought of his earlier attempts to create a past, a background, an ancestry—something that would tell him who he was. . . . He had always admired Kate's ability to live in the present, but he had also wondered at her lack of need to understand her past. Maybe she had the right idea; maybe it was the present that mattered, only the present. (p. 88)

Loney returns to thoughts of his surrogate mother for a year, Aunt "S," hardly known, now dead; the only real family he has had. Kate has chosen change through white knowledge, "learning as a kind of salvation, a way to get up and out of being what they were" (p. 90).

A few chapters later, Rhea asks, "What is it that troubles you?" Loney visibly tiptoes the line between individual psychology and tribal consciousness: "I don't even know myself. It has to do with the past. . . . I know it has to do with my mother and father . . . an aunt I lived with . . . who she really was and how she died." Then he suddenly tells her of the extraordinary white bird that appears "when I'm awake, but late at night when I'm tired—or drunk. . . . Sometimes I think it is a vision sent by my mother's people. I must interpret it, but I don't know how." The question of whether he will go to Seattle suddenly becomes, quite clearly, a choice between two cultures, two plots. Rhea asks, "'Did it ever occur to you that if you left you would leave these . . . visions behind? You might become so involved with a new life that your past would fade away—that bird would fade away for good.' 'I don't know that I want that to happen'" (pp. 104–106).

From the white point of view, the change of interests offered by a wandering plot might lay to rest Loney's troubling hallucination. From the Native American point of view, his vision-knowledge is inextricably tied to past and place, although he lacks the tribe ("my mother's people") to interpret it. That knowledge would be entirely lost if he moved away. The scene ends as they discuss his geographical place. The half-breed Loney has ambivalent responses:

This is your country, isn't it? It means a great deal to you.

I've never understood it. Once in a while I look around and I see things familiar and I think I will die here. It's my country then.

> Other times I want to leave, to see other things, to meet people,
> to die elsewhere.

Genetic determinism is troubling to liberals. Reading these books,
however, one sometimes wonders if the half-breed has two knowl-
edges in his bones.

The Death of Jim Loney cannot be read without Native American
context. The most obvious example occurs right away: "He walked
and he realized that he was seeing things strangely, and he remembered that it had been that way at the football game. It was as
though he were exhausted and drowsy, but his head was clear. He
was aware of things around him—the shadowy trees, the glistening
sidewalk, the dark cat that moved into the dark" (p. 4). In the white
world, we trace this "altered state" backward to tough drinking and
forward to trouble. Anyone familiar with Plains Indians, however,
will recognize a possible vision-quest state of mind, which would
suddenly make Loney the doctor instead of the patient. Sure
enough, seven chapters later, the bird appears in the book for the
first time, "And again, as he had that night after the football game,
he saw things strangely, yet clearly. . . . he saw the smoke ring go
out away from his face and he saw the bird in flight. . . . It came
every night now" (p. 20).

Loney did not "seek" the state of mind or the bird, as far as he
knows. Indeed, that is his situation throughout the novel: He thinks
white, would not mind being white, but he seems to have Indianness
visited upon him. He is the reluctant victim of a vision without
quest, of vague yearnings for family, past, and place that halfway
yield to white interpretation—this individual has a problem, "he
will not allow himself to be found" (p. 34), and "it had everything
to do with himself" (p. 134); and halfway yield to tribal analysis—
Loney needs to come home.

There are a number of tribal aspects to Loney's tale. The bird
vision is dramatically important although never explained, never
interpreted—we are offered an Indian with a spirit-helper as help-
less as he. Throughout the book, Loney yearns for family, with
dreams of a mother long dead, aching memories of one Christmas
with the kind "aunt," the tracking of a worthless father at last
brought to bay in his trailer. Loney's inability to find an adequate
father or elder stands in marked contrast to the other five novels

and seems indivisible from his downfall. Ike is an anti-grandfather, the perfect opposite of Betonie, Bull, and Yellow Calf. And he is white.

Beyond the bird and the family themes and Loney's obvious ties to place in the novel are some tribal fringes that become surprisingly central. Loney's sleeping dreams are prophetic. When Ike says, "You might need this" and hands Loney the shotgun with "a familiar grin" (p. 149), we and Loney remember Ike's identical words as he handed him a shotgun in a dream months before (p. 24). Not only does the book introduce dream epistemologies but several narrative intrusions or outside views of Loney are also decidedly "blood" in point of view. Most exquisite is the ancient Indian grandmother at the airport, welcoming home her soldier grandson whom "she had lost" to new experiences abroad in the white world: "And it filled her with sadness, for she knew that what he had gained would never make up for what he had lost. She had seen the other boys come home. And she stared past her soldier at Loney's wolfish face and she thought, That's one of them" (p. 58). Loney has never been off to war or anywhere else; but she knows that half of him has left for the white world, and cannot come home. Loney himself "never felt Indian":

> Indians were people like the Cross Guns, the Old Chiefs—Amos After Buffalo. They lived an Indian way, at least tried. When Loney thought of Indians, he thought of the reservation families, all living under one roof, the old ones passing down the wisdom of their years, of their family's years, of their tribes' years, and the young ones soaking up their history, their places in their history, with a wisdom that went beyond age.
>
> He remembered when the Cross Guns family used to come to town. . . . old Emil Cross Guns . . . sitting in the back seat. . . . Loney recalled going up to the window and touching his hand. . . . Now he [Pretty Weasel's father] was old, but in a white man way, thrown away. Not like Emil Cross Guns.
>
> Loney thought this and he grew sad . . . for himself. He had no family and he wasn't Indian or white. He remembered the day he and Rhea had driven out to the Little Rockies. She had said he was lucky to have two sets of ancestors. In truth he had none. (p. 102)

Loney's connection to this distant past is Amos After Buffalo, the little boy who helps him chip his frozen dog out of the ice and who is upset that the dog is not buried. Amos is from Hays on the Reservation, "way out there" (p. 54), and when Loney is ready to die ("It's my country then" [p. 107]), he chooses to do it in Mission Canyon of the Little Rockies, just past Hays and the Mission school. As he walks through Hays in the dark, his thoughts are of Amos and the real Indians: "Amos After Buffalo will grow up, thought Loney, and he will discover that Thanksgiving is not meant for him . . . and it will hurt him . . . and he will grow hard and bitter" (p. 166). Then, in a parallel to the deer conversation in *Winter*, Loney suddenly and quite seriously addresses the strange dog trailing him through town, and for a moment he has indeed leapt back into the tribe's distant past, when animals and men worried together over things like proper burials, a pouch on the grave: "'You tell Amos that Jim Loney passed through town while he was dreaming. Give him dreams. Tell him you saw me carrying a dog and that I was taking that dog to a higher ground. He will know' . . . The dog was gone" (p. 167).

Amos had said, "Do you know where I live?" (p. 54). Now Loney knows. Loney's own confidence and command, and the truth of his dreams throughout the novel, lead us to assume that the dog is off to deliver the message, but Welch's spare style and disjunct images almost hide, or rather force us to consider—to supply our own rhetoric for—the immense distance between the bars and trailers of Harlem and this dog-dream-messenger. Loney then walks to his death thinking of his past, which "brought me here," thinking of the old Indians in the canyon, "the warriors, the women who had picked chokecherries" (p. 168), and finally of the mother who "had given up her son to be free" (p. 175). But freedom hasn't worked for either the mother or the son who "would not allow himself to be found." The only thing left is not Boone's heaven of suburban isolation, or Catherine's tribal heaven of singing around the fire, but Welch's half-breed heaven, High Line grace: "But there had to be another place where people bought each other drinks and talked quietly about their pasts, their mistakes . . . like everything was beginning again" (p. 175).

What is this novel about? Welch considers the end positive because Loney has tried to understand his past, and because he has taken control of his life by orchestrating his death (*Dialogues* 1982:176). But that existential plot is hard to affirm in Loney. Unlike Bigger Thomas in *Native Son*, who has deliberately killed and has tried to escape, and who accepts his execution as the fitting end to his racist plot, Loney's decisiveness is almost gratuitously self-destructive. The white existential plot offers only the tiniest shred of affirmation: Loney accepts responsibility for accidental murder (arguably with unconscious intent, for Pretty Weasel has threatened him with intimacy, good memories, and success). When he shoots Pretty Weasel, "he sees death for what it is—a release from the realities that he cannot comprehend." (Thank you, Linda Weasel Head.) He then stages his own unnecessary execution. Many isolated events serve this weak white plot: Shooting Pretty Weasel, shooting at his father, and setting up the policeman's shot, are all acts of an indecisive loner in submission to his own arbitrary yet self-willed fate. But the refusal to leave his place, the mourning of lost ancestors, the bird vision, the prophetic dreams, the violence, and the scenes with Amos After Buffalo, all make a counter-pattern of Native American resistance to assimilation: This is *our* disaster, and I will make my stand on *our* ground in honor of my ancestry and ancestral knowledge. Like Old Bull in *Wind*, Loney has "received" the bullet from the Indian upholding white law, and "This is what you wanted, he thought" (p. 179). Loney's individuality, his "existence," and most of his conscious knowledge, in the white sense, may be isolated, but his dreams and desires and finally his resolution are not. These aspects of Loney constitute a loyalty to a tribe and tribalism he never individually knew.

The tension between the white and Indian plots *is* the tension in *Loney*. In Welch's work, the individual psychic drama is a kind of melody played against the pedal bass of tribal past. Much more than *Winter*, *Loney* forces us to hear the counterpoint of these competing strains. *Loney* takes us realistically to the blurred edge of consciousness of a High Line Indian who knows there must be something good in his people, past, and place, but who doesn't even know why he knows that. The book dares us to see Loney's final homing as not at all the perversion it seems to be, however much, like Kate and Rhea, we still want Loney to leave. In *Loney* more than in any other of the six novels, the reader is placed squarely in the breed's situation, unable to choose between a white realism that seems to offer at best lonely success or intelligent despair, and an Indian pride in tradition that must seem a dream. For the reader as well as the breed, the white and Indian plots are not good and bad opposites but simultaneous, inescapable forces, centrifugal and centripetal, that can leave one so stuck in orbit that even Loney's decisiveness—one jump back toward the center—becomes a quantum leap.

The breed's situation is not a comfortable one; like most readers, I found *Loney* at first a most uncomfortable book. So did Anatole Broyard in the *New York Times,* who sounded like a peeved Indian agent: "Is he threatening us with his unhappiness? Why do so many of our serious novels have to be read like unpaid bills?" (1979:37). Broyard's ignorance of the subject matter (he thinks Rhea improbable) and his distaste for guilt are beside the point; the novel doesn't even try to recover those vast debts, nor does it directly threaten us. The limbo itself makes Broyard whine; life without individualism plus life without tribe, creates the impression Kenneth Lincoln had of a "'breed's' novel, neither Indian nor white" (1983:168): "*Nothing* matters in this novel of small revelations" (p. 166). However, the novel is both Indian and white, and things do matter: Loney's refusal, like Bartleby's, has its large and mysterious (and very accurate) aspects; the *reasons* for his refusal, unlike Bartleby's, may not be so much existential as tribal, and that matters a great deal. Lincoln writes, "There is little, if any, older ethnology" in *Loney* (p. 168), and so he misses the positivism of the end. Tribalism gives dignity and honor to Loney's choice. In the political terms used by Krupat to discuss Indian "as told to" autobiographies, Loney's refusal to leave constitutes a resistance to "assujetissement," the adjustment of Indians as well as whites to the ruling mythology: individual advancement. Those who would have Loney leave (or rather that part of every one of us which would have Loney leave) are requesting another Indian biography depicting success through capitulation. Such "comedy," as Krupat points out, quoting Frye, would serve the status quo, the "moral norm" of the ruling class (1983:270). That is exactly why Cushman's comedy, *Stay Away Joe,* is a racist book: while realistically presenting Indian failure, it does so by complacently serving the white point of view. That makes the novel most readable, unfortunately, to whites and Indians alike.

In his article on "Poem, Dream and the Consuming of Culture," Karl Kroeber compares white Romantic poetry (and dreaming) to Indian poetry (and vision quests):

The Indian poem is fashioned otherwise. Its function is the transfer or utilization of tensions rather than their creation. It opens outward, away from itself, into ceremonial dance, into public activity, rather than concentrating into itself. "The Fall of Hyperion: A Dream" is characteristic of Western poetry, not just Keats's, in leading back into itself, returning us finally to the dreamer himself. . . . Such return of desire upon its origin makes a kind of frustration inevitable. . . . The articulation of the Ojebwa dream is a liberation of it from the dreamer's self. (1983:332)

All six novels present a Western "self" seeking to transfer energy to a tribal context. Loney dies two deaths: His white suicide is certainly a "return of desire upon itself," which "makes a kind of frustration inevitable." Yet his loyalty to Amos, the dog, his past and place is a transfer of energy "outward, away from itself . . . into public activity," the history of tribe. Thus, the articulation of his dream is also "a liberation of it from the dreamer's self"; Loney dies watching his past, "the beating wings of a dark bird as it climbed to a distant place" (p. 179).

The homing plots of McNickle, Momaday, Silko, Welch, and even Erdrich marry white failure to Indian pride, and if that marriage is "almost too real," it is not the fault of the novelists. They are not offering Indian answers, but reflecting continued respect for tribal identity while realistically depicting the disadvantages of non-assimilation. The challenge to whites is to appreciate how these novels present a single, eloquent argument against de-reservation and assimilation, and for the necessity of working out an identity in relation to one's past. These are neither formula nor protest novels. Welch had not read McNickle before writing his two books. Native American authors are writing clearly and effectively about experiences that began "when the buffalo went away" and "the hearts of my people fell to the ground," experiences which continue today in the proud and often tragic homings of these books:

Our narratives deal with the experiences of man, and these experiences are not always pleasant or pretty. But it is not proper to change our stories to make them more acceptable to our ears, that is if we wish to tell the truth. Words must be the echo of what has happened and cannot be made to conform to the mood and taste of the listener. (Eskimo to Knut Rasmussen, quoted in Swann 1983:xiv)

REFERENCES

Broyard, Anatole. "Books of the Times," *New York Times,* Nov. 28, 1979.
Chapman, Abraham, ed. 1975. *Literature of the American Indians.* New York: New American Library.
Crevecoeur, St. Jean de. 1782. *Letters from an American Farmer.* Quoted in Sculley Bradley, Richard Croom Beatty, E. Hudson Long, and George Perkins. 1974. *The American Tradition in Literature,* vol. 1, 4th ed. New York: Grosset and Dunlop.
Deloria, Vine, Jr. 1970. *We Talk, You Listen.* New York: Macmillan.
Dialogues with Northwest Writers. 1982. *Northwest Review* 20 (2–3).
Erdrich, Louise. 1984. *Love Medicine.* New York: Holt, Rinehart and Winston.
Fey, Harold E., and D'Arcy McNickle. 1959. *Indians and Other Americans.* New York: Harper.
Garcia, Andrew. 1967. *Tough Trip Through Paradise.* Sausalito: Comstock.
Guthrie, A. B., Jr. 1947. *The Big Sky.* Boston: Houghton Mifflin.
Kroeber, Karl. 1983. Poem, Dream, and the Consuming of Culture. In *Smoothing the Ground,* ed. Brian Swann. Berkeley, Los Angeles, London: University of California Press.
Krupat, Arnold. 1983. The Indian Autobiography: Origins, Type and Function. In *Smoothing the Ground,* ed. Brian Swann. Berkeley, Los Angeles, London: University of California Press.
Lincoln, Kenneth. 1983. *Native American Renaissance.* Berkeley, Los Angeles, London: University of California Press.
Linderman, Frank. 1962 [1930]. *Plenty-Coups.* Lincoln: University of Nebraska Press. (Originally published as *American, The Life Story of a Great Indian, Plenty-Coups, Chief of the Crows.*)
———. 1974 [1932]. *Pretty-Shield.* Lincoln: University of Nebraska Press. (Originally published as *Red Mother.*)
McNickle, D'Arcy. 1936. *The Surrounded.* New York: Dodd, Mead.
———. 1978. *Wind from an Enemy Sky.* San Francisco: Harper & Row.
Momaday, N. Scott. 1966. *House Made of Dawn.* New York: Harper & Row.
Silko, Leslie. 1977. *Ceremony.* New York: Viking.
Standing Bear, Luther. 1978 [1933]. *Land of the Spotted Eagle.* Lincoln: University of Nebraska Press.
Strelke, Barbara. 1975. N. Scott Momaday: Racial Memory and Individual Imagination. In *Literature of the American Indians,* ed. Abraham Chapman. New York: New American Library.

Swann, Brian, ed. 1983. *Smoothing the Ground*. Berkeley, Los Angeles, London: University of California Press.

Vittorini, Elio. 1949. *In Sicily*, trans. Wilfred David. New York: New Directions.

Welch, James. 1979. *The Death of Jim Loney*. New York: Harper & Row.

———. 1974. *Winter in the Blood*. New York: Harper & Row.

———. n.d. *Fools Crow*. Harmondsworth: Penguin (forthcoming).

Notes on Contributors

Paula Gunn Allen, a Laguna Pueblo, is currently Visiting Lecturer in Native American Studies at the University of California, Berkeley. Among several books her most recent are *Shadow Country* (poems, 1982), and a novel, *The Woman Who Owned the Shadows* (1983). She is the editor of *Studies in American Indian Literature* for the Modern Language Association (1983), and has most recently published *The Sacred Hoop: Recovering the Feminine in American Indian Traditions* (1986).

Donald Bahr is a longstanding student of Pima and Papago culture. His first and most important study in this field is *Piman Shamanism and Staying Sickness* (1974). He is Professor of Anthropology at Arizona State University, Tempe, and currently continues to work with Papago singers.

William Bevis is Professor of English at the University of Montana, where he has taught since 1974. He has published on Emerson, Wallace Stevens, Native American poetry and prose, and several Western authors from Cooper to Richard Hugo. He currently chairs the Western Studies Project at the University of Montana.

William Bright, Professor of Linguistics and Anthropology at the University of California, Los Angeles, has worked with Native American peoples in California and Meso-America since 1949, specializing in anthropological linguistics, sociolinguistics, and ethnopoetics. In addition to a number of scholarly articles and poems, his most recent publications are *Coyote Stories,* which he edited in 1978, and *American Indian Linguistics and Literature* (1984). He is also the editor of *Language,* the Journal of the Linguistic Society of America.

H. David Brumble has for some years been at work on the history of

American Indian autobiography, and is the compiler of *An Annotated Bibliography of American Indian and Eskimo Autobiographies* (1981). An Associate Professor of English at the University of Pittsburgh, he has also published a translation of a seventeenth-century Dutch comedy, as well as articles on medieval and renaissance art and literature.

Willard Gingerich has taught in Pittsburgh, Panama, and at Navajo Community College in Arizona. He currently is Associate Professor of English at the University of Texas at El Paso. A poet and translator, he has specialized in the criticism of Nahua (Aztec) literature, while also publishing on the work of contemporary Native American and Chicano novelists and poets.

Dell Hymes is Dean of the Graduate School of Education at the University of Pennsylvania, and also Professor of Folklore, Linguistics, and Sociology. Among many books, his most recent are *Vers la compétence de communication* (1984), *Essays in the History of Linguistic Anthropology* (1983), *"In Vain I Tried to Tell You": Essays in Native American Ethnopoetics* (1981), and (with John Fought) *American Structuralism* (1981).

Rudolf Kaiser is Professor of English and the Didactics of English at the University of Hildesheim in West Germany. He was a Fulbright scholar in California in 1963–1964, and has made research trips to the American Southwest in 1981, 1982, and 1983. Along with essays in various periodicals, he has recently published *Diese Erde ist uns heilig—Die Reden des Indianerhauptlings Seattle* (with his daughter, Michaela, 1984), *Gesang des Regenbogens—Indianische Gebete* (1985), and *This Land is Sacred—Native American Views and Values* (1986).

M. Dale Kinkade is Professor of Linguistics at the University of British Columbia. He has published numerous articles on Salishan narrative and languages, and is currently continuing work on dictionaries of the Upper Chehalis and Cowlitz as well as on Upper Chehalis and Columbian Salish texts.

Arnold Krupat teaches literature at Sarah Lawrence College. He has published a number of articles and reviews applying literary theory to Native American studies. His book, *For Those Who Come After: A Study of Native American Autobiography* appeared in 1985. With Brian Swann, he has edited *I Tell You Now: Autobiographies by Contemporary Native American Writers* (1987).

Anthony Mattina is Professor in the Department of Anthropology at the University of Montana. A specialist in Salishan languages, he is the author of many articles and monographs on Colville, Flathead, and Okanagan linguistics. Most recently, he has published *The Golden Woman: The Colville Narrative of Peter J. Seymour* (1985).

Duane Niatum, a member of the Klallam tribe, is a widely published poet whose work has appeared in many anthologies. His books include *Ascending Red Cedar Moon* (1974), *Digging Out the Roots* (1977), and *Songs for the Harvester of Dreams* (1981). He has also edited an anthology of Native American poetry, *Carriers of the Dream Wheel* (1975), and a follow-up volume, *Harper's Book of Twentieth-Century Native American Poetry* (1986).

Howard Norman is the translator of *The Wishing Bone Cycle: Narrative Poems from the Swampy Cree Indians* (1976), and *Where the Chill Came From: Cree Windigo Tales and Journeys* (1982); *Conversations with the Snow: Cree Trickster Narratives* is currently in progress. He is the editor of *Northern Tales* for the Pantheon Folklore and Fairy Tale Library, and has a novel called *The Northern Lights* scheduled for publication in 1987.

Carter Revard, an Osage from Pawhuska, Oklahoma, was a Rhodes Scholar at Oxford, and since 1961 has taught at Washington University where he is a Professor of English, specializing in medieval literature. He has published many articles in scholarly journals as well as books of poetry, among them *My Right Hand Don't Leave Me No More* (1970), and *Ponca War Dancers* (1980). He is currently at work on a collection of poems and a novel, while contemplating a collaboration with his cousin Carter Camp which would set straight some of the history of AIM and Wounded Knee.

Julian Rice teaches in the English Department at Florida Atlantic University. He has published articles on the Lakota oral tradition in many journals, and he has just completed a booklength manuscript, "Words to Reach the End: Lakota Language Literature," that is presently under review for publication.

Joel Sherzer is Professor of Anthropology and Linguistics at the University of Texas at Austin. His work has focused particularly on the Kuna Indians of Panama. His publications include *An Areal-Typological Study of American Indian Languages North of Mexico* (1976), and *Kuna Ways of Speaking* (1983).

Brian Swann is Professor of English at The Cooper Union in New

York City. He is the author of a number of books of poetry and fiction as well as the translator of ten volumes of poetry. His latest books are *The Plot of the Mice* (fiction, 1986), *Song of the Sky: Versions of Native American Songs and Poems* (1985), and *The Middle of the Journey* (poems, 1983).

Dennis Tedlock, a westerner by upbringing, is University Professor of Anthropology and Religion at Boston University. His books include *Finding the Center: Narrative Poetry of the Zuni Indians* (1972), *Teachings from the American Earth: Indian Religion and Philosophy* (with Barbara Tedlock, 1975), and *The Spoken Word and the Work of Interpretation* (1983). His latest work, *Popol Vuh: The Mayan Book of the Dawn of Life* (1985) was awarded the 1986 PEN Translation Prize in Poetry.

Barre Toelken directs the Folklore Program at Utah State University. During a lengthy period in the mid-1950s, he lived with the Yellowman family in Montezuma Creek on the Navajo reservation, and since that time has been engaged in recording and studying Navajo narratives about Coyote. A former editor of the *Journal of American Folklore,* and a past president of the American Folklore Society, he is the author of a number of articles about Native American traditions, and on various genres of folklore.

Andrew Wiget teaches in the Department of English at New Mexico State University. He has published articles on Zuni, Aztec, Eskimo, Navajo, and Hopi oral literatures, as well as on contemporary Native American writers. He has recently published *Native American Literature* (1985), and edited an anthology called *Critical Essays on Native American Literature* (1985). His monograph on the Acoma poet and fiction writer, Simon Ortiz, has just appeared in the Boise State Western Writers Series (1986).

Paul Zolbrod is Professor of English at Allegheny College. He comes to Native American poetry via an interest in classical, medieval, and renaissance literary theory and a curiosity about European and southwestern American oral literature. He has published many articles on American Indian literature and is the author of *Diné Bahaneʼ: The Navajo Creation Story* (1984).

Index

Art: communal, 462 n. 5; difference in, 14, 554–556; function of, 106. *See also* specific type

Arte para aprender la lengua mexicana (de Olmos), 95

Ashley, Rachel, 423

As I Lay Dying (Faulkner), 109

Aspect, defined, 259; Kuna tense-aspect system, 153

Association for American Indian Affairs, 42

Association for the Study of American Indian Literature, 44

Astronomy, 34; Mayan cycles, 489; temple observatories, 35

Athabacan, 31

Audience: affirmation by, 320–332; interaction with, 181; performing variables and, 152, 256, 315–318

Augustine, 537, 540–541, 547

Austin, Mary, 1

Autobiography: historian of, 546; Native Indian, 7, 537–551

Autobiography of a Winnebago Indian, The (Radin), 537–551

Autofellation, 357–358

Aveni, Anthony, 34–35

Aztecs, 31; calendars of, 35; Coyote tales, 339; theology of, 86, 96

Aztec Thought and Culture (León-Portilla), 86

Babies: care of, 185, 192; death of, 187, 281; euphemisms for, 185–186; socially inappropriate, 185, 189. *See also* Children

Bachelard, Gaston, 405

Badger, Coyote and, 367

Bagley, Clarence B., 506

Bahr, Donald, 3, 4, 6

Baja, California, 347

Balance. *See* Symmetry

Ballinger, Franchot, 247

Bass, Alan, 125 n. 2

Bateson, Gregory, 335 n. 22

Bauman, Richard, 314–315, 317

"Beadway," 20–21

Beans, 23

"Bear and Bee," 258

Bear stories, 257–258, 456

Beauty, reality and, 86

Beautyway, 573

Beaver, Coyote and, 394–395

Beckwith, Martha Warren, 436–437

"Beep Beep the Roadrunner," 340

Behavior, 181; anthropology and, 8

Bekoff, Marc, 346, 354

Benally, Little John, 389–390

Bennett, Bruce, 358, 370

Beowulf, 18

Berkhofer, Robert F., Jr., 561

Berman, Judith, 82 n. 1

"Berry Feast, A," 345–346, 376

Bertholf, Robert, 568

Bevis, William, 3, 7, 125 n. 3, 251

Bible: chants and, 181; as source of truth, 569–570

Bierhorst, John, 88

Big Sky, The (Guthrie), 595–597

Big Spirit, 392

Biography, 537

Birds, creation of, 483. *See also* specific tales

Birth defects, 185, 189

Black Bear, 456

Black Elk, 436, 438, 441

Blackfeet, 558–559, 595

Black folk narratives, 339

"Black Pig," 137

Blessing, Richard, 556

Blocking-out technique, 135, 145 n. 14

Blood, 96

Blowsnake, Sam, 537–551; confession and, 542; conversion of, 544; education of, 540, 545; as informant, 542

Blue Cloud, Peter, 44, 341, 359, 371

Blue Heron, 22

Bluejay stories, 72, 255–295, 341; alternative analysis of, 286–288; Heck version of, 256–280; other versions of, 291–294; pattern number in, 258; performance of, 288–289; structure of text, 282–286

"Bluejay visits the Land of the Dead," 260–280

Boas, Franz, 1, 3, 8, 44, 70, 119, 255, 257, 281, 291, 344

Boggess, E. K., 351

Bolivar, Simon, 182

Book of Chilam Balam of Chumayel, 478, 488

Born For Water, 18

Boudinot, Elias, 6

Monkeys, origin of, 489
Monogamy, 360; Peyotists and, 544
Monsters, 392. *See also* Giants
Monster Slayer, 17–18, 23, 574
Moon, 29; as Female Star, 447
Moral tales: chants and, 189; introjection and, 435; multiple interpretations of, 190; negative examples, 402–403
Morris, Wright, 555
Mothers: grandmothers, 441, 564–565; naming ceremony and, 456–458. *See also* Children; Women
Motherfathers, Mayan, 475, 478, 481–483
Mothers of the Word, 470
Mountains: clouds and, 477; sacred, 23, 30
Mouth, loss of, 71
Mulatuppu, San Blas, Panama, 151, 181
Multisong sets, 198
Museum of Northern Arizona, 16
Myth(s): abstract structures, 192; ambiguous figures in, 46; choice of words in, 117; cross symbolism in, 32; etiological, 192–193; folktales vs., 312; Indian vs. Anglo, 220 n. 2; pre-Columbian, 32, 85–111, 469–495; reenactment of, 13; shared features in, 184; songs as, 202; symbolic oppositions in, 187–188; transformational relationships in, 76; written versions of, 545. *See also* Stories
Mythography: constellation, 135; legitimate, 5; task of, 5, 133, 137, 142; verse and, 137
Mythologiques (Lévi-Strauss), 75–76

Nahuas: aesthetic vision of, 86; languages of, 85, 95, 469–495; Nahuatl literature sources, 110; pre-Hispanic poetry, 85–112; tecpillatolli style, 94, 100–101
Namedropping, 191
Naming: as cultural phenomenon, 464 n. 11; descriptive nature of, 443 n. 7; Heidegger and, 104–105; impoliteness of, 254 n. 1; Mayan, 491; Osage, 446–465; Puma, 448–461
Narratives, oral. *See* Oral narratives
Narrators: focus of, 293; kinesic features

of, 321–325; paralinguistic features of, 325–328; patterning choices of, 51; role-switching by, 319–320; skills of, 60, 297; women as, 49. *See also* Performance
National Archives, Washington, D.C., 502–503, 508
National Wildlife Federation, 512
Native American Church, 549 n. 12
Native American Literature (Wiget), 2
Native Americans: Anglo influences, 126 n. 5, 181, 220, 546–547, 557–558, 569–570; archaeoastronomy, 34–35, 489; bicultural, 560; bilingual, 547; canonization of texts, 121; contemporary authors, 43, 563–619; cultural maintenance of, 122; descendants of, 42; Mayan influence on, 31; medical system of, 209 (*see also* Healing); preservation, 102, 541; recorded oral performances, 118, 137; scholars, 43, 45, 220; stereotypes of, 497, 552–562; studies, 4. *See also* Oral narratives; Poetry; Tribalism; specific authors, tales
Nature: alienation from, 439; culture vs., 78; English poetry, 424; function of, 598–599; as home, 602; individuation of, 604; reciprocity in, 19, 391–392; as sacred, 497, 598–608; urban concept of, 601; as wilderness, 598
Navajo, 6; art of, 15–16, 19, 30; ceremonial poetry of, 13, 16; chantway system of, 395–401, 570–573, 577; Coyote tales, 348–349, 364, 388–401; creation myth, 16, 34, 37; credibility of, 30; cultural values of, 389; major deities of, 25; migration of, 31; order vs. disorder themes, 27–28; poetic world of, 254 n. 1; respect for privacy, 254 n. 1; Twin heroes of, 395; witches and, 394–399
Navajo Legends (Matthews), 16
Negative example, 402–403
Neihardt, John G., 436–437
Neo-Platonism, 547
Neopoetics, 345, 366
Neoteny, 354
Newberry Library, Chicago, 469
New York Times, 617
Nezahualcoyotl, 92

Parsons, E. C., 308

Particle(s), 135; initial marker, 55, 61

"Particle, Pause and Pattern in American Indian Narrative Verse" (Hymes), 135

Passages, 501

Patohil mountain, 494

Patterning, 133–136; chronological order, 548 n. 7; pause and, 135, 152; principles of, 51

Pauses, 130; line-framing elements, 152; patterning, 135, 152; pitch-pause, 288–289

Pecked cross, 35–37

Penises: Coyote and, 72; trading of, 69–70

Pepper, Chester, 380

Performance: analysis of, 318–332; anthropology and, 8; audience's role, 181, 315–318, 320–332; competence vs., 288; comprehension and, 5; cultural context of, 317; devaluation of, 249–250; emergent quality of, 317; environmental frame, 318–319; frame of communication in, 313–318; linguistic features, 329–332; kinetic features of, 138; metaphoric stacking in, 336 n. 49; paralinguistic features of, 133, 325–328; poetics of, 152–153; recording of, 5, 118, 129, 137, 193, 297, 316; rhetoric of, 193; role switching in, 319–320; song function in, 330–331; text and, 119–120; theory, 297–336; voice quality, 130. *See also* Oral narratives

Perry, Ted, 513–514

Pete, Maggie, 291–293

Petersen, Annie Miner, 47

Petit, Jean, 80

Peyote Cult, 198, 540, 542–544; ceremony, 572; transcendence and, 547

Philology, anthropological, 247

Philosophy, Western, 101

Phonology, Pima changes in, 198

Pima, Heaven songs of, 6, 198–244; devil songs, 209; dictionaries, 244 n. 10; Europeans and, 208, 220; funeral ceremonies and, 201–202; generalized celebrations, 201, 221 n. 4, 222 n. 7; literary studies, 245 n. 10; recorded, 204; song set norms, 217; subsistence ceremonies and, 221 n. 3; Yumas and, 220

Pindaric odes, ring composition, 295 n. 27

Pitch-pause combinations, types of, 288–289

Place, vision-knowledge and, 612

Place of Mystery, 89

Place Where the Waters Crossed, 21

Plains Indians, history of, 607

Plants, 25; healing, 392, 440–441; sacred, 23, 457

Plastic arts, 13–38. *See also* specific arts

Plath, Sylvia, 108

Pochoda, Elizabeth, 82 n. 1

Poe, Edgar Allen, 557

Poet(s): collaboration with, 253; Native American, 7, 247; as translators, 247–248, 250

"Poetic Retranslation and the Pretty Languages of Yellowman" (Toelken), 388–389

Poetry, 1–2, 129; advantages of, 15; aesthetic and, 555; animals in, 556–557; ceremonial, 13; contemporary, 345; contrast with other arts, 14; dramatic, 144 n. 5, 257; ethnopoetics, 41–84, 288, 344–345, 380; human knowledge and, 86; as language essence, 103, 106; narrative and, 38, 49, 126 n. 3, 142–144; nature in, 556–557; origin of, 91, 94; poet and, 93; pre-Hispanic, 110; vision and, 617–618. *See also* Verse; specific poems

Point Elliot Treaty, 502, 504; original manuscript, 533 n. 7

Polka-style music, 206

Pollution. *See* Ecology

Poor Sarah (Boudinot), 6

Pope, Bob, 292

Popol Vuh, 469–495; creation of humans in, 484–485; divinatory days in, 485; interpretation of, 476–494; Mayan calendar and, 480–482; patrilineage shrines in, 492

"Poppies in October," 108

Populism, 44

Porcupine, 218

Portrait of the Artist (Joyce), 123

Designer:	U.C. Press Staff
Compositor:	Janet Sheila Brown
Text:	Baskerville 10.5/12.5
Display:	Baskerville
Printer:	Edward Bros., Inc.
Binder:	Edward Bros., Inc.

This ground-breaking collection of essays brings to the study of Native American literatures a broadly interdisciplinary approach. While serious study of the subject by anthropologists and linguists is still less than a century old, such consideration on the part of students of literature began even more recently. Much has been accomplished, and now the time is ripe for a sharing of skills, a pooling of resources. Literary scholars must take note of the linguistic and cultural data their social scientist colleagues have amassed, while the social scientists must attend to the questions of rhetorical force and form which their literary colleagues have posed.

To this end, the present volume offers some of the best work now being done on Native American literatures from a variety of disciplinary perspectives. The editors offer a wide selection of essays by folklorists and theorists, anthropologists and linguists, poets and literary critics, all of which may deepen our understanding of American Studies and, in particular, of Native American Studies. These essays address the overlapping issues of the *presentation* and *interpretation* of Indian literary expression. How is one best to present in writing an art that is primarily oral, dramatic, performative? And how is one to interpret that art, both in its traditional forms and in its later, written forms? Contributors examine a range of materials from pre-contact songs and stories, to nineteenth-century, white-influenced autobiographies, to novels written by contemporary Native Americans.